INTERPRETING THE ENVIRONMENT

SECOND EDITION

Frontispiece: The resource, the visitor, and the interpretive medium; the basics for an interpretive program. Mount Rainier National Park, Washington. (Photo by Grant W. Sharpe.)

INTERPRETING THE ENVIRONMENT

SECOND EDITION

Grant W. Sharpe

Outdoor Recreation
College of Forest Resources
University of Washington
Seattle, Washington

175 YEARS OF PUBLISHING

1807 **JW** 1982

JOHN WILEY & SONS
New York   Chichester   Brisbane   Toronto   Singapore

Library of Congress Cataloging in Publication Data:

Main entry under title:

Interpreting the environment.

   Includes index.
    1. Natural history—Study and teaching.
2. Nature study. 3. Park rangers. 4. National
parks and reserves. I. Sharpe, Grant William.
QH51.I5 1981   790'.06'8   81-10391
ISBN 0-471-09007-7   AACR2

Printed in the United States of America

10 9 8 7 6 5 4 3 2 1

CONTRIBUTOR'S LIST

GORDON A. BRADLEY
Associate Professor of Outdoor Recreation
  and Resource Planning
College of Forest Resources
University of Washington, Seattle

VON DEL CHAMBERLAIN
Astronomer
Space Science and Exploration Department
National Air and Space Museum
Smithsonian Institution
Washington, DC

WILLIAM W. DUNMIRE
Superintendent
Coulee Dam National Recreation Area
Former Chief
Division of Interpretation
National Park Service
U.S. Department of the Interior
Washington, DC

DONALD R. FIELD
Regional Chief Scientist
Pacific Northwest Region
National Park Service, Cooperative Studies
  Unit and Professor, Outdoor Recreation
  College of Forest Resources
University of Washington, Seattle

INGER L. GARRISON
Consultant
Living Interpretation and Cultural Affairs
College Station, Texas

CHARLES P. GEBLER
Superintendent
Stephen P. Mather Training Center
National Park Service
U.S. Department of the Interior
Harpers Ferry, West Virginia

ANNE HARRISON
Public Information Officer
Rocky Mountain Forest and Range Experi-
  ment Station
USDA Forest Service
Ft. Collins, Colorado

RON W. HODGSON
Outdoor Recreation Planner
U.S. Army Corps of Engineers
Waterways Experiment Station
Vicksburg, Mississippi

RICHARD A. KUEHNER
Recreational Planner
Department of Interpretation and Recreation
Fish and Wildlife Service
U.S. Department of the Interior
Portland, Oregon

PAUL A. MCINTOSH
Interpretive Specialist
Forest Service
U.S. Department of Agriculture
Juneau, Alaska

A. SIDNEY MALBON
Landscape Architect and Supervisory Out-
  door Recreation Planner
Northwest Regional Office
National Park Service
U.S. Department of the Interior
Seattle, Washington

ROBERT MICHAEL PYLE
Consultant to International Union for Conservation of Nature and Natural Resources
Gray's River, Washington

LAWRENCE RAKESTRAW
Professor of History and Forestry
Michigan Technological University
Houghton, Michigan

PAUL H. RISK
Associate Professor
Recreation and Parks
The Pennsylvania State University
University Park, Pennsylvania

DONALD H. ROBINSON
Regional Interpretive Specialist (Retired)
Southeast Region
National Park Service
U.S. Department of the Interior
Atlanta, Georgia

GRANT W. SHARPE
Professor of Outdoor Recreation
College of Forest Resources
University of Washington, Seattle

SPENCER J. SMITH-WHITE
Senior Interpretation Officer
National Parks and Wildlife Service of New
  South Wales
Sydney, Australia

MYRON D. SUTTON
Assistant Chief (Retired)
Division of International Affairs
National Park Service
U.S. Department of the Interior
Washington, DC

J. ALAN WAGAR
Urban Forestry Research
Forest Service
U.S. Department of Agriculture
Berkeley, California

HAROLD E. WALLIN
Chief Naturalist (Retired)
Cleveland Metropolitan Parks and Adjunct
  Assistant Professor
College of Urban Affairs
Cleveland State University
Cleveland, Ohio

HOWARD E. WEAVER
Curator
Crossroads Village
Genessee County Parks and Recreation
Flint, Michigan

GARY B. WETTERBERG
Coordinator of Western Hemisphere Activi-
  ties
International Park Affairs Division
National Park Service
U.S. Department of the Interior
Washington, DC

"I'll interpret the rocks, learn the language of flood, storm and the avalanche. I'll acquaint myself with the glaciers and wild gardens, and get as near the heart of the world as I can."

John Muir
Yosemite Valley
March, 1871

FOREWORD
TO THE FIRST EDITION

Our restless population, faced with an increasingly complex society and troubled environment, is turning more than ever before to the nation's public lands for a leisure-time alternative to daily turmoil. In a single generation we have seen visits to areas of the National Park System alone swell from 33 million in 1950 to 217 million in 1974. That number increases manyfold when parks at all levels of jurisdiction are taken into account.

Park administrators at every level share a common objective: to improve the quality of experience that visitors may enjoy in their area. And, as administrators, we know that when people visit our parks, whether a world-famous national park or a local site with more modest credentials, their experience will be importantly shaped by the interpretive services and facilities they find there.

Today we view interpretation not as the luxury it may have been considered in the past, but as a cornerstone of good park management. For interpretive programs not only foster an awareness and understanding of park features, but they also present an opportunity to affect the attitudes of visitors about lands held in public trust and about their total environment.

Environmental interpretation has evolved into a discipline requiring its practitioners to be professional in the fullest sense. Interpreters must bring to their jobs a professional competence in subject matter; they must have a mastery of the increasingly sophisticated tools of the craft; and, above all, they must have a complete grasp of the art of communicating with people. For nearly a generation the profession has been guided conceptually and philosophically by the teachings of Freeman Tilden, through his classic, *Interpreting Our Heritage*. But until now, no single volume has addressed the need to make plain how interpretation is applied on a day-to-day working basis.

Resource managers, professional interpreters, and students and educators in this field have long waited for a book of this kind that would lay out the working methods of environmental interpretation. The editor and author of six chapters, Dr. Grant Sharpe, brings to this book a wealth of personal experience in interpretation, dating from his early years as a naturalist with the National Park Service to his present position as a distinguished educator. He wisely has drawn from nearly two dozen nationally recognized experts, men and women with experience at nearly every level of field and academic interpretation, to author many of the individual chapters.

The title, *Interpreting the Environment,* is most apt, for it establishes that park and outdoor interpretation must embody a total-environment approach leading to a greater appreciation of natural and cultural surroundings and an understanding of the processes linking each to the whole environment.

All who are concerned with communicating park and environmental values will applaud the authors and publisher in producing this comprehensive volume. The end result can only be a raising of the standard of interpretive excellence in our parks.

Gary Everhardt
Former Director
National Park Service

PREFACE

The principles and methods cited in this textbook have applications to many interests: the college classroom, the public recreation agencies at all levels, and the vast and varied private sector. Interpretive programs are no longer a novelty; the public expects such services and is able to judge the quality of these programs with growing sophistication.

The purpose of this book is to share ideas with the managers, planners, and interpreters of parks, forests, refuges, and equivalent areas, not just in North America, but on all continents. The authors recognize the impracticality of transplanting North American solutions to interpretive problems elsewhere in the world. Each country, with its own customs and traditions and multitude of unique problems, must develop its own interpretive program in a manner that best suits its needs. However, the practices herein can be adapted, with some modifications, to any country.

A brief look at the table of contents will reveal the variety of ideas to be shared. The titles should appeal both to beginning interpreters, wondering what it's all about, and to "old hands" looking for new ideas. The various authors were chosen because of their expertise in particular fields. They have presented traditional methods, along with the innovative and experimental.

Parks and equivalent areas are more than places to play, picnic, and camp. They are places to learn and to be inspired. Not all areas have superlative features, but ecological processes are taking place everywhere, and good interpretation can stimulate interest in some very ordinary areas, as well as save attractive areas from overuse and misuse. We hope, through this book, to further good interpretation.

The authors gratefully acknowledge the invaluable assistance given by many colleagues. We are particularly indebted to the following individuals who provided information, reviewed sections of this book, or helped in some other significant way:

Roger W. Allin, Katherine D. Athanas, James K. Baird, Dennis R. Baker, Paul L. Beck, Jacque Beechel, Kenneth Begay, Nelson Bernard, John W. Brainerd, D. Scott Brayton, C. Frank Brockman, David L. Brown, Harold C. Bryant, Wayne W. Bryant, James R. Butler, William H. Carr, Gabriel Cherem, Roger Contor, David A. Dankel, Ned Danson, William C. Dillinger, Toni Dutch, Roland Eisenbeis, Garrett C. Eppley, Gunnar Fagerlund, Rosco Files, Paul R. Frandsen, Glenn D. Gallison, Donna B. Gebler, Jack Geyer, Charles M. Goethe, John M. Good, Eva L. Gordon, H. Raymond Gregg, D. Robert Hakala, Robert A. Huggins, Glen Kaye, Ken and Lillian Harrison, Arthur A. Hathaway, Jean Hendered, Glenn L. Hinsdale, Mark Hogan, Neil Johannsen, Steven T. Karpiak, Jr., George J. Knudsen, Frank Kowski, Robert Lovegren, Bing Lucas, Ian Mahood, David McIntyre, Helene J. Malbon, Alan Mebane, Norman Messinger, Loye Holmes Miller, Patricia A. Milliren, William P. Mott, Roland Nagel, Chris Nelson, Jack Nicol, Charles H. Odegaard, Doris I. Omundson, E. Laurence Palmer, Adrian Phillips, Richard L. Perfrement, George Quimby, Louis Ritrovato, James Richardson, George W. Robertson, Ralph Rudeen, Ron Russo, Marc Sagan, Janice M. Schneider, Steve Starlund, Jim Stevenson, Dwight Stork, Lloyd E. Surles, Louise M. Testor, Dale Thompson, S. Ross Tocher, William G. Vinal, J. V. K. Wagar, Thomas R. Waggener, William Webb, Ralph White, Arthur Wilcox, George T. Wilson, Norman Wilson, Harold Wood, Don Yeager, and Bill Young.

In a project of this kind, many reviews and revisions are necessary, requiring close cooperation between the various authors and the editor. All must be patient, and the spirit of compromise is often invoked, while deadlines threaten and life presents its daily problems. I am grateful to the contributors for their cheerful cooperation and hard work.

This second edition incorporates the numerous suggestions made by users of the first edition. Of particular help have been the suggestions made by Leon Buist, University of Nevada, at Reno, John Hanna, Texas A. & M., and Paul Risk and Jerry Elliott, Pennsylvania State University. Most chapters have been revamped to reflect recent developments.

The most significant change is the addition of Chapter 24, "Historical Interpretation," by Dr. Lawrence Rakestraw. This becomes a companion to the chapters on sky and marine interpretation, representing previously neglected areas of specialized interpretive endeavor. Another contributor to the writing team is Dr. Ron Hodgson, who brings to the book his communications skills, particularly in Chapter 7, "Information Duty."

As in the previous edition, the book emphasizes the conventional approaches to interpretation, those methods that have been field tested and proven successful. Once these basic forms are mastered, the innovative interpreter can experiment with new ways to approach the interpretive task.

The imaginative chapter title illustrations were done by Richard J. Cliffton, Chief of Interpretive Services, Washington State Parks. The skills of the people in the Audio-Visual Photo Lab at the University of Washington were of tremendous help in the reproduction of many of the photos used in the book. A salute goes to the outdoor recreation students at the University of Washington, who contributed in numerous ways.

I also thank the participants of the International Seminars on Administration of National Parks and Equivalent Reserves who, over the years, opened my eyes to interpretive problems and approaches around the world, and thus confirmed the need for this book.

Finally, I give very special recognition to my wife, Wenonah Finch Sharpe, for her many hours of editing during all phases of the preparation of this book.

Grant W. Sharpe
Seattle, Washington

CONTENTS

PART I   THE INTERPRETIVE PROCESS

PART II   THE TECHNIQUES OF INTERPRETATION

Personal or Attended Services

Nonpersonal or Unattended Services

PART I
THE INTERPRETIVE PROCESS

Not having an interpreter in a park is like inviting a guest to your house, opening the door, and then disappearing.

William H. Carr

CHAPTER 1

AN OVERVIEW OF INTERPRETATION

Grant W. Sharpe

WHAT IS INTERPRETATION?

Interpretation is a service for visitors to parks, forests, refuges, and similar recreation areas. Though visitors to these areas come for relaxation and inspiration, many also wish to learn about the area's natural and cultural resources. These resources comprise the geological processes, animals, plants, ecological communities, and history and prehistory of humans. Interpretation is the communication link between the visitor and these resources (Frontispiece).

Interpretation has been defined in several ways, some of which are included here. *Freeman Tilden* describes interpretation in his book *Interpreting Our Heritage* as: "An educational activity which aims to reveal meaning and relationships through the use of original objects, by firsthand experience, and by illustrative media, rather than simply to communicate factual information." [11]

Harold Wallin, Chief Naturalist for the Cleveland Metropolitan Parks, tells us interpretation is . . . "The helping of the visitor to feel something that the interpreter feels—a sensitivity to the beauty, complexity, variety and interrelatedness of the environment; a sense of wonder; a desire to know. It should help the visitor develop a feeling of being at home in the environment. It should help the visitor develop perception." [12]

Yorke Edwards, of Canada, describes interpretation as being a combination, in different amounts, of at least six things:

"It is an information service . . . a guiding service . . . an educational service . . . an entertainment service . . . a propaganda service . . . an inspirational service."

"Interpretation aims at giving people new understanding, new insights, new enthusiasms, new interests . . . . A good interpreter is a sort of Pied Piper, leading people easily into new and fascinating worlds that their senses never really penetrated before. He needs three basic attributes: knowledge, enthusiasm, and a bit of the common touch."[5]

Don Aldridge, of Scotland, at the Second World Park Conference in Grand Teton National Park defined interpretation as ". . . the art of explaining the place of man in his environment, to increase visitor or public awareness of the importance of this relationship, and to awaken a desire to contribute to environmental conservation."[1]

According to *The Countryside Recreation Glossary* (England), interpretation is "the process of developing a visitor's interest in and enjoyment and understanding of an area, or part of an area, by describing and explaining its characteristics and their inter-relationships."[4]

These definitions agree in several aspects and are well-thought-out summaries of the interpretive task. This book will go a step further and also consider interpretation as a management tool. The management aspect of interpretation is often overlooked by the interpretive specialist.

THE OBJECTIVES OF INTERPRETATION

Interpretation seeks to achieve three objectives. The first or primary objective of interpretation is to assist the visitor in developing a keener awareness, appreciation, and understanding of the area he or she is visiting. Interpretation should help to make the visit a rich and enjoyable experience (Fig. 1-1).

The second objective of interpretation is to accomplish management goals. It can be done in two ways. First, interpretation can encourage thoughtful use of the recreation resource on the part of the visitor, helping reinforce the idea that parks are special places requiring special behavior. Second, interpretation can be used to minimize human impact on the resource in a variety of ways.

The third objective of interpretation is to promote public understanding of an agency's goals and objectives. Every agency or corporation has a message to convey. Well-done interpretation favorably promotes the image of the agency that supplies it. If it is overdone, the message is labeled propaganda, rather than interpretation or public information.

THE PHILOSOPHY OF INTERPRETATION

For centuries teachers and writers have been assisting people in "discovering" and appreciating the out-of-doors. In early writings there was an element of interpretation when the writer passed on his or her impressions or observations to the

FIG. 1-1. The primary objective of interpretation is to assist the visitor in developing a keener awareness, appreciation, and understanding of an area. In this scene interpretation is lacking, and the visitor's questions go unanswered. Big Sur, California. (Photo by Grant W. Sharpe.)

recipient, the reader, who may never have been near the feature being interpreted. In present-day interpretation we work more closely with the feature itself, are in direct contact with the recipient, and have a variety of media to rely on.

This book is not intended to be a philosophical approach to interpretation, but rather a practical one—a book concerned not so much with the *why* of interpretation but more with the *what* and *how*. The *why* of interpretation has already been dealt with by Freeman Tilden in his book *Interpreting Our Heritage*. Tilden's book is particularly useful to those with some experience in the field of interpretation. It is a statement on the ideology of interpretation, or as one of my students put it, "an interpretation of interpretation." The reader is encouraged to explore this recognized authority's work on interpretive philosophy.

INTERPRETIVE POLICY

Most organizations, in the course of their development, adhere either closely or loosely to some written or implied statement of policy. Agencies that become involved with interpretation should see that this aspect of their activities is covered in the general policy statement. All too frequently an interpretive program is based on the enthusiasm of an individual rather than developed from a well-defined policy. A policy statement is recommended if an interpretive program is to survive.

Depending on the organization, the statement of policy may be very general or it may be so detailed that it is regarded as the final word. A large organization, such as the United States National Park Service, has too diversified a program to cover all activities, and the policy statements are very broad. In a small organization such as a municipal park system, the policy statement may spell out exactly what can or cannot be done.

An agency with a high-quality interpretive program usually has a clearly established interpretive policy set forth in its administrative manual. In this way the objectives of the interpretive program are spelled out, monies are allocated when the budget is written, and long-range interpretive planning and implementation are made possible.

Two examples of policy statements follow:
Policy (National Parks of Canada, House of Commons, 1964)

1. *Educating the public in the purpose of national parks and how to use, know and enjoy them is recognized as one of our basic purposes.*
2. *Interpretive services and qualified naturalists are essential to encourage and assist the public to understand, appreciate and enjoy all forms of nature which are preserved in these sanctuaries.*
3. *Education and interpretation will involve planned and co-ordinated use of various aids, such as publications, photographs, special structures, etc., and the assistance of wardens and others.*
4. *Museums, where desirable, should exemplify and illustrate natural history and historical values directly related to the park and its purposes. Museums should be provided and administered by the Department.*[8]

Policy (Washington State Parks and Recreation Commission)

It is the intent of the interpretive program to acquire, preserve, interpret, and mark areas within the state embracing the field of history, geology, an-

thropology, and ecology. A significant part of interpretation is the development of interpretive centers, display shelters, interpretive trails and markers. All these activities are to preserve and interpret the heritage of the state through the state park system and to provide a learning experience for greater understanding and enjoyment by the park visitor.[9]

INTERPRETATION AND PUBLIC RELATIONS

As was pointed out in the third objective of interpretation, the public image of an agency or organization is important. Public opinion influences the gaining of approval for the master plan, obtaining of financial support, and acquisition of additional land.

The purpose of public relations is to inform the public of your programs and services. Without this, often the only matters that get into print are controversial ones. This frequently means that your image is being shaped by your critics. Once an unfavorable impression is formed in the public mind, it is difficult to eradicate, even though the facts of the case may be quite at variance with those reported.

Some organizations have public relations staffs who devote themselves exclusively to promoting good relations. Most park staffs are not so equipped and may depend on the interpretive staff to handle this function.

The public is more likely to accept a sound but controversial plan if they understand the reasons for it and the possible consequences of not adopting such a plan. An astute staff will communicate its plans and purposes and thus gain the public trust. This involves the use of newspapers, magazines, radio, and television, as discussed in Chapter 17.

THE INTERPRETIVE PROGRAM

The overall interpretive effort is known as the *interpretive program.* It includes the personnel, facilities, and all interpretive activities of an organization, agency, or individual area. The interpretive program relates the natural or cultural phenomena of a park or equivalent area to the visitors and utilizes a wide variety of methods to present this subject matter. The interpretive specialist and the media form the link between the phenomena and the visitor. Interpretation is more than mere identification (Figs. 1-2 and 1-3).

Much of the day-to-day interpretation is carried out by seasonal employees, persons who work only during the heavy visitor-use season. These persons translate human history and scientific knowledge of the earth sciences into easily understood terms. Although the seasonal staff does an excellent job, they are not expected to plan and develop the interpretive program. This is carried out by

FIG. 1-2. Interpretation is more than mere identification. The label above, unfortunately nailed to the tree, represents identification. (Photo by Grant W. Sharpe.)

more experienced, permanent interpreters in coordination with other staff members.

THE BENEFITS OF INTERPRETATION

Interpretation provides many benefits:

1. Interpretation contributes directly to the enrichment of visitor experiences.
2. Interpretation makes visitors aware of their place in the total environment and gives them a better understanding of the complexities of coexisting with that environment.
3. Interpretation may broaden the visitor's horizons beyond the park or forest boundary, giving a greater understanding of the total natural resources picture.
4. Interpretation informs the public and an informed public may make wiser decisions on matters related to natural resources management.

FIG. 1-3. A comparison with the label in Fig. 1-2. This example is brief, has a simple message that relates to familiar objects, and is supported on its own post. (Photo by Grant W. Sharpe.)

5. Interpretation may reduce the unnecessary destruction of park property, resulting in lower maintenance and replacement costs.
6. Interpretation provides a means of moving people subtly from sensitive areas to sites that can better sustain heavy human impact, thus protecting the environment.
7. Interpretation is a way to improve public image and establish public support.
8. Interpretation may instill in visitors a sense of pride in their country or in the region's culture and heritage.
9. Interpretation may assist in the successful promotion of parks where tourism is essential to an area's or country's economy.
10. Interpretation may be effective in preserving a significant historic site or natural area by arousing citizen concern.
11. Interpretation may motivate the public to take action to protect their environment in a sensible and logical way.

THE VISITOR

The visitor is the primary reason for the interpretive program. The fact that visitors vary greatly in age, education, cultural backgrounds, and experience presents a challenge to the interpreter. It is these *visitor characteristics* that establish the level and content of the interpretive message. The *visit characteristics* also have an influence on the interpretive program. For example, the number of people in the group, the number of repeat visits, and the length of stay all influence the cycle of interpretive offerings.[7]

Visitors come to parks and forests and other recreation areas for various reasons, but primarily for enjoyment. Researchers Field and Wagar tell us visitors want informality and social interaction.[6] Interpretation, therefore, should, along with its other functions, enhance social interaction.

The visiting public is a diverse group, and interpretation aimed at one group of visitors may not be effective with another group. Interpretive efforts, where possible, should be varied to meet the diverse interests and age levels of the visitors.

Consideration should also be given to the geographical origin of visitors. Some areas attract mostly "locals"; some have many visitors coming from great distances. The reasons for this include such factors as nearness of population centers and the availability of transportation and lodging facilities, as well as the inherent attraction of the site.

Local visitors may have a different attitude than visitors from great distances. People on the periphery of an area often believe that they know all about it, and seldom participate in interpretive activities except to tour the visitor center when they are showing friends or relatives the local attractions. Possibly living close to a natural feature tends to dull one's sense of wonder. In contrast, people who have spent considerable funds and time to reach a place often try to get the most out of their visit and participate more in interpretive functions.

The interpretive program is actually an educational program—but it must make its points more quickly and less formally than the usual educational offering. The visitors make the visit on their own time. When they participate in the interpretive program, they do so voluntarily, which is a significant departure from the traditional educational experience.

The knowledgeable interpretive specialist considers all aspects of visitor and visit characteristics and plans the interpretive program accordingly.

THE INTERPRETIVE SPECIALIST

Interpretation is only one aspect of the total management function of an area used for outdoor recreation. Although the administrator of an area is ultimately responsible for interpretation, a successful interpretive program needs a qualified supervisor, someone directly responsible to the administrator for all activities related to interpretation. This person, traditionally called the Chief Naturalist or Interpretive Specialist, is largely concerned with the development and coordination of the overall interpretive program.

The interpretive specialist, as we will call him or her, often has one or more full-time assistants, and this staff is augmented by several seasonals. During the heavy visitor-use season, as mentioned earlier, much of the day-to-day interpretive work is carried on by seasonal interpreters. The different resource management areas vary in their organizational structure, thus the lines of authority for the interpretive staff are variable.

It should be emphasized that every member of the agency staff, even concessionaire employees, can play an important role in interpretation when they come in contact with the visitor. Frequently, staff meetings are held to discuss division matters. It is up to the interpretive specialist to insist that he or she be permitted to participate in these occasionally to see to it that all employees are adequately informed of the basic methods of communicating with the public. This improves employee morale as well as public relations.

EQUAL OPPORTUNITY IN INTERPRETATION

As in most natural resource positions, men have traditionally dominated the field of interpretation. However, women have been directly involved in interpretation since about 1917 when Esther Burnell was licensed by the federal government as a nature guide in what is now Rocky Mountain National Park, in Colorado. Even before this, women were involved in the field as nature writers, illustrators, and natural scientists. Records show there have been a few women employed through the years as interpreters in local, state, and federal agencies (Fig. 1-4).

In earlier years, it was difficult for women to be accepted in most outdoor-related positions for a variety of discriminatory reasons. Women were stereotyped as being fragile and unable to carry out tasks such as forest fire fighting and law enforcement. Civil service exams for entry positions have traditionally been open only to men. This condition prevailed in some states as late as 1970. For these and other reasons it has been difficult for women to be accepted in the field of interpretation.

Opportunities for women interpreters opened up in the National Park Service during the mid-1960s. Omundson (1974) found that by 1974 there were 84 women in the field of interpretation compared with 421 men. In the U.S. Forest Service, women are employed in 17 of 112 permanent interpretive positions. With the rising demand for equal employment and new opportunities in a variety of interpretive areas, the number of women employed in interpretation appears to be rapidly increasing.[10]

FIG. 1-4. Ranger Naturalist Herma Baggley, an interpretive specialist with the National Park Service in 1929. (Photo courtesy of Yellowstone National Park.)

THE INTERPRETIVE ROLE WITHIN THE ORGANIZATION

Organizational structures and names vary among agencies, but the interpretive program is usually in a division or department separate from other functions.

Because administrators of outdoor recreation areas often do not have interpretive backgrounds, they may not fully understand the work of the interpretive division. Thus, the need frequently arises to "sell the program to the boss."

The interpretive staff has the problem of maintaining good working relations with other parts of the organization. Their combination of highly specialized training, great enthusiasm for their work, and close public contact may cause jealousy among other employees and create the impression that the interpreters are "getting all the glory." This situation presents a challenge to interpreters; they are specialists in communications and should be able to use this skill within their own organization.

The special nature of their work also provides interpreters with opportunities to assist other units of their organization. Since the interpreter is frequently the visitor's only contact with an official, visitors may air their grievances about many matters at the time of contact. For this reason it is essential that the interpreter have a sound understanding of park policy and a firsthand knowledge of the functioning of the park organization.

Visitor feedback is essential to good park administration, and interpreters in their day-to-day contact with the visitor are in an excellent position to receive this feedback and pass it along to their administrators and co-workers. If this is not done in a tactful constructive manner, it may do more harm than good.

OPPORTUNITIES FOR INTERPRETATION

Opportunities for on-site interpretation exist almost anywhere people congregate for leisure-time activities. Public lands used for outdoor recreation, such as parks, forests, and wildlife refuges, are prime examples. Interpretation is also utilized at historic sites, museums, nature centers, visitor centers, and other locations not necessarily related to land resources.

Many opportunities are neglected or overlooked. Lands owned and controlled by forest industries, mining firms, public and private utilities, and works of engineering are examples of areas where on-site interpretation could be utilized. Some of these groups are beginning to develop interpretive programs aimed at explaining their company's role in environmental matters (Fig. 1-5).

Interpretation is often neglected on vacation farms, rehabilitated stripmined lands, and youth-oriented camps. It is generally poorly done on transportation facilities and such sites as historical homes, castles, and fortresses. Interpretation is, unfortunately, lacking on most park lands supervised by local (county and municipal) government, except perhaps in botanical or zoological gardens.

Interpretation is also carried on away from the site itself. Contacts are made by the interpretive staff with school groups, clubs, and various other organizations who may or may not plan to visit the area being interpreted. Radio, television, newspapers, and magazines are other examples of off-site interpretation which will be discussed in greater detail in Chapter 17.

FIG. 1-5. A beginning has been made. Here a private electric utility has channeled people's activities to this platform on a cliff overlooking a waterfall. Future plans include interpretation from this overlook. Snoqualmie Falls, Washington. (Photo by Grant W. Sharpe.)

Most presently established interpretive programs could be upgraded by making use of current research and new techniques. Public demand and interest is high, and audiences are more sophisticated and critical than in former times. Interpretive opportunities should be fully exploited by the most modern and informed methods, which does not always mean more complicated and expensive media. Simplicity and fresh thinking are often the most effective ingredients.

INTERPRETATION AS A MANAGEMENT TOOL

In our discussion of interpretive objectives we noted that interpretation may be used to accomplish management goals. For our purposes here we will divide those goals into four parts: recreation benefits, resource protection, visitor protection, and law enforcement.

Recreation Benefits

A well-designed and managed interpretive program has the potential of both increasing the recreation benefits generated by recreation resources and of substantially reducing the costs of recreation resource management. Recreation benefits can be increased by better matching of available resources and visitor needs, reducing conflicts among competing uses, increasing carrying capacity by making unwanted encounters less likely, and influencing users to be less obtrusive. Interpretive services can help increase positive economic impacts on local communities by providing visitors with information on commercial services available. They can also improve public relations by directing users to avoid trespass on private lands or interference with other resource use such as logging and grazing operations. Recreationists are also kept informed of what is happening in their favorite recreation area when a castrophe occurs (Fig. 1-6).

Resource Protection

Interpretive specialists must realize that assisting the manager to protect the resource is part of their job, along with dispensing factual information about park geology, animals, and vegetation. Interpretive techniques can be used in attempts

FIG. 1-6. Exhibits in a temporary visitor center located near Mount St. Helens tell the public of the volcanoe's destructive force. Gifford Pinchot National Forest, Washington. (Photo by Grant W. Sharpe.)

to control problems such as an unauthorized fossil collecting, defacing Indian writings, littering, driving vehicles off park roads, and in camper etiquette matters dealing with, for example, leashes for pets, pets in swimming areas, alcohol consumption, noise disturbances, careless stock handling, misuse of fire, and destruction of park vegetation. Interpretation may also be used to inform the public of management objectives in situations such as timber harvesting, changes in fire management, or other controversial policy matters where public understanding is desirable.

Visitor Protection

Interpretation can also be used to warn visitors of dangerous situations, such as the presence of wild animals, poisonous snakes or plants, and danger from strong currents, rising tides, or flash floods.

Imaginative efforts to help reduce visitor discomfort, injuries, or deaths will be appreciated at all levels of agency management. Interpreters who ignore visitor- and resource-protection obligations are simply not doing their job properly.

Law Enforcement

Interpretation can provide substantial assistance to law enforcement through educational persuasion. Consider the example of rules and regulations. To be effective, rules and regulations must be publicized and enforced. This is ordinarily the task of the administrator and law enforcement personnel. Interpretation can, however, state the desired behavior and point out the ecological consequences of erosion from trampling, superfluous and impromptu trails, wildflower picking, carelessness with fire, and other aspects of depreciative behavior (Fig. 1-7). Interpretation can explain to visitors why rules and regulations exist. Most transgressions against rules, such as picking wildflowers, collecting rock or animal specimens, and "shortcutting" trails are done in ignorance rather than malice.

Visitors to recreation areas are often in strange surroundings. Frequently, their behavior is less than desirable from the manager's point of view, but from the visitors' viewpoint there may be nothing wrong with their behavior. After leaving home and often traveling great distances, getting into trouble is the last thing on visitors' minds. They want to enjoy themselves, and this may mean unknowingly breaking a few rules and regulations. Also, visitors often consider themselves to be above particular rules.[3] Basically responsible but ill-informed and temporarily inconsiderate people create many problems in public parks. An interpretive program that recognizes its opportunity to educate well-meaning but uninformed visitors and that clearly deals with the care and appreciation of the natural environment should have an immediate and positive effect.

FIG. 1-7. Interpretation informs visitors of the ecological consequences of leaving designated trails. The sign says, "PLEASE STAY ON THE TRAIL—The delicate mosses and other tiny plants struggling to grow here face complete destruction if trampled or disturbed." Mount Rainier National Park. (Photo by Grant W. Sharpe.)

OBSTACLES TO INTERPRETATION

Not every park or equivalent area has an interpretive program. It may be lacking because of inadequate funding, low or nonexistent employee interest, or a poor supply of talent on the staff. Also, agency policy may make no provision for it. There may have been no provision for it in the overall park plan, which is related directly to the fact that there may have been no stated objectives concerning interpretation. Planners of parks, park boards, commissions, or other guiding bodies need to better understand the scope and potential of interpretation. Too frequently interpretation is an afterthought rather than an integral part of a park planning and implementation process. Interpretation should be a part of the planning process because without it a park is not providing maximum benefits to the visitor.

A common excuse for lack of interpretation is the assumption by administrators that vandals lurk behind every tree. Vandalism and theft do preclude certain kinds of interpretation from being utilized in some situations, but the majority of interpretive devices survive for many years. This requires that the device be properly designed, routinely maintained, and strategically located. When these conditions are met, vandalism should not be a precluding factor. Vandalism is discussed in Chapter 25.

INTERPRETIVE PLANNING

Interpretation without adequate planning may result in an overlap or omission of pertinent information; or worse yet, it may lead to the deterioration of a feature through inappropriate use. The interpretive plan should be available when management decisions are made. In fact, a comprehensive interpretive plan should be a prerequisite to funding the interpretive program.

The interpretive plan should be worked out carefully by the interpretive planner and a team of resource management specialists with varied backgrounds. The interpretive specialist, if one is on the staff at this stage, should also participate for it is this person who will have the responsibility of carrying out the interpretive program.

Interpretive planning follows a series of seven logical phases or steps: determining objectives, taking inventory, analyzing data, synthesizing alternatives, developing a plan, implementing a plan, and evaluating and revising the plan.

First stage objectives should be feasible and specific. Once the objectives have been determined, one is ready to begin the inventory stage.

The second phase, or interpretive inventory, serves to identify and locate before any development takes place those natural and cultural amenities that are significant to the area's interpretive story. Every area has a natural history to relate. There may also be oddities, fragile or irreplaceable objects, rare or unusual species of plant or animal communities, ecological relics, or geological processes to be interpreted. These significant land and water resources, as well as evidence of human activities, must be located, identified, and described. The inventory determines their extent and number (Fig. 1-8).

A sound plan must be based on accurate information. Interpretive planners can seldom be knowledgeable in all disciplines; and, as so often happens, the area may be new to them. Still, data must be gathered if a plan is to mature.

Data on the area can be obtained from a variety of sources. By walking the area, keeping daily records, doing library research, and asking questions, the interpretive planner can learn quickly. Local biology teachers, historians, hobbyists, and members of bird clubs or garden clubs can contribute information.

For specialized input it is possible to seek out geologists, soil specialists, foresters, botanists, and other resource persons. Graduate students from nearby universities can be most helpful, particularly if they are looking for research projects on the natural and human history of an area.

Many features will be worthy of interpretation; however, not all are suitable. If adequate protection cannot be assured for a fragile object or area, it should not be considered for inclusion in the interpretive program.

The third phase, the analysis of interpretive opportunities, utilizes the information gathered in the inventory stage. The specific elements are examined carefully, and basic themes selected. The themes will be related to the area's ecological,

FIG. 1-8. The interpretive inventory serves to locate and identify those natural and cultural amenities that are significant to an area's interpretive story. Linville Falls, Blue Ridge Parkway, North Carolina. (Photo by Grant W. Sharpe.)

historical, geological, or archeological resources. The next step to consider is the selection of media—those facilities and services necessary to tell the interpretive story. Media include the many personal and nonpersonal means of communicating with visitors. At the conclusion of this stage the planner should know the limitations and opportunities of the area.

The fourth or synthesis phase starts with a review of the objectives, inventory, and analysis phases. After looking at present conditions and trends, environmental concerns, and organization and user needs, several alternative courses of action are proposed. These are different plans for the same area. The manager or other decision makers then weigh the positive and negative factors of each and select the most appropriate alternative, which becomes the plan.

The fifth phase is the alternative chosen from phase four. This is the *plan*—the assembling of the final document that discusses the purpose, objectives, principles, visitor data, and organization structure and includes supporting maps, lists, controls, development and operational details, and other basic data.

The sixth phase is plan implementation and includes the careful scheduling of details to insure the proper sequence of actions so that development may take place.

The seventh and final stage is plan evaluation and revision. This is essentially a monitoring program to evaluate user impacts on the resources and the effect of the program on the visitors. After the initial review is complete and revisions are made, periodic reviews are still necessary to update the plan.

Public involvement during the seven phases is strongly urged. The plan should not be a surprise to those who are supposed to benefit from it. Citizen participation in the decision-making process must be a reality rather than just a paper policy.

The planning phases will be discussed in greater depth in Chapter 4, "The Interpretive Plan," and Chapter 5, "Selecting the Interpretive Media."

INTERPRETIVE QUALITY

The success of an interpretive program often depends on the quality and appropriateness of the media in use. A heavy dose of detailed, lengthy, technical information will quickly bore most visitors. An uninspiring evening program, a deteriorating self-guided trail, or a poorly conducted walk will do little to encourage further visitor participation in interpretive activities. A poor program may even create an unfavorable public image. Thus, complete absence of interpretation may be preferable to a low-quality program.

FINANCING INTERPRETATION

Interpretation costs money. Insufficient funds seem to be a problem common to most interpretive programs, but there are still ways of carrying out the task.

First of all, the interpretive division must be identified within the organization and become a part of the budgetary process, as staff must be employed and equipment purchased. Without money nothing will happen.

The interpretive specialist must determine priorities. What gives the best visitor contact for the money? How does one weigh the importance of high visibility interpretation, such as installing a self-guided trail or providing some form of public contact, against that of gathering data, making study collections, or conducting long-range plans that have less visibility?

Interest in a program by politicians may also have some influence on the direction a program takes. A local politician with a pet interest could be a great asset

FIG. 1-9. Youthful volunteers carry the weight of the interpretive program at the Nature House. Thomas S. Francis Provincial Park, British Columbia. (Photo by Spencer Smith-White.)

in supporting a project. However, there are pitfalls. The political figure may be happy to cut the ribbon at the dedication, but uninterested in supporting the budget for upkeep.

Other support may be obtained from organizations with outdoor interests, such as garden clubs, scouting, or other youth groups (Fig. 1-9). The subject of funding and getting help from outside sources will be discussed in Chapter 6, "Management of the Interpretive Program."

INTERPRETATION AND COMMUNICATION

Interpretation is communicating ideas to visitors in outdoor recreation settings. Because communications material is interspersed throughout this book, only a few points are stressed here:

1. You must get and hold the attention of the visitor.
2. The experience of this communication must be rewarding to the visitor.
3. The visitor should be made to feel at ease.
4. Know with whom you are communicating.
5. The message must cater to diverse interests.
6. The message should touch people's lives.
7. The experience should be fun.
8. Do not assume that the visitor is always interested in what you have to say.
9. People in unfamiliar surroundings will tend to reject new ideas.
10. The size of the group has some effect on the learning experience.
11. Don't assume you will reach the visitor on first contact.

INTERPRETATION AND ENTERTAINMENT

Entertainment is not the primary objective of interpretive presentations, but good interpretation can and should be entertaining. Most interpretive audiences are free to leave at any time, and they may not stay if they are not interested. Excessive text material in an exhibit or a "lecture approach" to a talk will be associated with education, and the visitor may resist. In contrast, group singing or story telling at the beginning of a talk, or animation and innovative lighting in an exhibit, will be associated with entertainment. Washburne found that the dichotomy of education and entertainment parallels that of inertness and animation. An interpretive audience prefers those interpretive media that are more closely associated with entertainment.[13]

To hold the visitor's interest, interpretation must be more than routine explanation. There must be an element of excitement, "a feeling of expectancy, of surprise around the corner." As one interpreter put it, interpretation must have "snap, crackle, and pop." This presents the interpreter with a real challenge—that of educating and enlightening in a way that is entertaining while maintaining dignity and authority.

INTERPRETIVE RELEVANCY

Land managing agencies and corporations have their own stories to tell visitors. In the national parks of the United States, for example, interpretive programs focus on relevant natural and cultural history themes. By contrast, the interpretation in national recreation areas built on great reservoirs should deal with change brought about by the dams as well as the benefits, including recreation, that the stored water brings to people. Wildlife refuges should follow wildlife-related interpretive themes. In a commercial forest, the interpretation should be more concerned with the utilization of natural resources.

National forests, on the other hand, are utilized in a variety of ways, and many have superlative natural attractions (Fig. 1-10). Their interpretive themes, therefore, range from people's use of the forest to natural history, such as glaciation, erosion, cave formation, and tide-pool life.

In this way the visitors have a clearer understanding of the relevancy of each of these different land-managing institutions and their effect on, and relationship to, their own lives.

One cannot invite people to a park or forest for an interpretive experience and offer them only agency propaganda. If the intent is to hold the visitor's attention, the interpretive story must go beyond the agency message and include the significant natural and cultural features that the site offers.

FIG. 1-10.   A catastrophe occurred here, and the explanation of what happened is found in the interpretive program. Madison River Earthquake Area, Gallatin National Forest, Montana. (Photo by Grant W. Sharpe.)

FIG. 1-11. Environmental education and interpretation are difficult to separate. Here a young visitor on a field trip to a Quebec park is working on plant identification. (Photo courtesy of Quebec Government, Canada.)

ENVIRONMENTAL EDUCATION AND INTERPRETATION

Interpretive specialists and fellow employees in their respective outdoor recreation resource areas have long been involved in environmental matters. Even before the "ecology movement" gained prominence they were working with teachers and other groups in forest, wildlife, and soil conservation in what was collectively known as "conservation education."

Today environmental education includes all the traditional conservation disciplines plus such concerns as pollution, population, and energy problems. Interpreters must remember that the environmental problem of one group is all too often another group's employment base. The problem of air and water pollution, population control, and abusive land practices are all critical, complicated issues which should be handled in a constructive and objective manner. It is to be hoped that those in environmental education and interpretation will not take the easy route of condemnation of obvious mistakes, but will work to make everyone aware of the choices available and the costs that must be borne, whichever route is chosen.

Environmental education has been generally more to the forefront in environmental matters, as interpreters' tasks have kept them busy close to home both physically and politically. Too much isolation is to be deplored; interpreters must be concerned with local, regional, and national problems that require informed choices personally. They can no longer ignore what is happening upstream or downwind from the outdoor recreation resource. Even what is happening many miles away in crowded cities eventually affects his or her area in the form of urban visitor attitudes and behavior.

Separating interpretation from environmental education is difficult. In outdoor recreation we note that interpretation is mostly directed to visitors to natural resources areas, such as parks, forests, or wildlife areas, and is concerned with exploration of the resource in place as well as the management problems of such areas (Fig. 1-11). Environmental education, on the other hand, is largely directed toward school-age groups, and takes place in such widely diverse areas as schoolrooms, school yards, city streets, and on field trips to museums, parks, and forests.

Regardless of the technique, environmental education is not a substitute but should be regarded as an extension of interpretation. A more thorough coverage of environmental education and interpretation will be found in *Islands of Hope* by William E. Brown.[2]

REFERENCES CITED

1. Aldridge, Don. 1972. *Upgrading Park Interpretation and Communication With the Public,* Second World Conference on National Parks. Grand Teton National Park, Wyoming.
2. Brown, William E. 1971. *Islands of Hope,* National Recreation and Park Association, Washington, DC.

3. Campbell, Frederick L., John C. Hendee, and Roger Clark. 1968. "Law and Order in Public Parks." *Parks and Recreation.*

4. "Countryside Recreation Research Advisory Group" *1970 Countryside Recreation Glossary,* Countryside Commission, London, England.

5. Edwards, R. Y. 1965. "Park Interpretation," *Park News* **1** (1), 11–16. National and Provincial Parks Association of Canada, Toronto.

6. Field, Donald R., and J. Alan Wagar. 1972. *Visitor Groups and Interpretation in Parks and Other Leisure Settings,* Paper presented at Third Work Congress of Rural Sociology, Baton Rouge, LA.

7. Fischer, David W. 1966. "The Role of Interpretation," *Park Practice Guideline* **5** (66), 89–92.

8. National and Historic Parks Branch, 1969. *National Parks Policy,* Indian Affairs and Northern Development. Queens Printer for Canada, Ottawa.

9. Odegaard, Charles H. 1973. Director, Washington States Parks and Recreation Commission. Personal Correspondence.

10. Omundson, Doris I. 1974. *Women in Interpretation,* Presented at annual meeting of the Association of Interpretive Naturalists—Western Interpreters Association, Pacific Grove, CA.

11. Tilden, Freeman. 1967. *Interpreting Our Heritage,* The University of North Carolina Press, Chapel Hill.

12. Wallin, Harold E. 1965. *Interpretation: A Manual and Survey on Establishing a Naturalist Program.* Management Aids Bulletin No. 22. American Institute of Park Executives. National Recreation and Park Association, Arlington, VA.

13. Washburne, Randle F. 1971. Visitor Response to Interpretive Facilities at Five Visitor Centers. Unpublished master's thesis, University of Washington, Seattle.

CHAPTER 2

ORIGINS OF INTERPRETATION

Howard E. Weaver

GOETHE   COMENIUS   FREEMAN   CARR   TILDEN   Mather   PESTALOZZI

SOCRATES

BRYANT   MILLER

FROEBEL   Sir Izaak Walton

The roots of interpretation go deep into recorded history having been nourished by the fields of religion, philosophy, the natural sciences, education, literature, and the arts.

Undoubtedly it began through accounts of hunters, fishermen, and artisans of the Middle East and the Orient. Eventually Greek and Roman philosophers dared suggest natural causes for supernatural phenomena. Through application of scientific data, exploration and discovery, and record keeping, the profession and art of natural history interpretation has evolved.

Much of the early history of education compiled by Freeberg and Taylor for outdoor education is pertinent to natural history interpretation.[8] For example, Thales (640−546 BC) interpreted the water cycle and introduced practical astronomy; Democritus (584−500 BC) related sound to mathematics.

Socrates (469−399 BC) developed a method of questioning to seek out truth and form concepts, while Plato (429−348 BC) advocated the theory of unity and practice (the interrelationship of life and areas of learning, and learning by doing). Aristotle (384−322 BC) manifested great interest in the natural sciences and advocated the need for experience and discipline and emphasized the place of leisure in the educational process. He also attempted to utilize the objective, inductive method of reasoning.

Romans such as Cicero (106−43 BC), Horace (65−8 BC), and Quintilian (40−118 AD) influenced later educators by encouraging firsthand learning and sensory experience in learning. They also recognized the necessity of a desire to learn. Keatinge quotes Quintilian:

The acquisition of knowledge depends on the will to learn, and this cannot be forced. Through precepts the way is long and difficult, while through example it is short and practicable.[13]

More than a thousand years elapsed before scientists dared teach natural phenomena rather than a politically enforced religious dogma. Roger Bacon (1214–1294) popularized "useful knowledge" in his *Opus Majus;* Petrarch (1304–1372) revived the spirit of inquiry and promoted the sciences and arts; Erasmus (1467–1536) criticized empty verbalism and pleaded for a humanistic approach to learning. Nicholas Copernicus (1473–1543) provided a basis for modern astronomy, while Galileo (1564–1642) saw clearly the unchangeable relation between cause and effect.

Undoubtedly one of the most notable practitioners and exponents of nature and science education and interpretive methodology was John Amos (Komensky) Comenius (1592–1670) who championed sensory experiences and sense perception in imparting knowledge to children and facilitating understanding.[13] In his *Didactica Magna* of 1638, Comenius formulated a system of object teaching and urged that appeal be made to sight, touch, and the use of accurate models and pictures should the actual object be unavailable. He used a garden as a laboratory for learning, and his *Oribus Pictus* of 1658 was the first picture book for children. Comenius also demonstrated insight into what was to become the science of ecology.

Three centuries before Freeman Tilden presented six principles of interpretation in *Interpreting Our Heritage,* Comenius taught and practiced, as did others before him, the value of relating an object to the experiences of the student.[23] He also advocated a different approach when teaching children and adults.[13]

Sir Izaak Walton (1593–1683) interpreted stream conditions and cited the values of wholesome outdoor recreation in *The Compleat Angler* in 1653, while John Locke (1632–1704) insisted on the gaining of knowledge through experiment and observation in his *Essay* and *Thoughts Concerning Education.*

Keatinge further notes that Jean Jacques Rousseau (1712–1778), author of *Social Contract* and *Emile,* like Comenius, recognized that learning is facilitated by play and by direct experience through the senses. Likewise, John Bernard Basedow (1723–1790) championed informal education and less verbalization and utilized excursions into the neighborhood for educational purposes. Rousseau and Basedow greatly influenced Pestalozzi.

Gilbert White (1720–1793) of England set a standard of excellence in nature literature when he published his *Natural History of Selborne* in 1789. He keenly observed, described, and interpreted the flora and fauna of the English countryside.

Certainly one of the foremost early educators and methodologists was Johann Heinrich Pestalozzi (1746–1827) of Switzerland. Pinloche notes that Pestalozzi regarded sense perception as the supreme principle of instruction and the absolute foundation of knowledge. His pupils were taught to observe and form correct ideas on the relationship of things and express themselves clearly on what they saw and understood.[20]

According to White,[27] Frederick Froebel (1782–1852) of Germany improved on Pestalozzi's methods of object teaching. Gardening was the nucleus of Froebel's kindergarten that included the care of animals, native crafts, study collections, and visits to neighborhood workshops. Froebel taught the role of prey and predator and the responsibilities of humans toward animals. His book *The Education of Man* abounds in methodology and outdoor-related learning activities that influenced nature study and outdoor education.

EARLY NATURALISTS AND EXPLORERS

The geologic and faunistic wonders of America attracted European scientists and educators whose knowledge was indispensible in their cataloguing. They gravitated to Philadelphia, the earliest center of science in the United States. William G. Vinal[24] cites many early naturalists of the Philadelphia area such as William Penn whose *Green Country Town* in 1632 warrants Penn's reputation as a naturalist; Vinal also cites the work of early horticulturists such as Dr. Christopher Witt and Johan Kelpris who founded a botanical garden as did John Bartram (1699–1777) in 1728. Bartram and his son, William (1739–1823) are noted for their expedition into the Southeast. Their journals were published in William Bartram's *Travels* in 1791. Mark Catesby published the *Natural History of Carolina* in 1731, seven years before the great Swedish naturalist Carolus Linnaeus (1707–1778) published his *Genera Plantarum; Species Plantarum* was published in 1753. Sweden's Peter Kalm (1717–1779) also contributed much to American botany.

Benjamin Franklin (1706–1790) and Thomas Jefferson (1743–1826) set examples for scholarship, invention, and inquiry. Jefferson also encouraged the expeditions of André and François Michaux into the Ohio Valley and the western trek of Meriwether Lewis and William Clark.

Buley's excellent overview of early sciences in the United States includes mention of Philadelphia's botanical gardens and museums like those by Charles W. Peale in 1794, the Philadelphia Academy of Science led by Dr. Gerhard Troost of the Netherlands, and by Thomas Say (1787–1834), the first renowned American-born naturalist.[4] Philadelphia and the Ohio Valley attracted John James Audubon, Thomas Nuttall, the unique Constantine Rafinesque, and Scotland's William Maclure and Alexander Wilson who inspired Audubon to begin his *Birds of America*.

George de Cuvier (1769–1832) was the leading French naturalist of his time; other notable explorer–naturalists included Alexander von Humbolt (1769–1859), founder of the modern science of physical geology, and Françqis Michaux whose *The North American Sylva* was a classic for its time. Lewis and Clark and botanists David Douglas and John Coulter brought new knowledge of the American west. Other expeditions included Major Long's first exploration of the Rocky Mountains in 1819 with Thomas Say as zoologist, and the Cass-Schoolcraft Expedition of 1820 and 1832, which brought geology of the Great Lakes region to the attention of the public. These and other expeditions enhanced natural history interpretation and encouraged public and private support of the natural sciences.

New Harmony in southwestern Indiana on the banks of the Wabash followed Philadelphia as a notable center of scientific studies from 1826–1860. Here were found leaders such as William Maclure the father of American geology via his *Observations on the Geology of the United States* in 1809 and his *Essay on Formation of Rocks* in 1832; Thomas Say, the father of American entomology; Charles A. Leseur of France who first described the fishes of the Great Lakes and with François Peron had described the Australian fauna; Dr. Gerhard Troost, chemist and geologist; and idealist Robert Owen and sons.[4] They were joined by Joseph (Naef) Neef who was brought to America by William Maclure to introduce the Pestalozzian method of education. Other details of the New Harmony settlement may be found in Walter Hendrickson's *David Dale Owen* published by the Indiana Historical Society in 1943.

Expeditions that left a legacy of natural history interpretation must include England's Charles Darwin (1809–1882) and his circumpolar voyage on the Beagle from 1831 to 1836 and the explorations of Darwin's contemporary, Alfred R. Wallace (1823–1913).

Europe's gifts to America included Switzerland's J. Louis Agassiz (1807–1873) who authored *Etudes sur les Glaciers* and became a professor at Harvard in 1847, and John Muir (1838–1914), naturalist and conservationist.

Other explorer–naturalists included Paul DuChaillu in Africa; William Henry Hudson, the first native South American naturalist; and the popular American naturalists Roy Chapman Andrews, William Beebe, Carl Akeley, and David Fairchild. These and other explorers interpreted the natural history of the world and whetted an appetite for travel and science-related literature.

MEDIA OF INTERPRETATION

Botanical gardens, arboreta, zoos, and related organizations continued to grow in number and to play an increasingly important role in natural history interpretation. Early facilities included Bartram's Gardens, 1728; Philadelphia Botanical Society, 1806; Arnold Arboretum at Harvard, 1876; New York Botanical Garden, 1891; and the Brooklyn Botanic Garden, 1910. Early zoological parks were opened at Cincinnati, 1875; Philadelphia, 1876; the New York Zoological Park, 1888; National Zoological Park, 1890; and the New York Zoological Gardens, 1899.

Museums have long constituted one of the most important mediums of scientific investigation and education, and the museum movement encouraged and promoted the trailside museum and nature and science center movements of today. Early museums include the noted British Museum, the Smithsonian Institution, 1846; Agassiz's Museum of Natural History and Comparative Anatomy at Harvard, 1859; the Peabody Museum of Natural History at Yale, 1866; and the New York Museum of Natural History, 1870.

The museum movement made rapid strides with the founding of the American Association of Museums in 1906; the Association, along with the Carnegie Institute and the Laura Spelman Rockefeller Memorial, promoted the trailside museum programs of the national parks and to a lesser extent state parks through leaders such as Hermon C. Bumpus, John Merriam, Joseph Grinnell, Laurence Vail Coleman, and others.[3]

The Buffalo Museum of Science under the direction of Chauncey Hamlin developed natural science study groups that promulgated youth and park programs after the park movement had been facilitated through the leadership of Frederick Law Olmstead—father and son, Jens Jensen, John Muir, George B. Grinnell, Stephen T. Mather, Raymond Torrey, and others.

While the Buffalo Museum of Natural History had a highly developed children's museum program in 1879, the first children's museum was founded in Boston in 1889.

As the natural sciences were enhanced through growing support by major universities, other organizations encouraged the development of museums and related educational programs including park naturalist programs. Early organizations included the Philadelphia Academy of Science, 1812; the American Forestry Association, 1875; American Geological Society, 1838; Boston Society of Natural History, 1830; Buffalo Society of Natural Sciences, 1861; the Agassiz Association, 1875; and the American Humane Education Association, 1877. These were followed by the American Ornithological Union, 1883; National Academy of Science—General, 1886; National Geographic Society and the Geological Society of America, 1888; Society of American Foresters, 1900; Wildflower Preservation Society, 1902; and the American Nature Study Society, 1908.

Early European science educators influenced nature education in the United States. Pestalozzi and his students, for example, influenced early educational leaders such as Horace Mann, Louis Agassiz, and Edward Sheldon who was assisted at Oswego (New York) Training School for Teachers by Hermann Krusi, son of Pestalozzi's loyal assistant. Through Sheldon object teaching spread to many parts of the United States and reached its peak from 1860 to 1880; it was a forerunner of nature study and modern elementary science.[14]

Long after the teaching and varied field studies of Rafinesque, outdoor laboratories and field stations strengthened the natural sciences and facilitated the nature study movement. Louis Agassiz opened the first field science laboratory on the Island of Penikese in Buzzards Bay off Massachusetts in the summer of 1873. His

40 students included David Starr Jordan, H. H. Straight, and Henry Ward, the founder of Wards Natural Science Establishment in Rochester, New York, 1882. Agassiz is deserving of the title "father of nature study in America." He also influenced the teaching of natural sciences at Cornell. The Marine Biological Field Station at Woods Hole followed Agassiz's pioneer effort, and in 1876 the Harvard Summer School of Geology opened at Cumberland Gap with Jordan and Shaler in attendance.

In 1875 the Agassiz Association was founded by Harland H. Ballard to honor Agassiz and interest young people in nature study and research. By the 1890s high school science had shifted from natural history to morphology and anatomy. Wilbur S. Jackman (1855–1907) of Cook County (Illinois) Normal, however, helped to bridge the natural and physical sciences with his 1891 book, *Nature Study for Common Schools*. In 1903 he edited the third yearbook of the National Society of the Study of Education, an issue devoted to nature study.

Cornell University became the leader of the nature study movement in the late 1890s through the efforts of Liberty Hyde Bailey (1858–1954), Anna Botsford Comstock (1854–1930), and later by James G. Needham, E. Laurence Palmer (1888–1970), and others. Bailey's *The Nature Study Idea* in 1903 laid a philosophical base for the nature study movement, and Mrs. Comstock's *Nature Study Leaflets* formed the basis of the long-popular *Handbook of Nature Study* and the *Cornell Rural School Leaflet* that flourished under the editorship of Palmer and others. Bailey and Comstock were also helpful to Cornellian David Starr Jordan, the first president and chancelor of Leland Stanford University, making Stanford the "Cornell of the West" and thereby promulgating the teaching of nature study in California schools.

Leaders in other universities influenced natural history interpretation; these included John C. Merriam and Joseph and John Grinnell, University of California; Loye Miller, University of California and UCLA; Henry Cowles and John M. Coulter, University of Chicago; T. Gilbert Pearson, University of Tennessee; and Linde Jones of Oberlin College.

Nature pursuits both active and passive have been stimulated and enhanced by outstanding naturalists many of whom were excellent writers. Gilbert White led the way for such writers as Henry Thoreau, John Burroughs, Richard Jeffries, John Muir, Henry Van Dyke, Dallas Lore Sharp, Ernest Thompson Seton, Enos Mills, and the explorer–naturalists previously mentioned. The "nature fakir controversy" that embroiled Burroughs, Seton, Abbott Thayer, Theodore Roosevelt, and others was therapeutic; it not only stimulated public interest in nature literature, but also upgraded literature devoted to natural history and its interpretation.

Camps and voluntary youth organizations have served to promote awareness, empathy, and occasionally excellent instruction and leadership in nature-related activities. They include the early natural science camp of Edward Howe Forbush in New Hampshire in 1885, Professor Arey's camp of 1891, and Stanford professor William W. Price's Camp Agassiz at Fallen Leaf Lake near Lake Tahoe in California that ran from 1896 to 1916. William Gould Vinal (1881–1976) has long been a distinguished promoter of nature activities in organized camping. He organized the first of seven Nature Lore Schools of Cape Cod in 1920.

Youth-serving agencies have included Seton's Woodcraft Indians of 1896 (incorporated as the Woodcraft League of America in 1902), artist Daniel Carter Beard's Sons of Daniel Boone, Lord Baden Powell's Boy Scout troop in England in 1907 followed by Lady Powell's Girl Guides; the Boy Scouts of America and the Campfire Girls of America, 1910; and the Girl Scouts of the United States, 1912. These organizations have provided youth throughout the world with outdoor living experiences and activities in nature interpretation.

In 1918 the Museum of Natural History in New York sponsored and trained George Gladden's Boy Scout Troop to lead the blind through exhibits—one of the earliest nature programs in America for the handicapped.[9]

EARLY NATURE GUIDING

The origin of nature guiding is unknown, but many early naturalists were skilled in leading field excursions. The father of nature guiding is generally conceded to be Enos A. Mills (1870–1922) who prepared himself to be the "best guide in the Rocky Mountains."[11] In the summer of 1889 Mills conducted nature-oriented field trips up Long's Peak in what is now Rocky Mountain National Park[19] (Fig. 2-1).

Carl P. Russell in correspondence with Loye H. Miller (now in the archives of the University of California's Bancroft Library) identified such early park nature guides as Ranger Milton Skinner who began guiding at Yellowstone as early as 1898 and Lt. F. Pipes who conducted field trips of a botanical nature at Wawona, Yosemite in 1904. Park rangers led visitors through Mesa Verde in 1907, and Ranger John B. Flett lectured at Mount Rainier National Park in 1913.[21]

A nature trail had been established in Banff National Park, Canada, in 1915, but Alan F. Helmsley indicates that the location and source of the labels is unknown. Park naturalist programs started in Canada's National Parks in 1930.[12]

Stephen T. Mather, first director of the National Park Service in 1916, and his assistant Horace M. Albright sought to promote further congressional support for the parks. Mather personally financed and employed Robert Sterling Yard as chief of the Education Division to develop promotional literature including the *National Parks Portfolio*. Mather then created in June 1918 the National Parks Educational Committee consisting of 75 college presidents and other educators organized by Charles Walcott of the Smithsonian.[3] Mather, constantly pressured by special interest groups seeking to exploit the parks for financial gain, sought ways to build public support for preserving park values.

FIG. 2-1. Enos A. Mills, regarded as the "father of nature guiding," was conducting nature-oriented trips up Long's Peak, in 1889. (Photo courtesy of Rocky Mountain National Park.)

Enos Mills urged the employment of park guides in an article, "Guiding in the National Parks," that appeared in the January 1916 issue of *Country Life in America;* Mills also listed desirable qualifications for such guides. Likewise, Zoologists Joseph Grinnell and Tracy I. Storer of the University of California, urged in *Science,* September 15, 1916, the employment of a trained resident naturalist as a member of the park staff in every national park. Mills again justified the need for park nature guides in "Guides Wanted" for the Januray 6, 1917 issue of *Saturday Evening Post.* He cited the demand for such guides and urged their employment in the national parks.

Mather and Albright had been irritated by Mill's insistent prodding on park policies and failed to recognize his suggestions. They were determined to do things their own way.

Mills did, however, succeed in getting Esther Burnell, a homesteader, to become the first licensed nature guide in what is now Rocky Mountain National Park. They later married and together recruited Esther's sister, Elizabeth Frayer Burnell, to whom Mills dedicated *The Adventures of a Nature Guide* in 1920. Elizabeth helped Mills operate the Long's Peak Inn Trail School for both children and adults. Mills described the school in the March 1919 *Saturday Evening Post* article, "Children of My Trail School." Elizabeth became supervisor of nature study in the Los Angeles schools[19] (Fig. 2-2).

Dr. Loye Holmes Miller (1874–1970), a paleo-ornithologist, after teaching in Hawaii began teaching nature study and zoology at the Los Angeles Normal School (now UCLA) in 1904. He found nature study already well established in the Los Angeles area and led many field trips for teachers and students. In the summers of 1912–1914 he conducted nature study classes at the Forest Home Resort in the San Bernardino Mountains; in the summer of 1917 Miller and Prof. M. L. Maclelland held a summer school with lectures and field trips for teachers in Yosemite.[18]

Dr. Harold C. Bryant (1886–1968), the economic ornithologist from 1914 to 1927 for the California Game and Fish Commission and the University of California Extension Service and editor of *California Fish and Game* from 1916 to 1930, led numerous trips that included a popular program, "Six Trips Afield," for businessmen and students in the Berkeley area. In the summer of 1918 the Commission sent Bryant on a tour of the summer resorts in the Yosemite area to lecture and lead field trips. Later that summer the Byrants accompanied Sacramento philanthropists and nature enthusiasts Mr. and Mrs. Charles M. Goethe, both offspring of wealthy bankers and founders of the California Nature Study League, on a trip to Glacier National Park.[22]

Prior to World War I, Charles and Mary Goethe made trips around the world promoting recreational programs and facilities. During several trips to Europe they became enthusiastic about nature guiding in Germany, Switzerland, Norway, and Denmark that included field trips for the blind. They were determined to intro-

FIG. 2-2. Elizabeth Burnell during a 1919 visit to Grand Canyon National Park. (Photo courtesy of Enda Mills Kiley.)

duce nature guiding to parks, schools, and other settings in the United States. Apparently the Goethes were unaware of the extent of nature guiding by Enos Mills, Skinner, Muir, Miller, and others. The trip and resultant growing friendship of the Bryants and the Goethes led to the Tahoe Experiment in 1919.[10]

The Tahoe Experiment consisted of the Bryants and Goethes travelling by horseback to summer resorts in the Tahoe area where Bryant led field trips and lectured under the sponsorship of the California Game and Fish Commission.[2]

During the summer of 1919 Loye Miller and his family were also in the Tahoe area.[18] Miller was intent on making zoological collections and enjoying the summer with his family. Once a week he volunteered to lecture at the Fallen Leaf Resort auditorium. For a small fee he also led field trips.

On the evening of July 20, Stephen T. Mather stopped at Fallen Leaf Lodge and forgot his supper when he saw an enthusiastic overflow audience captivated by Miller's talk on "Voices of Birds" with owl calls. Miller, a superb lecturer, was also an expert in imitating bird songs. This is exactly what Mather was seeking in order to counteract those persons who would selfishly destroy park values. The following day he phoned Miller from the Tallac Resort and asked Miller to go at once to Yosemite. Miller declined and urged greater study and publicity so the program could be undertaken the following summer.[18]

During the Bryants' and Goethes' successful 250-mile (400-km) horseback trip from Yosemite to Tahoe, they stopped at the Fallen Leaf Resort from July 24 to August 1. Miller, a friend of the Bryants, met the Goethes for the first time.* Miller's diary makes no mention of his lecturing or leading field trips with Bryant; instead Miller compliments Bryant's activities that were similar to Miller's earlier program at the San Bernardino resort. Before Miller left on August 19 he promised he would return the following summer to lecture and lead field trips in exchange for lodging and a fee.[18]

In December 1919, Mather invited Goethe to his Christmas party for University of California classmates; Mather asked Goethe to transfer his Tahoe Experiment to Yosemite the following summer. Bryant and Miller were immediately contacted by Goethe at Mather's insistence and both agreed to come to Yosemite the summer of 1920, thus becoming the first official nature guides in the National Park Service.[17] (Fig. 2-3).

Bryant was on duty when Miller arrived in June 1920. Bryant's services were sponsored by the Game and Fish Commission, while Miller's salary was probably covered equally by Mather and Goethe. Bryant and Miller were designated tem-

---

*A plaque at Fallen Leaf Lake reads: Midsummer 1919, began National Park's interpretive program. W. W. Price, Stanford University biology graduate, owner Fallen Leaf Lodge, convinced reluctant proprietors of 5 other Tahoe resorts as to nature guiding movement "imported" from Europe by Mr. and Mrs. G. M. Goethe. National Park's Director S. T. Mather, witnessing its amazing popularity at Fallen Leaf, requested its introduction in 1920 to Yosemite. Thus began National Park Ranger Naturalist's Interpretive Program.

FIG. 2-3. Though nature guiding had been introduced in several national parks, its first official recognition came in 1920, at Yosemite National Park. Here, Dr. L. H. Miller (at left) and Dr. H. C. Bryant (at right) offered a summer public interpretive program. Within a few years a budget was provided for park naturalists and the program was extended to a year-round service. (Photo courtesy of Yosemite Museum Collection.)

porary rangers by superintendent Washington Lewis and assigned to "special work"—nature guides. They had the volunteer service of Mrs. Enid Reeve Michael, a student in Miller's first class at L. A. Normal. The guides alternated between field and "office" with field trips in the morning from Old Village or Camp Curry and afternoon classes for children. Evening lectures and campfire programs were given at Camp Curry or the Village, and all day trips were made on Saturdays. Mrs. Michael maintained the labeled wildflower exhibit where visitors asked questions of the guides during the "office" hours.[2]

Miller left Yosemite at the end of July to keep his commitment at Fallen Leaf Resort, but Miller and Bryant returned for the full summer in 1921—Miller's last summer at Yosemite. Bryant continued and initiated the Yosemite School of Field Natural History in 1925 using the newly completed Yosemite Museum as headquarters. Bryant continued his distinguished career with the National Park Service as assistant director of the Service in charge of the Division of Research and Education in Washington in 1930 and the superintendency of Grand Canyon.

Clark summarizes the importance of the 1920 program at Yosemite by stating:

While it is true that earlier work in the direction of nature guiding and public interpretive service had been carried on in several of the national parks, the Yosemite Program marked the beginning of carefully directed and planned public contact work which was to spread throughout the national parks and become the most direct and most important function of the service.[6] (See Fig. 2-4.)

Horace Albright, superintendent at Yellowstone in 1920, does not mention the service of Ranger Milton P. Skinner as a naturalist or nature guide; but Albright's annual report for 1920 does credit Ranger Isabel Bassett Wasson with giving free half-hour talks and lectures three times daily and campfire programs in the evening. Bryant and Atwood trace the development of the first official nature guide program at Yellowstone in 1921 as it kept pace with the Yosemite program and those of other national parks.[3]

Bryant and Miller, personally financed by Mather, traveled by train to the major cities and science centers of the eastern United States in January 1921 to lecture

FIG. 2-4. A guided auto caravan in Yosemite Valley in 1932. These were later discontinued because they became too popular and created traffic jams. (Photo courtesy of Yosemite Museum Collections.)

on the national parks and natural history subjects thereby promoting the parks and the nature guide service. As usual they were an unqualified success, and Miller's lecture on bird music, requested by Mather, continued to be popular. Their first stop was Des Moines, Iowa, where they attended the founding meeting of the National Conference on State Parks organized in part by Mather. The conference helped to spread nature guiding into the state parks via leaders such as Major William A. Welch and Richard Lieber. The trip enabled Bryant and Miller to meet the greatest names in science and to appear before prestigious organizations which were to give considerable support to park interpretive programs.[16]

While nature guiding was getting started in California, a similar program was underway in the Kanawauke Lake region of Palisades Interstate Park in New York. Here in 1919 Benjamin T. B. Hyde (Fig. 2-5), and Boy Scout William H. Carr had a tent nature center. In 1920 Hyde hired Carr to work at the American Museum,* and in the summer of 1922 they opened a nature museum in the Boy Scout camp headquarters at Kanawauke Lake and used materials "borrowed" from the American Museum. They also developed nature trails, trailside nature centers, and conducted campfire programs for the Boy Scouts. Park superintendent William A. Welch, Dr. Hermon C. Bumpus, Hyde, and Carr deserve much credit for the development of trailside museums at Harriman and Bear Mountain State Parks. Welch developed more than forty-five resident camps that were served by the world's first regional trailside museums. From 1926 to 1944 William H. Carr had the dual position of director and park naturalist at both Harriman and Bear Mountain State Parks and served as consultant for the first permanent trailside museum built at Bear Mountain in 1927 under the same sponsorship (Laura Spelman Rockefeller Memorial) as the first museum at Yosemite in 1924. The well-publicized Field Station for the Study of Insects developed by Frank E. Lutz in the Rampoa Mountain section of Harriman State Park from 1925 to 1927 constituted the first combination information and self-testing trail.[5]

Other developments in the East included William G. Vinal's Nature Lore Schools from 1920 to 1927, which led to his Nature Guide Schools of 1928–1930 at Western Reserve University and the Massachusetts State College (now University of Massachusetts). Vinal truly deserves the title "father of nature recreation." He and Palmer of Cornell pioneered in many currently used methods of natural history interpretation and environmental education.

William P. Alexander, director of education at the Buffalo Museum of Science, and Chauncey J. Hamlin, director of the Buffalo Society of Natural Sciences, had both developed extensive nature education programs. In 1921, Alexander developed a tent nature center and a mile-long nature trail—The Bear Cave Trail—in Allegheny State Park.[1] A nature study camp was also initiated by George R. Green primarily for the use of his classes at Pennsylvania State College in 1924.

*American Museum of Natural History, New York City.

FIG. 2-5. Benjamin Hyde, who in 1920, initiated what became a pioneer interpretive undertaking at Bear Mountain Park in New York State. The plaque (below), erected soon after his death, commemorates his actions on behalf of interpretation. (Photo courtesy of Palisades Interstate Park Commission.)

Miss Lucy Pitchler of Indianapolis served as a volunteer nature guide during her vacations at McCormick's Creek State Park in Indiana from 1923 to 1926 where she was provided room and board in exchange for her naturalist services. The program in Indiana was formally organized in 1927 through the efforts of Colonel Richard Lieber and the encouragement of Raymond Torrey who, from 1925 to 1927, had conducted the National Conference on State Parks and the American Planning and Civic Association.[7] Sidney R. Esten was appointed chief nature guide with headquarters at Turkey Run State Park, Indiana.

The naturalist program in the U.S. national parks was strengthened in 1921 by the appointment of Ansel Hall as Yosemite's first full-time naturalist; in 1923 he became National Park Service Chief Naturalist and, with the creation of the Educational Division, he had an office in Berkeley where the early master planning for park naturalist programs occurred. Advancements included the construction of the Yosemite Nature Museum in 1924, Bryant's Yosemite School of Field Natural History in 1925, and Directior Albright's establishment of the Branch of Research and Education in Washington D.C. in 1930, to be headed up by Dr. Harold C. Bryant, who by now was assistant director of the NPS. A noteworthy event took place in 1929 at the Forestry School on the Berkely campus of the University of California. Chief Naturalist Ansel Hall called together the entire permanent National Park Service naturalist staff for the First Park Naturalist Conference (Fig. 2-6). In addition to the eight full-time naturalists, the meeting was attended by many local professors, researchers, museum technicians, and others interested in interpretation. A more detailed historical study of NPS involvement in interpretation will be found in C. Frank Brockman's article on Park Naturalists, cited under General References at the end of this Chapter.

From 1926 to 1944 William H. Carr continued to experiment and develop the nature programs and facilities at Bear Mountain. His seven major bulletins on nature trails and interpretive methods were published by his employer, the American Museum of Natural History, and constituted the first and most important series on this subject. Carr was to culminate his creativity with the development of the Arizona-Sonora Desert Museum near Tucson, Arizona, and the Ghost Ranch Museum in New Mexico, which was supported, in part, by Arthur Newton Pack, director of the Charles Lathrop Pack Forestry Foundation.

Other early programs included the Allegheny School of Natural History from 1927 to 1940 under the leadership of Robert E. Coker; the Oglebay Institute of Wheeling, West Virginia—an outgrowth of the bird walks and other nature activities led by Alonzo B. Brooks in 1927; and the initiation in 1928 of the California State Park's Nature Guide Program sponsored by the Division of Parks and the California Game and Fish Commission, the latter withdrawing support in 1931.

Park interpretive programs were greatly expanded in both state and national parks in the 1930s through the availability of emergency federal funds and public works agencies such as the Works Progress Administration (WPA) and the Civilian Conservation Corps (CCC). The Branch of Recreation, Land Planning, and

FIG. 2-6. The National Park Service (NPS) permanent interpretive staff, photographed while attending the First Park Naturalist Conference, in Berkeley, California, in 1929. Back row left to right: C. Frank Brockman, Mount Rainier; John D. Coffman, NPS Fire Control Specialist (former naturalist); Frank Been, Sequoia; Edwin D. McKee, Grand Canyon. Front row, left to right: Dorr G. Yeager, Yellowstone; Carl P. Russell, NPS Field Naturalist; Ansel F. Hall, NPS Chief Naturalist; C. A. "Bert" Harwell, Yosemite. Missing from photo: George C. Ruhle, Glacier. (Photo by NPS photographer George M. Grant.)

State Cooperation of the National Park Service appointed recreation planners including Garrett G. Eppley and R. C. Robinson who helped seventeen states start naturalist programs. Most of these programs, however, were terminated with the onset of World War II. Despite heavy postwar attendance, park interpretive programs were slow in being revived. During the period of 1949 to 1951, Weaver found only nine states with state park naturalist programs—the most prominent being in California and Indiana.[26]

RESEARCH AND PROFESSIONAL TRAINING

More than twenty theses written at Cornell University under the direction of Dr. E. Laurence Palmer from the period 1931 to 1952 concerned conservation education and leadership training in camps, museums, outdoor laboratories, state and national parks, and wildlife refuges. Theses, mostly doctoral, devoted to park and park-related interpretive programs were written by Ann L. Steger, John R. Arnold, Babette I. Brown, Minter Westfall, George W. Howe, Wilson F. Clark, John Wanamaker, and Howard E. Weaver.[26]

While Bryant and Atwood analyzed research and education in the national parks, Professor J. V. K. Wagar of Colorado A&M State College studied and advocated nature interpretation in forest recreation.[25] The U.S. Forest Service, however, failed to develop its forest naturalist or Visitor Information Service until the period 1960 to 1962 when the Branch of Visitor Information Service was created under the leadership of Paul M. Kihlmire. A network of nature trails and visitor information centers and services were then established in the nine regions of the service. The Forest Service has an excellent potential to combine forest and wilderness interpretation with management and utilization practices; a good start has been made.

FIG. 2-7. Freeman Tilden (at left) and Grant Sharpe at an A.I.N. meeting in Ohio. This organization promotes professionalism among interpreters. (Photo by S. Ross Tocher.)

Most of the Cornell dissertations included the training of outdoor educators, but Weaver's concentrated on state park naturalists. His study was in turn updated by Phyllis Wells, a graduate student at the University of Michigan working under the direction of Dr. Grant W. Sharpe who, at Michigan, developed the first curriculum for the training of interpretive naturalists. Weaver followed by developing an option for interpretive naturalists within the undergraduate curriculum of Recreation and Park Administration at the University of Illinois, Urbana-Champaign. Similar curricula rapidly developed at other universities with the growing employment of interpretive naturalists by metropolitan, county, state, and national parks, the U.S. Forest Service, and National Wildlife Refuge program. Another factor was the opportunity for communication afforded by the Annual Workshop on Interpretation through the leadership of Professor Reynold Carlson of Indiana University. The workshop served to create the Association of Interpretive Naturalists in 1960.

One of the A.I.N.'s first publications was Jean Sanford Replinger's committee report, the "Preparation of the Interpretive Naturalist," which proved useful to colleges. This was followed by the more comprehensive and statistically reliable doctoral study of Benjamin D. Mahaffey at Texas A&M University in 1972.[15]

The training of preservice and inservice naturalists has been enhanced through workshops available through the A.I.N. (Fig. 2-7), the Natural Science for Youth Foundation, the educational division of the National Audubon Society, the Western Interpreters Association, Interpretation Canada, and the Stephen T. Mather and Horace M. Albright Training Centers of the National Park Service. Such courses and workshops continue to upgrade interpretive naturalist programs throughout the world through international cooperation. Prospective and professional interpretive naturalists or equivalent staff at museums and nature and science centers should join and become active in one or more of the following professional organizations:

Association of Interpretive Naturalists, 6700 Needwood Road, Derwood, MD 20855*

Interpretation Canada, Box 160, Aylmer, P.Q. Canada. J9H 5E5

Western Interpreters Association, c/o Doug Bryce, Executive Manager, P.O. Box 28366, Sacramento, CA 95828

REFERENCES

General References

Adams, A. B. 1969. *Eternal Quest—The Story of Great Naturalists,* Putnam, New York.

*The Association of Interpretive Naturalists is divided into numerous regions throughout the United States.

Bailey, L. H. 1909. *The Nature Study Idea,* Third Edition. Macmillan, New York.

Brockman, C. Frank. 1978. "Park Naturalists and the Evolution of National Park Service Interpretation Through World War II," *Journal of Forest History.*

Bumpus, H. C., Jr. 1947. *Hermon Carey Bumpus—Yankee Naturalist,* University of Minnesota Press, St. Paul.

Burns, Ned J. 1941. *Field Manual for Museums.* United States Department of the Interior. National Park Service. Washington, DC (Out of Print).

Cantu, R. 1973. *Interpretation: A Way of Looking at Things,* Association of Interpretive Naturalists, Derwood, MD.

Carr, William H. 1974–75. "Bear Mountain Trail Blazers." *The Conservationist.* State of New York, Department of Environmental Conservation, Albany.

Cloes, H. 1953. *Conversation with the Earth,* Knopf, New York.

Coleman, L. V. "Contribution of Museums to Outdoor Recreation," Report of the National Conference on Outdoor Recreation, Senate Document 158, U.S. Government Printing Office, Washington, DC.

Eppley, G. G. April 1940. "State Parks—Centers for Nature Recreation," *Recreation.*

Goode, G. G. "The Beginnings of Natural History in America," *Annual Report for the Year Ending June 30, 1897,* Smithsonian Institution, Washington, DC.

Gregg, H. R. October–November 1947. "A Perspective Report on the Program of Interpretation," *Yosemite Nature Notes.*

Hawkes, J. 1951. *A Land,* Random House, New York.

Jelinek, V. 1953. *The Analytical Didactic of Comenius,* University of Chicago Press, Chicago.

National Recreation and Parks Association. *1974.* "Trends in Interpretation," *Trends.*

Palmer, E. L. September 1950. "Nature Writings," *Cornell Rural School Leaflet,* Ithaca, NY.

Palmer, E. L. November 1957. "Fifty Years of Nature Study," *Nature Magazine.*

Peattie, D. C. 1936. *Green Laurels—The Lives and Achievements of Great Naturalists,* Simon and Schuster, New York.

Robinson, R. C. 1940. "Naturalist Programs in America," *The Regional Review,* National Park Service, Washington, DC.

Runte, Alfred. 1979. *National Parks: The American Experience.* University of Nebraska Press, Lincoln.

Russell, C. P. 1940. "A Forward Look at Naturalist Programs," *Proceedings,* Second Park Naturalists' Conference, Grand Canyon, National Park Service.

Russell, C. P. 1947. *One Hundred Years in Yosemite.* University of California Press, Berkeley.

Scott, E. B. 1957. *The Saga of Lake Tahoe,* Sierra-Tahoe Publishing Co., Lake Tahoe, NV.

Seton, J. M. 1967. *By a Thousand Fires—Biography of Ernest Thompson Seton,* Doubleday, New York.

Shankland, R. 1970. *Steve Mather of the National Parks,* Knopf, New York.

Swain, D. 1970. *Wilderness Defender—Horace L. Albright and Conservation,* University of Chicago Press, Chicago.

Terres, J. K. 1961. *Discovery—Great Moments in the Lives of Outstanding Naturalists,* Lippincott, Philadelphia.

Vinal, W. G. 1926. *Nature Guiding,* Comstock Publishing Co., Cornell University Press, Ithaca, NY.

Watts, M. T. 1957. *Reading the Landscape,* Macmillan, New York.

Watts, M. T. 1971. *Reading the Landscape of Europe,* Harper and Row, New York.

References Cited

1. Arnold, J. R. 1938. "Report of State Supported Agencies Other Than Schools Concerned in the Conservation of Natural Resources," unpublished doctoral minor thesis, Cornell University Library, Ithaca, NY.

2. Bryant, H. C. July 1925. "Nature Guiding," *Nature Magazine.*

3. Bryant, H. C. and W. W. Atwood. 1936. *Research and Education in the National Parks,* U.S. Government Printing Office, Washington, DC.

4. Buley, R. C. 1950. *The Old Northwest—Pioneer Period—1815–1840,* Vol. II, Indiana Historical Society, Indianapolis.

5. Carr, W. H. 1937. *Ten Years of Nature Trailing,* School Services Series, No. 11, American Museum of Natural History, New York.

6. Clark, W. F. 1949. "The Interpretive Programs of the National Parks; Their Development, Present Status, and Reception by the Public," unpublished doctoral dissertation, Cornell University Library, Ithaca, NY.

7. Esten, S. R. 1946. "History of the Indiana State Naturalist Training Sercice." Naturalist Training Institute, McCormick's Creek State Park. (Out of print).

8. Freeberg, W. H., and L. E. Taylor. 1961. *Philosophy of Outdoor Education,* Burgess Publishing Company, Minneapolis, MN.

9. Gladden, G. 1919. "Boy Scouts as Naturalists," *Review of Reviews.*

10. Goethe, C. M. July 1960. "Nature Study in National Parks Interpretive Movement," *Yosemite Nature Notes.*

11. Hawthorn, H., and E. B. Mills. 1935. *Enos Mills of the Rockies,* Houghton-Mifflin, Boston.

12. Helmsley, A. F. 1971. "Background Paper on Park Interpretation—National Parks of Canada," unpublished paper, National and Historic Parks Branch, Department of Indian Affairs and Northern Development, Ottawa.

13. Keatinge, M. W. 1910. *The Great Didactic of John Amos Comenius,* Adam and Charles Black, London.

14. Krusi, H. 1875. *Pestalozzi—His Life, Work, and Influence,* Antwerp, Bragg and Company, Cincinnati, OH.

15. Mahaffey, B. D. 1972. "A Study of Professional Recommendations for Curricular Guidelines of Environmental Interpreters," unpublished doctoral dissertation, Texan A & M University Library, College Station.

16. Miller, L. H. "Eastern Journal—January 1921—A Lecture Tour by H. C. Bryant and Loye Miller in Behalf of the National Parks Promotion," unpublished diary, Archives of the Bancroft Library, University of California, Berkeley.

17. Miller, L. H. "Fallen Leaf Lake, Tahoe Area in 1919," unpublished manuscript, diary from July to August 1919, Archives of the Bancroft Library, University of California, Berkeley.

18. Miller, L. H. "Fording the Sierras," unpublished manuscript, Archives of the Bancroft Library, University of California, Berkeley.

19. Mills, E. A. 1920. *The Adventures of a Nature Guide,* Doubleday Page, Garden City, NY.

20. Pinloche, A. 1901. *Pestalozzi and the Foundation of the Modern School,* Charles Scribners Sons, New York.

21. Russell, C. F. "A 40th Anniversary—Nature Guiding in the National Parks," *Yosemite Nature Notes,* **39.**

22. Sutton, A., and Myron Sutton. January 1955. "Harold Bryant, Pioneer," *Nature Magazine.*

23. Tilden, F. 1957. *Interpreting Our Heritage,* The University of North Carolina Press, Chapel Hill.

24. Vinal, W. G. May 1957. "Nature Recreation in William Penn's Country," *School Science and Mathematics.*

25. Wagar, J. V. K. 1947. *Nature Interpretation in Forest Recreation: Proceedings,* Society of American Foresters Meeting.

26. Weaver, H. E. 1952. "State Park Naturalist Programs; Their History, Present

Status, and Recommendations for the Future," unpublished doctoral dissertation, Cornell University Library, Ithaca, NY.

27. White, J. 1907. *The Educational Ideas of Froebel,* University Tutorial Press, London.

CHAPTER 3

PEOPLE AND INTERPRETATION*

Donald R. Field
J. Alan Wagar

*Adapted from "Visitor Groups and Interpretation in Parks and Other Outdoor Leisure Settings," published in *Journal of Environmental Education* **5** (1): 12–17, 1973.

A chapter titled "People and Interpretation" might seem unnecessary, or at best, redundant in a book on interpretation. Yet people are the beneficiaries of interpretation; people are the object to which our efforts are directed. However, the literature on environmental interpretation yields very few articles dealing primarily with people. Who are the clientele for whom we work? Why do they come to this particular recreation place? How can we adapt our programs to their levels of understanding?

Managers and interpreters do have opinions about people and why they are present in a recreation area. But these opinions are often different from the visitors' view of themselves and what they seek.[6] The *who, why,* and *how* questions, therefore, become central if an agency's interpretation is to be more than a somewhat cursory public relations effort.

The purpose of this chapter is to study the people visiting leisure settings and the factors associated with interpretation for such visitors. This information can then be translated into five general principles for interpretation.

A BASIS FOR INTERPRETATION

Understanding individual behavior and group influences on behavior is especially important for interpretive personnel. Effective interpretation requires a working knowledge of the clientele to whom the messages are directed so that appropriate means can be used to arouse interest and transmit information. A summary of the relationship of people to interpretation is illustrated in Figure 3-1.

Our primary criterion for the effectiveness of interpretation is the successful transmission of information to clientele groups. Media are the means to accom-

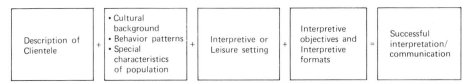

FIG. 3-1. The linkage between people, cultural background, and successful interpretation.

plish this end. Consequently, instead of beginning with media—such as a visitor center, amphitheater, or other familiar interpretive formats—interpreters must first define their objectives. Second, they must evaluate interpretive alternatives for reaching these objectives. Only then should procedures be selected for interpreting specific attractions or ideas for specific kinds of visitors or visitor groups. One must not rely on a limited set of time-honored techniques without examining their current appropriateness. Therefore, our focus is on two components of interpretation: (1) the visitor, and (2) procedures for transmitting information. Current knowledge about human behavior in leisure settings is used to suggest various interpretive strategies.

Unfortunately, interpretation often falls far short of its potential for enhancing visitor experiences. Major problems diminishing its effectiveness include:

1. *An inadequate emphasis on interpretation in resource management agencies.* Do resource managers overlook the benefits of interpretation and thus allocate insufficient human and physical resources to interpretive programs? Do they recruit, train, and encourage top-flight personnel for interpretive positions?
2. *Misdirected effort.* Is interpretation offered at times and places suited to the visitors? Is the same information presented over and over again to the large percentage of repeat visitors?
3. *Working against usual behavioral patterns.* Do we, as interpreters, harness within-group communication or work against it?
4. *Inadequate attention to visitor motivation.* Do we consider how interpretation will reward our visitors or only what we want them to know?
5. *Mismatching of messages to visitors.* Do we tailor presentations to the diverse ages, backgrounds, and interests of our visitors, or is all interpretation aimed at a "standardized" visitor?
6. *Not monitoring the effectiveness of efforts.* Are the goals and expected results of interpretation clearly stated? If objectives are clear, what feedback mechanisms are used to determine how well the interpretive efforts are accomplishing these objectives?

PRINCIPLES OF INTERPRETATION

Although research on visitor groups and interpretation is relatively new, results already suggest strategies for current interpretive situations. It is convenient to organize the search for these around five principles:

1. Visitors and leisure settings are diverse, and a variety of approaches will be required.
2. Visitors anticipate a relaxed, enjoyable and informal atmosphere.
3. Interpretive information must be rewarding to visitors.
4. Interpretive information must be readily understood.
5. Feedback (i.e., communication from visitors to the interpreter) is essential.

A discussion of interpretive options follows. Some ideas are new, others are being employed successfully in a variety of places. Each is related to one of the above principles of interpretation.

Diversity of Visitors and Leisure Settings

It would greatly simplify interpretive planning if all information could be directed in a standardized format to the "average" visitor (a mythical character). However, visitors differ widely in their ages, educational attainments, interests, and in the objectives they wish to achieve within an outdoor leisure setting. Although not all come specifically to enjoy a social outing, nearly all visitors have experiences influenced to some degree by sociability. Case studies of several special populations in the Northwest attest to the diversity principle (Fig. 3-2). In addition, the goals and objectives of recreationists are partially shaped by the frequency with which they visit an area. Visitors familiar with a specific place often seek experiences that build on knowledge from previous visits (Fig. 3-3).

Although outdoor recreation areas do attract new visitors each year, a majority of the visitation arises through repeat visits by groups who attend regularly.[7] Therefore, a re-examination of interpretive strategies is suggested. A seasonal as well as within-season rotation schedule might provide repeat visitors an opportunity to enjoy a greater variety of interpretive experiences. One reason for a disproportionate number of newcomers found in visitor centers might be that repeat visitors have previously viewed the exhibits and thus may spend little additional time there.

While parks and similar areas attract visitors from all parts of the country, many repeat visits are by residents in the immediate vicinity. Interpreters might consider having these local residents plan and maintain one exhibit which would be changed periodically. A theme might be park and community history, or park-community cultural and natural events.

CLIENTELE GROUP	CULTURAL BEHAVIOR PATTERNS ADDRESSED	INTERPRETIVE OR LEISURE SETTING	INTERPRETIVE OBJECTIVES AND FORMATS ADDRESSED
1. Disabled or handicapped (Beechel)[1]	Yes	Parks in general	Yes
2. Elderly (Renninger)[21] (Bultena, Field, Renninger)[2]	Yes	Northwest parks	Yes
3. Families (Machlis)[15]	Yes	Campgrounds	Yes
4. Children (Machlis, Field)[16] (Machlis, McDonough)[18]	Yes	Places in general	Yes
5. Hikers (Wolf)[27] (Wolf, Womble, Field)[28]	Yes	An Alaska trail	Yes
6. Foreign Visitors (Machlis, Field)[17]	Yes	Parks	Yes
7. Cruiseship Passengers (Koth, Field, Clark)[14]	Yes	Alaska cruiseships	Yes

Note: Authors cited by number can be located in references at end of chapter.

FIG. 3-2.   Case studies supporting the diversity principle.

If exhibits are self-contained and movable, an interpretive program can be modified with ease. Following a "modular unit" idea, a visitor center could be changed periodically to update the content, adjust to the time of year, or provide variety for repeat visitors. Modular units would likewise offer staff an opportunity to test, evaluate, and modify a proposed design prior to embracing it as a permanent part of their interpretation. In addition, modular units could be rearranged to accommodate different traffic flow patterns as visitor numbers change during different parts of the season. An interpretive staff would simply use flexibility of exhibit content, design, and spatial arrangements as additional means for enhancing message reception.

Exhibits might also be made modular in a slightly different sense. Equipment for presenting slides synchronized with sound is now available in a variety of forms. This allows quick substitution of one program for another, permitting presentations to be tailored to the needs of the moment.

Too often interpreters are assigned to visitor contact areas where only a small proportion of the total visitor public can be found. A reassignment of staff to areas

FIG. 3-3. Visitors to specific parks and other recreation areas often seek experiences that build the knowledge gained from previous visits. Yosemite National Park, California. (Photo by Grant W. Sharpe.)

of visitor concentration might be required. An examination of interpretive empha-sis—where, to whom, and at what time—is needed. A balance sheet could be developed to assess where the visitors are and where interpreters are assigned. Sightseeing by vehicles, for example, is one of the most popular activities found in large parks and forest areas. Interpreters who are available along major road systems have an increased contact opportunity, as do interpreters on public conveyances. Camping is a popular activity, and campgrounds are traditional interpretive sites. Yet interpreters are seldom found in campgrounds in the morning, midday, or afternoon. Because picnicking is the third most popular activity in parks, picnicking areas could be used much more intensively for interpreting natural and cultural features.

People usually visit recreational areas as members of social groups. Patterns include family groups of various types such as nuclear families, or multigeneration family groups (Fig. 3-4) and groups comprised of same-aged individuals, such as teenagers, young marrieds, or retired people. Although most resource managers recognize that people come to parks with others, managers often do not understand the influence of the social group upon the perceptions, attitudes, and behavior of individual members.[8]

Because so many of the visitors reached by interpretive programs arrive in social groups rather than as individuals, the social group is an important vehicle (or format) for the transmission of interpretive messages. One of the important aspects of group behavior is the shaping of information to the best level of understanding for children of different ages. It has also been found that group members who assume leadership roles as teachers or interpreters, rather than remaining as passive learners or listeners, tend to gain improved understanding of the information they present.

We must also consider opportunities for the group to gather together to share the information being received. For example, relief models showing the topography of an area are among the most popular exhibits in visitor centers.[26] One reason for this popularity is that they readily accommodate groups. When gathered at a relief model, members of a family or other group can discuss information of interest among themselves and can set their own pace. Social interaction with others outside the group is also possible.

Visitors Anticipate a Relaxed Atmosphere

Visitors consider parks and other outdoor leisure settings to be places where informality prevails, and group members are free to interact. Unfortunately, a great number of interpretive facilities are now designed to deal impersonally with the users as individuals, without opportunity for group interaction. Thus, under the pressure of serving increasing numbers of people, small and informal campfire programs have become formal lectures to large audiences seated in neat rows. Elsewhere, instead of a human naturalist, many visitors meet only audiovidual programs and message repeaters.

Limited opportunity budgets may severely constrain the amount of face-to-face interpretation that can be offered. However, informal contacts with interpreters are usually the most rewarding and should be retained and encouraged. A small informal amphitheater might be considered for settings in which small groups are the norm. There, the interpreter might move among the visitors while presenting

FIG. 3-4. People usually visit recreation areas as members of social groups. For example, this family reunion includes five generations. Olympic National Park, Washington. (Photo by Gary Machlis.)

the topic. By avoiding a stage as much as possible and allowing periodic interruptions, such as discussions or questions from visitors, the interpreter creates an atmosphere which encourages informality and participation.

As part of their informality, parks and other outdoor leisure settings are places where it is considered appropriate for strangers to interact with one another. This may be unique to leisure settings and should be encouraged.[3,4] Interpretive planners might capitalize both on this informality and the diversity among visitors by hiring interpreters from various age groups to initiate informal interpretive happenings. For example, in the Southwest where many retirees visit parks, retired persons should be hired to specialize in informal interpretive contacts with others of the same age (Fig. 3-5). Their discussions of opportunities for retired visitors would focus not only on park attractions, but also on the appropriate recreational and social opportunities available in nearby communities. In other settings where teenagers are predominant visitors, young people might be employed to present interpretive information to their own age group. Familiarity with the life styles of their colleagues might make retired and teenage interpreters especially effective in involving segments of our society often neglected in generalized presentations. In both instances, qualified people might be available on a volunteer basis.

Rewarding the Visitor

One of the verities of human behavior is that people tend to persist in doing the things they find enjoyable and rewarding. Yet this has often been overlooked in interpretation, especially by interpreters who have strong preconceptions about

FIG. 3-5. Off-season visitors to certain recreation areas are often retirees. Qualified retired persons should be considered for interpreting to visitiors of this age group. Grand Canyon National Park, Arizona. (Photo by Grant W. Sharpe.)

what people should know or find enjoyable. For example, Graves,[12] protested the use of tape players, movies, and exhibit systems designed for participation. Yet such dynamic presentations tend to hold visitor interest and become especially important when person-to-person interpretation is not possible. To enhance the quality of people's experiences and to help them understand the attractions they visit, one must reject the notion that the only worthwhile visitors are those whose values duplicate those of the professional resource manager.

Research has demonstrated a number of factors that contribute to visitor interest in interpretation. One of the most important is to provide for visitor participation and involvement. For example, at the Ohanepecosh Visitor Center in Mount Rainier National Park a recording quizboard was installed that simply presented four written, multiple-choice questions and permitted each to be answered by pushing electric buttons opposite the answers selected.[25] When a correct answer button was punched, a green panel reading "right answer" lighted up, the question panel just answered darkened, and another question panel lighted up. In addition, the quizboard made a rather satisfying clicking sound as relays snapped and hidden counters registered people's answers (Fig. 3-6). Although the other exhibits in the visitor center were extremely well done, the quizboard was the only exhibit that permitted participation and manipulation. Within seconds after it was installed it became, for children, the most popular exhibit in the center.

The "kid power" of participation should be further harnessed, as participation increases the retention of information received. Ecological float trips, for example, have been initiated at Yosemite National Park. Other possibilities might include

FIG. 3-6. The recording quizboard. The four large panels each contain one question with four answer choices. When the visitor selects the correct answer on the lighted panel, the next panel lights up, exposing a new question. Hidden electric counters record the correct and incorrect responses, giving the interpreter feedback on visitor understanding of other exhibits in the visitor center. (Photo by J. Alan Wagar.)

organized bike trips to interpret a particular topic. An organized game of litter removal can be more than a cheap way to clean up areas; it can be an interpretive device to instill a philosophy for "keeping America clean."[5] Interpretive programs for children only, combined with an activity such as a marshmallow roast (again, from Yosemite National Park), puppet shows, or reading of stories based on ecological principles are other examples (Fig. 3-7).

To capitalize on the principle of visitor participation, living interpretation, as

FIG. 3-7. Children's interpretation can include such activities as marshmallow roasts and puppet shows. The "Tree House Theater" illustrated here was built by the staff at Olympic National Park. It is used at schools and fairs as well as at evening campfire programs within the park. (Photo by Grant W. Sharpe.)

cited in Chapter 10, should be encouraged. In addition, opportunities for visitor groups to engage in activities like painting, shooting a musket, or throwing a pot might be developed where appropriate to the social, cultural, and natural history of an area. Nothing more convinces visitors of the complexities of skills and life styles of the past than attempting to recreate an object or event with family or friends.

A study of exhibits at four different visitor centers showed additional factors that were rewarding to visitors.[26] Complete stories and presentations that included cause and effect relationships were found to be more interesting to people than isolated facts.

As for subject matter, violence and violent events are of greater interest than any others, a fact well known by writers and entertainers for thousands of years. Fortunately, leisure settings abound in examples of violence that can be interpreted in good taste. For example, life in the ocean is so hazardous that, for most organisms, millions of young must be hatched to insure that a few will survive to maturity.

Interest was far above average for exhibits with dramatic or animated presentations such as movies, changing lighting (to direct the visitor's attention from place to place), and recorded sound. By contrast, interest was below average for inert presentations such as texts and mounted photos. Viewed another way, visitors find the media normally used for entertainment to be more rewarding than the less dynamic media that have traditionally been used for education[23] (Fig. 3-8).

As media commonly associated with entertainment, television, tape recorders, and radio have all been employed one place or another with varying degrees of success. However, their full potential has not been exploited.

Closed-circuit television offers enormous possibilities, especially now that relatively inexpensive videotape systems are available. For example, at a central control unit, one interpreter might interact with visitors at a number of consoles. By talking to visitors at any console, the interpreter could determine their interests and levels of knowledge, answer their questions, and show them selected videotapes. This would leave the interpreter free to interact with other visitors on other consoles. Where the construction of a theater in a visitor center would be questionable, television might offer a less costly alternative.

Portable cassette tape players also offer great flexibility (Fig. 3-9). During a recent study visitors could choose tapes of two different lengths for self-guided trail.[24] The choice could have been extended to tapes with different emphases, different levels of complexity, or even different languages.

Short-range radio transmitters are now being used in parking lots at a number of places to contact visitors through their own car radios. Use of transmitters at intervals along a road has also been considered as a means of presenting a sequence of information to visitors as they drive along. Costs per visitor contact

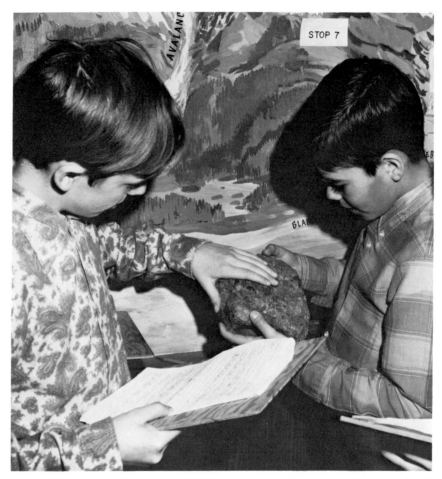

FIG. 3-8. Anchorage, Alaska school children in a portable visitor center from the Chugach National Forest put their heads together to discover the questions raised about a rock. (Photo courtesy of U.S. Forest Service.)

appear to be quite reasonable. At the moment, however, it is not certain that available equipment will provide adequate range from a simple antenna without exceeding the power output permitted for unlicensed transmitters. New limits for power output are under consideration by the Federal Communications Commission. An alternative (at a substantially higher cost) is the use of cables laid under the roadway to control the transmission zone.

FIG. 3-9. Visitors to a tide pool hear interpretation on a portable cassette tape player. Cape Perpetua, Siuslaw National Forest, Oregon. (U.S. Forest Service photo by Charles J. Newlon.)

Being Understood

As part of making interpretation rewarding, interpreters must use language readily understood by the visitor. As an extreme example, most Americans would not understand a lecture delivered in Chinese, but even in our own language subtle differences in word use can cause difficulty. For ready understanding, the terminology, examples, and analogies used for interpretation must be within the vocabulary and experience of the visitor. Ideally, examples should draw upon situations and experiences well known to the visitor. For example, it would be foolish to compare a smell to the aroma of new mown hay for visitors whose olfactory environment has been mainly factory smoke.

In addition to easily grasped language and examples, understanding depends on prior knowledge. Before understanding how DDT can threaten brown pelicans with extinction, one must understand food chains and the mechanisms by which DDT is passed along from species to species in increasing concentrations. Before one can understand a geyser, one must recognize that the boiling point of water increases with pressure.

When pamphlets or brochures are needed, as at park entrances or for trails, it may be a good idea to write several versions. A variety of styles oriented to

FIG. 3-10. The natural parent-child relationship is reinforced through interpretive media that permits parents and children to interact. Chugach National Forest, Anchorage, Alaska. (U.S. Forest Service photo by Robert Hakala.)

different visitor publics might be appropriate. Different versions or sections might be aimed at different age groups, different interest groups, or might assume different levels of prior knowledge. The National Park Service already has some materials for children, describing natural or cultural features in story form and including pictures that can be colored. This is an excellent way to orient children to natural resources. A question-answer series wherein parents and children could interact while discussing a park or recreational feature is another format which would reinforce the natural parent–child relationship (Fig. 3-10). If pamphlets or other materials were made more diverse, they would better serve new visitors, repeat visitors, youth, retired visitors, or even visitors who do not speak English.

Feedback

Perhaps no general concept or principle is more important for interpretation than that of feedback. In general terms, feedback is simply a set of signals indicating the extent to which an operation is going as planned and showing what corrective action would be useful. In interpretation, feedback is the flow of information from visitors that lets interpreters know how well they are achieving both their objectives and those of the visitors. Because different visitors will have different objectives, feedback is essential for tailoring presentations for a variety of people.

When an interpreter meets with small visitor groups on a face-to-face basis, feedback is readily available. Unless totally insensitive, the interpreter can tell from people's expressions, questions, and other behavior if they are interested or disinterested and if they understand the words and examples. Using this continuous flow of feedback, the interpreter can continually adjust the presentation to increase its effectiveness.

Once the easy and informal exchange of face-to-face interpretation is lost, obtaining feedback becomes much more difficult. Instead of direct interaction with a good cross section of visitors, the interpreter is increasingly exposed to fellow interpreters, to visitors who are especially receptive to interpretive presentations, or to visitors who are too polite to criticize shortcomings. More than one interpreter has had bad habits reinforced by compliments that were perfunctory rather than sincere.

When feedback is used to evaluate effectiveness, objectives must be clear. Surprisingly, many interpreters and interpretive planners cannot specify what it is they are trying to do. To be useful, objectives must be taken beyond vague generalities and must be stated in terms of behavior that the visitor could express as a result of interpretation.[19,20] An example of an objective that lends itself to evaluation would be to enable the visitor to describe food chains in general and the particular food chain which permits solar energy to be utilized by the cave cricket.

Once clear objectives are defined, feedback procedures can be devised to monitor the effectiveness with which objectives are being accomplished. These procedures can range from the interpreter's informal collection of impressions during face-to-face contact, to suggestion boxes, to formal studies in which visitors are asked to indicate how they enjoyed the interpretation and are then tested on their understanding of the information presented.

To avoid the many problems of attitude measurement, evaluation should be concentrated on objective information.[13] Not only are attitude changes difficult to measure, but attitudes are unlikely to change much in the short exposure provided by most interpretation. It is far better to measure effectiveness in transmitting basic concepts. If people understand these, their attitudes and behavior are quite likely to shift in appropriate directions.

Ideally, feedback mechanisms should be included in the design of interpretive programming. The recording quizboard mentioned earlier is not only an invitation to participate, but also a device to determine how well visitors understand the ideas presented to them. It lends itself especially well to determining whether a change in interpretation is increasing or decreasing comprehension by visitors.

We began this chapter by describing the relationship between people and interpretation. Feedback can be enhanced by the development of a formal visitor monitoring program. Such a program can provide information on: (1) the composition and key characteristics of people who participate in specific interpretive programs, and (2) a description of people present on a recreation site but who are not attending interpretive programs. Beginning in 1974 a team of researchers began experimenting with various forms of a monitoring program.[9,10,11,22] Building on the principles of interpretation noted earlier, a final visitor monitoring system was developed for the National Park Service (Fig. 3-11).

Designed to be employed by the interpretive staff, information systematically obtained can provide the interpreters with useful information to evaluate objectives and change programs as appropriate.

For greatest usefulness, feedback and evaluation should be concentrated during the development of an interpretive presentation before it has become "set." If the interpretation is not enjoyed or understood, the fault is usually with the presentation, not the visitor. When they are integrated into interpretive programming, feedback procedures can permit the evaluation of effectiveness and can indicate opportunities for improvement.

SUMMARY

The beneficiaries of a well-designed interpretive program are people. To communicate effectively with people or to transmit information to them requires that each audience be understood. Resource managers responsible for interpretation must understand both human behavior and resources sufficiently to inform various visitor publics and to enchance their experiences. For this task, five principles

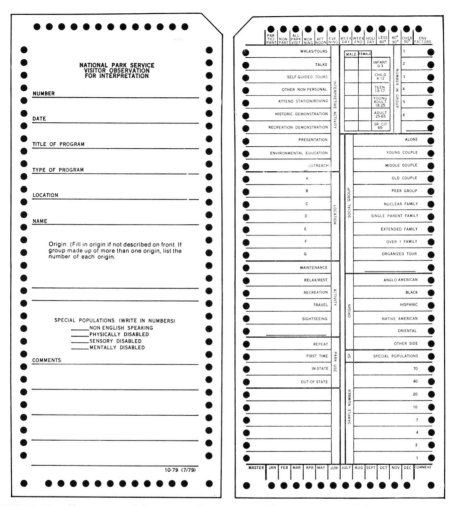

FIG. 3-11. Key sort card for visitor observation and interpretation. Information systematically obtained and conducive to specialized retrieval helps interpreters tailor their presentations to various groups.

of effective interpretation are suggested: (1) visitors are diverse, (2) visitors anticipate a relaxed and enjoyable atmosphere, (3) interpretive information must be rewarding, (4) interpretive information must be understood, and (5) the effectiveness of interpretation must continually be evaluated. In addition, alternative approaches are presented for achieving comprehensive interpretive programs attractive to a wide variety of visitors. However, the objectives of interpretation must be defined prior to the selection of an interpretive method or format.

REFERENCES

General References

Bultena, Gordon, and Donald R. Field. 1978. "The Effect of Social Structure on National Park-Going Patterns." In: *Proceedings of the First National Symposium on Outdoor Recreation Research and Planning,* Napier, T., and Pierce, J. M. (eds), Ohio State University, Columbus. [Also published in modified form in *Leisure Sciences* **3**(3), 221–240 (1980)].

Field, Donald R., and Joseph T. O'Leary. 1973. "Social Groups as a Basis for Assessing Participation in Selected Water Activities," *Journal of Leisure Research* **5,** 16–25.

McDonough, Maureen H., Donald R. Field, and James H. Gramann. 1977. "Application of Sociological Research to Interpretation: The Northwest Experience," *The Interpreter,* 7–11 (Fall). [Also appears in *Trends* **15,** 40–42 (Spring 1978)].

Machlis, Gary E., and Sally G. Machlis. 1974. *Creative Design for Bulletin Boards,* National Park Service, Cooperative Park Studies Unit, College of Forest Resources, University of Washington, Seattle.

Oltremari, Juan V. 1974. "A Survey of Desirable Preparation and Career Development of Interpretive Personnel," Master's thesis, College of Forest Resources, University of Washington, Seattle.

Renninger, Renee. 1977. "An Interpreter's Guide to Retired Visitors," National Park Service, Cooperative Park Studies Unit, College of Forest Resources, University of Washington, Seattle. Mimeographed.

References Cited

1. Beechel, Jacque. 1975. *Interpretation for Handicapped Persons: A Handbook for Outdoor Recreation Personnel,* National Park Service, Cooperative Park Studies Unit, College of Forest Resources, University of Washington, Seattle.

2. Bultena, Gordon, Donald R. Field, and Renee Renninger. 1978. "Interpretation for Retired National Parkgoers," *Trends* **15,** 30–33 (Spring).

3. Cheek, Neil H., Jr. 1971. "Towards a Sociology of Not Work," *Pacific Sociological Review* **14,** 245–258 (July).

4. Cheek, Neil H., Jr. 1972. "Variations in Patterns of Leisure Behavior: An Analysis of Sociological Aggregates." In: *Social Behavior, Natural Resources, and the Environment,* Burch, W. R., Jr., Cheek, N. H., Jr., and Taylor, L. (eds). Harper and Row, New York.

5. Clark, R. N., R. L. Burgess, and John C. Hendee. 1972. "The Development

of Anti-Litter Behavior in a Forest Campground," *Journal of Applied Behavior Analysis* **5,** 1–5 (Spring).

6. Clark, R. N., John C. Hendee, and Fred Campbell. 1971. "Values, Behavior and Conflict in Modern Camping Culture," *Journal of Leisure Behavior* **3,** 143–160 (Summer).

7. Field, Donald R. 1972. "Visitors to Parks in the Pacific Northwest," paper presented at the Pacific Northwest Region Superintendent's Conference, Portland, OR.

8. Field, Donald R. 1976. "Interchangeability of Parks with Other Leisure Settings." In: *Research in National Parks,* transactions of the National Park Centennial Symposium, NPS Symposium Series, No. 1, Government Printing Office, Washington, DC.

9. Gramann, James H. 1978. "History and Evaluation of the Interpretive Activity Inventory, An Observational System for Use in Parks," Master's thesis, College of Forest Resources, University of Washington, Seattle.

10. Gramann, James H., and Donald R. Field. 1977. *Interpretive Activity Inventory: Analysis of the 1976 Data from Mount Rainier National Park and Perry's Victory and International Peace Memorial,* National Park Service, Cooperative Park Studies Unit, College of Forest Resources, University of Washington, Seattle.

11. Gramann, James H., and Donald R. Field. 1978. *The Whitman Mission Data: Interpretive Activity Inventory,* National Park Service, Cooperative Park Studies Unit, College of Forest Resources, University of Washington, Seattle.

12. Graves, P. F. 1972. "Summation of the Forest Recreation Symposium." In: *Summary of the Forest Recreation Symposium,* USDA Forest Service Research Paper NE-235.

13. Hendee, John C. 1972. "No, to Attitudes to Evaluate Environmental Education," guest editorial, *Journal of Environmental Education* **3**(3).

14. Koth, Barbara A., Donald R. Field, and R. N. Clark. 1979. "The Cruiseship as a Leisure Setting: Implications for Interpretation," paper presented at the Northwest Association of Interpretive Naturalists Annual Meeting, Juneau, October. (Submitted to *The Interpreter,* Winter 1980).

15. Machlis, Gary E. 1975. "Families in Parks: An Analysis of Family Organization in a Leisure Setting," Master's thesis, College of Forest Resources, University of Washington, Seattle.

16. Machlis, Gary E., and Donald R. Field. 1974. "Interpreting Parks for Kids— Making it Real," *Trends* **11**(2), 19–25.

17. Machlis, Gary E., and Donald R. Field. 1979. "Foreign Visitors and Interpretation: A Sociological Look at the Japanese Tourist," paper presented at the Second Conference on Scientific Research in National Parks, San Francisco.

18. Machlis, Gary E., and Maureen H. McDonough. 1978. *Children's Interpretation: A Discovery Book for Interpreters,* National Park Service, Cooperative Park Studies Unit, College of Forest Resources, University of Washington, Seattle.

19. Magar, R. F. 1962. *Preparing Instructional Objectives,* Fearson Publishers, Belmont, CA.

20. Putney, Allen D., and J. Alan Wagar. 1973. Objectives and Evaluation in Interpretive Planning, *Journal of Environmental Education* **5**(1), 43–44.

21. Renninger, Renee. 1976. "Retirees in Parks: Implications for Interpretation," Master's thesis, College of Forest Resources, University of Washington, Seattle.

22. Silvy, Valeen, and John Hanna. 1979. *Visitor Observation for Interpretation,* National Park Service, Cooperative Park Studies Unit, College of Forest Resources, University of Washington, Seattle. (Also published by Hanna, Silvy & Associates, Bryan, TX.)

23. Travers, R. M. W. 1967. *Research and Theory Related to Audio-Visual Information Transmission,* U.S. Department of Health, Education, and Welfare, Washington, DC.

24. Wagar, J. Alan. 1972. "Evaluating Interpretation and Interpretive Media," paper presented to the Association of Interpretive Naturalists, Callaway Gardens, Pine Mountain, GA.

25. Wagar, J. Alan. 1972. *The Recording Quizboard: A Device for Evaluating Interpretive Services,* USDA Forest Service Research Paper PNW-139.

26. Washburne, Randel F., and J. Alan Wagar. 1972. "Evaluating Visitor Response to Exhibit Content," *Curator* **15**(3), 248–254.

27. Wolf, Wendy. 1978. "Incorporating Visitor Use Data into the Development of Interpretive Services (Case Study—The Chilkoot Trail)," Master's thesis, College of Forest Resources, University of Washington, Seattle.

28. Wolf, Wendy, Peter Womble, and Donald R. Field. 1977/1978. "Hiking the Chilkoot Trail: Implications for Interpretive Services," *The Interpreter* **9**, 17–22.

CHAPTER 4

THE INTERPRETIVE PLAN

Gordon A. Bradley

INTRODUCTION

The task of developing an interpretive plan requires an appreciation for and an understanding of planning, both as an activity and a process.

Considerable discussion has centered around the terms planning, plans, and planners. In professional journals, conferences and symposiums, and among citizen groups planning is a topic of current debate. As a result divergent views exist as to what planning actually comprises. Certainly with many successful and unsuccessful planning examples to be found, it is not unexpected to have different views as to its usefulness. Planning is viewed by some as a panacea for all problems and by others as an attempt to regiment that which should be left to evolve naturally. It is the intent of this chapter to place the concept of planning in perspective so that interpreters may recognize planning's value as a means for achieving interpretive program objectives with minimum difficulty and maximum efficiency. Initial sections of the chapter address planning from a general perspective. This involves a discussion of how planning is defined and general planning objectives, including the larger framework in which interpretive planning occurs. Latter sections concentrate on the systematic approach necessary for determining the interpretive potential of an area. This involves discussion of the role of planning in interpretation, interpretive planning objectives, and the interpretive planning process. To further illustrate, a suggested format for an interpretive plan has been included in an appendix to this chapter.

DEFINITION

The concept of planning, regardless of the discipline (social, transportation, interpretation); the level (site, area, unit); or the resource (water, land, timber) does not vary greatly from one entity to any other.

Planning by definition "refers to any detailed method, formulated beforehand, for doing or making something" (Webster).* Implicit in this is the notion of attempting to achieve desired goals. Additional aspects of planning are more thoroughly discussed in definitions found in the planning literature. It is useful to look at several definitions and to discuss those that most thoroughly address the concept of planning.[5]

1. Planning is orderly development.[3]
2. The planning process represents the self-conscious attempt by man to order his environment so as to realize common goals and values.[9]
3. Planning is a way of defining purposes and choosing means of obtaining them.[2]
4. Planning is the conscious and deliberate guidance of thinking so as to create logical means for achieving agreed-upon goals.[8]
5. Planning is that process of making decisions about future goals and future courses of action which rely on explicit tracings of the repercussion and the value implications associated with alternative courses of action. In turn, it requires explicit evaluation of choices among the alternative matching goal-action sets.[10]
6. Planning is the process of preparing in advance of action and in a reasonably systematic fashion, recommendations for policies and courses of action (with careful attention to their probable by-products, side effects, or spillover effects) to achieve accepted objects in the common life of society.[11]

As the definitions become more lengthy, we begin to discover the complexities involved in planning. Planning is more than the utilization of a detailed method; it is more than achieving desired goals, and it is more than orderly development. In Definitions 5 and 6 there are several key elements that best describe the total nature of planning.

The first is that planning is a *process*. There are logical and sequential steps in this process; and it is continuing and ongoing. Therefore in the development of a plan, it is important that it not be viewed as an end in itself. A plan is a dynamic tool. Because of new information, changing social attitudes and values, new technology, and new ways of approaching problems, it is imperative that a plan be flexible enough to respond to and reflect such changes. It must always be open to comment and revision and must not be a static document cast in concrete.

*Webster's New World Dictionary of the American Language.

FIG. 4-1. Planners, representatives of citizens groups, a park commission, and the press gather at an undeveloped state park to discuss its future. Leadbetter Point State Park, Washington. (Photo by Grant W. Sharpe.)

The decisions that are made in the development of a plan are based on reason. They are a conscious attempt, using the best available information, to substantiate and justify particular courses of action. To make planning decisions based purly on intuition, especially today when planning efforts are under such close scrutiny, would be the height of folly.

Planning is also concerned with future courses of action as a means of achieving established goals and objectives. Therefore, the rational planning process is in advance of action. To develop a plan to justify actions already taken is not planning. Also, the future courses of action must have a direction as indicated by the fact that we are attempting to achieve certain goals and objectives. Unless the goals are clearly defined in advance and readily understood by those affected, it is impossible to know whether or not the planning effort is successful or will be well received (Fig. 4-1). Therefore, measurable goals and objectives must be established.

Also, we must know what the repercussions of a particular course of action will be, both in terms of meeting the established goals as well as in the side effects, by-products, or spillover effects that may not be a desired result of a planning effort. This is increasingly important in the United States, given the requirements of recent environmental legislation such as the National Environmental Policy Act of 1969. Section 102(2) (c) of that act requires that the planner indicate the environmental impacts of a proposed action and any adverse environmental effects as well as any irreversible or irretrievable commitments of resources that would be involved in the proposed course of action should it be implemented. This directive includes not only the immediate or primary effects, but also requires that the planner look closely at secondary and tertiary effects of the course of action. Without a clear understanding of the implications of a particular course of action, it becomes difficult if not impossible to make rational and informed decisions.

We must also understand the values associated with a particular course of action in terms of who we are planning for as well as how the planner's values may affect the plan. Too often a plan is merely a reflection of the individual values of the person who is developing the plan. Unless the plan reflects broadly accepted social values it will be poorly received. To be successful the planner must know the publics affected by the plan—their customs, traditions, values, and other pertinent information. A great failing in many past planning efforts was the notion that the planner knew what was best. The only person who knows what is best for an individual is that particular individual, and it is the responsibility of the planner to become informed and maintain objectivity in using the planning process to reflect other people's values.

Planners must present alternatives. Regardless of the goals of a plan, there is always more than one way of achieving them. Alternatives imply that those for whom we are planning have a choice. Each alternative will normally have both advantages and disadvantages. To avoid severe side effects, decision makers may choose an alternative that falls short of the desired goal but incurs less undesirable by-products. Such judgements must be allowed for in the planning process and are basic to planning in a democratic society.

Consideration of the preceding key elements in a planning effort is essential to the viability of any plan.

OBJECTIVES

From any reasonable definition of planning, it follows that planning is conducted for a particular purpose. Objectives may vary considerably, but several general objectives are common to all types and levels of planning. The following planning guidelines have been found highly useful and are applicable to interpretive planning. They were developed for regional planning by Coleman Woodbury.[11] They have been modified to serve the discussion of interpretive planning.

1. *Livability:* In planning for interpretive programs, particularly developed interpretive facilities, reasonable conveniences for all persons in their normal activities should be provided. Special attention should be given to safety and the separation of incompatible uses or uses that detract from the conveyance of the interpretive message. Opportunities for interaction with the

interpretive subject, as well as with other people should be supplied but should not be compulsory.

2. *Efficiency:* Facilities should be arranged in patterns that make for reasonable efficiency in the provision of services, utilities, maintenance, and other operations necessary for the support of an interpretive program.

3. *Amenity:* Provide a setting including variety and unity as well as character, beauty, and a sensitive and imaginative treatment of the interpretive subject. The amenity objective applies equally to the message and the setting in which the message is presented (Fig. 4-2).

4. *Flexibility and Choice:* Because both planning and interpretation are dynamic processes, maintaining flexibility and choice must be an objective of interpretive planning. Facilities should permit the incorporation of new themes and new techniques as well as modification of the intensity of the interpretive program. The interpretive messages must be developed so that the recipients can receive, understand, contemplate, and evaluate them at their own pace. A successful program allows visitors some choice.

5. *Minimum Harm to Natural and Cultural Communities:* A major recurring dilemma faced by the interpretive planner is the possibility of destroying the very subject being interpreted. Changes caused either by construction or visitor usage should be minimally disruptive and should be estimated in advance to determine what offsetting steps could be taken (Fig. 4-3). This applies to plant and animal communities as well as to cultural settings. Visitors and facilities on a fragile meadow, a nesting ground, or in the territory of a primitive society can virtually destroy the interpretive subject. Measures

FIG. 4-2. The interpretive subject here is a pioneer cabin. The treatment of the scene is compatible with the rustic character of the historic setting. Blue Ridge Parkway, Virginia. (Photo courtesy of the National Park Service.)

FIG. 4-3. Seashore visitors following a boardwalk through planted beach grass. Cape Cod National Seashore, Massachusetts. (Photo by Grant W. Sharpe.)

must be taken to insure the early identification and means of protecting sensitive, and rare environments. For these reasons some areas may have to be excluded from visitor use.

6. *Optimum Use of Resources:* A continuing problem in planning is the allocation of human and capital resources among the various types of investments necessary for an interpretive program. There must be a choice between new developments and program revisions that represents some approximation as to their optimum use. This suggests establishing priorities among the needs for interpretation that will meet immediate needs first and will minimize future shortages of facilities and services.

7. *Public Participation:* The general public should take part in the planning process through regular rather than chance opportunities for criticism and voicing of preferences.

To expect to meet these seven objectives in a manner satisfactory to all concerned would be unrealistic. Rather, the point is to understand their existence, address them in all planning efforts, and attempt to maximize each to the extent feasible given a particular interpretive planning context.

ROLE OF THE INTERPRETIVE PLAN
IN THE TOTAL PROGRAM FRAMEWORK

Interpretation may be the primary purpose of a particular area, but it is usually only part of a larger framework. This is true at the city, county, state, regional, and federal levels as well as with private and semiprivate organizations. For example, plans and policies for a large national park involve many areas of planning and programming. In addition to interpretive planners who develop programs around the natural and cultural phenomena of the area, transportation planners are needed to develop the circulation network, recreation planners for the outdoor recreation activities, forest resource planners and wildlife managers for the general forest areas, and facility planners (architects, landscape architects, and urban planners) for the developed areas. All of these areas must be coordinated into a cohesive unit that may be referred to as the overall area plan. In some organizations this is called the Master Plan. Whatever term is used, this document is the guide for the development, operation, and preservation of the area. In addition to containing the plan for interpretation it also serves as a guide for acquisition, protection, development, operations, and management of the unit.

To be effective this document requires the integration of all elements. A typical mistake in attempting to utilize this multi-use concept is to bring together many separate plans and call the composite a master plan for the area. The weakness in this approach is that the first plan submitted usually becomes the dominant plan around which all other planning elements revolve and are subordinated. For example, a national forest may develop a multiple-use plan that in reality is a wilderness plan with remaining areas to be utilized for timber production, wildlife management, forage, or watershed management. Conversely a timber management plan may dominate rather than function in a compatible manner with recreation, wilderness, watershed, wildlife, and range management. It is therefore essential when initiating a new planning effort that coordinated direction be given to bring all known sectors of the plan together at the beginning of the planning process. This assures that all programs will be weighed equally in the development of an area. Once again we are faced with trade-offs and the probability that all participants will not be satisfied.

Interpretation is considered a luxury by some organizations—to be considered after the "necessities" have been taken care of. When this happens we often find that the interpretive features and opportunities have been destroyed or so severely damaged that a high-quality interpretive program is rendered impossible.

Although highly conceptualized, Fig. 4-4 illustrates the general framework in which potential uses for an area would be evaluated. Indicated is the suggestion of a larger framework within which all uses are considered. The initial phases are concerned with determining the resources of the area and the actual demands. The resource inventory would determine the feasibility of various types of uses. This would include an inventory of historic, archeologic, vegetative, geologic, soils, wildlife, social, economic, visual, and other factors. The determination of need would assess the demand for recreation, timber, interpretation, wilderness, and other uses technically feasible on a specific area as dictated by the resource conditions. Specific uses are then considered, utilizing all proceeding information. This ultimately results in a general development plan and a statement outlining the implications of the plan. The process is usually complex, and there are still other considerations necessary. All planning elements are considered together and the final master plan is a synthesis rather than an appendage.

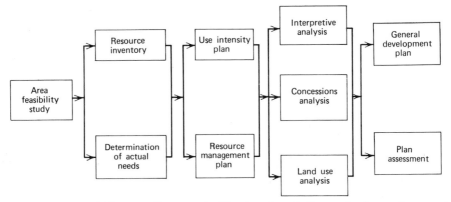

FIG. 4-4. General Planning Framework. The flowchart indicates the larger framework within which all uses, including interpretation, are included.

The need for team efforts in pursuing a planning program has been noted. The necessary expertise, however, varies according to the areas under study. A project coordinator (team captain or project planner) must fulfill important coordinating responsibilities. Other members could include an architect, landscape architect, engineer, historian, naturalist, ecologist, resource specialists (wildlife biologist, climatologist, soils scientist, geologist, forester, etc.), economist, and sociologist. The necessary technical staff to assist in report compilation and graphic aids would complete the planning group. This type of team is not always possible. Because of funding problems, available expertise, time limitations, coordination difficulties, or other constraints, it may be that only one person is available to complete the task. In such cases the limitations should be explicitly stated so that decision makers are aware of the shortcomings of the plan.

ROLE OF PLANNING IN INTERPRETATION

To establish the nature of interpretive planning it is necessary to examine the specific objectives of the interpretive discipline. It is then possible to determine how planning fits into the interpretive framework.

In Chapter 1 we discussed how interpretation seeks to achieve three basic objectives. The first is to assist the visitor in developing a keener understanding and enjoyment of the area visited.

The second objective is to accomplish management goals. Interpretation can encourage thoughtful use of the resource on the part of the visitor and can reinforce the idea that public spaces are special places requiring special behavior.

Interpretation can also be used to minimize adverse impact to the resource by keeping people and facilities away from sensitive areas.

The third objective is to provide public understanding of a particular organization and its programs.

It is important to note that interpretation does more than just convey a message. Beyond educating the visitor and developing an awareness and appreciation for a particular subject, interpretation also serves a management and public relations function. Herein lies the notion of the interpretive plan functioning as a multipurpose tool. The plan contains management principles for use, preservation, and operation of an area. The development of a successful program, the assurance of protection for areas of special interest, and the delineation of guidelines for efficient management, operations, and maintenance programs are all a part of interpretation and more specifically the primary objectives of interpretive planning.

The planning process is discussed in detail later in this chapter. To focus on the role of planning in interpretation, let us examine the relationship between our three primary objectives and the concept of planning.

Successful Program Development

Many factors contribute to the development of a successful interpretive program. The task facing the interpretive planner is to insure that all possible factors are addressed. By pursuing a systematic approach, one would hope that a successful program would be developed.

Planning must also address the organization's goals and objectives. What is it that the agency is trying to do? What is the nature of the organization for which the interpretive program is being developed? What type of message will best communicate to the visitor the desired image of the organization? A thorough understanding of the organization is prerequisite to interpretive plan development.

In addition to understanding the agency, the planner must also know the user. Who will experience the interpretive program? Where will they come from? What will be their background? How long will they stay in or around the area? The interpretive planner must have this information to insure the development of a successful program. This is discussed in greater detail in Chapter 3.

In addition to knowing the agency and the user, the interpretive planner must know the resource. This includes not only the primary resource or the focus of a particular interpretive program, but all resources associated with, contiguous to, or affected by the program. Obviously, one individual is not qualified or even expected to be technically competent in all of the resource areas that must be addressed in an interpretive plan. Therefore it becomes necessary to call on resource specialists. A team effort or multidiscipline approach is usually necessary for any measure of success.

Protection of Areas of Special Interest

A comprehensive inventory and analysis by appropriate specialists should identify areas that will require special protection. The responsibility of the specialists in identifying fragile, unusual, or sensitive areas should also include the identification of factors that may contribute to the degradation of such sites. In other words, if an area is going to be interpreted, how do we minimize the probable impacts? A good interpretive planner will insure the identification of the causal elements and will incorporate appropriate protective measures in the interpretive plan. The planner again is not expected to be an expert in all areas, further underlining the necessity for a multidisciplinary approach in the development of the plan. Protective measures can be suggested by the resource specialists as well as architects, landscape architects, and engineers. In as much as the resource, whether natural or cultural, is the focus of an interpretive program, it is imperative that planning insure its continuation rather than contribute to its demise.

Interpretation: A Complement to Management

Interpretive plans, like any plans, must conform to the structure and operational constraints of the administrative unit for which they are developed. Often area managers, superintendents, and operators contend that problems are created rather than solved by an interpretive program. Either because of increased maintenance costs or operational costs, an interpretive program can become a nuisance and drain the resources of a particular unit. Hopefully, careful planning will minimize these possibilities.

An interpretive program requiring a heavy staffing schedule may not be feasible for an organization with a small budget. An interpretive facility requiring continual maintenance may not be feasible if placed in an area already understaffed and with other maintenance obligations. Interpretive trails or facility layouts must be designed with maintenance criteria in mind or they will create numerous problems for the unit manager.

Obviously, there will be compromises to the interpretive program when attempting to satisfy all objectives. However, this should not be construed by the interpretive planner as a rationalization for doing a less than professional job. By the very nature of the planner's work he or she will undoubtedly be subject to criticism. Planning involves working wtih "grey areas," dilemmas, and trade-offs. One must strive to satisfy balanced objectives to the extent possible and feasible given a particular planning context. As an interpretive planner one wears many hats, functioning as expert, generalist, educator, decision maker, information generator, and a clarifier of alternatives (Fig. 4-5). One should not be defeated by this fact; on the contrary, the challenges presented are opportunities for developing new techniques, new approaches, and innovative methods of interpretation.

FIG. 4-5. An interpretive planner making a presentation of alternatives for an interpretive master plan. Rogue River National Forest, Oregon. (Photo by Grant W. Sharpe.)

THE INTERPRETIVE PLANNING PROCESS

The planning process tends to follow a universal pattern distinguished only by the specific planning objectives of the particular organization.

The process tends to be sequential, interactive (looping), and continual. The phases lead from one stage to another, and there is a need for inputs and the resultant feedback throughout the process. A plan is never complete. There will always be a need for revision and improvements in planning. Indicated below are a series of steps that comprise the planning process.[5] These steps have been modified slightly for this specific discussion of interpretive planning. They are as follows:

1. Anticipation
2. Appraisal of need
3. Establishment of goals and objectives
4. Delineation of areas of special interest
5. Identification of assumptions
6. Definition of evaluative objectives, criteria, and standards

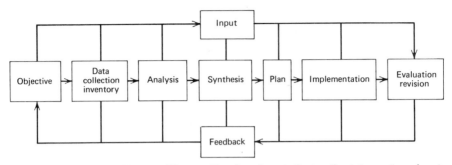

FIG. 4-6. Interpretive Planning Phases. The flowchart indicates the interpretive planning phases and the elements to be included in the study plan.

7. Preliminary identification of alternative courses of action
8. Reevaluation of objectives
9. Selection of alternative courses of action
10. Gathering of information
11. Evaluation of alternatives
12. Ranking of alternatives
13. Recommendations to decision makers
14. Policy articulation
15. Program/plan selection
16. Plan implementation
17. Plan evaluation
18. Revision

It is obvious that the planner is not necessarily a participant throughout the entire planning process. The public is the source of the expression of need. Elected officials respond with the formulation of policy objectives or goals. The planner's responsibility lies mainly in defining evaluative objectives, applying standards, gathering information, and developing alternatives in addition to evaluating the plan's effectiveness and making the necessary revisions. The organization administrators are responsible for plan implementation.[1,4]

Our primary concern is the responsibility of the interpretive planner. Fig. 4-6 shows the various phases of interpretive planning discussed below and also functions as a study plan outline.

Preliminary to any planning effort, the planner must determine a course of action. What are you going to do? How long do you have? Who will be doing what? How much funding do you have? What information is necessary before you proceed to the next phase? These are basic questions that should be resolved prior to beginning any work. Too often a planner muddles along without specific direction, apparently with the hope of developing such direction from an unknown source. Without adequate organization an interpretive planning effort is almost certainly doomed. Therefore, a preliminary study plan is needed (Fig. 4-7).

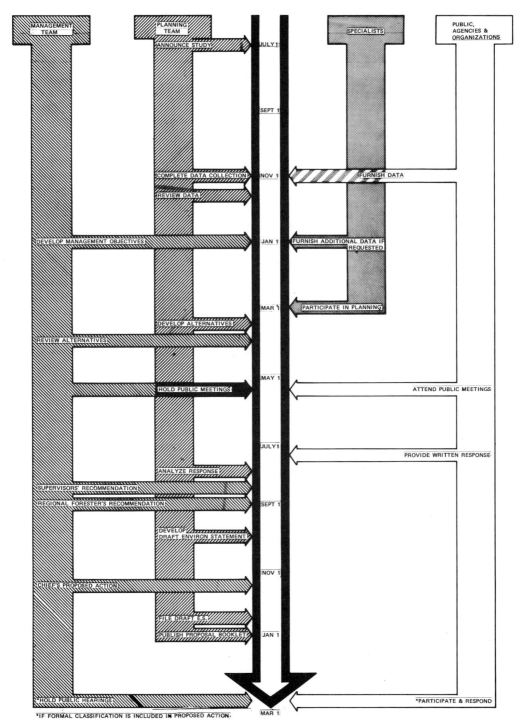

FIG. 4-7. A sample flowchart from a U.S. Forest Service study plan illustrating the relationship of time and the many actions and inputs by different groups.

The study plan should define all phases of the project, including a statement of the goals as defined by the responsible organization. Define within each phase the tasks to be accomplished. Information and the sources from which it is to be derived are identified, and personnel responsible for specific tasks assigned. The time frame for the specific interpretive planning project should also be clearly noted. The study plan thus constitutes a vital element in planning. It is similar to plotting an itinerary before beginning a trip. You must know where you are going, how to get there, how long it will take, and how much it will cost.

Objectives

Objectives are the guides to specific actions required in an interpretive plan. As indicated by Young[12] the guiding policy must:

1. State an overall purpose.
2. Indicate an awareness of the implications of that purpose or other purposes.
3. Provide a target that reflects the overall purpose and whose attainment appears feasible.
4. Imply a course of action.

Implicit in these requirements is a hierarchy with logical consistency among different levels of objectives. Putney and Wagar break these levels into policy objectives, objectives to guide selection of opportunities, and evaluation objectives.[6] Young prefers to define the levels as goals, standards, and objectives.[12] Regardless of the nomenclature used, there is a progression from the general to the specific.

The first level provides a purpose for the action. It is often an ideal that may be expressed in the abstract terms of values. It is essentially a policy statement that defines program direction and balance.

The second level is more specific and further guides us in selecting opportunities available for interpretation. For each of our first level objectives it may be necessary to develop several second level objectives.

The third level defines the desired outcome and permits measurement and evaluation pertinent to the first and second level. Several third level objectives may be needed for each second level objective.

An example of the three levels is as follows:

First level—Show visitors the positive and negative effects of environmental modification.

Second level—Show visitors the interrelatedness of parts of an ecosystem.

Third level—Enable each visitor to describe the life cycle of the Pacific Salmon, indicating (1) the conditions necessary for survival of the eggs and young fish, and (2) human activities that can upset these conditions.[6]

Essential to reaching the target is knowing where the target is. Objecties and their definitions are integral to plan development. Provided that objectives are developed with consistency, the measured success of third level objectives allows one to infer success of second and first level objectives.

Inventory—Data Collection

The object of the inventory phase is to identify and locate the resources and amenities—both natural and humanly altered—that make up the physical, biological, and cultural environment. This search for information is critical to successful interpretive plan development and must be carried out with a high degree of thoroughness and accuracy. Opportunities for interpretation and information that may shape an interpretive program should be identified during the inventory process. A good inventory provides basic data necessary for effective transmission of interpretive information, potential justification for acquiring additional land, and opportunity for retaining the interpretive integrity of the area. Inventory techniques vary as do sources of information, but searching the current literature, examining aerial photographs, reviewing mapped data, interviewing agency personnel, citizens, and professional experts, and analyzing the site are standard procedures (Fig. 4-8).

FIG. 4-8. An interpretive planner conducting a site analysis in the inventory data collecting phase to assess the interpretive resources before development takes place. Newhalem Creek, Ross Lake National Recreation Area, Washington. (Photo by Grant W. Sharpe.)

The type of information needed will vary from project to project; therefore it is difficult to provide a checklist that indicates all the necessary information. Any list should undergo examination and modification based on the requirements of the specific planning project. With this caution the following list suggests the type of information useful in plan development. The elements listed identify the major issues surrounding a planning effort, the opportunities available for interpretation, and the limitations imposed on the planner. In addition the elements identify the potential users and their characteristics, types of uses and their requirements, and the likely consequences of developing a particular program (see Table 1, opposite page).

As we discussed earlier one person will not have expertise in all areas and specialists are needed to provide and interpret the full range of information. The planner, as coordinator, must know the type of information needed and the best format for its presentation. These criteria must be specified and communicated clearly if the specialist is to provide information useful to the planner and understood by the decision makers. The planner must be explicit in requests for information as to subject detail and intended use.

If information is inadequate the result may be a low quality plan. In some instances this can be avoided; in other situations one must simply work with the best data available even if it is less than ideal. Also, some information may not be current, causing information gaps in the inventory. If those gaps cannot be filled with current data, decisions based on outdated information should be made with caution, clearly indicating the limitations of the data.

Analysis

Information derived from the inventory provides separate descriptions for all of the elements that comprise the natural and cultural systems. During the analysis these data must be examined and evaluated for information critical to interpretive plan development and assembled into interactive systems. The properties of a particular soil or vegetation type, for example, are not a sufficient basis for developing detailed interpretive proposals. Analysis should focus instead on holistic processes and responses to specific management alternatives. Interpretation should attempt to present a whole rather than a part, consequently the analysis should consider total systems.

Cultural information is used to construct a "picture" of the area in its historical context, its current context, and what may be anticipated in the future given specific management parameters.

The analysis phase also identifies potential interpretive themes. The basic theme may be centered around some significant feature of the area, or it may be more general. What was the reason the area was set aside? Was it historical, geological, archeological, or did the site possess unusual plant or animal life? It

TABLE 1

PUBLIC INPUT	INFORMATION NEEDS	
	NATURAL FACTORS	CULTURAL FACTORS
Source	Lithosphere	Regulations, Legislation
Public interest groups	Geology	Local
Private interest groups	Soils	Regional
Governmental agen-	Topography	State
cies	Hydrosphere	National
Information	Freshwater	Population
Issues	Lakes	Characteristics (demographic
Concerns	Streams	data)
Interest	Saltwater	Densities
	Marshes	Trends
	Estuaries	Grouping
	Bays	Interpretive uses
	Biosphere	Locational requirements
	Flora	Operational requirements
	Fauna	Compatibilities
	Atmosphere	Environmental impacts
	Climate	Media Options
	Microclimate	Communication effectiveness
		Operational requirements

Cultural Factors (continued):

Perceptual
  Auditory
  Visual
Historical
  Human use
  Customs—traditions
Archeological
  Ancient sites
  Artifacts
Land Use
  Forms
  Recreation
  Commercial
  Industrial
  Agricultural
  Urban
  Transportation
  Characteristics
  Patterns
  Capacities
  Densities
  Trends
  Ownership
  Value

may be a combination of these, or perhaps the reason was purely recreational. Some areas, of course, will be more noteworthy than others, but all sites have interpretive potential. The unexceptional area often presents the interpreter with the greatest challenge. Skillful interpretations of the ordinary scene enables visitors to identify with life processes in a manner not always possible in more spectacular areas.

Once themes are selected, methods of interpreting these themes must be considered. These methods comprise the media—those facilities and services necessary to tell the total interpretive story. Many have been field tested for over half a century in parks and equivalent reserves around the world. Some are simple modifications of these old methods; others are quite new.

The more traditional methods include personal presentations on boats, buses, and trains; evening campfire presentations; conducted walks or rambles; self-guided activities; the use of exhibits, signs, and labels; publications; and visitor centers.

A modification of old methods may be seen in mobile exhibitions, mobile information centers, and roving personnel in areas of visitor concentration. Living interpretation and cultural demonstrations, though not new, are reappearing with fresh impact. Audio devices add new dimensions as interpreters experiment with short-range radio, cassette tapes, closed-circuit television, inductance loops, and voice repeaters.

Because experience and research show us that visitors are remarkably diverse, we cannot expect a standard interpretive message to work with all visitors.

The planner should strive for the most complete analysis possible. Time, funds, and expertise will, of course, be limiting factors. The best available information should be obtained from sociologists, economists, ecologists, and other specialists. This should provide a reasonable understanding of the resource, the user, and the alternative management strategies and patterns. The ultimate goal is to provide sustained benefits at the least cost.

At the conclusion of the analysis phase the planner should have an accurate picture of the specific area. The raw data should be in manageable packages describing the resource, the interpretive opportunities, the users, potential competing uses, and the agency and cultural constraints and preferences.

Synthesis of Planning Alternatives

The Planner is now in a position to begin synthesis of several alternative courses of action, identifying the implication of each. At this point the design and imaginative ideas become important, providing both a range of choices among alternatives as well as a basis for program selection by the decision maker.

Depending on the particular project, there may be opportunities to develop greatly contrasting alternatives. On the other hand the planner may be so constrained that there exist only slight variations between feasible proposed alternatives.

In preparing alternatives, the planner must frequently review the interpretive planning objectives for guidance. The optimum mix of interpretive technology is sought, thereby providing the most effective interpretive media in conjunction with the appropriate intensity of facility development. Environmental capabilities, user needs, organization requirements, and contemporary values, trends, and conditions must also be reviewed.

Following synthesis the planner is able to present decision makers with alternative means of meeting the originally stated objectives. These are essentially different plans for the same area. The decision makers should be able then to study each alternative and to be able to determine the relative advantages and disadvantages of each.

The selection of a final course of action should represent the plan alternative that best satisfies the interpretive objectives.

The Plan

The final stages of the planning process focus on the preferred alternative—the one most satisfactory to all concerned. The planner at this point must make any necessary revisions and then begin to complete all aspects of the selected plan including a detailed estimate of its impact as well as the means for implementation. The content of the interpretive plan and a recommended format are presented in an appendix to this chapter.

Implementation.   Once a plan has been assembled there are many additional requirements to be met before the proposed interpretive program can become operational. Developmental phases must be scheduled carefully to insure proper sequence of actions.

Budgetary considerations are usually a primary concern. These may require a shift in agency allocations, and any change in priorities will produce resistance. The plan must be well received by those within the organization if friction and foot-dragging are to be minimized.

Purchase of land to acquire the area in total, or to consolidate areas is frequently necessary. Staffing needs must be considered and funds must be allocated for them. Costs and funding sources must be clearly delineated.

If the momentum of a planning effort is not maintained, the plan will probably end up on a storeroom shelf. Considerable investments of time, money, and effort are required to generate good plans. The public is increasingly unwilling to see large planning expenditures made without realization of the anticipated benefits. Therefore, the implementation effort must be well organized and executed with persistent tact and efficiency. No matter how fine your plan, or how well it will meet the need that called it into being, it will be a failure if it is never implemented.

Plan Evaluation and Revision

To insure that a plan continues to meet its objectives, a monitoring program is needed. This evaluates user and facility impacts on resources and the impact of the program on the users. A review shortly after implementation with periodic reviews at later times should insure program viability, thus requiring only occasional minor program revisions. Programs can be eliminated or substantially altered whenever the review indicates such a course of action.

It is essential that all members of the planning team participate in the review in order to contribute evaluative criteria and suggestions for program improvements. This review process is not only necessary for program administration but can serve as a guide to future program development.

CONCLUSION

The discussion presented in this chapter attempts to focus on the basics of planning as a process related to interpretation. No general review of planning can cover all of the problems one will undoubtedly he confronted with when developing an interpretive plan. In applying the basic planning concepts there is ample room for latitude in adjusting the process, objectives, and format of information. Each planning context will differ depending on the area, the interpretive theme, the time, staff, available expertise, and, of course, funds. By adhering to a systematic planning process the interpretive planner should develop programs that reflect the best knowledge of an area and lead to a quality interpretive experience.

APPENDIX: THE INTERPRETIVE PLAN—A DOCUMENT

Interpretive planning is essentially a process—an approach to a particular management activity. However, this process is generally embodied in a planning document. This document will guide the operation, preservation, and maintenance of the interpretive program. Contained within this planning document will be all the pertinent information that has been generated throughout the planning process.

The interpretive planning document discusses the purposes, the significance of the area, how we expect to maintain it, how we expect to use it, and the benefits to be derived as well as who will operate the area. The document also discusses how it is to be operated, the facilities, their layout and justification, and finally the information on which the plan is based. This is obviously a large undertaking, but there is virtually no shortcut in developing the systematic approach needed in planning a successful interpretive program.

The following is a suggested format for the interpretive plan that indicates the organization and the content. In this format the information will be most useful to the visitor, the agency administrator, the specialists, and the operational personnel. The format closely follows the general structure of master plans used for planning and development by the California State Parks and Recreation Department.[7]

The Plan Format:

A. Guiding Principles
   1. Introduction
   2. Purpose
   3. Objectives and policies
   4. Land management priorities
   5. Visitor use and characteristics
   6. Unit organization
   7. Unit operation
B. Supporting Plan Documents
   1. Inventory base maps
   2. Control documents
   3. General development documents
   4. Operational documents
C. Appendix

Moving from the general to the specific, we can see that the initial sections are concerned with the basic policy, its application, and what is to be expected at the operations level. The intermediate portion of the plan guides the operations, and the final section reinforces the plan with factual data. Each suggested section of the plan is discussed below.

Guiding Principles

Introduction.   A brief description of the area and its location, supplying the information necessary to acquaint the reader with the primary concerns of the plan.

Purpose.   States why the organization is interested in an interpretive program in the particular area. The justifications for the organization's interpretive program are presented.

Objectives and Policy.   Recognition of the area's values, both from a resource and human perspective. It is important to begin with a general statement of objectives and policy and progress to specific objectives ultimately allowing for the independent measurement of the success of the interpretive program.

Stated policies should similarly indicate the general preservation and use policy of the agency and progress to more specific guidelines and requirements necessary to insure proper use and protection of the interpretive resource.

Land Management Principles.   Should delineate all resource considerations including the plan development. Further significant precautions and techniques to protect and perpetuate interpretive values should be set forth.

Visitor Use.   Describe ways in which visitors will use the interpretive program. This section also details what themes and media are necessary to accommodate the interpretive program and the visitor. It should also state the kinds of visitors to be served.

Unit Organization.   Describes the functions and structure as well as responsibility for various activities within the organization. For supervisory purposes this section should also identify staffing necessary to operate the program and any supporting facilities.

Unit Operations.   Provides the plans for accomplishing the interpretive program. The necessary organization, scheduling, and phasing of all administrative, management, interpretive maintenance, and operations activities are clearly delineated in the unit operation section.

Supporting Plan Documents

Inventory Base Maps.   Information included in the inventory checklist should be represented in this section to the extent that it lends itself to graphic display. This may include boundaries, ownership, culture, physiography, flora, fauna, historical and archeological areas.

Control Documents.   Information concerning the ultimate area boundaries and general use distribution. Because of administrative, developmental, or protection needs (including maintenance of ecological integrity, watershed unity, or increasing area value) it is often necessary to acquire adjacent lands. Therefore, the control documents should indicate the ideal boundaries of the unit.

A general land use plan portrays the use areas to the extent that zones are delineated, indicating the major use areas and their relationship to one another. This is only a general depiction as the specific use information is indicated in the development documents.

General Development Documents.   Show the specific use areas if appropriate, including the type and extent of development indicated for all structures, trails, rest areas, parking areas, overlooks, maintenance areas, and the necessary utilities.

If the area is several thousand acres in size, it would be appropriate to have the general development documents illustrate the total unit on one map at a relatively large scale. For more specific areas the plan can be broken down into several sheets illustrating the various use areas on a smaller scale. These documents would include the design and interpretive analysis, which is a narrative justifying and describing all activities provided in the plan.

A general development document is what most people associate with planning. It is often a single-sheet illustration that "sells" the project and is usually found hanging on the office wall in a conspicuous place. The user, not versed in the total complexities of planning, the planning process, and the decision-making process usually wants to see what the area will look like when developed. The average user is not interested in all the data leading up to this document but will appreciate seeing the general development plan.

Operation Documents.   Detail the unit operation program discussed at an earlier stage in the plan. All details, including outlines for themes and illustrations for interpretive tours, should be included along with the important features that are critical to the interpretive program. Relevant historical sites, archeological features, and biological phenomena should be indicated.

The necessary information relating to visitor and staff services is also included in this category. These services may include preparation rooms, storage areas, workshop space, and involve general circulation patterns.

Appendix.   The basic data used in the development of the preceding proposal such as information on soils, geology, topography, flora, fauna, climate, hydrology, history; information concerning past public use and public sentiment; economic analysis; and any other information useful for planning, management, administration, and operations purposes.

REFERENCES

General References

Boulanger, David F., and John P. Smith. 1973. *Educational Principles and Techniques of Interpretation,* USDA, Forest Service, Pacific Northwest Forest and Range Experiment Station, Portland, OR.

Brockman, Frank, and Lawrence C. Merriam, Jr. 1979. *Recreational Use of Wildlands,* (3rd ed.). McGraw-Hill, New York.

Darling, Fraser F., and John P. Milton. (eds.) 1965. *Future Environments of North America,* The Natural History Press, Garden City, NY.

Gold, Seymour M. 1973. *Urban Recreation Planning,* Lea and Fibiger, Philadelphia.

National Park Service, 1965, *Interpretive Planning Handbook,* Washington, DC.

National Parks of Canda. September 1971. "Background Paper on Park Interpretation," National and Historic Parks Branch, Department of Indian Affairs and Northern Development, Ottawa.

State of California. 1973. *Planning and Development Guidelines,* The Resources Agency, Department of Parks and Recreation, Sacramento, CA.

State of California. 1972. *Interpretive Facilities Planning Guidelines,* The Resources Agency, Department of Parks and Recreation, Sacramento.

Tilden, Freeman. 1967. *Interpreting Our Heritage,* The University of North Carolina Press, Chapel Hill, NC.

References Cited

1. Altshuler, A. A. 1966. *The City Planning Process,* Cornell University Press, Ithaca, NY.

2. Banfield, E. C. "The Field of Planning." Updated mimeo.

3. Beyer, G. H. 1967. *Housing and Society,* MacMillan, New York.

4. Chapin, F. S., Jr. 1965. *Urban Land Use Planning,* University of Illinois Press, Urbana.

5. Driver, B. L. (ed.) 1974. *Elements of Outdoor Recreation Planning.* The University of Michigan Press, Ann Arbor; and Longman Canada, Limited, Don Mills, Canada.

6. Putney, Allen D., and J. Alan Wagar. 1973. "Objectives and Evaluation in Interpretive Planning," *The Journal of Environmental Education* **5**(1).

7. State of California. 1966. *Master Plan Handbook,* The Resources Agency, Department of Parks and Recreation, Sacramento, CA.

8. Trecher, H. B. 1950. *Group Process in Administration,* Revised Edition. Womens Press, New York.

9. Weaver, Robert C. 1963. "Major Factors in Urban Planning," M. L. J. Duhl (ed.) *The Urban Condition,* Basic Books, New York.

10. Webber, Melvin M. 1963. "The Prospects for Policies Planning," M. L. J. Duhl (ed.) *The Urban Condition,* Basic Books, New York.

11. Woodbury, Coleman. 1965. "The Role of the Regional Planner in Preserving Habitats and Scenic Values." *Future Environments of North America,* Natural History Press, Garden City, NY.

12. Young, Robert C. 1974. "Establishing of Goals and Definition of Objectives," *Elements of Outdoor Recreation Planning,* B. L. Driver (ed.) University of Michigan Press, Ann Arbor, and Longman Canada, Limited, Don Mills, Canada.

CHAPTER 5

SELECTING THE INTERPRETIVE MEDIA

Grant W. Sharpe

The Interpretive Media are herein defined as the means, methods, devices, or instruments by which the interpretive message is presented to the public. Media selection is the process of choosing the most appropriate method for delivering that message. It was pointed out in Chapter 4 that media selection is an integral part of the interpretive planning process. The intent of this chapter is to expand that part of the process.

How does the interpretive planner or specialist know which medium to select for a particular situation? One way to deal with the problem is to ask some questions:

Does this medium require a person to operate it?
Does it require electricity?
Could it be easily vandalized or stolen?
Will maintenance be a problem?
What effect will weather have on it?
Will it hold up with continuous use?
Can a substitution be made easily?
Is it to replace something already in use, or is it part of a new program?
At what audience is it being primarily directed?
Will it be a duplication of what someone nearby is doing?
Is the quality of the presentation in keeping with prescribed standards?
Has interpretive research discovered anything about the effectiveness of this
    medium?
What will be its cost?
If high visibility is needed, will this medium provide it?
Will it be accepted by the public, or will it appear too extravagant or intrusive?

What effect will the medium have on the visitor and the visitor on it?
What effect will the medium have on the environment in which it is to be used?

The answers to some of these questions may become obvious after initial investigation. On the other hand, some answers require considerable experience in interpretive work, and this experience may be something that the reader has not yet acquired. There is no set formula for media selection. To gain a better insight into the media selection process, let us consider those factors that directly influence the selection—namely, the visitor, the resource, and the interpreter. Finally the media themselves will be considered.

FACTORS INFLUENCING SELECTION

The Visitor

Most interpretation today assumes a homogenous audience in characteristics such as educational and cultural background, mental and physical capability, language, age, place of origin, and travel objectives. Those sometimes left out are the physically or mentally handicapped, senior citizens, youth groups, foreigners, ethnic minorities, and people with limited educations. The interpretive planner should select a media mix that will provide as wide a range as possible and include at least some of these "forgotten" visitors.

Visitor Orientation.   People in unfamiliar surroundings may reject your interpretive offerings if they have not been made to feel welcome to your area. What medium do you select to make visitors feel comfortable when they arrive? An information person at the entrance or at an information desk, one with a smiling face that says, "Welcome," creates a warm atmosphere. Certainly that is preferable to a sign that only gives directions.

Orientation to the area's lodging and other facilities must be available 24 hours a day. Once visitors are comfortably settled they are ready for exploration. Orientation provides a brief look at the opportunities that are available. The family then decides what activities are within their time frame, interests, and physical capabilities.

Orientation may be accomplished with signs, but answers may be needed for additional questions the visitors might have. If personnel are not available to supply that information, an interpretive services leaflet or a bulletin board can also give the visitor an overall coverage of times and places of interpretive activities.

Although not strictly interpretation, visitor orientation is important to the park experience. It is often handled by interpreters and should be considered in the media selection process.

Visitor Interaction.   It has been my observation that there can be considerable interaction among strangers when they are in an unfamiliar environment. If there is a desire to get visitors to interact, one medium may provide the opportunity better than another. For example, a guided trip has more opportunity for social interaction among strangers than does an exhibit.

Visitor/Media Relationships.   Another point to consider when choosing media is what Freeman Tilden calls "relating to people in a manner that touches them personally." At Mount Rainier National Park there is a simple label which reads: "You are standing on rock polished by glacial ice." (Fig. 5-1). This gives a feeling of immediacy and personal participation. Hands-on exhibits offer the op-

FIG. 5-1. Interpretation should involve the visitor. The label reads: "You are standing on rock polished by glacier ice." Mount Rainier National Park, Washington. (Photo by Grant W. Sharpe.)

portunity for the visitor to turn a switch, push a button, lift a rock, or stroke a pelt; all are means of producing an interaction between the visitor and the resource, via the media.

Visitor Protection.   Precautions to ensure visitor safety cannot be overemphasized. Suppose an interpretive medium such as a sign or a self-guided trail attracts a visitor into what could be a dangerous situation under certain conditions. Examples might include a swamp, a glacier, a precipitous cliff, or an area frequented by dangerous animals. If the visit results in injury or death, negligence may easily be proven. This is particularly true where the problem may be created by changing weather conditions. The interpretive medium may be at fault if it can be proven in court to be negligent in its warning messages. A guided tour, on the other hand, could be handled by a person who could reduce the incidence of accidents by checking for suitable wearing apparel, maintaining constant surveillance over the party, and repeating warnings to the visitors about the dangers involved.

The Visitor Season.   Seasons vary with an area's elevation and latitude, and this may have some influence on the medium selected. A park at sea level may have a longer summer visitor-use season than one in the mountains. Similarly, one close to the equator may have a visitor season of 12 months whereas one at a latitude closer to either pole may have a season of only 1 month.

An area with a very short season may have difficulty getting qualified personnel to work for such a brief period. When seasonal personnel are not available, nonpersonal services must be chosen. On the other hand a three-month season, if it coincides with the school vacation season, will facilitate the seasonal employment of school teachers and college students.

Variety.   To meet visitor needs, a well-balanced interpretive program with a variety of media is necessary. A family with five days available may wish to participate in two or three different activities each day. A family with a total of three hours available obviously cannot participate in an all-day hike or a four-hour boat tour. However, a tour of a visitor center and a walk on a self-guided trail would be possible. Length of stay is a factor to consider when planning an interpretive program.

The Resource: Selecting A Theme

Every park, forest, wildlife refuge, or other resource-oriented recreation land has interpretive potential. Some, of course, offer more than others. The inventory phase of the interpretive planning process will reveal one or more features which characterize that area's natural or historical resources, and assist in identifying a theme. It may be geological, ecological, historical, or a humanly modified environment. One area may be represented by several distinct features or themes. To provide a logical basis for selecting a theme the following list is suggested: [2]

Landforms of the Present (Used by the U.S. National Park Service)

Caves and springs
Coral islands, reefs, atolls
Cuestas and hogbacks
Glacial phenomena
Hot water phenomena
Lake systems
Meteor impact sites
Mountain systems
Plains, plateaus, mesas
River systems
Sand dunes
Sculpture of the land
Seashores, lakeshores, and islands
Volcanic activity

Geologic History

The Precambrian Era
The age of primitive invertebrates
The rise of verbetrates and the first forests
The great development of land life and changes in marine life
The age of reptiles
The golden age of mammals

Land Communities of Plants and Animals

Boreal forest
Chaparral
Coniferous forests and woodland
Dry coniferous forest
Eastern deciduous forests
Deserts
Grassland (Steppe)
Pacific forest
Tropical ecosystems
Tundra

Aquatic Ecosystems

Estuaries
Lakes and ponds
Marine environments
Streams
Underground ecosystems

Each of the above themes could be further broken down into subthemes. For example, a cave site located in a park would come under the landform theme *Caves* and the subtheme could be related to its origin, that is, limestone formations. An oak-hickory forest would be under the Land Community theme *Deciduous forest*. Each region would have to modify the list to make it locally adaptive.

It is necessary to incorporate historical themes into the interpretive program. The following are only suggestions since the list applies specifically to the United States. Each country has a unique history and, as with the above, must be treated accordingly.[3]

Historical and Archeological Themes

> Prehistory and Indian cultures
> Colonial history
> Political history
> Military history
> Advance of the Frontier and westward expansion
> Commerce, travel, industry, and agriculture
> Arts and sciences

Works of Humans

> Hydroelectric developments
> Irrigation developments
> Rights-of-way
> Canals and locks
> Bridges
> Nuclear plants
> Buildings, factories
> Observation towers

Resource Protection. Ask yourself, "What are the environmental consequences of bringing people to a certain area?" The key to environmental protection is to minimize human influence on that particular environment. Thus, a medium may be selected because it provides some protection for the resource it is interpreting. For example, in a cave with fragile stalactites or in an historical building with valuable artifacts a conducted tour may be the only way to protect the resource. At a seashore, collecting marine life may have to be prohibited, but a diver can bring specimens ashore for close examination by visitors (Fig. 5-2).

On the other hand, large groups of people gathering around a naturalist on a forested path would have a great impact on delicate plant materials. If the same number of users were more evenly distributed over the length of the path, as on a self-guided trail, the problems associated with large groups could be minimized.

A self-guided trail I built in the rain forest of Olympic National Park was de-

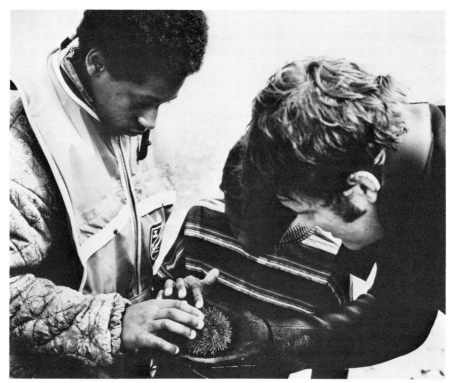

FIG. 5-2. To protect a resource, public collecting may have to be prohibited. In this example at a coastal park the interpreter brings the specimen ashore for visitor inspection then returns it to the sea. Deception Pass State Park, Washington. (Photo by Grant W. Sharpe.)

signed specifically for family-size groups. At a later period the use of the trail changed, and large groups were conducted over its length causing considerable site deterioration.

We can assume interpretive media attract visitors and increase the visitor's length of stay. Therefore, if visitor concentration becomes a problem, various interpretive media such as signs and wayside exhibits should be used to distribute the visitor load to less-used areas.

Finally, if interpretation helps a person appreciate the values of a resource, it can in turn lead to the protection of the resource. For example, an outdoor interpretive sign may point out that fragile plants are being damaged by visitor abuses. Visitors are thus encouraged to avoid further detrimental behavior (Fig. 1-7, page 17).

Site Disruption from Development

The interpretive planner recommending a specific interpretive medium must have some understanding of the impact that medium's development may have on the immediate environment.

Visitors are to be served, and this requires some site alteration. Suppose, for example, a modest building is proposed for a visitor center. The provision for utilities may be highly disruptive, particularly in remote areas. Roads and trails, parking areas, sanitary waste disposal systems, water systems, electrical lines, and provisions for drainage all require removal of vegetation and some grading.

A greater appreciation of the impact such developments will have on sites will be gained by reading Chapter 19, "Buildings, Structures, and Other Facilities."

Other Considerations

Media Availability and Cost. The availability of materials, machines, and people often dictates what medium is selected. If the equipment or replacement parts are unobtainable, you obviously choose something else. For example, you don't buy certain projectors if they or their replacement parts are difficult to obtain; you don't choose exhibits if exhibit designers are not available. Cost must be considered also. If you put too much money into one medium, you have to skimp on some other interpretive project. Obviously, some media are cheaper than others, and unfortunately cost is often a major criterion in media selection. One exhibit may cost the same as a seasonal interpreter; the making of one film the same as 50 exhibits; and a visitor center may be 10 times as expensive as the rest of the program.

In some countries labor may be plentiful, making personal services such as information duty and conducted activities easily available. On the other hand, the cost of salaries in another country may severely limit the number of people who can be employed. The alternative is to choose media having smaller labor requirements.

It is imperative that sufficient funds be available before attempting any interpretive project. Suitable plans and a contract for construction must be available as delays and mistakes are expensive. A cost estimate for the construction of an interpretive device can become obsolete in a few months.

Proximity to Subject. Whenever possible interpretation should take place at a site where the visitor can observe what is being interpreted. A discussion on "land shaping processes" or the birthplace of an important person is much more effective if the resource is near the interpretive medium (Fig. 5-3). Self-guided activities, wayside exhibits, and conducted activities are most appropriate. If the resource is not visible, visitor interest may be low.

Unfortunately, many artifacts cannot be left where they were discovered but must be removed for safekeeping.

FIG. 5-3. Cross-country cyclists pause before a roadside interpretive sign in Pepin, Wisconsin located near the birthplace of Laura Ingalls Wilder, a well-known author of children's literature. Such signs, near the feature being interpreted, contribute greatly to visitor understanding. (Photo by Senator Slade Gorton.)

Maintenance. "If you can't maintain it, don't built it." The originator of that piece of advice has been long forgotten, but the maxim is as true today as it was many years ago when first stated. Maintenance problems stem from a variety of causes—poor location, inadequate design, haphazard construction, and the effects of nature.

Building and putting media in place are only part of the project. Even well-designed and located interpretive media require a routine schedule of maintenance and care. If this schedule can't be followed, equipment and facilities deteriorate. Materials must be readily available for replacement. Knowledgeable repair people must be either on the staff or under contract.

Weather. Some media are used indoors where they are protected from the weather; some are placed outside where they are exposed to the elements. The location of the medium and the weather it will be subjected to must be considered in its selection. A typical indoor exhibit could never survive the inclement weather a sign of metal or treated wood can endure.

Although it may seem obvious, it must be said that an outdoor amphitheater is unrealistic where the weather is cold or rainy during the visitor season. I have seen them built and left unused at high elevations because wind and cold evening temperatures make them uncomfortable and impractical. Noise from wind or waves can make hearing difficult in amphitheaters built too close to the shore of a lake or ocean.

Shop the Competition.   Find out what others are doing. Write them numerous letters, visit their areas, and ask them what works and what doesn't. If you like what you see, take a photograph of it (Fig. 5-4) and later improve on it. Attend interpretive workshops, and subscribe to relevant publications.

FIG. 5-4. Recording interpretive ideas on film. A file of such photographs or slides is useful in the media selection process. Blue Ridge Parkway, North Carolina. (Photo by Grant W. Sharpe.)

If you have a cave to interpret, seek advice from other cave interpreters. If you have a marsh to interpret, study the approaches others have taken. Remember, too, what works in one park may not work in another; the conditions of each area must be carefully analyzed.

THE INTERPRETER AS A CRAFTSMAN

Every craft has the tools of its trade, each designed to do a certain job. Even without the correct tool you can operate effectively, but you can never quite gain the desired perfection. Marc Sagan of the U.S. National Park Service often uses the example of the carpenter and his tools to illustrate the concept of the interpreter as a craftsman. If the carpenter wants to smooth a piece of wood, he can use a hatchet, adz, axe, draw knife, plane, or spoke shave. All do approximately the same thing, but some are better than others in certain circumstances. What happens if he pulls the wrong tool out of the box? Suppose he pulls out the draw knife instead of a plane. According to Sagan, the carpenter can still do surprisingly well, but he never quite reaches the desired level of perfection.[4]

So it is with interpreters. Communicating is their craft, and they too have a "bag of tools" (their media) with each tool specialized for a certain part of the job. What happens if they select the wrong medium? The job gets done, but no doubt it could have been done better.

Discussing this same problem, Roscoe Files of the U.S. Forest Service takes a slightly different approach. He points out that craftsmen begin as apprentice and master the simpler tools of the trade by first learning their purpose, proper use, limitations, and maintenance; they then progress to more complicated tools. With experience, creative ability, and enthusiasm apprentices may eventually become master craftsmen.[1]

Because new media are continuously entering the interpretive field and modifications are frequently made to existing forms, one can never learn everything there is to know about interpretive media. Aside from this difficulty, it is apparent to this writer that there is not sufficient time spent in the apprentice stage learning the basics of each medium—when to use and when not to use it. It is for the apprentice interpreter, forced to make decisions without adequate experience, that this chapter is offered. It may also serve as a review or summary for the master craftsman.

Media selection is a task that is usually carried out by the interpretive planner. If there is no interpretive planner, the task is undertaken by the interpretive specialist. (There are times when whoever is responsible for the assignment may feel inadequate, for every area presents different problems.)

Planning media for a new area and adjusting portions of an existing area's program are both very challenging. In either instance the planner goes through essentially the same analysis. The total program is outlined by utilizing the inventory, writing themes, and carefully selecting a medium for each part of the story. Good planners consider all of the opportunities within their reach to develop an interesting and varied experience for the visitor.

To select the media properly you have to know a good deal about it. You must have a knowledge of the advantage and disadvantages of each medium. Though the media cited here will be dealt with in greater detail elsewhere in this book, a brief introduction to each is presented here.

MEDIA CHOICES

Interpretive media are traditionally divided into two categories—personal (attended) services and nonpersonal (unattended) services.[5]

The Personal or Attended Services

Here the visitor comes into direct contact with the interpretive specialist through the medium of (1) information duty, (2) conducted activities, (3) talks to groups, or (4) living interpretation and cultural demonstrations. Personal services are considered the ideal interpretive medium for reasons of their warmth and flexibility. The person on duty can make the visitor feel welcome and develop two-way communication. At the same time that person can handle situations beyond the scope of interpretation, that is, police action or first aid. Though there are advantages to personal services, there are also disadvantages (all to be discussed in greater detail in Chapters 7 through 10).

Information Duty.   The interpreter (or other employee) is stationed at a particular location, and the visitor seeks out him or her. The location could be at an entrance station, an information desk in a visitor center, a roadside information booth, or at a point of visitor concentration, such as an overlook, waterfall, trail head, or campground office.

The Conducted Activity.   This includes walks, hikes, cave tours, auto caravans, train and tram tours, and bus and boat tours. In this instance the visitor joins the interpreter for a guided tour from a beginning location and moves along a preselected route to several points of interest. Here the natural or human environment is interpreted, questions may be asked, and the visitors can enter into the discussion. The interpreter can vary the narrative to fit the needs of the audience, and since he or she is in a position of surveillance over the visitors, they may be taken to locations normally off limits to individuals for reasons of safety or possible depreciative behavior (Fig. 5-5).

FIG. 5-5. The leader of a conducted walk prepares to enter an historical building, once used as a lighthouse on Puget Sound. Because of the surveillance offered by a tour guide, such an activity permits access to areas that may normally be closed to visitors. Fort Casey State Historical Park, Washington. (Photo by Grant W. Sharpe.)

Talks to Groups. These are presentations made at announced times and places, such as amphitheaters, campfires, and auditoriums. The campfire program is usually presented to small audiences where two-way communication with visitors is possible. The presentation is structured in such a way that there is a close visitor—interpreter relationship. The site often lacks electricity; the interpreter must rely on personal skills and talents to carry the program.

The amphitheater or auditorium presentation is much more formal. Both sites have greater seating capacity than campfires and are usually equipped with electricity, making slide presentations possible. Answering peoples' questions should be part of these programs.

The subject matter of the personal talk should relate to the area's natural or human history. Such settings provide the opportunity to develop within the visitors an understanding and appreciation of the values of the area they are visiting. As convenient as it might be to a harried employee, showing a movie of a Detroit auto assembly line or a maritime fish cannery cannot be considered good interpretation, especially when the state or provincial park in question is hundreds of miles or kilometers from such activities. As stated earlier, every park or forest has its own interpretive potential. Do something with it.

Living Interpretation and Cultural Demonstrations. In living interpretation the interpreter introduces the visitor to the cultural heritage of the area. It may include a historical activity such as panning for gold (Fig. 5-6). The interpreter may be an indigenous craftsman demonstrating some native or pioneer implement or musical instrument. Such interpretation may also include the hand craft-

FIG. 5-6. A high point on the conducted walk in Westland National Park, New Zealand. An interpreter shows how gold was panned in the Waiho River. (Photo courtesy of New Zealand National Parks Authority.)

FIG. 5-7. An interpreter, at left, demonstrates the shaping of a dugout canoe. In this example of living interpretation the visitors are encouraged to participate in the demonstration. Oconuluftee Indian Village, North Carolina. (Photo by Grant W. Sharpe.)

ing of jewelry, baskets, quilts, canoes, early hunting paraphernalia, or the preparation of food, soap, or candles (Fig. 5-7). These activities may be presented as a life scene, incorporating costumes, dialect, and historical artifacts and buildings. The interpreter may be an artist demonstrating music, drama, dance, or other art form. The living or cultural interpreter usually allows a question and answer period; marketing of the handmade objects may be permitted (see Chapter 10).

The NonPersonal or Unattended Services

In this approach visitors come into contact with the interpretive specialist only peripherally, if at all. Instead, they are informed by the device that takes the place of the interpreter. These are important interpretive services with numerous advantages and, of course, some disadvantages. They should be considered not as a replacement for personal contact but as a means of expanding the interpretive program beyond the capabilities of individual interpreters.

Audio Devices. These are devices that have human voices or other sound effects carrying the message by means of stationary tape repeaters, portable cassettes, closed-circuit television, or individual car radio reception. The sound may be channeled to reach one person or a group of people. The message can be enhanced through the use of authentic voices, accents, various languages, suitable music, and natural sounds. The audio device is often used in conjunction with other media, such as motion pictures, slide programs, exhibits, and self-guided trails. The advantages and disadvantages are discussed in Chapter 11, "The Use of Audio Devices."

Written Material.   This includes signs, labels, and publications. They may be reread for clarification, and their message is silent. (There are times and places where an audible message is undesirable.)

Signs.   The interpretive sign is a quick method of presenting the story. The message must be simple and easily read; the sign must be made of durable materials, since it is usually placed out-of-doors. The cost of signs is relatively low.

Labels.   These are usually used in conjunction with another medium such as an exhibit. Generally, the principles that apply to signs also apply to labels. Both are treated in Chapter 12, "Signs and Labels."

Publications.   Interpretive publications include everything from self-guided trail leaflets and single-page checklists to extensive books on flora, fauna, geology, and other subjects. Publications may be used as a source of information and interpretation prior to a park visit as well as during the visit itself. After the visit the publication becomes a valuable reference and souvenir. The detailed presentation and the opportunity for home use are the publication's main advantage over other media. Publications are covered in Chapter 13.

Self-Guided Activities.   These are intended to put visitors usually in family-sized groups, in direct contact with the resource at the visitors' convenience. The visitors are on their own, and the interpretive message is provided by a variety of unattended media summarized below.

Self-guided trails.   The self-guided trail (SGT) is usually a walking activity—one that permits large numbers of people in small groups to come in direct contact with park or forest features in their natural setting. The trail is available at any time, and the group or individuals can move at their own pace. The location can be in any nonfragile site where the resource does not require continuous surveillance. Interpretation is usually handled by one of the following options: (1) the leaflet and marker, (2) the sign-in-place, or (3) an audio device. Each has advantages and disadvantages. These and related materials are mentioned in greater length in Chapter 14, "Self-Guided Trails."

Self-guided auto tours.   Most visitors arrive at park areas by automobile. Although it is challenging to try to get people out of their autos and onto trails, many simply are not interested. The Self-Guided Auto Tour (SGAT) often becomes their only interpretive experience. An important feature of the SGAT is that it encourages family participation. It also provides the interpretive specialist with an opportunity to interpret a larger area than would be possible with other media. It may even stimulate visitor interest in other interpretive opportunities. SGATs utilize the same options as self-guided trails. These are considered in greater detail in Chapter 15.

Exhibits (Indoor).   Exhibits are usually an indoor interpretive medium. The building in which they are housed and the exhibit area should both be well-lit, attractive, and uncluttered. The building should be a place people *want* to visit. The exhibits themselves must be designed to communicate quickly. The visitor should get much of the message at a glance and by lingering briefly get the full message before moving on to the next exhibit (Fig. 5-8). If extensive detail is necessary, an exhibit is probably the wrong medium.

In this park you have a matchless opportunity to see wildlife as the early explorers saw it.

FIG. 5-8. To be effective an exhibit must be designed to communicate its message quickly. Note the brief, simple message accompanying this mounted Red Squirrel. Yellowstone National Park, Wyoming. (Photo by Grant W. Sharpe.)

A common fault is putting too many exhibits in one room. Here they compete for attention and reduce the visitor's ability to grasp the essential message.

When used properly the exhibit is a highly effective method of interpretation. Through the judicious use of text, photographs, and objects, an exhibit should be able to arouse interest and stimulate curiosity any time, not just on rainy days.

Exhibits (Outdoor).   Often called wayside exhibits, outdoor exhibits are placed near the point of interest. At an overlook the point of interest may be the entire scene beyond (Fig. 5-9). At the edge of a river, the base of a waterfall, or along a roadway, the exhibit may interpret the feature immediately behind it. At a trail head it may interpret several aspects of the trail.

Wayside exhibits do not have to compete with other exhibits because they usually stand alone. The interpreter can add a bit more detail and assume that the visitor will linger to absorb the message. The principles of design cited in Chapter 16, "Exhibits," and Chapter 19, "Buildings, Structures and Other Facilities" should be adhered to carefully.

Visitor Centers.   The visitor center, usually the interpretive headquarters for the area, is a major installation. The decision to include one or more must be made carefully. (A single park may have more than one depending on the size and requirements of the park.)

The visitor center serves both the visitors and the park staff. The visitors' part ideally includes a lobby, exhibit room, and auditorium. The staff unit may include offices, workrooms, library, collection area, and maintenance and storage spaces. Rest rooms and drinking fountains are needed for both the public and the staff, and frequently are the primary reason visitors stop and enter.

The visitor center utilizes most of the media cited above. Orientation of the visitor is one of its prime functions. Since it is a focal point for visitor activities, it should outline the entire park story through its media. Interpretation during poor weather conditions is also a major function of the visitor center. (See Chapter 19 for further information on visitor center design and use.)

Off-site Off-season Media.   As the name implies, this type of interpretation takes place away from the park, often during the nonvisitor season. Talks are frequently given to school groups and other organizations. Interpreters may give regularly scheduled radio or television programs, work with school teachers on environmental study programs, and meet with conservation and civic organization. Interpreters also utilize several nonpersonal approaches, such as preparing and mailing out audiovisual programs and exhibits for schools and writing articles for newspapers and magazines. (See Chapter 17 for ideas on off-site off-season interpretation.)

FIG. 5-9. Outdoor exhibits that interpret the scene beyond are popular with visitors. Grand Teton National Park, Wyoming. (Photo by Grant W. Sharpe.)

A Summary of Choices—The Media Matrix

Some media will work better than others for your situation, but how does one know which to select? A suggested method for getting started is to use a media selection matrix (Fig. 5-10). Such a matrix permits the assigning of certain media to specific themes and sub-themes, lessening the chance for either omission or extensive overlap. Each theme is assigned a primary interpretive medium. Some themes might have a secondary or tertiary method of interpretation.

During the planning process the planner completes the inventory of park features and develops an interpretive theme for each feature to be interpreted. These features and their themes are entered on the matrix. Note that in the media matrix example of Granite Valley Park, there are opportunities for several themes.

In our hypothetical example, visitors entering the park will be given a basic orientation at the entrance station followed by further information at the information desk and campground office.

The first features listed in the matrix under Story Inventory are a waterfall and potholes whose theme is Sculpture of the Land. Since the distance to the site is

Name of Area *Granite Valley* Date *7-21-87* Interpretive Planner *B. Wilson*

INTERPRETING THE ENVIRONMENT
MEDIA SELECTION MATRIX

		PERSONAL OR ATTENDED SERVICES																		NON-PERSONAL OR UNATTENDED									
		1						2							3			4		5			6		7		8		9
STORY INVENTORY	INTERPRETIVE THEME AND SUBTHEME	Entrance Station	Information Desk	Roadside Info Booth	Point Duty	Roving Duty	Campground Office	Walk	Hike	Bicycle	Auto Caravan	Train/Tram	Bus	Boat/Float	Campfire Talk	Amphitheater Talk	Auditorium Talk	Living Interpretation	Cultural Demo	Audio Stations	Portable Cassette	Auto Radio	Signs and Labels	Publications	Self-Guided Trail	Self-Guided Auto Tour	Indoor Exhibits	Outdoor Exhibits	Visitor Center
Visitor Orientation		P	S				T																						
Waterfall and Potholes	*Sculpture of the Land*								P																				
Homestead Farm	*Advance of the Frontier*																			S								P	
Cedar Grove	*Coniferous Forests Sub Theme: Forest Giants*																						S		P				
Abandoned Beaver Pond	*Lakes and Ponds Pond evolution*																						P						
Indian Petroglyphs	*Prehistory and Indian Culture*																						P						
Dam and Reservoir	*Works of Humans Uses of Water*				S															P									
Limestone Cave	*Caves and Springs*							P																					
Wildflowers	*Woodland Plants*															P											S		

Order of Desirability
P = Primary
S = Secondary
T = Tertiary

1. Information Services
2. Conducted Activities
3. Talks to Groups
4. Living Interpretation
5. Audio Devices
6. Written Material
7. Self-guided
8. Exhibits
9. Visitor Center

FIG. 5-10. The Media Selection Matrix.

two miles by trail, the interpretive planner has chosen a conducted hike as the interpretive medium.

The second feature under the story inventory is a homestead farm, which fits the theme Advance of the Frontier. It would relate the story of a pioneer family who settled in the area before it became a park. The primary interpretive device chosen by the planner is a series of outside exhibits showing photographs and drawings of the early buildings. Audio stations are to assist in the interpretive story.

The next feature, a cedar grove, is under the theme Coniferous Forest. A subtheme could be Forest Giants. The grove is superb, and in order to protect the trees from site compaction people will have to be carefully channeled through it. The interpretive medium chosen here is a self-guided trail with secondary assistance coming from a series of signs-in-place.

A small abandoned beaver pond, easily seen from the roadway, comes under

Lakes and Ponds. This particular pond has a marshy shoreline and could have a sub-theme entitled Pond Evolution. The site would be interpreted with a roadside sign located at the edge of a small parking lot. Indian petroglyphs were found in our hypothetical park and can be placed under the theme Prehistory and Indian Culture.

At the parking lot overlooking a dam and reservoir the interpretive planner follows the theme Works of Humans and the sub-theme, Uses of Water. The planner has chosen short-range radio broadcasting devices to reach visitors. If visitor concentration warrants it, an interpreter on point duty will be assigned the overlook at peak visitor hours.

A limestone cave is the next feature on the inventory. Its theme is Caves and Springs. This is a very fragile resource and will be off limits to visitors without a guide; therefore, the interpretive device chosen is a conducted walk.

The last topic on the media selection matrix of our hypothetical park is Wildflowers, with the interpretive theme Woodland Plants. Note the planner has selected the amphitheater talk as the primary means, and an indoor exhibit as the secondary means of interpreting wildflowers.

The interpretive planner has only pointed out themes and media that the on-site inventory suggested. Actual programming will, of course, be based on funding, personnel, time of year, number of years of operation, land added to the park, and other factors. As the park is developed, visitation increased, and facilities and personnel added, the program will be expanded, and media presently not being considered will be brought into play.

CONCLUSION

Interpretive media selection will be greatly facilitated if the selector has had several years of experience in a wide variety of interpretive situations. This may not always be possible, of course. As has been pointed out, what works in one area may fail in another for a variety of unforseen reasons. An interpretive program must be flexible as conditions will change. New acreage may be added to an area, transportation systems may change the use pattern, or new funds may suddenly become available or former sources fail. A final word: move cautiously on ideas that have not been field tested. Some of the biggest interpretive failures have been with things never tried on the public. That's why some interpretive media have become traditional—because interpreters know the visitors like them. However, some innovative methods are eventually well accepted. Interpreters should travel, take note of new ideas, and keep up with interpretive research.

REFERENCES

General References

Aldridge, Don. 1972. *Upgrading Park Interpretation and Communication with the Public,* Second World Conference on National Parks. Grand Teton National Park, WY.

Helmsley, A. F. 1971. *Background Paper on Park Interpretation—National Parks of Canada,* unpublished paper, National and Historic Parks Branch, Department of Indian Affairs and Northern Development, Ottawa.

Mahaffey, Ben D. 1972. "Effectiveness and Preference for Selected Interpretive Media." *Interpreting Environmental Issues* (Clay Schoenfield, ed.), Madison Denbar Educational Research Service.

Sagan, Marc. 1963. *Interpretive Planning Handbook—Appendix One,* unpublished paper, U.S. National Park Service, Washington, DC.

References Cited

1. Files, Roscoe. 1972. "Selecting the Interpretive Media," unpublished paper presented at short course Principles of Interpretation in Outdoor Recreation. College of Forest Resources, University of Washington, Seattle.
2. National Park Service. 1972. *Part Two of the National Park System Plan: Natural History,* U.S. Department of the Interior.
3. National Park Service. 1972. *Part One of the National Park System Plan: History,* U.S. Department of the Interior.
4. Sagan, Marc. 1964. "Selecting the Media," unpublished notes, Association of Interpretive Naturalists Annual Meeting, Pokagon State Park, Angola, IN.
5. Sharpe, Grant W. 1973. "Principles and Methods of Interpretation in Outdoor Recreation," unpublished paper presented at Association of Interpretive Naturalists Annual Meeting, Salt Fort State Park, OH.

CHAPTER 6

MANAGEMENT OF THE INTERPRETIVE PROGRAM

Donald H. Robinson

The term "management," as it relates to the interpretive program, could conceivably include every activity in which managerial skills are required. But a generally accepted concept of the term, particularly as it refers to the technical and professional fields, is the one that will be considered here—the administration and supervision of the "noninterpretive" functions of an interpretive program, such as funding and financial administration, personnel management, and the relation of the program to other agencies and activities. To properly visualize the place of the interpretive program or division in the overall management structure, we should start by considering possible organizational structures that show the appropriate place of the interpretive program in relation to other functional or service activities.

THE INTERPRETIVE DIVISION WITHIN THE ORGANIZATION

Every organization that manages land or natural and historic resources must, of necessity, have functional or service responsibilities assigned to various individuals or groups of individuals. In larger organizations these may be referred to as "divisions" or "departments." In smaller organizations these varied responsibilities may be assigned to a few individuals or even to a single person. Division of responsibilities within an agency organization is basic to its function; and the responsibility for interpretive functions, if such is to be included, is one of the more important.

The divisional responsibilities may cover only a few functions, or they may include a wide variety of duties and responsibilities. In the typical agency setup for the purpose of land or recreational management, division of operational responsibilities may include fields such as maintenance of facilities, engineering and planning, equipment maintenance, road and trail maintenance, construction of facilities, visitor protection, fire protection, wildlife management, timber management, and last but by no means least, interpretation of the area to the visitors. Along with these operational responsibilities go service functions such as personnel management, finance, budget, mails and files, and other activities designed to serve or facilitate the function of the operational divisions. These and other necessary divisional responsibilities may require a large organization or may be simple enough to be grouped under only a few major divisions. Again, in the smallest parks or agencies these divisional responsibilities may involve only one or two people. But the responsibility for their function still remains, and the place of the interpretive division or function must be on a level of importance equal to that of any of the others.

The organizational chart, a diagrammatic rendering of an actual or proposed administrative structure, is the first step in setting up any organization. In the planning stages, it insures the proper positioning of all staff along a coordinated line of command. In this chart the interpretive supervisor must have a direct line of communication with the administrative supervisor and assistants and be on an equal footing with all of the top supervisors of other departments or branches of administration.

In practice, the organizational chart should create a well-defined and compatible work force. It informs staff members of their exact position within the hierarchy and defines their major field of responsibility. Through this, employees will not only be aware of the overall structure of their organization, but will also know for what and to whom they are responsible. It will also channel their efforts into regions where they are most effective and thus prevent overlap or unnecessary repetition of duties.

The organizational charts on the following pages illustrate examples of structure that may be set up or modified to meet individual needs for three parks of differing sizes and complexities (Fig. 6-1, 6-2, 6-3). These charts are intended merely

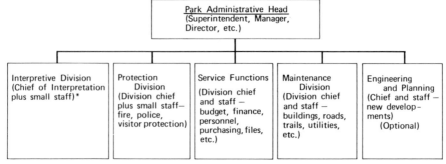

*The division <u>could</u> consist of only one or two people, but still maintain divisional function.

FIG. 6-1.   Example of organizational structure of a small park.

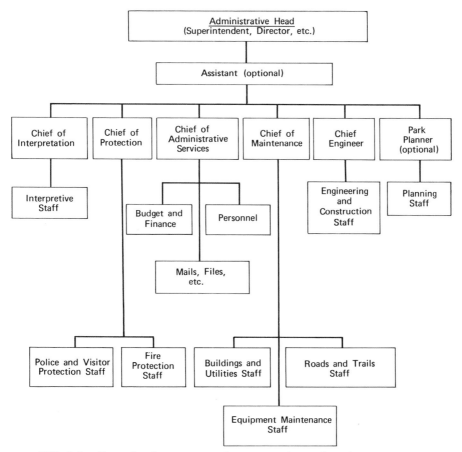

FIG. 6-2. Example of organizational structure of a moderately complex park.

as illustrative examples of what *can* be done, not necessarily as recommendations. Every organization will, of necessity, be arranged according to its particular needs and circumstances, but the relative importance of the interpretive function should always be kept in mind.

In the typical, small organization all divisions usually report directly to the top administrator, and the heads of the various divisions serve as his or her operational staff and advisors. Each division head may have one or more staff members to carry out divisional functions. In a very small or embryonic organization, the division head may be the entire divisional staff. But regardless of the particular situation or size of the organization, it is vitally important that the functions of the interpretive division be given status and responsibility equal to that of the other divisions, and that the level of responsibility of the chief of the interpretive division be the same as that of other division chiefs. He or she should be a full member

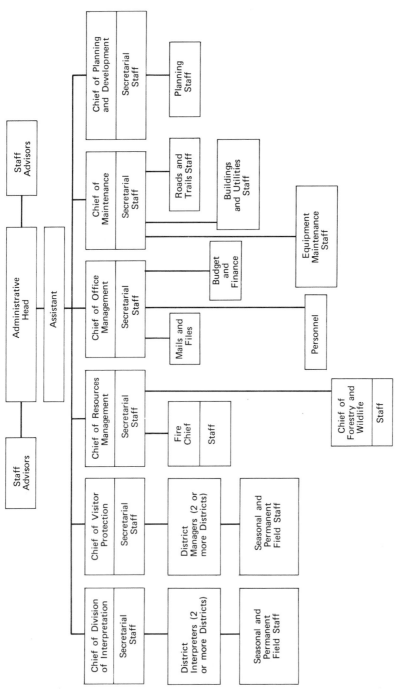

FIG. 6-3. Example of organizational structure of a large park. This structure may be oversimplified, and many positions could be added or eliminated to fit specific needs; but the general structure places interpretation in its proper relation to every other park function.

of the administrative "cabinet," representing the interpretive function as chief of staff for the interpretive division. Only in this way can the interpretive division operate as an integral, functional unit of the park, assuming its rightful place in the total organization.

Another feature to be noted in these organizational charts is the line of authority from the chief administrator or superintendent directly down through the division chief to the people "on the front line." It is vitally important that the interpretive manager or division chief be in the direct line of command between the functional staff and the top administrator. Attempts to place the professional interpreter on the side as "advisor" to the superintendent while noninterpretive managers run the program in the field have been tried in a number of instances; in only a few rare examples have they been totally successful. The professional interpreter *must* be a physical link in the "chain of command" so that interpretive expertise can be skillfully blended with management of the program.

The illustrated organizational charts can and should be modified to fit the particular needs of the organization. But, to reiterate, there are certain specific fundamentals that are important to any organizational structure involving interpretive functions. First, the interpretive division should be a separate entity functioning as a coordinated unit of the whole park. Second, the division chief must assume "cabinet" status in the superintendent's staff equal to that of other division heads. And third, the interpretive division chief must be in a position of line authority between the top administrator and the field operational level.

THE CHIEF INTERPRETER AS AN EFFECTIVE MANAGER

The titles for this person may vary with agencies, but for our purposes we will refer to the person in charge of the interpretive program as the "chief interpreter," regardless of agency title. But whatever this person's title, he or she is a *manager,* and the importance of effective management of this program cannot be minimized. This manager may have ample professional staff, adequate facilities, and a wide technical and professional expertise, but the program can fail miserably if the financial situation is bungled, personnel are not handled properly, or enmity develops between the interpretive staff and outside or in-house departments.

Proper handling of these and other managerial functions requires far more of the manager than professional knowledge or expertise. First and most important, the chief interpreter must develop the faculty of seeing the relationship of the interpretive program to that of the overall agency operation and goals and be able to fit this program into it. The manager must also have or develop the ability to get along with people; to lead others, rather than force them to reasonably and clearly understand the rationale of the program. Total agreement with the administrator's ideas and concepts may not be achieved, but an "understanding disagreement" is at least an acceptable working relationship.

The effective interpretive manager must keep firm control of the finances, records, and reports necessary for operation. Not only is this important for the functioning of the operation, but it also shows the manager's superiors that he or she is capable of running the program. As a result the manager will probably be given a freer hand in the activities and will have better success in obtaining what is needed from top management. Adequate financing always seems to be an illusive goal. A common complaint is, "If I only had more money, I could . . ." All too often this is only an excuse. A close scrutiny of the operation may reveal that administrative weakness or even waste is the basic problem and can be corrected with little or no additional funding.

Two common failings of a program manager are undue emphasis on program function and too little on administration, or just the reverse, both of which have an adverse effect on the program and morale of subordinates. To be properly effective a good interpretive manager must be a sort of "balance wheel" between top management and the functional program. The manager must know what is going on at the administrative levels as well as in the interpretive program and why. In fact, this should be *his* or *her program,* designed to fit into the parameters defined by top management and dictated by local circumstances. This tends to emphasize the previously mentioned importance of placing the chief interpreter in direct line of authority between the administrator and the interpretive program, rather than at some staff level with no direct authority over the program.

The interpretive manager is a key position in any organization and as such must be carefully selected, both for knowledge of the professional field and the ability to manage and direct the program. This is a monumental task and a professional challenge.

SELLING THE PROGRAM

For those in the process of setting up an interpretive program there are certain management functions imperative to its success, and one of the most important before any program can get off the ground is "selling" it to top management. If you are fortunate, top administrators may be fully cognizant of the interpretive functions and their results. But all too often the uninitiated land manager views the interpretive program merely as "frosting on the cake," something that can be done without until surplus time and money are available. This is the first challenge for the interpretive manager, and the following suggestions may assist in this selling process. They have worked effectively in the writer's experience and observations.

The first step is to produce a definition of the program as envisioned by the interpreter and an outline of its proposed scope. This is usually referred to as the "Interpretive Plan." If top management is to understand what is proposed, this plan must be quite definitive (and incidentally, this little exercise can also be an eye-opener for the preparator!). This plan must include, among other things, the reasons why such a program is needed, what the benefits of the program will be, what types of activities and developments it will include, types and numbers of personnel needed, and annual cost figures. It may be necessary to present the program on an expanding scale; that is, what will be required at the start and what the needs will be as it expands to a plausible optimum.

The value of a well-developed interpretive plan cannot be overemphasized. Several of the national parks in Chile have interpretive programs today because interpretive plans put together by Peace Corps volunteers were later adopted by the government and used to develop their parks.

Accompany the above-mentioned plan with well thought-out justifications; list and explain the benefits that can be derived from interpretation. One benefit that can be appreciated by administrators is that of increased public support of the agency as visitors become better informed about its operation, policies, resources, and other values. Explanation should show how public interest can be created through subtle but accurate, objective information in talks, publications, and exhibits. As stated, this should be subtle as the obvious "propaganda pitch" can be very distasteful and may even turn people away. Probably the most effective support for an interpretive program comes as a result of the people's enjoyment and appreciation of what the area has to offer and how thoroughly it has been interpreted and presented to them. For example, people who have discovered the fragile beauty of the alpine tundra, the complex ecology of the seashore or desert, or the fascination of a historical site on an effectively presented conducted walk or tour will be the first to get up in arms if these particular features are threatened in any way (Fig. 6-4).

In presenting the plan to administration, you should explain that effective interpretation of an area is one of the best means of protecting it from exploitation, vandalism, and other destructive human elements. The strongest body of law enforcement officers can never equal the protective efforts of several thousand visitors who understand and appreciate the natural and historical resources of an area. Most people are very protective of what they love and regard as a part of their heritage, and woe unto the vandal whom the dedicated park visitor catches in an act of destruction! The informed and enthusiastic friend of the park can be a forceful ally at times when outside forces such as overambitious or poorly informed legislators, overzealous developers, or logging and mining interests threaten the area or its integrity. The more visitors reached by an effective interpretive program, the more supporters that administration can call on in times of need.

Aside from the aforementioned support and assistance that can be provided by properly informed visitors, use of the program by public schools for outdoor study and environmental education can also be a strong factor in building public support for the area and its programs.

FIG. 6-4. Through this interpretive presentation, support is being developed to assist in the protection of the area. Hurricane Ridge, Olympic National Park. (Photo courtesy of National Park Service.)

Stress the importance of resource protection through education. Some of the greatest damage done to park resources, such as trampling of vegetation, short-cutting of trails, roadside and trailside littering, man-caused fires, and other depreciative behavior, is not so much the work of vandals as it is the result of thoughtlessness and carelessness.

In short, every effort should be made to convince the administration of the importance of a well-informed visitor when it comes to administrative and legislative support and park protection.

Another important facet to be included in selling a program to top management is the cost factor. This should be broken down by years or other major time periods from its inception to an optimum level of development consistent with the stated goals of the program. This portion of the presentation should include all the monetary needs with well-justified reasons for them, including a logical, realistic buildup of staff, both seasonal and permanent, and their estimated costs. It should also include estimates of needed investments, such as trails, exhibits, visitor centers, personnel housing, and equipment and a realistic time frame for development of facilities.

Two common faults in the presentation of such a program are what might be termed "over-conservatism" and "shooting-for-the-moon." In the former, interpretive managers may say to themselves, "This is what I actually need, but maybe if I cut it down here and there, I'll be more apt to get it." This attitude is self-defeating. A conservative administrative head will invariably take this to be the optimum program and any reductions will be made from this base, leaving little chance of justifying the previously unstated needs.

The other fault, asking for "the moon" in hopes you will get something less that will still fit your needs, can also backfire. Top-level administrators did not reach their positions by being foolish! They will very likely see through the subterfuge and may lose confidence in the entire presentation. It is far better to present a realistic program, one that can be defended in all its facets, thereby showing your superiors that you are well informed. Then if you do not get all you requested, you still have justifiable grounds for a later request.

Finally, show what is being done in other areas and agencies, including data on the effectiveness of their programs. Most agencies that have developed successful interpretive programs are only too glad to furnish supportive material and information.

ESTABLISHING THE PROGRAM

Following the "selling" of the program to top-level management comes the hard part, that of establishing a program that will be functional in the shortest possible time and still keep within the aims of the established interpretive plan. The first thing that comes to mind at that point is money. If you have been adequately persuasive in selling your program to the administration, you may have little or no trouble obtaining the funds to hire personnel, purchase supplies and equipment, and initiate the interpretive plan. Unfortunately this is a dream that is seldom realized. More commonly there is some management "foot-dragging," or inadequate funds for the desired needs, or both. Here is where the interpreter's ingenuity and ability are put to the test.

The first, and probably the most important step, is to keep in mind the planned goals of the program and gear every step from start to finish toward this end. This will result in fewer wasted efforts and unplanned deviations. This statement may appear elementary, but it is surprising how many times developing interpretive programs stray onto an unplanned tangent, resulting in wasted effort, time, money, and damaged credibility with the administration.

The second step is to set up a budget and program funds consistent with your financial resources. Here the resourcefulness of the manager comes into full play. All too frequently there is little or no funding available for the new program.

If the parent agency is capable of providing funds, a firm budget should be developed that will provide realistic annual buildup as the program matures. This budget should include personnel salaries; equipment and supplies; travel; developments such as trails, visitor centers, and exhibits; and funding to maintain these facilities when they are completed. The first year might only include the salary and travel funds necessary to start a one or two-person operation. Plans for continuing the development of the program toward its ultimate goal should be included.

Where monetary resources are limited, funds for initial development are frequently supplemented by private foundations, grants, gifts, or endowments. Within the U.S. National Park Service, the resources of Cooperating Associations are frequently called on. (See page 141 "Cooperating Associations.") Commercial firms can sometimes be prevailed on to assist with such things as exhibits and audiovisual equipment. Local service clubs, garden clubs, natural history and historical associations, and educational institutions are frequently the source of funds, personnel, advice, and assistance. The organizations may continue their assistance long after initiation of the program, so early and frequent contacts with them are important.

There are many innovative ways to secure funds for developing a program, aside from agency resources. Listed below are a few that have been used at one time or another, and a bit of ingenuity and thought will probably suggest others.

1. Federal Aid programs for housing and developments.
2. Working with other agencies, such as service clubs, local clubs, local parks, conservation clubs, and schools for both funds and personnel.
3. Use of Neighborhood Youth Corps, Peace Corps, and other such volunteer or federal agencies for development work, personnel, and even funds.
4. Students from colleges and universities with interpretive courses may be prevailed on to assist in planning and development of facilities and programs (Fig. 6-5).
5. Garden clubs like to prepare or maintain features such as interpretive trails, arboretums, plantings, and outdoor exhibits.

FIG. 6-5.   Outdoor recreation students provide volunteer labor to build an outdoor amphitheater. Horseshoe Cove Campground, Mt. Baker-Snoqualmie National Forest, Washington. (Photo by Grant W. Sharpe.)

6. Local historical societies or natural history associations can be very helpful with funds, personnel, and technical advice, if the program is in keeping with their goals.
7. Conversion of unused buildings, even if they are old, into temporary interpretive centers can help launch a program.
8. Local fund-raising projects, such as craft sales, sale of produce or publications, and scheduled guest speakers are good sources of funds provided they can be continued as long as needed (Fig. 6-6).
9. Cooperation with county, state, or private park departments can elicit assistance, particularly in the line of technical expertise and planning.
10. Admission charges to certain interpretive features are a steady source of income, provided the feature is of sufficient interest and attraction to warrant such a fee.
11. There are countless other sources of aid, such as government surplus equipment, exchange of films and exhibits with other agencies, sale of publications and photos, local service clubs, "friends of the park" organizations, and so on.

FIG. 6-6. A miller at work in an historical grist mill. The corn he grinds is sold in an adjacent craft shop to park visitors. The income assists in paying the salaries of those participating in the living interpretation demonstrations. Cades Cove, Great Smoky Mountains National Park, Tennessee. (Photo by Grant W. Sharpe.)

A few words of caution are in order at this point. First, be careful about starting a program without planning for adequate financial assistance to continue it. A big drive for funds to get a program off the ground can build up much local, cooperative enthusiasm. But if provisions are not made to keep it going, this enthusiasm and interest will soon die, and the program will be in trouble. Plans for funding or assistance should provide for the continuation or replacement of those funds. For instance, where local fund-raising projects are on a one-time basis and will soon cease, further operational and maintenance funds must be derived from other sources. Fortunately, budgeted funds from the parent agency are often available after the first or second year.

There are other fund-raising and assistance programs that can be continued over longer periods of time, some indefinitely. Craft sales, assistance from educational institutions, use of local historical or natural history resources, and cooperation with other agencies can be of long-term or continuing benefit and should be approached with this expectation.

Park concessionaires are another continuing source of assistance. Their employees are in constant contact with the public and can perform a valuable service for both the park and the concessionaire by being well-informed and capable of passing on interpretive information to the visitors. A number of National Park Service concessionaires have taken steps to have their public service employees well-trained and informed. This is probably most dramatically illustrated by the training course given to drivers of the sightseeing buses in Glacier National Park. They are highly trained prior to entering on duty and are required to continue studying and to take periodic examinations on park information. The informational source manual for many years was required text not only for the drivers but also for the Park Service interpreters and rangers. Another example of concessionaire involvement in interpretation is in Grand Teton National Park. Here the concessionaire provides a float trip on the Snake River for park visitors. The interpretation on the modified WW-II pontoons is done by college students, who work for the concessionaire in the summer (Fig. 6-7).

A second caution about getting an operation under way is not to start off too strongly. Even if you realize the dream of unlimited funds at the beginning, it is best to start slowly, to feel your way for a while to determine what is feasible. Unless the interpretive manager has had wide experience in this field and knows exactly what is needed, a slow start, letting momentum build up as one goes along, and learning just what is needed and where, is strongly recommended.

More typically the program will start on a "shoestring" using existing personnel, homemade devices, and self-guiding facilities. Existing buildings and trails can be put to use for exhibit purposes; neighborhood craftsmen and artists may be qualified to design temporary exhibits in an old warehouse, office, or other building. At one time three British Columbia provincial parks were supervised by one naturalist who traveled from park to park during the summer months, living in his pickup camper, thereby spreading his services thinly but widely.

FIG. 6-7. Interpretation courtesy of the park concessionaire. This example, a float trip on the Snake River, shows two concession employees steering the raft and interpreting park natural history to visitors. Grand Teton National Park, Wyoming. (Photo by Grant W. Sharpe.)

In one of the major U.S. parks the embryo interpretive program was literally "lifted by its bootstraps." With a two-man permanent staff, one man designed and made all the wayside and trail exhibits, hauled logs into place for temporary campfire circle seats, and participated actively in the summer season nature walks and evening talks. The other man, in addition to planning and manning the program, wrote publications and had them printed by a local printer. He even set the type himself. The publications were contracted on a delayed payment basis and were offered for sale at ranger stations, concession stores, and similar outlets. In a matter of just a few years this effort created enough interest to bring about increased agency funding, and it is now a large, effective program.

Another small U.S. park with no interpretive facilities assigned an interested ranger to develop some interpretation. Despite almost total lack of funds aside from his salary and an overburdened work load on all park personnel, he initiated evening programs using the help of knowledgeable local volunteers. He devised some simple seats using the area behind an old concession building for an amphitheater, made his own trail labels and holders, and converted existing sections of trail into self-guiding trails. With the assistance of local talent he even developed a simple interpretive center in a small space adjacent to his office, where he could serve it when he had time.

These are just examples of how personal effort and ingenuity can be utilized to get something started. In most instances a "shoestring" effort will result in more substantial assistance as those who manage the finances realize and appreciate the effort devoted to the program and its potential for development with minimum assistance.

PERSONNEL MANAGEMENT

Personnel management is one of the interpretive manager's important day-to-day functions. The term as used here includes commonly associated activities such as selection and training of personnel, supervision on the job, and evaluation of employee performance. But to be most effective, it must also include studied techniques for understanding and handling people to obtain the highest and most dedicated performance of which they are capable. This involves the use of applied psychology and ability to get along with subordinates as well as superiors.

Selection of personnel, both permanent and seasonal, is an important and sometimes difficult task. When applicants are few and the choice is restricted, the selection may be simple even though the final results may be far from satisfactory. But as the number of applicants increases, it taxes the manager's astuteness to make the best selection. The ideal interpreter at the same time is a teacher, a leader, and a friend. He or she must have, first of all, at least a basic knowledge of the subjects or area to be interpreted. The interpreter must be able to accurately and adequately present the subject to the visitors, answer their questions, and give them a meaningful interpretive experience. It is not essential that the interpreter have a Ph.D. in some particular field or that he or she can converse learnedly with any expert on any subject. Interpretive audiences are mostly common people with an average (or less) knowledge of what is being presented. If the unanswerable question is encountered, the interpreter can always look it up or find the answer from the expert before the next such encounter.

To a degree the interpreter is a teacher, not in the sense of the classroom tutor, but to the extent that he or she can lead the audience into learning experiences, challenge them to find out what they can on their own, and help them when they cannot. In this same sense the interpreter is also a leader, to whom the visitors look for information and guidance.

The professional interpreter must at all times be an effective communicator. This is one of the most important attributes of the successful interpreter. He or she may be brilliant in a chosen field, a natural leader, and a great person, but if unable to communicate ideas to the listeners or viewers, these abilities are useless. Some managers tend to put the quality of communication ahead of professional knowledge. This may be going to the extreme, but there is a degree of validity in the contention that a person can more readily learn the basic background information necessary to interpret a subject than to develop the ability to communicate effectively. The more acceptable qualifications probably come closer to including a balance of both knowledge and communication skills.

When dealing with people, whether it be on conducted tours, formal or informal talks, or the one-to-one informational encounter, the interpreter must remember that people react to leaders, teachers, and interpreters in much the same manner that they are "reacted to." The friendly, outgoing interpreter not only leaves a good impression of the agency but is far more successful in getting the message across than the gruff, authoritative "nonperson."

In personnel selection it may be difficult to evaluate all of these qualifications, particularly from a written application or letter, although these may give certain leads that can be helpful. The most effective combination is always the personal interview backed by references from discerning and knowledgeable former employers or others in a position to know. Through these the prospective employer can look for the above qualities and is in a better position to evaluate them than from the written application only. It is sometimes difficult to arrange for personal interviews with a prospective employee because of location. In this case it may be possible to set up interviews through other capable people in or near the prospective employee's location. Whatever the complications, the more the interpretive manager can learn about the prospective employee, the better informed the choice will be, and the end result should be a more effective interpretive program.

Another phase of personnel management that is too often overlooked in the interpretive field is training tailored to fit the particular job or situation. All too often the manager or the trainee feels that his or her education or training is adequate for the job at hand without further instruction. Unless the person undertaking the interpretive task is known to be wholly familiar with the job, training is in order. There are no two interpretive agencies without their differences in procedures and interpretive approaches. For this reason, if for no other, it is imperative that all new interpreters be trained, either prior to the job or on the job, preferably both, in all aspects of their assignment. The top-notch botantist may be thoroughly familiar with botany but in need of considerable training in interpretive communication. The new historian may be an excellent speaker but may have little or no knowledge of how to lead a conducted tour. Poorly informed interpreters may be the result of their own lack of interest, but lack of adequate training is a fault that lies solely at the door of their supervisor or manager.

And last, but by no means least, good personnel management includes evaluation of the employee's performance. Periodically, by some systematic process, the interpreter's supervisor should be able to put down on paper an objective evaluation of how each of the staff members is doing and how each is progressing in relation to past performance. How this is carried out is immaterial, just so long as it presents an accurate picture of the employee's progress or lack of it.

Employee performance can be observed in a number of ways, the most common of which is observation or monitoring by superiors. There are also other signs that point to an employee's competence. Unsolicited reactions by the visitors who attend the programs can be very revealing, particularly if there are a number of them along similar lines. Unfortunately when a person does a mediocre job, comments to "headquarters" are few or nonexistent. If there are problems, however, you will soon hear about them, directly or indirectly. In like manner, the exceptionally good interpreter is often praised by letter or the spoken word. But the employee in between can literally go on forever, in a mediocre way, with neither praise nor condemnation. That is the person to watch, as he or she may be in need of help.

The popularity of an individual's programs may be another mark of his or her capabilities. After discounting such factors as travel count, weather, and the appeal of the subject, program attendance can be an evaluating factor. Word of an individual's prowess does get around, even among transient visitors, and the attendance factor should be considered in evaluation.

And finally, an indication of an individual interpreter's possible success is enthusiasm and energy. These factors are contagious, and the enthusiastic interpreter always engenders a like response in his or her audience.

On-the-job supervision of personnel can involve many of the manager's talents, not the least of which is that of being able to get along with people and still get them to do what is wanted. A contended and happy staff is usually a hard-working staff. This situation can often be obtained by including them in the goals and problems of the operation. If subordinates do not understand what is going on, or why, resentment and ridicule may result, with disastrous consequences for the effectiveness of the program.

The effective manager must be firm where firmness is called for, sympathetic where sympathy is needed, and knowledgeable and understanding of subordinate's needs. There are many little devices that help morale in any organization and produce better performance. The following is a short list of ideas that help keep employees contented and aware that they, too, are a functioning part of the program. This list is only a start—there are many other ways:

1. Occasional staff meetings to keep key personnel informed of what is happening "upstairs" can be very helpful, particularly if the staff is large.
2. In-house news letters or informational leaflets keep personnel informed of current happenings.
3. Rotation of duties is often practical and advisable. Prepare work schedules with variety to minimize the danger of boredom.
4. Delegate certain minor supervisory duties to the better qualified interpreters. This will provide incentive for greater effort.
5. Give full responsibility to those qualified to take such responsibility. The best means of invoking subordinates' top performance is to assign them to challenging situations.
6. Special duties, such as needed research projects, can be an incentive to better efforts and will provide a change of pace from the day-to-day interpretive program.
7. The "fun" aspect of the interpretive program can be enhanced by off-duty parties, picnics, game competition, and other such activities that tend to

bring their families together and allow them to see the boss as a person, not a superior being.
8. Pre-arrival information to new employees on weather, housing, and household equipment needed.

These are just a few of the many little things that add up to an effective, fired-up staff and topflight performance. When you find an outgoing, enthusiastic supervisor with unbounded ideas and energy, you will most certainly find a park with an enthusiastic, eager, hard-working staff. This is a contagious situation that can only work for the good of the program.

COOPERATING ASSOCIATIONS

Although mentioned previously as a means of financial assistance to both new and on-going programs, cooperating associations offer such potential for interpretive assistance that they should be treated in some depth as to their formation, operation, and values.

Cooperating associations, as the term is used here, can refer to anything from the local Boy Scout troop to a natural history association or park historical society directly connected with the interpretive program. This discussion will cover two facets of the subject: (1) suggestions for organizational structure of cooperating associations set up as a direct assistance to the interpretive program; and (2) ways in which any such association can be of assistance in furthering the program.

Undoubtedly the most effective and valuable cooperating association is one similar to those set up by the National Park Service to assist their interpretive programs. These associations are authorized by Congress to make use of governmental services and facilities. They are chartered with the state as private, non-profit organizations, whose purpose is public service through the advance of the National Park Service's research programs and its educational, interpretive, and conservation activities. They are known variously as natural history associations, history associations, library associations, museum associations, or other pertinent titles. They are usually governed by a board of directors consisting of both agency and nonagency personnel acting within the provisions and limitations set forth by Congress and their respective state charters.

Since these organizations are quasi-public, operating directly for the benefit of the National Park Service, their responsibilities and participation in Service activities must reflect Service policies and regulations, despite the fact that they are chartered by the state and their membership may be mainly from the private sector. Legislation authorizing establishment of these organizations is largely confined to the National Park Service, but there is no reason why they could not be similarly set up under any other governmental unit.

These associations assist the Service in many ways, such as buying, publishing, and distributing appropriate interpretive literature and other suitable material. The latter may include books, posters, cards, and certain selected souvenir objects. From the proceeds of such sales the associations assist the parks in obtaining equipment and supplies for interpretive or educational purposes, developing libraries, and establishing research programs. Some associations even assist in acquisition of nonfederally owned lands that may be obstructing conservation or interpretation of park values. Some associations have provisions for the acceptance of donations or, to a lesser extent, membership dues. But the bulk of their financial resource is derived from the sale of interpretive literature and publications.

Other organizations that can function as cooperating associations if they are properly motivated are youth organizations such as the Boy Scouts, Girl Scouts, Camp Fire Girls, 4-H Clubs, and church affiliated groups. These organizations have been helpful in many ways such as trail construction and maintenance, environmental cleanup, interpretive demonstrations, information duty, and other types of volunteer work in keeping with their specific capabilities. Local service clubs can also become cooperating associations if they can be properly directed. There are limitless areas wherein local clubs, schools, or other outside organizations can be of assistance to the interpretive program if the proper attitude is engendered between area management and the local communities. This type of cooperative effort can be generated in large urban areas, but it is more desirable and productive in small town situations where a feeling of personal involvement in park activities is possible.

For agencies with limited resources or those just getting their interpretive program off the ground, cooperating associations and agencies can be most helpful and should be enthusiastically encouraged. This is one place where the effective manager can get the most assistance with the least effort, provided that these organizations can be properly formulated and motivated. Assistance in forming cooperative associations such as those in the National Park Service can be obtained by calling on the Service or one of its larger associations.

RELATIONSHIP WITH OUTSIDE AGENCIES

Aside from the cooperating associations and agencies mentioned above, there are many other sources of assistance in the interpretive program that can be called on under certain circumstances. In North America the facilities of federal agencies such as the National Park Service, U.S. Forest Service, and the Canadian Department of Indian Affairs and Northern Development can be tapped for advice, guidance, and information, as well as those of many very fine state and provincial park organizations. These larger agencies can often assist in cooperative

FIG. 6-8. A park executive from Sweden studies a photoelectric cell used to determine the number of visitors utilizing the self-guided trail. James River Interpretive Trail, Blue Ridge Parkway, Virginia. (Photo by Grant W. Sharpe.)

training programs, advice on technical problems, and even give personnel assistance in some instances. Colleges and universities with interpretive and outdoor education courses should be contacted for training and informational aid.

"Shopping the competition" is a recognized and accepted practice with interpreters the world over. Every opportunity should be utilized to stop in and see what others are doing in the interpretive field and how they are able to function in a particular direction. Most interpreters are pridefully eager to share their successful accomplishments with others. This is one of the common methods of spreading interpretive information and techniques throughout the country (and even the world), enhanced by coordinated meetings and workshops of interpretive organizations (Fig. 6-8).

Membership in groups such as the Association of Interpretive Naturalists, the Western Interpreter's Association, and Interpretation Canada, is almost a must for the progressive interpreter on the North American scene. Their publications, workshops, programs, and professional contacts can be a valuable aid to any interpreter, old or new.

A close working relationship between agencies, organizations, and even nations is a necessity in this modern era of rapid, worldwide communications. A common community of interagency and international interpretive interest and knowledge is a necessity if modern management principles are to be fully developed and utilized in the interpretive field. After all, no matter who we are or where we are, the ultimate goal of our interpretive programs is the same—to enhance public knowledge and appreciation of our natural and historic heritages.

GENERAL REFERENCES

Doell, Charles E., and Louis F. Twardzik. 1973. *Elements of Park and Recreation Administration.* Third Edition, Burgess Publishing Company. Minneapolis, MN.

Rodney, Lynns. 1964. *Administration of Public Recreation.* The Ronald Press Company. New York.

PART II
THE TECHNIQUES OF INTERPRETATION

The interpretation of the environment should have upon the visitor an influence or stimulus which, in turn, should have a beneficial influence upon the landscape and park values through the visitor's awareness, understanding and appreciation.

National Parks of Canada

Personal or Attended Services

Successful interpretation is a balancing or juggling act, a graceful and smooth ballet of interaction between your interpretive presentation and the mind of the listener.

Paul H. Risk

CHAPTER 7

INFORMATION DUTY

Grant W. Sharpe and
Ron W. Hodgson

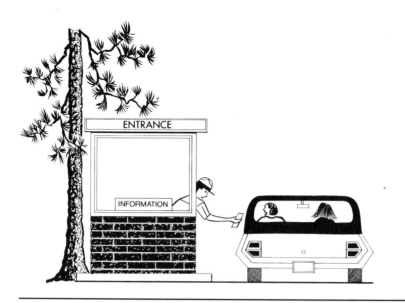

Communicating effectively with visitors is vital to sound resource management. Recreationists need to know what kinds of recreation opportunities exist and where they are located; they need information in order to enjoy their visit in comfort and safety; and they need to know the rules that govern behavior in the park or forest. Visitors also need information to enhance their understanding of the experience and to help them conserve the resource and avoid annoying other users.[2]

Few visitors are likely to have all the information they need. Most are from urban and suburban communities where the rules of behavior, as well as the attendent hazards, are different from those of a park or forest. In some areas, visitors may well be strangers making their first visit. They do not know what they need to know to use the area effectively and appropriately and cannot be expected to acquire that information without assistance. Even in urban parks, visitors cannot be expected to know the rules of appropriate behavior or how to get the most out of their experience.

Certain people are employed specifically to answer visitors' questions. The rationale here is that the information giver provides a necessary service and also relieves interpreters and others of this task. This activity usually takes place at a site readily accessible to the visitor.

Information duty is regarded as a service to the visitor and is an essential element of the recreation management program. The main objective of this service is to provide a pleasant welcome to the visitors and to disseminate information. A second objective is to present, through appearance and manner, a favorable image of the agency while explaining its goals and activities. These uses of information duty are not always fully recognized, but should be kept firmly in mind when hiring for and managing information services.

Although the position does carry considerable responsibility, it is often filled at an entry or beginning salary level. People filling these positions usually do so with the understanding that it is a temporary assignment, perhaps only a seasonal job, or that if it becomes permanent, they will eventually move into another position. It is considered by some to be the first rung in a career ladder.

THE DUTIES

Visitors expect every employee of a public recreation area to be able to answer questions. Therefore, all employees must be instructed in how to handle these contacts, even if all they can do is direct the visitors to the proper source for answers. Some employees may view these questions as interruptions in their work and may be curt, yet a smile and a pleasant reply are most important to the agency's image.

Information duty differs from typical interpretive activities in several ways. One is that it is not quite the same as speaking before a group. Information duty is the information giver and the visitor conversing on a one-to-one basis (Fig. 7-1). Another difference is that the questions asked frequently do not pertain to natural or human history. Finally, the information duty person may or may not be a member of the interpretive staff. Interpreters are sometimes involved, however, and for this reason information duty is considered here.

The person handling this activity must be genuinely pleasant, friendly, and enthusiastic. He or she must be able to keep these attributes in evidence for several hours at a time. Although the person who stands information duty must be prepared to answer almost any question, most questions will be somewhat repetitive.[4]

To determine the kind of person needed for information duty one needs an accurate description of the job.

As stated above, the purpose of the position is to greet people and to answer questions. The duty station is usually indoors. The person involved may have other duties such as typing, issuing permits, answering the telephone, or operating a two-way radio. The duty may be for several hours at a time. Maintaining a sales counter may be a part of the task as may be assisting other staff members during slack hours. In some instances the person at the desk may be responsible for the entire building, including the maintenance of rest room facilities, overseeing of exhibits, and even running the first aid room. Information duty may require the services and skills of a very special kind of individual. On the other hand, this duty is in some circumstances monotonous, and the variety of tasks assigned information personnel creates some special communication problems. These problems are discussed in following sections about interpersonal communication and on information service management.

FIG. 7-1. Information duty differs from other interpretive work in that the employee often meets the visitor on a one-to-one basis. Note the temporary outside information booth. Yosemite National Park, California. (Photo by Grant W. Sharpe.)

THE LOCATION

Information duty usually takes place at one of the following sites:

Entrance Station. The usual purpose of the entrance station is to provide a place for the collection of entrance fees. Unfortunately, the press of traffic seldom allows time for conversation. Visitors, however, seeing a person in uniform, expect to have their questions answered. This problem is commonly solved by a general information handout and a map issued by the person at the entrance station. Since this station is typically small, visitor access is not encouraged. If further information services are available in another place, this fact should be communicated to the visitor.

Visitor Center. One of the main functions of a visitor center is to provide an opportunity for visitors to have their questions answered. This is usually handled by a person on duty in the lobby at a desk easily seen by visitors when they enter the building (Fig. 7-2). Aids to assist the person on duty include a bulletin board,

FIG. 7-2.   The information desk is a place to provide a pleasant welcome to the visitor and to disseminate information. Mount St. Helens Visitor Center, Gifford Pinchot National Forest, Washington. (Photo by Grant W. Sharpe.)

mounted maps, and a nearby relief model. These aids will be discussed later in the chapter.

Campground Offices.   Some outdoor recreation areas maintain an office in the larger campgrounds, and although its primary function is to assist visitors with campsite assignments, it also serves as an information outlet. The size of the building usually determines whether or not visitors are welcomed inside or greeted through an information window.

Movable Information Booth.   When conditions warrant, a movable booth should be considered. This could be a structure of poles and canvas, a wooden building built on skids, or a small trailer or caravan on wheels. These are used only during peak visitor seasons (Fig. 7-1).

Point Duty. During peaks of the visitor season, such as holidays and weekends, it may be appropriate to station a person at a point of known concentration. Such sites could be scenic overlooks, waterfalls, or other areas, usually with parking facilities. In these circumstances, it becomes a matter of taking the information station to where the people are. A booth may not be necessary unless the weather is often inclement. The duty hours should coincide with heavy-use periods of the day, which vary from place to place and season to season.

The presence of the information duty person in uniform is all that is necessary to attract visitors. Most questions, as one would expect, will be related to what is in sight; maps, models, and other aids are usually not necessary. A spotting scope or telescope is often provided (Fig. 7-3). The duty person should be well acquainted with the area, for here is a station in the middle of the natural environment where interpretation as well as general information can be disseminated.

Roving Duty. This type of duty is similar to point duty except that the duty person moves about, either on a bicycle, on horseback, or on a motor vehicle, looking for concentrations of people. Rangers on horseback are particularly attractive to visitors. Although use of horses requires special skills, more use of horses by interpreters and information rangers should be considered. Both point and roving duties are an effective means of reaching large numbers of people. The questions during these duties are related heavily to the nearby scene. Of course, if the site is located on a major road, there could be questions related to distances and available services.

FIG. 7-3. A naturalist pointing out a wildlife feature. The visitors are lined up to use the spotting scope. Mount Rainier National Park, Washington. (Photo by Grant W. Sharpe.)

Roving duty also provides the opportunity to reach visitors with current information about hazards such as avalanches, high water, and fire danger.

This type of duty is popular with interpretive employees as it provides variety and the opportunity to exercise initiative and creativity (Fig. 7-4).

COMMUNICATION

Information duty almost always involves face-to-face communication between the information person and the visitor. This can be the most effective kind of communication when it is properly conducted. During the interchange, the visitor can express the specific kind of information he or she wants, and an information person skilled in interpersonal communication can select and tailor messages to meet the visitor's needs precisely. Immediate feedback permits both the information person and visitor to correct their communications until a satisfactory exchange has been achieved.

Information media such as brochures, books, and recorded messages are not flexible enough to meet individual needs exactly. No mass-produced messages will achieve the quality of communication that a skilled interpersonal communicator can achieve. These media are important, however, and they will be described later.

Interpersonal Communications

Each of us has a different set of experiences. We grow up in different environments and different social and cultural communities. We share many experiences with those who are our companions and neighbors. We share less with people who grow up and live in different places and who do not share our work or lifestyles. These cultural differences are most noticeable when the people we meet are from other nations with languages and customs very different from our own. Yet, the cultural differences between a Californian who grew up and lives and works in the farming country of the Sacramento Valley and a Californian who grew up in urban Los Angeles can be as great as those between a person from urban Los Angeles and one from Mexico City.

Differences in our experiences and background are important because communication depends on shared meanings for symbols such as words and gestures. We learn meanings for symbols through our experiences. Even common words have slightly different meanings for people of similar backgrounds. Sometime ask a group of acquaintances to draw a tree. You will find that some draw conifers, some draw deciduous trees in leaf, others draw bare branched deciduous trees, and some may even draw palm trees. Words such as "wilderness" and "park" will have even more widely divergent meanings.

FIG. 7-4. An interpreter on roving duty goes where visitors are. This bison and prairie dog community is popular with visitors in Theodore Roosevelt National Memorial Park, North Dakota. Here the roving interpreter talks informally with visitors at the site. (Photo by Grant W. Sharpe.)

When we attempt to communicate, we try to stimulate an image or meaning within the other person that is like the one we have in our own mind. If we give directions on how to find a trail head or a store or a rest room, we try to cause the receiver of our message to imagine our mental map with enough accuracy that he or she can follow it successfully. When we describe how an ecosystem operates or relate how the Lewis and Clark party lived and worked as they searched for a route to the Pacific, we also try to create visual and emotional images. Our success depends on how accurately we predict the images and sensations that our chosen symbols (words, gestures, etc.) will arouse in our receiver.

To make accurate predictions, we need to know quite a bit about how each individual visitor will interpret the symbols we use. We can make fairly accurate predictions if we know about their experiences and background, and if we know how they are related to meanings for symbols either through our own similar experiences or through communication with others.

We can make some predictions about how people will interpret our symbols if we know something about their cultures or social groups. For example, the word "snow" may have little or no meaning for a person from Costa Rica who has never traveled outside Central America before. However, there is much variation in experience among people from the same culture. Although people from Chicago almost all know what snow is, to some it is a cold, wet, dirty slush that causes falls, snarls traffic, and ruins expensive footware. To others it is cold, clean, powder in which they can enjoy themselves skiing. In the first example, "snow" may arouse negative feelings and images whereas in the second, it arouses positive feelings and images. If you choose to use the word "snow" to describe clusters of calcium sulfate crystals on cave walls, the images that come to mind for the Costa Rican and the two Chicagoians will be quite different; none of them may correspond to your image.

The more we know about an individual's social and cultural group, the better we can predict responses to symbols. The best predictions, however, are made on the basis of what we know about the person as an individual, apart from his or her culture or social group, and about the experiences we share with that individual. If we share many things, our predictions are likely to be relatively accurate and our communication effective. If we have less in common, we will have to be careful about our predictions, trying them out tentatively and revising them as we get feedback.

Whenever practical to do so, information persons should actively learn about each individual with whom they communicate to improve predictions and, therefore, communication effectiveness. One should not simply wait for questions and then provide the most obvious answer. To do so is to waste the potential that makes face-to-face visitor contact superior to other informative media.

Communicating with each visitor as an individual different from other visitors is not a simple task. A complete explanation of how to develop effective interpersonal communication skills is beyond the scope of this chapter. Well-written texts are available, however. One, by Miller and Steinberg, is cited among the references for this chapter. All information duty people should seriously study the principles of interpersonal communication.

Although an intensive discussion of interpersonal communication is not possible, some guidelines can be given. These should be supplemented by reading and training.

GUIDELINES FOR COMMUNICATIONS

Information Staff Should Approach Visitors Whenever Possible Rather Than Waiting for Visitors To Approach Them.   Visitors are new to the communication situation. They don't know the rules. By approaching them you clearly indicate you can be talked with. The approach also communicates interest in the visitors and puts them at ease more quickly. An approach says "welcome" and offers assistance. Note the stiff and apparently uncomfortable communication relationship between the visitor and the seated information person in Figure 7-1.

Information Staff Should Try To Come out from Behind the Desk Whenever Possible.   To some people the desk is a physical and psychological barrier between the visitor and the interpreter. Even if there is a sign above the desk clearly indicating that the information person dispenses information, the nonverbal message of the desk may overpower the verbal one. A desk or counter can be a useful place to store materials but it should not anchor the interpreter in one spot (Fig. 7-2).

Observe the Visitor.   One can learn a great deal about visitors that will improve communication predictions simply by being a careful observer. The sort of clothing worn and its condition tells something about the kind of recreation the visitor is engaged in. It may tell if they are just starting their visit or have spent several days at the area already. One can predict something of the visitor's physical and emotional state by their posture and other body cues. A camera, binoculars, books, can all say something. One can even note the kind of soil on footwear or the existence of mosquito bites to predict recent activity.

Don't Wait for the Visitor To Initiate Conversation.   This is another way to get useful information to help you tailor your communication. It is easy to verify predictions made from observations with a few conversational questions. Conversation is an important source of information.[5] Ask questions. "Where are you from?" can tell you about something in the personality or experience of the visitor to which you want to direct your communication. "Did you just arrive?" can tell you something about how tired or refreshed the visitor might be. "Where did you stay last night?" can give you important data. Was it a campground or a lodge? Were you in the campground where the bear was trapped? Did you see the evening program? What parts of the park have you seen? These kinds of questions can help you fit your messages to the visitor's experiences and needs. All this useful information is collected through natural, casual conversation, not a formal survey.

Identify How the Visitor You Are Talking with Is Different from All Other Visitors.   What are the interests and experiences this visitor has had that makes him or her unique? You want to address your messages as much as possible to that unique person. Being careful to view the person as an individual will help prevent stereotyped responses. Not all photographers want to talk about lenses, film speeds, and filters.[5]

Identify Ways the Visitor Is Like You.   If you have shared similar experiences, visited the same places, lived in similar areas, enjoy the same activities, you and the visitor will be able to communicate effectively, even about things you do not share, by relating your messages to things you have in common. You and the visitor are going to be different, perhaps more different than you imagine. People who work and live in parks may come from different subcultures than their visitors who live and work in cities. It is important not to assume that the visitor shares your values, beliefs, and knowledge. However, visitors and rangers are not completely different; some things are shared in common. Find out what those things are for that one, particular visitor.[5]

Avoid Distractions. Effective communication is impossible unless you can focus your attention on the other person and the communication situation. Telephones, radios, and other things that interrupt the visitor contact seriously impair communication effectiveness. Information duty personnel should not have other duties that cannot be ignored while talking with the visitor.

When an interruption cannot be avoided, be certain to break off your conversation with the visitor in a way that is positive and contributes to the experience. Do not simply drop the conversation to answer the telephone or radio. Continue until the visitor can study a map or look at a publication while you deal with the interruption.

This is a problem for management and design more than for the person who is assigned information duty. However, sometimes the on-duty person must accommodate for poor design or less-than-enlightened management. Remember the effectiveness of information duty depends on focusing on the visitor.[5]

Treat Each Visitor Contact as a New Situation. Information duty is not always pleasant. In spite of your best efforts, some visitors will behave in insulting or annoying ways. This frequently occurs when a visitor is making a complaint. It requires a great deal of energy and character to put up with such behavior, to accurately record the complaint, to correct the problem if possible, and to sooth the visitor's feelings as much as possible. Experiences of this kind may leave the information person angry, hurt, and aroused. This is not a good state of mind to be in when greeting the next visitor.

When such situations occur, the information person should take some time to compose himself or herself before meeting another visitor. Unless one is really expecting a positive experience, one will unintentionally and unconsciously communicate dislike or distrust that will make effective communication difficult.

At a less dramatic but equally important level, do not assume that the new visitor knows what the previous visitor knew, or that this next person is interested in the same things. Each new person must be individually researched through observation and conversation. Visitors are *not* "pretty much all alike."

Be Rested. Frequent and continuing contact with strangers is psychologically stressful. Learning about each new person in sufficient detail to communicate effectively in a short time requires a great deal of energy. You can't face the public and communicate well if you are tired or ill.

THE QUESTION AND ANSWER GAME—KNOW THE RESOURCE

Prior to beginning the job, information duty persons should read everything available on the area. This would include popular natural and human history guides. As both time and interest permit, employees should also peruse the more technical publications. They must also acquaint themselves with the general policy of the organization: what are its objectives, why does it exist, and so forth.

A knowledge of nearby features of interest, including other parks, forests, and refuges, and the significant features of each, is important. Distances to nearby towns and cities and the services available in each must be checked out and noted (see Information Checklist, pages 163–166).

Questions will be asked about a variety of subjects. Most information duty people on the job for the first time (especially those with a background in interpretation) are disappointed by the simplicity of the questions asked. Keep in mind that the visitor might be asking a mundane or thoughtless question to establish rapport with the person on duty. In any instance consider every question important to the visitor, even when they are of this type:

When does the nine o'clock walk leave?
Does it ever get this windy here?
Which end of the lake is the highest?

Answering these questions without embarrassing the visitor can be quite a challenge. Unfortunately, information duty doesn't always offer challenges. The questions are usually routine and can be easily categorized. A sampling of the common questions asked at information desks shows that most are directional. Consider these samples:

Where are the rest rooms?
Where is the campground?
Where can we buy food (gasoline)?
Where is the best place to fish around here?
Where can we pick berries?

Many questions will be area specific. An area with a prominent lake would generate questions such as these:

How deep is the lake?
What kind of fish are found here?
Do I need a license to fish here?
Do they stock the lake with fish?

A height of land nearby might prompt questions like these:

Where does the trail to the top of that hill start?
How long does it take to hike to the top?

A restored fort with an information desk in one of the buildings might receive these questions:

What were these buildings used for?
Can we go inside the other buildings?
How many men stayed here?
Were the guns ever fired in anger?
When and why was the fort built?

Mixed in with the area-specific questions will be directional or "where are" types. Frequently the visitor will take a personal interest in the duty person or the job and ask:

Do you get lonely here?
How did you get this job?
What do you do in the winter?

Other questions will relate to the organization's work, particularly those dealing with some aspect of natural resources management, such as soils, forests, or wildlife.

Some questions, but very few, are related to the natural history of an area. Examples include:

What's that tall, orange flower with the black spots on it?
How come all those trees outside are dead?
What's the topic of the talk tonight?
That bird with the red patches on its wings—what's its name?

There may be a marked distribution of the kinds of questions asked during the day. Time of day and day of week both influence the number and type of questions asked. Wilcox, in his study at a visitor center in Minnesota, found that when people were just arriving in the late afternoon most questions were related to camping, lodging, and food availability. Questions relating to policy matters and to human and natural history were asked mostly during the morning hours. Questions of a geographical nature (place, location, and how to get there) were asked in early afternoon. A noticeable correlation between the day of week and type of questions asked presumably related to day use and backcountry travel patterns and distance traveled by visitors.[6]

INJECTING INTERPRETATION

Although most questions are of a "where-is-it?" nature, some questions allow you to include some interpretation in the answer you give. For example:

Visitor: "How come all those trees outside are dead?"
Information person: "They were killed by beetles."
Alternative: "Five years ago we had an outbreak of beetles. Did you notice the new trees coming up outside? Just before they died, the old trees put on a huge crop of cones and now seedlings are growing everywhere. Take a look when you leave."

Visitor: "What's that tall, orange flower with black spots and green leaves?"
Information person: "Tiger lily."
Alternative: "You say it's tall and orange with black spots? Let's look in our park flower guide in the orange section. Here's one that looks like it; see the drawing? Could this be it?"
Visitor: "That looks like it. Tiger lily. This is a nice little flower guide. Is it for sale?"

Visitor: "Are there really rattlesnakes around here?"
Information person: "Certainly."
Alternative: "We're very lucky to have rattlesnakes here although we seldom see them. This is one of the park's most interesting animals. In the next room we have an exhibit on the life history of the rattlesnake that you might enjoy. Are you concerned about your safety on the trails? There is not much danger from snakes if you take the simple precautions discussed in the exhibit."

In this instance the visitor feels a need to talk about an alarming subject. The duty person, by expressing a calm, accepting attitude, can lessen this person's fears and arouse an interest in the reptile's life history.

Visitor: "What's that brown bird with a yellow breast we keep seeing?"
Information person: "That's the meadowlark."
Alternative: "It's a meadowlark. People quite frequently ask us about this bird because we see it along the roadside on fences or power lines, and it has a lovely song. By the way, the illustrated program at eight o'clock tonight will be on animals of the prairie. You might find this quite interesting. Here's a handout stating the time and place of our interpretive activities."

THE COMPLAINTS

Occasionally a visitor will wish to register a complaint, and the information desk is the logical place to do it. Most of the time the visitor will be content to just let off steam, so listen carefully and take it all down in writing: the time, place, name, and circumstances. If it is a policy matter, tactfully explain the policy, but don't get into an argument with the visitor, for that is a game that you cannot win. Remember: "The visitor is always right."

The procedure for handling complaints varies with areas. Give the visitor assurance that the matter will be looked into, and pass it along in writing to your supervisor for proper disposition. You've been a good listener and have assured the visitor that action will be taken. Usually, that will be the end of it.

GIVING DIRECTIONS

Be precise and to the point. Don't throw in unnecessary conversation. The visitor to a strange area will be confused enough without you adding unnecessary details.[3] Here is such an example:

Visitor: "Can you tell me how to get to Silver Falls?"

Information person: "Get in your car and go north out of the parking lot and go for about two miles until you come to the intersection marked with the notations, 'Route Four' and 'Route Six.' Take Route Six to the left and go for about three-quarters of a mile and turn right past the sign saying 'Jones Lake.' I caught six fish there last night, or was it the night before? Anyway, as I was saying, in about one and a half miles you will come to the trail head to Silver Falls. It's on the right and will say 'Silver Falls.' "

The best way to give directions is by first orienting the visitor on a map, preferably one the visitor can take along.

Alternative: "You are here (showing position on map). This is north. Follow this road west two miles to this intersection and turn south on Route Six. Just past Jones Lake take a right and watch for the sign saying 'Silver Falls.' "

Remember to keep the answer simple and avoid too many turns and directions. Let the map do the work for you.

AIDS

There are several devices that will make answering questions easier: the information checklist, counter map, and handouts are a few. Some, such as relief models and other exhibits, work effectively for you when you are very busy or tied up with repetitive questions. Others, such as bulletin boards and after-hours audio devices, work for you after the station is closed.

Information Checklist

The information checklist is a list of things visitors will ask about most often. Although you may remember some of the answers to questions asked, you cannot be expected to remember all of them. Develop a notebook or an indexed card filing system, perhaps using the following entries as headings or subheadings. Keep your file up-to-date and accurate, cross-reference some entries if that is necessary. Write clearly and legibly so that others also may use the system. The most important headings or subheadings would include the following:

A. *Automotive*

Automobile club offices
Gas stations (with hours, and types of fuel sold)
Mechanical services (repairs, supplies)
Motorcycle service
Towing services

B. *Cultural*

Art galleries
Libraries
Museums
Radio, TV stations
Theaters

C. *Emergency Services*

Ambulance
Fire stations
Hospitals (clinics)
Police (local, county, state)
Veterinarians

D. *Food Services, Suppliers*

Grocery stores
Organic health food stores
Restaurants

E. *General Information*

Chambers of commerce
Churches
Fraternal organizations
Interpretive services—times and places
Local agencies
Offices (government)
Newspapers

Postal offices
Senior citizens' organizations
Telegraph offices
Weather forecasting services
Youth organizations, groups

Also be prepared to know the following information:

Distances
Fishing, hunting regulations
Local, state history and lore
Industries (business)
Maps (where to obtain)
Points of interest
Monuments
Tides

F. *Medical-Health Services*

Clinics
Dentists (list)
Doctors (list)
Druggists
Hospitals
Veterinarians

G. *Miscellaneous Services, Suppliers*

Animal boarding (kennels)
Appliances (repairs)
Baby sitters (nurseries)
Banks
Barbers
Cleaners
Department (variety) stores
Electricians
Hairdressers
Hardware stores
Ice vendors
Law firms (list)
Liquified petroleum (propane-butane) dealers
Liquor stores
Locksmiths
Marine hardware dealers
Motels (hotels)
Novelty (souvenir) shops

Oxygen (tank) suppliers
Pet shops
Plumbers
Realtors
Rental firms (miscellaneous)
Social service agencies
Stove fuel suppliers

H. *Recreational Needs*

Art supply stores
Arts, crafts stores
Boat launching ramps
Boating services, supplies
Bowling alleys
Campgrounds
Diving air station
Diving (snorkel, scuba) shops
Docks
Fairs (fiestas, local celebrations)
Golf courses
Harbors (moorages)
Horse rentals, instruction
Lapidaries
Marine supplies, equipment (fishing, bait)
Park (local, state, national)
Rental agencies (especially boats, recreation equipment)
Resorts (private)
Sewage disposal areas
Sightseeing tours
Skates, rental
Skating rinks (ice, roller)
Sporting goods stores
Swimming pools, areas
Tennis courts
Theaters

Also familiarize yourself with the various forms of recreation indigenous to your area. Know where to send people in accordance with their particular interests and where equipment may be rented or purchased for that pursuit.

I. *Transportation Services*

Airlines
Buses

Car, truck rental firms
Ferries
Railroads
Steamship agencies
Taxi services
Travel agencies, bureaus

Other listings, or ways to organize a list, may suggest themselves, according to the area in which you work.

Maps

"Do you have a map of this area?" This is one of the most commonly asked questions. If you don't have one to offer, find out why. The cost of maps is relatively low, and visitor interest is high.

Maps vary from simple mimeographed versions with limited copy, which are given away, to the very elaborate productions in multicolor with considerable copy, which are salable items.

A wall or counter map of the area is very useful for visitor orientation.

Handouts

A handout should not be considered as a replacement for oral answers but, instead, as answers that the visitor can carry along. If, for example, you answer a family's inquiry about an interpretive activity, you should also give them a complete list of activities. This encourages further participation in the interpretive program.

Examples of handouts include bird and mammal checklists, common plants, trees, things to see and do in the area, photo hints, fishing regulations, free maps, and mileages to other points of interest. Printed checklists are not necessary and should be considered only after less expensive methods, such as mimeographing, have been utilized for a few seasons to obtain as complete a list as possible. The least expensive reproduction method possible should be acceptable for something that is distributed free.

Relief Models

The relief model, described in greater detail in Chapter 16, is a useful device for answering questions related to the specific administrative area's trails, roads, boundary, and other features. The model gives an aerial view of the total area—this is of great interest to most visitors. The model is most dramatic (and necessary) in hilly or mountainous terrain or in an area containing numerous lakes (Fig. 7-5).

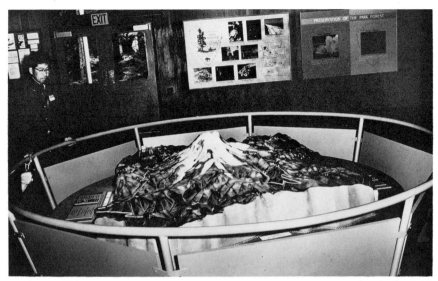

FIG. 7-5. The relief model as an interpretive aid. Visitors are intrigued with the opportunity to plan activities through the use of such a model. Mount Rainier National Park, Washington. (Photo by Grant W. Sharpe.)

Other Exhibits

Commonly asked questions can often be answered or elaborated on in an exhibit. Suppose, for example, that resource utilization such as tree harvesting or mineral extraction is taking place nearby, and visitors frequently ask about it. An exhibit of useful products garnered from this raw material will illustrate how the material touches the lives of humans.

Visitors greatly appreciate personal attention. When one comes to the information desk and describes a flower just seen, invite them to look at the layman's herbarium with you (shown in Fig. 21-4, page 480). If it is an animal they are describing show them a photo of what you assume it is, or better yet, project a slide on the wall or through a rear-projection screen (Fig. 7-6).

Bulletin Boards

The bulletin board is used for posting current notices and announcements. Properly cared for it can work effectively for you 24 hours a day, and it is particularly helpful to visitors arriving after your station is closed.

Obviously, the bulletin board would be too cluttered if it contained everything in your information checklist. Keep material brief and to the point.

An effective method of displaying information on an after-hours board is shown

FIG. 7-6. Illustrating the answer. If a visitor asks about an animal, the duty person listens carefully to the description, then rotates a selector dial (under the counter) to a number corresponding to the name of the animal it is inferred to be. A slide then appears on the screen. The projector, located behind the screen, is a random access Kodak Ectagraphic Model RA-960. Rocky Mountain National Park, Colorado. (Photo courtesy of National Park Service.)

in Fig. 7-7. Each category is laid out with clear titles. The following are suggested headings: rules and regulations, where to stay, what to do, and personal messages. Visitors may use the bulletin board to rendezvous with other families or friends. Provide 3 × 5 in. (7.6 × 12.7 cm) cards, and request that the messages be dated, so that they may be removed after a reasonable length of time. Bulletin boards tend to become "rat's nests," cluttered with faded, obsolete material unless they are frequently updated.[3]

After-Hours Audio Device

This device adds a human touch to a closed station. A word of welcome and the statement that "we are sorry the information station is closed" are appropriate. List immediately the answers to common after-hours questions, cite the fact that further information is available on the bulletin board, and close.

The button label should read, "Push button for brief message." Stating that the message will be brief encourages the visitor to listen to the end of the tape.

The audio device should be in good repair. It is unfortunate enough for the visitor to find the information station closed, but to find the badly needed answers unavailable because of a malfunctioning machine will put the visitor in an even worse frame of mind.

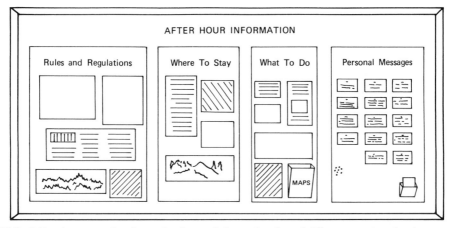

FIG. 7-7. An example of an after-hours information board. The categories clearly separate information for easy retrieval by visitors. Blank cards for visitor messages and maps of the area are available.[3]

SUPERVISING INFORMATION DUTY EMPLOYEES

The employee at the information desk is the organization's public image; often he or she is the initial contact and sometimes the only contact your organization has with visitors. The public relations impact of this position cannot be overemphasized. Don't assume that the employee understands this connection. In fact, don't assume that new employees know anything about the position and its responsibilities. This is especially important in greeting visitors, answering the telephone, and handling complaints and emergencies. Care must be taken to train every new employee in all aspects of visitor contact.[1]

After the employee is on the job it is necessary to monitor that individual periodically. Observe the manner in which the employee treats visitors. Does the employee look so busy that visitors pass by the information desk? Does he or she give disinterested answers? How well does the duty person handle complaints, and does his or her voice contain a helpful tone or an official tone? Meet with the information duty personnel during slack periods; be as receptive to them as they should be to visitors. Show a genuine interest in them by seeing if they have any criticisms to air, questions to ask, and comments or suggestions to offer. If personnel do not feel good about their work and their organization, they will not be effective in accomplishing their jobs. A few minutes' conversation with the boss can often resolve minor problems.

Remember, too, that skill in public relations does not come automatically to new employees, but must be learned. Employees should be made to feel that they are serving the public rather than just working for the agency. Citizens expect a return in services for their taxes, and being able to ask questions of an information duty person is a visible return for their investment. This fact is often difficult for visitor contact people to understand unless it is emphasized during the job-training program.

Information duty is not easy duty. The constant contact with strangers, the complaints, the often repetitive nature of the job all create stress. Stress may lead to impatient replies to visitor questions, attempts to reduce contact by occupying oneself with minor activities and not noticing visitors, daydreaming, or excessive reliance on publications. A stressed visitor information person will eventually respond in an angry or insulting way to a visitor, resulting in potentially serious public relations problems.

No one should be assigned continuous visitor information duty. Although the optimum duration for visitor contact has not been researched and probably differs depending on personalities, four hours may be a maximum shift. Duties should be varied. Information duty should be mixed with other park or forest management work involving little visitor contact. Examples might be trail maintenance, assistance with research activities either in the field or in the library, and preparation of materials for interpretive publications or programs.

Information duty people can only be effective if they know what is going on. They should be frequently briefed on management activities. They should occasionally ride with patrol rangers, work campground duty, do interpretation, assist at a prescribed burn, and even work with the concessionaire if possible.

People are not automatically qualified communicators. Information duty people should receive specific training in interpersonal communication. Interpersonal courses in college might be a requirement for seasonal employment. Several well-written texts are published and copies should be given to information duty people to read before they begin to work and to review as they gain experience. Slide-tape or videotape training programs might be prepared and made available.

A check with personnel managers of large organizations reveals only slight differences of opinion as to the qualities they look for in applicants for an information duty opening. Several of the qualifications appear repeatedly; the first three listed below were on every list. Grouped together, these qualities included the following:

1. Appearance.
2. Personality.
3. Politeness.
4. Knowledge of the organization's functions.
5. Ability to meet the public and to communicate articulately.
6. Ability to perform minimal clerical functions.
7. Ability to organize and to make good use of time.
8. Ability to control emotions and to exhibit patience.

9. General knowledge, poise, and maturity.
10. Loyalty and trustworthiness.
11. Self-confidence and assurance.
12. An ability to work closely with other people.
13. An ability to work alone under loose supervision.

In the past women were found in informational positions in greater numbers than men, due ostensibly to lower pay scales and the fact that the type of work required was considered demeaning or unchallenging to men. Today, however, with the equalization of pay scales and opportunities, and changing attitudes about sex roles, men are being attracted to these positions in ever-growing numbers. The recent emphasis placed on ecology and conservation have also helped to attract greater numbers of men into information-oriented positions with land management or park agencies.

Despite the equal opportunities available for advancement and similar pay, marked differences remain between how men and women performing this kind of duty perceive themselves and their roles, in how the visitors may in turn perceive them, and also in the problems faced by each.

Criteria for selecting personnel for information duty vary from one agency to another, and it is therefore impossible to select one absolute method for determining who may be right for the position. In many instances these criteria are weighted toward the particular interests of the agency providing the service.

One problem experienced by both men and women in these positions is unwelcome personal attention from visitors who seek to dominate the information person's time and perhaps to go so far as to make physical advances. Although the problem is more frequently experienced by women, in either case it is necessary for the personnel involved to be forewarned of the possibility and to be ready to handle it in a firm, though diplomatic, manner. Managers should be aware of the need to support information personnel should these occasions arise.

Despite the varied duties (i.e., information dissemination, light clerical work, visitor contact, and so forth) and the usually hectic schedule faced by most individuals in information duty, boredom can and frequently does set in. When regularly assigned duties have been discharged, it is expected that the employees will use their initiative to find additional work with which to occupy themselves. Frequently there are lulls between visitor contacts, and it becomes necessary for personnel to be creative and self-starting. These lulls can be used for training and the acquisition of new information or to assist with the preparation of new information or interpretive messages and media. Managers should plan important but not urgent work that information people can do when there is no pressure.

The following are a few suggested do's and don'ts for information duty employees.

Do

Maintain a neat, clean appearance at all times. Be equally pleasant and courteous to everyone. Smile and greet visitors cheerfully; maintain good eye contact.

Make a sincere effort to be helpful and responsive to the needs of others.

Get plenty of sleep before your duty as rest increases your responsiveness and interest in the job.

Maintain your enthusiasm about the job.

Arrive at your post ahead of your scheduled starting time.

Wear your name badge while on duty.

Keep your duty post (information desk) tidy and organized.

Keep your Information Checklist up to date.

Remain at your assigned duty post until you have been relieved—notify your supervisor promptly when it becomes necessary for you to leave your post unattended.

Put out only a limited number of brochures or printed materials at any one time as this discourages visitors from taking more than their share.

Report rule infractions immediately to the proper authorities.

Turn in all lost items to your supervisor.

Report any visitor illness or accident at once to your supervisor.

Don't

Eat, drink, smoke, or chew gum while on duty.

Talk to friends or co-workers while visitors are present.

Talk down to visitors—but *do try to make allowances* for differences in culture, language, and age.

Be abrupt, no matter how busy you may be.

Read, knit, or write letters while on duty—this tends to discourage the visitor from asking questions.

Try to remember everything; refer to your Information Checklist.

Bluff—do admit it if you don't have the necessary answer, then get it as soon as possible.

REFERENCES

General References

Lewis, William J. 1980. *Interpreting for Park Visitors,* Eastern National Park and Monument Association, Eastern Acorn Press, Philadelphia, PA.

References Cited

1. Artz, Robert M., Temple R. Jarrell, and Adah Parker. 1968. *Staff Public Relations Handbook,* National Recreation and Park Association, Arlington, VA.
2. Lime, David W. 1973. *An Exploratory Study of the Use of Two Forest Service Visitor Information Centers: Voyageur and Sylvania,* North Central Forest Experiment Station Office Report, St. Paul, MN.
3. Machlis, Gary E., and Sally G. Machlis. 1974. *Creative Design for Bulletin Boards,* National Park Service, Cooperative Park Studies Unit, College of Forest Resources, University of Washington, Seattle.
4. Manvey, Albert. 1968. *Say, Ranger . . . Or How to Perform in the Information Center,* Visitor Services Training Series, National Park Service, Government Printing Office, Washington, DC.
5. Miller, Gerald R., and Mark Steinberg. 1975. *Between People: A New Analysis of Interpersonal Communications,* Science Research Associates, Inc., Chicago.
6. Wilcox, Richard Arthur. 1969. "Information Desired by Visitors at the Voyageur Visitor Center," unpublished thesis, University of Michigan, Ann Arbor.

CHAPTER 8

CONDUCTED ACTIVITIES

Paul H. Risk

Conducted activities are a special form of interpretation in which the interpreter and the visitor move sequentially through a series of on-site experiences involving actual objects and views. In its best developed form the conducted activity brings into play all five senses permitting the visitor to see, touch, smell, hear, and even taste the subject of interpretation.

Such activities take many forms in park and recreation areas, and it is only for imaginative interpreters to conceive new and innovative types.

Common activities include nature walks and hikes which vary from an hour or two to several days; trips through caves; tours of historical and archeological sites; automobile caravans; bus and tram tours; and boat, canoe, and raft trips.

All of these activities have in common the movement of a group of visitors led by an interpreter whose goals are to develop sensitivity, awareness, understanding, appreciation, and commitment in the members of the group. In essence the conducted activity has the same framework as a talk.

Five points are inherent in all effectively conducted activities.

1. Arrive early.
2. Start on time.
3. Describe what you plan to do.
4. Do it.
5. End it.

As pointed out in Chapter 9, tell the visitors what you are going to do, do it, and then tell them what you did.

Let's look more closely at the five points above.

1. ARRIVE EARLY

At least 15 minutes prior to the announced starting time you should be present to identify the fact that "this is the place." Since they are usually unfamiliar with the park and often not listening or reading as carefully as they might, the visitors quite often are uncertain as to the exact beginning point of the activity.

Also, your presence will allow time to meet members of the group as they arrive, providing the first threads of rapport that will ultimately weld all of you into an effective interpretive unit. Be friendly: smile. Your face won't fracture. This isn't the time to tug your hat brim down to within two fingers of the bridge of your nose, don mirror-finish sunglasses, and do an impersonation of a Marine drill instructor. An officious bearing will erect a wall between you and your group and doom your efforts before you even start.

As people arrive greet them warmly and find out a little about them. Show an interest. People like people who like them. Where are they from? How long have they been traveling? What do they do for a living? What other guided trips have they been on? Are they enjoying their stay in the park? But, remember, this isn't an interrogation. It is designed to help you get bits of information that can be skillfully woven into the fabric of your presentation later as you tailor your style to meet the needs of your people. This customizing is one of the important factors that makes you more versatile and effective than a message repeater.

Don't devote all your attention to one family or a single person. Undivided attention directed to a particularly comely woman or handsome man to the exclusion of others will not only limit your effectiveness, but will cause resentment in the rest of the group.

Groups attract. Others who observe the growing cluster of people will often stop out of curiosity and provide the opportunity for you to add them to your entourage.

2. START ON TIME

When the time comes to begin, do it! Don't make excuses that you had better wait for latecomers and thus inconvenience all those who were there on time. However, it isn't necessary to actually *leave* on the second. Turn your attention from individuals to the entire group and with a smile conversationally welcome them to the activity and introduce yourself. "Hi! I'm John Doe, the Park Naturalist here, and on behalf of Tubagurra National Park I'd like to welcome you on our beach walk." But be careful. An interpreter in a large park who had done everything well until this point suddenly shifted from a personable demeanor to a formal, automatic, "museum guide" tone, reciting a standard welcome and altering the whole feeling of friendliness he had built before the activity.

3. DESCRIBE THE ACTIVITY

While providing a beginning that satisfies the group with your punctuality, the brief introductory statement and description of the activity that follows will allow a few moments to elapse before your actual departure and will serve the purpose of allowing latecomers to arrive without calling attention to the fact.

Clearly and concisely explain what will be involved in the proposed activity. The visitors have a right to know what they are in for. Also, if special skill or equipment is needed this should be carefully explained. "I assume that all of you who are going to accompany us on the tour of this active volcano have your asbestos suits and breathing gear."

Establish *where* the activity starts and ends. Be sure the visitors understand how long they will be out. Time is the important factor, not mileage. Most people don't relate distances to anything familiar. "We begin right here and we will be out about 2 hours, ending up, after walking a loop trail, over there on the other side of the parking lot. We'll cover a little over a mile, but it's leisurely and pleasant. The trail is smooth, and I'm sure you'll enjoy it."

On walks or hikes make your first stop close enough to the point of departure that your group can be seen. This gives a final chance for late arrivals to catch up (Fig. 8-1).

Then tell them your theme. But, don't do it by saying, "my theme today is . . ." Rather, "today I'd like to take you on a walk into the past. Let your imag-

FIG. 8-1. This interpreter has planned her first stop carefully so that her group can be seen by latecomers. Shenandoah National Park, Virginia. (Photo by Donald H. Robinson.)

ination guide you as we step back 700 years to a time when household chores were the same as now, but their solutions were somewhat different. As we tour the ruins I think you'll begin to see many similarities to life today, and one of the goals of this walk is to help you develop a kinship with that not so distant or alien past.''

If possible, foster an atmosphere that elicits questions. "If you see something that interests you which I don't comment on, call it to my attention. I may have missed it.''

4. DO IT

Having finished all of the preliminaries, you are now ready to actually conduct the activity. However, for your efforts to be effective you must have laid a great deal of groundwork. The type of preparation will depend largely on the kind of activity. But, there are many commonalities regardless of the activity type. For the purposes of this chapter the guided walk will be used to illustrate many of these universal principles.

Developing the Walk

Inventory the Area.   Like an effective salesman, it is imperative that before you give a good walk you must "know your territory." Familiarize yourself with what the area has to offer. If you are limited to an existing trail or other route, walk it carefully from both ends, examining and listing each potential subject. If your route has yet to be determined, criss-cross it in a rough grid, marking on a piece of graph paper the location of things you may want to include.

In areas that have a lengthy history of interpretive activities, the route as well as the points to be interpreted are all too frequently selected on the basis of tradition rather than rationale. To interpret a particular object just because the person who taught you did is no reason at all. However, the underlying basis may be firm, designated by the type of area. An archeological site has a particular story that must be told, and there are several different and equally effective ways of approaching it. Just because you are in an historical or archeological area doesn't mean that every single word you speak must refer to artifacts of bygone ages.

Define a Theme.   The inventory should have suggested numerous themes or central threads that could be skillfully woven through your walk, lending a unifying reinforcement and facilitating the development of visitor comprehension.

The variety of flowering plants encountered may suggest a wildflower walk.

But, a flower walk based solely on identification can be a bore even to a botanist. A search of the literature may show that many of the currently blooming species had pioneer or native uses; and the theme, while still identifying the plants, could be shifted to include this aspect.

It is possible to randomly wander along talking about whatever you locate, but it is difficult for the average visitor to sustain interest unless some direction and point is indicated.

An exception is the "discovery walk." Advertised as this, each visitor is given a field guide for some aspect of the trip, and a random walk ensues during which the group does its own identification and gleans information about each new discovery.

Gather Facts.   An inventory is a very dry document, and interpretation presented in this style is very likely to serve only as a means of promoting sleep. People tend to be interested in things that relate to their own experiences. Facts must be gathered on each of the items you plan to incorporate in the interpretive presentation. The more things you know about the subjects of your activity, the more likely you will be to touch responsive chords in your group and to carry out a successful trip. For that matter, the more facts you have at your fingertips, the more your mind, like the computer it is, will make correlations that will enable you to present your inventory in a manner calculated to stimulate.

Don't be afraid to use experiences about which you have personal knowledge.

"I remember a friend of mine who was climbing near Yosemite Falls with a team of mountaineers. Reaching for a ledge above his head, he felt a "thorn" prick his finger. Levering himself up to the ledge he found he was eyeball to eyeball with the "thorn," a rattlesnake just like the one you see here. Bitten, he cooly climbed back down with his team, walked into the hospital, announced his predicament—and fainted away. He's fine today but has quite a vivid memory of that climb."

Outline the Walk.   Just as in your preparations for a formal talk, make a topic outline to determine the order you plan to use in discussing each point along the way. Committing the outline to memory will help you make smooth transitions from one stop to the next. But, allow flexibility so that unforeseen occurrences or discoveries can be blended into the walk.

Finally, be willing to change any or all parts if you feel *yourself* losing interest. If *you* aren't interested, it is difficult to conceal it, and the walk will soon lose vitality.

Duration of Stops.   It's difficult to cite figures, since each interpreter will have his or her own ideas on this. Also, group size will dictate proper length. But, with groups of 35 or less, stops should probably not exceed 5 to 7 minutes and often will be far shorter. On the other hand, there may be occasions when you want the group to experience tranquility or discuss a story with philosophical overtones. Then stops may last as long as 15 to 20 minutes.

As group size increases, the number of stops should be reduced and the time spent at each location correspondingly shortened. Larger groups not only become unwieldy but seem more subject to boredom; their attention span drops.

5. END IT

Few things are as disconcerting as a walk that comes to an uncertain end.

Having just led one of the finest walks possible, an interpreter in one of the western U.S. National Parks stopped, looked over his group, and announced somewhat hesitantly, "Well, I guess this is about as far as we'll go . . ." And, turning to a couple near him, he began to carry on a conversation. His group shuffled uneasily, looked at each other, and waited to see if they had heard him correctly. But, minutes passed and obviously nothing more was going to happen. One by one in small clusters, the people began to trickle back down the trail. It was unnecessarily awkward.

Plan a concluding statement that will neatly wrap up any loose ends, summarize what you hope to have accomplished, and notify the visitors that the trip has ended. In other words, you told them what you were going to do, you did it, and now you are telling them what you did—and goodbye.

"From this viewpoint you can get a very nice picture of the entire series of changes we have shown you today. As I mentioned, temperature and moisture are the two key factors that cause this modification. Our trip ends here but yours will continue, and as it does, I hope you'll notice with new perspective similar changes across the country. I've surely enjoyed being with you, and I hope we'll see you at some of our other activities."

SOME GENERAL COMMENTS

Stay in the Lead

By being in front you not only can control the pace but will be able to see spots to stop far enough in advance to allow you to group your people in the most advantageous way (Fig. 8-2).

Arriving at a stop, especially with a large group, walk past it almost half the length of your party. Stop, inform the people at the head of the line to stay where they are, and walk back halfway. In this way you will have automatically distributed the crowd so that they can all hear and see.

FIG. 8-2. The interpreter should stay in the lead to control the pace of the group. A beach walk in Acadia National Park, Maine. (Photo by Grant W. Sharpe.)

When you finish interpreting a stop, your group may move off without you, and on narrow trails it can be very awkward to catch up. Ask them to wait until you get back to the head of the line before they begin walking.

Face Your Group

There is a strong temptation while walking between stops to engage in conversation with those nearest you. This is fine. However, those behind will be stretching to overhear your gems of wisdom, and if you are discussing things relevant to the rest of the group, you should brief them at the next stop. Whatever you do, don't attempt to walk and interpret. Your voice will be carried away and only those nearest will hear. This applies equally well at viewpoints or other spots that tempt you to look toward the vista and talk away from the visitors.

Provide Visibility

The group's viewpoint is different from yours. Objects near or on the ground are difficult to show groups, since only those closest to you can really get a good view. When dealing with more than a dozen people, it's best to limit yourself to points of interest that are large enough to be easily observed. Clustering around you, a tightly packed mass of people can obscure the view of almost anything. Keep your people back. Urge them to form a large circle or semicircle a few feet away to increase ease of viewing for all. One interpreter giving beach walks simply draws a line in the sand with the stick he carries for a pointer and asks visitors to stay behind the line. Carried out pleasantly and with finesse his "stay behind the line" carries no air of officiousness and is well received.

Be especially sure children in the group can see. Their perspective is considerably different from yours or the rest of the group. Invite them to step to the front. The adults will be able to see over them (Fig. 8-3).

Visibility can also be obscured by the sun. On stopping, your group should be faced so that their backs are to the sun. Not only will they be able to see, but their attitudes will be better.

Limited access structures in historical and archeological sites pose unique problems of visibility. In some cases it will be impossible to move a large group into a building, and relays of smaller clusters will have to be used.

Speak Loudly Enough

An observant interpreter can tell by tilted heads, strained positions, and expressions when those at the back can't hear. The key word is *observant*. Continuously monitor your group for feedback of all kinds, and most difficulties can be overcome before they really develop.

All questions addressed to you should be repeated for the benefit of the entire group. Too frequently, those speaking will do so in small voices that don't carry, and your reply will be meaningless to those who didn't hear the original query. Not only will this practice keep your entire group aware, but it will remind those few who might take unfair advantage and monopolize the activity that you have responsibilities to all and can't provide a private walk.

Be careful to adjust your volume to the group size. A bellow calculated to reach the back of an amphitheater filled with 600 people is a little hard to take in a group of six. The gentle conversation adequate for the half dozen won't quite make it with 600.

Know When To Be Still

There appears to be a myth which promotes the idea that an interpreter must unceasingly fill the air with well-chosen verbal gems. All too often, a conducted activity becomes an almost uninterrupted barrage of information with pauses only long enough for the interpreter to catch a breath.

What can you really say about the beauty of a sunset, the magnificence of a star-filled sky, or the grace of a leaping buck? Freeman Tilden[2] suggests that there are times when silence and inactivity are the most appropriate form of interpretive message. These things surely speak for themselves far more eloquently than you or I, and they do so directly to the heart. Plan a stop at a particular awesome or thought-provoking spot. Build up to it before you actually get there, and then

FIG. 8-3. An experienced interpreter will consider the group members carefully, stopping with the sun at their backs. Children should be invited to step to the front. Jasper National Park, Alberta. (Photo by Grant W. Sharpe.)

give your group time to simply sit or stand quietly to absorb and meditate. Let them make the experience theirs in their own way.

Use Teachable Moments

No matter how well-planned your activity, there will always be occurrences that take place spontaneously. Be flexible and alert enough to interpret them. If an eagle swoops down, scoops a baby out of the arms of its mother, and flies off into the blue, don't gnash your teeth at this unwarranted interruption and doggedly pursue your description of bark beetle life history. Shift gears and interpret this serendipitous happening. This is a teachable moment. *Now* is the time to interpret eagles, not down the trail five more stops where you planned to show your people an empty nest. (Obviously, it's also the time to talk about science fiction a bit!)

In one area an interpreter discussing the delicate balance in the flora of the alpine community was interrupted by an uncouth little ground squirrel which picked that moment to do a little broken-field running right through the legs of his startled group. But, did he take advantage of his cue to talk about this fleet-footed little rodent? By no means! Casting a baleful glare at the fuzzy little upstart, he completed his comments on alpine ecology—mostly to the backs of the visitors who were watching the squirrel disappear up the slope.

A truly skillful interpreter, like a virtuoso musician, can alter pace and blend into the presentation, almost without a perceptible break, any spontaneous situation.

Use All the Senses

Most interpretation takes advantage only of sight and hearing. Visitors stand looking at a particular view or object while the interpreter explains it. Show and tell!

Occasionally, people are hesitant to participate in activities that incorporate more senses because it requires a loss of anonymity. If they can merely accompany a group but not enter into active interaction, they maintain a kind of neutrality. For example, mature ponderosa pines have a characteristic fragrance, especially when their bark has been warmed by the sun. It is usual practice for interpreters in areas where they grow to urge their groups to smell the bark. "The bark of this tree has a pleasant fragrance. Feel free to step up and smell it." Few do. A giggle or two can be heard and one or two innovators sniff self-consciously. The group moves on.

It could be different. Walking up to the tree, the interpreter places his nose against its orange bark and draws a deep breath. Exhaling a satisfied "Ahhh!" he says, "Boy! That smells *great!* It's especially good today. Come on up and try it. What do you think it smells like? Oh, come on, don't be hesitant. You're missing one of the most important parts of your visit. You're just afraid of what your friends will think if they see you sniffing trees."

A little cajoling and good humored urging designed to overcome the inertia of self-consciousness will result in most of the group's smelling the tree and finding to their amazement that it has a delicious aroma. Coupling this experience with the description of the bark as a source of synthetic vanilla will complete a very successful minipacket in your interpretive series.

The enlarging of one's environmental awareness through extended use of the senses is limitless. If you are intrigued, read Steve van Matre's little book entitled *Acclimatization.*[3] You'll find it full of good suggestions.

Set a Reasonable Pace

Start out briskly. This will give you a chance to spread the group out a bit and permit you to see how well they move. Then set a pace that will not tire those who seem slower. Too fast a pace will create large gaps in the group, promoting clusters of people who may do their own interpretation as they go and slow even further those behind. Too slow a rate builds impatience and boredom.

Keep a Head Count

On short walks where lost visitors are a virtual impossibility the necessity for head counts is minimal. But, on extended hikes, especially in rough terrain, they become imperative. It's very difficult to explain later how you left one of your people "out there."

Emergencies

Heart attacks, bee stings, asthma episodes, sprains, bruises, and simple exhaustion sometimes compounded by heat or cold: all these can and do happen. Develop contingency plans to cover all possible emergency situations. On hikes of any great distance or duration radio communication should be mandatory. Speed in securing help in critical illness, injury, or searches can save lives. Some would argue that a radio is too expensive to send out with each group, and that it isn't needed all that often. But, it could also be argued that today, when such modern communication devices are available, the park agency that does *not* use them is simply negligent in its responsibilities to the public. Needless to say, that kind of legal decision can have repercussions far in excess of the cost of radio equipment.

Realities will dictate, however, that many activities will be undertaken without adequate communication units. In these instances a visitor may have to be sent out for help or be used as leader to take the remainder of your group back while you stay with the ill or injured party. Perhaps, if your group includes a doctor, it would be faster for you to go for help. Individual situations vary and only you can make the on-site decisions that will be required.

Whatever the case, there is no excuse for your failure to plan ahead and to know enough first aid measures to take action. A small first aid kit represents little bulk and should be included on all walks and hikes.

Children

Youngsters are usually attracted magnetically to the group leader. They constantly vie with each other to see who can remain closest to the interpreter, invariably stepping all over that individual in their zeal. Lost shoe heels are a hazard of the occupation. Younger children, usually less inhibited than their slightly older peers, often will unabashedly slip their hand into yours to lock their relationship. So, like the Pied Piper, you move along the trail, a seething mass of small people bumbling along behind and on you.

These youngsters can be a great asset. They are likely the most observant and alert people on the activity, seeing things that you and others miss. Certainly, they can become a nuisance if uncontrolled enthusiasm permits them to take over the activity. But, properly balanced and utilized they can be a real blessing. Above all, be careful to avoid doing or saying insensitive things (unless dire circumstances warrant it) to children. To them you are a hero. If they like you and you obviously like them, you have won their parents as a bonus.

Conducting a walk in one of the U.S. National Parks, the interpreter had just passed a rotting log. A girl about 10 years old found a little frog beside it. Picking it up she then spent the next two stops unsuccessfully attempting to get the interpreter's attention. Finally, tired of her interruption, he looked down, saw at long last her prize, and responded with, "Where did you get that! It's against park regulations to disturb any living thing! Now, you take that right back where you found it and keep your hands off things from now on!"

Crestfallen and in absolute disgrace, under the eyes of the whole group, whom she undoubtedly thought sided with the ranger, she walked back down the trail, eyes brimming with tears, and replaced the animal.

With one lead-footed move, displaying total ineptitude for dealing with people, this interpreter destroyed the activity for all who were with him as well as altering, perhaps permanently, this young girl's and probably her parents' image of rangers and the Service.

A far better response would have been to squat (kids are smaller than adults) down to her level, look at the frog, show it to the rest of the group, and tell them something about it while complimenting the young lady on her sharp eyes. He would then be free to put the frog back by a log with a *gentle, sensitive* comment that, "we want to be sure it can find its way back home, don't we?"

Probably a warning is in order. There are parents who view conducted activities as a baby sitting service. They deposit their youngsters at the trail head while they go off on their own activities. Not only is this a questionable practice in terms of parental responsibility, it also poses serious potential problems for both the interpreter and the park agency. By the nature of your duties you cannot be constantly aware of the actions of unescorted children and any injuries that occur would place both you and your agency in an unfortunate position. In addition, there is the simple fact that the children may become a nuisance. Unless young people seem quite capable and mature, it is best to decline to take them without parents.

SPECIALIZED ACTIVITIES

Bus and Tram Tours

For quite some time larger zoos and a few other agencies have provided motorized guided trips through their facilities. More recently and due largely to increasing visitor impact and congestion, still more areas, including some of the national parks in the United States, have instituted this mode of park use (Figs. 8-4 and 8-5). In areas otherwise restricted to foot travel, the bus or tram tour permits access for those visitors unable or unwilling to go on foot.

FIG. 8-4. The Yosemite Valley shuttle bus, where the driver has the opportunity to interpret to the passengers. Yosemite National Park, California. (Photo by Grant W. Sharpe.)

FIG. 8-5. The view from the top of the shuttle bus (opposite page). Riders turn to look at the feature being interpreted by the driver below. Yosemite National Park, California. (Photo by Grant W. Sharpe.)

Carried out either by the driver or an assistant, interpretation can present a smooth, sequential story of the park while the vehicle moves along.

Of course, the most economical method of information presentation is for the driver to provide interpretation. However, with attention split between interpretation and driving, there are questions of safety. A lavalier or head-mounted microphone will allow both hands to be free for driving and reduce the hazard factor, but the driver is still forced to speak with his back to the group. Lacking the eye contact desirable in effective communication seriously impairs the driver's ability to develop rapport and monitor nonverbal feedback from the visitors. This style of presentation is likely to become mechanical and memorized until it becomes difficult to know whether the words emanate from the driver or a recorder.

From the standpoint of interpretive effectiveness, the use of a second person, facing the group, is more desirable. A far more personable approach is possible even though the interpreter will find it necessary to look ahead from time to time to synchronize the presentation with points of interest.

Although at first glimpse it would appear most desirable for the bus or tram to move continuously, such may not be the case. It is entirely appropriate for a few stops to be made, allowing visitors to leave the vehicle to take pictures. In some areas visitors leave and reboard as they desire. In this way they may ride as far as they care to, leave the tram for a walk or hike, and reboard a subsequent vehicle.

Automobile Tours

An auto caravan is only practical in cases of minimal visitation where relatively long distances must be covered. Visitors drive personal vehicles, following a park interpreter. In the more usual format it is necessary at each stop to wait while passengers disembark from their cars and walk to the interpreter's position. Following the interpretive message, all walk back to the cars, reenter them, and the procession begins again. It is easy to visualize the problems encountered when 20, 30, or more autos attempt to participate in such a trip. It becomes total chaos at stops as everyone tries to find a place to park. Often the result is a partly or entirely blocked roadway.

With smaller groups the technique can be effective. Be sure that drivers signal turns as they see the car ahead do so and that speeds are kept slower than normal. There is a tendency in caravans to follow too close for safety and sudden stops can easily create a chain collision.

In a few areas radios are being used to permit interpretation to be broadcast to each vehicle in order to make stops unnecessary. A small radio converter is attached with tape to each vehicle's radio antenna. For cars with aerials in the windshield the unit is merely taped on the glass over the wire. The interpreter in the lead vehicle speaks over the park radio frequency. This transmission is received by the converter, changed to a standard broadcast station to which each of the car radios has been tuned, and rebroadcast through them. In this way each car has its own interpreter. But, as the length of the caravan increases, it is not uncommon for the interpreter to be talking about something so far in advance of the following people that they can in no way make sense of the message. Furthermore, in looking around to figure out what they ought to be seeing, the driver may drift off the road or into oncoming traffic.

Last of all, the converters often do not function as well as they might.

However, even with all the potential problems, this approach has much promise.

Boat, Canoe, and Raft Trips

Boat and bus trips are very similar. On smaller craft, interpretation is provided by the captain who narrates as the boat progresses (Fig. 8-6). Larger boats ordinarily use the services of an interpreter who can work more closely with the passengers.

It is not necessary to talk constantly. Periods of interpretation can very nicely be interspersed with time for the interpreter to walk about making personal contact with individuals and families. As with the informal pretrip contacts prior to walks, this time can be spent building rapport, finding out more about passengers, and gathering information that can make subsequent messages more personal.

FIG. 8-6. On smaller boats like the one above, the interpretation is provided by the captain. On larger vessels an interpreter can work more closely with passengers. Maligne Lake, Jasper National Park, Alberta. (Photo by Grant W. Sharpe.)

Canoe and paddleboat tours are waterborne excursions where one craft follows behind another. Periodic stops are made or the group "rafts up" in a large cluster to hear interpretive messages (Fig. 8-7). Some of the same problems found in auto caravans exist here as the number of participants rises. For success this activity requires small groups. But given a gentle river, a few boats, and an efficient interpreter, it can be a high-quality experience.

A few agencies are operating interpreted raft float trips. Either rubber or wooden rafts may be used, but the key is a leisurely pace.

Wild rivers do not lend themselves well to interpretation, and perhaps that is just as well. Some aspects of wild nature are best discovered on one's own without anyone attempting to interpret them.

Floating slowly along at a pace governed by the current permits a unique atmosphere of unhurried give and take interpretation (Fig. 6-7). Rather than relying solely on prepared, formal presentations, it may be appropriate to lead the group into discussions of various points of interest. Some of the U.S. National Parks are now encouraging "rap sessions" on management policies to help users gain a clearer insight into the problems facing administrators and the reasons behind management decisions.

Archeological and Historical Sites

The ideal thing about both types of areas is that they have built-in relevance if the interpreter will just take advantage of it. The works of humans are, by the

FIG. 8-7. A guided paddleboat tour. At selected places the group "rafts up" to hear the interpretive message. The interpreter is standing at far left. Fairy Stone State Park, Virginia. (Photo courtesy of Virginia State Parks.)

FIG. 8-8. A conducted tour through native dwellings abandoned several hundred years ago. Visitors are permitted to visit the ruins only when on a guided tour. Mesa Verde National Park, Colorado. (Photo by Grant W. Sharpe.)

very nature of the site, at the heart of everything (Fig. 8-8). Comparisons of ancient with modern practices make natural reference points. There is no hard and fast rule that states that interpretation of these sites must always deal exclusively with architectural facts. Technology, health, clothing, and plant uses for dyes and fibers logically fit into the picture and lend variety.

Since extensive coverage of living interpretation (Chapter 10) is encountered elsewhere in this book it will be sufficient to comment here that it is a difficult subject to make live for the average visitor. Every effort ought to be used to develop innovation and flexibility so that neither the interpreter nor the visitor becomes bored.

Cave Tours

Caverns present a unique challenge to the interpreter. On the one hand, they have a magnetic attraction for visitors because of the mystique of dark, dank underworlds coupled with whisps of folklore and terror tales. A cave is automatic excitement. On the other hand, it may be automatic boredom to an interpreter. Apparently unchanging year after year, subject to none of the variety imposed by seasonal changes, it can seem a sterile field for innovative interpretation. All too often the interpreter, settling on a comfortable sequence of stops, solidifies the presentation into a mechanical patter replete with tired puns and worn-out names. How many caves contain a Devil's Basin, a Bottomless Pit, a stalactite called Elephant's Trunk?

Maximum leeway for change must be permitted in cave interpretation if it is to remain vital. Walk the route looking for new formations on which to comment. Revise the wording and phrasing of messages. Change the order of your topics. And never forget that the visitor has never seen this before. For your group there still is an aura of excitement, and you have a great opportunity to maximize the experience.

Hikes

For the purpose of this section, the difference between a hike and a walk lies chiefly in increased length and/or severity. Requiring more stamina and perhaps special equipment and skill, the hike also calls for modification in interpretive style.

The most important change is reduction in message. You can't talk the whole time. If you take a group out for a full day or even half a day and talk "at them" the entire time, there is grave doubt about your ever returning. Someone is likely to do you physical harm or at the very least place some large object in your mouth just to get a little peace and quiet. Richard Shew in a doctoral dissertation entitled "Visitor Types in the National Parks"[1] has shown that many people join guided hikes mostly for the security of accompanying a competent leader. He mentions nothing about going along to hear an unceasing barrage of words.

In one sense a guided hike is really an outing on which an interpreter just happens to be along to serve as a resource person, injecting gems of sparkling information periodically and answering questions. More planning and finesse is needed to successfully carry out this type of interpretation than at first may be apparent.

Rest stops should be spaced at reasonable intervals, often determined by a watchful eye on the slower members of the party. *Some,* but not *all,* of these stops may be times when interpretive information can be presented. A proper inventory can allow you to select rest stops with interpretive potential.

Be especially sure that you maintain and continually update a count of your people and that contingency plans have been worked out to take care of emergencies.

Overnight hikes impose logistical problems which may require that you help visitors select and pack gear. Be sure that all members are prepared for the undertaking physically. Those who appear to be ill-equipped or in questionable physical condition should diplomatically be urged to undertake less taxing activities, but don't embarrass them in front of the group.

Without doubt conducted activities offer as many challenges to the interpreter as he or she is willing to accept. However, the rewards are many. The deep satisfaction resulting from a successful conducted activity goes a long way toward making the effort worthwhile.

REFERENCES CITED

1. Shew, Richard L. 1970. Visitor Types in the National Parks: A Q-Study of Public Wants and Needs in Outdoor Recreation, unpublished Ph.D. dissertation, Ohio State University.
2. Tilden, Freeman. 1967. *Interpreting Our Heritage,* The University of North Carolina Press, Chapel Hill.
3. Van Matre, Steve. 1972. *Acclimatization, A Sensory and Conceptual Approach to Ecological Involvement,* American Camping Association, Bradford Woods, Martinsville, IN.

CHAPTER 9

THE INTERPRETIVE TALK

Paul H. Risk

Interpretation, whether through talks or other means, is almost exactly what the word states. It is the translation of the technical and often complex language of the environment into nontechnical form, with no loss in accuracy, so as to create in the listener *sensitivity, awareness, understanding, enthusiasm, and commitment.*

Sensitivity is a prerequisite to perception and leads to the development of awareness of the many facets of existence that may have escaped notice. Through effective interpretation an understanding is fostered. Born of sensitivity, this new-found awareness and understanding can build a thrill of enthusiasm. Finally, this bubbling appreciation may initiate a desire to take an action new to the individual—a commitment—as new insight prompts a changed approach to life.

The interpretive talk takes advantage of one of humankind's most potent tools, the power of speech. Through the spoken word and its associated nonverbal mannerisms we may shape and mold the understanding and the reaction of our audience. Even more important, we may touch the human heart.

If it is anything, *effective interpretation is an affair of the heart*—the heart of both the interpreter and the listener. Certainly, effective interpretation is an intellectual exercise also, but it is not *just* an experience in education.[4]

In this sense, successful interpretation is a balancing or juggling act, a graceful and smooth ballet of interaction between your interpretive presentation and the mind of the listener.

But, if this performance is to be what you desire, your sensitivity to and understanding of the audience must be at a high level. This is only possible if you are able to "read" them.

READING YOUR AUDIENCE

Reading or analyzing the audience begins the moment you set eyes on them and continues during the entire time you are in contact throughout both formal and informal phases of the talk.

To successfully gather useful information from your audience requires a high degree of sensitivity on your part. You must be observant. Some of the information will come from data directly acquired in conversation; other information will be garnered indirectly through observation.

Information you can obtain includes data on origin of their trip, native state, town, length of trip, number of people in their party, enjoyment of the trip, emotional state, response to you, response to others, age, occupation, and much more.

How do you get all this information?

Your Audience

Before examining the mechanics of talk construction and development, it is important to have some understanding of audiences. Audiences are composed of people whose ages vary from 2 months to 90 years; their educational attainment levels range from kindergarten to Ph.D. (regardless of age); and their interests and experiences include every facet of life from playing bridge to antique collecting, from tropical fish breeding to electronics, gardening, and television viewing. It is possible through careful planning to touch momentarily chords of relevance in each and every person in your group. Tilden has indicated that the visitor's first interest is himself. "Any interpretation that does not somehow relate what is being displayed or described to something within the personality or experience of the visitor will be sterile".[4]

Yet, it has often been suggested that a talk ought to be scaled to appeal to a tenth grader since this is the average level of attainment in most public audiences.

Certainly, if you do this you will be guaranteed of holding the interest of all the tenth graders. But what about all the other people in the group? Rather than setting a particular *level* for your talk, it is far more appropriate to plan a presentation that follows a wavelike pattern (Fig. 9-1).

10th Grade Level

FIG. 9-1. The wavelike pattern of a presentation whose level fluctuates above and below tenth-grade comprehension. Such a presentation periodically reaches people with higher or lower experiences or attainments than those achieved in the tenth grade.

The wave form described is simply the trace of your talk level as it occasionally reaches the heights (or depths?) of the M.D. and Ph.D., trends toward the middle of the road at tenth-grade attainment level, and dips below to reach periodically those whose experiences or attainments are less.

First, you must realize that talks are not just standing in front of a group, beginning to speak, speaking, and concluding. Before the formal starts, you can talk with visitors, eliciting a great deal of information both from their comments and the nonverbal cues you perceive in intonation, facial expression, and gestures.

People generally like to give information about how far they have traveled and the quality of the experience thus far. It gives them an opportunity to brag a bit. Later, it will be shown how to use this information to increase the talk appeal.

Indirect or Nonverbal Cues

There are many nonverbal cues that will help you assess the continually changing state of your audience throughout both the formal and informal phases of your presentation (Fig. 9-2). These include facial expressions, head nods, shaking the head, eye contact or its absence, body movement including nervous shuffling of

FIG. 9-2. The speaker and his audience. As a speaker gains experience he or she watches the audience for nonverbal cues to determine how well the talk is going. This indoor presentation is at Wright Brothers National Memorial, North Carolina. (Photo by Grant W. Sharpe.)

the feet and body, and outright walking out. Occasionally, feedback will be very direct and easy to assess when it comes in the form of heckling.

Generally, audiences respond in fairly predictable ways. An enthralled or awed audience is a silent one. "You could have heard a pin drop." Well-balanced and appropriate humor should elicit laughter, smiles, and head nods. Nodding of the head also can indicate agreement (or slumber).

The receptive interpreter will sense all these indicators and take appropriate action. Incongruities of response are generally cause to modify your approach or style of delivery.

However, there is some danger in relying too heavily on audience feedback. Occasionally, you may notice a particular individual who appears not to respond to *anything*. To all your modification this person responds with a poker face. Frustrated, your confidence shaken, you bend every effort to gain some response. In this nerve-wracking rush to affect one person you can easily lose track of the rest of your audience and thus fail.

Never lose sight of the fact that the art is in balancing the talk to meet the needs of the *majority* of the group. To cater exclusively to a particular individual to the exclusion of the rest is to court disaster.

You would be well advised to read one or more of the references related to interpersonal and nonverbal communication in order to prepare as fully as possible to use this important source of data.

YOUR IMAGE

As you consider the methods of reading audiences, you must also realize that they are continuously assessing you, and that this evaluation commences at the same time yours does of them. These assessments include your credibility and personality and result in a composite that determines how favorably the audience will respond to you.

INITIAL CREDIBILITY

Although the presentation characteristics of your talk will have an important effect on how you and your message are perceived, you have the advantage of beginning from a rather high level in terms of acceptance.

By virtue of your position, the audience already accepts that you are a person of some worth, a credible source. But how worthy, how credible remains to be determined. Of course the level of your perceived credibility will vary depending on what agency you are associated with and its particular image in the minds of the visitors.

Additionally, your personal appearance will cause them to make an assessment about personality and credibility. Good grooming and erect posture help create positive attitudes; slouching and sloppiness have the opposite effect.

The knowledge that most of the audience regards you as worth listening to even before you open your mouth should increase your confidence.

A NOTE ON STAGE FRIGHT

A supervisor of mine once said, "The day you can walk out in front of a group to speak and remain entirely calm and unmoved will be the day you commence to fail as a communicator. . . ."

An elevated adrenalin level—that feeling of butterflies in the stomach and tremors in the hands—is perfectly normal for speakers. Actors and professional speakers alike all acknowledge that they have been afraid throughout most of their careers. Each time they walk out to speak, they are seized by nervousness. In extreme cases, some feel nausea and even vomit before public presentations. Others develop diarrhea or a great need to urinate. The key is to maintain control and not allow the symptoms to become apparent to your audience.

Frankly, the heightened sensitivity and drive associated with stage fright is probably beneficial in that it tunes you to a pitch most likely to increase your dynamism and success as a speaker.

YOUR COMMUNICATION SKILLS

These skills that must be successfully brought to bear to present an effective talk may be categorized as verbal and nonverbal.

Verbal Skills

High on the list of recommended verbal skills are articulation and pronunciation.

To articulate is simply to pronounce distinctly and clearly. Understandable speech is necessary if the audience is to comprehend and appreciate what you have to say. If you mumble or slur words into an irretrievable jumble, you can easily lose the audience. If you are not sure how well you articulate, tape record your talk. And then, *listen* to it. Recorders, however unflattering, do not lie.

Pronunciation should be correct. A mispronounced word, or worse, a series of them, seriously affects the audience's perception of your credibility. They begin to wonder whether you really know what you are talking about or are merely parroting memorized facts.

Although it may not be precisely classed as a verbal skill, the use of technical jargon deserves to be mentioned here. Scientists have for years produced massive quantities of written and spoken messages dealing with their subjects. Much of it has been couched in language so technical that even the scientists themselves have difficulty understanding it. There has almost been perpetuated a belief that the more obscure and difficult the language, the more profound the message.

Your audiences are unlikely to be committed enough to suffer through a barrage of jargon. Steer clear of it. Where it is necessary to use a technical word, explain it. But, do so with finesse and good taste. Don't make the listener feel like an idiot. "The mountains around us are composed almost entirely of metamorphic rock. For those of you who don't understand the word, it means. . . ." It would have been far more subtle to say, "The mountains around us are composed almost entirely of rock which has been changed from its original form and composition by great heat and pressure, called metamorphic, which in fact, *means* changed."

If you have a tendency to use big words you would be well advised to read a fascinating little book entitled, *To Know a Fly* by Vincent G. Dethier (1962)[1] and to take to heart the following brief statement:

Never fear to use little words
Big words name little things,
Big things have little names, such as life, death,
Peace, dawn, day, night, hope, home.
Use little words in a big way,
It is hard to do but they say what you mean,
When you don't know what you mean, use big words,
They sometimes fool little people.

Major General Bruce E. Kendall
Industrial College of the Armed Forces

Nonverbal Skills

Nonverbal skills include vocal nuances such as pitch, rate, and volume. Although more will be said about each of the three, a single statement can very well be used as a rule of thumb. BE CONVERSATIONAL. This sounds like the simplest thing imaginable. Unfortunately, many speakers seem to find it difficult to attain.

To determine whether or not you are being conversational may or may not be easy. But, in essence, you must ask yourself if you sound as though you are lecturing *at* or speaking *with* your audience. Do you sound as though you are carrying on a conversation with someone you know? Or is there a formal, stilted manner about your presentation. Probably, the most obvious example of the latter is what might be called "the museum guide syndrome." We all have been exposed to that type of individual who sounds as though a tape recorder had

FIG. 9-3. The knowledgeable interpreter avoids lecturing to the audience but communicates best by using a conversational approach. The speaker at this outside presentation is utilizing a portable amplifier. Note the informal seating arrangement. Coastal area, Olympic National Park, Washington. (Photo courtesy of National Park Service.)

been implanted in the skull for playback of the interpretive message on audience demand.

An audience that perceives that it is being lectured *at* is not as likely to respond as well as one spoken *with*. *People like people who like them.* The conversational approach tells the audience that you consider them worthwhile human beings, not merely objects of your trade (Fig. 9-3).

Pitch is largely a matter of your vocal anatomy and your emotional state. Stage fright tends to cause many people to speak in higher pitch than normal. Practice until you determine what is normal for you and then with the aid of a tape recorder determine if this is the pitch you use in public.

Pitching your voice at other than a normal tone will only strain your vocal cords and result in hoarseness and laryngitis. Practice until you are able to find a pitch that is natural and produced without effort.

You should also realize that pitch should not be an absolute constant throughout the talk. Constant pitch produces a monotone that not only is unpleasant to listen to, but also reduces listener retention of the material presented and may even reduce credibility. Studies have also shown that monotonic presentations lower listener comprehension.[3] So, vary your pitch throughout the talk in an appropriate manner to get across the emotional and contextual shadings inherent in your message.

In fact, there are a series of factors that may be strongly tied to perceived speaker credibility and retention and comprehension of the material presented. These are rate, force, pitch, and quality. Generally, varying these elements increases the persuasiveness of the speaker.[3]

However, be careful where rate is concerned that you do not habitually speak either too slowly or too rapidly. Chronic slow speech can drive listeners to utter distraction as their minds leap far ahead of the speaker and frustration mounts as they wait for the interpreter to catch up.

Rapid speech, especially when it comes in bursts, can be just as distracting and can result in loss of comprehension as it causes words to run together and become unintelligible. Normal speaking rate is between 125 and 190 words per minute.[3]

Pauses and breaks in the flow of the talk tend to lower the perceived credibility of the speaker. "Communicators with 'good delivery' are consistently observed to have higher credibility."[3]

Memorizing and Use of Cue Cards

Memorized talks usually sound mechanical. To put it simply—don't memorize anything but major section headings or perhaps the beginning and ending statements.

Two examples stand out as mortifying in the extreme and will serve to illustrate the point.

The first is the interpreter who has memorized exactly the entire text of the talk. The presentation has been practiced over and over until there is not a flaw present. Then comes that fateful day of reckoning. Stage fright interrupts his or her smooth flow and suddenly a complete mental blank develops, followed by an embarrassed silence while the interpreter attempts to continue. Finding this impossible, the mental computer is reset to some previously stated part of the talk, and the interpreter begins again.

Not only does this type of difficulty indicate a certain lack of competence on the part of the interpreter, it is also easily preventable by memorizing only the major section headings and speaking around these.

Note cards are another matter, equally inappropriate. If notes are required, either the interpreter is unprepared or incompetent, or both.

This author, one evening, had the opportunity to watch an interpreter at a lighted lectern READING his talk from small cards. About 15 minutes into the program, in flipping through the cards, they suddenly all fell to the floor in a chaotic pile. Apparently they were not numbered, because after much apologetic shuffling, the interpreter had to *call off* the talk! The whole terrible experience could have been avoided if he had followed the procedure recommended in the following paragraphs.

A TALK FRAMEWORK

Whatever type of interpretive talk is planned, there are some guidelines that can assist in efficiency.

In schematic form, the framework of the entire presentation might look like this:

PRE-TALK PERIOD

Turn on equipment and *briefly* check function
Informally greet visitors on arrival; chat with them

WARM-UP OR INTRODUCTION

Welcome the entire audience; give them your name
Make announcements
Lead singing (if appropriate)
Lead into talk topic

THE TALK

Opening statement
Body
Concluding statement

Pre-Talk Period

It is very important that the interpreter arrive at the site from 20 to 30 minutes before the talk is to begin. This period is largely for the purpose of informal contact with the members of the audience as they arrive. A few minutes may be used to turn on and quickly check necessary equipment, but major checkout of equipment, including volume adjustment of the public address system, should take place at some prior time. The main purpose for this pre-talk period is to enable the interpreter to establish rapport with the audience members.

As each person or group of people arrive they should be greeted and welcomed. Walking from group to group, the interpreter strikes up a brief conversation. Especially in state and federal parks, not only are the visitors strangers to each other, but the area and you are strange to them. This time period gives you the opportunity to break the ice of unfamiliarity. Smile, be natural, be conversational. Do you sound as though you are really interested in each person, or as though this is a required part of your duty? Are you official and officious or are you pleasant and pleasing? Is your tone the same you would use if one of your friends dropped in to chat, or is it something else?

Not only does this informal period allow you to establish ties of friendship, it also permits you to gather bits of information about each of the people with whom you speak. This information can be skillfully woven into parts of your talk through oblique comments. "I'll bet the cool weather today is nothing new to you folks from New York, but it really ought to be warmer here this time of the year."

Often, while talking to one family, you will be joined by others as they find common interests. Not infrequently, groups find that they are from the same area of the country or have other things in common. Each word exchanged can be an effective break in the armor of uneasiness, newness, and strangeness and will improve the climate of receptivity necessary to successsful talks.

As the time for your talk approaches, this informal period can be smoothly and professionally blended into the introductory phase of the program.

Talk Warm-up and Introduction

Remember, you are talking to a group of your friends. During the pre-talk period you have spoken to many of the members of the audience and now you can begin to use these contacts. "I've really enjoyed talking to many of you. You are an unusually warm and friendly group."

The introductory or warm-up period might be termed a semiformal part of the overall talk framework. Although there is less opportunity for feedback directly from the audience, there is still an easy, less formal tone to the proceedings than will be the case when the talk is actually begun. It is during this time that announcements and songs may be included. In the federal parks it has become traditional to lead a few campfire songs and engage in some light, humorous antics. Whatever the approach, there most certainly is no reason why various parts of the program must stand apart, separated awkwardly from the other components. Using well-chosen, smooth transitions, various portions of the talk frame can be quite gracefully attached.

A Note About Campfire Singing

Some people enjoy it and some do not. However, whether or not singing is a success seems to depend on your enthusiasm far more than anything else. It is certainly not necessary that you have any particular talent as a singer. The only skill that is recommended is the ability to move your arm and hand up and down in time with the music with wide enough gestures to be seen and followed (Fig. 9-4). Never mind that you don't know the exact pattern your hand should describe for a particular beat. Just beat and let the rest take care of itself. Yes, it takes a certain amount of nerve to stand in front of a group and lead singing, but so does standing in front of a group talking. Remember, interpretation is largely

FIG. 9-4. This evening program starts with a campfire and group singing. In some instances lyrics are projected on the screen, in others song sheets are used. Slide presentation at George Washington National Forest, Virginia. (Photo courtesy of U.S. Forest Service.)

a form of recreation, not an academic exercise designed to produced total anesthesia. Develop and cultivate a sense of humor and give it a try. But, whatever you do, NEVER TAKE YOURSELF TOO SERIOUSLY. RELAX.

Normally, singing is engaged in at outdoor talks rather than those given indoors, but this need not be a hard and fast rule. You will simply have to use your own judgment as to whether or not it would be appropriate in your setting.

If your decision is to sing, it is recommended that the songs have something to do with your topic or the setting you are in. Inappropriate songs should be avoided.

Unless the songs you use are old favorites which the majority of your audience is familiar with, it is advisable to provide the words. There are two ways to do this.

The first is to project the lyrics on the screen using a slide that is easily made by photographing typed copy. If you have access to a typewriter with extra large type, use it.

The second way to provide assistance is to pass out song sheets. However, the lighting in many outdoor interpretive sites may be limited and reading impossible. Also, it is very awkward to try to read a song sheet while keeping your eye on the person directing. In addition, there will be some loss involved each time the sheets are used since there are always those who will keep them as a memento. So, unless your budget allows you to continue to reproduce sheets, the slide technique is best.

If you want additional information on proper song leading a good reference is *How to Lead Informal Singing* by Robert O. Hoffelt.[2]

THE TALK

The Subject or Theme

Obviously, before you can begin to structure your talk, you must have something about which to talk. When at all possible, pick a topic that interests *you*. It is difficult or impossible to transmit an enthusiasm you don't feel. And if you aren't enthusiastic, your audience isn't likely to be either.

Unfortunately, it isn't always possible to pick your topic with total freedom. Perhaps your agency or supervisor assigns topics. For example, the policy in the past has been that there will be talks on birds, mammals, wildflowers, and human history. You have been assigned the topic of wildflowers. Although your basic topic has been given to you, there is still great flexibility available in the *way* you approach the subject. One approach guranteed to thoroughly bore most of your audience is the cataglog technique. In this, you simply name and show a picture of all the flowers currently blooming. To really frost the cake, you are careful that the only name you give is the scientific one—genus, species, subspecies, and variety.

Chances are, this approach wouldn't even hold *your* interest. Why do you think it will appeal to your listeners?

Perhaps a better way would be to give a talk on historical uses of the plants in your area. You can still select only those plants flowering currently. But the inclusion of information on uses of the plants for medicine, dyes, and other purposes will touch many chords of relevance in your listeners. Chances are they'll remember more of what you said, too.

Now that you have determined your subject or theme you are ready to move into the actual structuring of the talk. As has been said, talks are generally made up of three sections:

1. Introduction.
2. Body.
3. Conclusion.

The introduction essentially tells the audience what you are going to talk about. It is a kind of lead-in summary that ought to attract the audience's attention, stimulate their curiosity, and commit them to a desire to hear you out.

In the talk body you will follow through in detail on the information given in the introduction.

The conclusion wraps up all the loose ends, perhaps summarizes what you said, and ends your talk.

More concisely, the three parts could be summed up as:

1. Tell them what you are going to do.
2. Do it.
3. Tell them what you did.

Lead into your talk smoothly from the warm-up. "Some of the songs we have sung tonight tell the tale of the westward-bound pioneers—their trials and tribulations. Today, we seem to have lost many of the abilities and much of the knowledge that made our pioneer forefathers successful. This evening I would like to take you on a journey of recollections, of reminiscences. Come with me on a desert walk as we stroll through a great outdoor supermarket, scanning the shelves of Nature's General Store in search of those same commodities the pioneers of this great land used for food and medicines." (A lead-in for a talk on the pioneer uses of native plants.)

Thus, with a minimum of bother, the introduction has taken place.

Introductions should be attention-getters, drawing everyone toward the theme of the talk and the same time explaining the subject. However, it is *never* proper to begin by saying, "Our topic for this evening is . . ." This approach tends to create abrupt transitions.

The point is that *all* transitions should be made to avoid segmenting the talk framework. Don't make announcements; don't announce your talk topic. Rather, blend the segments one with another, relating one portion of the talk to all others.

Body

Determination of what to include in the talk body will have been partly decided when you selected your theme or topic. The key to success is logical organization, and this is best accomplished by outlining your program.

However, at the outset it isn't important that your outline be logical. In fact, after you determine what your theme will be, it is quite usual to simply list random ideas as they come to mind. A handy way to do this is on small file cards. These are easy to shuffle into order later.

Let's look at an example. The talk topic is "Fire in the Forest."

Phase I—Random Ideas
> (What things do I want to include?)
> Fire fighting
> > Ground crews and equipment
> > Fire retardant drops
> Awesomeness of fire
> Fire ecology
> Regeneration after burn
> Fire finding
> Causes of fire
> Myths about fire

> (As you can see, the order is not particularly orderly.)

Phase II—Organize Outline

A logical way to organize a fire talk is to start at the beginning. What starts fires? How are they located? etc.

Causes of Fire
  Human
  Weather
Locating Fires
  Fire Towers
  Air Surveillance
Fire Suppression
  Mobilization of Ground Crews
    Equipment
  Mobilization of Air Drop
    The drop
  Fire Fighting
    Ground crews
    Awesomeness of fire
  Mop up
Appearance of forest after burn
Myths of Fire
  Fire Ecology
  Regeneration after burn
Thought-Provoking Ending

In other words, the fire starts, is located, suppression commences, the fire is extinguished, the forest regenerates, end.

As a general rule it is not a good idea to write out everything you hope to say; this leads to memorization. Rather, as stated previously, commit the major section headings to memory and talk around them. Your talk will be far more conversational, and flexibility will be maintained, allowing you to make modifications as audience feedback dictates.

Illustrated Talks

To illustrate a talk often clarifies and enhances your points. But be especially sure that you are indeed illustrating a talk and not talking about illustrations. An error commonly made by speakers using slides is to make direct references to the illustrations. "This is a picture of . . ." and "This slide shows . . ." are two good examples of the type of comment to strictly avoid. The audience is already aware that it is a picture. There really is no question in anyone's mind as to whether or not you have mysteriously produced the real thing on the screen. Just keep talking and let the illustrations appear as they are needed to assist your presentation.

Another problem often noted in talk development is that the interpreter works backwards. Instead of developing a talk and then selecting illustrative slides, he or she first examines the slide file and then builds a set of slides about which to talk. Usually the talk sounds like it was produced in just that manner.

The storyboard technique is a procedure that will assist you in organizing your talk in conjunction with the illustrations. It is merely a modification of the plan just described. File cards are used on which random ideas for inclusion are written or typed. About a third of the card is left to allow either a sketch or a brief description of desired illustration to be included. These cards are then placed on a large table so that they can be shuffled into proper organization, or they are inserted into a large wall board into which slits have been cut or to which envelopes are glued. In this way, the sequence can be shifted and revisions made until the interpreter is satisfied.

A Few Hints for the Use of Slides

There are four important DON'TS that you should consider:

1. Don't use a slide too long. A good rule of thumb is to plan for two to three slides per minute of presentation time. A Kodak specialist once recommended that the maximum time a slide ought to be on the screen is about 6 seconds. Certainly, any longer than half a minute means that visual boredom is likely to be setting in on your audience. If you must talk longer than this about a particular segment of the subject, use several slides taken from various vantage points or distances to liven the presentation.
2. Don't use a slide when you are talking about something else. If the illustration is no longer needed, it should be changed. If the talk is well-planned and you are really illustrating a talk rather than the other way around, this will not be a problem.
3. Don't use a slide when it is irrelevant. There is a great temptation to put illustrations in just because they are pretty or spectacular. Uncontrolled, this can easily lead you into the "family vacation syndrome" in which 20,000 slides are inflicted, for no apparent reason, on trapped viewers.
4. Don't use a slide of poor quality. Those who shoot their own illustrations seem to be most likely to succumb to this pitfall. They just have to get it in even though it is slightly out of focus, underexposed, or tipped in the mount. Become heartless as you examine your slide file and destroy those which are substandard.

A Note About Unforeseen Circumstances

Murphy's Law states that if anything can go wrong, it will. In interpretation, this is an absolute guarantee. Project bulbs burn out, projectors mysteriously chew up slides and gag on them, public address systems fail or develop motorboatlike popping sounds. "Be prepared" is more than the Boy Scouts' motto. It should be the byword of every interpreter.

If the whole electrical system goes up in a mushroom cloud, you must be able to continue. Go to "Plan B." Ideally, you ought to be able to continue the talk without benefit of illustrations if the projector dies. But, if the talk relies too strongly on illustrations to permit this—for instance, a plant talk—then you should have an alternative plan so that only the *approach* has to be modified, not the entire theme. Certainly, there is no reason to call off the talk because of a mechanical malfunction.

Long before talk time, give in-depth consideration to every possible difficulty that might occur and devise a backup approach. Know where extra bulbs are located (right next to the projector). Be aware of where the circuit breakers are and how to reset them. Understand how to extract a jammed slide quickly.

The Talk Conclusion

For many interpreters, this is the toughest part of the talk. Unfortunately, this is often rather evident. Talks go along fine until it comes time to end; then they either finish indeterminately and awkwardly or so suddenly that it takes the listeners' breaths away and leaves them wondering what happened.

Plan your ending carefully. This is one of the two parts of the talk you may want to write entirely. (The other part is the opening statement.)

The purpose of the conclusion is to wrap up all the loose ends and indicate clearly, smoothly, and *definitely* that the talk is over.

It may be a summary statement. However, it is never appropriate to summarize in academic fashion—"To briefly review this evening's presentation . . ." Rather, use one or two sentences or a phrase to quickly restate the key concepts and then end.

For example, "Fire is older than the human race. For eons the bolts from the sky have kindled our forests and grasslands. Yet, somehow, even without suppression the forests still endure. Tonight we have shown that contrary to Smokey the Bear, fire is not all bad. It is responsible for some of our most beautiful stands of aspen and for matchless grasslands. In fact, it is often a management tool. Perhaps as you travel during the rest of your vacation and occasionally pass burns you will see this natural ecological recycler through different eyes."

ANALYZING YOUR PERFORMANCE

Analyzing your performance is not always easy. Abraham Lincoln, after delivering the Gettysburg Address was convinced that the talk was a disaster. Apparently, he was wrong.

On the other hand, it is also possible to evaluate incorrectly in the other direction. One of the greatest aids to misinterpretation is audience comments and contact after the talk. There are always those who for numerous reasons want to talk with the interpreter after the program. Often, it is only to get information on route finding. Since it is awkward to approach a speaker on a subject that has nothing to do with the topic so soon after the talk, people almost always preface their remarks by telling you what a great talk it was. It may have been rotten, but there will always be a few who will compliment you.

So, it is wise to have more objective methods available from which to get feedback.

Recording

One of the best methods of self-evaluation is the tape recorder. Get in the habit of recording your talks *and of listening to them.* Few people like the sound of their own voices on recordings. Grit your teeth and listen anyway. You will be able to get a great deal of information on the quality of your delivery and whether or not there are inaccuracies.

Peer Evaluation and Coaching

If you have someone whose advice and criticism you value, have them come to the talk and discuss it with you afterward. Also, group coaching can evolve into a very productive aid if a number of interpreter friends systematically attend each other's talks and exchange helpful suggestions.

Lastly, this "Self-Appraisal Chart for Oral Presentation" used by the National Park Service can be of considerable assistance to you.

SELF-APPRAISAL CHART FOR ORAL PRESENTATION
(National Park Service Training Aid)

The purpose of this chart is to encourage those speaking to groups to review their performance, to be their own critic in detecting rough spots that need polishing.

Preparation of the Talk

Do you schedule your time so that you have the opportunity regularly to prepare for your subject?

Do you organize your thoughts so that the important points are covered in an orderly, concise manner?

Do you vary the outline of your talk with new concepts and new illustrations occasionally?

Do you find yourself using too much technical language?

Do you memorize your talk? (A practice that is generally not encouraged).

Do you have a planned beginning and a planned end to your talk, even though it is a brief and informal presentation?

Delivery of the Talk

Do you use a friendly, conversational tone?

Do you speak loud enough to be heard with ease? How do you check this?

Do you talk with enthusiasm? Do you talk distinctly?

What words do you slur? Do you run your sentences together with "and uh" or "ah" instead of having clean breaks between sentences?

Do you pause to emphasize important points?

Do you open your mouth and use the tongue and lips for clear enunciation?

How is your eye contact—front row, one or two people, or do you cover the field and make everyone feel included?

Do you periodically check your rate of talking?

Do you vary the rate of talking (from 125 to 190 words per minute) as a means of keeping visitor interest and stressing important ideas?

Do you modulate your voice so as to avoid a monotonous tone?

Are you over-serious in your talk?

Is your manner friendly?

Do you use objects, or exhibits in your talks? If so, how effectively do you use them?

Do you use a tape recorder or other mechanical device periodically to check on your rate of speech, enunciation, and modulation?

Do you listen regularly to the better radio or TV speakers to note in particular their style of delivery?

Do you read aloud regularly so as to get accustomed to the sound of your voice and also to improve your enunciation?

Do you invite someone (fellow employee, wife, husband, or friend) interested in your self-improvement to give you candid criticism?

Do you conscientiously try to improve your use of the English language?

Attitude Toward the Audience

Do you enjoy speaking to people?

Do you enjoy talking about the features of the area?

Do you keep the attention of the visitor?

Are you more interested in the subject matter or the audience?

General Appearance

Is your uniform well-fitting, clean, pressed, and in good condition?

Do the accessories conform to Service regulations?

Do you stand erect and poised before the group?

Do you have nervous mannerisms that distract attention?

It requires many hours of practice to incorporate in your talks all the skills and techniques advocated in this chapter. The interpretive talk is perhaps the severest test of an interpreter's ability, so perfect your delivery by enlightened practice; there is no other way.

REFERENCES

References Cited

1. Dethier, Vincent G. 1962. *To Know A Fly,* Holden-Day, San Francisco.
2. Hoffelt, Robert O. 1963. *How To Lead Informal Singing,* Abingdon Press, New York.
3. Knapp, Mark L. 1972. *Nonverbal Communication in Human Interaction,* Holt, Rinehart and Winston, New York.
4. Tilden Freeman. 1967. *Interpreting Our Heritage,* University of North Carolina Press, Chapel Hill.

Recommended Additional Reading

Barnlund, Dean C. 1968. *Interpersonal Communication: Survey and Studies,* Houghton Mifflin Company, New York.

Bettinghaus, Erwin P. 1968. *Persuasive Communication,* Holt, Rinehart and Winston, New York.

Boulanger, F. David, and John P. Smith. 1973. *Educational Principles and Techniques for Interpreters,* USDA Forest Service General Technical Report PNW-9, Pacific Northwest Forest and Range Experiment Station, Portland, OR.

Gregg, H. Raymond. 1968. (Revised, Douglass Hubbard and William W. Dunmire), *Campfire Programs, A Guide for Leaders of Campfires in the National Parks,* National Park Service, U.S. Dept of the Interior, U.S. Government Printing Office, Washington, DC.

Eastman Kodak Company. 1974. *Effective Lecture Slides.* S-22, Rochester, NY.

Eastman Kodak Company. 1968. *Producing Slides and Film Strips,* Audiovisual Data Book, S-8, Rochester, NY.

Harrison, Randall R. 1974. *Beyond Words, An Introduction to Nonverbal Communication,* Prentice-Hall, Englewood Cliffs, NJ.

Hovland, Carl I., Irving L. Janis and Harold H. Kelley. 1966. *Communication and Persuasion,* Yale University Press, New Haven, CT

Lewis, William J. 1980. *Interpreting for Park Visitors,* Eastern National Park and Monument Association, Eastern Acorn Press, Philadelphia, PA.

CHAPTER 10

LIVING INTERPRETATION

Inger L. Garrison

Interpretation of history and heritage through personal demonstration may have several almost synonymous descriptive titles: living history, living interpretation, folk culture. All of these titles have the theme of human life experience as their base. Living interpretation, to choose one, is a means of bringing humanity, reality, and depth to the interpretive function.

TYPES OF LIVING INTERPRETATION

There are at least four types that can be distinguished under the general title *Living Interpretation.*

1. First-Person Living Interpretation

An interpreter, usually working alone, plays the role of an individual who lived, or was at the site, at a particular time or era. Usually, this is a representative "common person," rather than a famous character. The language, dress, mannerisms, tools, techniques, attitudes and mores of that time are adhered to in an attempt to recreate a time in the past and draw the visitor into it. This sort of character is often called "the visitor from the past," as this person purports to know nothing of events that have occurred since his or her time, but will discuss events current to the period portrayed.

First-person living interpretation may make use of self-generating monologue, but more often it relies on visitor interaction to allow explanations to unfold naturally, and to create the atmosphere that gives this sort of presentation its peculiar cogency.

2. Performance Living Interpretation

Interpreters, drama students, or nearby residents play the roles of people who might have lived in, or occupied the site, at a particular era in the past. As in first-person interpretation, these performers are not trying to recreate a specific event, but are attempting to present, in a performance setting, a glimpse of the past. They either have a prepared script to follow, at least in outline, or discuss their activities and situation informally with one another. There is no visitor interaction required, although it is not precluded.

3. Craft and Skill Demonstrations

Interpreters, dressed in suitable garments, and using authentic tools, or reproductions of such tools, demonstrate a period skill or craft. This would include musket and connon firing, cooking, sewing, metal work, weaving, pottery, playing a musical instrument, and other activities of this type, which are obsolete or rare in the modern world. No attempt is made to create a realistic or performance setting.

This type of interpretation would include demonstrations of still viable crafts and skills of native artisans, who may or may not dress in traditional garments for the interpretive event.

4. Cultural Festivals

These include pageants, exhibitions, parades, day- or week-long activities, or festivities marking a political event or the folk culture of ethnic groups.

Portrayals may run the gamut from the prehistoric time of the ancestral Creek Tribe at Ocmulgee in Georgia, through Williamsburg during the first century of the English in America, the Spanish adjusting liturgical music to the Indian tongue in a California mission, to work in the farm fields at Booker T. Washington National Monument, or a troop of Sea Scouts hoisting a full suit of sails on the historic whaling ship *Charles W. Morgan* at Mystic Seaport, Connecticut.

Contemporary scenes could include a commercial fishing camp on Lake Superior at Isle Royale National Park, or latex making in Malaysia (Fig. 10-1): or Navajo weavers at Hubbell Trading Post National Historic Site in Arizona.

Action at each of these sites may draw on the full circle of human culture: food and life-style, dress, leisure pursuits, industry of factories, home, music, religion, education, cottage craft, and science and politics; these suggest myriad facets of indigenous life that may be used to create the desired scene.

In essence, living interpretation involves on-site re-creation of the lives of a people, wearing their clothing, speaking their dialect, reviewing their decisions. If it is a daily program of the homely things done, such as household chores or a schedule of work in the fields or care of animals, it suggests a continuum of similar events (Fig. 10-2). A visitor would find the event a friendly and natural experience

FIG. 10-1. Living interpretation: a latex-making demonstration on Penang Island, Malaysia. (Photo by Myron Sutton.)

and might join the dance or the farm work or share the corn pone or the military rations.

This stream of continuing action that characterizes living interpretation differentiates it from historical episodes, which may be reenacted through pageants, folk festivals or fiestas, musical programs, ethnic ceremonies, political anniversaries, or combinations of these events. Examples would be the Sir John Simcoe Day in Toronto, Ontario, Mardi Gras in New Orleans, Louisiana, or perhaps the Canadian Dominion Day and U.S. Fourth of July celebrations each July. These latter events are authentic and exciting, but are obviously periodic in nature. These parts of living history and its pageantry will be mentioned under "Cultural Festivals" but the major theme here is living interpretation.

A park interpreter developing an interpretive plan for a site must look for the best methods to communicate the message of that resource. Living interpretation is one of the options to be considered.

Does the site and situation lend itself to living interpretation? Can it be done naturally? Are the resources for research, and the money and personnel available to mount and sustain a high-quality program? Should it be first-person, or performance living interpretation?

FIG. 10-2. An insight into life on a frontier farm can be gained by visitors to Lincoln Boyhood National Memorial, Indiana. The National Park Service maintains the Lincoln farm as it was when Abe was growing into manhood. (NPS photo by Richard Frear.)

This is the first decision for the interpreter doing the planning, and he or she must be convinced that it is not only a possible way to interpret that aspect of the park but the best way to carry the interpretive message. Enthusiasm and commitment are essential for an interpretive adventure of this sort.

Management of a resource must be a part of the planning team from the beginning of the project. Today managers have many disciplines at their disposal to assist them in decision making. Final program decision to use living interpretation as well as its details must be guided by research in the appropriate fields. This includes the participation of the maintenance, fiscal, and engineering departments as well as historians and scientists. All will have a part in the success of the project.

ADVANTAGES

When well done, living interpretation is fully communicative and involves the totality of physical senses, as well as inducing emotional involvement.

The smell of new-mown hay or bread baking in an outdoor oven, the sound of taps across the parade ground or the quickstep of a fife and drum corps, the color flash of costumes or the harmony of silver and turquoise jewelry (Fig. 10-3), the incredibly soft smoothness of a highly polished ceramic piece or the rasping tex-

FIG. 10-3. A native American craftsman demonstrating jewelry making. Monument Valley, Navajo Tribal Park, Arizona-Utah. (Photo by Grant W. Sharpe.)

ture of a fisherman's net, the elusive thread of sweetness in the first sample of maple syrup boiling, or the acrid fumes of black powder that clutch the throat of an observer—all of these experiences are communicated with the five physical senses. Above them all is the derivative emotional involvement and response by each visitor.

Living interpretation offers historical, cultural, and ethnic understandings that cannot be achieved as well in other ways and, when minority populations are involved, it is particularly fruitful in opportunities for self-expression and fulfillment, both for the demonstrators or interpreters and the park visitors.

The interpreter, always mindful of budgetary restrictions, will find that living interpretation, *particularly the first person role,* is generally moderate in cost and often superior in quality to other methods of interpretation. In some instances, such as Plymouth Village in Massachusetts, Hopewell Furnace National Historic Site in eastern Pennsylvania, and Lincoln Boyhood National Memorial in Indiana, everyone working in the area is part of the interpretation. The farmer, the maintenance man, the garbage man, the cook, weavers, and other workers are all regular staff and, for the most part, extra expense is for costuming only. It provides a high level of communication, an effective medium for program message, easy monitoring of quality, a pleasant experience, and an opportunity for creative involvement with visitors.

Part of the visitor reward is the opportunity (in many situations) to "step on stage" and become part of the scene. This may be a little girl quilting, or a mountaineer strumming an old zither. Sometimes visitors are recruited as members of a team to fire a cannon: with three minutes for advance drill this team carries out orders to aim, load, and fire and is taught how to clean the canon. Visitor participation offers a touch of humanity and fun if the procedures do not appear to be contrived but are a simple and honest sharing of skills with the demonstrator.

DISADVANTAGES

A good living history program requires a great deal of lead time. Research, assembling needed materials, and recruiting and training staff are not done quickly. Are seasonal employees available locally or must they be recruited elsewhere? This aspect can be particularly difficult if the program involves native peoples whose tribal base is no longer their home, such as at Ocmulgee, Georgia, where the formerly indigenous Creek Tribe was relocated to Oklahoma.

Another possible adverse factor is the impact of heavy visitor use or abuse of fragile historical resources. Examples are the constant wear on authentic rugs and floors in historic houses, or trips through Montezuma Castle in Arizona, where overuse required that it be closed and viewed from a distance.

Another disadvantage lies in the limited time span of most living history demonstrations. Can it be a day-long program? Or is it more properly an occasional performance for afternoons or evenings or weekends? If it is episodic in nature, how can this fit the time schedule of the major flow of park visitors? The "visitor from the past" mode of interpretation can be difficult when the audience is not familiar with, and does not comprehend the situation. They may feel threatened, or be uncomfortable when brought into the conversation. Unless there is a knowledgeable member who will participate with the interpreter, the group may fail to realize the full potential of this interpretive device, and perceive the visitor from the past (no. 1) as a part of performance living interpretation (no. 2, above).

Obviously, in spite of the glow and promise of living history and a determination to use it, the interpretive program must also encompass a number of the more traditional kinds of offerings, such as exhibits, publications, and self-guided trails so that there is something for visitors to see and do at those times when the living history is not offered.

Lastly, interpreters must be sure they want to make the commitment to total immersion in the life and times of the historical resource. This will be necessary if living interpretation is to be authentic and meaningful for the visitors. If a high-quality program cannot be sustained, the project should be discontinued because both the visitor and the resource will be the losers.

RESEARCH

At this point the interpreter rereads the historical notes and again concludes that living interpretation is the one technique that will do justice to the resource. Then comes the selection of the exact site and historical data to be used.

How much research has already been completed and how does it respond to the interpretive story requirements? Where are the reports? Can the interpreter or a staff person research the available data to select the materials that fit these requirements?

Most historical sites, at least in the United States, have a background file. It may be with an agency or it may be in the local historical society or library records. An emerging source of information is found in folklorists' teaming up with historians, archeologists, and basic scientists. In some areas library/computer techniques with retrieval capability provide information to the interpreter on the availability and location of materials. Ideally these kinds of data are already on hand so that preparation of an interpretive plan and story narrative can proceed.

In some instances advance preparations are greatly simplified because native peoples or local historical committees already have completed the preliminaries, and the interpretive program may simply follow existing patterns. There are historic sites where the past cultures carry over to the present time: Hubbell Trading Post National Historic Site, Arizona, the Great Smoky Mountains National Park, Tennessee, Denali National Park, Alaska, Pu'uhonua o Honaunau National Historical Park, Hawaii, Nez Perce National Historical Park, Idaho, and Sitka National Historical Park, Alaska, where the descendants of former peoples still reside. However, the interpreter must verify the authenticity of these conclusions from primary sources.

Authenticity is essential, particularly for simple items such as the types of clothing worn and how they were made, dyed, and decorated. For example, a search of old store records at Hopewell Village revealed some of the basic food and cloth purchases of early residents. The language, tools, clothing, and furnishings used in the interpretive period for the area as well as the product of the inhabitants' labors should be as authentic as possible. Rebuilding, repairing or actually making new tools in the old manner can be a part of the interpretive message. Many times the old objects are fragile and cannot be used so that authentic reproductions are the only answer to this dilemma.

Authentic maintenance of structures and artifacts is too often neglected. A simple question as to the care of a buffalo robe may reveal a dozen answers but most often receives no response at all. Care of artifacts from the crude to the sophisticated is a major part of living interpretation routine. Daily maintenance is a necessity and often can be done as part of the living interpretive demonstration.

A firm decision must be made on the selection of all objects, events, and incidents to be included in a living interpretation scene. Often these materials are not ideal but are the best available, and their display or use must be researched carefully before talking about them. Usually, there is more information known than can be used, and it is important to screen it carefully. The message must be authentic, simple, and clearly understandable: to many artifacts or too many words will be confusing.

A living interpretation program must have a tentative story outline, but response to visitor inquiries and sharing of interests will later shape the script. Visitor groups will vary, and the program should respond to these differences. The onsite interpreters, through their own research and reading, should become authorities on the life and times of the former inhabitants of the site, and should make

FIG. 10-4. A Cherokee woman tells the history of her people. Note the artifacts used as furnishings. Oconuluftee, North Carolina. (Photo by Grant W. Sharpe.)

suggestions for innovations. This will keep the interpreters' interests lively and renewed, too.

The whole research and editing program must be done with great sensitivity and empathy so that the results are correct but are expressed in everyday language and not obscured by professional jargon. In generalities about this kind of program, it is necessary to keep in mind the wide variety of possible participants such as farmers, soldiers, statesmen, craftsmen, or ethnic groups or persons.

For on-site "Indian" programs the Native Americans themselves are often the authorities/interpreters/communicators (Fig. 10-4). Once a successful program is established, they can be relied on to carry it through with pride, and to maintain a high level of quality. In the last ten years more than 100 museums and interpretive centers have been built by various tribes across the United States and Canada.

SITE

Site preparation is the next major action as the interpreter considers the actual source of props or artifacts, their specific location as part of the scene, and their condition and possible need of repair. The girl doing the knitting may require contact lenses if period glasses are not available. Firewood for the bake oven must be obtained. The peel (the shovel-like implement used for removing bread from the oven) may need to be polished.

The preferred location for any living history program is the actual place where the real events occurred. It may have been modified by changes in use or ownership, and a decision must be made as to restoration of the site or accepting a substitute. If an alternative site must be used, it is always desirable to have some bond between the alternative site and the original such as proximity, similarity of environment, or relationship of events.

Tumacacori Mission, Arizona, is a good example of an original site. A High Mass with Mariachi music and a fiesta are held annually at the mission on the anniversary of Father Kino's birth. The solemn processional in which ceremonially dressed Pimas swing their smoking censer pots as their ancestors did three centuries ago is particularly appealing. The fiesta aspects do not seem irreligious but colorful, unique, and apt.

The Ozark Folk Center at Mountain View, Arkansas, a state program in the heart of the Ozark Mountains, could be considered as an example of an alternative site. The native mountain culture is interpreted in a specially built demonstration area for crafts cottages (Fig. 10-5). A theater for dancing and music, a sales shop, and a motel and restaurant are a part of the complex. There is a conference center for training and workshops in mountain culture that is not far from the small farms and homes where the activities originated, and where they continue to some degree.

FIG. 10-5. A broom maker at work at the Ozark Folk Center in Mountain View, Arkansas. Crafts are interpreted in specially built cottages. (Photo by Inger L. Garrison.)

Spatial requirements for the interpreter are important in planning a site, and the nature of the demonstration dictates the space allotments. A weaver must have room for a loom and materials and, perhaps, for dye baths for yarns. A blacksmith must have a ventilated area specifically for his work—the noise and smoke rule out proximity to other activities. Some demonstrations like cooking, pottery, and washing need a water supply. Routine maintenance of a home or building site also requires water.

Thought should be given to the visitors. Is there enough room to stand or sit and view a demonstration in comfort? (Fig. 10-6). Are there rest rooms? Is a limit on number of visitors indicated for particular days or events? Should there be some control over the number of viewers at one time and the length of time given to each person or group? The visitor should not feel pushed along and should come away from the experience with satisfaction. A planned traffic pattern will be needed. Energy saving should also be a consideration both for the park administration and the visitor.

Also, particular attention should be given to the safety of both visitors and performers. The most effective safety strategy is to develop an attitude of safety consciousness and responsibility that guides the planning and is ever present in the minds of the staff.

A chapter on living interpretation is not complete without mention of the epitome of this type of interpretation—the living village or town. In the United States, Colonial Williamsburg in Virginia is the prime example. It gives the visitor a rich and varied experience of life at the beginnings of this nation. The portrayal ap-

FIG. 10-6. Visitor comfort is essential to successful living interpretation. Note the audience observing the firing of pottery. San Ildefonso Pueblo, New Mexico. (Photo by Inger L. Garrison.)

peals to all of the senses—color, sound, taste, viewing, touching and, best of all, the feeling of participating in the world of Colonial America.

East historical community or district had a special reason for being, which was to be found in the environment, the resources, the people whom it served, and their total existence. Hopewell Village, in Pennsylvania, sold only iron and iron products but its total story includes economics, technology, military history, environment, social structure, culture, religion, and education. The living interpretation of history must respond in all of these dimensions.

Other similar living interpretive communities or districts are found worldwide and at all levels of ownership. They are particularly well done in privately financed situations.

In the interpretation of native American culture special consideration about the authenticity of the program, both as to site and tribal ancestry, is essential. We have mentioned the Creek Tribal site at Ocmulgee, Georgia where assistance in living interpretation must come from a tribal base in Oklahoma. At Walnut Canyon National Monument in Arizona, the original Pueblo people are gone. In such instances, substitutes should be selected only after a real search for native people with similar cultural ancestry. This problem requires a special sensitivity in planning, since the contemporary neighboring tribes may not be of the original ancestral group, and will not take part in a program that is alien to their culture.

PERSONNEL

The staff to carry on the daily program at a site with full living interpretation may be no more than one permanent employee, particularly if it is a seasonal presentation. This employee is usually the coordinator of the program and may or may not be a part of the presentation. One place where the coordinator is also the presenter is at Pea Ridge National Military Park where he presents the views of the Union soldier and then later reverses roles and becomes a Confederate soldier. The seasonals, who are the real talent pool and working group, may come from varying sources. Sometimes it may be desirable to employ professional actors for key roles, but this is seldom necessary except for special events, anniversaries, and dramas. However, some parks employ drama students from nearby universities such as Golden Spike National Historic Site, Utah. Every university with an active outdoor recreation or park management program will be eager to place their students seasonally so that they can gain interpretive experience. Volunteers in parks (VIP) are another good source of help.

Nearby residents may carry much of the work load as at Catoctin Mountain Park, Maryland, where many neighboring people participate regularly in craft demonstrations. If a program is built around a live-in homely drama such as at Great Smoky Mountains National Park, or Lincoln Boyhood National Memorial, local residents often have a strong feeling of identity with events and become creative participants (Fig. 10-7). This may be particularly true if the local resident is also a member of a family with local ancestral roots so that the role playing has deep personal meaning.

Wage rates may present some difficulty, since comparable job titles and position descriptions usually do not exist. Generally, wage rates are established as comparable to hourly labor pay, with some supplemental position title such as "Cultural Demonstrator," "Craftsman," "Potter," or "Weaver," to justify premium pay for special skills. Occasionally, management may use the technique of calling the workers "labor-leadman" or something similar. In some parks a classified Civil Service rating system is used, assigning grades with salaries comparable to premium labor jobs. In other parks, job or product contracts may be used; still others employ craftsmen or demonstrators through contracts with third-party cooperating associations which, in turn, employ the weaver, silversmith, basketmaker, blacksmith, glassblower, or candlemaker.

Buying a piece of art directly from the creator is one of the special joys of possession. One-to-one contact is important both to the craftsman and to the viewer who purchases the work, as it establishes a rapport and respect between them.

FIG. 10-7. Local residents often have a feeling of identity with events and become creative participants in cultural demonstrations. Lincoln Boyhood National Memorial, Indiana. (NPS photo by Richard Frear.)

TRAINING

Training is another essential part of this interpretive method. As much training as possible should be given the new employee by the managers of the program: background reading, contact with experienced demonstrators, and practice with the medium. The interpretive goal should be established. Alternatively, some interpreters do their own research because it is their special interest. As the result of such research, one of the interpreters at Many Glacier in Glacier National Park depicts, at evening camp fires, an old miner early in the century before the establishment of the park. Each program participant in the living interpretation scene should naturally and easily carry a role as part of a reenacted, on-site, living adventure. The player must be sincere, having read widely about the period and studied the real people who lived there, and having adopted a suitable pattern personality and speech pattern as one of the historical persons. The demonstrator must become that individual for the term of the public appearance. If there are hand crafts to be demonstrated, the craftsman should be skillful at this craft.

Occasionally, participants can be found who bring with them an understanding of life in the times portrayed or some skill in craftsmanship, repair work, gardening, or cooking. More often this experience is gained on-site, on the job, and on-stage in full public view.

To support the illusion of an alternate identity, each player must extend the details of the new identity to language, bodily movement, and all parts of daily attire such as shoes, stockings, hair arrangements, rings, watches, cosmetics, and the form of tobacco used. A package of modern filter cigarettes beside a kitchen hob with a kettle of garden beans is most incongruous and destroys the image that has been laboriously established.

Special mention must be made of the skill of any craftsman/demonstrator as a communicator, both through action and speech. A silent craftsman may produce superb baskets, but the program as well as the pay scale is based on *communication* with visitors. The craft worker should stimulate questions through the techniques used and then should lead into the broad story of what is being made, how it was utilized, and the particular reasons for that type of work in the community.

NATIVE AMERICANS

The author's experience has been that it is necessary to build a highly personal relationship of mutual respect before you succeed in negotiations for a living interpretation program. You must exhibit confidence and integrity, and convince others of the dignity of the program. Some native Americans have become very sensitive about their personal image as well as that of their tribe. The native people have much to teach us about their relationship to the land, the environment,

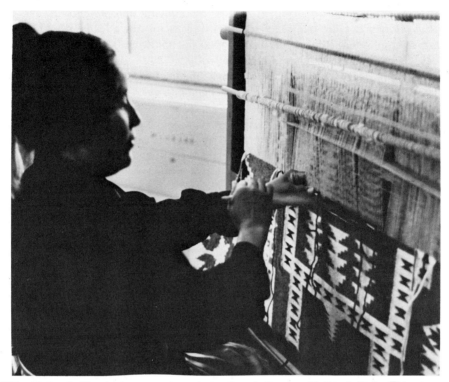

FIG. 10-8. A Navajo weaver at work in Grand Canyon National Park. This weaver started carding and spinning at the age of eight. (Photo by Inger L. Garrison.)

their folklore, and traditions. Almost all historical sites in the western two-thirds of the United States have some relationship to native Americans who were there before the coming of other peoples.

Retention of the old crafts, foods, farming methods, and folklore becomes difficult as their life-style changes in response to the pressures of modern living. This may mean training like that given to young native students in traditional skills at Sitka National Historical Park, where sewing of costumes and bead work are taught to Tlingit girls and totem carving and canoe making to the men. If such classes are a public display, it is proper to pay the students for their services.

Many tribes have almost disappeared except in name, and others have been moved so that they are no longer knowledgeable about their own history. The remnant populations or the relocated people are often eager to be retaught their own ways. The Hopis and Navajos are active in furthering the continuation of their own culture and crafts through their guilds (Fig. 10-8).

It must be remembered that an 8 to 5 routine, five days a week does not allow time off to attend rituals of seasonal advent: planting, harvesting, training of the young, puberty ceremonies, pleas for good hunting or rain, marriage rites, or the well-established times of social gatherings. Since living interpretation is partially for the retention of the native folkways as well as for our education and enjoyment, several federal offices have developed the third-party employment procedure. A typical example is for a cooperating association to agree to provide the living interpretive program for a park where native Americans and their cultures are involved. Under this contract, the association employs the Indians and manages all of the details of wage rates, time off, housing, and daily schedules. This arrangement provides flexibility in arranging hours and days of work that accommodate the employees' requirements for tribal responsibilites. Either the park interpreter or a particular staff or association representative should be available as a person to whom the native people can turn for information and assistance.

Another special employment situation may exist with certain artists such as a Navajo rug maker who supplies the raw wool from her own sheep, the equipment and materials and labor to clean and dye the wool and to process it into yarn. She then uses her own loom and tools and talent to weave it into a rug. Payment under these circumstances is for demonstrating the work and talking to visitors about it.

The accepted rationale is that because of her ownership of materials and tools and her traditional design skill and weaving art, she is employed to perform her usual tasks at a public place, and payment is for demonstration services only. Through ownership of all of the materials, ownership and sales rights remain with her, and she sells the product through normal commercial channels. This type of arrangement is usually most satisfactory on a contract basis with a cooperating third party.

A living interpretive program in cooperation with native Americans is indeed a special kind of experience and challenge. However, the rewards are high for visitors as it acquaints them with the various tribes and their knowledge of living with the land. It also reinforces the identity of the native Americans through awareness of their own heritage.

Tribes such as the Alabama Coushatta and the Tigua del Sur of Texas have set up their own cultural interpretation programs. At the Alabama Coushatta a drama is presented in the summer months. The Tigua del Sur have built an interpretive center and museum. Both are tribally operated. In Niagara, New York a building constructed in the form of a turtle is the Indian cultural center for the northeastern part of the continent. There is already a strong museum association, and a group known as Atlatl is an advocacy organization for Indian arts.

CULTURAL FESTIVALS

Cultural demonstrations are an ancient and highly visible form of interpretation that is growing in popularity. These demonstrations are usually regional in scope.

FIG. 10-9.   Kiowa dancers perform at Chamizal National Memorial, El Paso, Texas at an annual folk festival. Such a cultural demonstration includes the music, art, food, dance, and costumes of the region. (Photo by Inger L. Garrison.)

The music, art, food, dance, and costumes of a region become part of a festival, although music can and does hold its own fest on many occasions.

A cultural demonstration or fiesta often occurs at locations where visitors are most numerous and can readily attend. The events are usually ethnic in theme but often are multinational in character. Chamizal National Memorial in Texas (Fig. 10-9), the National Folk Festival in Washington, D.C., and the Northwest Folklife Festival in Seattle are good examples of interpretation of our regional heritages.

Many of the general conclusions about living interpretation are equally valid for cultural demonstrations (which may later become established parts of the festivals, fairs, or exhibitions). Their scope may vary from rural to urban, regional to local, and their mood may range from fun and frolic to the solemnity of poetry reading or the dignity of music and dance.

CONCLUSION

In a balance of interpretive potentials the concept of living interpretation must always be considered as an option. In all situations that involve people who did things great or small, a living sequence may well be the most significant and creative method of expression. A substantial investment of time is required in basic research, and in adapting authentic events to the site and equipment available.

This must be followed by careful selection of the crew, creative leadership, and training to stimulate natural role playing. A total immersion in the events brings rich returns to both visitors and participants.

GENERAL REFERENCES

Bibliography, Indian Arts and Crafts Board. 1979. U.S. Department of the Interior.

Drury, Clifford Merrill. 1963. *First White Women over the Rockies,* 3 volumes, Arthur H. Clarke Company, Glendale, CA.

Edwards, Ralph, and L. G. G. Ramsey (eds.). 1968. *The Connoisseur's Complete Period Guides to the Houses, Decorations, Furnishings, and Chattels of the Classic Periods,* Bonanza Books, New York.

Kay, William Kennon. 1970. *Keep it Alive: Tips on History Demonstrations,* National Park Service, Visitor Services Training Series, U.S. Department of the Interior.

Langdon, William. 1965. *Everyday Things in American Life, 1776—1876,* Scribner's, New York.

Langdon, William. 1965. *Everyday Things in American Life, 1607—1776,* Scribner's, New York.

Mercer, Henry C. 1923. *Dating of Old Houses,* Bucks County Historical Papers, Vol. V, October 13, Doylestown, PA.

Noel-Hume, Ivor. 1970. Archeology, Doorway to the American Past, *The Athaneum Annals,* **41**(2) 154th Annual Meeting Address, Philadelphia, PA.

Reed, Bernice. 1973. Culture Comes of Age in America, *Trends,* July—August—September, Park Practice Program, National Conference on State Parks, Arlington, VA.

Schiff, Bennett. 1973. Arts in park and recreation settings, The Parks, Arts and Leisure Project, sponsored by the National Endowment for the Arts, The National Park Service, the National Recreation Association. (Copies from any of the above.)

Sherfy, Marcella. 1977. "Interpreting History," *Trends,* January—February—March, Park Practice Program, National Park Service and the National Recreation and Park Association, Arlington, VA.

Tunis, Edwin. 1965. *Colonial Living,* World Publishing Co., Cleveland and New York.

Tunis, Edwin. 1965. *Frontier Living,* World Publishing Co., Cleveland and New York.

White, Elizabeth Q. 1964. *No Turning Back,* Polingaysi Qoyawayma. (As told to Vada F. Carlson.) University of New Mexico Press, Albuquerque.

SPECIFIC REFERENCES

Buildings

Davidson, Marshall B. 1971. *History of Notable American Houses,* American Heritage Publishing Co., New York.

Sloane, Eric. 1967. *An Age of Barns,* Funk and Wagnall, New York.

Cooking

Carson, Jane. 1968. *Colonial Virginia Cookery,* Williamsburg, Virginia, Colonial Williamsburg.

Randolph, Mary. 1860. *The Virginia Housewife or Methodical Cook,* E. H. Butler and Co., Philadelphia, PA.

Simmons, Amelia. 1958. *American Cookery,* Oxford University Press, New York.

Costumes

Laver, James. 1963. *Costume Through the Ages,* Simon and Schuster, New York.

McClellan, Elizabeth. 1969. *History of American Costume, 1607—1870,* Books I and II. Tudor Publishing Co., New York.

Crafts, Skills

Bridenbough, Carl. 1950. *The Colonial Craftsman,* Phoenix Books, University of Chicago Press.

Marcus, Margaret F. 1952. *Period Flower Arrangement,* M. Barrows and Co., New York.

Schneider, Richard C. 1972. *Crafts of the American Indians,* A Craftsman Manual. Published by Author. 312 Linwood Ave., Stevens Point, WI.

Tunis, Edwin. 1965. *Colonial Craftsmen,* World Publishing Co., New York.

Wigginton, Brooks Eliot. 1972. *The Fox Fire Book,* Two volumes. Doubleday, Garden City, NY.

Dying, Needlework, Weaving

Adrosko, Rita J. 1968. *Natural Dyes in the United States.* Smithsonian Institution Press, Washington, DC.

Amsden, Charles Avery. 1949. *Navaho Weaving,* University of New Mexico Press, Albuquerque.

Brightbill, Dorothy. 1958. *Quilting As a Hobby,* Bonanza Books, New York.

Landon, Mary T., and Susan B. Swan. 1970. *American Crewelwork,* Macmillan, London.

Sterling Publishing Co. 1969. *Wool in Pictures,* New York.

Thorpe, Azalea and Jack Larsen. 1967. *Elements of Weaving,* Doubleday, Garden City, NY.

Farming, Gardening

Agricultural History (Quarterly Journal of Agricultural History Society). University of California Press, Davis.

Fox, Helen M. 1970. *Gardening With Herbs,* Sterling Publishing Co., New York.

Randolph, John. 1826. *A Treatise on Gardening.* Reprinted in 1924 from American Gardener. Richmond, VA.

Tabor, Grace. 1913. *Old-Fashioned Gardening,* McBride, Nast and Co., New York.

Firearms

Peterson, Harold L. (ed.). 1964. *Encyclopedia of Firearms,* Dutton, New York.

Peterson, Harold L. 1961. *A History of Firearms,* Scribner's, New York.

Tunis, Edwin. 1965. *Weapons,* World Publishing Co., Cleveland and New York.

Furniture

Nutting, Wallace. 1954. *Furniture Treasury,* Macmillan, New York.

Ormsbee, Thomas H. 1951. *Field Guide to Early American Furniture,* Little, Brown, Boston, MA.

Ramsey, L. G. G. (ed.). 1962. *The Complete Encyclopedia of Antiques,* Hawthorn Books, NY.

Transportation

Beales, Joan. 1968. *The True Book of Travel by Land,* Children's Press, Chicago, IL.

Ensminger, M. E. 1963. *Horses and Horsemanship,* Interstate Printers and Publishers, Inc., Danville, IL.

Tunis, Edwin. 1965. *Oars, Sails, and Steam,* World Publishing Co., Cleveland and New York.

Tunis, Edwin. 1965. *Wheels,* World Publishing Co., Cleveland and New York.

ADDITIONAL ASSISTANCE

The American Crafts Council, 22 W. 55th St., New York 10019. Research library on contemporary crafts; film rental; inventory of craftsmen of the United States by state and region; member of the World Craft Council; advisory to the National Park Service, many states, individuals, and industry.

Embroiderers Guild. Information at 73 Wimpole St., London, WIM 8AX. Handwoven Materials Information, William Cox, Historian, Kings Mountain National Military Park, Kings Mountain, NC.

Indian Arts and Crafts Board, Room 4004, United States Department of the Interior, Washington, DC. General and regional publications lists as well as contemporary information on the status of the Native American Arts. (Excellent source.)

National Endowment for the Arts, Washington, DC. Source for grants and advice to state Art Commissions, individual artists, artists and craftsmen in residence, crafts centers and schools.

National Folk Festival Association, Inc., 1346 Connecticut Ave., Suite 710, Washington, DC.

National Recreation and Parks Association, 1601 N. Kent St., Arlington, VA.

The Silver Thimble, Embroidery supply source. Gay St., Bath, England.

Smithsonian Institution, Washington, DC. 20560.

Nonpersonal or Unattended Services

Because of the inquiring nature of the human mind, interpretation enables us to enjoy a park to the fullest and to appreciate its values.

Paul E. Schultz

CHAPTER 11

THE USE OF AUDIO DEVICES

Spencer J. Smith-White

Many of those involved in the development and operation of interpretive programs would agree that the most effective interpretation results when a knowledgeable and enthusiastic interpreter establishes stimulating two-way communication with his or her audience. Yet, the cost of maintaining a large staff of trained interpreters makes it virtually prohibitive to operate a complete interpretive program on this basis alone.

In devising substitute methods for these personal services, the interpretive specialist should note the important part sound plays in interpersonal communication. More than 60 percent of human intelligence is transmitted through sound.[5] Most interpretive methods, however, emphasize the written or printed word. Leaflets, brochures, handbooks, exhibits, signs, and labels present visitors to areas such as national parks with an overwhelming assemblage of text. It would take average national park visitors several days to read all signs, labels, and publications—even if they were inspired to go about the task systematically.

Our society is thoroughly conditioned to receive its information through sound.[2] We can pick up the telephone and call almost anywhere in the world. At the twist of a radio or TV dial we can have the news, weather report, and local traffic conditions. Interpretive specialists must be aware of the many ways in which sound can be incorporated into their programs.

As instruments capable of reproducing sound, audio devices include:

(a) The wavy-groove method of sound reproduction used in making phonograph records;
(b) The optical method of sound reproduction used in the making of sound movies; and
(c) The magnetic method of sound reproduction used in the making of tape recordings.

Our attention here is focused on this last method of sound reproduction.

Until recently, small organizations could seldom afford audio devices for communication with the public. Rapid developments in the magnetic recording field in the last few years, however, have resulted in reliable equipment at reasonable cost. These devices have already been installed in parks, forests, and museums throughout the world. They are used to interpret trails and overlooks, in exhibits, and at points of interest, such as historic buildings. Teamed with short-range radio transmitters, magnetic tape now makes it possible to tune in park information on your AM car radio.

This chapter states the advantages and limitations that are involved in the use of audio devices, surveys the variety of equipment available, and discusses a number of situations where they can be used effectively (Fig. 11-1).

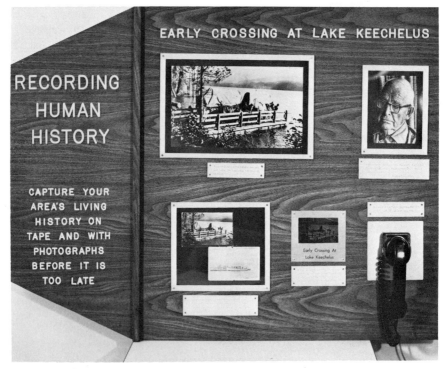

FIG. 11-1. A student-made exhibit showing various uses of early-day photographs as well as a pioneer's voice. A message describing the crossing is heard automatically when the handset at right is placed to the ear. University of Washington, College of Forest Resources. (Photo by John Spring.)

THE ADVANTAGES OF AUDIO DEVICES

In general, the advantages of audio devices are:

1. An audio message is usually less visually and aesthetically distracting than a printed sign or label.
2. The audio message allows viewers to concentrate their visual attention on the features of the exhibit, diorama, relief model, or scene before them without interruption.
3. The visitor's attention span is significantly longer for audio messages than for printed labels.[1] Within reasonable limits, the longer the message the greater the advantage audio devices have over other media.
4. Audio devices can serve large or small groups, using loudspeakers or handphones as the occasion demands.
5. An audio device can relieve a live interpreter in situations where the frequent repetition of a message is necessary. A taped voice maintains enthusiasm—even at the end of a long day.
6. Audio devices facilitate the communication of messages in foreign languages or to visitors of various ages. This can be a very economical and efficient means of reaching different groups with your story.
7. Sound effects can be included in audio messages. These are of particular value in adding authenticity and interest. The calls of birds and other animals, historical voices, and the sounds of past events enhance a message and give it a dramatic impact.

THE DISADVANTAGES OF AUDIO DEVICES

1. As they are both mechanical and electrical, audio devices are subject to breakdown. When the "out of order" sign goes up, the interpretive story is out of business. Regular maintenance and standby tapes and machines are essential when audio equipment is used.
2. Messages on loudspeakers may be obtrusive and annoying, particularly after they have already been heard a number of times. To visitors who wish to linger at a point of interest or to employees working within earshot, the endless repetition of a loudspeaker message may become nerve-wracking.
3. Although battery-powered audio devices are available, most equipment requires a regular 110-volt A.C. power supply, which is not always available in outdoor areas.

In summary, audio messages often communicate more effectively than signs or labels, and they are normally more economical than maintaining "live" interpreters.

AUDIO EQUIPMENT

The various types of equipment used in audio installations include recorders and playback units, speakers and handphones, remote switches, proximity switches, inductance loop devices, and radio transmitters.

1. Recording and Playback Units

The basic units of the audio installation are the magnetic tape recorder and the playback unit. The recording unit is used to record tapes and can serve many playback units. The playback device (often called a slave unit) does not have the recording circuits and is therefore cheaper. Some recorders are also used as playback units. The different types of tape recorders are identified by the different methods of tape "packaging." The three main formats are the reel-to-reel, cartridge, and compact cassette (Fig. 11-2).

(a) The Reel-to-Reel Format. Standard reel-to-reel equipment is the original type and continues to be widely used. Generally reel-to-reel machines reproduce the best quality sound, but they have limited application in audio installations. Their principal disadvantage is that many models will not operate continuously. When the tape runs out, it must be rewound before the message can be played again. Some models can be operated by remote control, and a few are equipped to play in both forward and reverse directions automatically or at the touch of a remote switch.

One method of effecting the continuous repetition of a message on standard reel-to-reel machines is to use an extra-long tape [standard play is 1200 ft (366 m); double play, 2400 ft (732 m); and triple-play tape, 3600 ft (1097 m) long] combined with a slow tape speed. A triple-play tape, for instance, played at 1⅞ inches per second (ips) (4.76 cm/s) will have a playing time of six hours per side. While this would allow one to switch the unit on in the morning and rewind the tape each evening, recording the tape would be a lengthy business. It would require the recording of a one-minute message, for instance, 360 times.

An alternative method involves joining the ends of the tape to form a loop. If the message is short, one minute or less, it is quite practical to place the tape recorder on a shelf with the reels vertical and having the long loop of tape falling from them. A one-minute message played at 1⅞ ips (4.76 cm/s) will require a loop containing almost 10 ft (3 m) of tape. Tape tangling may result if longer loops are used.

(b) The Cartridge Format. To overcome the limitations of reel-to-reel equipment, various endless loop cartridges have been developed. These specially made plastic cartridges contain a drum on which specially lubricated tape is wound.

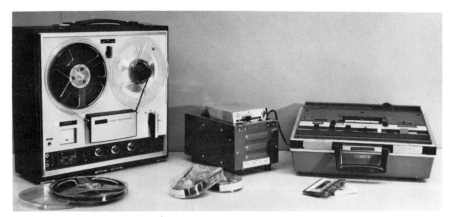

FIG. 11-2. The three main formats of tape-playing devices: at left, reel-to-reel (Sony); center, continuous tape cartridge (Cousino); right, compact cassette (Wollensak). (Photo by John Spring.)

When properly placed on the tape recorder, the tape transport mechanism pulls the end of the loop protruding from the center of the drum. After passing the heads, the tape is wound back on the outside of the tape spool. Although the endless loop cartridge has the advantage of continuous operation, it has inherent problems. The constant slipping of the tape over itself, and the tension it is under as it is pulled around the tape guides results in more rapid deterioration of the tape and poorer sound quality than is experienced with reel-to-reel tapes.

Endless loop cartridges are available with prewound tapes in a variety of lengths for most reel-to-reel machines. The length of such loops is usually expressed in minutes of playing time at a particular playing speed.

The earliest types of special cartridge units were called "message repeaters" and were used in advertising. These machines, which employed the type of cartridge described above, were small and their sound reproduction was generally poor.

Recent developments, spurred on by the interests of the broadcast industry and the demands of the home market for tape formats simpler to use than phonograph records have resulted in several variations of the basic endless-loop cartridge.

The 8-track cartridge system, popular for use in automobiles, employs a cartridge with a built-in pinch wheel. The 8-track machines, constructed for domestic use, do not have sufficient durability for use in audio installations. Equipment is available today, however, that has been specially designed for use in audio installations. The cartridges used employ the continuous tape principle cited above. These continuous-play machines are ruggedly constructed and are available with automatic stop, remote start, and projector and light synchronization.

(c) The Compact Cassette Format.   The development of the compact cassette was an important advance in tape recording. Originated by the Philips Company of the Netherlands, this format has been licensed to about 60 other companies and has therefore become a worldwide standard. All cassettes, both monaural and stereo, are interchangeable and will play on any cassette recorder or player.

The compact cassette is simply two small reels inside a plastic case. The small size is possible because the tape is less than ⅛ in. (3 mm) wide, and the tape building up on the take-up hub occupies space just vacated by tape unwinding from the feed hub. The tape speed on cassette machines is only 1⅞ ips (4.76 cm/s), and since it is basically a reel-to-reel system, it avoids the excessive wear associated with endless loop cartridges.

Cassette technology has developed very rapidly, and cassette machines designed for a variety of uses in audio installations are now on the market. So far, however, the most widespread use of these machines in interpretive situations has been where portable machines with prerecorded cassettes are rented or loaned to provide a *self-guided* tour. The tape players are easy to operate and are usually powered by batteries or from the cigarette lighter receptacle on an automobile dashboard.

2. Delivering the Message

Audio messages can be delivered to the prospective listener in several ways; each has its advantages for particular situations.

(a) Loudspeakers.   Loudspeakers provide the best method for delivering the sound in many circumstances—particularly where it is necessary or desirable for a group, even a large group, to hear the message at one time. Some tape machines have a built-in speaker, and this may be satisfactory; but it does mean that the machine itself has to be located on the site where it will be exposed to theft or vandalism. However, a separate speaker placed at the interpretive site can be connected to a remote audio device in an office or other supervised location. Centrally located machines can be easily checked for correct operation. Separate speakers have to be chosen carefully to match the power output characteristics of the tape recorder or playback unit. In general, the larger the speaker, the better the sound quality (Fig. 11-3). Frequently the speaker will be hidden from view, or used in a sound shell.

For individual listeners or small groups, an 8-in. (20 cm) speaker mounted in a suitable enclosure is adequate. Where the message is to be heard by a large audience, a horn-type speaker may be required. Always be sure that the speaker is beyond harm by vandals and the weather.

If speakers are to be used in an enclosed area, for example, an exhibit room,

FIG. 11-3. Several simple loudspeakers used in delivering interpretive messages. The two in the foreground are built-in or hidden from view; the white, round speakers may be used both indoors and outdoors; the larger, square speakers are for indoor use in exhibits. (Photo by John Spring.)

it is advisable to take the acoustics of the enclosed space into account. A room with bare walls and a hard floor is said to be acoustically "alive," for sound will bounce and echo off the sound reflecting surfaces. In such situations, it may be advisable to carpet the floor and cover the walls with sound-absorbing acoustical tile or wall hangings.

(b) Handphones.   Where sound from loudspeakers would be impractical or undesirable, the use of a telephone hand receiver may be preferred. Special units, incorporating a telephone receiver and a remote control switch, are available. When properly connected to an audio device with the facility for remote operation, the message will be heard through the hand receiver as soon as it is lifted from its wall-mounted cradle. Although other listening devices, such as earcups, are available with the same function as the telephone receiver, the latter is recommended because of people's familiarity with its use (Figs. 11-1 and 11-7).

(c) Sound Chairs.   The sound chair is another means of delivering sound to individuals or perhaps small groups in indoor situations where sound spillage is undesirable. As its name implies, it is a specially designed chair with a high back that forms a semicircle around the head of the person seated in it. Two small speakers are mounted in the top section of the chair. When these are operating, only the person seated in the chair will hear the message. Sound chairs are particularly useful in places like visitor center lobbies where people are waiting or resting, and where there is usually a high ambient noise level.

(d) Inductance Loops. Inductance loop (hidden loop antenna) equipment delivers sound by a magnetic field. The sound signal is taken by wire from the audio output of a tape unit to the site of the interpretation. Here the wire is connected to an "inductance loop" which creates a modulated magnetic field. When the visitor walks into this magnetic field wearing a special wireless headset, or carrying a hand-held radio, electric currents are generated and converted into audible sound. The volume is simply adjusted by the wearer moving further into or out of the magnetic field. There are no knobs to be fiddled with or broken (Fig. 11-8).

This method has several other advantages. The size of the magnetic field can be varied from an area the size of a football field to an auditorium in which each seat may be wired with its own inductance loop. Hence, it would be possible for individual seats to have different programs, or alternatively, the same program in different languages.

One of the limitations of the inductance loop method is that it can be used only in supervised interpretive situations where the wireless receivers can be distributed to visitors and collected after use.

(e) Radio Transmitters. The majority of automobiles today have AM radios. These radios have great potential as receivers of interpretive messages and have until recently been neglected by the interpretive specialist. In Yellowstone National Park it has been reported nearly 80 percent of visitors in vehicles fitted with an AM radio tuned in to park broadcasts, whereas it is known that only about 4 percent of those who passed a roadside exhibit stopped to read it.[3,4]

The transmitters available for this purpose have a low power output and are connected to an appropriate audio device such as an endless loop cartridge slave unit (Fig. 11-4). The message can then be broadcast either by an aerial type antenna or by the recently developed buried cable antenna. The latter has specific advantages, for instance, greater field strength, stability, and less interference with the broadcast signal.

Although the initial cost of installing radio transmitting equipment might seem high, this promises to be a most effective means of delivering a message. Where you have a large number of visitors, the cost per contact is very low.

Situations where the use of transmitters has been tried include park entrance stations, where the latest accommodation and safety information can be broadcast; parking lots at the entrance to self-guided trails (see Script No. 1 at the end of chapter); trail heads, where safety and protection suggestions can be relayed to those preparing for overnight trips; and at sites of accidents or road hazards, where traffic can be advised of the reason for the delay and how long it will be before the road is cleared. Limited range broadcasting can also be used along the

FIG. 11-4. The Driver Information Service radio transmitter, power supply, and playback unit. The transmitter is a low-power AM radio station that beams repetitive messages directly to car radios over a designated frequency. (Photo by Grant W. Sharpe.)

routes of self-guided auto tours at points of interest. As a visitor drives into the range of the broadcasting device a small sign points out the frequency where information is available (Fig. 11-5). The device has also been tried on guided auto tours where the person in the lead vehicle broadcasts to radios in the vehicles following.

Technical Systems, Inc., of Bozeman, Montana, has been instrumental in developing this device in cooperation with the staff at Yellowstone National Park. Because devices like this increase visitor contact significantly, their rapid incorporation into park and forest information systems can be expected. However, those interested in pursuing the use of transmission systems should familiarize themselves with Federal Communications Commission rules.

Citizens Band (CB) radio transceivers can also be considered potential devices for interpretation. Small low-cost portable units are readily available and, unlike the use of AM transmission, the CB units provide the opportunity for questions and answers. Because of the likelihood of interference, their use is probably best restricted to remote locations.

3. Activating the Message

In many interpretive situations it is convenient for the audio message to be repeated continuously, whereas in others it is desirable for the visitor to be able to

FIG. 11-5. This simple sign points out that information on the park is available without stopping, by tuning to the indicated frequency. Yosemite National Park, California. (Photo by Grant W. Sharpe.)

trigger the device to begin the message. The remote switch permits the visitor to activate the tape machine.

(a) Push-button Switches. A simple push-button will normally suffice as a remote switch, provided that the equipment is designed for remote operation. Push-buttons can be obtained in a great variety of sizes and styles and should be strongly constructed, vandal-proof, and weatherproof if they are to be used-out-of-doors. Push-buttons should be mounted so that they can easily be seen and operated by visitors, including children.

(b) Foot-mat Switches. In certain circumstances, it may be desirable for visitors to trigger audio devices without actually being aware of it. In such cases, a foot-mat switch can be placed under a carpet or rug, or even under the cushion or leg of a chair. When somebody stands or sits on the place where the foot-mat switch is hidden, the tape machine to which it is attached will play its message. Foot-mat switches should also be installed in such a way that they cannot be vandalized.

(c) Photoelectric Eyes. Photoelectric eyes perform essentially the same function as the foot-mat switch, but they can be used where it would be impossible to use a foot-mat; for example, on an exposed concrete floor or along a trail. They do, however, require a power supply. (See Fig. 6-8, page 143).

THE MESSAGE

1. Preparing the Script

Remember that spoken language is quite different from language used in descriptive writing. Don't let your audio message sound as if it is being read out of an administrative manual. Write so that it will sound as if you were having a relaxed, person-to-person chat with your visitors. Wherever possible, use the first person (I and we) and second person (you) and keep the sentences short. It is also important to keep the message short. A maximum of three minutes is a good guide in most situations.

When typing the script, make it easy to read and be certain there are no mistakes in spelling or punctuation. Double space the lines and keep them short so the narrator can easily skip from the end of one line to the beginning of the next. This leaves plenty of room on each side to note necessary instructions or sound effects. (See Script No. 2 at the end of chapter.)

Always make several copies of the script and be sure to file the original. You never know when you might need it again.

2. Sound Effects

One of the great advantages of audio is the interest that can be added by the use of authentic sounds. A great variety of background effects are available on record. In addition, consider using voices in dialect, if appropriate. Natural sounds, particularly those of animals, are also useful. Many of these are on record and inquiry will often lead to someone who makes recordings of sounds such as earthworms chewing and woodpeckers pecking.

Background music might be considered, but it should not be distracting.

3. Making the Recording

If professional results are required, it is best to have the recording made at a local recording studio or radio station. They are usually well equipped for recording and, for public service efforts, may keep fees reasonable. They can also arrange for a narrator if one is required.

An alternative is to get assistance from the radio–TV department of the nearest university. These departments usually have facilities for making professional recordings. You may get help with the narration and even the dramatics of your script from students majoring in radio or TV.

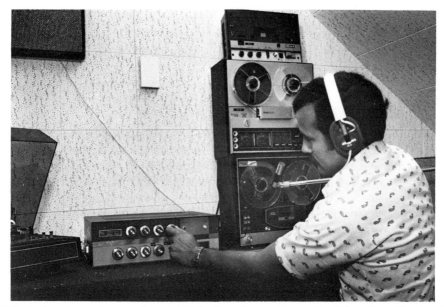

FIG. 11-6. A simple recording booth built under a stairway by the author. The booth contains a turntable, amplifier, reel-to-reel tape decks, a compact cassette recorder, and microphone. Note wall and ceiling insulation. University of Washington, College of Forest Resources. (Photo by John Spring.)

There may be many occasions when you will want to make your own recordings. When you do, find the quietest room possible because the microphone will pick up all the background sounds, such as traffic noise, ringing telephones, humming light fixtures, barking dogs, and children playing outside.

A simple recording booth, housing only a microphone, may be made by lining a wooden frame with acoustical tile or industrial soundproofing material. A booth 2 × 2 ft (60 × 60 cm) would be about minimum size.

Equipment needed for making the recording varies, but basically, it starts with a microphone, tape recorder or cartridge system, and a turntable for adding sound effects and background music (Fig. 11-6).

SOME APPLICATIONS FOR AUDIO DEVICES

1. Audiovisual Presentations

The most widespread use of audio devices for interpretive purposes has been in combination with slide projectors for the presentation of audiovisual programs.

Compared to making movies, the equipment and materials required for slide-sound productions are relatively inexpensive. They are easier for the amateur to prepare and also are easier to update than movies.

In most circumstances the type of equipment used will be determined by the purpose of the program, the degree of sophistication, and the level of automation required. For single-projector on-off programs a simple cassette or reel-to-reel recorder and a synchronization device may be all that is required. However, if variable dissolve rates, multiple screens, stereo sound, and regular performances are required, the latest in audiovisual technology is a must.

The application of the silicon chip and integrated circuit to audiovisual machinery has added a new dimension to the world of the "slide-show." The range of equipment that is available will meet the dictates of the most fertile imagination and, for the results, the cost is not unreasonable for most agencies. The Audio-Visual Equipment Directory, published by the National Audio-Visual Association, Inc., of Fairfax, Virginia is perhaps the best source of information on the range of equipment available.

2. Exhibits

Sound can add an extra dimension to exhibits. The most popular equipment used is the endless loop cartridge format discussed previously. Indoors, a convenient method of delivering the sound is by handphones (Figs. 11-1, and 11-7).

FIG. 11-7. Visitors listen to an ecological food chain message over a handphone. The audio device substitutes for labels in the exhibit. Peaks of Otter Visitor Center, Blue Ridge Parkway, Virginia. (Photo by Grant W. Sharpe.)

Exhibits with audio that involve the visitor in answering questions seem to be very successful. An exhibit on the historical development of computers in the Lawrence Hall of Science, University of California at Berkeley, regularly keeps visitors fascinated for a period of 20 minutes.

The Smithsonian National Museum of Natural History and the Milwaukee Museum among others have found the hidden loop antennas (cited earlier) to be

FIG. 11-8. A rechargeable hand-held radio device that receives its message from a hidden wire loop antenna placed near an exhibit or other point of interest. Historic Ships, San Francisco. Courtesy of By-Word Corporation. (Photo by David Black.)

FIG. 11-9. A class of school children listen attentively to sounds of convict court cases played through 10 hidden loudspeakers in the Hartley Historic Site Courthouse, N.S.W., Australia. (Photo by K. Gillett.)

popular with visitors. Recorded messages are heard by visitors as they approach the hidden antenna, through a lightweight handheld radio receiver. An advantage to this device is that it can be used both indoors and outdoors (Fig. 11-8).

Concealed loudspeakers have been used effectively to interpret historic buildings. In one such example, at Hartley Historic Site, N.S.W., Australia, 10 loudspeakers have been carefully hidden under desks and behind chairs in the convict era courthouse (Fig 11-9). Sound tape, on an endless loop cartridge player is programmed to switch sound from one loudspeaker to another, or several in combination. The audio consists of dramatized re-creations of actual courtroom proceedings taken from the old bench books. When visitors trip the photoelectric switch, the tape player turns on and the visitor hears cell doors clang, a convict ushered into the dock, the constable call for order, and the magistrate pronounce sentence. Through the automatic switching of speakers by the control track on the tape, each sound appears to come from the appropriate location in the courtroom.

Loudspeakers can also be used effectively to interpret outdoor exhibits, allowing family groups to listen to the narrative together.

3. Trails

Audio devices have been effectively used in self-guided trails. They have been especially useful in historic areas and are widely used to interpret the sequence of events at battlefield sites. Authentic voices and sound effects heighten their appeal.

Trails through caves provide another opportunity for the use of audio equipment. However, the replacement of a personal guide by audio equipment may expose delicate features to depreciative behavior and vandalism. If the significant features are vulnerable, the use of a guided tour may be mandatory.

The use of audio devices along self-guided trails is not as widespread as it is on sites of historic interest (Fig. 11-10). Yet, the sounds of natural things can be just as fascinating to people as are the doings of our forebears. Bird calls have been used in some instances, such as on the Bear Lake Self-Guided Trail in Rocky Mountain National Park.

The type of audio device best suited to a trail depends on factors such as whether 110-volt power is available, what supervision the trail will receive, and level of visitor use. When power is unavailable, portable cassette tape players along with the appropriate cassettes can be rented or loaned to visitors.

When power is available, the use of cartridge units obviates the need for close supervision of the trail. If power is only available at a central location, it is necessary to run speaker and remote control wires to each interpretive station. Where any type of audio device is used, protection from theft, vandalism, and weather is essential.

4. Auto Tours

The audio device that has become most widely used for auto tour interpretation is the portable cassette tape player. These players are available for rental at many of the national parks and historical areas in the United States. They have not, however, received overwhelming response from park visitors mainly because of the nuisance associated with the return of the machines.

The use of limited range AM radio transmitters seems to offer many advantages where auto tours are concerned. First, they can be used for tours when the lead car is fitted with such a transmitter. This allows visitors in following cars to tune their car radio and receive the interpretive commentary as the group moves along.

Transmitters can also be placed at points of interest along auto tour roads and visitors traveling them can be advised of the radio frequency by sign. As mentioned previously, for such installations as this the transmitter is used only to deliver the message and, except where it is used in the conducted situation mentioned above, it must be teamed with some type of tape-playing unit.

Citizens Band radio transceivers have been a particularly popular interpretive device at the remote Sturt National Park in the far northwest of N.S.W., Australia. During vacation periods, the ranger-in-charge of this 300,000-hectare desert park leads regular auto tours of up to six vehicles to particular points of interest. Each

FIG. 11-10.   An audio station placed in a historical area. A button is pushed to activate the three-minute message. The station incorporates a simple label showing a drawing of a former cabin. The extended metal frame serves as a bird perch, reducing droppings on the label. Whitman Mission National Historic Site, Washington. (Photo by Grant W. Sharpe.)

vehicle is provided with a portable CB radio, the novelty of which induces a continuous stream of questions about the park and its wildlife.

PROTECTION OF EQUIPMENT

Audio equipment needs special protection from theft, vandalism, moisture, and dust. The message repeater should be under supervision at all times. If this is not possible, it should be locked in a sturdy concealed location. Even remote speakers need sturdy covers to protect them from both weather and vandalism. Wires should be buried or hidden. Audio equipment is very expensive, and readily converted to cash if stolen, so prodigious efforts must be taken to protect it.

SUMMARY

Audio devices can be effectively utilized to communicate information and to dramatize a park or site story.

While the cost of audio and audiovisual hardware can be quite high, the cost of changing the message or the story is extremely small. However, the technology continues to advance rapidly, and units available this year may be only second-best next year.

The interpretive situations where the use of audio devices will increase the effectiveness of communication are many and varied and are limited only by the imagination and funding resources of the interpretive specialist.

APPENDIX

Sample Script No. 1

This script is in use in a limited range broadcasting device at the Mud Volcano parking area in Yellowstone National Park:

Mud Volcano, Black Dragons Cauldron, Sizzling Basin, and Mud Geyser all give a hint of the fascinating and different array of thermal features found in this area.

Hear what Lt. Doane had to say when the Washburn-Langford-Doane Expedition explored the area in 1870.

In a ravine over the ridge, hot vapors pour out in every direction. A small stream of green water flows down the ravine having its source in a rocky cave in the bank. . . . A perfect grotto, lined with brilliant metallic tints of green, red, and black, and from which steam escapes in regular pulsations to a distance of 40 feet, forcing the water out in waves which break over an outside horizontal rim about one in ten seconds.

A self-guiding nature trail about ¾ of a mile long leads you safely through this weird landscape, and tells you about these unusual features. Be sure and pick up a trail guide from the dipenser box at the trail head and follow the trail directional signs. Allow about a half hour for the trip.

Boiling water, steam and unstable ground are encountered along this trail. Please tour the area safely by always staying on the designated trails. Keep children under physical control at all times.

Sample Script No. 2

Subject: Logging Locomotive
Author: Spencer Smith-White
Narrators: Peter Smith and Fred Brown
Time: Three minutes
Date: x/y/z

Voice	Narrative	Sound Effects
DAVE	"Hi! I'm Dave Jones, engineer. Me an' my offsider, Bill . . . say 'hullo' Bill . . ."	Fade steam locomotive, then bring under and hold
BILL	"Hi!"	
DAVE	". . . We've been working Number 36 here for 15 years—hauling logs down from the mountains. Doug-fir and spruce mainly. Ol' Betsy here is what we call a 2-6-6-2-type of locomotive—have a look at her wheels and you'll see what I mean. Two little wheels at the front—they're called bogies; two lots of six driving wheels and two more bogies right back here under the cab."	Steam escaping, brakes screaming, and couplings straining
BILL	"Brakes Dave, a log on the line. . ."	
DAVE	"If we take it slow, we'll push it out of the way with the cowcatcher . . . often gets trees blown over the tracks. Ol' Betsy runs on oil . . . we've got about 3000 gallons of it back there in the tender, 'nuff for about 800 miles.	locomotive moving slowly.

Voice	Narrative	Sound Effects
DAVE	Any of you folks know how a locomotive works? Well, the oil is burnt down under the boiler and heats the water in the boiler to steam—she carries about 6000 gallons of water. This steam goes to the pistons under high pressure and forces the pistons back and forth. The driving wheels are turned because they're connected to the pistons by all those connecting rods. Well, guess most of these ol' steam locos been turned into scrap iron by now. Sure glad they saved ol' Number 36 here tho' so you young folks can see what they were like . . . Bye now.''	Blast on whistle

Sample Script No. 3*

Subject:	Historic Barn
Author:	Jonathon S. Schechter
Narrators:	George Wilson and Will Price
Time:	Three minutes
Date:	x/y/z

Voice	Narrative	Sound Effects
NARRATOR	The year is 1872 and from out of the west rode Peter French and a small band of buckaroos. With them is a herd of cattle. The barn you are now in was constructed and the growth of the Blitzen Valley cattle empire had begun.	Horseback riding, whistles, cattle mooing
	Land was quickly acquired and before long French *ruled* over 135,000 acres of land! Homesteaders resisted his growth and many felt threatened by his very presence in the Blitzen Valley.	More cattle noises, cowboys shouting

*From: Interpretation As a Management Tool for Sections of the Malheur National Wildlife Refuge, Harney County, Oregon. Unpublished masters thesis, University of Washington, 1975, by Jonathon S. Schechter.

VOICES	"That French will drive us all out. We don't stand a chance. Something must be done." (All voices in hushed tones).	Hammering, sawing, men working
NARRATOR	Most lands from the P-Ranch, on up the Blitzen River were drained as his cattle empire grew. What he built was built to last . . . miles of fencing, the Long Barn, and the unusual round barn near the town of Diamond. By the 1890s Peter French had built one of the best managed cattle empires in the West.	
	As his holdings increased, his enemies also increased. Ed Oliver, a homesteader, soon found his small tract of land surrounded by French interests.	
SIMU-LATED VOICE OF ED OLIVER	"My own land, I can't get to it. This has got to stop."	Cattle sounds, men talking
NARRATOR	Oliver successfully petitioned the Harney County Court for a right of way into his property . . . But tensions grew as French resisted the court's action. And then . . . during a cattle drive, on the morning after Christmas, in 1897, Oliver and French met head on in a field about 5 miles south of here. What happened next is disputed, but French's whip cracked through the air at Oliver . . . Oliver aimed his pistol and fired and Peter French fell from his saddle.	cracking whip: one clear loud shot
VOICES	"He's dead! Oliver killed him! Get the sheriff!"	Horses galloping, men shouting
NARRATOR	Oliver was arrested and brought to trial.	Judge's gavel sounds
JUDGE VOICE	"Does the jury have a verdict?" Yes, your honor . . . Not guilty."	Cheers in the court-room

Voice	Narrative	Sound Effects
NARRATOR	To many, Oliver was a hero, . . . The life of Peter French and his cattle empire had come to an end, but his legacy lives on. The town of Frenchglenn bears his name and the Long Barn stands as a monument to that colorful and controversial cattle baron of the Blitzen Valley.	Western music, horses galloping

REFERENCES

General References

Audio-visual Communications—journal, United States Business Publications, New York.

Audio-visual Communications Review—journal—Association for Educational Communications and Technology. Washington, DC.

Haynes, N. M. 1957. *Elements of Magnetic Tape Recording.* Prentice-Hall, Englewood Cliffs, NJ.

Salm, W. G. 1969. *Tape Recording for Fun and Profit.* TAB Books, New York.

Sharpe, Grant W. and Robert R. Searles. 1969. Directory of Interpretive Materials. Interpretive Aid No. 1. The Association of Interpretive Naturalists, Inc., Derwood, MD.

References Cited

1. Mahaffey, Ben D. 1969. *Relative Effectiveness and Visitor Preference of Three Audio-Visual Media for Interpretation of an Historic Area,* Department Report 1, Texas Agricultural Experimental Station, Texas A & M University, College Station, TX.

2. McLuhan, Marshall. 1964. *Understanding Media,* Routledge and Kegan-Paul, London.

3. National Park Service. U.S. Department of the Interior. *News Release,* April 16, 1971.

4. Starobin, Sidney S. 1973. "Yellowstone National Park Radio Broadcasts Survey," Unpublished report, Yellowstone National Park.

5. Zettl, Herbert. 1976. (Third edition). *Television Production Handbook.* Wadsworth Publishing Company, Belmont, CA.

CHAPTER 12

SIGNS AND LABELS

Paul A. McIntosh

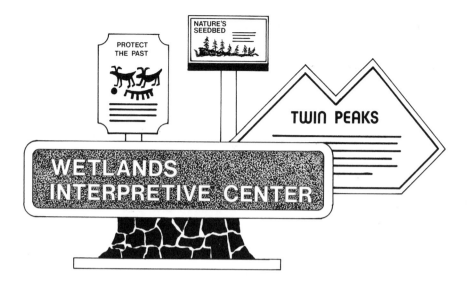

Two types of signs are commonly used in interpretive programs: interpretive signs and administrative signs. Entrance, orientation, information, and directional signs are classified as administrative signs. One of their functions is to bring the visitor in contact with the interpretive program. The purpose of interpretive signs, on the other hand, is to interpret on the site the natural processes, historical events, or physical features of an area, thereby providing visitors with a feeling of participation and personal discovery unstructured by interpretive personnel. Labels are a type of interpretive sign. They are used to interpret and to identify objects, for example, individual plants on a self-guided trail. The wording is usually brief and simple.

This chapter deals specifically with interpretive signs. However, many of the guidelines are applicable to administrative signs as well.

The Advantages of Signs

Interpretive signs have a number of advantages over other media.

1. They can be relatively inexpensive. Frequently, interpretive signs can be designed, built, and installed by "in-house" personnel. While this is often cheaper than buying or contracting for professionally designed signs, these homemade signs must not appear amateurish.
2. The operation and maintenance costs of signs are usually quite low provided that the signs are well designed and constructed.
3. Signs are self-pacing. That is, readers can go at their own speed and read only what they are interested in. Thus, people in a hurry can check the headline, subheadings or illustration to see if they are interested in reading further. If they decide not to read the complete text, they have at least

received an outline of the message content. An audio station message or a live interpreter's talk cannot be skimmed in this way. Conversely, if the interested readers miss a word or thought, they can reread a sentence or paragraph without interrupting a talk or listening through an entire message to hear it again. The self-pacing feature of signs is also helpful to teachers and parents as they can explain things to their children without disrupting a talk or missing part of a taped message.

4. Signs are in place at all times. Hence, they provide interpretation before and after normal working hours, on weekends, and whenever emergencies create heavy demands on an organization's interpretive staff. This feature is of real value to the visitor passing through at these times. Most people go to parks and forests with their families or close friends.[2] Because signs are in place at all times, they can serve individuals and small groups as they arrive. Visitors do not have to wait for scheduled or conducted activities with large, organized groups. This may be advantageous in high-use areas.

5. Finally, the sign itself provides the photographer with information about his or her pictures and may serve as a caption or title for the visitor's own slide programs (Fig. 12-1).

The Disadvantages of Signs

The disadvantages of interpretive signs can be divided into two groups. The first deals with the effect a sign has on the visitor.

1. A sign is passive and requires mental effort on the part of the reader. In contrast, audio stations and live interpreters do not require this same level of effort from the visitor. Since people are used to getting a large portion of their information from radio or television, they may be unwilling to read educational material.

2. Signs cannot have special sound effects such as bird songs or authentic voices "dubbed in" as can audio stations. This is a disadvantage only if the message could benefit from such effects.

3. Interpretation with signs is one-way communication. Therefore, visitors cannot ask for more detailed information as they can from an interpreter. A sign cannot adjust to the interest, age, or education level of the reader, nor can it respond to shortlived interpretive opportunities such as the occurrence of unusual weather phenomena or the sighting of a rare animal.

4. The sign has no souvenir value except possibly the visitor's photograph of it.

The second group of disadvantages affects the manager more than the visitor.

1. The sign may draw attention to a perishable resource which, in turn, may be lost through the depreciative behavior of visitors. Explaining how native

FIG. 12-1. Signs serve the visitors in many ways including titles for their own slide programs. Signs should be professionally designed, as is this entrance sign at Great Smoky Mountains National Park. (Photo by Grant W. Sharpe.)

Americans used birchbark for canoes may suggest to visitors that bark can be peeled off, resulting in the disfigurement of an area's birch trees. This problem is most severe in areas where employees are not present to protect the resource.

2. Signs are vulnerable to damage and depreciation by weathering, decay, wildlife, and vandalism. Ultraviolet rays in sunlight break down the finish and the wood, and windblown ice and sand erode surfaces. Fungi attack organic components, and in some areas bears and porcupines damage signs by gnawing on them. Birds use them for perches and defecate on them. Jackknife artists carve on signs and souvenir hunters often steal them.

Use of Interpretive Signs

Interpretive specialists have several media from which to choose. Each medium has inherent capabilities that enable it to do a particular job better than any of the others. In deciding which medium to use, consider program objectives and the unique capabilities of all the alternatives. Is personal contact with the visitors desirable and economically feasible? Does the message involve an object that can be exhibited? Can the message be enhanced with recorded authentic voices, bird songs, or other sound effects? Will the majority of visitors be near their radios? Do you want to provide something for the visitors to take home with them? A "yes" answer to any of these questions indicates that signs may not be as effective as an interpreter, exhibit, audio station, or brochure. On the other hand, if the interpretive situation can be served by a medium that is self-paced, photogenic, in place at all times, and inexpensive to operate and maintain, a high-quality interpretive sign or label should be considered. By keeping the objectives, audience and message in mind, the selection of a medium will be simplified.

The Message

The label for an object may need only the common name to identify it. However, if it is accompanied by the scientific name, phonetic spelling, and a map illustrating its geographic distribution or range, the educational value and retention factors may be greatly increased.

Interpretive messages are more complex. Regardless of their length, they must perform a number of functions. They must gain the visitors' attention, hold their interest, provide them with an understanding of the subject, and in some instances evoke a behavioral response. In a short message, these functions must be performed by the headline and possibly one paragraph. In longer messages, they are performed by the headline, lead paragraph, interior paragraph(s), and closing paragraph. The facts, spelling, grammar, and word choice must be accurate, concise, and appealing to a variety of readers.

Headline

The headline is a vitally important part of the message. Its main job is to gain attention. It also gives a hint of the message content and induces further reading. A good headline is usually short and the letters are larger than those of the rest of the message (Fig. 12-2). It should contain verbs or verb forms that add action and create movement, life, and vitality. For example, a sign near a beaver pond might read: "Caution—Logging Ahead." Quotations in headlines can be effective, but should be used correctly and sparingly. "Thar she blows!" might be an appropriate headline for a sign on a whaling ship. Don't be afraid to try unorthodox headlines. Some of the best headlines do not follow any of the standard guidelines. Be sure they are effective, though, before you put them on display.

FIG. 12-2. A well-designed and written interpretive sign illustrating the use of the headline, lowercase letters, and two drawings. The letters and drawings were cut into the wood with a hand router. Rocky Mountain National Park, Colorado. (Photo by Gunnar Fagerlund.)

Lead Paragraph

When more than one paragraph is used, the lead paragraph usually determines if the visitor will read on. Its job is to hold the visitor's interest and provide a transition from the headline into the interior paragraph(s). The lead paragraph should be short, fast paced, and interesting. This means few details and lots of action.

You can hold visitor interest by one of several approaches. One way is to establish an antithetic element in the lead paragraph. This is an apparently contradictory or illogical statement created by a partial disclosure of the facts. For example, a sign in a volcanic area might describe pumice as "rock that floats in water." The purpose is to get visitors to read on to resolve the contradiction. Another, though often overused way, is to pose an intriguing question that will prompt the visitors to read further. You can also involve them by using a direct address, for example, "Notice the 'bowl' carved in the rock at the base of the waterfall." Quotations, excerpts from original sources, and vernacular can generate interest in a subject. For example, a sign on the mountain where Daniel Webster spoke during the Whig Convention might begin with: "From above the clouds I address you . . . ," the first line of his speech. Sections using these techniques should be easily understood and not so long as to lose the reader in a quagmire of details or unfamiliar language.

Interior Paragraph

The job of the interior paragraph(s) is to develop an understanding of the subject and create an appreciation for it. Any antithetic elements established earlier should be resolved here, and any questions should be answered. The interior paragraph is frequently the last section of the message, but where an action or behavioral response is desired, a closing paragraph follows. If the interior paragraph ends the message, be sure the closing neither hangs nor stops abruptly.

Closing Paragraph

The closing paragraph makes clear what action or response is desired. It may summarize the pertinent points of the message and then encourage the reader to do something. For example, if the message is about alpine ecology, the closing paragraph may encourage visitors to protect the fragile alpine meadows.

ACCURACY AND CLARITY

The text must be accurate. If visitors notice the slightest error, their confidence in the whole message will be shaken. Research the subject thoroughly, consult current literature, and have experts in the field review the message when you think it is finished. Check the spelling of words in a dictionary. Use a thesaurus and a composition handbook or style manual to insure proper word choice, style, punctuation, and grammar (Fig. 12-3). Review each phase of the sign production process word by word to see that errors have not been made in typesetting or stencil cutting. Putting even minor errors on public display may detract from the interpretive message and reflect in a negative manner on the program's administration. In projects representing substantial investment in time, energy, and resources, a small-scale model or mock-up may avoid costly mistakes and needless errors.

Fraction of Selection

Whether or not a visitor reads an interpretive sign depends on what Wilbur Shramm has called the "fraction of selection"[7]:

$$\text{Fraction of Selection} = \frac{\text{Expectation of Reward}}{\text{Effort Required}}$$

The larger the fraction for a particular sign, the greater the number of visitors who will read it. Hence, the interpretive specialist must strive to maximize the fraction. This can be done by increasing the Expectation of Reward or decreasing the Effort Required.

FIG. 12-3. This sign is hard to read. It lacks a title, is not punctuated, and capital letters are used throughout. (Photo by Grant W. Sharpe.)

Increasing the Expectation of Reward

Expectation of reward is greater when readers can identify with the message. If the subject is physically or psychologically close to the readers or if it is related to their roles in society, expectation of reward will be increased.

Some subjects such as wildlife or native people are popular with a wide variety of visitors. You can take advantage of this popularity by building your messages around them whenever possible.

Writing style can also affect reader interest. If your style is very formal and you use unfamiliar words, your readers' interest and expectation of reward will be low. Hence, your messages should be written in a conversational style (second person), using personal words and sentences.[4]

Decreasing the Effort Required

A long block of continuous text is uninviting and discouraging (Fig. 12-4). Therefore, if you want the average person to even consider reading a message, it must be short and appear easy to read.

FIG. 12-4. This potentially interesting sign may be discouraging to readers because of the large blocks of print, the length of the message, and the capital letters. Perhaps another medium should have been chosen for some of this information. Grand Teton National Park. (Photo by Grant W. Sharpe.)

Never sacrifice clarity for brevity. Improve the clarity of the message by using common words or by defining any unfamiliar terminology. Analogies drawn to things in the experience of the reader also improve the clarity of the message. When using words of other than the commonly spoken language, you should include the phonetic spelling the first time they appear. This will be especially appreciated by parents who must read signs to their children.

Although brief messages are desirable, some subjects require more text than others. The psychologically discouraging effect of seeing a long block of text can be minimized by using generous margins, large type, short lines, and short paragraphs. Subheadings should also be used to "break up" the text and help carry the story along. The reading ease of the text is also improved by shorter words and sentences.[4]

Remember the old saying that a picture is worth a thousand words. It is especially true for interpretive signs and labels. Pictures not only help carry the message but are strong attention getters. Simple line drawings or diagrams are best for maximum clarity and understanding (Fig. 12-5).

Research studies of typographical factors affecting legibility have provided guidelines for decreasing the effort required to read print.[6] Though most of the research was done for reading at normal distances of approximately 15 in. (38 cm), several of the guidelines can be safely generalized and applied to interpretive signs, which often require greater viewing distances.

Through morning air comes the shriek of a young rabbit, food for the blue racer. Bird eggs fall victim to night-prowling racoons.

"What a shame!" you say.
Not really. In nature's scheme of things, there is little concern for the individual plant or animal. The well-being of the community is most important.

FIG. 12-5. Simple illustrations greatly increase visitor interest in signs and labels. The paper label is dipped in hot paraffin to protect it from the weather. This example is from Kensington Park, Huron-Clinton Metropolitan Park Authority, Michigan.

Although wide margins may reduce the psychologically discouraging effect of a long block of text, they do not increase the legibility of print. When the sign material is expensive, wide margins can be very costly. Narrow margins reduce both the material costs and the blank spaces that often attract a variety of unwanted inscriptions.

The color combinations for best legibility are those with high brightness contrast between letters and background. For labels, black letters on a yellow background are better than red letters on a green background. Also, dark letters on a light background are better than light letters on a dark background. Hence, black on white is better than white on black. However, where a sign is to be used in subdued light such as in a forest or to be read at night, the light letter on a dark background will be easier to read (Fig. 12-6).

Although no real difference in legibility exists between dull and glossy reading surfaces, people judge that dull surfaces promote legibility, and prefer them to

FIG. 12-6. Sign design is important. Color of letters and background, texture of surface, and simple artwork increase visitor interest. As sentences are short, capital letters are acceptable in this administrative sign. Yosemite National Park, California. (Photo by Gunnar Fagerlund.)

glossy surfaces. By providing signs with dull finishes, you can eliminate reflections and glare and meet the expectations of visitors.

The optimum angle of the reading surface to line of sight is 90°. A deviation of as little as 15° from this optimum can significantly decrease the efficiency of reading.[9] Hence, interpretive signs should be oriented at 90° to the line of sight of the average visitor (Fig. 12-7). Steps should be provided at podium-style interpretive signs, horizontal display cases, and other interpretive devices where children may have trouble viewing them (Fig. 12-8).

Most interpretive signs are used outdoors and natural illumination is sufficient. However, the lighting in exhibit and display rooms is often insufficient for easy reading of labels, and supplemental lighting should be considered. Twenty to thirty footcandles are sufficient in most reading situations.[9]

SIGN DESIGN

First impressions are important. This is true of signs as well as people. Though unrelated to the message itself, the quality of design and maintenance of signs may be equated with the quality of the message. Presumably, the sign with the

FIG. 12-7. The angle of the reading surface of a sign or label should be about 90° to the reader's line of sight. Banff National Park, Alberta. (Photo by Grant W. Sharpe.)

best appearance will have the best message and the greatest expectation of reward. Hence, the design of the sign is an important factor in determining whether or not visitors will read it and accept its message.

General Appearance

Signs should be designed to minimize their intrusion on the site. The use of local materials for the sign and its supports can make the sign more aesthetically acceptable and will help promote the theme of the area. For example, lava rock can be used in volcanic areas, driftwood on coastal sites, and massive posts in old-growth timber.

The height of a sign can also be designed to fit the environment. In desert or plains settings, low-profile signs are most appropriate; in a forest setting taller signs may be appropriate.

Type Styles

All modern uncluttered typefaces or letter styles such as Helvetica Medium, Scotch Roman, Garamond, or Antique are equally legible. For maximum legibil-

FIG. 12-8. Are children forgotten visitors? A step is needed at this roadside rest interpretive sign near Yakima, Washington. (Photo by Grant W. Sharpe.)

ity, avoid American Typewriter and the very decorative or highly ornamented styles, such as Cloister Black (Old English), particularly in long blocks of text. Some letter styles are most appropriate with certain messages—historic, scientific, artistic, or other.

The most legible type form for interpretive signs is lowercase, boldface. Messages written totally in capitals or italics are harder to read and they should be used only to give special emphasis to a word, phrase, or sentence (Fig. 12-4).

Certain typefaces or lettering styles are frequently used to help characterize the theme of an area. The National Park Service[5] uses Barnum or heavy block Roman for Civil War, frontier, or western expansion subjects, and worn type Roman or Classic Roman for colonial and Revolutionary War subjects. Heavy block gothic is used for Indian, prehistoric, and historical subjects, and modified gothic for natural history subjects.

Color

Different colors are commonly associated with different natural and historical subjects. The National Park Service uses dark blue on light gray for Civil War subjects, and black on white for frontier, colonial, and Revolutionary War subjects.[5] Colors traditionally associated with natural areas are blue for marine or coastal areas, tan for desert areas, and dark green and brown for forested areas. These colors not only characterize the theme of an area but in natural areas, help the signs blend with their surroundings. Colors also have psychological effects on people and can be used to enhance a message by putting people in an appropriate mood. For example, red is exciting while blue is subduing.[1]

Methods and Materials

Producing the actual sign can be a big job, but there is help available. Many companies are in the business of casting, printing, routing, or painting signs. A graphic designer or landscape architect can also contribute to the success of a sign's design. However, a variety of materials and aids are available to those who prefer to make their own. Lettering can be done by machine, press-on letters, stencils, or ready-made three-dimensional letters in a wide variety of materials. Chalk, ink, paints, and stains come in all colors. Many of these items can be found in art and drafting supply stores or catalogs and in college or university bookstores. *Directory of Interpretive Materials*[8] lists many of the suppliers of materials and equipment for making your own signs and labels.

In selecting sign materials, the designer should consider their durability with respect to local weather, decay, insects, wildlife, theft, and vandalism. These factors help determine the useful life of the sign. Where the occurrence of theft and vandalism is low, the extra expense for a durable sign may save you several times that amount in lower maintenance costs. On the other hand, an inexpensive but less durable sign may be best in areas of high theft and vandalism where frequent replacement of signs is necessary.

Metal

Sheets of anodized aluminum are very durable and can be used for an entire sign or label or for the illustration on a large sign. Prints of the desired illustration or label are made on aluminum from black and white negatives. Line drawings and good black and white photographs reproduce very well with this process. The signs can be scratched, but they are unaffected by weather, decay, or insects. A plastic sheet can be mounted over a metal sign to protect it from scratches, but it must be sealed to keep moisture from condensing on the inside of the plastic and obscuring the sign. A single sign with text and illustration is expensive, but once

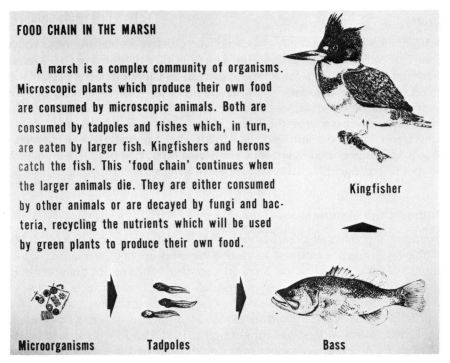

FOOD CHAIN IN THE MARSH

A marsh is a complex community of organisms. Microscopic plants which produce their own food are consumed by microscopic animals. Both are consumed by tadpoles and fishes which, in turn, are eaten by larger fish. Kingfishers and herons catch the fish. This 'food chain' continues when the larger animals die. They are either consumed by other animals or are decayed by fungi and bacteria, recycling the nutrients which will be used by green plants to produce their own food.

Kingfisher

Microorganisms   Tadpoles   Bass

FIG. 12-9. A label utilizing the metal photo process. Anodized aluminum is used in the darkroom instead of photo paper. Example from the University of Washington's Waterfront Nature Trail, Seattle. (Photo by Grant W. Sharpe.)

the negative is made, additional copies cost only the price of the anodized aluminum blanks and the darkroom time (Fig. 12-9).

The silk screen process on metal produces an attractive and durable sign. This sign will be expensive if only one is made, but the unit cost goes down as additional signs are produced. Because silk screen signs are made with paint or ink, they are less durable but potentially more colorful than signs made by Metalphoto or Permaloy processes.

Interpretive messages and simple line drawings can be routed or etched on heavy aluminum plates. They are expensive to produce but withstand a tremendous amount of abuse.

Signs can also be cast in aluminum or bronze. Like routed aluminum, these signs are highly durable. Both routed and cast metal signs can be accented with baked-on enamel.

FIG. 12-10. A park official from South America tries out a hand router on a wooden entrance sign. Blue Ridge Parkway, Virginia. (Photo by Grant W. Sharpe.)

Wood

Wooden signs have universal appeal, but can be expensive to maintain. The message can be hand painted, stenciled, silk screened, carved, branded, or cut with a router. (Fig. 12-10). Wood is always vulnerable to jackknife vandalism, as well as weathering, decay, and insect attack. However, wooden signs are less popular gunshot targets than are metal signs. If you are considering rustic wooden signs for your area, you should obtain *Durable Rustic Wooden Signboards,* a Forest Service Research Paper by Glenn A. Cooper, which is available from the North Central Forest Experiment Station.[3]

Plastic

Signs can be printed on opaque sheets of plastic, or routed on a "sandwich" of two different colors of plastic. With this latter technique, the underlying layer shows up in the bottom of the groove and produces a letter that contrasts with the background without the use of paint.

Paper

For less expensive sign and label materials, consider printing signs on paper. Protection is provided by laminating them between plastic or fiberglass, or dipping the label in hot (high-melting point) paraffin (Fig. 12-5). Where vandalism is prevalent, numerous copies should be run off at one time and stored for use as needed. Remember to avoid American Typewriter typeface if you have a choice.

Hardware

Signs or labels made of lightweight materials require rigid holders and posts on which to mount them. The posts should have a plate or anchor at the bottom to keep them from being pulled out, as well as cross arms several inches below the soil surface to keep them from being worked back and forth and loosened.

Beware of rust. Use aluminum, stainless steel, brass, or bronze where possible. Ferrous metals should be galvanized, plated (cadmium) or painted with rust-inhibiting paint. Painting the hardware also makes it less obtrusive than bright unpainted metal.

Location

In planning the location of an interpretive sign you should look for safe and easy visitor access to the site. If it is a roadside sign, ensure adequate distance for deceleration from either direction and sufficient parking space to keep cars from stopping on the road. Do not require visitors to risk natural hazards such as steep trails, low branches, or poisonous plants in approaching the sign. The sign should be easy to find and view without stretching, stooping, or overexertion. It should also be visible without intruding on the scene. The subject of the message contained on the sign should be clearly and unmistakably in view. The site for the sign should not be near distracting or inappropriate features. Consider the photographers. Can they photograph the subject easily without getting unwanted buildings, utility poles, and wires in the picture? Do they have a choice of including or excluding the sign?

Protect the site by paving where necessary. Provide litter receptacles and mount signs on their own supports, not on trees or natural rock formations (Fig. 12-11).

FIG. 12-11.   Signs should be mounted on their own supports and never on trees. Gold-stream Provincial Park, British Columbia, Canada. (Photo courtesy of British Columbia Department of Recreation and Conservation.)

Maintenance

Use signs that can be maintained by "in-house" personnel whenever possible. Keep duplicates of vulnerable signs on hand for immediate replacement. If your signs are of a weathered, rustic nature, you should have a supply of weathered stock available so replacements will not look raw.

Maintenance of signs involves not only repainting, repairing, and replacing of signs but also checking the message for clarity, legibility, and visibility. Are the facts still accurate and relevant? Is there a better specimen or example to interpret or a better site from which to interpret the same one? Has the site deteriorated? Should it have a rest? All personnel in an organization should be alerted to look for and report any sign maintenance needs to the supervisor of the area.

REFERENCES

General References

Forest Service. *Sign Handbook,* USDA, FSH 7109.11. Washington, DC.

Park Practice Program. *Design.* (numerous entries). National Recreation and Park Association, National Conference on State Parks, and National Park Service. Arlington, VA.

Park Practice Program. *Grist.* (numerous entries). National Recreation and Park Association, National Conference on State Parks, and National Park Service. Arlington, VA.

References Cited

1. Birren, Faber. 1961. *Color Psychology and Color Therapy,* University Books, New Hyde Park, NY.
2. Cheek, Neil. 1972. "Today's Park Visitor: Who Is He, and What Facilities Does He Need?" paper presented at National Park Service Meeting, Denver, CO. February 1972.
3. Cooper, Glenn A. 1969. "Durable Rustic Wooden Signboards," Research Paper NC-29, North Central Forest Experiment Station, USDA Forest Service, St. Paul, MN.
4. Flesch, Rudolf. 1974. *The Art of Readable Writing,* Harper and Row, New York.
5. National Park Service. *Sign and Wayside Exhibit Handbook,* Part 2.
6. Paterson, D. G., and M. A. Tinker. 1940. *How to Make Type Readable,* Harper and Brothers, New York.

7. Schramm, Wilbur. 1971. *The Process and Effects of Mass Communication,* University of Illinois Press, Urbana.

8. Sharpe, G. W., and R. K. Searles. 1969. Directory of Interpretive Materials, The Association of Interpretive Naturalists, Derwood, MD.

9. Tinker, M. A. 1963. *Legibility of Print,* Iowa State University Press, Ames.

CHAPTER 13

INTERPRETIVE PUBLICATIONS

William W. Dunmire

Most of us in the field of park or forest interpretation have been strongly stimulated and influenced by the writing of natural history authors of the past. Who has not felt the mark of Darwin, Muir, Sigurd Olson, or Edward Abbey, to name a few, all of whom were or are interpreters *par excellence* in their own right. It is only natural for modern interpreters to turn to the medium of writing as a way of communicating with their visitors—whether it be producing a large volume about the wonders of a great natural area or a simple handout sheet on some plant or animal of their park. A further nudge toward publication comes from the prospect of having a visible interpretive product that can be fairly quickly produced and placed in the hands of park visitors.

PUBLICATION LIMITATIONS

In planning any well-rounded interpretive program, it is a cardinal rule to evaluate the media available and to select the one that most effectively can communicate each part of the park story. Publications are just one of the many tools an interpreter has to convey the message, so knowing the limitations as well as the advantages of the printed word is very important.

First, let us consider a few disadvantages of publications compared with other media.

1. Publications are a "cold" medium, lacking the warmth of a personal contact, seldom demanding visitor involvement with what is being read or, more to the point, the subject that is being taught. Yet, involvement is a critical ingredient of the learning process, especially if the learning is on a voluntary basis as is true for most park interpretation.

2. Dynamic concepts, such as geologic forces over a period of time, are difficult to convey through this static medium. Films or animated exhibits usually can do a better job when the story involves dramatic movement.
3. Publications are a one-way form of communication. Direct feedback is lacking; the interpreter has no way of evaluating on the spot whether the reader actually understood and has no possibility of changing the message to fit the audience.
4. Finally, publications too often become an overused panacea. While the public is being bombarded with self-guiding handouts, the interpreter is somewhere in the back office—preparing another publication, no doubt.

WHEN TO OPT FOR PUBLICATIONS

On the other hand, interpretive publications do have some real advantages over personal services and other media. Consider the following:

1. Publications have a potential for offering the greatest interpretive depth and detail. After all, words are read and comprehended many times faster than they are heard, and space (as for signs and exhibits) or time (as for talks) is invariably limited. Therefore, if your park story is long and complex, a booklet or book is likely to be the single best way to communicate it.
2. Publications have a take-home value; they can be read and reread at a visitor's leisure. And they can provide a handy reference during the time a visitor is in your park—especially advantageous for informational material such as maps and schedules of ongoing events (Fig. 13-1).
3. Through publications your interpretive message can be distributed widely beyond the park or forest by taking advantage of commercial outlets or local information centers. When read in advance, publications can orient and sensitize visitors to a park, helping visitors make the best use of their time after they arrive.
4. Manuscripts can be reviewed by outside experts before being committed to print. Through such scrutiny, errors are avoided and the message is improved. Yet, even after they are printed, leaflet and booklet type publications are easy to revise and update—improvements that are much more costly when dealing with films or exhibits.
5. Valuable staff time is saved at the information desk whenever publications are available that provide answers to regularly asked questions.
6. Publications sometimes are the cheapest tool in the interpreter's mixed bag. If the publication is produced for sale, it may pay for itself or even provide a small income to support some other aspect of the interpretive program. Even complimentary publications can be remarkably inexpensive per copy if the printing volume is great enough.

FIG. 13-1. An exhibit showing examples of interpretive publications in recreation areas. Interpretive Laboratory, University of Washington. (Photo by John Spring.)

7. Compared with signs, outdoor exhibits, and visitor centers, publications have virtually no adverse impact on the park environment, a factor of growing concern today on the part of park managers and the public alike in our precious natural areas. Environmentally, publications are sound, unless, of course, the information sheet or pamphlet has so little value that it ends up littering the trailside.

Publications, then, when not used as a crutch or as a substitute for more effective media are invaluable tools that can support any interpretive program. Knowing *what* they can do best, the interpreter must next be aware of the kinds of publications appropriate for distribution in a park—either those available through outside sources or those produced in conjunction with a local interpretive program (Fig. 13-2).

TYPES OF PARK-RELATED PUBLICATIONS

Information Publications

These are usually produced locally, and more often than not are given free to park visitors—free because they contain the kind of information that should be

FIG. 13-2. The publications and other materials available at this counter are keyed to the area's human history. Custer Battlefield National Monument, Montana. (Photo by Mary Minton.)

available to all visitors; and a price tag, however nominal, will automatically screen out at least a few. Informational literature should be brief, to the point, and easily understood by those who are unfamiliar with the area.

Most parks and other land-managing organizations beyond the community level have developed descriptive brochures of their area, and for good reason. Managers and interpreters alike know that the prime concern of most visitors is orientation to their unfamiliar surroundings. Visitors need to know the location of picnicking or camping sites, food service and other facilities, what there is to see and do—how best to spend their time. Brochures also should contain rules and regulations, pertaining specifically to the area, that are couched in as positive a tone as possible, for nothing turns visitors off more quickly than a barrage of formidable "don'ts" just after they arrive. The agency or organization that runs the park usually likes to have a description of its function in the brochure. This is best kept down to a brief paragraph.

A good summary of the park interpretive story also belongs in the descriptive brochure, but it should be in capsule form, just long enough to tease the visitor into wanting to learn more. Finally, if the area is large or the least bit confusing, a map is indispensable. Surveys conducted by the National Park Service have shown that visitors want a map above all else, and Park Service folders now devote up to half their space to area maps and inset maps of developed sites.

Sometimes schedules of activities conducted in the park—nature walks, film showings, museum hours, and other recreational programs—appear in the descriptive folder, but more often than not these events are subject to such frequent change that a separate handout is advisable. This can take the form of a mimeographed or printed sheet, depending on volume required and regularity of change. A number of larger parks have successfully employed a weekly or biweekly newspaper format for their activity schedules (Fig. 13-3). Whatever form the activity schedule takes, it can have a dramatic influence on program attendance and is usually much more effective than reproducing the same information on a poster or bulletin board.

Specialized information such as hunting, fishing, or boating regulations, descriptions of what to expect in the park during other seasons, or statistics relating to some park feature often is conveyed in a separate handout. Checklists of the common plants, mammals, or birds of the area are welcomed by many visitors and can best be covered on separate sheets or in pamphlets (Fig. 13-4). Here a word of caution is indicated. Don't place these special gems out where everyone can help themselves. Visitors will do so because they are free, whether or not they are interested in the subject, and they will end up unread in the trash bin. Keep a supply out of sight but handy; many will ask about such publications, and

FIG. 13-3. Many areas now use a newspaper format for describing current interpretive activities and other up-to-the-minute park information. (Photo by Charles V. Janda.)

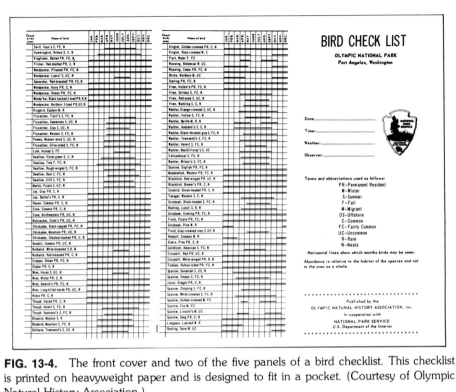

FIG. 13-4. The front cover and two of the five panels of a bird checklist. This checklist is printed on heavyweight paper and is designed to fit in a pocket. (Courtesy of Olympic Natural History Association.)

the interpreter can always follow up a visitor's questions with a handout if there is one on the subject.

Interpretive Publications

Interpretive handbooks, theme booklets, self-guiding trail and road booklets, and publications directed at a selected audience such as school children or backcountry users have room for a much more detailed treatment than do strictly informational publications. They may incorporate photographs, artwork, and other visual aids, and they often employ more than one color. Since these refinements and the characteristic greater length of text result in higher production costs, interpretive publications of this kind usually must be sold rather than given away. But the fact that they are sold gives the interpreter a solid piece of feedback; you *know* that a sales publication is going to be read if people are willing to pay for it; you can get an idea of what subjects are of most interest to your visitors when they must make a choice through their pocketbooks.

Interpretive or natural history handbooks usually present the principal themes or subjects relating to the park and cover these in separate, detailed sections. It is necessary to identify the relative importance of the various pertinent subjects, such as geologic evolution, forest succession, animal life, or human history of the area and to organize the text accordingly. If the park has one principal interpretive theme, that thread should be woven throughout the various chapters in order to communicate an overall understanding of the area.

Theme booklets focus on a specific subject such as "Wildlife of Jones Park." They have an advantage over the handbook approach in that visitors with specific interests can be selective in their reading. If native tribes of the area are their main interest, they may be unwilling to purchase a more expensive handbook containing only a single chapter on this subject, but they will cheerfully put out a dollar or two for a slimmer booklet specifically on "Indians." A further advantage is that an author for a specific subject may be easier to locate than one who is knowledgeable about the entire park story. Large parks with diverse themes do well to offer a series of subject-related natural and cultural history booklets.

Self-guiding booklets provide sequential interpretation for a specific trail or road. Descriptive paragraphs that identify the various features to be interpreted usually are keyed to numbered markers planted along the path or roadway (see Chapter 14). Another approach is to tie the text to obvious features seen along the route, such as a stream crossing or dramatic view, omitting artificial markers. Road guides sometimes use mileage distances as reference points.

The most successful self-guiding booklets incorporate a general theme that threads through the various stops along the way rather than employing a shotgun approach with unrelated subjects. A typical theme for a seacoast trail might be. "The Influence of the Ocean on the Land and Its Life." Whenever possible the text would relate each feature being described, whether it be a plant, an unusual landform, or evidence of ancient human habitation, to the effects of the ocean and its marine climate. Employing a theme has the advantage of stimulating the readers to think for themselves about the general subject as they approach each stop; it also tends to result in a more cohesive text.

The greatest pitfall in preparing self-guiding literature is allowing texts to become too wordy. Remember that, in the typical situation, one family member will be reading the text aloud to others on the trail or in their car. This takes a great deal longer than reading silently, and most groups prefer to keep moving without long stops in any one place. If the text for any one station cannot be read aloud in less than a minute, it probably is too long. Since the aim usually is to entice every group taking the self-guided route to use a booklet, it should be produced as inexpensively as possible and sold at a nominal cost (with the choice of merely borrowing the booklet), or it should be given away.

Don't Forget the Kids

Most park interpretive programs include exhibits, nature walks, and other events specially aimed at children. But too often all the literature on display at the information desk is "R-rated," restricted to adult interest only. In publications as in other interpretive media there ought to be some options for different ages. Your youngest visitors will prize coloring books on the area or subjects relating to it. The art for coloring books should be very open with lots of blank space to color in and only the barest detail that might confine or even frustrate the budding artist. Texts must be brief and simple (Fig. 13-5). Older youngsters also deserve some interpretive literature aimed at their level of reading and understanding.

salmon are sometimes caught by hungry bears

FIG. 13-5. Materials for children are lacking in most interpretive programs. The page from the coloring book above is aimed at 5- to 8-year-olds. The page from the book at right is designed for 10- to 12-year-olds. This amount of detail would prove frustrating to most younger children. The drawing above is from *Life of the Salmon;* the drawing at right is from *Fort Vancouver Discovery Book.* Both were written and illustrated by Sally Graves and Gary Machlis for the National Park Service.

The Indians of the Northwest enjoyed living here and many tribes lived good productive lives. Rivers were important routes of travel and several tribes settled by a large river upstream from where it flowed into the Pacific ocean. Among these were the Chinook and Klickitat. The Chinook traded with the Indians to the north and south. The area became a central meeting place for trading skins, shells and salmon.

Ten- to twelve-year-olds and their parents invariably are pleased when they find a booklet on the park written for fifth or sixth graders.

Writing for children is an art in itself. As Freeman Tilden has so aptly counseled, interpretation aimed at youngsters below the age of twelve should take a fundamentally different approach and not be a mere dilution of that presented to adults. When it comes to interpretive writing for kids, it is best to review your material with a grade school teacher or other educator who has professional know-how in communicating with the young.

Other Types of Publications

Postcards typically do not offer much beyond souvenir value unless the graphics and captions are carefully selected to portray and describe a scene or object especially pertinent to the park story. On the other hand, color slides of hard-to-photograph objects such as museum displays, plants, wildlife, or remote natural features are welcomed by professional educators and the general public.

Recently, demand has grown in parks for supplementary educational aids that may be purchased and taken home or to the schoolroom. Charts showing geologic time scale relationships or plant and animal life zones and distribution have their place, as do posters with a graphic interpretive message. Environmental handbooks and teaching guides that foster awareness of the world of nature and the place of humans in it are desirable for adjuncts to a collection of interpretive publications; most interpreters today recognize that their park can be a starting point for "discovering" nature.

Although phonograph records and cassette tapes go beyond the usual definition of publications, they too should be considered. The bugling of an elk, the song of a thrush, and many other sounds of nature can never effectively be described in print; yet sounds often are an integral part of the interpretive experience. Since few visitors are equipped to make their own recordings, a record or tape of park sounds with accompanying narration or text is a much appreciated sales item at the visitor center.

PUBLICATION PRODUCTION

Selecting an Author

Assuming that you have identified a real need for producing a new publication for your park, your first step is to locate an author. If the work is to be a trail guide or other brief piece of writing relating to the local area, most likely you or another staff member will be the author.

If more comprehensive work is intended, it may pay to look outside your own shop. A search in the surrounding community, paying special attention to local institutions of learning, often will reveal an expert who knows the subject, who can write effectively, and who is more than willing to make a contribution to the park by supplying a manuscript. However, it is always best to ask for a sample of the prospective author's previous writing before becoming committed. A clear understanding between the interpreter and author as to objective and style is essential, and periodic review of the manuscript wards off possible conflict after the manuscript is completed.

No matter who does the actual writing, the final responsibility for insuring accuracy, readability, and acceltable appearance of the publication always must rest with the park interpreter. That means ensuring that the subject has been thoroughly researched and that the writing is directed toward the correctly identified audience. It also means seeking impartial editing counsel once the manuscript has been prepared. The most successful authors, no matter what the field, keep tuned to suggestions of others about their writing, especially suggestions from readers who have the same general background as those who will become the final audience.

Unless the agency for which the publication is produced has an absolute rule against it, the author should be credited in print. The same is true for an illustrator or photographer. Recognition is one of the psychological rewards all people seek, and identifying the author in print provides that recognition with full credit for excellence of writing as well as responsibility for accuracy.

Effective Writing

Unfortunately, no good books or manuals exist that instruct the novice in the subject of natural history writing. Perhaps it is just as well, for good writing is an art that cannot be reduced to a mechanical formula. The best advice for a fledgling author is to read and analyze the styles of the published works of others, particularly the great natural history classics. Some general reference works on writing are found at the end of this chapter. A few ideas on writing effectively for park audiences follow:

Make a detailed outline in advance.
Arrange facts in logical order, first things first, and related things together.
Show your reader the way from one idea to another with smooth transitions.
Simplify difficult concepts by introducing them in a familiar context.
When appropriate, try to involve your readers through emotional impact.
Use personal and live verbs to convey warmth and action wherever possible; use active rather than passive words.
Don't assume that your readers have the same understanding of ecological concepts that you do and beware of using too many technical terms (which must be defined).

Break sections and paragraphs into digestible chunks.

Relate what you write to the experience and understanding of your readers.

Above all, strive for verbal crispness and an economy of words, trimming out the loose language and verbosity that always crop up in a first draft.

Your text should be in tune with contemporary interests and thinking; for example, the growing international concern for energy conservation.

Design of Publications

Too often the format and design of an interpretive publication is overlooked, and a fine piece of writing goes unread by a park visitor because of its unattractive appearance. Good design involves a clean, uncluttered look with carefully integrated text and illustrations and the conscious use of open space. A common failing of the novice is the use of too many type styles and sizes in a single publication. It is as important to seek the advice of a professional graphic designer (and to pay for it if need be) as it is to have a thorough editorial review of the text.

The appearance of the cover will have a great influence on potential buyers. We can take a cue from professional booksellers who know that eyecatching cover appeal is what puts a book in a buyer's hands (Fig. 13-6). Of course, literature that doesn't get into their hands for scanning never gets purchased—or read.

Printing

The surest way to evaluate and to select a printer is to see examples of the firm's work comparable to what you are about to publish. Always get quotes on a job from more than one printer and make certain that each quote is for an identical product.

You will have decided in advance how many to print based on your estimate of visitor demands for the publication. But it is wise to ask for quotes on a range of printing runs. You may find that the per copy cost will lower substantially if you are willing to purchase an inventory that will last several seasons. But you must take into consideration the possibility of the publication becoming obsolete or requiring updating.

Discuss with the printer in advance the options in selecting paper stock as this choice will affect both the appearance of the final product and the cost of the job. If the publication is to be carried in the field, consider using a water resistant paper. Use of recycled paper (and stating that fact somewhere on the publication) gives your reader an added message: that your park has a special concern for the conservation of natural resources.

FIG. 13-6. Eye-catching covers are very important to the success of the sales of interpretive publications. Cover courtesy of Awani Press, Fredericksburg, Texas. (Photo by John Spring.)

Use of more than one color of ink will add to production costs but may increase eye appeal and be an aid to the interpretive objective, particularly if diagrams are to be included. Although the cost of full-color illustrations has been drastically reduced over the years, few parks can afford the luxury of full-color printing. Consider the use of colored paper stock and perhaps an ink other than black if you want to give the appearance of a multicolored publication for virtually the same price as black on white.

In any case, publications must compete with other media in your interpretive budget, so keep the cost down whether it is to be sold or given away. Certainly one objective in producing a publication is to get it into the hands of as many visitors as possible, and a charge, however nominal, always has the effect of screening out potential readers.

When the printing firm has been selected, insist on reviewing a proof after it has been first typeset and also the final type and layout before the job goes into production. If the publication will have lasting value, you probably will want it copyrighted to protect you or the author from unauthorized reproduction.

Copyrighting is an inexpensive and simple process that should be accomplished promptly after your publication comes off the press. The printed publication must bear a copyright notice including the word "copyright" or symbol © followed by

FIG. 13-7. Publication sales cases must be well lighted, uncluttered, and provide easy access to the items on sale. Fort Raleigh National Historical Site, Manteo, North Carolina. (Photo by Grant W. Sharpe.)

the name of the owner and the year of publication. Normally the owner would be your agency (except for Federal agencies) or organization that produced the work. Send two copies along with an Application for Registration and a small fee to the Register of Copyrights, Library of Congress, Washington, DC 20559. For complete information, request a free copy of *General Information on Copyright* from the above address.

YOUR PUBLICATION MIX

Most park visitor centers or information stations have display space for a number of publications. Your job is to select a mix that both satisfies the reading appetite of your clientele and relates to the various interpretive themes of your park. Besides those publications that the park has produced, a well-rounded mix might include other literature that describes the park or nearby areas as well as field guides and natural and human history publications that will help enrich a visitor's understanding of the area. Some literature on general environmental themes is always appropriate. But screen out substandard items; don't let your visitor center be transformed into a bookstore.

Publications on display should be out in the open where visitors can make their own review and selection (Fig. 13-7). Visitor centers that have converted their sales counter space from glassed-in to open displays have experienced doubling and even tripling of sales, which more than offsets the occasional loss to pilferage. Displays should be well lighted and uncluttered so that visitors will be enticed into taking advantage of this important complement to park interpretive programs.

Your goal, after all, is to help visitors achieve a rewarding, meaningful, and inspirational park experience. You accomplish this through communication— communicating an understanding of the values of your park or forest area. One of the most effective tools in your bag of communication media is the printed word.

GENERAL REFERENCES

Bernstein, Theodore M. 1967. *The Careful Writer, A Modern Guide to English Usage,* Atheneum, New York.

Follett, Wilson. 1970. *Modern American Usage,* Grosset and Dunlop, New York.

Strunk, Jr., William, and E. B. White. 1978. (3rd ed.). *Elements of Style,* Macmillan, New York.

White, Jan V. 1974. "Editing by Design," *Word-and-Picture Communication for Editors and Designers,* R. R. Bowker, New York.

CHAPTER 14

SELF-GUIDED TRAILS

Grant W. Sharpe

The self-guided trail, in natural and human history interpretation, is a device that places visitors, usually in family-sized groups, in *direct contact* with the park or forest resource. A self-guided trail, in contrast to a conducted tour, means that the visitors are on their own; there is no one to guide them through the trail experience. The self-guided trail (SGT) is a meandering footpath along which the visitors' attention is drawn to interesting or unusual features that might otherwise be overlooked or not fully appreciated. Although the interpretive device used with the SGT has traditionally been a printed message, either in booklet form or on fixed signs, some SGTs are being successfully interpreted by means of audio devices.

Any short trail that provides access to a natural setting could be termed a "nature trail," even though it may lack interpretation. Adding the *in-place means of interpreting the trail-side environment* puts the trail in the self-guided category. Since not all self-guided trails deal with nature, the word has been omitted here from the chapter title. In practice the word *nature* or *history* appears in the title of most self-guided trails. Because of budget problems, lack of personnel, and its special adaptation for certain sites, the SGT has come into its own as a major component of the overall interpretive program. The SGT should not be regarded as a substitute for the conducted tour but rather as a supplement.

What is the role of the SGT in the interpretive program? What are its advantages and disadvantages? Where should it be used? Where should it not be used? This chapter will attempt to answer these questions.

ADVANTAGES OF SELF-GUIDED TRAILS

1. There may be no substitute for the friendly tutelage of the conducted tour, but personnel for such tours are often limited. The SGT releases interpretive personnel for other duties, including conducted activities in more appropriate areas. Thus, the SGT becomes a reasonable alternative to the conducted tour.
2. Visitors may use the SGT at their own convenience. There are no schedules or places to be at a certain time. This is particularly desirable for those visitors who may find it difficult or distasteful to "be on time" when on vacation. Once there, visitors can walk the trail at their own pace. This is advantageous to those with very young children, those who wish to devote time to photography or those escorting disabled visitors, as well as to those who simply prefer a leisurely pace and the company of their own thoughts.
3. The self-guided trail provides interpretation in out-of-the-way areas where it is impractical to station personnel, such as short trails leading to waterfalls, bogs, or other points of interest. Thus, the SGT serves to spread the interpretive program to remote areas.
4. Whereas the guided activity functions only when personnel are available, the SGT functions during several seasons of the year. A visitor arriving at off-seasons, such as spring or fall, or during emergencies, such as forest fires or rescues, finds some interpretation available.
5. The SGT puts large numbers of people over a trail in small groups. In the conducted walk, on the other hand, large groups of people are led over a trail week after week, and there is certain to be some detrimental site impact. Large groups cannot hear a tour guide without bunching up and overflowing the trail onto surrounding vegetation.
6. Visitors with younger children may feel the conducted walk is pitched too high for children's interest level. On the SGT parents can interpret the written words along the trail and answer questions the children may have.
7. The SGT is a simple means of admitting people to and channeling their movements through a sensitive area, such as a spectacular stand of trees, with a minimum of site alternation or development.
8. Interpretation assists in winning public support. Once established, the SGT is a quick, inexpensive way to interest and educate the public in the special values of a natural or cultural feature. Inexpensive devices such as the self-guided trail may help gain support for more ambitious programs.

DISADVANTAGES OF SELF-GUIDED TRAILS

1. The SGT story can't reveal everything, and the communication is in one direction only. There is no chance to clarify complex points. The inquisitive

visitor may be frustrated when he or she can't get an answer to a specific question.

2. The SGT with its fixed story has the impossible task of adjusting the presentation to fit the needs of all individuals. It must be geared to an average audience. Thus, it will be too elementary for some and too sophisticated for others.

3. It may be difficult to enlist and hold the interest of the visitor, as a conducted-tour guide might do.

4. There may be very little control over vandalism.

5. On the SGT vandalism may go undetected for many days, much to the annoyance of the visitor, so interpretive media on the trial must be checked and repaired frequently.

6. Because of natural phenomena, such as storms, washouts, dying trees, or even natural plant succession, a once relevant story becomes obsolete—perhaps at a faster rate than a busy interpretive staff can promptly handle.

7. The SGT has the inherent problem of having to interpret features as they appear along the trail rather than in an orderly manner as an exhibit sequence might do.

WHERE TO LOCATE THE SELF-GUIDED TRAIL

The SGT is generally located near campgrounds, lodges, visitor centers, outdoor education centers, or other places of visitor concentration. Such trails are also found along a park or forest roadway between major points of interest, giving motorists a chance to stretch their legs during the drive.

The SGT must have reasonable visitor access. Suitable parking is important, since the entrance to most trails of this type is reached by vehicle.

The best trail has features or structures that relate to significant natural history or a cultural story. A variety of habitats enhances the trail experience.

A trail's value is increased if it has a feature of special interest. Such a feature could be any of the following:

A bog, marsh, or swamp
A lake, pond, or stream
A waterfall
A sand dune
A rock outcrop, cave, or other geological formation
A fossil bed
An area with rare or unusual plants or animals
A woodland or forest with special significance
A desert community

A historical area
An archeological site
A spectacular view
An area showing human impact on the environment

The significant feature can be used as bait to lure the visitor into contact with the trail environment. The interpreter can subtly introduce the subject of plant succession or other ecological principles. The trail interpretation, if done properly, will develop an awareness of what makes up that environment.

The exciting feature is not absolutely necessary, however. By using a little imagination, the interpretive specialist can, with reason, locate an SGT almost anywhere.

The trail may have to start at a ranger station, visitor center, or other point of visitor concentration since this gives better protection from vandalism to the interpretive devices. Because of this, the best features an area has to offer are not always the ones that are interpreted.

WHERE NOT TO LOCATE THE SELF-GUIDED TRAIL

Not every site is adequate. The site may simply be too limited in resources, or it may be too isolated and too difficult to be easily reached by both visitors and staff. Perhaps the topography is too rough or parking is not available.

The SGT should not be placed in areas with fragile or irreplaceable features where constant protection is necessary or where rare wildlife species may be disturbed. Some sites prove too dangerous to use. Steep cliffs, proximity to heavily used roads, or other factors may rule out certain areas. Sites in close proximity to schools, universities, or other institutions that have physical fitness programs may also present problems as there will be those who wish to run on the trail rather than walk. Locating an SGT near a riding stable would also create difficulties if horseback riders were to use the trail. While the rider is reading the label, the horse may eat the feature being interpreted. Excessive mud or dust and manure also result from horse use of a trail, and none of these is acceptable on a foot trail used for interpretation.

All too frequently the SGT has been located on a route that ties in with another trail or road currently in use for other purposes. This often puts the users in conflict. Such sites make poor SGT locations because they are usually too wide, have exotic plants growing along them, and probably will lack the natural meandering quality of an interpretive trail. A completely new trail built specifically for interpretation is preferable. Such a trail has its own reason for existence, and that reason is to interpret natural or human history without interference from other activities.

SELF-GUIDED TRAIL THEMES

Self-guided trails usually can be classified into two main types—the general subject and the special subject trail.

The General Subject Trail

Such a trail interprets nearly everything in its path—the trees, flowers, animal dens, geological features, and even historical subjects—as they appear along the trail. It is possible to tie some of the points together, but generally the intent of this trail is primarily to bring the user's attention to features they might otherwise overlook. This is the simplest and most common type of self-guided interpretive trail.

The Special Subject or Theme Trail

Here a specific theme is followed. A fully developed interpretive program could call for several theme trails, each different, scattered throughout the area. Themes vary with the resources available: geology, plant succession, human history, marine environment, spectacular tree stands, swamp or bog habitat, and rare species are a few examples.

The decision of whether or not to make a trail a general subject or special subject trail depends on the resources available. It may be that there are several thematic trail opportunities available within the park or forest. Having a broad picture of the resources available and a plan showing where future trails might be located would assist the interpreter in choosing a theme. This avoids the task of interpreting everything that occurs along each trail. It also presents a variety of trail experiences, avoiding the claim that "if you've seen one self-guided trail, you've seen them all."

TRAIL POLICY

The self-guided trail is an educational trail designed for people who are walking. Activities such as jogging, bicycling, motorcycling, and horseback riding are incompatible. Even dog-walking creates problems. Inappropriate uses should be discouraged at the outset before conflicts arise as it may be difficult to evict nonconforming groups once they have established their use of the trail. Any promotional material related to the trail should clearly point out its purpose and objectives.

The Parking Lot

Locating the beginning or entrance to the trail may require assistance from the engineering staff. Most SGTs are reached by vehicle, which means suitable parking facilities must be considered.

A trail starting from a visitor center, picnic area, or other public site may not require new parking facilities. However, increased use of the area resulting from the SGT itself may require an expansion of existing parking space. For example, an SGT built near a campground where visitors can walk to the trail may not need its own parking lot. As other visitors discover the trail, however, additional parking may become necessary. The size of the lot has an effect on the amount of use a trail receives. Big lots not only cost more but allow more people on the trail. The trail, however, is for people to use and enjoy and should be designed to accommodate as many people as possible without causing serious impact on the resource. A decision must be made that attempts to keep these factors in balance.

Finally, thought should be given to the impact the parking lot may have on the visitor. It is the *transition* between the fast speed of the roadway or highway and the slow pace of the foot trail. Its layout requires help from the design specialist in order to help create the mood for the trail experience. Ease of entry, flow pattern, designated parking slots with suitable separation, safety for children, and general appearance must all be considered. The trail entrance should be conspicuous enough to be easily located in a sea of autos. Rest rooms, a drinking fountain, and garbage cans may also be necessary. (See Chapter 19 for further information on parking lots.)

The Entrance Sign

The materials and design of the entrance sign may be dictated by the sign policy of the agency. The sign itself should contain the name, length, walking time, and schematic drawing of the trail.

The sign should be handsome and substantial enough to convey the time and care that went into the planning of the trail. A routed wooden sign is generally most adaptable and compatible with other recreation structures as well as landscape variables.

If leaflets are used to interpret the trail, the leaflet-dispersal box and information regarding its use may be incorporated into the sign structure.

LAYING OUT THE TRAIL

The Trail Length and Design

Certain principles should be followed in laying out the self-guided trail. Visitors are usually in a strange environment and depend on the trail designer to guide them safely over the trail and back to the starting point. Such a trail should be less than a mile (1.6 km) in length, preferably a half-mile (0.8 km), but this will vary with the topographical features and the size of the available area. A short trail prevents fatigue and keeps visitor interest high. An SGT should seldom take more than 45 minutes for the visitor to complete.

A self-guided trail should, where possible, form a closed loop with the beginning and end at or very near the same location (Fig. 14-1). There are several reasons for this. First, since a loop trail brings visitors back to the starting point without retracing their route, monotony is reduced as every station is a new en-

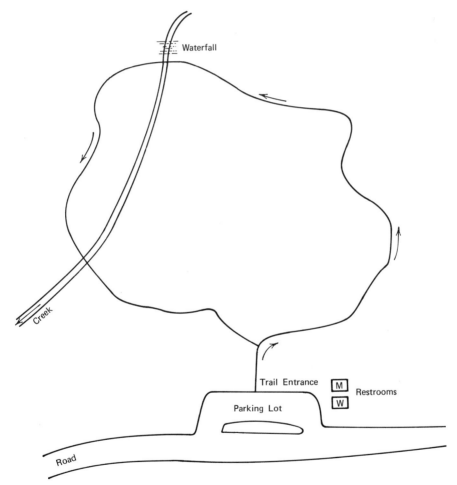

FIG. 14-1. An illustration showing a parking lot, the beginning and end of a one-way loop trail, rest rooms, and the featured resource. Note that the trail does not cross other trails, roads, or railroad tracks.

counter. Second, people are dispersed along the length of the trail without coming in contact with those who have already been to the end and have started back. Third, when the trail is of the leaflet-marker type, the leaflet is in continuous use to the end of the trail and, it is to be hoped, will be returned to the leaflet box in good condition. The trail should be one way only, the direction depending on the decision of the person writing the story.

Finally, a self-guided trail should not come in contact with any other trail. Children, often less interested than their parents, may wander ahead, and if they can't or don't read, they may take the wrong trail. For the same reason, such a trail should never cross a road or a railroad track. Cliffs and other points of danger should also be avoided. Parents should rightfully assume the trail designer has avoided dangerous features. Every effort must be made to avoid litigation because of poor trail layout.

What To Interpret—Selecting the Stations

Regardless of which kind of trail you select (general subject or special subject), you will need to assess the contents of the area carefully. Which features have visitor appeal? It may be the ordinary things that every trail can offer such as local trees and shrubs, evidence of some former occupation or use of the land, animal dens, and normal ecological influences. Perhaps it is something which only that trail can offer. A disfigured tree damaged in its youth by insects or misshapen by an ice storm in its later years might be the main interest point, or it may be a tree growing in an unusual place, such as in a crack in a cliff or on top of a large boulder. An oddity mixed in with the commonplace keeps visitor interest high. The station selected should also be permanent, that is, there should be some guarantee that the subject will be around for several years (Fig. 14-2). This rules out stations with annual plants, which have short blooming periods. These plants should be identified with temporary labels. A good rule of thumb would be: if it isn't conspicuous during the entire visitor season, don't make it a permanent station.

How do you locate the features that have potential as stations? Start at your trail entrance and head off in the general direction you feel the proposed trail will go. Then wander back and forth through the area looking for interpretive possibilities. Not all will be used, but when you finally know what the area has to offer, you can choose the best. During the reconnaissance survey make a crude map showing the locations of your interpretive subjects and identify each on the ground with a tag or stake.

Tying the Features Together

From your map you can see how these features tie together physically and perhaps gain insight into how you might put a story together, one that will unfold

FIG. 14-2. Station subjects should be permanent features, as is this western redcedar stump, a remnant from early logging. A station on Seattle City Light's self-guiding Trail of the Cedars in the Ross Lake National Recreation Area, Newhalem, Washington. (Photo by Grant W. Sharpe.)

logically as the visitor moves from station to station. Aim for 20 to 25 appropriately spaced stations in a half-mile (0.8 km) trail. This puts the stations an average of 100 ft (30 m) apart. Stations too close together cause crowding if the trail is heavily used (Fig. 14-3).

On the ground, rough-in the location of the trail with flagging ribbon; never mark the trees along the route with paint or axe blazes. This practice disfigures the trees and exposes them to insects and disease. Also, you may find later you will want to change the location of part of the trail, and these markings present a problem. A trail lined with blazed or painted trees inspires respect for neither the forest community nor the interpretive facilities, and may invite vandalism.

FIG. 14-3. Permanent stations should not be crowded together as in the above example, but should be at least 75 to 100 ft (23 to 30 m) apart. Visitors will ignore some stations when the trail gets crowded. (Photo by Grant W. Sharpe.)

Trails are more exciting if you can see only short segments at any one time. Wind the trail around rock outcrops, trees, or other features, picking a route where construction will be the easiest. Extended steep grades are undesirable. Avoid natural hazards, sensitive areas, low places where water might accumulate, and places that might easily erode. Also, avoid sharp turns where unthinking users might cut across. Keep each side of the trail loop as far from the opposite side as possible, thus discouraging short-cutting across the loop.

The trail will be used by people of all ages and should not be so steep that physical discomfort conflicts with the interpretive message. The grade, up or down, should be less than 10 percent. If disabled people will be using the trail, its grade should be less than 6 percent.

CLEARING AND CONSTRUCTING THE TRAIL

The standards for the SGT are quite different than those for hiking or horseback trails. A clearing right-of-way of 6 to 8 feet (1.8 to 2.4 m) is usually wide enough for a one-way trail. The width may need to be increased for very heavily used trails.

The trail designer must mark everything to be removed along the right-of-way and must go with the clearing crew and work directly with the foreman so that there is no misunderstanding. Clearing crews accustomed to working on horse or hiking trails or on roadside clearing may have difficulty adjusting to the SGT standards. Brush and overhanging branches must come out, but the trail designer must keep telling the foreman to "remove nothing you don't have to." Insist that the clearing crews carefully prune all limbs flush with the trunk with a pruning saw rather than with an axe. Get the point across that this is a special kind of trail and requires special treatment. The appearance of the trail will be enhanced by sawing logs which have fallen across the trail with a sloping cut that forms a wide "V." Cover up or remove all evidence of trail construction such as tree felling and clearing.

Once the clearing stage is completed, the trail tread should be considered. The actual tread width should be wide enough for two adults to walk side by side. On a one-way trail 4 feet (1.2 m) should be wide enough, but again, this will vary with use. Provision for dry footing is important to keep people from stepping off the trail in order to avoid a puddle. A layer of bark or wood chips, possibly on top of gravel, reduces soil compaction and root damage and subtly tells people where you want them to walk. The chips blend in with their surroundings much more than does a paved surface. Paving with asphalt, concrete, or soil cement may become necessary in some areas of extremely heavy use or on trails designed for persons in wheelchairs. Water bars, culverts, and drainage ditches will be needed to reduce water erosion. For wet sites corduroy, a boardwalk, or simple log bridges may be necessary. The boardwalk has been successfully used over the full length of some trails (Fig. 14-4). Should the need arise to reroute part of the trail, the boardwalk is easily removed to the new location. The old site should recover quickly, since there is little disturbance compared with the impact made by surfacing materials.

The interpretive specialist should ask for engineering help in difficult situations.

NAMING THE TRAIL

Once you have decided on the general location of the trail, have found a suitable location for the entrance, and have determined the kind of trail you want (general subject or special subject), you should think about the trail's name.

The name should add to the interest and appeal of a trail. Visitors may even show more respect for a named trail, but this is only speculation. We do know, however, that it is easier for the visitor to identify the various trails in an area if they have descriptive names.

If a trail has a particular identifying feature, this highlight should become part

FIG. 14-4.   The boardwalk is a means of giving people access to difficult-to-reach areas. It nicely defines the area where people are to walk. Bellville Municipal Park, Bellevue, Washington. (Photo by Wenonah Sharpe.)

of the name. Some examples would be: Beaver Pond Self-Guided Trail, Hogback Ridge Self-Guided Trail, Butternut Canyon Self-Guided Trail, or Old Limber Pine Self-Guided Trail. The word "nature" could be added to any of these trail names, but is not necessary.

There are times when it is suitable to name a trail after a person. This is often done to honor a local or national conservationist. When an endowment is involved, naming the trail after the benefactor may be prudent.

CHOOSING THE TYPE OF INTERPRETATION

The interpretive planner must decide which type of trail interpretation he or she will use. This decision will be most appropriate and effective after answering these questions: What has been our traditional policy on the type of interpretation? Who will be our audience? What can we expect in the way of vandalism? How much money do we have for the interpretive media? Can a leaflet box be supplied and checked frequently? What weather problems do we have? Will the sign-in-place be obtrusive? Do we feel a souvenir of the park or forest is important? Can we accommodate the renting or loaning of audio devices? What types of interpretation will best fit our story to our audience?

The next section will outline and explain several of the options available to the planner.

THE INTERPRETIVE OPTIONS FOR SELF-GUIDED TRAILS

The interpretive specialist has three main options in trail interpretation: (1) the leaflet and market trail, (2) the sign-in-place, and (3) the audio trail. Each method has advantages and disadvantages.

The Leaflet and Marker Trail

On this trail the interpretation is presented in a printed leaflet carried by the visitor and is keyed to numbered or lettered markers along the trail (Fig. 14-5).

Advantages.   Because there is only a simple marker on the trail at each station, there is less likelihood of vandalism. Also, the marker is less obtrusive. If a marker is removed, the information in the booklet is still available to the visitor. An attractive, factual, and well-organized booklet has a souvenir value and serves as a follow-up reference guide after the visitor returns home. When it is necessary to conduct a guided tour over the self-guided trail, the leader and visitors can ignore numbers or letters more easily than signs; therefore, there is less interference and distraction from a route with markers if it must also be used for conducted walks. Finally, the overall interpretive costs are usually lower on this type of trail.

Disadvantages.   In spite of its many advantages, this type of trail also has some disadvantages. A leaflet-dispersal box is required (Fig. 14-6). The leaflet box must be kept stocked, and this could require several visits from the interpretive staff each day. The funds to continue the supply of booklets may not always be available. If a charge is made for the booklets at the trail head, the coin box, unfortunately, offers a temptation. Also, if a drastic change takes place on the

FIG. 14-5. The leaflet and marker trail. The leaflet, carried by the visitor, is keyed to numbered stations along the trail. Olympic National Park, Washington. (Photo courtesy National Park Service.)

FIG. 14-6. A leaflet dispersal box at the beginning of a self-guided trail. The raised-top design protects the leaflets from the weather. Blue Ridge Parkway, Virginia. (Photo by Grant W. Sharpe.)

trail, the guide leaflet cannot be corrected until the next edition is printed. Finally, there is the possibility of theft of the leaflets as well as their potential for litter.

The Leaflet

The leaflet contains a sequence of paragraphs and illustrations. The writing should follow the principles of publications cited in Chapter 13. Leaflet quality is important if the souvenir value is to be realized and if the interpretive message is to be well received. A poor quality leaflet may create a negative attitude toward the trail.

Most SGT users are permitted free use of the trail leaflet which is returned to the box at the end of the trip. A provision is often made for purchase. Sales of the leaflet may actually help pay for the interpretive costs of the trail. Production costs will vary from a few cents per copy to about 30 cents.

The leaflet should contain a brief paragraph of welcome, a schematic drawing of the trail, perhaps a brief environmental message, and the text material. Resist the temptation to put too much material in the individual paragraphs.

Illustrations, if they are well done, can enhance the leaflet and help break the visual monotony of the text. They also can present the object being interpreted in an interesting and idealized aspect, thus arousing interest. It is possible that the visitor may not be clear about what is being discussed or what it looks like, and an illustration can be helpful (Fig. 14-7). Be careful to have clear, appealing drawings. A sophisticated text illustrated with crude drawings is a combination all too frequently encountered.

An effective way of reaching more than one age group is to write leaflets for two age levels, juniors and adults. However, naturalists on the Blue Ridge Parkway in Virginia noted that adults were using the junior guide in preference to the one for adults because it was easier to understand.

Most leaflets are approximately 5½ × 8 inches (14 × 20 cm) in size and contain three to five folded sheets of paper plus a cover.

Initially, an inexpensive mimeographed leaflet gives you a chance to experiment with wording, illustrations, and leaflet shape and may prove valuable where rapid changes are anticipated in the message. After a trial period, any confusion of word meaning could be discovered through visitor feedback. The next, corrected version can be more refined, with printed text, illustrations or photographs, and possibly the use of color.

The Marker

The marker is used with the leaflet and identifies the stations on the trail. The simplest kind is a 4 × 4 inch (10 × 10 cm) treated wooden post standing about 2 feet (0.6 m) out of the ground. It has a routed or painted letter or number on a sloped face. Where termites are found, a concrete post or galvanized pipe may be needed. Some markers are made of metal; large, smooth, rounded boulders with painted surfaces have also been used. However, the treated wooden post is generally preferred as it is inexpensive, stands out above the invading trailside vegetation, and yet seems the least obtrusive.

By using a combination of letters and numbers, the interpreter has much flexibility. The letters can be used to identify the individual stations and corresponding

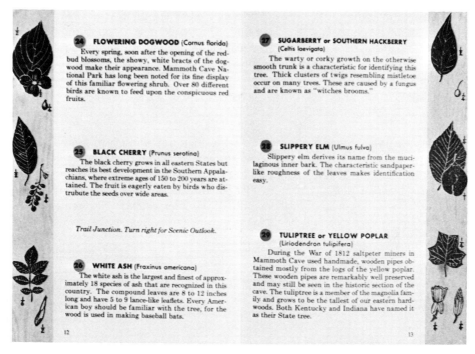

24 FLOWERING DOGWOOD (Cornus florida)

Every spring, soon after the opening of the red-bud blossoms, the showy, white bracts of the dog-wood make their appearance. Mammoth Cave National Park has long been noted for its fine display of this familiar flowering shrub. Over 80 different birds are known to feed upon the conspicuous red fruits.

25 BLACK CHERRY (Prunus serotina)

The black cherry grows in all eastern States but reaches its best development in the Southern Appalachians, where extreme ages of 150 to 200 years are attained. The fruit is eagerly eaten by birds who distrubute the seeds over wide areas.

Trail Junction. Turn right for Scenic Outlook.

26 WHITE ASH (Fraxinus americana)

The white ash is the largest and finest of approximately 18 species of ash that are recognized in this country. The compound leaves are 8 to 12 inches long and have 5 to 9 lance-like leaflets. Every American boy should be familiar with the tree, for the wood is used in making baseball bats.

12

27 SUGARBERRY or SOUTHERN HACKBERRY (Celtis laevigata)

The warty or corky growth on the otherwise smooth trunk is a characteristic for identifying this tree. Thick clusters of twigs resembling mistletoe occur on many trees. These are caused by a fungus and are known as "witches brooms."

28 SLIPPERY ELM (Ulmus fulva)

Slippery elm derives its name from the mucilaginous inner bark. The characteristic sandpaper-like roughness of the leaves makes identification easy.

29 TULIPTREE or YELLOW POPLAR (Liriodendron tulipifera)

During the War of 1812 saltpeter miners in Mammoth Cave used handmade, wooden pipes obtained mostly from the logs of the yellow poplar. These wooden pipes are remarkably well preserved and may still be seen in the historic section of the cave. The tuliptree is a member of the magnolia family and grows to be the tallest of our eastern hardwoods. Both Kentucky and Indiana have named it as their State tree.

13

FIG. 14-7. Short paragraphs, open space, and good illustrations enhance the appearance and readability of a trail leaflet. This example is from Mammoth Cave National Park, Kentucky. (Photo by John Spring.)

paragraphs in the guide leaflet; numbers can be used on smaller markers to identify plants keyed to a list at the end of the leaflet.

The Sign-in-Place Trail

On this trail the interpretive story appears permanently on fixed signs along the trail at the selected stations. The wording and artwork are usually on treated paper, plastic, wood, metal, or a combination of these. With frequent inspection and modest maintenance, signs should last several years. The message should be brief and easy to read with only one subject per sign. Follow the principles for signs cited in Chapter 12.

Advantages. When well done, interpretive signs are impressive and give the trail a high-quality appearance (Fig. 14-8). The visitor may respond more to the importance of the trail and its purpose. Should a change in the message be necessary, only that station needs to be altered. The same correction may not be so easily made in a leaflet.

The sign-in-place trail may be necessary if there is no means of keeping a leaflet-dispersal box supplied.

Disadvantages. Signs are more subject to theft and vandalism than a station marker. Weathering is a problem in most climates but certainly must be taken into consideration in severe climates if the sign is to be left out all winter. A sign that is removed or damaged leaves that station without interpretation. The trail must be inspected regularly if the integrity of the interpretation is to remain high. On the sign-in-place trail, interpretation is generally more expensive to install and maintain than on a leaflet trail.

Finally, there is more environmental impact at the station itself, since groups of people will bunch up to read the sign. In the leaflet and marker system the message can be read without standing in a particular spot, and this helps to lessen visitor impact on the site.

Design and Construction

All the interpretive signs along the trail should be of the same material, shape, and size. A standardized format keeps costs down and creates a sense of unity and coherence. The posts should be made of metal or of wood treated with preservative. The sign and post should complement the trail environment. The post can be stabilized in the ground with cross rods and lifting can be made difficult by attaching a flange to the bottom.

Identification Labels

As stated above, only the permanent stations should have interpretive signs. Seasonal features, such as blooming wildflowers, should be cited with simple, temporary labels that are changed frequently to correspond with the blooming period. The common and scientific names are usually sufficient for identification labels.

The Audio Trail

The audio trail is an interesting innovation. It currently offers two methods of interpretation, and no doubt others will be forthcoming.

One of the present methods is the fixed-listening station or talking label trail where each station is equipped with an audio device. The visitor activates the

FIG. 14-8. The sign-in-place trail, utilizing a metal post placed 3 ft (0.9 m) in the ground. A well-designed label and holder give the trail a high-quality appearance. Seattle City Light's Trail of the Cedars, Ross Lake National Recreation Area, Newhalem, Washington. (Photo by Grant W. Sharpe.)

station by pushing a button or inserting a rented key. This talking label essentially replaces the sign-in-place.

In the second method, visitors carry a hand-operated cassette player which they activate when they reach the appropriate station. In a sense the cassette player is a substitute for the printed leaflet.

Advantages.　The audio trail has numerous advantages over other interpretive options. One can interject special voices, music, and sound effects. A well-done listening station creates a mood, involves the listener, and can be heard by sightless persons. It is particularly effective on historical trails. Not only is a greater volume of interpretive information possible, but the interpreter's voice continues to stay fresh after many hours of use.

Disadvantages. With this type of interpretation there is no opportunity for illustrations. Breakdowns, thefts, or damage to the equipment can be a problem. If fixed-listening stations are used, the cost is quite high, since each station must have a message-repeating device. If cassettes are used, the initial cost is reduced considerably, but there is the nuisance of equipment rental and maintenance. This subject is treated in greater detail in Chapter 11, "The Use of Audio Devices."

Which Type To Choose

Through the media selection process you have decided to use a self-guided trail. Now you must choose a specific method of interpretation for that trail. Your options are: (1) leaflet and marker, (2) sign in place, (3) audio trail (talking labels), and (4) audio trail (portable cassette). The advantages and disadvantages of each can be quantified relative to one another. Figure 14-9 is a means of comparing the four trail media. The values cited are for a temperate zone, forest trail in northwestern United States. These values may change from region to region, making a reevaluation necessary.

WRITING THE INTERPRETIVE TEXT

Whichever of the above options is selected, someone has to write the interpretive text. The wording of self-guided material may sound simple and look easy to write, but it isn't. First, the interpretive specialist cannot be an expert on everything found along or seen from the trail. Second, the easily understood, precise language needed cannot be forthcoming without numerous rewrites. Considerable time must be set aside for the research, formulation, and completion of artwork needed for each station.

Once you have settled on your route and station locations, visit each stop and rough out notes on the site. Why did you select *this* station? Probably the reason you wanted to stop at this particular spot is your title or headline for the station. Here are some examples of station titles:

LIGHTNING STRUCK HERE!
EASTERN HEMLOCK
GLACIAL ERRATIC

	Leaflet and marker	Sign—in—place	Audio (talking label)	Audio portable cassette)
Initial cost	4	2	1	3
Vandalism	3	1	2	4
Subject to weathering	3	1	2	4
Litter potential of the media	1	4	4	4
Potential for site deterioration	3	1	1	4
Aesthetic intrusion	4	2	1	4
Souvenir value of the media	4	1	1	2
Maintenance problem	4	1	1	2
Illustrates progress	2	4	3	1
Easily modified	1	3	4	2
Stocking	1	4	4	4
Distribution	4	4	4	1
Availability (sunup to sundown)	3	4	4	1
Attention span of visitor	3	3	4	4
Self—pacing factor	4	4	1	2
	49	39	37	47

Interpretive Trail Options

Scale
Worst — 1   2   3   4 — Best

FIG. 14-9. A numerical comparison of several factors to be considered when choosing one of the four trail media options. In this hypothetical example the leaflet and marker type trail was the first choice.

ARIZONA ROSE
FOREST GIANT
PORCUPINE DAMAGE
HOMESTEADERS LIVED HERE
NATURE'S SOIL FACTORY
LIFE IN A SWAMPY POND

Next, what can you tell the visitor that is interesting or unusual about the stop? It is best to stick to one broad subject area at each station. One or two facts will do. Remember also to avoid duplication with other stops along the trail. Limit yourself to 40 or 50 words.

The material must be accurate in every detail—facts, spelling, punctuation— and must avoid technical jargon and clichés.

Unfortunately, it is not always possible to have the story unfold in the order you wish, since the material does not always occur in the appropriate order. Then too, the interpreter does not always know in advance what the visitors will find most interesting; nor will he or she be sure what the visitor wants to know about each station.

A simple technique to get visitor reaction is to invite them over your roughed-out trail, read the material you have written, and ask for comment. See if they easily understand what you are trying to say. At this stage you still have time to make changes in the trail's interpretation.

Errors creep in, even in the final version of your text material. Get others in your own organization to review your writing (Fig. 14-10). Even after several

FIG. 14-10. The interpretive specialist cannot be a specialist in everything. Here a team of Forest Service personnel assist in the final wording of a label on a new self-guided trail. Ottawa National Forest, Michigan. (Photo by Grant W. Sharpe.)

reviews some errors may remain undetected. Find someone with editorial skills for a final proofreading.

FILLERS

Occasionally you will need a filler station to plug a long gap in the trail where there is not a major feature to interpret. Visitors need assurance that they are on the right trail, and fillers are used to give them the reinforcement they need. Here is a good opportunity to mention local animals even though visitors may have only a slight chance of seeing them along the trail.

One filler could be on larger mammals, another one on the smaller mammals frequenting the area. Just knowing that they, the visitors, are temporarily invading the habitat of a particular animal enhances their experience.

An interesting filler can be made on birds even though there may be no obvious evidence of their presence. The bird filler may do one of several things: it may ask the visitor to stop and listen, it may list and illustrate a few common birds found along the trail, or it may indicate that this place is the spring nesting site of birds that winter hundreds of miles from there.

Still another filler could be on climate and weather; for example, a description of what a station looks like in the middle of winter would intrigue summer visitors.

PLACING THE MARKERS OR SIGNS

Again, the trail designer must be there when the holes are dug and markers or signs are planted (Fig. 14-11). Their location is important in telling the story. They must be oriented perfectly so there is no misunderstanding about what is being interpreted. The height above ground of the markers or signs should be uniform throughout.

TRAIL FURNITURE

Many people appreciate an opportunityhto sit and rest somewhere along the trail. This may be at a view station, a bird listening point, or at the top of a rise.

There is also good evidence to show that people remember the information at those stations where they were able to sit while reading. Obviously you cannot provide a seat at every station; however, if you have a point that you wish to emphasize, it should be made at a station where a bench is provided.

Simple benches of hewn logs are appropriate, although more formal designs are sometimes used (Fig. 19-9 page 434).

FIG. 14-11. The trail planner, at left, instructs the trail crew in the exact location of the first station on a self-guided trail. Entrance to Seattle City Light's Trail of the Cedars self-guided trail, Ross Lake National Recreation Area, Newhalem, Washington. (Photo by Grant W. Sharpe.)

MAINTENANCE

After the trail is built someone must be responsible for it. Though this may sound obvious, it is a task that frequently gets slighted. Maintenance on a self-guided trail includes more than the clearing of interfering brush and fallen trees and the upkeep of the tread, drainage devices, and footbridges. It should include once-a-day inspection of the trail to pick up litter and to look for any evidence of vandalism and other depreciative uses of the trail. Evidence of shortcutting should be erased with barriers and plantings. Defaced signs and markers should be replaced immediately. Daily patrol of the trail is mandatory if the trail is to fulfill its proper role as an interpretive device. Ease of maintenance is another reason the trail should be less than one mile (1.6 km) in length.

INTERPRETIVE TRAILS AND DISABLED VISITORS

The terms "disabled" and "handicapped" cover a wide spectrum of disabilities and a bewildering range of attitudes and capabilities. A specialized trail set aside

FIG. 14-12. By the addition of a few simple features the self-guided trail becomes available to several user groups. The special fence shown here makes the trail available to sightless people, and the paved surface and easy grade make it available to people in wheelchairs. (Photo courtesy of Pocahontas State Park, Virginia.)

for those visitors will seldom be successful. There are several reasons for this. The title may offend some and embarrass others. More importantly, the needs of the mentally or physically disabled vary greatly and are sometimes in direct conflict with one another. For example, sightless people do not want to be overprotected. (This cry is heard frequently from other special user groups as well.) Persons in wheelchairs, on the other hand, must have a paved surface on which to travel, increased trail widths, decreased grades, and special rest room access and facilities. Drinking fountains of the correct height should be available also.

Find out the potential use of your trail by these different types of users and check to see if other trails that incorporate features helpful to the disabled are available in your region (Fig. 14-12).

Supporting groups might be willing to help with both research and financing, but be sure that they are well-informed in addition to being well meaning. For instance, the use of braille comes to mind when considering interpretation for the sightless, yet only 5 to 10 percent of the blind can read braille. Another common mistake is remote location; these trails should be near urban areas or in an area of very high visitation if they are to receive much use.

You can make your trail suitable for most of the disabled by simply modifying some of its features. Perhaps you will have the funds and know-how to construct an innovative trail, a "special" trail, such as the "Touch and See Nature Trail" in the National Arboretum in Washington, D.C. It is strongly recommended that the interpreter planner for such a specialized trail seek professional guidance to serve the particular group in the best way possible. Remember also, this type of trail receives considerable publicity and for this reason also should be most carefully planned.

In any case, inform yourself of the needs of this group of users and keep abreast of the current developments in this field.

GENERAL REFERENCES

Ashbaugh, Byron L., and Raymond J. Kordish. 1971. *Trail Planning and Layout,* National Audubon Society, New York.

Beechel, Jacque. 1975. *Interpretation for Handicapped Persons, A Handbook For Outdoor Recreation Personnel.* National Park Service Cooperative Park Studies Unit, College of Forest Resources, University of Washington, Seattle.

Cooper, Glenn A. *Durable Rustic Wooden Signboards,* North Central Forest Experiment Station, St. Paul, Minnesota, 150 pp., illus., USDA Forest Service Research Paper NC-29.

Sharpe, Grant W., and Paul McIntosh. 1970. *Esthetics VS Athletics on the Arbo-*

retum Nature Trail, Arboretum Bulletin, University of Washington Arboretum Foundation. Seattle.

USDA Forest Service. 1964. *Developing the Self-Guiding Trail in the National Forests,* Superintendent of Documents, U.S. Government Printing Office, Washington, DC, Miscellaneous Publication 968.

CHAPTER 15

SELF-GUIDED AUTO TOURS

Gary B. Wetterberg

The self-guided auto tour, as used in interpretation, is a device that permits family-sized groups to experience *widely distributed* park or forest resources in the privacy of their own automobile. This device can be used by the interpretive specialist to satisfy visitor objectives such as orientation, heightened awareness, or enjoyment. It can also be used to achieve management goals such as distribution of visitor use patterns over a large area.

Self-guided auto tours (SGATs) take advantage of the fact that we live in a highly mobile society. The ORRRC Report showed that automobile driving for sightseeing and relaxation was the major recreation activity of the American public and that it would probably remain as one of the most popular recreation activities at least until the year 2000.[4] The SGAT capitalizes on this fact for relatively little cost to the interpretive specialist.

As the name implies, a self-guided auto tour is one in which the visitors, in their own car and at their own pace, experience an area together. Interpretation is carried out by use of leaflets, signs, or audio devices that the visitors either take along with them, or that are placed at strategic locations along the route they travel.

What are the advantages and disadvantages of a self-guided auto tour? What kinds are there, and what are the options available for use by the interpretive specialist who wishes to employ this device? These are some of the questions this chapter will attempt to answer.

ADVANTAGES AND
DISADVANTAGES OF SELF-GUIDED AUTO TOURS

Many of the advantages and disadvantages mentioned in the chapter on Self-Guided Trails apply equally to the self-guided auto tour. Motor tours, however, have some of their own characteristics.

Advantages

1. The SGAT is nondestructive of resources if existing roads are used.
2. A self-guided auto tour can fulfill a primary visitor need by providing initial, broad exposure to an area. By utilizing this device, the interpretive specialist can reach a very high number of visitors, and provide a low-cost substitute for face-to-face contact by salaried personnel.
3. The SGAT would be easy to inspect for vandalism, since all of the markers or signs would be seen from a motor vehicle during routine site inspections.
4. The SGAT encourages family participation and provides the opportunity for the social experience of being together.
5. Visitors can use the SGAT at their leisure. They can stop to take photographs or to picnic along the way. They also can haul all of their creature comforts such as their hibachi grills and portable tables with them.
6. Handicapped visitors can participate.
7. A SGAT, either with audio devices or with brochures, can be multilingual. This is especially important if used in countries where a large percentage of the visitors do not speak the national language, yet may visit by car.
8. The visitors are comfortably seated in their cars, rather than on hard benches or standing on their feet.
9. Often, it is possible to utilize the same tour by snowmobiles or cross-country skiers during the off-season.
10. The SGAT provides an opportunity for a holistic approach to interpretation. For example, varied glacial or volcanic features that are spread over a wide area can be described. Items of interest outside of your area of jurisdiction can be mentioned, if seen from the road and needed to complete the story.

Disadvantages

1. Roadside marker posts or signs are subject to vandalism.
2. Brochures, if used, may cause a widespread litter problem, especially if unimaginative or poorly written.
3. If the visitor is made aware of potentially hazardous attractions such as an

old mine shaft, or birds' nests along steep cliffs, the agency that provides the SGAT may be liable for injuries incurred. Warnings about hazards must be included.

4. Winter snow removal may knock down marker posts.
5. If stopping points are used, traffic congestion may occur.

KINDS OF SELF-GUIDED AUTO TOURS

As in self-guided trails, there are two categories of self-guided auto tours; the general subject tour and the special subject tour.

General Subject Tour

The general subject tour provides a broad orientation for the visitor. It may include descriptions of geologic, historic, and scenic highlights. Examples of this category would include the Beartooth Country Tour in Montana and Wyoming, the Ajo Mountain Drive in Arizona, and the Cades Cove Tour in the Great Smoky Mountains National Park. General subject SGATs are by far the most commonly used type of motor tour.

Special Subject Tour

The special subject tour has information points oriented around one theme. Examples of this category would include the Bessey Nursery and Plantation Tour in Nebraska, the Georgia Leaf Tour, the Tour of Handmade Glass Factories in West Virginia, and the Ruby River—Gravelly Mountain Range Tour in Montana.

The choice of tour type depends primarily on local conditions, visitor needs, and administrative objectives.

DESIGNING THE SELF-GUIDED AUTO TOUR

First Considerations

Objectives. In the overall interpretive plan for an area, the use of a SGAT may or may not be desirable. The interpretive specialists must first define what they want to accomplish. Examples of some objectives might include: (1) to demonstrate the relationship between altitude and vegetation types, (2) to encourage visitor use of certain roads, and (3) to describe an area's mining history to visitors. The specialists should search for the optimum combination of interpretive devices available to achieve their objectives.

In several of the U.S. National Parks, the use of the private automobile has become a major problem.[1] In many other recreation areas the use of the automobile is becoming less and less compatible with management goals. In instances like these, the specialists should carefully weigh their objectives. If, for example, one objective is to provide a broad orientation to the great majority of park visitors who simply wish a quick drive-through to say they have "been there," the SGAT, if well designed, could easily and efficiently be utilized. If the automobile is eliminated in parts of some parks, the interpretive resource inventory, which should be the basis for all interpretive work, can be adapted to use in conjunction with mass public conveyances such as monorails or buses. Although these would not be self-guided, in terms of the visitors driving themselves, the objective of broad orientation could still be met.

Maintenance. If you can't maintain the self-guided auto tour once it is built, don't build it. Little maintenance is required for a SGAT compared to a major facility such as a visitor center. Still, signs or marker posts, if used, must be kept in good condition. Fast growing vegetation may require monthly clearance to keep views open. As nature tries to cover up small roadside markers, it is often necessary to remove brush. If audio devices are employed with the SGAT, it is necessary to keep the equipment and tapes in good condition.

Location. How does the interpretive specialist locate a SGAT? One method of auto tour location has been described in detail for Eagle County, Colorado.[8] Although the inventory checklists in that study are particular to that area, the procedure followed is broadly applicable, and includes the following:

Inventory. Investigate, map, and tabulate resources such as waterfalls, caves, sand dunes, ghost towns, petroglyphs, legends, and volcanic craters. This inventory can also be a basis for other interpretive work and should form part of the overall interpretive master plan.

Overlays. A good way to visually collate the inventory is to categorize the resources (water, historical, geologic, etc.), and plot them on overlays of a base map. This will help determine concentration zones of interpretive resources.

Road Selection. In contrast to trails, roads can seldom be constructed for the sole purpose of interpretation. Reliance must usually be placed on existing roads. Parking pulloffs, if necessary, frequently do not coincide with features to be interpreted, or else they are located where vehicles must cross on-coming traffic to reach them.

The length of the road selected is important. Depending on the terrain, SGATs that are greater than 100 miles (161 km) can easily fatigue visitors. It's better to keep visitors interested with a lively presentation than to physically and mentally wear them down. Remember, they will not just be reading or listening to your presentation, they will also be driving and watching out for other vehicles.

If the drive is to be a *general subject* type, an existing road that transects a good variety of the concentration zones as determined on the overlays, should be selected.

If it is to be a *special subject* tour, such as one dealing only with ghost towns, select the road that provides the most opportunity to see these features.

Roads Not To Select.   Not all roads or highways have a potential for self-guided auto tours. Some simply do not have features which can be interestingly interpreted. A SGAT should not be considered on a freeway or in areas where heavy traffic congestion already exists. Roads with heavy trucking and dust are only marginally acceptable.

Features To Interpret

Which features along a selected road should be interpreted to visitors? This is perhaps the most subjective decision interpretive specialists will have to make when preparing a SGAT. In general, the interpretive planners must use their professional judgment to select those features that best tell the complete story in accordance with the tour objectives. Since local conditions and objectives may vary widely, no specific guidelines can be set. The superlatives (tallest, smallest, highest, etc.) will often be included. However, the specialists should remember that if the auto tour attracts users from other parts of the country, items that are commonplace to local residents may be of great interest to visitors.

Wherever possible, the features should appeal to more than just the sense of sight. People who can smell the rotting logs of a trapper's cabin, hear the continuous whirring sound of mine air vents from deep within a mountain, or taste the crystalline salt of a natural sodium chloride bed, are apt to remember them.

If stops are used, they should not be encouraged in ecologically fragile areas. For example, along portions of the Trail Ridge Road Auto Tour in Rocky Mountain National Park, visitors heavily trampled the delicate alpine flora and as a result special footpaths had to be constructed.

Naming the Tour

Self-guided auto tours should have a name that will help the visitor remember the area and, ideally, serve as a reference for tying the interpretive story together.

If it is a general subject tour, this gives a wide range of possibilities. Some examples would include: The Round-the-Island Guide to Oahu in Hawaii, and the Elkhorn Drive in Oregon.

The name of a special subject tour would most likely include that subject. For example: the Cactus Forest Drive in Arizona, the Petroglyph Loop Trip in California, and the Battlefields-Around-Fredericksburg Tour in Virginia.

INTERPRETIVE OPTIONS FOR THE SELF-GUIDED AUTO TOUR

Several alternatives are available to interpretive planners designing a self-guided auto tour. The options are: sign and pulloff, leaflet and marker post, and various audio devices. The ultimate choice depends on the available finances and local suitability.

Sign and Pulloff

This type of auto tour has been the traditional approach and utilizes interpretive signs at roadside pulloffs. It is probably the least desirable method of auto tour interpretation.

Advantages.   A flashy set of signs may be an impressive showpiece and indicate that someone is doing something. Since signs certainly arouse awareness, this may be a good way to gain public credibility in a newly established area. The pulloff for parking and reading the sign provides a place for the visitor to rest (Fig. 15-1).

FIG. 15-1.   An elaborate roadside interpretive sign and pulloff in Wind Cave National Park, South Dakota. (Photo by Grant W. Sharpe.)

Disadvantages. Signs, especially those along roadsides, present several problems to the interpretive specialist. They may obscure the scenery, they are costly, and they are particularly subject to vandalism. Visitors stopping to read the signs during peak hours can cause traffic congestion.

Although signs may arouse public awareness, they are not necessarily read. In a study made in Yellowstone National Park, it was estimated that only about 10 percent of the visitors stopped at wayside exhibits and less than half of these read the signs.[2]

The Sign. Materials, methods of construction, and texts are described in the chapter on Signs and Labels.

The Pulloff. The tour should be designed so that the pulloffs are either on the side of the road of normal traffic flow, or that the pulloff be so located as to minimize the risk involved for the visitor in crossing traffic lanes.

The interpretive specialist, except when in the fortunate position of advising in the design of a new road, may have to depend on existing pulloffs. The pulloff should accommodate between 2 and 10 cars, depending on the popularity of the feature and its distance from the road. The interpretive signs should be placed so that they are not obscured by visitors in several cars stopping simultaneously to read them.

At some parking pulloffs, sighting devices may be necessary. Simple devices could include a length of brass pipe on a swivel (Fig. 15-2) or lines or arrows on a flat board (Fig. 15-3).

Leaflet and Marker Post

The most common type of auto tour in use today involves a printed leaflet or brochure that is keyed to numbered posts along the road. In some instances, pulloffs are available for parking.

Advantages. This method of SGAT has several advantages. It is the least expensive to prepare and to operate. More detail can be provided in the pamphlets than on the signs, and the visitor can keep the leaflet as a souvenir of the trip (Fig. 15-4). It is nonrestrictive in the sense that the interpretive specialist does not have to rely on interpretive features that correspond to existing pulloffs. In large areas, such as a national park, one booklet can be distributed that describes several SGATs, from which the visitors can select one that meets their needs and interests.

Disadvantages. This method of SGAT has many of the same disadvantages described in Chapter 14 for the leaflet and marker trail including a potential litter

FIG. 15-2.   A sighting device made of brass pipe mounted on a swivel. The far side of the pipe is brought to rest on notches that are identified with the name of the feature in the distance. Grand Canyon National Park, Arizona. (Photo by Grant W. Sharpe.)

problem and the impersonal coldness of a written message. In addition, an employee or some device must be used to distribute the leaflet.

The Leaflet.   The text in the leaflet should present more than isolated facts. It should adequately answer the standard five W's (Who, What, Where, When, Why), as well as point out features that appeal to the five senses. In doing this, analogies and questions can be utilized to break up the reading or listening, yet an attempt should be made to tie together principles and present a structure or framework for the whole story.

The cover of the leaflet should be attractive, utilizing either drawings or photographs that illustrate the theme of the tour (Fig. 15-5). The message in the brochure should be accurate, provocative, and of interest to the whole family. Research has shown that visitor interest is high when dramatic or violent events, such as lightning fires, mine disasters, and volcanic activity are presented.[7] If the

FIG. 15-3. A simple flat board sighting device. The arrows and names of peaks are cut into the wood with a hand router. Waterton Lakes National Park, Alberta. (Photo by Grant W. Sharpe.)

mother and younger generation find the message interesting and intriguing, the father will be encouraged to participate.

A map is usually essential. It serves as a continuous source of orientation during the tour, and as a handy reference for the visitors to take with them.

The Markers. The markers designating stopping points, or features to be interpreted without stopping, should be unobtrusive yet readily visible. Ideally, they will in some way be tied in with the drive theme. For example, the Moffat Road Auto Tour in Colorado follows an old railroad grade, and the stops are marked by small, numbered, locomotive profiles, each bolted to a post (Fig. 15-6). The route of the Old West Trail, which covers portions of five states, is marked by an easily recognizable buffalo head profile. Markers along the Elkhorn Drive, which

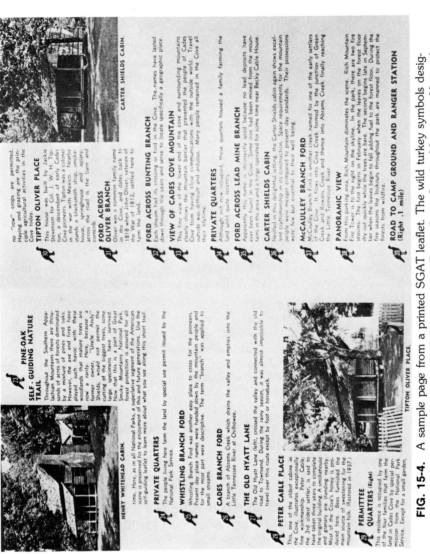

FIG. 15-4. A sample page from a printed SGAT leaflet. The wild turkey symbols designate each stop. Cades Cove Self-Guiding Auto Tour, Great Smoky Mountains National Park, Tennessee. (Photo by John Spring.)

FIG. 15-5. Four SGAT leaflets illustrating the use of photographs or drawings on the cover. (Photo by Gary B. Wetterberg.)

was designed to interpret the scenery, history, and geology of Oregon's Elkhorn Range, are readily identified by visitors because each has a simple, yet bold, elkhead outline.

If the markers are used to indicate a stopping point at a roadside pulloff, they should be placed at the approach of the pulloff and not within it, since one car could obscure the stop indicator (Fig. 15-7).

Audio Devices

Studies have shown that visitor interest is greater when information is heard than when it is read.[3, 6] Interpretive specialists can take advantage of this fact in designing the SGAT.

Audio devices, their advantages and disadvantages, and the equipment available today, are described in Chapter 11. They offer the interpretive specialist who is preparing a SGAT the closest possible approximation of personally conducted interpretation.

Cassette Tapes. Cassette tours have met with varying degrees of success. They have been tried in several cities, as well as some of the heavily visited

FIG. 15-6. Stop number 7 on an historical railroad route in Colorado which is used as a SGAT. Each stop is identified with the appropriate number and the railroad engine motif. The simple illustration is bolted to a post. (Photo by Gary B. Wetterberg.)

national parks. There are even "package" auto tape tours now available that enable the visitor to cover extensive areas in the state of California and include car rental and accommodations. Most interpretive specialists, however, will not be involved in such a grandiose setup.

Since traffic conditions may vary, it is unrealistic to have the tape continuously playing while the visitor tries to maintain an even speed. Marked posts along the route should remind the visitors to turn on the player, and the narrator should tell them to turn it off when each segment of the message is completed.

Advantages. A cassette tape SGAT in which the visitor uses a portable tape player has many advantages. Because the tape does not have to be read, visitors can look at the attractions (and, pay attention to the road), while they are being

FIG. 15-7. A SGAT marker identifying the site and station number. The marker is placed at the approach to the pulloff so that a parked auto cannot block the sign. Seventeen-Mile Drive, Carmel, California. (Photo by Grant W. Sharpe.)

described. The tapes can be tailored to specific interest groups such as rock hounds, birdwatchers, or special language groups. Character voices can be used to add a touch of historic reality, and sound effects can be used. Cassette tapes are easier to update than a printed brochure, and a substantial amount of detailed information can be presented without fatiguing the visitor. What is more, conscious visitor involvement is necessary as they turn the tape player on and off at each marker along the SGAT route.

Disadvantages. The biggest disadvantage using the cassette tape player for a SGAT is distribution and collection. If you wish to have an auto tour of this type you will probably need salaried personnel to handle this function. In an experimental SGAT in the northern Cascades of Washington State, equipment was returned to a ranger residence after-hours, and in some cases, kept overnight but handed in the next day. This had not been anticipated in the experiment. It seems visitors are often capricious and resent the structuring of their time that the return of the cassette tape player imposes. Since they may suddenly become involved in a long hike, or decide to spend the night, provision must be made for after-hours return.

Taped SGATs have additional disadvantages. The visitors can't skim a tape to pick out the main points and then move on as they might with a brochure or sign. The players are subject to breakdowns and battery failure. Also, the visitors cannot ask the tape questions. Unless sales arrangements are made, the visitors cannot take the tapes home with them as a reference or souvenir.

To avoid unnecessary risks with the tape players and tapes, cassette auto tours are best suited either to dead-end roads or else to loop roads, which do not offer the temptation of leaving the area before returning the equipment. Additionally a deposit could be required that would be sufficient to replace what is lost.

Theft does not seem to be a problem if common sense is used. In an experiment on the Siuslaw National Forest in Oregon, the Forest Service issued tape players, without charge, hundreds of times on a self-guided nature trail without losing any. A member of each group was asked only to sign a receipt and give his or her car license number. On the Mt. Baker—Snoqualmie National Forest in Washington, the Forest Service used the same procedure in a SGAT situation where the visitors could have easily driven by the distribution point without notice, yet none of the tape players was lost or damaged.[6]

Sequenced Radio Transmitters. Low-power radio transmitters are now commercially available. These transmitters can be operated manually by using a microphone, or automatically by using tape repeaters. The entire apparatus, including its 12-volt battery, occupies about two cubic feet (.06m³), and is capable of transmitting signals directly to car radios on the standard broadcast band. If the transmitters are located at intervals along a road, or at turnout points, the visitors can be alerted by signs to the correct frequency and tune in the interpretive message while driving along. Since the broadcast radius is quite limited, the maximum length of the message would be inversely proportional to the traveling speed of the vehicle.

Advantages.   Radio transmitters, as used in a self-guided auto tour, have many of the same advantages as cassette tape players. If the transmitters are well concealed, vandalism would be negligible. The necessity of distribution and collection of equipment, which is the biggest disadvantage with the cassette tape players, does not exist with the interval transmitter SGAT.

Although the initial purchasing and installation cost of radio transmitting equipment may seem prohibitive, it is not as expensive in the long run as one might expect. In an area studied on the Black Hills National Forest in South Dakota, the cost per visitor contact of the interval transmitter SGAT would be only slightly more than that of the leaflet and marker posts, yet the radio would probably reach more visitors.[5]

Disadvantages.   Radio transmitting equipment as utilized in the self-guided auto tour has certain disadvantages. Climate fluctuations and physiographic features can seriously affect transmission. The ranges of the spaced transmitters must not be allowed to overlap. This may be a problem in flat country and could result in the simultaneous reception of two or more messages. Finally, the interpretive story does not reach visitors who do not have car radios or other portable receivers with them.

SUMMARY

The self-guided auto tour is an interpretive device that permits family sized groups to experience an area in the privacy and comfort of their own automobile.

The interpretive specialist, when using a SGAT, takes advantage of the fact that the automobile is the conveyance of most visitors to parks, forests, and cities. The SGAT can help to penetrate the automobile's relative isolation without disrupting its privacy. As a result, visitors using the SGAT, especially for their initial broad orientation to an area, may become interested in participating in other more localized interpretive activities.

REFERENCES CITED

1. Conservation Foundation. 1972. *National Parks for the Future,* Conservation Foundation, Washington, DC.
2. McDonald, Arthur L. 1969. "Final report to the National Park Service, Yellowstone Park," Mimeographed paper from Psychology Department, Montana State University, Boseman.
3. Mahaffey, Ben D. 1969. *Relative Effectiveness and Visitor Preference of Three Audio-Visual Media For Interpretation of an Historic Area,* Dept. Report 1, Texas Agr. Exp. Sta. Texas A. & M. University, College Station.
4. ORRRC 1962. *Outdoor Recreation for America—An Introduction With Summary of Recommendations,* Outdoor Recreation Resources Review Commission, U.S. Government Printing Office, Washington, DC.
5. Putney, A. D., and Wagar, J. A. Cost Per Visitor Contact—A Step Toward Cost Effectiveness in Interpretive Methods. Unpublished manuscript.
6. Wagar, J. Alan. 1972. "Evaluating Interpretation and Interpretive Media," paper presented to Association of Interpretive Naturalists, April 7, 1972, Callaway Gardens, Pine Mountain, GA.
7. Washburne, Randel F., and J. Alan Wagar. 1972. "Evaluating Visitor Response to Exhibit Content," *Curator* **15**(3).
8. Wetterberg, Gary B. 1967. "Self-Guided Auto Tour Location," master's thesis, Colorado State University, Fort Collins.

CHAPTER 16

EXHIBITS

Grant W. Sharpe

In interpretive practice an exhibit is a device that publicly displays text, photographs, and objects. As with all interpretive media, the purpose of the exhibit is to inform. While doing so, it may enhance visitor enjoyment and appreciation of a natural or cultural entity. It may also be handsome or decorative in itself, creating a feeling of warmth and welcome in a public place. The intent of this chapter is not just to show how to build an exhibit, but to illustrate how the exhibit may carry its share of the interpretive message.

There is no limit to the kinds of materials that can be exhibited. However, brevity is essential. The viewers will be standing, rather than sitting, and you must consider the fatigue factor. It is necessary to arrest their attention. An exhibit should, if possible, employ more than one of the senses to tell its story. The most effective combination employs both visual and sound stimuli.

Exhibits are often expected to do too much. They are sometimes too technical or too abstract. Some have an overload of information, too many unrelated components, or have more than one theme; these faults can be summarized by the word "clutter." The exhibit audience is not a captive one. If an exhibit doesn't sell its message immediately, people will simply move on.

ADVANTAGES

1. As an interpretive tool, the exhibit has several advantages over other media. Its chief advantage is that it can display original objects, that is, the *real thing:* the object of discovery, an artifact of human history, or a specimen of natural science. There it is in all its fascination before the viewer. Can anything approach the effectiveness of the original? A well-executed facsim-

ile, reduced or enlarged as the need to change scale arises, is often necessary and acceptable. It's all in how you look at it—or rather—display it.

2. Another advantage to the exhibit is that valuable artifacts can be publicly displayed and still be protected. Instead of being buried in the archives, out of view except to the researcher, the valuable object, with certain safety precautions, can be made available to public view (Fig. 16-1).

3. Another advantage of the exhibit is the freedom it gives visitors to move through an interpretive experience at their own pace. Assuming the story is properly presented, visitors linger until they have grasped it, or become fatigued, then move on. Visitors on tight schedules have the opportunity to examine those exhibits that are of greatest interest to them and to pass over the rest.

4. A further advantage of this medium is the ability of the exhibit preparator to bring the out-of-doors indoors. By reducing objects (as in dioramas), it is possible to reproduce huge features in small scale to tell the story. Examples include battlefields, forts, towns, and other pieces of real estate. One can exhibit large man-made objects such as dams and ships, simply by reducing

FIG. 16-1. An important feature of exhibits is that original objects can be made available to public view. Humpback Rocks, Blue Ridge Parkway, Virginia. (Photo by Grant W. Sharpe.)

the scale. The preparator can also provide perspectives not otherwise available to the visitor in aerial views and cross sections.

On the other hand, the exhibitor can expand tiny objects to sizes much greater than the original. Insects, plant parts, and hundreds of other objects can be expanded or "blown up" in size through a variety of techniques.

Exhibits have still other advantages. Once in place, they are continuously available, telling the story in the absence of live interpreters. They can be designed for comprehension and appeal to all age levels. Telling the story in the out-of-doors, such as on a self-guided trail, may be difficult because the objects of nature must be utilized where they occur, and this brings problems with weather and site deterioration. The exhibit sequence, on the other hand, can be arranged to permit the story to logically unfold in a protected environment.

DISADVANTAGES

An exhibit can't do everything, nor should it be expected to. The exhibit is frequently used to present something that would be better assigned to another medium. For example, an exhibit cannot explain policy, nor present detailed information or abstract ideas nearly so well as a publication. People generally do not wish to stand and read a lengthy text. Also, the exhibit has no souvenir value, and seldom can it compete with moving objects or living things.

No one disputes the place of exhibits in the art of interpretation. Properly conceived and executed they are vital to the interpreter in many situations. However, it must be remembered that the desired effects of exhibits are often lost, or lessened, because exhibits are poorly designed or incorrectly used.

WHERE TO USE EXHIBITS

Display of informative or educational materials is possible in many situations—sports shows, county fairs, small ranger stations, elaborate and permanent museums, and visitor centers—all make use of this technique in some form. Exhibits serve as a means to show not only the natural history and culture of an area, but also the work of an agency or organization and its importance to the community or region. A portable exhibit may be taken to meetings, trade fairs, serve as background for TV programs, and appear periodically at schools, airports, store windows, public buildings, and shopping malls.

The exhibit planner should remember that the objective is to get the visitor (1) to stop in front of the exhibit, (2) to remain long enough to look at the material, and (3) to be stimulated to immediate or future thought or action (Fig. 16-2). To

FIG. 16-2. An exhibit is usually viewed by standing people. To be effective the exhibit must get people to stop, look at the material, and be stimulated to immediate or future thought or action. Cumberland Falls State Park, Kentucky. (Photo by Grant W. Sharpe.)

do this, the exhibitor must provide fresh ideas and present them with a sense of showmanship. Perhaps nowhere is there greater opportunity in interpretation for creativity and imagination than in designing and constructing exhibits. These must be guided by careful planning if they are to be translated into a creative, imaginative exhibit.

THE EXHIBIT THEME

Identify Your Audience

You must know the characteristics of your visitors. Are they rural or city people, local inhabitants or people from foreign countries? Do they arrive as individuals, in families, or large groups? What is their length of stay? What age classes are represented? What is their education? What is the purpose of their visit; are they curious, or do they just want to use your toilets?

Each group has different needs and interests. The wise exhibit planner will study the characteristics of these groups carefully and where possible design an exhibit to appeal to them.

Define Your Objective

What is your exhibit supposed to accomplish? Ask yourself these questions. Are you telling the viewers something new? Changing their minds about something? Showing them how something operates? Are you trying to stimulate them into action, or merely to entertain them on a rainy day? Perhaps you want to do all of these but (we hope) not all in one exhibit. Define your objective and keep this decision firmly in mind, and your exhibit will have a greater likelihood of getting quickly and clearly to the point.

Obtaining Permission

Subject matter planned for some exhibits may need clearance. Controversial topics and matters related to organization policy are two examples. The use of certain materials, such as rare or valuable specimens, endangered species of plants and animals, or what may appear to be excessive use of more common species, may cause concern to some visitors. Therefore, the appearance of "robbing nature" should be avoided. Approval for use of the material gives the designer and preparator protection from public or administrative wrath. Some judgment is needed to determine when approval is necessary.

Choosing a Theme

If the audience is *who* and the objective *why*, then the theme is *what*. For example, what information would most enhance a visit to this area? What questions are commonly asked by visitors? Perhaps these will yield an exhibit theme. Or should you inform them about something not readily evident?

The individual exhibit theme should present only one message, idea, or mood. In restricting your theme the best rule is to *keep it simple,* leaving out any elements not related to that theme. This avoids confusion, both on the part of the designer and the viewer, and your exhibit will be less time consuming and expensive to build.

Once you've selected the theme, list its components to see if it's an exhibitable item. Does it lend itself to graphic presentation? Will it depend too heavily on words? It is too complicated? If the idea is too abstract, it's possible another medium such as a publication should be considered.

To determine if you have a valid theme (one lending itself to an effective exhibit), organize your subject material. Can your desired story be told with visuals and limited text?

KINDS OF EXHIBITS

There are numerous ways to categorize exhibits. Most are used indoors, but some are designed for outside use. The majority of exhibits use inanimate objects though some incorporate animation. Some exhibits utilize simple art and photographs (two-dimensional) whereas others make use of objects that give the exhibit a third dimension. Some are directly related to natural history or human history, while some depict ideas. Some are simple in their message. Others such as didactic (teaching) exhibits may be detailed. Some use a recorded sound sequence instead of printed text. Participating exhibits, where the viewer is involved, ask for action such as stroking a pelt, lifting a rock, or pushing buttons on a quizboard. Exhibits may utilize any combination of the above. Another approach to categorizing exhibits is by subject matter. This could include historical, geological, ecological, archeological, and philosophical topics, each having many subcategories.

Another way of categorizing exhibits is by design. This includes flatwork, objects, dioramas, and models, and is the method used here.

Flatwork (Two-Dimensional Exhibits)

The flatwork exhibit is usually a *flat panel,* contains narration, and lacks a protective case. It utilizes illustrations ranging from simple sketches, diagrams, and graphs, to elaborate maps and detailed artwork (Fig. 16-3). The use of compatible color combinations becomes important to the success of flatwork. Coordination between the scientist-specialist and the artist is necessary. Photographs are grouped in the flatwork category also, though in some instances they are original objects.

The *narrative panel,* with words only and no objects, is another example of the two-dimensional exhibit. The narrative panel, however, is seldom able to compete with other types of exhibits.

Flatwork exhibits can take on the appearance of a third dimension when the illustration or photograph is mounted on a plane raised a few inches from the main panel.

Objects (Three-Dimensional Exhibits)

Here depth becomes an integral part of the presentation, and the object itself is used to create depth. Objects serve the purpose of letting visitors see for them-

FIG. 16-3. An example of a flatwork or two-dimensional exhibit. The flat panel lacks a protective case. Great Smoky Mountains National Park, Tennessee. (Photo by Grant W. Sharpe.)

selves. In this "visible storage" approach, the artifact, though protected, is exposed to public view. This could be a single object, such as a piece of pottery, a basket, a piece of sculpture, or an object of nature. It may be an exhibit where every piece is closely related. Examples would be stone axes of a native tribe, cones of California conifers, shorebirds of the Maine coast, or fossils of Ontario. Too many specimens in a small space become confusing, however. A few specimens set off by plenty of open space are most effective (Fig. 16-4).

Techniques of displaying objects are numerous, and it seems as if new ones are dreamed up every time an exhibit is built. They include hidden fasteners, glass or plastic supports and containers, wire supports, blocks of wood carefully painted or covered with fabric, mirrors for side or rear viewing, and magnifying devices.

Drawing the viewer's attention to the object may be done by installing a miniature spotlight whose beam shines on the specimen, or by installing tiny lights next to the specimen. In either instance, the lights may be wired to push-button switches on individual labels that identify or describe the object, and are controlled by the viewer.

FIG. 16-4. A three-dimensional exhibit showing a few objects, few words, and plenty of open space. The enclosed box gives the objects protection. Yellowstone National Park, Wyoming. (Photo by Grant W. Sharpe.)

Dioramas

A diorama is another kind of three-dimensional exhibit. Dioramas employ a group of carefully molded or carved figures and objects in the foreground which merge into a curved, painted background to give the illusion of depth. Viewing is usually from the front only. The purpose of the diorama is to dramatize a scene. It usually depicts historical events, close-ups of a violent activity, an ecological setting (Fig. 21-5), or an overview of a large section of landscape such as a town or city.

Dioramas are usually in miniature, although where space is not limited, full-size animal or human exhibits are possible. These life-size habitat or historical scenes usually employ the same painted curved background and carefully planned lighting techniques.

The use of an audio device in the diorama eliminates the need for labels, and adds greatly to the realism of the scene. However, when an audio device fails to function, it is very frustrating to a visitor, so reliable equipment is important to the success of the exhibit. Audio equipment is discussed in greater detail in Chapter 11.

Unfortunately, dioramas are expensive to build and dioramists are becoming scarce (Fig. 16-5).

FIG. 16-5. A dioramist at work in a National Park Service museum laboratory. Although dioramas have great visitor interest, they are expensive when compared with other kinds of exhibits. (Photo by Grant W. Sharpe.)

Models

Models are representations, usually in miniature, which show the construction of, or serve as a copy of something. They may be viewed from all sides as there is no attempt to create an illusion of depth, as is done with the diorama. Materials are usually wood, plastic, and metal.

1. *Equipment* models reduce the size of machinery, locomotives, automobiles, airplanes, ships, and other vehicles. They are used to save exhibit space, and effectively to portray the original in miniature.
2. *Architectural* models are commonly used to illustrate buildings in close detail. The miniature structure is often surrounded by appropriately scaled people, vehicles, and vegetation.
3. *Topographic* relief models are maps on which elevations are shown dimensionally to scale. Such models show the visitor the terrain of a park, forest, or other large land area. The topographic model usually lies flat and normally is in alignment with the cardinal points of the compass. Roads, streams, lakes, mountains, valleys, and points of known visitor interest are

FIG. 16-6. A topographic relief model illustrates the terrain of a park or other land area. Roads, streams, lakes, mountains, and valleys are shown on this plaster model in Great Smoky Mountains National Park, Tennessee. (Photo by Grant W. Sharpe.)

illustrated on the model (Fig. 16-6). For greatest visitor interest the entire park, forest, or refuge should be portrayed. The larger the scale, the more detail is permitted, adding greater interest. Models beyond a certain size, however, place the viewer too far from the center to see much detail.

Topographic relief models have many uses. Planning bodies have found these models indispensable in informing citizen groups, commissions, and political figures of their development plans for parks, towns, highways, and other land uses. In a park or forest situation, the topographic model assists viewers to orient themselves to places they may wish to visit. The construction of a topographic model is seen in Figs. 16-7 and 16-8.

EXHIBIT PLANNING AND DESIGN

Before an exhibit can be built, it must be subjected to the planning process, followed by the design stage. Planning is broad in scope, whereas design is more concerned with the specific and the exact.

FIG. 16-7. The before and after of a simple topographic model. Plywood, cardboard, composition board, or styrofoam is used. Detail comes from topographic maps. They may have to be projected for enlarging or reducing, or a pantograph may be used. Tracing the map's contour lines provides the boundary of each layer. The lines are cut with a jig or band saw, or with a hot wire in the case of styrofoam. Relief is built up by stacking and gluing the layers. The vertical scale is usually exaggerated, often doubled, to give the landscape a more dramatic look.

FIG. 16-8. For certain uses, topographic models are left in the terrace stage, as in Fig. 16-7. If a more natural slope is desired, the steps are filled in with clay-mache or similar material. Here is the same model after adding trees, painting, and lettering. Supplies are available at hobby shops. (Photos by John Spring.)

Factors To Consider in Planning

Location. Exhibits too often lack visual separation, that is, individual exhibits appear too close together. What kind of space will be provided for the exhibit? This will tell you something about the size and shape you should design for. Will the exhibit stand on the floor, sit on a table, lean against a wall, or be suspended from a strip of molding? What lighting is available? Will it require additional lights, for example, spots from above, or will it need built-in lights?

Mobility. Will the exhibit be moved frequently? If so, how will it be transported? Should it be designed to fit into a station wagon? Will it receive rough treatment? Perhaps it will need a shipping container for longer trips. Who will put it in place, the person who built it or someone else? If strangers erect it, it will have to be relatively easy to put together. Complexity, and the resultant problems of setup, may have to be considered in the design.

The Competition. Exhibits displayed by themselves are the most successful. If your exhibit is but one of dozens, say at a convention or trade fair, it will need to convey its idea quickly, with even fewer specimens and labels, than a single exhibit with no competition. Exhibits in a poor setting, with labels that are difficult to read, and a cluttered, messy appearance will be passed over quickly or totally ignored. Another point to remember is that an exhibit can seldom be expected to compete with moving things, giveaways, or attractive people in a booth.

Vandalism and Theft. Valuable objects must be under glass or kept out of reach of the viewer. If available to the public, the display objects must be expendable. Surveillance by guards or protection with electric alarm devices may need to be considered. Damage or theft may occur despite these precautions. A well-designed, soundly constructed, high-quality exhibit usually discourages vandalism, however.

Style and Color. Exhibit styles change with the years. The exhibit that endures is the simple one. Look at other people's exhibits for ideas. Take copious notes and photographs when looking, but don't be lazy. Modify—don't copy. Make a visit to an old-fashioned, amateur museum, and you might learn what *not* to do.

Color is a valuable tool and can pull the components of an exhibit together but should be used carefully or it may overwhelm the exhibit. Neutral colors may be used to lessen distractions. Psychedelic colors may date an exhibit. Keep your color combinations simple.

Viewing Distance. The viewing distance is another important factor, one which may determine the size of the exhibit elements, particularly the labels. A viewing distance of 4 to 8 feet (1.2 to 2.4 m) is considered average, but this differs with the exhibiting circumstances. Adjustments in sizes of both objects and labels will be necessary if the vewing distance is much over 8 feet (2.4 m). Available lighting may have some effect on size requirements also.

Special Equipment Needs

Electrical Needs.   Will the exhibit require electricity? If so, what wattage will be used? Lighting on the exhibit should be artificial, since daylight varies during the day and sunlight will fade exhibit colors. Fluorescent tubes may be used in some exhibits. Hidden spotlights may be useful to emphasize detail.

Switches for push-button exhibits should be durable and readily replaced (Fig. 16-9).

Radio or electronic supply catalogs are good sources for ideas on the kinds of switches available. If motors or other mechanical devices are required, use standard equipment, since it is much easier to obtain parts. However, it may be easier to replace an entire motor than to get a part repaired.

Check with the fire marshal to see if there are different electrical regulations for

FIG. 16-9.   A quizboard exhibit utilizing labels, electric switches, and calendar pictures of birds. When the correct name and bird switches are energized, the owl's eyes light up. The switches must be durable and readily replaced. (Photo by Grant W. Sharpe.)

different kinds of exhibits. Electrical conduits, for example, may be required for a permanent built-in exhibit but not for a portable exhibit.

Water. Will your exhibit require fresh or saltwater? What provisions will you need for waterproofing the surroundings in case of spills? Such exhibits may be restricted to the ground floor of buildings.

Materials to Use

The variety of exhibit materials seems endless. Compatibility with the central theme is important, of course. Plywood, particleboard, pegboard, masonite, plastics, fabrics, glass, metals, and paint are all important items in exhibit construction, and most are available in local hardware stores or lumber yards.

Other materials include fastening devices, label stock, and lettering materials. Uneven printing is very distracting. Lettering guides or press-on letters should be used on the labels unless one is an expert at printing.

Glass should stop infrared rays and be shatterproof. Even lucite or other clear plastic is preferable to plate glass (which readily shatters), but choose a plastic sheet that can be polished with scratch remover. The mirrorlike surface of glass or plastic may present reflection problems. In these cases nonglare glass may be used to good effect.

Titles and Labels

Titles. Titles serve as headlines and are used to get the viewer's attention. They should be brief, put the theme across, and utilize no more than six to eight words.

Raised letters give a title a third dimension. Letters made of cardboard, plastic, or plaster of paris are available in most commercial display houses or can be ordered through the mail. They come in a variety of styles, sizes, and colors. Wooden letters are also available commercially or can be cut on a jigsaw if time is not a factor. Plastic letters can be ordered on cast sprues thus reducing the cost of individual letters. Whatever the material, plain white is recommended. Colored letters can then be made by using spray-can paints of various colors.

Letters should be glued in place rather than nailed unless a special effect is desired. Mounting the letters on a strip of wood or masonite, and elevating this strip 1 or 2 inches (2.5 or 5.0 cm) from the exhibit panel's main surface gives the title further emphasis. Capital letters are acceptable for titles, and two different sizes can be used to differentiate the main and secondary headings. The size depends on the space available and the viewing distance. One-, two-, and three-inch (2.5-, 5.0-, and 7.5-cm) tall letters are most commonly used.

The title usually appears at the top of most exhibits leaving the lower area for the objects to be displayed (Fig. 16-10). Visualize what the exhibit will look like

FIG. 16-10. An outdoor exhibit illustrating the use of titles and labels. Note the location of the title at upper left, the logical place for a viewer to begin reading text. Old Fort Townsend State Park, Washington. (Photo by C. R. Jensen.)

when people are standing in front of it. If the title is inconspicuous because it is too low, the exhibit may get passed up by potential viewers.

Labels. The main purpose of the label is to serve as the bridge between the exhibit elements and the viewer. Labels are the text; they can enhance or clutter an exhibit, depending on how they are used. Keep the label brief and to the point. Few people will bother to read a lengthy label. Plain lettering is best; fancy lettering may detract from the message of the exhibit.

Letter sizes of labels vary with viewing distance. A ¼-inch (0.6 cm) letter at 3 feet (0.9 m) is about right. At 6 feet (1.8 m) use a ½-inch (0.12 cm) letter and so on. The spacing between letters and words becomes important and should be checked at appropriate distances for effect.

Ordinary typewritten copy is usually too small for exhibit labels. Such copy may be expanded photographically, but the enlarged type may appear somewhat irregular. An agency or organization with considerable label work should investigate the purchase of a "labeling typewriter," a machine that has extra-large size type. Some brands are available with carbon ribbons in several colors. A provision for expanded spacing between letters and words is an important feature to look for in these machines.

Lettering instruments should also be considered. Koh-I-Noor pens and templates are one satisfactory brand; another is the ever-reliable K + E Leroy lettering set. The Varityper is another good lettering device. Consider press-on or transfer letters, or even small three-dimensional plastic letters glued in place. Silkscreen letters are often used successfully.

Label colors must be used carefully as they may detract from the rest of the exhibit. Also, certain color combinations of letters and background may themselves clash and become difficult to read. Labels are considered in greater detail in Chapter 12.

Specimens

A specimen of some sort is usually the main element of an exhibit, and it should be displayed with ingenuity and imagination. Wire, wood, plastics, and adhesives are important ingredients for holding down rocks, fossils, plant materials, evergreen tree cones, and other specimens.

Animals are always popular subjects, since they are not available for close scrutiny in their natural state. A mounted specimen is usually more impressive than a photograph and certainly is superior to a study skin. The exhibit is greatly enhanced if the mounted specimen is placed in a habitat scene.

Photographs

The exhibit designer should never underestimate the power of a photograph. Large photos are best, and color photos are preferable, though not always available. The color transparency, illuminated from behind, always attracts attention. Though photos play strong supporting roles in exhibits, they can be distracting if not used intelligently and mounted properly.

SKETCHING AND LAYOUT OF A SINGLE EXHIBIT

After reviewing the above sections on exhibit planning and the exhibit theme, you you are ready for a few sketches. Have lots of sketch paper. For purposes of illustration, let's say your exhibit will be a panel. Using a reduced scale, lay out its approximate dimensions (the space your exhibit will occupy). Now locate the title somewhere near the top of the exhibit.

Start your information flow from left to right (unless the language you are working with dictates otherwise).

Locate your attention getter. It may be the title, subtitle, an actual object, a piece of art work, or a photograph. At this point you may not know what this will be, but at least provide for its location.

Next, locate your supporters; those statements or objects that tell your exhibit story.

First attempts at sketching usually produce an unorganized mess. Admittedly, layout is a difficult step for the beginner. There are a myriad of ways in which an exhibit story can can be portrayed. But you have to make a start. If help is needed take your problem to someone skilled in exhibit design or consult the reference list at the end of this chapter.

It is in the layout stage where the exhibit theme and related elements are pulled together. Test your sketches on someone who is unfamiliar with the subject matter. Can they understand the message? If it is properly done, the viewer will be guided through the exhibit theme with a minimum of confusion.

We have concerned ourselves here with the layout of a single exhibit. Layout also includes organizing the exhibit sequence, that is, a series of exhibits in place. This may be for use in the entranceway, corridor, or exhibit room itself.

BUILDING THE EXHIBIT

One of the ways of getting the exhibit built is to contract for the construction with someone skilled in this work. A secondary possibility is to find someone on your staff or in the nearby community who is willing and able. The third means is to do it yourself. For the inexperienced exhibit builder the book by Arminta Neal, *"Help! For the Small Museum"* is strongly recommended.

MAINTENANCE AND CLEANING

A wise person once said, "If you can't maintain it, don't build it." Though the reference probably wasn't directed toward exhibits, it does apply.

No matter how well they are cared for, exhibits deteriorate with time. Components fade, crack, fall off, become damaged or vandalized. Such parts should be replaced immediately, or the entire exhibit should be removed. The exhibit designer must allow for reasonable access to the case for replacement of lights, motors, screws, and other parts. Exhibit cases containing organic materials, such as paper, fabrics, fur, or feathers need protection from insects and mold. Use of insecticides and fungicides is mandatory in exhibit maintenance.

Preventive maintenance is possible through frequent and careful cleaning. Tender care is required, and preferably by someone with an interest in the task. Carelessness in the use of cleaning materials and equipment can be damaging.

Glass should be cleaned frequently. If a case is covered with plexiglass or other plastic, abrasive cleaners cannot be used.

STORAGE

Exhibits not in use represent considerable capital investment and must receive proper care. The exhibit in storage faces new dangers. Mold, insects, rodents, dust, light, and air pollution are constant hazards, and periodic inspection is necessary.

What To Look For

Mold is able to consume the organic components of an exhibit and is a formidable enemy. It is best controlled by avoiding a poorly ventilated, warm, damp storage environment. Mold can be expected if temperatures exceed 70° F (21° C) or the relative humidity is more than 65 percent.

Damaging insects include silverfish, cockroaches, clothes moths, powderpost beetles, and carpet beetles. They will eat anything in the exhibit made of organic materials—paper, wood, cloth, hair, or feathers. The powderpost beetle is capable of burrowing into the dry wood parts of the exhibit.

Rodents, particularly mice and rats in search of nesting material, can do considerable damage in a very short period.

Dust soils exhibits and becomes an abrasive while it is being wiped off. Cloth or plastic covers are recommended.

Light causes damage mainly by the fading of colors, though there may be some deterioration of textiles from photochemical activiy. A dark storage room is essential.

Pollution from contaminated air may cause harmful chemical reaction and physical damage to exhibit components made of organic materials. Leather becomes brittle, fabrics weaken and disintegrate. Even metal becomes tarnished or encrusted from air pollutants that corrode or oxidize. Fumes, exhaust, and heating by-products need to be filtered, if the air intake draws in contaminated air.

The ideal storage space is dark, insect and rodent proof, well ventilated with clean filtered air, and has controlled temperature and humidity.

OBSOLESCENCE

Exhibits, no matter how well designed, built, and maintained, will eventually become obsolete. New generations of visitors, with different interests, tastes, and backgrounds, will find the exhibit uninteresting, for various reasons. It may be that the style of design has become antiquated, or perhaps the theme is no longer relevant, or the exhibit may be simply too familiar. Perhaps new discoveries have been made or new theories propounded. Replacement then becomes necessary, and from the exhibit designer's and builder's point of view, this has its advantages, for it keeps them employed, and enables them to try out new techniques and ideas.

OUTSIDE EXHIBITS AND EXHIBIT SHELTERS

The outside exhibit or kiosk (also known as the wayside, trailside, or roadside exhibit) differs only slightly from other exhibits cited in this chapter, in that new environmental factors enter in, namely light, moisture, and other climatic problems.

Light, for example, fades color photographs very quickly out-of-doors, and the reflection on glass or plastic presents a problem for the viewer. Moisture, heat, and cold make some materials (particularly paper) difficult to use. On the other hand, wood and metal weather quite well. (Fig. 16-11).

A partial solution to these problems is the use of an exhibit shelter, discussed in Chapter 19. Although this may add considerably to the total cost of the exhibit,

FIG. 16-11. An outside exhibit made of wood and aluminum. The titles are hand routed letters. Isle Royale National Park, Michigan. (Photo by Grant W. Sharpe.)

the shelter is essential in many instances. The shelter must fit the theme and mood of the site. (Figs. 16-2, 16-10, and 19-12.)

The outside exhibit usually stands alone, therefore has no competition from other exhibits, and more detail may be included. Normally the outside exhibit is located near the feature being interpreted and, thus, has the advantage of interpreting the scene behind it. This adds interest and immediacy to any exhibit.

GENERAL REFERENCES

Bergman, Eugene. 1961. "Exhibits That Flow," *Curator,* **14**(4), 278–286.

Burcaw, G. Ellis. 1975. *Introduction to Museum Work,* The American Association for State and Local History, Nashville, TN.

de Borhegyi, Stephan F. 1963. "Visual Communication in the Sciences Museum," *Curator,* **6**(1), 45–57.

de Borhegyi, Stephan F. 1965. "Testing of Audience Reaction to Museum Exhibits, *Curator* **8**(1), 85–93.

Erickson, Harvey D. 1977. *Preservation of Wood Artifacts,* College of Forest Resources, University of Washington, Seattle.

Hayett, William. 1967. *Display and Exhibit Handbook,* Reinhold, New York.

Lewis, Ralph H. 1976. *Manual for Museums,* U.S. National Park Service. U.S. Government Printing Office, Washington, DC.

Mahaffey, Ben. D. 1969. *Relative Effectiveness and Vistor Preference of Three Audiovisual Media for Interpretation of an Historical Area,* Dept. Report 1, Texas Agr. Exp. Sta. Texas A. & M. University, College Station.

Neal, Arminta. 1965. "Function of Display: Regional Museums," *Curator,* **8**(3), 228–234.

Neal, Arminta. 1969. *Help! For the Small Museum,* Pruett Publishing Co., Boulder, CO.

Parr, A. E. 1959. "Designed for Display," *Curator* **2**(4), 313–334.

Parr, A. E. 1962. "The Obsolescence and Amortization of Permanent Exhibits," *Curator,* **5**(3), 258–264.

Parr, A. E. 1962. "A Nice 'Gooky' Exhibit," *Curator* **5**(2), 118–119.

Vonier, Thomas V., and Richard A. Scribner, 1973. *Community Information Expositions,* American Association for the Advancement of Science, Washington, DC.

Wagar, J. Alan. 1972. *The Recording Quizboard: A Device for Evaluating Interpretive Services,* USDA Forest Service Research Paper PNW-139, Pacific Northwest Forest and Range Experiment Station.

Washburne, Randle F., and J. Alan Wagar. 1972. "Evaluating Visitor Response to Exhibit Content," *Curator* **15,**3.

Wittlin, Alma, S. 1971. "Hazards of Communication by Exhibits," *Curator* **14**(2), 138–150.

PART III
SUPPORTING ACTIVITIES

The interpretive dollar is the best dollar we spend.

Irving C. Root

CHAPTER 17

OFF-SEASON, OFF-SITE INTERPRETATION

Charles J. Gebler

Off-season interpretive programs provide activities at unusual times of year, frequently in unusual settings. They reach visitors not ordinarily contacted during the main season and open up excellent opportunities for working with residents in the surrounding communities. Off-site interpretive programs extend the park into the surrounding communities, directly or indirectly. They take the talent of the park staff and some of the richness of the park resources outward, bridging gaps that may exist between local people and the park.*

Over the years most interpretation has been cyclic—both in use patterns and psychologically. And so, when the subject of "off-season, off-site interpretive programs" is introduced it may be met with some disdain, especially if budgets, personnel, facilities, and other interpretive management ingredients are geared to one main season.

Traditionally established interpretive programs consist of a series of activities during that time of the year when the majority of visitors are in the park. For many areas this is the summer season. It is the time when interpretive managers expect and handle most of the visitor use. Then suddenly summer is over, visitation drops off dramatically, the seasonal staffs go back to their full-time occupations, and the permanent park staffs breathe a sigh of relief. In southern and desert areas the cycle may be reversed.

Since the off-season, off-site interpretive program is not usually in the tradition of the seasonal program, implementing it becomes a matter of management priority. Budgets and personnel play heavy roles in how much can be done. Success also parallels the imagination of the park manager and the interpreter (who is also a manager). Such expansions of the park program call for an attitude that consid-

*The term "park" is used in this chapter to represent all types of parks, recreation areas, and forests.

ers all visitor use patterns in the park and that views the park as part of an overall community rather than an isolated unit people visit.

This chapter discusses some of the rationale and possibilities of off-season, off-site interpretation. It suggests a break with tradition, but if it is practical and logical to extend and expand the interpretive program in this manner, the dividends could be high for the park, the park staff, the visitors, and the residents of the surrounding communities.

THE BENEFITS

Through visitor centers, self-guiding devices, conducted trips, campfire programs, publications, and other activities, visitors become better acquainted with the park. As a result they may understand and enjoy their stay more. They may take more pride in the park and, in a sense, become an extension of the park staff by protecting the resource. They may be more cautious of their own actions and those of others. When they return to their home communities after a good interpretive experience, they should have greater appreciation for their everyday living and working environments. If all is not well, they may be more willing to do something about it. The same is true of issues that directly affect the fate of the park itself. Those who are acquainted with and appreciate the park are going to support it. With off-season, off-site interpretive programs the positive effects on people, parks, and the total environment are continuous.

Surprisingly, many elements of off-season, off-site interpretive programs may be implemented without a serious increase in funding and manpower. They can be a source of great creative satisfaction to park staffs if these programs are accepted as a vital part of park management. At least they are worthy of consideration, if just on an experimental basis. You will never taste the success of the new and the original without such experimentation.

THE LOGIC

There are still very definable visitor seasons. Yet as the seasonal patterns of society change, particularly the traditional school year, we can expect more year-around or "off-season" use.

Senior citizens and others without families or children in school are often seen in parks and recreation areas during the off-season (Fig. 17-1). The crowds are gone. Travel can be accomplished at a leisurely pace. Parks can be enjoyed in dramatic seasonal settings. In addition, sports enthusiasts and families flock to sites with winter recreation facilities, particularly those sites adjacent to metropolitan areas.

FIG. 17-1. The off-season period often sees a new clientele in parks and other outdoor recreation areas. Senior citizens and visitors without children in school become the off-season visitors. Interpretive programs need to be adjusted to meet these off-season needs. Lake Chelan National Recreation Area, Washington. (Photo by Grant W. Sharpe.)

If the park or other outdoor recreation area is to serve the community, it should be a part of that community and the community should be a part of it. "Off-site" could mean a group of small towns or a major metropolitan area of millions of people. Park staffs have a great deal to offer these communities. Communications can extend over a broad spectrum of audiences, including minority and disabled groups. Many groups in these communities can be encouraged to use park resources creatively during the off-season. Examples are special field trips for senior citizens or the extension of the school curriculum to include environmental study areas within nearby parks.

Parks and people go together. Creative management gives positive direction to both.

THE STAFF

This is logically the most critical element of any park management program, and staff is equated with funding. When a program expands, more funding is needed. However, a program can expand somewhat by shifts in priorities. If the use of a park is increasing during the off-season and a definite trend or pattern is noticed, then it is logical to determine the need for serving these visitors with an interpretive program.

One solution to the staff problem is to adjust work schedules. For example, there are many possibilities for manning a basic visitor information facility during the winter season. Assume that winter visitation of a park suddenly increases, and you decide to use a ranger station for expanded information and interpretive services. If permanent interpretive personnel are not available, other staff members may serve in this capacity. Rangers in a ranger station may be able to handle these duties along with other responsibilities. If permanent interpretive personnel are available, a shift in the work week may be all that is necessary to provide weekend service.

Another solution is to hire part-time or seasonal personnel. They usually live in nearby communities and could be some of the same seasonal staff employed during the main visitor season. The summer program might be altered slightly to provide funding for this personnel.

Some governmental organizations have formal volunteer programs. They seek out volunteers of all ages with a desire to serve people and to work in a park with its staff. Volunteers can be found among college or university students, who may even get credit for their services in an internship program. Senior citizens have a great deal of knowledge and experience to offer. These programs usually offer fringe benefits to the volunteer such as modest payments for room and board, travel, uniform, and insurance protection. Volunteers are not a complete solution as they sometimes require more supervision than paid employees and their availability may be irregular. They should not be considered as replacements for professional park staff. But they can supplement and enrich park programs while gaining valuable experience and personal satisfaction. A good balance between paid staff and volunteers is desirable.

THE PRIORITIES

This will be dependent on the visitor demand in the park, the genuine need to work with communities and, of course, the funding and personnel. In the case of off-season in-park programs, build them as needed based on visitation and use. Unless a sudden increase in funding becomes available, you will want to develop your program on a priority basis. Apply the question, "What is needed, when, and where?"

For example, visitors using a park during the off-season would ordinarily use a standard route in and out of that park. If an established information-interpretive facility is not within that travel route but a ranger station is, then it would be logical to use this station. Should the park activity be concentrated in one area during the winter, the operation of facilities and interpretive activities in that area would be a practical first step.

The same logic is used in determining priorities for off-site programs. Where are the markets? Is it more important to work vigorously with the media to reach a great many people or with the schools in nearby communities? Is it desirable to concentrate on one type of activity and do it thoroughly or to do a modest amount with several activities?

The facts and consequent priorities are then specific for each situation. Priorities are necessary and should assist the park manager and staff in achieving overall goals. A great deal of creative insight can be gained by gathering together the park staff for brainstorming sessions on observations and needs. This should lead to an interpretive management plan that lists by priority the various off-season, off-site options in light of the available personnel and funding. List the goals of the program along with the suitable interpretive tools available. Then select those that can be realistically programmed. A program that is developed carefully with progressive, realistic steps is far better than a dramatic plunge with a few sustaining values.

OFF-SEASON INTERPRETIVE PROGRAMS

Information Facilities and Visitor Centers

In addition to providing the routine face-to-face information, be imaginative in meeting visitor needs. If established visitor centers are available, use them with a sense of experimentation. Weather may be poor during the winter months and campgrounds closed. Visitors will likely use facilities, such as visitor centers, for longer periods and in more depth than during the summer. They will appreciate all the activities that occur during the summer, such as information services, exhibits, publications, and audiovisual programs.

Try short talks or tours of the exhibit area and special exhibits and programs on the off-season aspects of the park. If a temporary information situation is used, such as a ranger station, concession facility, or private winter sports lodge, consider installing some innovative temporary facilities. These may include a portable information desk, a bulletin board, or several small exhibits.

Roving Interpretation

The roving interpreter is an increasingly common sight in major areas during the main visitor season. Interpreters go where the people are, meeting them at lookout points along roads, on trails, or in picnic areas or campgrounds. The spring, fall, and winter also offer excellent opportunities for roving interpretation. Wildlife may be more in evidence, and the changing seasons may bring a special quality to certain scenes. One-to-one communication is always effective and especially so during the uncrowded relaxed time of off-season.

Illustrated Programs and Demonstrations

Illustrated programs and demonstrations on park features, skill subjects, and living history may be especially appreciated during the off-season. If you have a facility for programs, for instance, an audiovisual room or auditorium, these activities would be a natural step in building an expanded program for both park visitors and nearby residents.

If such facilities are not available, consider improvising them in an exhibit room or spacious lobby. It may be logical to take the programs to where visitors are staying. If you decide to experiment in facilities that are not park owned, use care in the type of commitments you make until you are sure of the success and staff availability. Build your program around an interest in providing interpretive services rather than an evening's entertainment for overnight guests.

Try out special programs on weekend evenings with invitations to park guests, people in nearby lodging facilities, and local communities. Programs by the park staff or guest speakers, either as single events or a series, featuring demonstrations, slides, or appropriate motion pictures are possibilities. Film festivals on a variety of subjects or a particular theme are often well received. Programs on activities and skills such as winter hiking, backpacking, camping, or photography with demonstrations of equipment may draw surprising numbers of guests and residents. The rising interest in living interpretation opens the door to many possibilities including costumed demonstrations of everything from spinning to musket firing, from old-time ski gear to hiking clothing. These and other programs may be conducted in cooperation with local historical societies or individuals with appropriate background and skill.

People must be aware of upcoming events if they are to participate. Use all appropriate means for getting the word out, including newspapers and bulletin boards in public places.

Conducted Trips

Seasons other than the main visitor period should present many occasions for interpreting the park environment under unusual and striking circumstances. The seasonal changes in plant cover and wildlife present outstanding interpretive opportunities—some even better than during the main visitor season. Photography and wildlife hikes or automobile caravans work well in certain situations. Consider modes of transportation in keeping with the season, such as a haywagon in the fall and a sleigh during the winter. Snowshoe trips and cross-country skiing provide visitors with a new look at the park and perhaps give them an opportunity for a new experience (Fig. 17-2).

An interpreter with imagination can experiment with an almost endless array of possibilities. The secret of success is to fit the activities to the season and the conditions rather than trying to make summer-type activities work in nonsummer circumstances. This means a break with tradition, but real success is often nontraditional.

Environmental Education

More and more parks are being used by organized groups, particularly schools, scouts, and environmental organizations, for off-season field trips and other activities. Agencies have responded in a number of ways but generally agree that the greatest success comes when the leaders or teachers are familiar with the park resources prior to their trip. Pretrip training could be provided by workshops giving leaders an opportunity to learn the location and significance of features and, perhaps, by specialized training sessions on subjects like winter survival.

FIG. 17-2. The winter season also brings sports enthusiasts to parks. An interpreter with imagination can provide visitors with a new park experience. Here a park ranger is conducting a winter snowshoe tour along the rim of Crater Lake National Park, Oregon. (Photo courtesy of National Park Service.)

If on-site workshops or training are not possible, consider meeting with leaders elsewhere at their convenience. If the plans of schools or groups are known in advance, a packet of interpretive and informational material, along with a letter of welcome (with an offer to provide assistance), can pave the way.

The National Park Service has developed a unique approach to bridge the gap between parks and schools. One or more National Environmental Study Areas have been earmarked in certain parks for use by schools. These areas possess characteristics that are rich environmentally and provide opportunities for a broad range of school activities from the study of ecology to the relationship of the fine arts to the environment. A training program is worked out between the park and the schools with the schools doing most of the organizing and training and the park staff serving as resource people. The materials developed are an integral part of the school curriculum rather than an extracurricular activity.

Much of the National Park Service educational emphasis is based on the NEED concept (National Environmental Education Development). This curriculum package was produced under the sponsorship of the National Park Service and the National Park Foundation, and is now published and distributed commercially. The program approaches the environment naturally and logically by using *strands:* variety and similarities, patterns, interaction and interdependence, continuity and change, and adaptation and evolution. One of the major keys to the program's success is that it does not require a scientific background but does emphasize observation and logic.

A unique approach to off-season park use is through the *environmental living* concept. This has been most successful in historical parks where school groups spend a day, or perhaps stay overnight, going back into time. Through teacher and parent workshops and extensive classroom planning, the students relive a day in the lives of their forebears. These workshops emphasize the historical period and events of the area through food preparation, work and play activities, and even costumes. The historical use of the environment, as well as our ancestors direct dependency on it, is emphasized.

These techniques are far more productive for all concerned than having an unannounced school bus appear and take the park staff by surprise. Furthermore, they provide an opportunity for park staffs to use park resources to increase an understanding of the environment by bringing the community and the park together.

Special Programs

This category of off-season interpretive activities includes a number of ideas. It is dependent on many circumstances, including the proximity of the park to nearby communities, the size of those communities, the communication lines established between the parks and the communities, the physical facilities of the park, and the weather. Included in the possibilities are tours for local residents, programs for senior citizens and other special groups, after-school activities for children, open house programs, potluck dinners, interpretive activities commemorating a historical event, year-end bird counts, arts and crafts exhibits, folklife festivals, and radio and television specials.

Generally the potential of these special activities is not well realized, principally because of costs, lack of personnel, and the inertia of tradition. However, many park staffs have found that one or more of these special activities each year brings together the park and the community. You may be surprised to learn just how much the residents of these communities are willing to do to make these activities a success.

OFF-SITE INTERPRETIVE PROGRAMS

The What, The Who, The How

The rationale behind off-site programs is stated near the beginning of the chapter in the section entitled "The Logic." In addition, in developing a strategy for off-site programs the following should be considered:

What is the park's sphere of influence?
What are the guidelines for time, personnel, and funding?
What are the messages that need to be carried to the community?
Who are your audiences?
How are the messages to be carried?

The concept of "sphere of influence" is an important part of making value judgments in park management. Just as "no man is an island," neither are parks usually isolated from the surrounding communities. A good share of the National Park System, parts of many national forests, and most state parks are adjacent to communities. Many are within reasonable driving distances of major metropolitan areas. The sphere of influence is merely a way of looking at the various surrounding patterns of population radiating outward from a park.

The guidelines for time, personnel, funding, and what the messages are to be, are dependent on the overall management objectives of the park. Some of the techniques for carrying these messages will be discussed later. Information about where park visitors reside, their age levels, the most effective grouping through which they may be contacted, and their uses of the park resource is vital if the off-site programs are to be aimed at particular user groups.

In many parks a major portion of visitor use originates from surrounding metropolitan areas even though the park has national and worldwide interest. Thus, if it is important to reach as many potential park visitors as possible with messages about particular safety issues, resource protection, and vandalism problems, it would be logical to seek out these local user groups.

An example of the significance of local use was found through an analysis of the backcountry use permit system for the North Cascades National Park Complex in Washington State. Permits from one summer were analyzed as to visitor origin and other factors. During the busiest part of the season it was found that nearly 60 percent of the users were from western Washington, with 23 percent from Seattle alone.* Messages to backcountry user-groups to aid in management objectives could well be given in the Seattle area. Similarly ORV users, hunters, horseback recreationists, and other special interest groups can be sought out via their club meetings, and presented with a program tailored to their interests and to the park's management problems with their group and its activities.

One of the unfortunate facts of many off-site interpretive or general public relations programs pertinent to park management is that they are not directed toward the proper audience. In many instances, research is not available as to where the user-group originates; yet much of this information can be obtained from simple observations such as zip codes, license plates, surveys, and permits, as well as through professional analysis by colleges and universities.

Mailouts

Off-site interpretive programs also encompass materials sent out from the park. A great deal can be accomplished through the mails with comparatively little personnel and funding. Many park agencies encourage potential visitors to phone or write the park in advance for information and literature. The National Park Service, Forest Service, and some state park agencies have established information offices in cities, usually in conjunction with a regional operation or management unit. These offices are designed for drop-in visits and are well prepared for telephone and mail requests. They are staffed with trained information specialists and are supplied with a wide variety of literature.

Literature packets, together with letters of explanation, can be mailed to schools or groups in advance of visits and can pay dividends for all. These assist the leaders in making the best possible use of time as well as in developing plans for trips that relate to the curriculum or group's interests. Special materials may be developed, such as simple hints for teachers or youth leaders on field trip opportunities or safe hiking practices. Material mailed to schools and libraries may be displayed with information stating how individuals can obtain copies. Several large metropolitan park systems have regular newsletters on park interpretive activities, specific natural history or history topics, and leadership techniques for use in the outdoors and environmental education.

---

*Data analyzed by the Sociology Studies Program, National Park Service Cooperative Park Studies Unit, University of Washington, Dr. Donald Field, Regional Chief Scientist.

Park environments offer excellent opportunities for photography. The results might be incorporated into packets of mounted photographs with short captions. These could serve as mailout exhibits. Sets of 35mm slides or slides converted into filmstrips may tell a number of stories including history or wildlife, staff activities such as the life of rangers in winter, visitor activity opportunities, or safety messages. They should be accompanied by scripts geared to the age levels of the audiences. Consult with local school teachers when preparing such material for various age levels and adapting them to the school curriculum. Simple captions may be photographically reproduced on the slides or filmstrip frames themselves by a number of processing laboratories. In addition to the script, tapes with signals that inform the projectionist when to change the slide or filmstrip frame may also contain the voices of the park staff and actual sounds from the park. Some school systems have automatic filmstrip equipment that uses tape cartridges with signals that change the frames. The tapes must be specially prepared for these systems.

Motion pictures of the park can be distributed in the same way. Commercial films on the park or related park features and activities may be included. Consider the production of a film leader to show sponsorship by the park or agency. Caution should be used in establishing a motion picture loan service unless personnel and funding are available to maintain it. Consider providing the various audiovisuals, including motion pictures, to school curriculum centers or libraries. Many will publicize, circulate, generally maintain them, and furnish you with use reports. Commercial film-loan companies provide this service for a fee.

Community Programs

Schools, clubs, and organizations welcome special programs by park personnel. If the communities surrounding a park are relatively small, park personnel may easily contact every child in the schools and present programs to all interested clubs and organizations without any severe taxing of an off-season work program. On the other hand, larger communities may necessitate production of an operating plan before it becomes general knowledge that a "Ranger" is available to appear. In many areas it may be practical to visit more than one school a day (Fig. 17-3). If long driving distances are involved, it is good business to block out a number of days for school and club programs, making arrangements in advance. Most school districts require advance planning for their programs, and service clubs, environmental, and other organizations often prepare printed notices, or programs in advance.

In developing programs it is especially important to discuss the ideas and subject matter in advance with school officials, teachers, or club leaders. The basic stories of the park often fit in with the school curriculum, camp programs, or club's interests. Subjects may also be designed to prepare students for trips to the park. Consider group size in school classrooms or assemblies, age or grade levels, program length, advance student preparation, and follow-up.

FIG. 17-3. An example of an off-season, off-site program. Here a park interpreter visits a grade school assembly, and answers questions on the park's natural history. (National Park Service photo by Don Cornell.)

Unless you have an unusually large budget and staff, it is best to concentrate on a few program types. The production of custom programs is a costly business. Yet most requests seem to be individual in nature. More often than not, these requests can, with some modest changes, be effectively handled through the programs already prepared. This is one of the advantages in offering a selection of programs in a printed announcement. There are exceptions to this, however, such as short courses, seminars, and special groups. If a number of staff members are available to present programs, each may want to concentrate on a topic appropriate for his or her interest and may even be available on a scheduled day each week. It is no great revelation that one or two programs, well prepared and presented, are far better than a large selection that does not meet good standards and imposes undue strain on the staff.

In working with schools, it is wise to have the school system make the program arrangements for the interpretive staff with agreement in advance on available time and program types. Be sure that the descriptions of the programs are available with the subjects, available dates, age levels, group size minimums, and other information.

In larger communities where school demand is high, group size may be significant. In these instances, assemblies with a large attendance are a more efficient way of using park staff time. It may be possible to arrange special appearances on educational television. If the school system has its own television facilities, it might be possible to produce a videotape or motion pictures for use in classrooms; but these are expensive.

Technique is important in off-site programs. Unless you have had experience with these situations, seek counsel from those who have. If this is not available, sit in on a class or assembly program and attend a program meeting of a club. Also, observe the facilities and the interest areas of the group.

Consider supplementary materials that are specific to your mission and reinforce your program. Simple guidelines for the teacher for discussion before and after the visit can be very useful. Material on the features of the park, backcountry information, wilderness-camping pocket cards, hiking-safety folders and posters, and even buttons symbolizing an environmental message are possibilities. These educational mementos are genuinely appreciated.

It is impossible to suggest what age level benefits most from these school programs. This is dependent on the interpreter, the community, and the subject, among other factors. There are benefits in working with all ages from preschool to high school and university levels. However, it is generally conceded that children in approximately the fourth to sixth grade level gain a great deal from guest presentations. They are old enough to understand and young enough to be freely enthusiastic.

Time length is another important factor. School administrators and teachers usually prefer a one-period program, limited to less than an hour. Service clubs and other organizations have time limitations, too. When businessmen gather for a luncheon and give you 30 minutes for a program, they mean 30 minutes. Allow for questions and answers. This could be the most valuable part of the program. Arrive in plenty of time to meet the school staff or organization hosts, properly set up equipment, and relax for a few minutes.

Equipment is usually furnished by the interpreter, and this is by far the safest procedure. You are familiar with the gear and know its reliability. Take into consideration all of the rules for good interpretation in the park—proper amplification so that all can hear without strain; adequate projection lighting and extra lamps; images large enough for all to view comfortably; well-focused images for slides and motion pictures; good quality slides that tell stories (including slide series that show progressive close-ups or various angles of the same object); professionalism in using slides, such as right side up and sensible viewing times; motion pictures in good repair. Do not take anything for granted such as the availability of a projection screen, extension power cords, or the capability to darken a room. In some rural situations or at school camps a few surplus blankets or a roll of black plastic, a package of tacks, thin nails, a hammer, and some masking tape, may save the day. If your equipment power cords have ground plugs, be sure to carry adapters that permit the use of sockets without the ground plug feature.

Audiovisual equipment is not essential. A well-planned and presented program using artifacts, historical or natural objects, or even puppets can be just as successful in the final analysis as an elaborate audiovisual production (Fig. 17-4). Demonstrations on backpacking or life-saving techniques or living interpretation skills and crafts can often be held outdoors and involve the viewer in the action. Some of these may be presented in costumes appropriate to the subject.

FIG. 17-4. Off-site programs can utilize artifacts, historical or natural objects, or even puppets. Here an interpretive specialist gets a point across to his young audience with a hand puppet. East Bay Regional Park District, Oakland, California. (Photo by Martin J. Cooney.)

Do not neglect the possibility of hiring seasonal employees who reside in a nearby community. They may be able to represent your agency off-site.

Environmental Education

Much of this chapter discusses techniques and situations that can be applied to environmental education activities off-site. In a broad sense almost all of the interpretive techniques described are a form of environmental education, particularly if they concern the natural and cultural aspects of the park. In the off-season section of this chapter a number of ideas are presented concerning the use of the park by groups, the specialized training of teachers and youth leaders, and other activities. Off-site workshops and programs may be the prelude to planned use of the park for environmental education activities.

In light of the richness of park resources it is always preferable to work things out so that groups can benefit from them directly. Thus, many off-site environmental education activities, such as teacher workshops or programs in schools or school camps, should be designed to link the teacher and student with the park resources. In the park the interpreters are on their own ground, know the resources, and can impart their knowledge and enthusiasm. If the training is well planned and executed, many professional educators will be ready to conduct their own activities with some specialized guidance from the park staff.

The presentation of environmental education teacher workshops is perhaps one of the most profitable activities that an interpreter can engage in off-site. Your time with each teacher will be multiplied many times as they, in turn, teach their own students.

It would be unusual if such workshops did not lead to more cooperative use of park resources and to better understanding of the environment. In larger school systems there may be opportunities to assist with, and participate in, educational television programs on pertinent subjects. Many park resource people serve on local, town, city, or regional environmental education committees to assist in planning curriculum materials and coordinating educational efforts, including those with the park.

Park people have a great deal to offer the educational community in environmental education fields. You need not have a formal, teacher-training background. You do need a desire to plan, work, and follow through with an understanding of the park resources and the school community and a desire to bring the two together.

Exhibits That Travel

There are many kinds of traveling exhibits used regularly by agencies and private enterprise. They have value in that they carry illustrated interpretive messages to

FIG. 17-5. A portable lightweight exhibit used by interpreters when talking to off-site groups. The exhibit can also be loaned to schools or libraries. The side panels of this exhibit fold back. Note the carrying handle at top. East Bay Regional Park District, Oakland, California. (Photo by Martin J. Cooney.)

FIG. 17-6. A forest naturalist meets with her group in front of the portable Tongass Visitor Center. The center, pictured here at its summer site at Ward Lake Campground on the Tongass National Forest, Alaska, has a reception area, exhibits area, and audiovisual theater. (U.S. Forest Service photo by Fred Harnisch.)

FIG. 17-7. The portable Tongass Visitor Center at a school site in Ketchikan, Alaska. The center is moved to several schools during the winter season. (U.S. Forest Service photo by Fred Harnisch.)

FIG. 17-8.   Children viewing the slide presentation in the audiovisual theater in the Tongass Visitor Center during its visit to a school. (U.S. Forest Service photo by Robert Hakala.)

many peoples in diverse situations. A portable, lightweight exhibit can be used as a part of a program given at a school or organization, or loaned to schools and libraries (Fig. 17-5). The same exhibit, or those of more elaborate construction, can be used in public situations such as store windows, bank lobbies, libraries, shopping centers, at conventions, and special shows. Consider photo and art shows featuring the park as possible traveling exhibits.

Some areas have developed mobile exhibit units, including trailers, that can be easily moved from one site to another. These serve as walk-through visitor centers in the park or forest during the summer season, and as off-season, off-site facilities, with different exhibits and audiovisual programs, during the winter (Figs. 17-6, 17-7, and 17-8).

Working with the Media

Newspapers, periodicals, radio, and television are vital means of off-site interpretation. In determining how you are going to work with the media, first know the policies of your agency. Many agencies have their own specialists in media relations, usually at a regional or comparable level. Most parks do not. Consult when possible with the specialists in developing media possibilities.

By their very nature the various media touch the lives of many people. They are readily accepted as a part of daily living and reach people immediately and intimately. There are many interpretive possibilities. Park stories, including the features, activities of visitors and staff, and unusual occurrences, all have wide human-interest appeal.

Stories.   Determine what your stories are. Make a checklist of possibilities with categories appropriate to your operation. One method of organizing might include major programs, important developments, significant events, general interest items, occasions needing public support, and specials. These will vary from the opening of a new interpretive facility to an unusual wildlife occurrence or an archeological or historical discovery. The checklist should also include descriptions and listings of interpretive programs in and out of the park. Stories fall under *hard news,* that which is immediate and gets to the public the same day as it occurs, and *soft news,* that which does not have pressing immediacy but is of broad interest. Much off-site interpretation falls into the soft news category. All stories, including the soft news types, have a time factor.

Media Outlets.   Know your outlets and the media people, if possible. In small or medium-sized towns the staffs of newspapers (usually weeklies) and radio and television stations are generally well acquainted with the park staff. This promotes immediate and informal handling of information. These media are generally supportive of the park and its activities, including interpretive activities and schedules, so detailed coverage is usually possible. The large city newspapers, radio and television stations are of necessity fast moving, and there is a great deal of competition for space and air time. However, the park stories often have appeal as refreshing breaks from the general run of big city news. When dealing with large newspapers, send or deliver material to the news or city editor or to the specific editor (such as the outdoor editor) in charge of the subject you are handling. For radio and television, your best first contact is usually the assignment editor, who determines which of the staff members should handle and process the story. Note and get acquainted with the writers and personalities that would have interest in your type of material. In all cases express your appreciation to the media for their efforts.

Files.   Good files are important whether you work with the media on an occasional or regular basis. File cards should list the media sources with details on publication and contact times, specific titles of key people, personal contacts made with staff, interest in certain stories, past experiences, and other pertinent data. This should be coupled with a systematic approach to contacting the media.

Approaches.   There are many ways of furnishing the media with news or stories. These include news releases, feature stories or columns, interviews, press conferences, public service announcements, periodicals, and books. Your story may fit into a regular commercially sponsored newscast or interview program, or may be a part of public service programming.

The Federal Communications Commission requires that all radio and television stations provide a certain amount of free air time. Competition for this time is keen. Before going ahead with a project, talk with the specialists in the media. You will save time and expense.

News releases.   The most common method of furnishing material to the media is through a news release (a press release is for newspapers only). Check the established format of a release for your agency. Some have custom-designed letterheads that add distinction to the material. If not, be sure to clearly indicate your agency's name and full affiliation. Include a date and information as to whether the material is for immediate release or for a specified date. Identify a personal source with a telephone number for follow-up. Use a good, descriptive title. In writing the story use a style that is simple, active, and explicit; avoid bureaucratic jargon. Generally follow the outline of "what, where, when, who, and why." Newsmen use the inverted pyramid style with the important things first, followed by other information in descending order of importance. Be careful that this does not produce irritating confusion, rather than the desired interest, however. Use standard size paper. Type double-space and produce clean, neat copy.

Gear your mailing so that the release arrives on time. Know the publication deadlines of newspapers. Weeklies have a weekly due day. Dailies have a deadline for copy depending on publication time. Television stations have due times determined by the schedules of newscasts. Generally, you will have most success discussing a story or getting a camera crew up to midday. Radio is less specific, particularly stations with newscasts throughout the day.

Photographs for use with releases are useful in certain instances, but there are some guidelines that will pay dividends. Most newspapers prefer to take their own photographs, but often staff is not available, and travel time is prohibitive. They will sometimes use the photographs you send, particularly if they show good contrast, emphasize detail, and have human interest appeal.

Television stations prefer 35mm color slides of horizontal format with the main subject off-center so that the slides can be projected in back of a newscaster. Check whether the stations prefer the center of interest to the left or right. If you send more than one slide to accompany a story, try to select them with a similar color balance and density. If you send or use a series of slides accompanied by a narrative, make sure that they illustrate the major points at the rate of about 10 seconds per item. If photographs are sent, stations prefer larger sizes, horizontal format, color if possible, and dull surfaces, although they can dull a glossy surface with spray.

Use of motion picture film requires very specialized techniques. Stations have various preferences as to length, raw or edited film, sound tracks, and other factors. Check with them if you are not regularly using motion picture film for television stories.

Emergency or special news stories are exceptions to all the foregoing. They can often be handled by telephone, or media representatives will come to the park. In most instances the media will contact you.

Feature stories or columns.   Most of the foregoing applies here also. Talk over the feature story proposal with the media people in advance, particularly if coverage in the park is necessary. Frequently, the media professionals prefer to design, write, and develop these stories themselves with park consultants. Occasionally park staff members do a weekly column on park features, activities, and related subjects. These may include descriptions and schedules of interpretive activities.

A few interpreters have radio programs. Some specialized departments do regular radio broadcasts with mass duplication and distribution of tapes to a number of stations. If you undertake these kinds of projects, be sure you have staff and funding available to follow through with your commitment.

Press conferences.   Staff personnel involved with interpretation often arrange press conferences. Follow the guidelines for timing and contact. If the park is convenient to most media, it may be possible to hold the conference on location.

Inquire in advance as to the best place and time if a routine has not been established. Morning is usually best. Send background material ahead to the media and have copies available at the conference. Have one spokesman. If this person is not a dignitary, and you have a choice, select a person with a pleasing personality. Use props and other visual aids if they enhance the story. If all media cannot send representatives, and the material covered is important, see that information is sent promptly to those not in attendance.

Interviews.   These can take place in or out of the park. Television and radio interview programs and newscasts offer excellent opportunities for interpretation. Check the listings, talk with the program producers and decide where you can best present your message. Consider all possible audiences, including preschool children (Fig. 17-9). In-person interviews on timely topics, such as backcountry-use permits, fire dangers, vandalism, or more general interest subjects such as visitor activities or research, all work well on television and radio. Interviews usually run 5 minutes, but some may last up to 30 minutes. For television, wear your uniform if appropriate, or dress in colors other than black and white and avoid contrasting patterns. Arrive ahead of time and have a suggested series of questions and answers ready, keeping in mind that on most interview shows little time is spent in discussion prior to air time. Have visuals and props. Relax and talk informally. Look at the camera (your audience) as well as at the interviewer.

FIG. 17-9. Two National Park Service interpreters appear with J. P. Patches on a children's show on KIRO-TV in Seattle, Washington. During the show the children were encouraged to write in for a kit of materials on hiking safety. (National Park Service photo by Mark S. Hogan.)

Public service announcements. A large share of public service time on radio and television stations is taken up with prepared material furnished by agencies and organizations with a message in the public interest. The material may be produced in the park and furnished to stations on a local basis or professionally reproduced in quantity for regional or national use. Included are copy scripts for reading by station personnel or tapes with prepared messages; 35mm slides with or without captions, accompanied by a script or tape; motion picture films with a script or sound track and video tapes. The video-tape medium is the most commonly used, however. Consider furnishing television stations with a slide featuring the agency insignia for many possible uses.

If you do not have professional media people on your staff, listen to and watch public service announcements and consult with professionals in the business. Know the policy of the various stations as to the type of material most suitable for them. Be sure to check on the acceptable lengths for announcements. These generally fall into 10-second lengths up to 60 seconds. Live copy can be prepared in various lengths, with reading times indicated. Stations in more sparsely populated areas may accept a variety of materials.

Use a cover letter addressed to the person in charge of public affairs. Enclose all copy and materials, explaining the mission and the audience sought. Label the packets of material with description, agency, and date. Allow about two weeks lead time for programming. You may have greater opportunity for better time on television during the summer and right after the first of the year, when competition with new shows and holidays is less. Some agencies program regular documentary films, but these are the exception rather than the rule.

Public or educational television presents another opportunity. Since there are no commercial sponsors, there is frequently opportunity for interviews and specials on the park resources. However, even educational television is getting much more programmed than in the past, so it is again a matter of working your material into the most appropriate slots. Public television stations do not use public service announcements.

Periodicals and books. Periodicals and books often offer opportunities for stories and photographs by the park staff. Quite frequently the authors and publishers of periodicals and books seek the assistance of park staff for proofreading information, and photographs. It pays to have fact sheets, lists of basic features and facilities, and a photographic file on hand for all uses. These avenues offer possibilities for communicating your important messages to large audiences.

SPECIAL PROGRAMS

This category includes everything not included elsewhere. Like all other activities in this chapter, the extent of participation is based on need, personnel, and funding.

Below are some possible areas of activity, that you should consider.

Scout Activities

Provide leadership training in outdoor survival techniques as a special single activity or a seminar series; participate in scout shows or camporees with exhibits and demonstrations such as backpacking and mountain climbing (Fig. 17-10).

Colleges and Universities

Participate in classes and public seminars as guest lecturers; cooperatively organize and present evening programs on the current activities of your agency with a variety of speakers and audiovisual presentation.

Community Celebrations

Provide exhibits; give living history demonstrations that fit with the celebration theme.

Festivals

Represent the activities of your agency with living interpretation and craft demonstrators of cultural groups (native craftspeople and dancers).

FIG. 17-10. An example of a spectacular form of off-site interpretation. Here the Pacific Northwest Region, National Park Service and Recreational Equipment, Incorporated, of Seattle, Washington, cooperate in a series of mountain climbing—mountain safety demonstrations at the National Scout Jamboree, at Farragut State Park, Idaho. Exhibits, literature, and a rescue vehicle were part of the program. (National Park Service photo by Bob Pace.)

Outdoor Shows and Related Events

Provide and staff information booths (such as a mock-up of a ranger station); exhibits; mini-theaters for interpretive programs; demonstrations of skills (mountaineering safety); and audience participation activities (do-it-yourself elementary climbing techniques, indoor snowshoe run); exhibits of equipment (ranger rescue vehicle and first-aid equipment). These are excellent opportunities for providing information on your park in advance of visitor use.

Touring Programs

Work with local libraries and schools sponsoring special tours in programs and demonstrations like family backpacking, history programs using artifacts and facsimiles, and puppet shows illustrating proper park use and behavior.

Special Groups

Summer interpretive personnel may be able to assist with special programs in nearby communities. These could include training of counselors and environmental awareness programs for the disabled, disadvantaged, youth, minority, or senior citizen groups; or participation in programs such as in nearby summer camps, conducting trips and campfire programs on a once-a-week basis.

SUMMARY

The park and staff are important and expensive resources belonging to all the people. For this reason, as well as for targeting special audiences with special messages for management purposes, the park staff should attempt to gather in people off-season, and to reach out to people off-site. Good handling of relations with radio, television and newspapers will greatly facilitate this broadening of park efforts.

REFERENCES

General References

Field, Donald R. 1973. Analysis of Backcountry Use Permits for North Cascades National Park Complex by Sociology Studies Program, National Park Service Cooperative Park Studies Unit, University of Washington. Unpublished data.

Gebler, Charles J. 1980. "Resource Preservation Through Interpretation," *Proceedings of the C.S.P.R.A.-W.I.A.-P.R.A.C. Workshop and Convention,* Santa Cruz, CA.

Gebler, Charles J., and Richard S. Tousley. 1967. "Leading Children in the Field," *Park Practice Guideline,* Publication 26, The Park Practice Program, National Recreation and Park Association, Arlington, VA.

Gilbert, Douglas L. 1971. *Natural Resources and Public Relations,* The Wildlife Society, Washington, DC.

National Park Service, U.S. Department of the Interior, July 12, 1968, *Superintendents' Guide to Media Relations.* Duplicated handbook.

National Park Service and National Park Foundation. 1971–1977. *Adventure in Environment* (classroom books, outdoor books, and teacher's guides for various grade levels), NEED-National Environmental Education Development, Silver Burdett, Morristown, NJ.

Northwest State-Federal Resources Information and Education Officers' Council. January 29, 1972. *Conference Workshop on TV News,* State of Washington Department of Natural Resources, Olympia. Duplicated conference procedures.

Seattle Federal Executive Board, Community Services Committee. 1972. *When You Want Media Time.* Duplicated handbook.

CHAPTER 18

URBAN INTERPRETATION

Harold E. Wallin

With only a few exceptions, the services of interpreters of urban communities in the past were limited to encouraging better understanding of the environment through a knowledge of natural areas surrounding the city. This knowledge included an appreciation of the need for protection of these areas from the multiple pressures exerted on them. This was understandable, since the number of interpreters employed directly by cities has been few. Under these circumstances, little was done to interpret the urban environment itself, until recently.

In the 1960s and 1970s cities and their problems became the focus of national attention. Fostering identification with, and pride in, the urban community were objectives interpreters could assist with. Although the task might have seemed dismaying at first, interpreters were often excited by the prospect of a relatively untouched field of endeavor, and were eager to turn their talents to these challenges.

In addition, the concept that a city is a biotic community has recently gained favor. As such, it should be interpreted. Sudia, in his Urban Ecology Series notes that:

> The factors that tend to control the living organisms in the urban environment are the same ones that influence the behavior of living organisms in the natural environment. All biological communities—man-dominated or not—are affected by three sets of factors: climatic, biotic, and edaphic (soil and topography). Man's activities constitute the engineering and the management factors.
>
> What is obvious is that man controls the biological relations of the urban environment. How he exercises that control will be largely dependent upon his understanding of the urban ecosystem itself.[8]

There was a time when we felt we had to remove ourselves and our constituents from the urban situation before we could begin to interpret the environment. The fact is that an awareness of our immediate environment, no matter where we are located, is the bridge to understanding the total environment, and with this realization, urban interpretation has come into its own and is the object of much creative thinking. Not only is the city now a legitimate topic, but urban parks and recreation departments, city schools, universities, art commissions, historical societies, and youth groups, are interpreting facets of city living and environment to both its residents and visitors.

An exhibit in the American Museum of Natural History encourages children to take a more perceptive look at the things around them and to try to determine how these were wrought from nature. A construction exhibit, for example, shows how building materials like brick, steel, glass, concrete, and terrazzo come from materials found in the earth. It points out that 170 different minerals have been found in the city and that Manhattan schist, the rock that Wall Street is built on, contains minerals such as quartz, mica, garnet, and feldspar.

A cross section of a New York street corner from above ground to deep underground shows a fire hydrant, water and sewer mains, an electrical conduit, a natural gas line, and a telephone cable, all sharing the same environmental niche.[4]

Two factors must be considered in comparing the natural and urban systems. In the natural ecosystem, diverse organisms are governed by a slowly evolved system of checks and balances. In the city, the checks and balances are dominated by one organism—the human one.

The second factor to be considered is that the urban community cannot exist by itself. Many solutions to the ecological problems of cities transfer these problems to other parts of the earth's ecosystem. The realization of the interdependence of urban and rural areas and an understanding of the role of each in the welfare of its inhabitants is an important theme in urban interpretation.

To assist in the interpretation of this interdependence, the National Park Service has established areas near urban concentrations, such as the Gateway National Recreation Area in the New York harbor area, Golden Gate National Recreation Area in and near San Francisco, and the Cuyahoga Valley National Recreation Area, which links the urban centers of Cleveland and Akron, Ohio. State parks are utilizing areas close to urban centers as well. The need for fuel conservation as well as reduced travel budgets have augmented this nationwide trend.

Another impetus to urban interpretation has been the awakening of interest in the past. Cultural and historical interpretation are integral parts of urban interpretation and here a richer and deeper mine of information is often available than in nonurban areas. Historical information cannot be separated from a consideration of natural resources, and the evidence of their union in the past can lead to a consideration of their relationship in the present. "Why is there a city here?" is always a fascinating question.

As population increases so must the services of interpreters increase and diversify. Cities present socioeconomic problems, noise, air, and pollution problems, transportation needs, and here the problems of waste disposal and the need for recycling resources is demonstrable. These topics are often interpreted in environmental programs.

TYPES OF AREAS

All types of areas and situations should be interpreted to increase our understanding of the urban environment. Even above the evening noises of the city the cry of the nighthawk is heard. Bright lights that attract insects and flat gravel roofs that provide nesting sites have enticed these interesting birds to large cities. Cities on large bodies of water are frequently visited by waterfowl of various kinds. Cities on well-established migratory flyways often boast a dozen species that settle into an area of greenery or open space for a day of feeding and rest before taking wing again.

Railroad rights-of-way become favorite spots for unusual plants that are not native to the area. Large freeway interchanges that are not too closely manicured become spectacular with the blooms of introduced species.

Sidewalks, parking strips, parking lot edges, vacant lots, and alleys are all habitats for living things. Those whose attention has been alerted to *seeing* what they are looking at will find much of interest here.

Opportunists, animals that have adjusted to the human habitat, are more abundant than we generally realize. Park and museum workers are bombarded with questions such as "how do we get raccoons out of our chimney?" or "there's a big gray animal in our garage; it has a long, naked tail." We can assure the latter caller that the animal is an opossum and the former that the situation can be controlled by capping the chimney with heavy screening.

City park lands, large or small, can provide some surprises. The lighted Christmas trees on the public square of a large city may shelter a small flock of wintering white-throated sparrows—almost completely undetected by the thousands of passersby.

Most towns and cities have some open space where seasonal events of nature can be experienced. The National Audubon Society, Nature Centers Division, encourages American cities, towns, and villages to set aside areas as green islands of nature. Both private and governmental groups are aided in establishing on these lands community centers for nature appreciation, conservation knowledge, and understanding (Fig. 18-1). They are located as close to centers of population as possible.

Commenting on their ecological values, Shomon says:

> The city is often viewed as organization rather than an organism; its mission is to serve man the biological entity. If the urban world is to function properly

FIG. 18-1. The Little Red Schoolhouse Nature Center near Willow Springs, Illinois. The center serves school groups, families, organizations, and individuals seeking knowledge of ecology, wildlife, and natural environments native to the Chicago area. This well-known center has an annual visitation of nearly one-half million people. (Photo courtesy of Forest Reserve District of Cook County, Illinois.)

as a suitable living environment for the people, then it is logical to expect that in planning the city either in reshaping an old one or building a new one, the principles of applied biology and ecology should be taken into consideration.[5]

Thus, an attempt to understand the total urban environment seems imperative. A basic tenet of ecology is the concept of change, and an awareness of the changes in our metropolitan areas and technologies becomes essential.

Perhaps a half century from now the population of the United States will exceed 500 million. Approximately 95 percent of the population will reside in large metropolitan areas. If these conditions occur, naturalists will be useful in providing a sense of relationship between the inhabitants of such monster cities and the natural world—hidden, but nearby.

To quote Cantu.[1] "The interpretive role becomes applicable in all settings—natural, urban, historical and cultural—if we regard 'environment' in its broadest sense, for man is definitely a part of all these complex areas."

RELEVANCY

Urban interpretation will not be successful unless it is tied into the life and experiences of the city dweller. It must meet the needs of various ethnic and racial groups. It is important that the cultural aspects of these groups be kept alive in a new environment. This is not always easy in an urban setting of diffuse cultures. The interpreter must be able to recognize areas of similarity so that old customs can be adapted to new circumstances.

The needs of children, the disabled, and "golden agers" must be met. Children, at a very young age, need to become aware of their environment and of the role they must play in the protection of that environment. Golden agers can contribute the vast experience acquired through a long life of changes. The physically and mentally disabled, too, can be given roles in improving environmental quality. All these groups must be made to realize that they have an important role to play in helping others adjust to inevitable changes.

Many youth organizations have in the past been geared mainly to rural living; they can be guided to activities related to everyday living in the city.

SUBJECT MATTER FOR INTERPRETATION

When we consider the urban community to be an ecosystem, then the subject matter for interpretation is limitless.

Geology

Often the geography, geology, and mineral resources of the region are the principal reasons for the existence of the city. Cleveland, Ohio, is located at the mouth of a river that empties into Lake Erie. This city is convenient to the sources of iron ore and limestone, both of which can be transported by water and the boats unloaded at docks along the river. Coal is located in the neighboring states of Pennsylvania and West Virginia as well as in southern Ohio and is transported by rail. Thus, Cleveland became a major manufacturing center for iron and steel as a result of its location; it is a practical meeting place for the three principle ingredients for this manufacturing process.

Since the underlying rock of Manhattan Island is of Pre-Cambrian igneous material, the erection of towering skyscrapers has been possible. Cleveland, on the other hand, is located on a filled, preglacial valley. Its buildings of 20 or more stories must be built on massive concrete foundations or on piers that penetrate the deep glacial fill 200 feet or more.

The origin of construction materials such as brick used in buildings and roads can point to the significance of a local deposit of clay or shale; if building blocks are of sandstone or limestone then how far away is the quarry? If most houses are of frame construction, is there a local source of lumber? Why are the houses in most parts of the country kept painted whereas many of those in New England towns remain unpainted with the wood in a good state of preservation?

Cultural and natural history

It is important that interpreters research evidence of the prehistoric inhabitants of an area. Archaelogical research may have been done revealing an ancient village site, a kitchen midden, a burial site, or evidence of a travel route. These findings should be woven into the interpretative message dealing with the modern city.

Historical research methods are required when older buildings are being restored or replaced. Priceless bits of early history are often found. The history of these projects will be of interest if imaginatively presented.

Types of architecture and the placement of homes on their lots often tell the story of the early settlers' place of origin. Homes in older southern Ohio towns are narrow, very close to the street, reminiscent of older sections of Philadelphia or Baltimore. Conversely, homes are set well back with wide lawns and garden patches in northeastern Ohio. The towns resemble those in New England; towns in both regions have prominent village squares. Northeastern Ohio was the Western Reserve of Connecticut, and many of its early settlers emigrated from New England.

Natural history, too, can be revealed by historical records as well as by reading the landscape. What was the area like when early settlers first began to build their homes? A study of old surveying records will reveal the nature of the original vegetation. In the eastern United States particularly, "witness trees" were named as corner markers for properties. A plotting of these trees can indicate what the native forest was like.[2,11] Such information is also available in most communities if old trees are present. Were old trees in the city introduced, or were they part of the original forest? Certain trees can tolerate specific atmospheric pollutants and diseases: what are they and what is there in the makeup of these trees that permits this tolerance?

The weeds that appear in flower beds and vegetable gardens usually had their origin in other parts of the world.[10] Why they should be more tolerant of altered environments than indigenous species has long been a research subject of botanists and agronomists.

Similarly, the altered human environment is attractive to birds and mammals from other lands. Starlings, house sparrows, and pigeons are at home in our cities, sometimes to the detriment of native species. Agricultural practices like single crop culture have increased dangerously the numbers of red-winged blackbirds. Urban and suburban plantings have led to a remarkable increase of common grackles.

City mammals can become a problem, but a study of their habitats and require-ments can help to control them and even lead to sociological reforms. A study of the life history and food habitats of the Norway rat could lead to its control by eliminating its supply of food and its source of shelter.

A review of the adaptability to changes in environment of "city bred" animals can bring into focus the possible reason for the increase or demise of animal species. The house sparrow, for instance, was introduced into North America in Brooklyn in 1850 when horse-drawn vehicles were in use. The food and drop-pings of horses in city streets provided an ideal diet for the sparrow. As transpor-tation became mechanized, the house, or English sparrow as it is more familiarly known, did not decrease in numbers; it was able to adapt to other sorts of food and spread westward with human migration. It is now found in towns and cities throughout North America.

The passenger pigeon, on the other hand, was not able to adjust to civilization. These birds nested in dense colonies containing millions at a single site, often with trees so heavily laden with birds and nests that even giant oaks crashed to the ground. Such habitats made them exceedingly vulnerable. They were shot, clubbed to death, captured in huge nets, and burned out of trees. Wagon loads of birds were shipped in barrels to New York and Chicago markets where they were served at fine restaurants.

Compare this history with that of the domestic pigeon which has in recent times outwitted humans in their every effort to discourage it from nesting and roosting in buildings, or of the starling that during the winter months in our northern cities migrates in tremendous numbers to the suburbs to feed in the morning and then returns to the warmth of tall city buildings or chimney tops to spend the night.

Compare the increase in the number of red-winged blackbirds as a result of corn planted year after year providing a source of food much more abundant, and perhaps more reliable, than the normal, marsh-edge food they originally de-pended on. Human alteration of the environment has also benefited many animal species beyond the city limits. The opening up of solid stands of timber has pro-vided the kind of habitat needed by the Virginia white-tail deer so that there are probably more deer in our eastern states than there were during the time of the early settlers. Coyotes survive and increase in suburban woodlands across North America. The interpretive story could include the myths that circulate about these animals.

METHODS OF INTERPRETATION

Through Schools

Encouraging children to use all their senses is stressed in modern teaching, and the city school yard is far from sterile in providing opportunities.[9] Even those school yards that are largely paved with asphalt will have hardy plants in the cracks, under the fence, or along the sidewalks. Certain insects will also tolerate this inhospitable habitat. Studies can be carried out comparing the temperature of pavement surface with that of a plot of grass nearby.

In school yards where there is a bit of lawn or a shrub border, the opportunities, though perhaps more obvious, are often overlooked. Can not a square yard of lawn represent a miniature jungle where things will live out their life span? Watching and recording a few moments each day during the early spring and late autumn will reveal a number of changes. Plotting the yard into strips or meter quadrants will give youngsters a hint of the diversity of a small habitat and show them a few of the methods used by scientists who study larger, more elaborate habitats. Observations made while traveling to and from school can produce a wealth of phenological information (those changes wrought by the seasonal advance)—the swelling of buds in the spring, the first of the migrant birds, the first insects, the activities of parents and neighbors in response to the season in preparing lawns and planting gardens, the flowering of bulbs.

During the fall the children can observe the preparations by humans and by the natural world for the winter to come. Is something being done by plants? In the north trees are beginning to turn color, and soon the leaves will fall. The daylight hours are decreasing, twilight comes sooner, and the nights are cooler. What factors of nature are at work?

In other sections of the country other events are producing their effects. Is there a rainy season and a dry season? How does each change the appearance of the landscape? The concept of stream formation can be illustrated in the schoolroom by watching rain drops gather and form rivulets down a dusty windowpane.

It is not necessary to have access to large areas of wilderness to teach ecological concepts. Many important lessons in environmental awareness can be taught in the most hostile urban environments.

A school class study of an old cemetery will dramatically tell the early history of the community. Rubbings of gravestones can open up genealogical research. The names may recall associations and events of the community, and early history can come alive. Why are the gravestones made of stone that would erode easily? Could it be that harder and more durable granite was not available locally and that transportation was not available at that time to import it from other areas?[7]

A wealth of teaching material is available in the urban community. Interpreters can assist teachers by offering workshops on an informal basis. Perhaps they can participate in short courses that offer credits from a local college or university. Sometimes the school administration will offer inducements to the teacher to participate in these educational opportunities.

One large city school system has developed a Supplementary Education Center in which a relief map of the city has been constructed. The various periods of the city's development, different forms of transportation during these various periods, the city as it is today, and as it will probably be in the future are shown. All of this is done on a scale large enough to allow children to walk through the exhibit. The human and natural history of the city then becomes very real.

Some university courses in interpretation take advantage of the potential of the urban setting to provide experience for students. School groups, disabled groups, senior citizens and community action groups, all have possibilities for student education and experience as well as for public service. Contact with people and the realization of the difficulties and rewards of this contact cannot come too early in a budding interpretive career.

Field Trips

Teaching opportunities outside the classroom should be utilized where available. Akron Metropolitan Park naturalists lead field trips in the regional parks located throughout Summit County, Ohio. Emphasis in the Deep Lock Quarry Park is on the abandoned standstone quarry from which grindstones were manufactured and building stones fashioned. These were then shipped on the Ohio Canal (Figure 18-2).

Employing the simple theme of water as used in the home and school can lead

FIG. 18-2. This regional park preserves the deepest of the locks between Cleveland and Akron. The entrance sign above utilizes a grindstone from an abandoned sandstone quarry. (Photo by Harold Wallin.)

to some very dramatic experiences. Visiting the source of the city's water supply and following it from its origin in a stream, lake, or underground source to its treatment for human consumption will demonstrate forcibly the need for conservation of water.[6] Following this with a trip to the sewage disposal plant to see what is done to the water once it is used and to see the problem of waste disposal will be most impressive.

The interpreter can help the teacher prepare children for a field trip to the museum, park, or nature center. A short presentation of what to expect can be given in the form of a visit to the classroom, or an outline or short brochure can be prepared explaining the relationship of the classroom lessons to the field trip (see Chapter 17).

Through Organized Groups

Often leaders of urban youth groups find it hard to discover within the urban situation ways to implement recommendations of the parent organizations such as Boy Scouts, Girl Scouts, or Campfire Girls. Here again the interpreter plays a most vital role—that of showing the leaders of these groups how to use the environment that surrounds the child to help the child to understand not only the immediate environment but also the forces of nature at work. Children's historical heritage and their part in preservation of the total environment are also potential topics for such group programs. Much can be done using the excellent format of these national organizations. Changes are taking place in many of the national youth organizations as they come to recognize the needs of urban youth. Both Boy and Girl Scout organizations are recommending activities that relate directly to the large city, with older youths becoming involved in community projects, being introduced to local problems, and sampling various career opportunities and responsibilities.

An example of the change of emphasis is the success of 4-H. This youth organization was originally geared to the needs of farm youth. It still plays an important role in this respect by giving the rural youngster a feeling of pride and achievement in producing quality farm products. With the movement from rural to urban living the 4-H program has not diminished, instead it has become more active than ever in promoting projects that interest urban children in living and growing things.

Schools can also help the city child understand that vegetables are not generated in supermarkets and that milk does not originate in cartons. This can be done by means of school gardens, small home garden plots, and participation in garden fairs.

Children's farms are being developed in many locations that are within easy reach of the central city (Fig. 18-3). The emphasis varies from place to place. Generally, however, they afford children a chance to become familiar with farm animals, to participate in milking cows, shearing the sheep, and collecting eggs. The children are given an opportunity to participate in or to observe the early farm family activities of spinning, weaving, candle making, and preserving of farm produce.

Cooperation with Farm Bureau and Agriculture Extension Service has led to the establishment of demonstration farms to tell the story of modern farm practices dealing with the mass production of food products. Both types of teaching farms are important. Both can be established close to urban areas.

By cooperating with the proper city agency, youth groups can help beautify their city by raising flowers from seed and planting them around their homes, parking strips, and roadsides, thus fostering a sense of pride. Projects of this kind may help eliminate the litter problem and reduce vandalism through involvement in community affairs.

The interpretive staff of the East Bay Regional Park System in the San Francisco—Oakland, California region has developed a number of urban-oriented activities that can be geared to all age levels and groups. One is called a *Gutter Walk* (Fig. 18-4). Here the interpreter leads a walk along a city sidewalk and uses the things found along the edge of the street to tell the story of the city, much as the historian reconstructs scenes of long ago. What was this discarded piece of rope used for? Where might it have originated? Is it the product of a living plant? If so, where might that plant have been raised, and what had to be done to the plant to make a rope? Was it synthetic? In that case how might the synthetic product be superior to the natural product? The discarded tool handle—to what was it attached? How was it used?

By tracing the origin of the material used in the manufacture of a discarded bottle cap, a steel or aluminum can, a gum wrapper, or a Styrofoam ™ cup, the complexity of world resource supply and the need for the conservation of these natural resources is emphasized. The need for energy conservation could also be a part of this discussion.

There is a weed growing in a crack in the cement along a curb. A dramatic story can be told about the force exerted by something as seemingly powerless as a seedling. What will happen if the street is abandoned? What has happened to ancient cities that were abandoned, cities that in their own time were as elaborate as ours?

The second innovative program of this interpretive services department is the *Supermarket Walk*. Here a group is taken through a large market and encouraged to explore the sources of food items. The dairy counter tells the variety of products that come from milk, the attempts to substitute a manufactured product—margarine for butter, or nonfat topping for whipping cream—the reasons for various food fads and merchandisers' capitalizing on these fads.

The meat counter reveals a whole industry that was once familiar to the farm family but that is completely unknown to city dwellers. The market can dramati-

FIG. 18-3. The children's farm, located within easy reach of the central city, offers a chance for urban children to become acquainted with farm animals. Here the animal is temporarily placed in a narrow pen for viewing. East Bay Regional Park District, Oakland, California. (Photo by Martin J. Cooney.)

cally illustrate the energy flow through the food chain from the producer to the consumer and the ultimate lesson of the source of all energy—the sun. Subtle lessons can be brought home through this very interesting technique. Care must be exercised, if course, to make careful plans for the trip: picking a slow period of the marketing day, briefing the market manager as to the purpose of the activity, limiting the size of the group, urging the group to respect the store and its customers, and perhaps making at least a token purchase to show appreciation to the management.

FIG. 18-4. The urban activity known as the *gutterwalk* is demonstrated here by Josh Barkin. Upon finding bits of glass, bottle caps, pieces of rope, wire, or plastic, he asks his audience "What was it's origin?" Demonstrated at Pacific Grove, California. (Photo by Grant W. Sharpe.)

THE RECREATION DEPARTMENT

The interpreter faces much the same problem in his or her relationship with the city recreation department that the outdoor educator encounters in the relationship with a strictly classroom-oriented school system. Interpreters have the job of convincing those in power that they have an important role to play and that the recreation department is a vital source of enrichment to the community because of the services interpreters can render.

Probably the approach should be "don't fight them, join them." The kite flying contest can be turned into a study of aerodynamics. Perhaps "Exploring the Sky" might be a more appealing title than just "Kite Contest." Preparation can be made by observing the prevailing winds, the times of day when currents are best, when updrafts are good, and why they are present. If a lake or larger body of water is present, would it be better to take advantage of the off-shore or the on-shore breezes? Are thermal currents different close to the masses of large buildings than in less built-up sections of the city? Observing the flight of soaring birds that may be present can lead to some ingenious modifications of the traditional form of the kite. While the kite is aloft, the participant can get a feeling of the lifting power of the air currents on the instrument he or she has created. The kite string allows contact with otherwise unattainable heights and unseen forces.

Bike trips can become more than marathons of endurance and distance. While riding silently under one's own power, the role of a nonpolluting form of transportation, the sights, sounds, and smells (good or bad) of a city can be noted. Rest stops can become exercises in observation and in the use of all of the senses in a shady spot or grassy plot. Even a stone wall can become a rewarding object of scrutiny as riders rest and catch their breath before continuing on.

The canoe trip led by an interpreter is also possible in some urban areas. The design of the craft and how it is adapted to travel on water, how flotation chambers help keep it afloat, what safety precautions should be taken, and why they must be rigidly observed can all be pointed out. The actual trip itself can be one of exploration as well as providing good physical exercise. Water creatures seem to be much less disturbed by a person in a canoe than one on foot or swimming. Gliding silently along a stream or even along the shores of a city lagoon will reveal interesting glimpses not only of animals but of plants adapted to water habitats.

Fishing derbies can lead to identification of fish, food, and feeding habits of fish. Familiarity with fishing laws can lead to an understanding of conservation and sportsmanship (Fig. 18-5).

FIG. 18-5. Interpreters can work with the recreation staff of the City Recreation Department in many ways. A fishing derby, for example, can lead to discussions of the feeding habits of fish. Chesapeake and Ohio Canal National Historical Park, Washington D.C. (Photo courtesy of National Park Service.)

Through activities of this kind the interpreter not only becomes accepted in the program of the park and recreation department but will be looked to for advice in the overall program. The interpreter then begins to exert influence in the planning of programs, to introduce aesthetic appreciation and sensory perception, and to stress the idea that "recreation" is more than physical exercise, paved playgrounds, and equipment.

COMMUNITY PARTICIPATION

The urban interpreter must be prepared to encourage, participate in, and initiate all manner of community activity. The celebration of a historical event can be highlighted by the possibility of locating something alive in the city that was in existence when the event took place. Locating old trees might capture the interest of a historical society or a natural history club.

These organizations might also be interested in highlighting special features of the town by providing a self-guided historical tour of the older section of the city, or of an especially colorful display of shrubs or trees such as the azalea tours of some of our southern cities or the lilac tour of Rochester, New York. Hinckley, Ohio has become famous for its celebration of the return of the turkey vultures to a well-established roosting area; Monterey, California is famous as a wintering ground of monarch butterflies; the return of swallows to the Mission of San Juan Capistrano, California attracts national attention.

Seasonal events such as bird walks can be featured during the height of migration either in spring or fall, whichever is the more spectacular. Fall coloration is exciting in many sections of the country; this is the time to concentrate on identification of trees. Expeditions to a nearby feature such as a desert in bloom, colorful alpine vegetation, or tide pools on the day of a minus tide will emphasize local special attractions.

Park and recreation departments need to encourage ethnic preferences or local practices. Parks in Cincinnati, Ohio and Milwaukee, Wisconsin can expect to have beer consumed as a regular part of the family picnic or the group gathering. Western towns will need to provide pits or other facilities for barbecues. Cities with large populations of varied ethnic origin should encourage the perpetuation of the various heritages through encouragement of "old country" or religious festivals and cultures. One large city has devoted sections of its public parks to the development of formal gardens depicting the backgrounds of various ethnic groups. The German Garden has statues of Goethe and Schiller; the Shakespeare garden was provided by the people of English descent. The interpreter can enter into this program very actively by first assisting in the research and planning of such areas, and later by using them in guided or self-guided historical tours for the public at large or for school classes.

New towns that are being developed form exciting opportunities for the interpreter. Encouragement is needed to include open space, trees and other vegetation, and provision for wildlife. During construction, as well as when it is finally built, interpreters should have a role in the administration. They can guide the planning and siting of the school so that environmental education can become an integral part of the curriculum.

Special Urban Opportunities List

Urban interpretation does not require a natural setting as a place to initiate programs. The *Gutter Walk,* the *Supermarket Walk,* and the *Kite Contest,* described in this chapter, are examples of interpretive programs that require nothing in the way of on-site natural land areas. However, most cities, even those with populations in excess of half a million, have semi-natural areas either within their limits or nearby. Dave McIntyre provides these examples of areas to look for within cities: [3]

1. *Military bases.* Some obsolete bases are being turned over to the park departments of cities in which they are located. Military reserves usually have some accessible undisturbed area.
2. *Arboretums and botanical gardens.* These areas may offer a diverse floral community and may harbor many birds and other animals.
3. *Waterfront parks.* Subject matter can include wave action, waterfowl, and aquatic and terrestrial plant and animal life. Even a dock sidewalk can bring new insights, especially if the interpreter knows something about ships and shipping as well as the tides.
4. *Private woodlands.* Landowners near the city may allow the use of their lands for conducted interpretive activities. Plants, animals, forest ecology, and forest practices are possible topics.
5. *Rocky outcroppings or areas with unstable soils.* These areas may defy the construction of buildings and thus serve as natural "islands" amid a sea of shopping centers or residences. Geophysiology and soil studies are possible.
6. *Marshes.* Marshes offer tremendous interpretive potential. Plant succession, fresh water ecology and the making of a marsh are possible themes. Marshy areas typically have more visible forms of wildlife than do other habitats.
7. *Golf courses.* Golf courses, because of their use by golfers, may be difficult areas in which to initiate interpretive events. They do, however, provide large areas of semi-natural landscape in the hearts of most metropolitan areas, and sometimes woodlands on their periphery are available for use by the interpreter and group.

FIG. 18-6. A hands-on exhibit with lots of appeal to visitors of all ages. It is in these asphalt beds where skeletons of the extinct saber-toothed tiger are found. George C. Page Museum of La Brea Discoveries. Hancock Park. Los Angeles, California. (Photo by Marilyn Hartley.)

8. *Cycling, hiking or riding trails.* These kinds of areas offer the potential of both guided and nonpersonal interpretive activities.
9. *University grounds.* Many university campuses have grounds that provide interesting plants and, at least, some animal species.
10. *Zoos and aquariums.* Such areas offer great opportunity, yet few could be called interpretive showcases. Urban interpreters can prepare their own interpretation for these areas through observation and study beforehand. Zoos usually have a surrounding green area also.
11. *Historical estates.* The homes of early settlers, politicians, or folk heroes offer special opportunities. Architectural styles are also of interest for study and comparison.
12. *City parks.* Not all city park spaces are devoted to playgrounds or other intensive recreation activities. There may be areas suitable for interpretive activity, perhaps even some unique sites (Fig. 18-6).
13. *Islands of green.* Some cities possess areas of steep topography where development has been impractical. These green areas contain an interesting mix of plants and animals. Cemetaries often contain remnants of plant associations which have been disrupted elsewhere, as well as old, large specimens of trees.

The city offers many other objects for interpretation. Consider transportation depots, buildings, especially those with stone facades, fountains and other works of art, open-air markets, industrial sites, and views from tall buildings.

The concentration in cities of diverse ethnic groups also offers an opportunity for interpreters. To attract an audience from all groups, to prepare programs that appeal to a varied clientele, to outwit the latent vandalism of any young urban population and to try to redirect this energy, is a challenging task.[3]

CONCLUSION

Urban interpretation requires preparation and dedication. The people who form your audience frequently have not come to your area seeking recreation or interpretation. They may be disinterested in the natural history of a parking lot, or in the architectural landscape. Finding ways to create interest and concern in all aspects of urban living can be a stimulating change from traditional interpretation. Certainly the urban clientele has been overlooked in the past, but now, for several reasons, it is receiving deserved attention from interpreters.

REFERENCES

General References

Kieren, John. 1959. *A Natural History of New York City,* Houghton-Mifflin, Boston, MA.

Moore, Raymond C. 1958. *Introduction to Historical Geology,* McGraw-Hill, New York.

Palmer, E. Laurence, and H. Seymour Fowler. 1975. *Fieldbook of Natural History,* McGraw-Hill, New York.

Shomon, Joseph J. 1962. *A Nature Center for Your Community,* Manual of Outdoor Conservation Education, National Audubon Society, New York.

USDA Forest Service. 1977. *Children, Nature, and the Urban Environment: Proceedings of a Symposium-Fair,* General Technical Report NE-30, Upper Darby, PA.

Van der Smissen, Betty, and Oswald H. Goering. 1968. *A Leaders Guide to Nature-Oriented Activities,* Second Edition, Iowa State University Press, Ames.

Wallace, George J. 1959. *An Introduction to Ornithology,* Macmillan, New York.

Williams, A. B. 1940. *Geology of the Cleveland Ohio Region,* Cleveland Museum of Natural History, Cleveland, OH.

References Cited

1. Cantu, Rita. 1973. "Interpretation—A Way of Looking at Things," unpublished research paper, University of Arizona, Tucson.
2. Gordon, Robert. 1969. *The Natural Vegetation of Ohio in Pioneer Days,* Ohio State University Press, Columbus.
3. McIntyre, David M. 1980. Assignment 17 of the Study Guide *Interpreting the Environment,* Office of Independent Study, University of Washington, Seattle.
4. Moffitt, Donald. 1974. "A Museum's Peek into Urban Ecology Is All Too Realistic," *The Wall Street Journal,* May 8.
5. Shomon, Joseph J. 1971. *Open Land for Urban America—Acquisition, Safekeeping and Use,* The Johns Hopkins Press, Baltimore and London.
6. Stapp, William E. 1970. "Environmental Encounters," *Journal of Environmental Education* **2**(1).
7. Stranix, Edward L. 1974. *The Cemetary: An Outdoor Classroom,* Project Kare, Con-Stran Productions, Philadelphia, PA.

8. Sudia, Theodore W. 1971–1977. The Urban Ecosystem, A six-part Urban Ecology Series with these titles: *Man, Nature, City; The Vegetation of the City; Ecology of the Walking City; The River in the City; The City as a Biological Community; The City as a Park; Technology Assessment of the City;* and *Ecological Engineering of the City,* National Park Service. Superintendent of Documents, U.S. Government Printing Office, Washington, DC.

9. Van Matre, Steven. 1970. *Acclimatization, A Sensory Approach to Ecological Involvement,* American Camping Association.

10. Watts, May Thielgaard. 1967. *Reading the Landscape—An Adventure in Ecology,* Macmillan Company, New York.

11. Williams, A. B. 1949. *Original Forests of Cuyahoga County, Ohio,* Cleveland Museum of Natural History, Cleveland, OH.

CHAPTER 19

BUILDINGS, STRUCTURES, AND OTHER FACILITIES

A. Sidney Malbon

Most interpretive planners agree that interpretation *on-site* is an ideal that should always be sought. Indeed, there is no completely satifactory substitute for authenticity. When the topic of an on-site experience is skillfully presented, most planners would agree that successful interpretation is assured.

However, when more than a few visitors participate in an interpretive program, very pragmatic and inescapable communications, management, financial, health, safety, and environmental problems arise. Buildings, other structures, and outdoor areas can partially, if not wholly, provide solutions to these problems. Structures and areas can provide *mass* interpretation in lieu of the pure on-site experience, or can supplement it. They can also furnish indispensable support services in a controlled and often more hospitable substitute environment.

As an example, the overhead and vertical planes (roof and partial walls) of an exhibit shelter may simply afford a degree of protection from the elements for an exhibit and its viewers. In contrast, the visitor center performs many functions.

ADVANTAGES

Regardless of the scope and scale of the facility, whether a visitor center or an exhibit shelter, it will have distinct advantages depending on the skill and care exercised in the preparation of its program, design, construction, and subsequent maintenance and operation. Some advantages apply only to the enclosed space of a building; others also apply to certain kinds of exterior spaces.

1. Shelter and Comfort

As with any building, at least rudimentary protection is afforded the occupants and its contents. Adverse atmospheric conditions can be controlled or eliminated in an enclosed structure.

In a manner similar to an enclosed structure, roads, trails, and other well-designed outdoor spaces also afford a degree of shelter and comfort. They may provide a firm surface over terrain that would otherwise be difficult if not virtually impossible to traverse. The surface may be graded to facilitate linear movement and to provide lateral drainage. It may be covered with any of a variety of materials to increase the traction of feet or vehicular wheels. Thus it indicates a prescribed route or place relatively free of the hazards of cross-country travel. It may create or take advantage of microclimates by the clearing or planting of vegetation, choice of surfacing materials, and location and orientation with respect to sun, wind, and air drainage. It may afford cooling shade or warming sun as desired.

2. Initial Contact and Identity

In the interpretive plan of an area, a building can purposely be the dominant feature of the landscape as initially seen by the visitor. Through the subtle design details of the structure and the site plan, it can beckon visitors. They subconsciously know where to go, thereby dispelling any feeling of disorientation.

3. Circulation

Controlled circulation plays a vital role in the interpretive experience. A predetermined circulation pattern can help lead visitors sequentially from one interpretive site to another. The major pause can occur at a structure or outdoor space during the initial phase of their visit. The design of the structure may offer optional experiences for the visitor.

All structures and their links, the roads and trails, are designed as sequential components rather than isolated entities. However, there are instances when the interpretive experience is confined to a single structure and its immediate environs.

4. Transition

When well done there is a dramatic change from the clamor of a crowded parking area to a structure or other outdoor space designed to direct one's attention to features ahead. Any view or sounds of the typical loading and unloading activities in the nearby parking areas are screened; only the scenes to be interpreted are revealed.

5. Concentrated Use

By incorporating design features, a small portion of a total area can be devoted to intensive interpretive services within a structure or outdoor space. The adverse environmental impacts of crowds can be concentrated within a designated structure or space. In especially fragile areas, the benefits of this are substantial.

6. Exhibit Display

If the exhibits are fragile, a structure to protect them from damaging elements is a necessity. Aside from vandalism, the usual culprits are humidity, moisture, rot, and ultraviolet light.

As the complexity and sophistication of exhibits increase, the need for a controlled display area also increases. The sequential display of exhibits to achieve an integrated interpretive experience is accomplished by their placement in relationship to each other and by controlling the circulation of visitors.

7. Interpretive Support Services

Many interpretive programs provide facilities for collecting, storing, and preserving specimens and artifacts. On a selective basis the public may be allowed to study those collections. All this requires building space.

Exhibits may be seasonal and require periodic change or rotation. Exterior interpretive exhibits and signs may need winter or off-season storage. This, too, requires additional enclosed space.

Orientation and information not dealing directly with area interpretation may account for much visitor interest. Large-scale relief maps or other maps of the area or region can assist, if there is building space for their display.

A small theater or auditorium for lectures, films, and demonstrations scheduled as part of the interpretive program may also be located in the visitor center.

8. Other Support Services

Sanitation facilities are essential wherever people congregate. Provisions for food services may be incorporated to meet visitor needs. The noises, odors, and litter associated with these services must be controlled.

Offices and work areas for the administration, protection, and maintenance of the noninterpretive aspects of the area's outdoor recreation program are often incorporated with interpretive facilities. Personnel can perform interpretive as well as noninterpretive functions. This is a significant factor in reducing personnel requirements. In off-seasons particularly, one individual can provide a variety of services. This can eliminate closing a structure because of the lack of personnel.

However, careful design to assure that there is no conflict between these conveniences and interpretive activities is essential.

9. Security

Visitor and resource protection facilities and activities are often enhanced and made more efficient by a building. The interpretive program, especially appropriate exhibits, can teach the visitor to appreciate the need for proper use and protection of resources. The presence of personnel in or about a structure can help discourage vandalism and theft.

10. Focus for Financial Support

A building is a highly visible element, other structures and outdoor places are somewhat less visible. All can come to symbolize the total interpretive program of which they are but one element. However, because of its conspicuousness, a building elicits the financial support of a constituency, including politicians. This support can underwrite other program elements that alone might be more difficult to finance.[5]

DISADVANTAGES

Interpretive structures have several disadvantages. Some of them are substantial and require serious consideration.

1. Inflexibility

A major disadvantage is inflexibility. Most structures and *improved* outdoor spaces cannot be altered, moved, or obliterated without considerable effort. Site restoration to the condition that existed prior to the construction of the facility is difficult. Unless the structure is designed to be flexible, its permanency tends to define future programs.

Program changes are generated by three ongoing activities not given to easy forecasting: research, interpretive technology, and staff and visitor needs and interests. Research may discover new areas and items of interpretive interest that require a change in the location or function of the interpretive structure or space. Advances in interpretive technology and changes in visitor use patterns may necessitate major alterations.

2. Conflict for Attention

It may occasionally be necessary to transfer the visitor's attention from authentic objects to reproductions. The visitor may then focus on the interpretive techniques and facilities and fail to perceive the objective of the interpretation. For this reason the purist interpretive philosophy recommends on-site experiences; however, this is not always possible.

3. Architectural Dominance

Akin to the above disadvantage, the visitor's attention is continually diverted to an edifice. This involves aesthetic preference and, more importantly, principles of perception. Does the structure dominate the landscape to the exclusion of visitor interest in virtually everything else? This has occurred where elaborate visitor centers have been constructed.

4. Cost

Any decision to allocate financial resources must consider the available options. Unfortunately this is seldom based on a clear understanding of both original and continuing costs. Costs are usually not well defined until the project is nearly underway. When this occurs and the cost exceeds available funds, a typically irrational effort is made to eliminate hastily defined *luxuries*.

Continuing costs need an especially careful analysis. The history of most legislative bodies empowered to authorize expenditures indicates a relatively receptive attitude to requests for appropriations for the first cost of capital improvements. There is, however, a reluctance to provide for the continuing costs of operation and maintenance. A modest structure, well operated and maintained, has obvious advantages over a more costly structure that is poorly operated and maintained.

Remote location and design standards imposed by a severe climate tend to raise original costs well above those of the same facility located in an urban environment.

5. Provision of Utilities

Frequently an interpretive structure is well removed from access to conventional utility service. In remote and especially high-altitude locations it may not be feasible to extend existing utility services to the facility. However, a high visitation necessitates the provision of potable water and the disposal of sanitary waste. This frequently requires electricity for the operation of pumps.

In providing these necessities the site may be inordinately altered. A self-contained sewage disposal system that uses a septic tank and drain field may require a drastic clearing of vegetation. Extensive grading to establish controlled grades for drain tiles may strikingly contrast with the contours of the existing topography. In an arid climate, lush green turf on the surface of a drain field surrounded by parched brown vegetation can motivate more questions than the interpretive program itself, as well as being an aesthetic distraction.

Small impoundments to divert water from streams for a gravity water system may alter the flow of the stream or even cause the stream to run dry. Shallow wells may lower the water table sufficiently to cause discernible vegetative changes.

Generating facilities for the production of electricity may also necessitate impoundment of small streams to divert water to operate turbines. Diesel- or gasoline-powered motors to drive generators can produce distracting noise.

Utility lines, if buried, require clearing of vegetation. Unless extreme care is taken to carefully separate, preserve, and replace the topsoil after the excavation has been backfilled, the location of the line will long be evident from the change in succeeding vegetation. Utility pipes placed on supports in very wet sites that preclude easy burial, or utility wires carried on poles, standards, or trees will usually be conspicuous.

An independent water supply of sufficient capacity and pressure to protect structures from fire will require a certain minimum size. At times a fire protection system can be more expensive and disruptive to the site than the structure itself. In these situations the risk and legality of eliminating or decreasing fire protection warrants thorough consideration.

In recent years the technology of solar energy collection and conversion has been greatly improved. Properly designed buildings in some climates can derive 90 percent of their heating requirements from solar energy; some cooling can also be provided. Water can be heated and electricity generated. Some new interpretive and other facilities in remote locations are incorporating this technology and are now less dependent on conventional utility service. Facilities such as these provide an excellent example of solar energy use. Certain existing facilities can be remodeled to accommodate this technology.

6. Site Disruption

Some site disruption is caused by the structure itself. Grading and clearing associated with the construction of a major facility affect the site drainage, water table, and vegetation. In brief, they alter the ecology and produce a new microecology. Programs that interpret the site's natural history could be adversely affected.

Some visitors may be disturbed by the mere presence of a structure. The scenic impact of a structure on an unaltered natural site needs careful evaluation before the final decision to construct it is made.

7. Vandalism

In today's social climate, vandalism of public structures must be expected and prepared for. Damage not promptly repaired seems to invite more vandalism (see Chapter 25).

8. Maintenance

Regularly scheduled maintenance is indispensable if the structure or space is to fulfill its function. Waste must be removed, disposable supplies must be replenished, and damage and deterioration must be repaired.

A more extensive maintenance program will incorporate preventive care. In addition to repairing past damage and deterioration, the structure is routinely checked and maintained.

Locations subject to the extremes of wind, rain, snow, and humidity require special maintenance. The structure may have to be *winterized* each fall and *opened* or dewinterized each spring. Winterizing may include installing storm windows, closing shutters, caulking seams, and marking the location of critical utility valves. Snow removal may require herculean efforts to provide access to the structure if it remains in use during the winter. It may sometimes be necessary to remove snow from the roof of the structure.

DESIGN AND LOCATION

Ideally, any interpretive structure would be a major consideration in a master plan for an area. However, the specificity of master plans vary. Some include detailed site plans with statements specifying objectives, goals, functions, and priorities of all the area's activities. Others present only generalized concepts. They indicate the use of land by broad classifications and perhaps show the location of roads and major trails.

Decision-making by a three-step process is a convenient and direct way to arrive at the design of a specific interpretive facility when the general location has been previously selected. These steps are:

1. Written prospectus.
2. Schematic or diagram.
3. Construction plans.

Much of the information for the first two items may be available from the master plan.

The *prospectus* is a concise narrative statement of the interpretive structure's objectives. It describes the structure's function, its relationship to its site, and provisions for operation and maintenance.

The *schematic* or *diagram* will express graphically in two dimensions the relative relationship of space allocated to certain functions and the circulation of visitors through these spaces (Fig. 19-1).

Construction plans are developed from the two preceding items. For buildings and other complex structures the services of an architect or engineer and land-

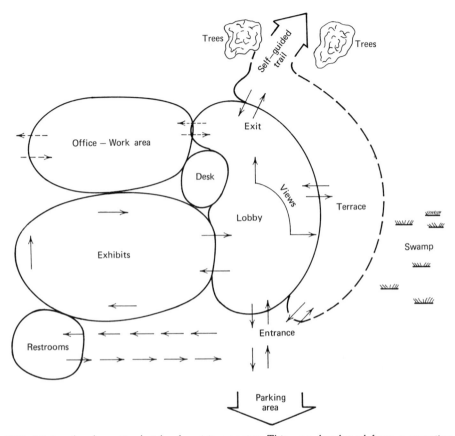

FIG. 19-1. A schematic sketch of a visitor center. This was developed from a narrative prospectus and would be the basis of a preliminary plan drawn to scale. Relative size of areas are roughly shown. Solid arrows indicate the circulation of visitors in, out, and within the building. Key features of the site are shown in their approximate location.

scape architect are required. A design team with representatives from each profession is preferable.

In many countries today a variety of interpretive structures are used (see Chapter 28). These range from the multipurpose visitor center to an exhibit shelter containing a single exhibit. The principle features of each follow:

1. The Visitor Center

A visitor center is a public use building where visitors congregate.[1] The term "visitor center" has supplanted the more traditional "administration building," "park museum," "park headquarters," or "ranger station," and the more contemporary "nature center" or "information center."

Originally the term "visitor center" implied a modern museum. Many visitor centers exemplify the museum concept admirably with ample and highly effective exhibit spaces, auditoriums, laboratories, work spaces, rest rooms, and information centers with related educational material for sale. However, in some newer visitor centers the administrative uses predominate with visitor facilities confined to a large lobby and modern rest rooms.

Functionally the visitor center has a distinctive interpretive rationale. It will subtly entrap visitors soon after they arrive in the area. Rest rooms and a drinking fountain, familiar things needed immediately, are the initial bait, but in a period of less than an hour visitors are launched into discovering the area's interpretive story. Their awareness of the experience that awaits them, the ways to achieve it, and their responsibility for protecting the environment is increased.

Distractions imposed by the close proximity of a coffee shop, restaurant, store, cocktail lounge, or lodging are under most conditions unacceptable. However, the proximity of these facilities can increase visitation.

The Site.   Site selection is a matter of sensitivity and values. One can argue that the visitor center should exploit scenic or historical views. Then from the building itself the scene can be interpreted. This usually places it near the focal point of activities (Fig. 19-2). Conversely, one can argue that a visitor center with its attendant roads, parking areas, and utility lines is an unwarranted intrusion in many sensitive sites. The construction of a modern structure can irreversibly alter these sites and ruin their inherent natural, scientific, and aesthetic values.

A major consideration is visitor ease in locating the center. Maximum visitor use is essential but the visitor center need not dominate the landscape in order to

FIG. 19-2.   A visitor center should be located so as to exploit the scene yet not dominate it. This visitor center overlooks the Mendenhall Glacier, Tongass National Forest, Alaska. (U.S. Forest Service photo by Malcom Greany.)

encourage use. Careful design of attendant walks, parking areas, and clearings can channel a flow of visitors to it even though the building itself is quite inconspicuous (Fig. 19-3).

Some visitor centers must command a rather dominant location to attract visitors. They otherwise risk being lost in the vastness of the landscape.

A visitor center astride the entrance and exit of a loop interpretive trail functions much as a gate. Provisions for bypassing it when the building is closed are essential.

Rest Rooms.   All visitor centers, regardless of the site, have two common essentials: rest rooms and drinking fountains. Provisions must be made for their use when the visitor center is closed. This suggests exterior entrances to all rest rooms and exterior locations of drinking fountains. More importantly these locations reduce the crowding and distractions associated with an interior location. These facilities help attract people who otherwise might forego the opportunity of exploring the visitor center.

Lobby.   Lobbies set the stage for the interpretive experience. They present a transition from the more hurried travel involved in getting there to a leisurely empathy with the interpretive theme. The lobby should be large enough to accommodate the average maximum visitation. To some extent the lobby can be flexible, expanding and contracting as the visitation changes with the seasons. Lounge furniture can be rearranged and temporary or movable exhibits shifted.

FIG. 19-3.   Careful clearing has kept this visitor center inconspicuous, yet easily accessible to visitors. The rest rooms at left are reached from the outside. Hoh Rain Forest, Olympic National Park, Washington. (National Park Service photo by Glenn Gallison.)

In any instance, visitors are made to feel welcome as soon as they enter. A sense of openness and a well-located information counter with free literature, maps, and friendly, competent personnel contribute much to this feeling. Public telephone booths and drink dispensers should be excluded from the lobby's public use areas.

An ideal space standard for the lobby is 12 sq ft (1 m²) per person though costs must often reduce this to 10 sq ft (0.9 m²) or even less.

Exhibit Area.   An exhibit area is a necessity in any visitor center. If the apparent lack of interest by some visitors is to be overcome, the exhibit area must have an inviting atmosphere. Particularly avoid narrow entrances and any sense of compartmentalization. Plan the exhibit area as an extension of the lobby with only enough separation to avoid real distractions. Dramatic lighting and imaginative use of background colors in addition to arresting exhibits can help entice the jaded or uninterested. Refer to Chapter 16 for the preparation of exhibits.

Clockwise circulation of visitors through an exhibit area is preferred. Individual exhibits must bear a logical spatial as well as interpretive relationship to each

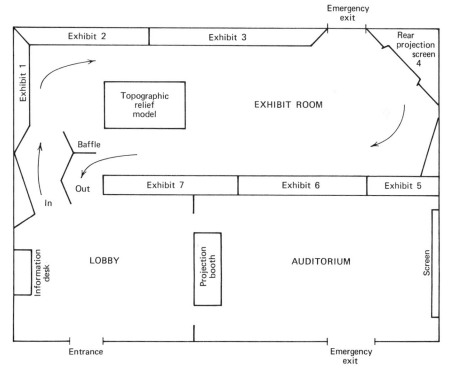

FIG. 19-4. A simple floor plan showing the exhibit room, auditorium, and lobby. Note the exhibit sequence showing the clockwise direction of the preferred flow pattern (in countries where people read from left to right).

other. Though they are planned as sequential exhibits, the visitor must have the freedom to bypass some exhibits and still grasp the theme. The first one or two exhibits, the introductory ones, receive the most attention and for this reason are usually the most effective. Attention span diminishes as the number of exhibits increases.

A standard of 20 sq ft (1.8 m²) per person is minimal to provide exhibit and viewing space (Fig. 19-4).

Auditorium.   Automatic audiovisual presentations are relatively more effective than exhibits in presenting the interpretive story. However, cost and problems of installation are formidable. Equipment failure is a potential problem particularly in remote locations where prompt service may be difficult to obtain.

Major visitor centers usually provide an auditorium off the lobby. The introduction to the auditorium may be the concluding topic in the exhibit area. This off-the-lobby arrangement permits easy access and also provides an option to the visitors if they are not interested in the exhibit area or if it is crowded.

However, this location carries the disadvantage of intruding noises. Lobby sounds enter the auditorium and vice versa with resulting distraction. Total acoustical insulation is possible, but it would destroy the open, casual relationship of the lobby and auditorium in which visitors are encouraged to wander.

Auditorium programs use automatic slide projecting equipment synchronized with accompanying tape narrative or films and are designed to operate nearly continuously during the visitor season. Front screen projection has been largely replaced by rear screen projection equipment utilizing mirrors and a translucent screen. Rear screen projection eliminates equipment at the rear and shadows on the screen. However, it is more costly and difficult to operate. It is desirable to design the auditorium for easy conversion at a later date to rear screen projection although front screen may be used initially. With a zoom lens the distance for front screen projection is quite flexible.

As with any auditorium, there are some minimum design standards. Ten sq ft (0.9 m²) per viewer is ample for seats and aisles. Clearly marked exits and low-level aisle lighting are essential for safety. An 8 to 12 degree slope of the seating area allows each row a clear view over the next. The angle at eye level in the front row from the horizontal to the top of the screen should not exceed 30 degrees. The best seats for viewing the screen fall within a 40 degree central angle projected from the center of the screen; an angle of 60 degrees is acceptable. Beyond that the image becomes too distorted. Main aisles are a minimum of 4 ft 6 in. (1.4 m) wide. Aisles between the seats are 2 ft (0.6 m) wide. The alternative continental seating arrangement with all ingress and egress from the sides utilizes seat aisles of 4 to 5 ft (1.2–1.5 m) with no main aisles. With this arrangement, a larger percentage of the area can be devoted to seating than is possible with the more common American seating arrangement.

Collection, Work, Storage, and Miscellaneous Areas. Areas for preparation, cataloging, storage, and study of specimens; exhibit preparation, library, general storage, and work areas are necessary to support an ongoing interpretive program. Standards for these are nonexistent. Rather, they are custom designed to meet the functions of the particular visitor center. The same is true of any administrative offices not related to the interpretive program.

Certain objects, particularly artifacts, that might be displayed or stored have minimum and maximum tolerance levels for their preservation. Some of these levels are well defined; others have a broad threshold and are often variable. Accurate climatic records are essential to determine these levels. Because interpretive programs are often developed in areas subject to extreme climatic conditions, these records are imperative in programming the preservation functions the visitor center will provide.

Circulation Patterns. Ideally, a visitor center creates a circulation pattern emanating from the lobby. When this is achieved there should be no sense of regimentation. Visitors move freely but according to a carefully planned sequence. In outline this would consist of:

1. The visit to the rest rooms and drinking fountain (outside access).
2. The transition and reorientation of the visitor.
3. A casual tour of the exhibit area.
4. A visit to the audiovisual program in the auditorium.
5. Detailed instructions on where to go now from the manned information desk, plus the purchase of any literature or slides, and pickup of free maps and brochures.
6. Departure through the lobby through which the visitors entered.

At any point in this six-point sequence, visitors may secure additional information from personnel who will be at or near the information desk. A floor plan of a visitor center incorporating these opportunities appears in Fig. 19-5.

Older buildings have been remodeled for interpretive purposes with considerable success. They have ranged from former residential structures to lighthouses (Fig. 5-5, page 113). The key to conversion rests with the structural limitations of the building coupled with the program requirements. The major elements are spatial arrangements and circulation requirements.

Space Allocation. Square feet standards per visitor have been suggested for major space allocations. However, a much more significant point is the determination of the anticipated visitation. Traditionally this has been a simple process of determining the number of private passenger vehicles and any commercial buses that could be accommodated in an adjacent parking area. Using a factor of approximately three for the former and a factor based on local observation for the

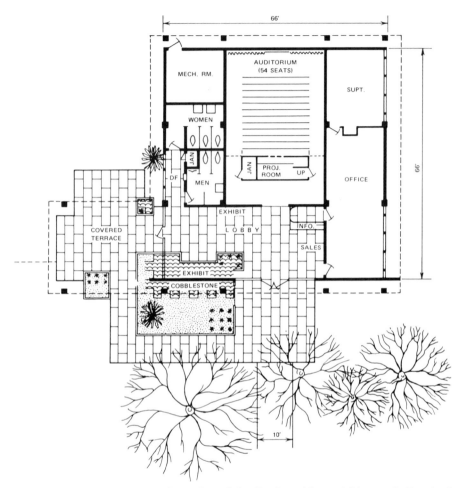

FIG. 19-5. The visitor center floor plan of the De Soto National Memorial, Florida. In this plan no separate exhibit room has been provided. Rather, exhibits are incorporated within the lobby. (Courtesy of National Park Service.)

latter, the maximum number of visitors that could be accommodated at one time is easily calculated. Conversely, the parking area could be designed to accommodate a specific number of visitors. By reasonable estimates based on study of similar situations elsewhere, a distribution pattern for the visitors throughout the area (including the visitor center) is assumed. By this process of deductive reasoning, the capacity of the visitor center lobby, exhibit area, and auditorium is determined. Applying the spatial standards, the square footage of each area is determined.

Changing patterns and modes of transportation may alter visitation. Smaller vehicles, more passengers per vehicle, and more reliance on public transportation could significantly increase visitation without altering the size of the visitor center parking area.

2. The Amphitheater

Interpretive programs in amphitheaters are primarily for visitors who spend the night in a nearby lodge, motel, or campground. Presumably they have more time and interest than the transient day visitor. They are also present when most outdoor photographic projection systems produce the best visual image on a screen—at twilight or night.

Some interpreters prefer the term "campfire circle" to indicate a less formal arrangement than "amphitheater" might suggest.[7] To some visitors the latter may have overtones of theatrical productions. A well-chosen site and appropriate design will dispel this confusion. A campfire circle may have simple audiovisual equipment or none at all.

The Site. An ideal site utilizes a naturally shaped bowl requiring little or no grading to accommodate a seating area and a screen or stage. The background beyond the stage area reveals no view of man-made elements, rather it should be neutral or complementary. A curtain effect created by a cluster of tall, lean tree trunks or the wall of a cliff is desirable (Figure 19-6). This arrangement gives some assurance that the visitor's attention will not be diverted during the program by backstage or off-screen movements. Very informal arrangements utilizing portable projection equipment and screens and having no seating facilities other than sand or driftwood have worked admirably in beach locations. The water is then the background for the screen.

Light must be avoided during periods when projection equipment is in use. Use of rear screen projection equipment can mitigate this difficulty. (Refer to the discussion on auditoriums under the section Visitor Center.) The light of the setting sun can be avoided by orienting the facility on a north-south axis. If the axis is located in a north-south valley, the effect is even better. Any light from passing vehicles, structures, campfires, or reflections off water that would strike the screen must be avoided. Sound from roads, door closures, electrical generators, campsites, and boat traffic can be especially disturbing.

Proximity to activities that could cause visitors to leave the audience in midprogram needs careful evaluation. Motels, restaurants, lodges, and coffee shops are some examples of this type of distraction.

Avoid severely exposed locations subject to strong winds or those downwind from disagreeable odors, for example, garbage disposal sites and corrals. High-

FIG. 19-6. A simple amphitheater in a small campground (27 units), designed and built by the interpretive specialist shown in the photo. The screen at left, in the shelter, is outdoor plywood painted white. The seats (which accommodate 60 people) are half-rounded logs on log supports. The projection stand at right is a vertical log with a hole cut in it to provide support and protection for the projector. Electricity comes from a small 110-volt gasoline generator. Ross Lake National Recreation Area, Washington. (Photo by Grant W. Sharpe.)

altitude sites that are comfortable during the day may have frigid temperatures once the sun has set.

Some source of electricity is needed to operate audiovisual equipment. In remote locations without access to a conventional supply system, motor-driven electrical generators are the usual supply. Storage batteries are sometimes used but must be frequently recharged. Electric generators, whether portable or fixed, must be prudently located and muffled.

Design Criteria. The amphitheater size varies with the size of the expected audience. The simple 60-seat amphitheater in Fig. 19-6 serves a small 27-unit campground. In contrast, a campground, lodge, or motel of 100 units requires a 250 seat amphitheater as a minimum.[7] This ratio is reduced slightly as the number of units served increases. It assumes all the overnight guests are bona fide visitors attracted to the area by its interpretive features and are not simply seeking convenient lodging or camping space for incidental reasons. Assuming the subject matter is not repeated nightly, most visitors spending more than one night nearby will repeatedly attend the program if there are no competing attractions.

If the audience source is in close proximity to the amphitheater, most visitors will walk to it provided there is a trail system for this purpose. However, a good program and facility will also attract an audience from distant lodges, motels, and campgrounds and will require additional parking space for these visitors.

Basic design criteria are essentially the same as those for visitor center auditoriums. The slope of the seating area is much steeper but should never exceed 30 degrees from the horizontal as measured from the bottom of the screen. Otherwise the image, as seen by the viewer, will be distorted.

Amphitheater programs are somewhat different from those of a visitor center auditorium. They are not as fully automated and depend to a high degree on the personal skill of the interpreter presenting the programs. In remote locations and for smaller amphitheaters this usually means one person will present the entire program and serve as both the projectionist and the host. With a front screen projection system, remote controls at both the left side of the stage and at the projection booth are required. The loud speakers are always ahead of the microphone location on the stage to avoid voice feedback.

Most programs traditionally feature a wood fire located in a pit alongside the stage to create a sense of camaraderie among the visitors. Be careful the fire does not illuminate the screen. A source of firewood secure from visitors is essential.

The screen needs protection. This is easily accomplished if it is a roll-up type that can be locked. If fixed, it may be protected by sliding or folding doors. Recessing of the screen into a stage structure and surrounding it with a dull black finish will reduce incidental glare and improve the projected image.

When the stage is occupied by the interpreter, before or after the audiovisual presentation, some lighting of the stage area is necessary as it makes it more convenient for the interpreter to mount the stage and to be seen by the audience.

The seating area may need some low level aisle lights. This need will increase with the number of visitors. The seating area surface must drain well, have good acoustical absorption, and not reflect light. A porous dirt or compacted crushed gravel surface may suffice but over long periods will erode, necessitating some periodic major maintenance. A bituminous pavement is more stable and if left to weather with dirt and duff (but not litter) can take on a very natural appearance. A surface of loose, round gravel creates noise as visitors walk in or out during the program. It also provides convenient projectiles for vandals to throw at the screen.

Seats may be constructed of half-logs or dimensional lumber. Seat backs are optional but are not common. Stone or concrete seats are too cool and damp at night for use in colder climates.

The location of a projection booth in the audience area presents some problems in addition to that caused by the interruption of the projected image by visitors' shadows. The noise of the equipment is difficult to muffle. If the equipment is stored in the booth, security is a problem. A generous supply of conduits between the stage and projection booth is advisable to allow for easy adoption of new projection equipment and controls in the future.

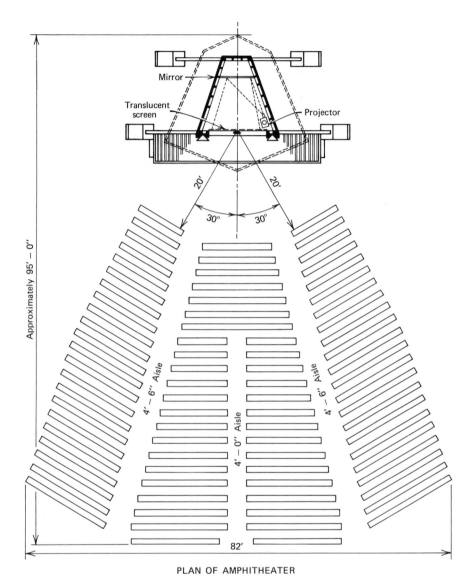

Mirror

Translucent
screen

Projector

20'   20'

30°   30°

Approximately 95' – 0"

4' – 6" Aisle

4' – 6" Aisle

4' – 0" Aisle

82'

PLAN OF AMPHITHEATER

FIG. 19-7. The plan view of a rear screen projection booth and 500-seat amphitheater in Acadia National Park, Maine. The projector, which is aimed at a mirror, is housed to the right of, and behind the translucent screen, eliminating a booth in the audience area. (From Park Practice Design.)

FIG. 19-8. The rear screen projection booth illustrated in Fig. 19-7. The soft translucent screen is protected by a garage-type door which slides down and under the stage when the screen is in use. One of the two speakers is shown unlocked at the right of the screen. (Photo by Grant W. Sharpe.)

Rear screen projection eliminates these problems. However, its use requires a substantial structure compared with a simple stage with a screen. See Figs. 19-7 and 19-8 for an illustration of an amphitheater that incorporates many of these ideas.

3. Trails and Roads

An interpretive foot trail connects individual scenes and objects to be interpreted in place through self-guiding signs, exhibits, leaflets and markers, or a conducted tour. It is frequently in close proximity to a visitor center and must always have ample parking at the trailhead. Self-guiding auto tours utilize roads for interpretive purposes in much the same manner as interpretive foot trails use paths. A detailed discussion of each appears in Self-Guided Trails (Chapter 14) and Self-Guided Auto Tours (Chapter 15).

Design Criteria for Trails. It is easier to construct a trail with motorized equipment and is usually less costly than one constructed with hand tools. Commonly available motorized equipment will require an effective clearing width of 8 ft (2.4 m) and leave a graded base of 6 ft (1.8 m) on which to construct the trail itself. A 6-ft (1.8 m) wide trail lends itself to easy maintenance by conventional vehicles. If the trail is surfaced with bituminous material, it can accommodate vast

FIG. 19-9. A section of the paved half-mile (0.8 km) trail to the observation tower on Clingmans Dome, Great Smoky Mountains National Park, Tennessee-North Carolina. The trail receives very heavy use. (Photo by Grant W. Sharpe.)

numbers of visitors and be fairly easily maintained (Fig. 19-9). However, it is difficult to relocate and obliterate evidence of its previous location.

Some visitors and interpreters may find a 6-ft (1.8 m) wide paved trail aesthetically offensive in an area featuring interpretation of natural history. A narrower, unpaved trail, which may be less offensive, can also be constructed with special motorized equipment, but miniature equipment may be difficult to obtain. Allow turning areas for any equipment. If carefully planned, these can later be assembling or viewing areas.

The width of a trail may be varied. The wider portion in flatter terrain may be constructed with conventional, motorized equipment. A narrower portion through a steeper area may then be constructed with hand tools.

To avoid the loss of topsoil and sod during grading, these should be salvaged and stockpiled, then replaced when the grading is completed. If certified native seed can be obtained, newly graded slopes can be seeded with native vegetation, especially grasses and wild flowers.

Though a varied trail grade is preferred, some consideration of maximum grades is necessary. For short stretches most people can maintain their stability on grades of up to 20 percent. For longer stretches, a maximum of 12 percent is more tolerable. If grades in excess of 20 percent are unavoidable, short steps cut into rock or cast in concrete are satisfactory. However, if cut into the soil, erosion will invariably result. Steps make use of the trail by the handicapped difficult if not impossible.

Should the trailside environment show the impact of overuse by visitors, it may be necessary to have an alternate trail available. Then the two trails can be managed as a system. When one is overused, it is closed for a few years to allow regrowth of trailside vegetation, and the other trail is used.

Because of the cost, roads are rarely constructed primarily for interpretive purposes. Rather, existing roads are utilized and adapted as well as possible. However, there may be opportunities to modify an existing road or design a new one. The amount of land devoted to the construction of a road is a function of three factors: the cross section design, the horizontal alignment, and the vertical alignment. To a large degree these are in turn a function of design speed.

For example, the 500-mile (805 km) long Blue Ridge Parkway in the eastern United States, one of the few roads ever constructed solely for scenic and interpretive purposes, was designed for a vehicle speed of 45 miles per hour (72 km/h). This speed is probably the maximum for interpretive purposes if driver and passengers are to perceive more than a fleeting impression of the roadside (see Fig. 19-10). The design, construction, and maintenance of roads are nor-

FIG. 19-10.   A section of the Blue Ridge Parkway, Virginia and North Carolina. The 500-mile (805 km) road was designed exclusively as a scenic drive with campgrounds, picnic areas, and interpretive facilities spaced approximately every 50 miles (80 km). The right-of-way averages 800 ft (244 m) wide or approximately 100 acres per mile (25 ha/km). Access is fully controlled. (National Park Service photo by R. G. Bruce.)

mally not within the purview of the interpretive staff. Engineers and maintenance personnel have this responsibility, although at some point interpretive input might be sought.

4. Overlooks, Viewpoints, and Assembly Areas

Visitors can be saved the time (though they forfeit the pleasure) of locating the best point to view a particular scene or object by careful selection and design of a facility for this purpose. This process is usually a compromise, the many seasonal variables being subordinated in order to agree on a site. The location is an integral aspect of the circulation of visitors through an area. Most often it is a specific location on a trail or a road or is an extension of a visitor center. An overlook may be a point on a loop trail which presents an overview of the trail that is not possible from any other point.

When access to the site is by auto only, ample parking is imperative and rest rooms may be necessary. Assembly areas at the beginning of an interpretive trail or at points on the trail where people tend to congregate are needed to protect the environment though they may not serve interpretive purposes.

Design Criteria. Clearing of vegetation to create a view is perhaps more of an art than a science. As any good photographer is well aware, landscapes are best perceived when depth is apparent.[4] Careful retention of some foreground vegetation will help achieve this. Often a branch hanging from a taller tree or careful pruning of branches to leave a tree trunk to the side will suffice. Clear vegetation slowly and carefully. Pause frequently to evaluate the effect.[10]

Parapet walls, fences, and railings to confine the movement of people are designed either to suggest the confinement desired or actually to prevent movement into restricted areas as much as possible. Considerable judgment is required to discern the appropriate circumstances for the use of either. Unless there are very definite safety considerations, a strong suggestion of a restraint may be ample. Young children are the most prone to falls from heights. A wire mesh fence from ground level to about a 2 ft (0.6 m) height will usually discourage them (Fig. 19-11).

If management policies permit, thorny shrubs and trees that inoffensively but effectively restrain visitors can be used. However, the planting of exotic shrubs and trees in natural areas is undesirable.

A low wall can serve as a barrier and a casual seat. This, or a railing, makes a very satisfactory base on which to mount easel-type exhibits or signs. They should be mounted nearly flat and low enough so they don't block the view.

In locations where deep snow fields form, extreme care must be exercised in locating any wall or fence. If the snow field moves appreciably as it thaws, it can easily displace a solid wall. A fence with large horizontal openings is not so easily displaced, provided it is well anchored.

FIG. 19-11. A protective fence at an interpretive overlook. The welded pipe and wire mesh fence serves to restrict visitor movement to the paved areas. Hurricane Ridge Road, Olympic National Park, Washington. (National Park Service photo by Louis Kirk.)

The section on amphitheater design discussed bituminous pavement as a surfacing material. Some additional points need to be made respecting the advantages and disadvantages of hard surfaces and the relatively softer gravel, wood chip, and similar surfaces whether used on trails or assembly areas. The softer surfaces are subject to water erosion and displacement by the treading of visitors' feet; the hard surfaces are not. The former will require periodic maintenance including the replacement of surfacing material.

A seldom-used material that is essentially a hard surface but has little of that appearance is soil cement. If the soil is friable enough so that it can be worked without lumping, it can be mixed in place with Portland cement to form a stable surface not subject to erosion and differing little in appearance from soil.

The parking area should never appear as one unbroken sheet of pavement. A few fundamental principles can be incorporated to avoid this. One should separate routes of vehicle circulation and rows of parked vehicles with islands of unpaved areas, retaining or replanting natural vegetation. Some islands may simply be resistant rock outcrops.

A roadside parking area is sometimes designed to orient the axis of the parked vehicle with the scene being viewed so that passengers need not leave their vehicle. Regardless of the medium used for the interpretive message, the interpretive planner can then assume that all visitors will have the same orientation from their vehicles.

The approach view to a visitor center should be uncluttered by parked vehicles. Simple but explicit directional signs and walkways are needed to assist visitors after they leave their cars.

5. Exhibit Shelters

An exhibit shelter protects both the exhibit and the viewer from the adverse effects of weather. Exposed seashores, alpine locations, and areas of frequent rain or burning sun often require exhibit shelters. They are usually an integral part of a viewing area or trail head assembly area and often provide interpretive and orientation functions. A trail head can be aesthetically improved by consolidating its miscellaneous signs into a single exhibit shelter.

The Site.   When used as a trailside or roadside interpretive facility, an exhibit shelter needs a well-drained surface where visitors can assemble and view the contents. If the contents can be viewed from two sides, the shelter logically is placed in the center of the surfaced area (Fig. 19-12).

An understanding of the purpose of the shelter is essential to optimize placement on the site. Protection from the sun requires an orientation of the display panels so that the information or exhibit displayed are in the shade of the structure most of the day. It also suggests a one-sided display panel. A structure to provide protection from wind or rain will have to be carefully oriented with regard to the prevailing wind during the visitor season. The roof must be big enough to cast shade and to protect the exhibit from rain, and sturdy enough to deflect falling limbs if located in a forest.

An exhibit shelter functions to a limited extent as a kind of a miniature visitor center. When used in an attempt to provide on-site interpretation of an object or scene only a few feet away, the size of the shelter may preclude direct viewing of the object. It should not disrupt the view of the interpreted object. However, when placed at a trail head, at trail junctions, in the midst of a parking area, or to supplement a closed visitor center where there is usually no direct interpretive relationship to the immediate site, then the problem does not exist, and a shelter may be used to house the exhibit without regard to the adjacent scene.

When located in close proximity to a comfort station—that social center of the campground—an exhibit shelter is assured a captive audience. It can be designed into the circulation pattern in and about the comfort station and become an expansion of the architectural character of the rest room by use of common materials, color, and detailing. As with any light-weight structure at high altitudes there is the problem of lateral displacement by the movement of snow fields. An additional hazard in seashore or lakeshore locations is damage from wave-tossed gravel and driftwood or inundation by wind-driven sand during winter storms.

FIG. 19-12. A massive exhibit shelter designed to withstand heavy snow loads, which often exceed the height of the structure. The site is the flattest portion of a glacial-scoured rock outcrop. The exhibits are removed during the winter. Box Canyon, Mount Rainier National Park, Washington. (Photo by Grant W. Sharpe.)

Design Criteria. Placement of display panels at convenient viewing height for most adults assumes an average eye level of 4 ft 10 in. (1.5 m). The upper third of a vertical exhibit or other graphic material is centered near this line of sight. If the display panels are mounted horizontally, tilting them approximately 15 degrees enhances viewing from a standing position. Some provision for viewing by children is desirable. The area below the display panels should be open so windblown litter and snow will not collect (Fig. 16-10, page 357).

Because of its relatively light weight, provisions for anchoring the shelter are necessary if it is to withstand horizontal wind pressures. A post and rail frame with burial of the posts directly in the ground is quite satisfactory provided that the posts are treated with adequate wood perservative and set deeply. If a bottom sill is framed, anchoring it to a concrete foundation with bolts allows easy relocation.

Few exhibits in an exhibit shelter are intended for permanent display. Some provision for removal of the exhibits and other displayed material is necessary. If a number of exhibit shelters are used throughout an area, standardization of the size of exhibits and display panels allows for easy exchange. A stock of reserve display material for prompt replacement of vandalized material is worth consideration.

Displays of delicate materials, such as relief models or preserved specimens, present special problems of protection and security if in exterior locations. If there is no special problems of protection and security if in exterior locations. If there is no alternative to their display, that is, an interior location or the substitution of flat work for three-dimensional objects, they can be placed in glass cases. The glass must be heavy gauge and shatterproof. Ample ventilation to avoid condensation within the case is necessary.

6. Lifts and Railways

Because of their cost these specialized transportation devices have seldom been used primarily for interpretation. However, once in place, interpretation can enhance the transport experience without great additional cost. Some of these devices function in this manner in the European Alps, and also in the North American mountain ranges.

Helicopters have revolutionized the construction of many facilities in alpine areas (Fig. 19-13). These "flying derricks" can airlift into place towers, cables, building materials, and the equipment and workers to erect them without the clearing and grading formerly required. As little of the disturbance of road or trail construction is created, adverse environmental and scenic impacts are reduced; yet, large numbers of people, including the disabled, can enjoy the view into the remote areas and make use of the facilities year-round.

Most aerial cable lifts move skiers from a lower to a higher location on a ski slope. They also move sightseers in summer and are easily incorporated into an interpretive program. Recorded interpretive messages played in a gondola during its most noiseless, birdlike journey through the air immediately capture the attention of passengers. Fixed exhibits at the terminals of lifts have a ready audience.

Narrow gauge railways that incorporate a rack or cog drive on steeper grades are superior to vehicular roads in several respects. The cross-sectional designs of the roadbed is narrower and the vertical and horizontal alighment is more flexible. Consequently, much rougher terrain may be traversed with less environmental impact. The spatial requirements of passengers in coaches is less than those of passengers in private vehicles.

Several narrow gauge railways operate in Europe, in particular in the Welsh Cambrian Mountains and the Austrian and Swiss Alps. These scenic trips offer outstanding interpretive opportunities but, unfortunately, few of them have been developed. They have the potential to provide mass interpretation efficiently in alpine areas while creating minimal environmental disturbance.

A funicular railway differs from an aerial cable lift in only one respect—the carrier vehicle rides on a ground track rather than an aerial cable.[9] Both employ

FIG. 19-13. A helicopter lifting a tower for transport up the mountain in the distance. Helicopters have revolutionized the construction of many facilities in high elevation areas. Mount Hood National Forest, Oregon. (Forest Service photo by Roland V. Emetaz.)

a cable driven by an engine at one of the two terminals to haul the carrier. Though there are many variations, a typical funicular railway is a system of two pairs of coaches (or series of coaches); one pair counterbalances the other. As one pair ascends the narrow gauge track, the other descends. They pass at midpoint where a siding track permits parallel passage. A funicular railway can traverse a very steep grade but it must be nearly uniform. Hence, most are quite short. They are best suited to moving a large volume of people a short distance to an otherwise inaccessible location. Most are found in Europe.

As an alternative to these fixed and relatively permanent ground railways and aerial lifts, helicopters can accomplish some of the same functions. They have greater flexibility but substantially reduced capacity and require favorable flying weather. Although they produce no long-term adverse environmental effects, other than a minimal flat clearing or "heliport" of 250 ft. (76 m) diameter, the air turbulance and noise when close by are unacceptable to most people. Even at a great distance the noise can be disturbing.

Design Criteria. All specialized transportation devices require complex engineering analysis and design. Some would qualify as contemporary engineering marvels. Universally applicable design criteria are simply not available. Major considerations in the design of aerial cable lifts vary with the cable diameter and the nature of the metal used. These affect the horizontal and vertical distances between towers, clearance between cable and ground including any required clearing of vegetation, and the horizontal and vertical deflection of the cable. Rack railways can achieve a maximum grade of nearly 20 percent. Narrow gauge railways can accommodate a 10-degree curve at 20 miles per hour (32 km/h). A realistic maximum grade for a funicular railway is probably 15 percent.[9]

FACILITIES FOR THE PHYSICALLY DISABLED

Designers have underestimated the mobility of disabled or handicapped persons, and most buildings (until recent years) have been constructed in such a way as to make use by the physically handicapped difficult and often impossible. Interpretive facilities have been no exception.

However, in the United States a turning point occurred in 1968. The Congress enacted Public Law 90-480, sometimes referred to as the Architectural Barriers Act. This requires that all buildings and facilities, other than military ones, constructed in whole or in part with funds from the federal government must be made accessible to and usable by the physically handicapped. Other provisions of this law provide for the establishment of standards for the design, construction, alteration, and use of buildings. The current standards now in use are those of the American National Standards Institute.[2]

Adoption of interpretive facilities to assure use by the physically disabled, though relatively easy in concept as it relates to buildings, is usually difficult because funds are seldom budgeted for the purpose. As the Standards referred to above describe in detail, the main requirements are:

1. Elimination of stairs wherever possible (Fig. 19-14).
2. A grade of less than 8 percent on all traveled surfaces.
3. Doorways of at least 32 in. (0.8m) horizontal clearance.
4. Handrails or grab rails in all critical places at 32 in. (0.8m) above grade.
5. Nonslip surfaces.
6. Extra wide parking spaces, preferable 12 ft (3.6m), reserved for use by the physically disabled.

"Barrier Free Site Design" by the American Society of Landscape Architects and the U.S. Department of Housing and Urban Development is a well-illustrated publication that applies these specifications to a variety of situations.[8]

Provisions for use of foot trails and exterior assembly areas require special considerations. The number of danger spots where safety may become a paramount

FIG. 19-14. This paved ramp now provides wheelchair access to the Mendenhall Glacier Visitor Center, complementing the original stairway seen in Fig. 19-2. Tongass National Forest, Alaska. (Photo by Grant W. Sharpe.)

consideration increases, and a greater degree of visitor protection is imperative. This must be done as subtly as possible, since disabled visitors often resent apparent overprotection.

Short interpretive trails specifically for visitors in wheelchairs can be provided adjacent to a longer trail for the general public; or the initial portion of a trail may be designed to facilitate such use. A nonslip, hard surface is required for passage of wheelchairs (Fig. 19-14).

In all cases the eye level on the wheelchair visitor, approximately 44 in. (1.1 m) above grade, needs careful consideration in the placement of signs and exhibits. Where the tactile sense is appropriately employed to enhance the interpretive experience, an arrangement that allows the wheelchair visitor to conveniently approach the object to be touched is a necessity.[6]

Interpretive facilities for use by the blind depend on a keen awareness by the interpretive planner of the senses of smell and hearing as well as touch. These have been effectively utilized to provide a self-guiding experience for the blind, either on a nature trail or within a visitor center.[3] Audio devices can assist substantially.

RECONSTRUCTION AND RESTORATION OF HISTORICAL SITES AND BUILDINGS

The dominant consideration in preservation or restoration work is the degree of authenticity desired in the reconstruction. The highest degree is the most expensive. It may require extensive research to determine the true conditions at some past time, the services of an architectural historian to devise detailed reconstruction plans, and the training and careful supervision of craftsmen in the techniques and materials used in the original construction (Fig. 19-15). This is a formidable undertaking. Modern plumbing, heating, and electrical service will also have to be subtly incorporated to avoid destroying the historical character.

Living interpretation demonstrations of reconstruction using the original construction techniques and materials can provide an interim but long-term activity pending complete restoration.

In the eastern United States several historical places from the beginning of the country's history have been restored. These range from small one-room cabins to mountain farms and a colonial capital.

CONCLUSION

This chapter is not intended to deal with the infinite technical aspects of the design of the facilities discussed. Such is the work of the architect, engineer, and land-

FIG. 19-15. Mabry Mill, Blue Ridge Parkway, Virginia, is an example of a restored facility. The old mill was in operation until the early 1930s. It was later acquired by the National Park Service and restored as an operating water-powered grist mill. Today visitors watch stone ground flour produced, and may purchase small packages of it. (National Park Service photo by Fred Bell.)

scape architect, and they should be consulted as necessary. Local building codes impose specifications that vary widely.

Rather, this chapter has dealt with the basic design criteria that any interpretive planner should take into consideration when developing an interpretive plan. These criteria are intended to be applicable regardless of the location.

More detailed information has been included where appropriate. This has been done to emphasize the particular site conditions that can be expected where interpretive strutures are common located. These are typically non-urban locations, often in a remote wildland environment. Materials that can withstand the rigors of these sites are obvious imperatives. Buildings and the array of other facilities that have been described in this chapter are tools of the interpretive planner. When used cautiously and thoughtfully, they can assist substantially in providing the visitor with a greater appreciation of the resources of an area. Realization of this goal depends largely on the ability of the interpretive planner to decide where and when they should be used and to clearly specify the various details necessary for their successful interpretive function.

REFERENCES

General References

Ashbough, Byron L. 1963. *Planning a Nature Center,* Information Bulletin Number Two, National Audubon Society, New York.

Beechel, Jacque Marlene. 1974. "Interpretation for Handicapped Persons," master's thesis, University of Washington, Seattle.

Department of Museum Studies, University of Leicester, 1969. "Conference on Countryside Centres," *Museums Journal* **69**(2).

Doerr, John E. 1957. *Summary of Conference of Visitor Centers.* National Park Service, U.S. Department of the Interior, Washington DC.

Eckbo, Garrett. 1963. *The Landscape We See,* McGraw-Hill, New York.

Lamoureux, John L. 1965. Planning Interpretive Centers, Sixty-seventh Annual Conference of the American Institute of Park Executives, Milwaukee, WI.

Litton, R. Burton, Jr. 1968. *Forest Landscape Description and Inventories-A Basis for Land Planning and Design.* USDA Forest Service Research Paper PSW– 49, Pacific SW Forest and Range Experiment Station, Berkeley, CA.

Lynch, Kevin. 1971. *Site Planning,* Second Edition, The M.I.T. Press, Cambridge, MA.

The Park Practice Program. *Design, Grist, Guideline, and Trends.* Four publications with structures, plans, and ideas for all types of recreation area situations. National Recreation and Parks Association, 1601 North Kent Street, Arlington, VA.

Rutledge, Albert J. 1971. *Anatomy of a Park,* McGraw-Hill, New York.

Simonds, John Ormsbee. 1961. *Landscape Architecture,* McGraw-Hill, New York.

Snow, Bruester W. (ed). 1959. *The Highway and the Landscape,* Rutgers University Press, New Brunswick, NJ.

Swiss Office for the Development of Trade, 1980. *Transportation and Communications,* Lausanne and Zurich, Switzerland.

Washburne, Randel F. 1971. "Visitor Response to Interpretive Facilities at Five Visitor Centers," master's thesis, University of Washington, Seattle.

References Cited

1. Alberts, Edwin C. 1965. Planning Visitor Centers, Sixty-seventh Annual Conference of the American Institute of Park Executives. Milwaukee, WI.

2. American National Standards Institute. 1971. *American National Standards*

Specifications for Making Buildings and Facilities Accessible to, and Usable by, the Physically Handicapped, New York.

3. Bureau of Outdoor Recreation, U.S. Department of the Interior. 1967. *Outdoor Recreation Planning for the Handicapped,* Washington DC.

4. Highway Research Board. National Research Council, National Academy of Science, 1959. *Selective Cutting of Roadside Vegetation,* Special Report 43.

5. Kuehner, Barbara (ed). 1976. "Visitor Centers—What Works and What Doesn't," *The Interpreter,* Vol. VIII, No. 3, Western Interpreters Association.

6. Mills, Emerson D. 1973. "The Design of Public Outdoor Recreation Facilities to Accommodate the Handicapped," master's thesis, University of Michigan, Ann Arbor.

7. National Park Service, U.S. Department of the Interior. 1961. *Special Park Uses Handbook,* Washington DC.

8. Office of Policy Development and Research, U.S. Department of Housing and Urban Development. 1977. *Barrier Free Site Design.* HUD-PDR-84(3), Washington, DC. Also as Stock No. 023-000-00291-4, Catalogue No. HH 1.2:B27, Superintendent of Documents, U.S. Government Printing Office, Washington, DC.

9. Schneigert, Zbigniew. 1966. *Aerial Ropeways and Funicular Railways.* Pergamon Press, Long Island City, NY.

10. U.S. Department of Agriculture. 1945. *Reducing Damage to Trees from Construction Work,* Bulletin No. 1967, Washington DC.

CHAPTER 20

PHOTOGRAPHY AND INTERPRETATION

Richard A. Kuehner

The interpretive specialist and the camera are inseparable. Virtually every interpretive program uses photography as a medium of communication. Photographs are used to illustrate talks, publications, and exhibits. They can magnify tiny things or reduce the size of large things. They save words by exhibiting complex relationships such as those between plants, animals, soils, weather, and other environmental components. Photographs are understood in any language and are, therefore, a very useful interpretive tool.

The interpreter uses photos to convey or reinforce a specific message. The photos selected must be free of distracting elements. Good photos are obtained by following the rules of composition and having wide knowledge of cameras and films. Although an inexpensive camera can produce good pictures, a broad array of expensive equipment is necessary for specialized photos such as extreme close-ups, telephoto shots, or crystal-sharp enlargements.

TYPES OF PHOTOGRAPHY

35-mm Photography

35-mm slides are probably the most widely used photographic form in interpretation. They are employed extensively in magazine and book illustrations and are more versatile than movie films for interpretive presentations. The sequence of the slides or the slides themselves can be changed to fit the personality of the speaker, the interests of the audience, or the particular climate or environment. The interpreter can also assemble slide exhibits that are operated by the visitor (Fig. 20-1). Synchronized sound, or title slides are used to carry the message (Fig. 20-2).

FIG. 20-1. A visitor-activated slide exhibit that utilizes horizontal 35-mm slides. Federation Forest State Park, Washington. (Photo by Grant W. Sharpe.)

Black and white enlargements can be made from sharp color slides. Many of the photographs in this book were made from 35-mm color slides.

Slides are easy to sort, label, catalog, and store because they are small, but they require careful handling as the film surface is easily scratched. To avoid scratches, lint, and fingerprints the slides can be mounted between glass covers and bound with aluminum or plastic holders. Many good mountings are available at photo shops. Another solution is to file the originals and project duplicates. This eliminates the time-consuming job of mounting the slides in glass. Eventually slide collections grow to considerable size; therefore, it is important to start the collection correctly (see Chapter 21).

Motion Picture Photography

Motion pictures, though less commonly used by interpreters, have certain advantages over still photography. Capturing and conveying the dynamics of animal movements, cloud formations, or wind in the trees is nearly impossible with still photography. Through time-lapse motion picture photography the day-long unfolding of a flower and other forms of hidden motion can be revealed.

Motion pictures can be used as supplements to the interpretive program. To

FIG. 20-2. Making title slides with a copy stand. White plastic letters are placed over a color photograph and copied with a 35-mm camera equipped with a wide angle lens. Letters can be added in successive photos to develop a progressive disclosure sequence. (Photo by Grant W. Sharpe.)

maintain credibility a slide-show commentary needs the smoothness that comes from familiarity with the subject. New or seasonal interpreters, who are not yet familiar enough with an area to assemble and present slide shows, can provide interpretation through the use of existing motion pictures. If well done, these movies can provide trainees with examples of effective interpretation and give them and the visitors valuable information about the area and its resources.

Although perhaps more convenient than sending a speaker when an interpreter is requested for an off-site program, loaning a motion picture is a questionable alternative. Film borrowers may not know how to operate projection equipment properly. The result is often poor projection and damaged film, and motion picture prints are expensive. It is suggested that an agency representative accompany the film even if that person does nothing more than identify the organization, introduce the film, and operate the projector. If a movie is to be used for this purpose, it is best to have it professionally made. Few interpretive programs have the money and expertise required to produce a high-quality nature movie. W.E.D. (Walt E. Disney) Enterprises, National Geographic Society, Canadian Film Board, and company-sponsored films (Humble Oil, United Airlines, etc.) have accustomed the public to excellent and expensive nature films.

Video Tape Recordings

Since the early 1970s, video tape recordings have become increasingly popular for interpretive and home use. The tapes can be played over many television sets by adding an inexpensive converter.

Video tapes can be replayed immediately after filming and could be used in the visitor center to show current activities. Everyday events such as plant and animal activity as well as more unusual events like flash floods and volcanic eruptions could be available for immediate viewing. Almost anything that can be photographed on standard movie film can be video taped.

Video tapes can be used in interpretive training. An interpretive talk or other program can be video taped and then reviewed privately by the chief interpreter and the interpreter-in-training, or perhaps with a group of peers undergoing the same scrutiny. This allows the new interpreter to more effectively evaluate his or her own presentation as discussed in "Video Tape, a New Tool for Seasonal Training."[7] Companies who sell video tape equipment may assist in organizing a video tape program.

Video tapes, like slides, can be sold to visitors for home use.

COMPOSITION

Photos used in interpretation must be carefully composed. Because the eye has broad and rapid focusing powers it is important to include only those elements that reinforce the interpretive message. The angle of view of the human eye and of normal camera lenses is about 45°. A normal lens on a 35-mm camera has a focal length of 45 to 55 mm, usually 50 mm. Lenses of shorter focal length cover more than a 45° view, whereas lenses of longer than normal focal length cover a field of view narrower than 45°.

Too complex a photo may confuse the visitor. Crowding too many images into a single photo may visually reduce the importance of each element. The interpreter must decide whether a single complex photo or a series of simpler photos will better support or explain the message.

Framing the topic is an important aspect of composition. Some photographers follow the rule of thirds. The main feature is located one-third up, down, or in from any side (Fig. 20-3). If a subject appears to be looking out of the photo, the viewer may be led to do the same. If an object is located too near the edge, it may draw the eye outside the photo. Similarly, several objects in a row may direct the eye out of the photograph. It is useful to learn rules of composition. With practice and constant attention, one learns to recognize what is regarded as the most pleasing and effective arrangement of subject matter for a picture. The recognition of such subject matter can become an automatic response while looking through the camera view finder.

FIG. 20-3. The "rule of thirds," whereby the main features of the photograph are located one-third from any edge has been followed here. Note, too, the person is looking into the scene, not into the camera. Tenedos Bay, British Columbia. (Photo by Grant W. Sharpe.)

Much can be learned about photographic composition by studying good photographs. Publications like the Sierra Club pictorial books, Time-Life books, or National Geographic magazines feature an excellent variety of high-quality photographs. These photographs are usually selected as the best of numerous possibilities. Studying various photography books will also help you learn. *Photographic Seeing, Successful Color Photography,* and *Principles of Composition in Photography,* all by Andreas Feininger[2,3,4] and *The Here's How Book of Photography* by Eastman Kodak[1] are good self-teaching aids.

Depth of Field

The depth of field is the distance from the nearest point of sharp focus to the furthest point of sharp focus in a scene. The objects in that area are emphasized by their sharpness. Depth of field depends on focal length of the lens, lens stop (aperture), and distance from lens to subject. Although sharpness in the whole picture area is usually desired in landscape photographs, a shallow zone of sharpness may be preferred in a close-up photograph of a flower. For example, by focusing on an individual flower we can render the background leaves and the twigs out of focus, lessening the conflict with the subject. This is most easily done at close range where the depth of field of most cameras is the least. Wide-angle lenses capture greater depth of field than do telephoto lenses used the same distance from the subject. All good lenses have a depth of field scale. In addition, a depth of field preview device permits the photographer to see the depth of sharpness in the viewfinder of single lens reflex cameras.

The greatest depth of field for a particular lens and aperture (f/stop) is obtained by setting the lens at the hyperfocal distance. The hyperfocal distance is the nearest point of sharpness when the lens is focused at infinity. This point depends on the focal length of the lens and the aperture used. For example, the hyperfocal distance is 30 ft (9 m) for a 50-mm lens at f/8 aperture, focused at infinity. This is read from the depth of field scale engraved on the lens. At a 30 ft (9 m) hyperfocal distance everything from one-half that distance [15 ft (4.5 m)] to infinity will be sharp.

Depth of Perspective

Human eyes see in three dimensions (because we have paired vision) but a camera lens produces an image in two dimesions only. The missing dimension, depth, is suggested by the relative size and position of various objects in the picture. A view across a still lake appears shorter than the same distance through a forest. An object in the foreground looks larger than the same size object farther away. The more overlapping objects we see, the greater the sensed perspective depth. Depth can be stressed or overemphasized by photograhing a large object in the foreground and similar smaller objects in the middle and distant view (Fig. 20-4). Equidistant spacing of similar size objects also increases the apparent depth. A classic example is a photo taken looking down a railroad track.

Perspective can also be used to stress height or steepness. A photo shot across a slope usually makes it appear steeper than one shot up the slope. Placing the camera parallel to the slope decreases the apparent steepness. It is like placing the camera parallel to a flat scene.

FIG. 20-4. Depth can be stressed by the arrangement of similar objects in the foreground, middle, and distant view. Baja California, Mexico. (Photo by Richard Kuehner.)

FIG. 20-5. The massive circumference of this western redcedar is emphasized by comparison with the two people posed nearby. Gifford Pinchot National Forest, Washington. (Photo by Grant W. Sharpe.)

Size is usually meaningless unless a comparison is included. The width of a tree is more effectively shown when a person stands beside it (Fig. 20-5). The frame of the photograph also provides a good height standard. The illusion of height can be created or increased by crowding the top of a mountain or tree against the top of the photo. Visually cutting off the top of the tree also achieves this effect.

Lighting

The subject and the mood desired in the photo suggest the appropriate lighting. Film manufacturers can supply data on the light-sensitive characteristics of your film, but you must decide on the technique that best suits your interpretive objective.

Back or side lighting can be used to silhouette and emphasize individual elements of the picture or to create a greater feeling of depth (Fig. 20-6). Back

FIG. 20-6. Using back or side lighting emphasizes individual elements of a picture. Indian paintbrush and pinyon cone. (Photo by Richard Kuehner.)

lighting can draw attention to a flower or other object by creating a halo of light around it. Cross lighting reveals texture.

Lighting can also help create moods. Nearly white direct sunlight suggests a hot day. Midmorning blue light can imply a clear, exhilarating atmosphere. Fog, smog, and dust particles block the blue light waves and emphasize greens, reds, and yellows. The film being used also determines which light colors will be em-

FIG. 20-7. Lighting helps create moods. Here the somber mood of a storm is conveyed by dark and light contrasts. Schulman Grove of Bristlecone Pines, Inyo National Forest, California. (Photo by Richard Kuehner.)

phasized. The somber moods of a storm are conveyed by dark colors with a few bright areas for contrast (Fig. 20-7).

Negatives respond to a greater range of light intensities than most print papers. Thus you may want to expose negatives for shadow areas and later print for the lighter areas. A shadow detail that is not adequately exposed cannot be added in the darkroom, but a slightly overexposed negative can be darkened by printing for a longer time.[6]

To insure at least one properly exposed shot, some photographers take one picture at the light meter reading and one at the next f/stop larger and smaller (a process known as *bracketing*). If an exposure record is kept, the accuracy of the light meter can be tested in this manner also.

EQUIPMENT SELECTION

Cameras

The camera most commonly used by interpreters today is the 35-mm single lens reflex. It is light enough and small enough to be easily carried, and adapts to a wide variety of specialized lenses.

Composition and framing are precisely controlled when the single lens reflex (SLR) is used because the subject is viewed through the same lens that forms the image on the film. This arrangement also insures against leaving the lens cap on while shooting the picture. With press or twin lens reflex cameras the viewer sees an image slightly above or to the side of what the camera lens sees.

A 70-mm SLR camera provides larger film sizes for smaller-grained enlargements. However, the film is more expensive than 35-mm film, not as readily available, and the transparencies fit only special projectors. The 70-mm SLR camera and its lenses are also more expensive than comparable 35-mm equipment.

Other smaller-format cameras are adequate for general scenes; some have high-quality lenses and can be used quite effectively. They are less expensive but are seldom used for telephoto or close-up photography.

Shutter speeds should be considered when selecting a camera. Be certain that the range of shutter speeds is appropriate for the lenses required in your particular type of photography. Most *good* cameras have an adequate range of shutter speeds and, therefore, this is not a problem.

Before purchasing any camera, it is advisable to review the buyers' guide in current camera magazines or consumers' guides, and to talk with experienced photographers.

Lens Selection

Lenses represent the major part of the photographer's investment in equipment. Although one can take a picture with a pinhole camera (no lens at all), refined lenses allow photographers to capture scenes in specialized light conditions at varying focal lengths. They also compensate for various degrees of perspective distortion throughout the entire range of focus.

The f/stop (aperture) scale on a lens indicates its light-admitting range. Each f/stop number is related to the next larger one by a factor of two. For example, f/8 admits two times as much light as f/11. The smaller the number, the larger the aperture. (In other words, the size of the aperture varies inversely as the squares of the f/stop numbers.) A lens whose largest aperture is f/2 is said to be "faster" than one whose largest aperture is f/4. But it is not necessarily a better lens in other optical characteristics. Aperture, f/stop, and lens opening all refer to the same thing.

The three most essential lenses are normal, wide angle, and telephoto. The normal lens is 45 to 55 mm focal length with approximately a 45° angle of view. Wide angle lenses are available from 21 to 35 mm and have about 75° of view. Telephoto lenses range from 85 to 1000 mm. Lenses longer than 200 mm are used primarily in wildlife photography. There is the risk of blurring the image when long lenses are hand-held unless the shutter speed is very fast (Fig. 20-8). To use sufficiently fast shutter speeds, highly light-sensitive (fast) films must be used.

FIG. 20-8. An interpreter using a telephoto lens. The film speed or shutter speed must be fast when such a lens is hand-held. Jasper National Park, Alberta. (Photo by Grant W. Sharpe.)

A special lens that is becoming increasingly popular is the zoom lens. It has a wide range of focal lengths, such as 50 to 250 mm, and allows the photographer to select the correct focal length without changing lenses. Because one zoom lens can do the work of two or three lenses, there is the added advantage of less weight and bulk to carry. However, the wider the range of focal lengths, the greater the complications in obtaining optical quality throughout that range.

Some lenses have a macro-adjustment. That is, they can be focused much closer than normal lenses without extension tubes or bellows. These allow a great range of focus without time-consuming lens changing. Now, even some zoom lenses have macro-focus options.

Filters

Filters are placed in front of the lens to block certain light colors or qualities. For color film, which is frequently used in interpretive work, haze filters and polarizing screens are often employed. Haze filters reduce the haze or ultraviolet light that can wash out bright sunlight scenes. Unwanted water or window reflections can be lessened or eliminated by polarizing filters. Other filters balance the color of outdoor film for indoor use and vice versa. Skylight filters, which reduce bluishness, are sometimes left on the lens to protect it from scratching.

With filters as with lenses, buying cheap optics is false economy. Filters should be dyed-in-the-mass optical glass, carefully ground, and coated on both sides.

Close-up Accessories

Most normal lenses on modern 35-mm cameras cannot focus any closer than 18 in. (45.7 cm). In close-up photography this distance is shortened. Again, the single lens reflex camera is preferable for this type of work.

The simplest way is to use supplementary lenses that are special magnifying glasses made to fit on the front of your camera lens. They are inexpensive, compact, and do not require additional exposure calculation.

Extension tubes of variable length or various lengths from 15 to 45 mm can be used concurrently to focus down to 2 or 3 in. (5 or 7.6 cm). They are inexpensive and sturdy but may require special exposure calculations unless through-the-lens light meters are used.

Bellows, which have a continuous focus down to 2 or 3 in. (5 or 7.6 cm), are quite flexible. They are not as durable as extension tubes and may be difficult to hold in the wind. As with extension tubes, bellows may need special exposure calculations.

Light Meters

Light meters are essential for consistently high-quality exposure. Because the human eye adjusts automatically and gradually to a wide range of light intensities, the photographer may not always be able to judge accurately the correct exposure setting.

Most SLR 35-mm cameras measure light levels through the camera's lens. Some light meters electronically control the shutter speed to precise tolerances. Others simply indicate the desirable f/stop. The electronically controlled shutter speed models are probably the simplest to use.

Some photographers prefer light meters that are separate from the camera. There are two types: reflected-light and incident-light meters.

The most common, the reflected-light meter, is held near the camera and pointed at the subject. It measures the light that is reflected from the subject to the meter. All through-the-lens meters are of this type.

The incident-light meter is held near the subject and pointed at the camera and light source. Regardless of the type of meter, one utilizing a solenium cell is preferred because of the quick readings and lack of memory (ability to adjust to new settings without retaining any of the previous reading). If a through-the-lens meter is used, it may be desirable to have available an extra meter as an emergency replacement.

Artificial Light

Photographs may be totally or partially exposed by artificial light. Some interpreters prefer to photograph wildflowers at night with an artificial light so the background will be black. Wildlife can also be photographed at night by using remotely triggered flash or strobe units.

Strobes.   A strobe unit consists of a glass tube containing xenon gas through which an electric charge is released. The electric charge can be built up by batteries or a transformer that runs on household current. Rechargeable battery units should be kept charged most of the time so that the batteries do not lose their ability to take a charge. If the strobe is used infrequently, a nonrechargeable battery pack may be the best choice.

A more sophisticated strobe employs a sensoring device that automatically controls the light output needed for proper exposure. Some models mount the sensor on the camera so that it points directly toward the area seen by the camera. Other strobe units require estimations and manual settings of the camera f/stop.

Strobes are available in a wide range of light intensities. Your specific requirements are determined by the type of photography anticipated. You would not need high light output for close-up photography, for instance.

Flash Units.   Flash gun units are smaller and lighter in weight than most strobe units. The flashbulbs come in various designs and can be synchronized with a variety of exposure speeds. They are fired with simple, relatively inexpensive batteries that have long-storage potential as each flash causes little drain. The primary disadvantages are the cost and inconvenience of purchasing and carrying the flashbulbs. Blue bulbs are required for color film but can also be used for black and white.

Floodlights.   Special floodlights with proper color balance are available expressly for photography. They are more economical for indoor use than either strobes or flash guns.

Reflectors.   Additional light can often be added outdoors with reflectors. This reduces detail-masking shadows. A white or foil-covered piece of cardboard can be used to reflect additional light onto the scene or a more elaborate silver or white umbrella can be purchased.

Steadying the Camera

As a general rule a camera can be held steady enough at shutter speeds that approximate the reciprocal of the focal length of the lens: 1/50 second with a 50-mm lens, 1/200 second with a 200-mm lens. With practice you may be able to hold the camera steady at slower speeds.

It is often necessary to have the camera steadier than can be achieved by hand. This is especially true when telephoto lenses or slower shutter speeds are used. Three basic steadying devices are tripods, unipods, and clampods.

Elevator tripods position the camera quickly to the desired height with a simple adjustment. They are usually too heavy [5 lb (2.2 kg)] to be carried on long hikes. Tripods that weigh less are usually not very steady. Some outdoor recreation areas provide specialized tripods for visitor use (Fig. 20-9).

A unipod, a straight pole of variable length to which the camera is attached, allows you to hand-steady the camera against solid ground. Some photographers believe that holding the camera in both hands with arms and elbows firmly against the chest provides the same degree of steadiness.

Clampods are short [6 in. (15 cm)] devices that can be clamped to almost anything. They are convenient and light weight and come with a screw attachment for use on logs and stumps.

FILM

Film Selection

The selection of either black and white or color film should depend on the message you intend to convey. Night scenes, or patterns and shapes in nature may indicate the use of black and white film. Colors may at times compete with the interpretive message, but this does not mean that black and white is always preferable for interpretive work. Flower identification photos and similar type pictures should certainly be in color. In fact, most interpretive pictures are taken with color film.

Purchasing and developing costs are about the same for small black and white prints, small color prints, and color slides. Large color prints cost two to three times as much as comparable black and white prints.

Infrared film is also used for interpretive photography. It is very effective in showing thermal pollution of air and water and has also been used to inventory wildlife at night. False-color infrared film shows the degree of vigor in vegetation.

Film Processing

Establishing a darkroom requires allocating building space, usually for exclusive use as a darkroom. However, if you are proficient in darkroom chemistry and

FIG. 20-9. A modified tripod (on wheels) provided for visitors to use in photographing dioramas in the visitor center. Mesa Verde National Park, Colorado. (Photo by S. Ross Tocher.)

techniques, you can probably produce consistently higher quality photos than commercial labs. Commercial labs use automatic machines, often overextend the life of their chemicals, and seldom carefully adjust the color balance and focus of each print. Developing your own photos is time consuming, but you have the added advantage of being able to experiment with the size and cropping of your prints as well as with exposure times, and other controls.

Before starting your own darkroom you should be familiar with the darkroom guides produced by darkroom equipment companies and with photo magazine buyers' guides. Numerous books on the technique of developing photos are available.

SPECIAL INTERPRETIVE IDEAS

The uses of photos and photography in interpretation are limitless. Numerous publications provide interesting and imaginative ideas (see especially Eastman Kodak[1]). Even multivolume photographic encyclopedias have been written (Time-Life[8]).

Photo Aids for Visitors

Through trail signs, booklets, and talks the interpreter can offer many picture-taking tips for visitors. Some suggestions that might be offered are:

1. Personalize photographs by including friends in the scene. Add to the photo by having them wear bright clothing.
2. Make title slides by photographing park or forest signs.
3. Photograph Lake Pleasant in the morning. Make sure the shoreline is horizontal.
4. Photograph Feather Plume Falls between 2 and 4 PM for best sunlight.

Such suggestions are best conveyed to the visitor by paired photographs showing both desirable composition and lighting and less desirable technique and timing.

Special nature-photography guided walks can be designed for visitors who carry cameras. On these walks the interpreter assists the visitors in improving their photographic skills as well as directing their attention to facets of natural history.

Photographic instruction naturally flows into interpretation. An interpreter giving advice on how to photograph sunsets could explain the factors that create colorful sunsets and how different films and exposure speeds affect those factors. The same approach could be applied to an explanation of mirages or shadows.

Photo walks can also be self-guided. Numbered posts keyed to a booklet or series of signs could direct visitors to photograph certain subjects at different angles and times. In both guided and self-guided walks the visitors focus their cameras and thus their attention on important features, and they return home with photographic reinforcement of the interpretive story.

Geological, Historical, and Seasonal Changes

Looking at Mount St. Helens in Washington State today, few would believe that it was ever a nearly symmetrical cone. But, photos taken of the mountain before it erupted in 1980 dramatically reveal the cataclysmic geological changes that have occurred. A series of dated photos showing the changes from dormancy to its present uneasy quiescence could enliven geologic interpretation. Geological forces seldom manifest themselves so dramatically.

An exhibit utilizing historical photographs could be made showing logging methods of the 1800s and ending with modern helicopter or balloon logging. Another use of photography in interpretation might be illustrations of land use on a certain tract from its early occupation to the present time. Sepia tones could be followed by black and white prints, which would be followed by color prints for the present-day scenes. Here, the medium would reinforce the message.

Photos can also be used to illustrate shorter segments of time. A series of photos taken from the same location during different seasons of the year can illustrate the changing aspect of a tree or other part of the environment. Series of color slides can be effectively projected through the use of a fade-in fade-out dissolve unit. With this device, one season seems to blend into the next.

Environmental Monitoring

Photography is an ideal medium to record the life history of an ecosystem or biologic feature. However, this takes foresight. It is often desirable to establish permanent photo stations in a diversity of ecosystems to form a baseline record for later comparison. Photographs should be taken annually or at other systematic intervals to observe and exhibit the rates and increments of plant growth, erosion rates, or other environmental changes.[5] Human impact can also be recorded in this manner.

A camera set on a leveled tripod can be used to take a 360° series of these photos at a photo station. A series of this kind makes it easy to relocate the photo station again even if the reference post is destroyed. A special panorama unit can be purchased that allows the subdivision of the 360° into equal-angle photographs.

For panoramic views, it is best to mount the camera on the tripod so that the optical center of the lens (rather than the camera body) is directly over the panning tripod head. One way to do this is to mount a focusing rail between the tripod and the camera. This will permit racking the camera back so that the lens is over the tripod head. The segments of the panorama picture will then fit together properly.

Size or Quantity Demonstration

Comprehension of the size of an area can be enhanced by a series of scale photographs. You might wish to show that 15 percent or 885,000 acres (354,000 ha) of a management area is covered by juniper woodland habitat. Such figures are meaningless, especially when you cannot see all of the area from one vantage point. A photo series might start with a satellite photo, followed by a high-level aerial photo, then a low-level, large-scale photo of only a part of the tract; the final shot would be the view from the interpretive site.

Photo Murals

Photo murals used as backdrops for exhibits can set the mood of the visitor center. A large photo can substitute for the actual scene, which may be inaccessible or distant from the visitor center. Some exhibit manufacturers and photographic stores can produce large murals in black and white or color from negatives. A pastel, single-tone print such as sepia (light brown) is very effective and neither dominates nor conflicts with the exhibits.

Back-lit 8'' x 10'' or larger color transparencies have been used in exhibits and murals for years. But until recently they appeared washed-out if there was much light in the viewing room. Now, the major photography companies produce a transparency film with a built-in diffuser that is even more brilliant when lit from both the rear and by the room light simultaneously.

Screened Photos

An overly contrasty negative can often be salvaged and enhanced by printing through one of a variety of screens (messo, dot, line, etc.) available at custom photo processors. Screening lightens the dark areas and darkens (sometimes) the light areas, creating a "soft" background photograph. Dark titles or text can be effectively printed over screened photos to tie the mood of the geographic or conceptual title with the appropriate scene. A crisp, detailed photograph would be less desirable in this situation because it could call attention to irrelevant detail in the scene. Screened photographs in an exhibit or leaflet intermingled with other photographs, can help avoid the monotony of too many of the same type or size of photos.

People in Photos

A photograph of people enjoying a scene is usually more desirable than a photograph of the scene alone. Also, fishing, hunting, interpretive touring, and other uses of an area can be more precisely conveyed by photos than words. Numerous ideas for including people can be gleaned from a magazine like *National Geographic.*

Locating Photos on a Limited Budget

Even though you may be an excellent photographer, you may not be able to obtain photos when needed. During the winter, you might have to finish an exhibit on spring wildflowers, or you might be illustrating a fall waterfowl hunting brochure which must be completed by spring. Perhaps, you have an interpretive talk planned that requires some specialized scenes.

Photos from professional photographers can be utilized but are usually quite expensive. Of course, if the budget allows, contacting a professional photographic studio in any major city will give you many valuable leads for procuring high-quality photographs for almost any subject needs.

If you have more time, a photography club or school photo class may be able to take the photographs you need or produce them from their files. They might include in a contest a prize for the photograph that best conveys your subject. The prize would normally be seeing their photograph in print or on an exhibit. As an extra incentive, you might donate some film to the class or club, or even offer a cash prize.

Nonprofit historical societies and governmental resource agencies will often make valuable photos available for the cost of reproduction.

CONCLUSION

The uses of photographs and photography, like the equipment available, are many and varied. Their application and suitability to interpretive media must be carefully considered. To do so, the interpreter must keep abreast of the changes and advances in both interpretation and photography.

Good photographers never stop learning. They are always trying new angles and techniques and refining their style. Constructive criticism from colleagues and other audiences is helpful and should be welcomed.

As an interpreter, you have an opportunity to add something of your own creativity to the permanent photo collection of an interpretive program. Your vision of the environment is unique. Through the camera, you share it with others.

REFERENCES

General References

Blaker, Alfred A. 1976. *Field Photography Beginning and Advanced Techniques,* W. H. Freeman and Company, San Francisco, CA.

Burk, Tom. 1974. *Do It In the Dark: Using the New R.C. Paper,* H. P. Books, Tucson, AZ.

Eastman Kodak Company. Annual. *Index to Kodak Information,* Rochester, NY. Describes specific publications on every aspect of photography.

Eastman Kodak Company. 1976. *Adventures in Color-Slide Photography,* Rochester, NY.

Hedgecoe, John. 1978. *The Art of Color Photography,* Simon and Schuster, New York.

Jacobs, Lou Jr. et al. 1978. *Petersen's Basic Guide to Photography,* Petersen Publication Co., Los Angeles, CA.

Jacobs, Lou Jr. 1974. *How To Take Great Pictures With Your SLR,* H. P. Books, Tucson, AZ.

Maye, Patricia. 1974. *Fieldbook of Nature Photography,* Sierra Club, San Francisco, CA.

Shipman, Carl. 1974. *Understanding Photography,* H. P. Books, Tucson, AZ.

References Cited

1. Eastman Kodak Co, 1971. *The Here's How Book of Photography,* Kodak Publication AE-100, Eastman Kodak Co, Rochester, NY.

2. Feininger, Andreas. 1973. *Photographic Seeing,* Prentice-Hall, Englewood Cliffs, NJ.

3. Feininger, Andreas. 1973. *Principles of Composition In Photography,* American Photographic Book Publishing Co., New York.

4. Feininger, Andreas. 1966. *Successful Color Photography,* Fourth Edition, Prentice-Hall, Englewood Cliffs, NJ.

5. Hastings, James R., and Turner, Raymond M. 1965. *The Changing Mile,* University of Arizona Press, Tucson.

6. Haveman, Joseph. 1971. *Workshop in Creative Photography,* Sadhana Press, Tomales, CA.

7. Sharpe, Grant W. 1974. "Video Tape, A New Tool for Seasonal Training," *Grist* **18**(1).

8. Time-Life Books. 1971. *The Life Library of Photography* (especially *Photographing Nature, Caring for Photographs, and Travel Photography*), Chicago, IL.

CHAPTER 21

COLLECTIONS AND FIELD NOTES

Robert Michael Pyle

For park visitors there is a step in understanding to be made between seeing the bird in the bush and recognizing or really knowing it. Sometimes it helps to have the bird in the hand. Collections enable curious visitors to see specimens and artifacts first-hand and may aid them in taking that perceptual step from mere seeing to real understanding. Collections do not always achieve this, however, because few of them apply interpretive principles. The application of such principles is the concern of this chapter, as well as the determination of when collections are desirable, and how, as systems, they may be augmented by field notes.

THE RATIONALE FOR COLLECTIONS

Collections usually gain justification in a park on one of four grounds. First, some naturalists and visitors desire to have a collection on hand with which to compare their field observations. For them, seeing an actual specimen up close is the most satisfactory way to bridge the transition between field observation and identification and a fuller knowledge of the organism.

Second, scientists studying certain regions, groups of organisms, or geological, historical, or archaeological questions may find park collections to be among their most valuable resources. In the past, these specialists came to rely on park-owned collections to provide necessary data, especially since personal collecting is prohibited in many park areas.

Third, the acquisition and curation of collections provides a means of acquainting novice naturalists with the park resource. Even experienced interpretive specialists frequently return to the collections to refresh their memories or for help with material that may be new to them.

Fourth, and most relevant to this chapter, collections are used with widely varying effectiveness for interpretive purposes. The rationale for collections has been changing and should be freshly examined in light of new interpretive developments.

TRADITIONAL COLLECTIONS

Collections of natural history and human-related materials have traditionally occupied a conspicuous role in outdoor recreation areas with interpretive programs. National parks especially tried to provide very extensive collections with floral and faunal representation as complete as possible. Large storage facilities were filled with geological and archeological specimens. These aggregations found use only by occasional enthusiasts and specialists and by the staff people themselves who often indulged their own hobbies in this way. However, in some instances, they were the definitive collections for whole regions and could certainly be justified on scientific grounds.

Exhibits made from these study collections were not usually very appealing. Trays of study skins and cases of mounted specimens offered little inherent excitement for visitors unless special talent was available for realistic and imaginative taxidermy and diorama manufacture. Also, there were ethical problems with exhibiting dead specimens in areas that purport to protect all wildlife (although many specimens thus displayed were found dead or seriously injured). It was also clear that exhibits of specimens simply did not interest many visitors.

Maintaining the collections was the responsibility of the naturalists. Sometimes these persons were trained curators and did a magnificent job. Much time, labor, space, and money were expended for disproportionately little public benefit. Worse, due to job turnover, many collections came under the jurisdiction of untalented or uncaring managers who allowed them to deteriorate.

These traditional park collections had a definite place and purpose. But as both interpretation and field science matured, change in emphasis was bound to occur.

EVOLVING TRENDS IN COLLECTIONS

The detectable revolution in collections has transferred more of the responsibility for definitive collections to universities and city museums. Simultaneously, as interpretation has become more sophisticated, the function of collections in parks has diminished in favor of more appealing exhibits and more advantageous use of time, money, and space. With the rise of field guides, which are now available for many regions in most specialties, and with the expanded roles and duties of interpreters, big and esoteric collections cannot usually be justified today. In their place, truly interpretive assemblages of original materials can be implemented to serve the continuing demand for real specimens.

This basic change reflects a broad and general shift in values and emphasis. It does not, however, presume to criticize resource managers or interpretive specialists who still desire to maintain large, museum-type collections nor to declare that these collections are anachronisms in parks. The principles of both traditional and small interpretive collections will be discussed.

TRADITIONAL MUSEUM-TYPE COLLECTIONS OF SPECIMENS

Categories

Each of the categories of original material collections has its own contingencies and characteristics. *Bird, mammal, and other vertebrate* collections are perhaps the most difficult kinds to acquire and maintain. There may be a danger of depleting natural populations, depriving visitors of the resources they came to see or offending the visitors by committing what they may interpret as a hypocritical action. If wildlife is protected, sensitive visitors expect everyone to obey the rule. Conversely, if less sensitive people see agency employees killing animals for specimens, they may be encouraged to neglect protective laws, thinking they can do it, too, for target practice or hunting. This can be avoided by pointing out clearly that only specimens found dead or injured have been included in the collection. In this way, several national wildlife refuges have been able to provide full displays of the creatures under their protection without offending visitors or setting a bad example.

There remains the problem of mounting and preserving specimens. Taxidermy and habitat-groupings are discussed below. Briefly, for a standard collection of study skins, birds and mammals are stuffed and kept in fumigated trays; reptiles and amphibians are usually stored in liquid preservatives. Skeletons may be mounted separately. The special problems involved in performing these procedures are not appropriate to this discussion, but relevant how-to-do-it sources will be found in the bibliography. Vertebrate collections are very taxing in time, energy, space, and materials. They have considerable scientific, but little interpretive value. Collections of this sort are usually best left to museums and universities with specialists in residence and adequate funding.

Microfauna collections involve many of the same problems. Hard-bodied invertebrates such as insects and the shells of mollusks can be stored in comparatively little space, but they still require extensive curation. Notably, all aggregations of animal tissue-bearing specimens must be fumigated against dermestid beetles. Otherwise, a valuable collection can disintegrate rapidly. Many valuable regional collections have been lost in this way. Soft-bodied invertebrates should be stored in fluids, and in this condition they have little, if any, interpretive potential.

Fewer obstacles are presented by *plant collections*. A herbarium requires less space than bird or mammal tray cabinets and less curation than insects. But if a really extensive herbarium with long series of each species is kept, it may not attract enough visitors to merit its existence. More interpretive, less extensive layman's herbariums will be discussed in a later section. One good thing to be said for relatively complete plant collections is that they do provide on the spot the last word in identification (if they are properly labeled). Flower and shrub guides, unlike those for birds and mammals, are usually selective and leave out many species. A full herbarium can settle, therefore, difficult identification problems that cannot be resolved by field guides. Of course the same can be said for insects, but generally there is more visitor interest in plants.

Space, once more, is the major problem with *historical and archaeological* collections. These items possess the additional liability (or asset, depending on how one looks at it) of uniqueness. Since living organisms are self-generating, they may usually be replaced, with the exception of extinct species or type specimens.* But human artifacts are far more likely to be one-of-a-kind and irreplaceable if burned, lost, stolen, or allowed to deteriorate. Prevention of the latter requires special staff skills. Human artifacts made of paper, cloth, or leather are especially subject to the ravages of time, moisture, and light, unless treated by preservation specialists.

Finally, traditional collections often contain *mineral* components. Geological specimens cannot be eaten by beetles, nor will their absence (usually) be missed from the park mountain range. But they do take a lot of space to store and even more to display. That fact summarizes the major problem of museum-type collections in outdoor recreation areas—storage and display space. Modern interpretation has little patience with storage problems and, in many instances, even less enthusiasm for plain display of artifacts; there are so many other exciting things to be done which really involve the visitor's imagination. Having said that, let us retrench a bit and explain that there are certain occasions when traditional collections may be appropriate and desirable.

When Museum-Type Collections Should Be Used

In the absence of a nearby university or city museum, an outdoor recreation area might well take on the task of providing specialized collections. Yellowstone and Grand Teton National Parks would have, therefore, a greater mandate to maintain large collections for scientists and interested lay persons than would Mount Rainier or Olympic National Parks, which are very near colleges and universities (Fig. 21-1).

The original specimens from which the species was described.

FIG. 21-1. Parks near large universities which maintain extensive study collections have less need to keep their own collection than isolated parks. Burke Memorial Museum bird skin collection, University of Washington. (Photo by John Spring.)

Another justification for a museum-type collection occurs if the artifacts involved should stay in the resource area but cannot be left for general public viewing due to the dangers of deterioration or vandalism. Consider the example of Mesa Verde National Park, where some of our most valuable traces of ancient peoples occur. An on-site museum is perfectly defensible here, with selective displays separate from the research collection. Other resource recreation localities that belong in this category include Ginkgo State Park in Washington, where visitors can view selections from the site's vast fossil flora, and Florissant Fossil Beds National Monument in Colorado, where an existing concession collection was incorporated into a new public recreation area. This latter example also illustrates the third justification for a large collection. When a really significant assemblage of specimens and/or artifacts already exists in a resource area, managers may be reluctant to dispose of it. The collection may be financially endowed, or the park may have assumed a responsibility to its clientele or donors to maintain it. Then the interpretive manager will probably decide to keep the collection. But that decision will have been a mistake if the collection cannot be properly curated and is allowed to deteriorate.

Acquiring, Curating, Cataloguing, and Disposing of Material

In acquiring specimens, a park manager or chief naturalist can enlist the help of staff and realize a double advantage. As material comes in, employees gain valuable knowledge of the organisms, artifacts, or minerals they encounter, and of the sites in which they find them. Collecting is not a random activity; it requires both advance preparation and background knowledge. Novices without direction can neither find what is desired nor identify it, and they can often damage specimens unless taught how to handle them. Expect to spend time learning techniques, preferably from an experienced collector. Anyone setting out to collect specimens is urged to spend time observing the creatures in the field beforehand. The interpretive specialist-cum-collector and the park's information bank both benefit tremendously if there is a little watching and learning before the nabbing.

When collecting, tell visitors who happen to see you that collecting is prohibited but, in this instance, is being done for scientific purposes. Better yet, restrict collecting to districts not frequented by visitors. Private collectors, if permitted, should observe this practice as well. The chief of interpretation is often confronted by collectors who want to be exempted from the regulations. All of them purport to have scientific reasons; some of them are bogus, the applicant simply desiring choice specimens for his or her personal hobby use. Authentic scientists and serious amateurs engaging in research can be distinguished from the rest by interview. If a permit results, the manager can exploit the occasion to the advantage of the park's collection. The private collector can be required to turn over all material to the park on completion of the research for which it was granted. Alternatively, a one-for-one policy may be prescribed: for every specimen the collector takes back to the laboratory, the park retains one. This is a very useful technique, but obviously it only works if someone can take care of the material thus received. The same may be said for the practice of soliciting significant collections to be willed or donated to the park.

Sometimes, cooperation may take the form of collectors actually developing interpretive exhibits of the material they study. In this way a small exhibit collection can be developed in an expert manner, and the collector-scientist can exchange time, labor, and advice for the opportunity to collect in the park. This approach may be taken a step further with the collector donating time to curate the study collection as well as to aid with interpretation.

A few other methods of obtaining collections material should be mentioned. Exchanges of duplicate items can be arranged with other parks, institutions, and collectors, and numerous scientific supply firms will fill specimen needs. However, the most economical and conservative method of collecting involves the retrieval of dead or severely injured animals in the park and its vicinity. In this way unfortunate roadside casualties serve a useful purpose. A short-stretch of highway near North Cascades National Park provided nearly perfect specimens of short-tailed and long-tailed weasels and a porcupine on the same morning. This method of specimen retrieval has been shown to be applicable even to insects. One collector in New Jersey retrieved over 100 species of butterflies, most in perfect condition, along a 5-mile (8 km) stretch of country road.

As for curation, it has already been noted that different groups of organisms require different means of protection. Without it the collection may become worthless. Another way to render a potentially valuable collection void is by keeping inaccurate, incomplete, or zero data with the specimens. The section on field notes presents the form that required data should take; generally, the date, specific place, and collector will be sufficient. Both material and data should be catalogued. Most museums employ a large ledger in which an entry accompanies every accession. This includes a number, the common and scientific names, the precise data, and any appropriate remarks. The same information, abbreviated, appears on the specimen label.

If a traditional collection satisfies one of the justifications given, can be enlivened through growth, and receives proper care, it may prove to be a valuable asset to the outdoor recreation area. Most resource areas, however, will probably find some of the following types of interpretive collections more suitable to their needs and resources.

INTERPRETIVE COLLECTIONS

In marked contrast to the standard museum assemblages discussed above, the several types of collections that we will consider now are designed to communicate directly to the typical park visitor as well as the specialist.

Exhibits

The simplest kind of collection that can be termed interpretive is the exhibit of specimens. If the arrangement, graphic art, and labeling are imaginative and involving, simple exhibits may work. Showy minerals, fossils, and the shells of mollusks use the disply case to reasonable advantage. This is the standard approach for butterflies, too, whose beauty can stand on their own. Generally speaking, arrangment should be taxonomic or ecologic, rather than merely by color, proportion, or some other parameter devoid of scientific meaning. An exhibit of butterflies can be dramatically improved through a background composed of life zones, habitats, or bio-geographical regions. Similarly, shell collections profit visually and educationally from a layout defining their phylogenetic relationships or distributional history.

Not only permanent objects are exhibitable, but also the carefully prepared remains of fragile organisms or ephemeral spoor. Animal tracks, for example, can be set in plaster molds for comparative exhibits. Media have been developed for fixing snowflakes and spider webs "trapped" in nature; these are indeed effective as exhibits. The Buffalo Museum of Science employs freeze-drying to create noted mushroom exhibits, while other mycological displayers rely on striking spore-prints garnered from the fresh mushroom.

Survey Collections

The survey collection presents the objects visitors are most likely to see during their visit to the park. By selecting and displaying those organisms most commonly encountered, the naturalist can save a great deal of time and the tedium of answering repetitive questions. Survey collections, to be maximally useful, should stay small and simple (Fig. 21-2). The visitor should be able to peruse them quickly to make rapid (if approximate), identification of the type of thing

FIG. 21-2. A survey collection of butterflies devised by Chip Taylor at the Organization of Tropical Studies in Costa Rica. Here the upper and lower wings are sealed between two sheets of plastic. Both the ventral and dorsal surfaces may be easily seen. (Photo by David Inouye.)

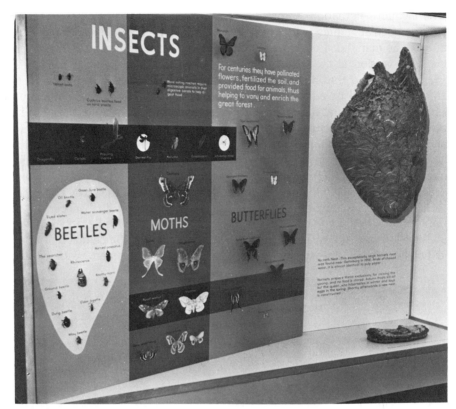

FIG. 21-3. A survey collection makes identification of common organisms relatively simple for visitors. Insect exhibit in Great Smoky Mountains National Park, Tennessee. (Photo by Grant W. Sharpe.)

seen in the field (Fig. 21-3). Most visitors gain a special sort of satisfaction from finding out the name of something they have seen and wondered about. The survey collection provides this kind of opportunity without undue burden on the staff.

One popular form of the survey collection is the *layman's herbarium*. This can be a box or filing cabinet, kept close to the front desk of the visitor center, which contains common plants mounted under plastic sheets and framed with aluminum or wood. The frame can be painted to correspond with the flower color, and a photograph of the living plant can be included beside the specimen. The layman's herbarium is so-called because it is selective (for lay observers) instead of complete. It will be more important to most travelers in the Rocky Mountains to know that they are seeing Indian paintbrush flowers than to know exactly which one of the 20-odd species of *Castilleja* is in view.

The layman's herbarium should be labeled with both scientific names and all of the vernacular names with which visitors might be acquainted. Some plants may have as many as a dozen common names in different regions. Visitors often think their version is the only name for a plant, so they should be given the opportunity to find that name among others by which it may be known. If the plants are arranged by color, their family name, and an interpretive summary of each specimen's natural history should be included in the write-up; thus, the layman's herbarium can actually reveal and provoke, rather than just dispense information. These qualities make it truly interpretive. Both the curious visitor and the interpretive staff significantly benefit from a well-kept and accessible layman's herbarium (Fig. 21-4).

Other groups of living things lend themselves equally well to survey collections. Insects, in particular, occur in such diversity that keying individual specimens can be an arduous and complex task. Displaying the most prevalent species enables the visitor to locate the object of interest quickly and easily. Since different insects and flowers appear through the seasons, survey collections can be made even

FIG. 21-4. The layman's herbarium is an easy way to make plant collections accessible to visitors. Each frame is color-coded to the flower color for easy referral. Craggy Gardens, Blue Ridge Parkway, North Carolina. (Photo by Grant W. Sharpe.)

more useful by changing the display to feature each month's specialties. Finally, every effort should be made to make survey collections accessible and attractive and to bring them to the attention of visitors.

Habitat Groupings

Realistic habitat groupings involving actual specimens make for startling and effective interpretation. These assemblages are often called dioramas, but that term is properly reserved for *miniature models* arranged against a painted scene. Instead of being faced with synthetic presentations, the visitor sees mounted specimens in actual situations—a resurrected truelife adventure. But the technique of creating such an illusion with hides, feathers, and paints is a difficult one, and artisans possessing it are rare (Fig. 21-5).

If the talents for taxidermy and authentic arrangement are available, their products can vastly enhance an interpretive program. One of the best examples of this type of artistry and ecological expertise greets visitors to the Denver Museum of Natural History. There the denizens of each of Colorado's life zones and biotic situations, as well as communities of creatures and plants from various world ecosystems, have been viewed by multitudes of appreciative visitors over several decades. One of the most involving and, hence, interpretive exhibits shows the process by which these groupings are created. Since all of the vegetation is handcrafted in the studio, a great deal of effort must be expended independent of the animal's preparation.

FIG. 21-5. A habitat grouping of Whooping Cranes. The foreground of the diorama is natural materials; the background is a painted scene. Saskatchewan Provincial Museum, Regina. (Photo by Grant W. Sharpe.)

Other fine examples of the genre may be seen in the Yale Peabody Museum of Natural History, the U.S. National Museum of Natural History in the Smithsonian Institution, and the Los Angeles County Museum; the grandest habitat groupings reside in the American Museum of Natural History in New York City.

Obviously, few outdoor recreation areas will have such talents represented on their interpretive staffs. Even the National Park Service can seldom afford the expense involved. Nonetheless, habitat groupings should not necessarily be rejected on that account alone. Much simpler exhibits can be prepared by imaginative interpreters with a modicum of skill and awareness. The small, rustic visitor center at Longmire, Mount Rainier National Park, has a simple one-case habitat grouping that was produced long ago at little cost by careful workers. It continues to show park guests the common creatures they may expect to see outside if they are observant. The bywords on habitat groupings are quality and realism. Mountings that place the visitors in the wildlife community as participants, so that they can feel the bobcat's breath on the cottontail's neck, command interest, curiosity, and respect.

When the central attraction in an interpretive collection is so impressive that it needs no surround, simplicity may be the most effective approach. Such is the case with the Hope Diamond, the blue whale, the bull African Elephant in the National Museum of Natural History, and the model Orca (killer whale) in the Whale Museum at Friday Harbor, Washington.

High-quality animal groupings must concentrate on authenticity as well as involvement. The designer should be well-versed in the ecological stories being depicted. If you presume to illustrate not only the organisms' appearance but also something of their interrelationships, then you take on the obligation to tell the story honestly. Predators must not be cast in a hateful light, or prey in a pitiful role. Discover the correct vegetative associations for the setting and include small wonders (beetles and bees) as well as superstars (pumas and deer). The visitors should be able to see more subplots each time they gaze into the small stage of the exhibit. But stop short of implying that it's all there; the inference should be that all this and more is available outdoors in the real setting. In that sense, habitat groupings are previews of the larger drama outside.

Human "Habitat Groupings"

Interpretation in outdoor recreation areas involves human happenings as well as wildlife activity. The same kinds of concepts applied to wild community exhibits in the previous section can sometimes be effectively extended to human history.

Many historical societies and "frontier villages" persist in offering visitors a diet of colorless collections of relics lacking in selectivity and organization. These masses of flotsam are interesting—for a while. But by the time the once-curious visitor peruses the thirteenth case of letters, old postcards, bullet molds, bonnets,

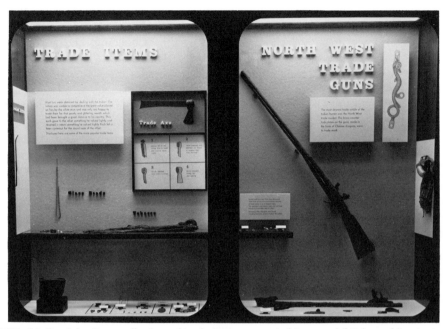

FIG. 21-6. A heritage collection of trade items presented in an exhibit for public viewing. Spokane House Interpretive Center, Riverside State Park, Washington. (Photo by C. R. Jensen.)

and wooden nails, fascination turns to boredom. Fortunately, energetic and imaginative interpreters are implementing new and exciting ways of presenting heritage collections (Fig. 21-6).

One approach being used by some museums (British Columbia Provincial Museum in Victoria and the Milwaukee Museum, for instance) consists of re-creating pioneer scenes indoors. The visitor can walk through whole sequences of shops, offices, homes, and other faithfully reconstructed facades and interiors, complete with furnishings and mannequins in period clothing. Within these sets, collections of artifacts may be displayed in a meaningful manner.

A variation on this theme is outdoor restoration. Buildings are now receiving extensive care in restoration for use as interpretive stations. Thus the old jail serves a new function in Silverton, Colorado. Disused railway stations furnish train and locomotive preservationists with beautifully appropriate headquarters, and the faithful re-creation of a Haida longhouse interior, again in Victoria, provides a superb cultural demonstration center.

Beyond functionally and attractively housing collections, buildings themselves may constitute collections. They may be already there, as in the classic Williamsburg colonial village complex. In Shropshire, England, an entire district comprising several "museums" illustrate the breadth of eighteenth-century industrial archaeology.[5] Called Ironbridge after the first cast-iron bridge, the centerpiece of the museum town, this "collection" employs wealth of buildings and artifacts already *in situ* and once derelict. On a lesser scale, Seattle has taken advantage of a former eyesore by preserving old industrial structures for their visual and historic interest in its innovative Gas Works Park. Alternatively, buildings may be dismantled, transported to the interpretive site en masse and rebuilt in an authentic fashion. Examples of this dramatic type are the Henry Ford Museum in Dearborn, Michigan, the Folk Museum in Oslo, Norway, and the superb Weald and Downland Museum in Kent, England. Perhaps the form reaches its apex at the famous Old Sturbridge Village in Massachusetts. The designers of each of these projects succeeded in re-creating whole villages of period dwellings—farm buildings, schools, churches, stores, and other endemic structures—and fitting them authentically with artifacts that might otherwise have been "exhibited" in oppressive heaps.[1]

Folk customs as illustrated by dancers in native dress augment the interpretive program at the Oslo village. Old Sturbridge goes so far as to populate the village with dozens of residents, each of whom dresses, works, and basically lives after the fashion of eighteenth-century villagers. The making of barrels by the cooper, the weaving and cooking, the forge, and the mills are all real and interrelated. This is a collection of experiences as much as objects, and it vastly enriches the recreationists' visit.

Creative presentation of valuable collections could and should be employed much more often to enliven historical recreation sites. If traditional dress, food, music, and folkways can be used with such success in the Great Smokies and Blue Ridge Mountains by the National Park Service and local residents, they can be emulated elsewhere. Military buffs seem to enjoy mock battles more than dark armories full of old uniforms. Likewise, jousting à la medieval tournaments outside the Tower of London holds more interest for visitors than all of the empty suits of armor within.

Experiences not usually classed as outdoor recreation, but certainly filling major time slots on the recreationists' itinerary could gain much from more creative interpretation. In Europe, castle-prowling is a very popular pastime for natives and tourists, yet castle interpretation is often turgid and musty. Caernarvon Castle in North Wales is an exception, having come into the public eye as the site of a royal pageant. But one of the most important Elizabethan manors in England, possessing a fabulous art collection and great quantities of unique artifacts and furnishings, manages to stultify rather than edify the visitor. With centuries of material to organize, the job is a big one. But with severe editing and the right mixture of intelligence and imagination, those centuries could come alive for the visitor. The German historical monuments agency appreciates this fact, and the result shows in King Ludwig's Bavarian castles.

Special Collections

Industrial tours also attract recreationists. The dry manner in which many corporations attempt to cultivate visitor interest, in spite of available funding, need not be retold. Mines, factories, and plants in this country could learn from the efforts of certain woolen mills and whiskey distilleries in Scotland. Customer relations are important to them, since the Scottish economy depends heavily on these industries. Their main thrust of interpretation is usually through *collections* of products and equipment, usually the older forms, deployed in graphic and involving ways. Distillers, brewers, and vintners are in the forefront of this kind of application throughout the world. In breweries from Milwaukee to Munich, collections of raw materials, bottles and casks, products (with samples), and all the other paraphernalia of brewing are exploited in exciting ways. England has three excellent museums of brewing, in London, Stamford, and the famous brewing town of Burton-on-Trent. Even the wine-tasting offered in California wineries can be called interpretation. In fact, it represents a whole field of the art that might be called *sensory collections*. Few interpretive collections are yet keyed to senses other than sight, but there are some noteworthy examples. Most of them are in museums, but they might apply equally well to outdoor recreation areas. The sense of smell is featured in an olfactory collection at the Yale University Peabody Museum. This exhibit presents interpretation on natural substances used in the perfume industry—musk, ambergris, civet oil, and castoreum—and provides fresh samples of each so that each visitor can get a whiff. Musical instruments on display in London's Victoria and Albert Museum can be heard as well as seen, thanks to visitor-activated audio-devices. Blind visitors are, on occasion, treated to a special textures collection at the University of Washington Henry Art Gallery. It is not difficult to imagine how each of the senses could similarly be accommodated in resource-oriented interpretive centers through collection of scented, tasty, and textured objects and tapes of natural sounds.

Dynamic Collections

A special interpretive collection for which the opportunity seldom occurs is that which involves an ongoing process. In Dinosaur National Monument, Colorado and Utah, fascinated visitors watch as park paleontologists excavate dinosaur bones and other fossils from a rock wall—all in the comfort of a visitor center built up against a mountainside! Surely this is a collection, but it is a far cry from the standard, gloomy dinosaur hall of a museum.

At Cape Alava, Washington, westernmost point in the lower 48 states, another dig is underway. In this situation a native village of great antiquity is emerging from the mudslide that engulfed it hundreds of years ago. Cooperation between the Makah Tribe (who own the site), Olympic National Park officials, and anthropologists from Washington State University enables hikers to visit the dig. Excellent interpretation augments the unusual experience furnished by this ongoing collection. Now many of the artifacts may be seen at the new Makah Museum in nearby Neah Bay. Authentic settings and the ability to handle reproductions of artifacts make for extremely effective interpretation of this specialized collection.

Dynamic interpretive collections will not work everywhere; there must be a suitable resource and work in progress, or some sort of continuum. Not every dig can accommodate this kind of attention, which may not be consistent with the work-load or resource fragility. However, this approach should be considered where it looks like the conditions may be right. The idea of a dynamic, ongoing process can sometimes be implemented indoors with static collections, through imagery and atmosphere. When the King Tutankhamen Egyptian treasures came from Cairo to the British Museum on loan, the London staff recreated a virtual experience of walking into the tomb and making the actual discovery for hundreds of thousands of visitors. The same could be accomplished on a smaller scale with park areas that have exciting collections to show.

Replica Collections

Groups of models set in realistic exhibits sometimes take the place of the real item in many interpretive situations. Dioramas, as these are called, may be applied where the genuine articles are not available, or the scale of things to be interpreted is either too vast or too minute for illustration with real objects. Since

FIG. 21-7. Full-scale replicas of native Mexican dwellings, complete with furnishings and utensils. Museo Nacional de Antropologia, Chapultepec Park, Mexico City. (Photo by Grant W. Sharpe.)

dioramas are discussed elsewhere in this book, they are not elaborated on here. Admirable jobs with dioramas have been carried out in many eastern U.S. National Historic Parks and in Mesa Verde National Park, Colorado. Large-scale dioramas can be built around or intermingled with artifacts or specimens that would in themselves be inadequate for telling the story. Fine examples are to be seen at the Museo Nacional de Antropologia, Chapultepec Park, Mexico City (Fig. 21-7).

Artificial plants and animals, when well crafted, may be desirable for a permanent interpretive collection. Perishable organisms such as colorful nudibranchs (sea slugs) lose their beauty in formaldehyde; amphibians cannot be mounted with relative ease and fidelity as can other vertebrates; and flowers quickly fade when pressed and exposed to light. Excellent imitations, such as glass flowers in the Botanical Museum of Harvard University, can be made if the skills are available. Replicas offer interpretation that should not depreciate and requires little curation. If the visitors come away amazed by the workmanship as well as by the subject, so much the better. Their sensitivities will have been reached on two levels.

Living Collections

The complete opposite of a replica is the living organism. Living collections place the visitor face to face with the specific resource being interpreted. They share some characteristics with self-guided trails but differ in that the resource is arranged in a way to enable the visitor to see it unconditionally. The element of chance is removed. This can be accomplished easily with plants, less so with animals.

A living collection of plants occurs at the famous Wicken Fen nature reserve in Cambridgeshire, England. There, the National Trust has cultivated a garden of common shrubs and herbs to be found in the fen just outside the visitor center. The chief problem with living plant collections is the need for a rather critical manipulation of soils and moisture conditions, which itself should be related to the visitor as part of the interpretive experience. Living plant collections lie somewhere between nature trails and herbaria in realism. They lack the wild, natural arrangement found in nature, but avoid the pallor and dryness of dead specimens. Not far from Wicken Fen, in Cambridge, one finds another variation on the theme. University botanists, in the Cambridge Botanic Garden, nurture collections of native plants arranged by habitat (e.g., chalk downland) and by genetic variation (e.g., geographic subspecies, ecotypes, and polyploid plants). Of course, all botanic gardens and arboretums fall within this category to some extent. They differ in their specialities, and in the degree of interpretation offered. Thus Kew Garden in London excels in rhododendrons among many other things, whereas the University of Papua, New Guinea welcomes visitors to one of the finest living orchid collections. The Botanical Garden of Ashkhabad, Turkmen, SSR, offers a look at current botanical research as well as furnishing the town with a green and quiet place to walk.

Living collections of animals present considerably greater technical problems. Of course, zoos may be considered to be in this genre, but they are not considered here. Zoos definitely serve an important role in outdoor recreation interpretation, but they are a discipline unto themselves and have their own body of literature. The sorts of living collections cited here are a step removed from zoos in the direction of wild communities. Under this concept, managers try to keep the creatures visible to the public, but in their natural habitats and usually within their normal range.[6]

A fine example of an interpretive living animal collection may be seen in the Bavarian National Park in Germany, near the Czechoslovakian border. Here lies one of Central Europe's larger forest wildernesses, managed cooperatively by West Germany and Czechoslovakia. Many large mammals that had become extinct in Central Europe have been reintroduced to the park from wild populations in Poland and the USSR. These rarities can be seen in the wild, but only by experienced hikers and observers; and the border presents difficulties. Since the introductions were made in the public interest, the authorities wanted the people to be able to enjoy them. A series of enclosures were constructed near the visitor center. There is one enclosure, unobtrusive though expansive, for each species being interpreted: wolf, bison, lynx, red deer, and otter. Via trails marked with the images of the animals, visitors can walk past the several enclosures and view the animals at relatively close range. The beasts are neither so tame as to ruin the image nor so secretive as to elude sighting. Of course, this sort of living collection robs the purist of the pursuit necessary for the satisfaction of real wildlife watching, but it provides at least a look at rare wildlife for the walking public (Fig. 21-8). The purists can always seek their deeper satisfaction in the backcountry, where they might see the same animal species unenclosed.

This kind of strategy has been emulated on a large tract of once cutover forest land in Washington State. Known as Northwest Trek, this facility is one of the few "habitat zoos" in North America concentrating on native species of mammals.

Great Britain provides several specialized examples of living animal collections. The well-known Wildfowl Trust on the River Severn estuary in Gloucestershire is home for 200 species of ducks, geese, swans, and flamingos. Although British species may be observed in the wild there, exotics are penned in continental habitat groups.

Sir Peter Scott has developed seven wildfowl centers of this kind in Britain since the original site at Slimbridge became famous. Along similar lines, Philip Wayre's Otter Trust in Norfolk seeks to exhibit and breed various species of otters, for eventual re-release into the wild where they have become rare. Both

FIG. 21-8. A living collection of Canada geese maintained for visitor viewing. Kensington Park, Huron–Clinton Metropolitan Authority, Detroit, Michigan. (Photo by Grant W. Sharpe.)

trusts furnish first-class interpretation on the animals, their needs, habitats, and conservation.

The Forestry Division of Northern Ireland has converted an old walled garden into a butterfly interpretation site called the Drum Manor Butterfly Garden. This popular forest park attraction contains larval and adult food plants for nearly all Irish butterflies. The insects are free to come and go, but on most days from March to October, visitors can see many more native butterflies clustered in the garden than they might see randomly in the countryside.[4]

The Arizona-Sonora Desert Museum, a sophisticated and richly diverse interpretive center, heightens visitors' experiences through the use of desert animal communities viewed along trails and from indoors. Underground rooms with glass walls expose the daytime activities of many of the nocturnal desert creatures from ants to kit foxes. For nearby Tucson school children, as well as for college students and other visitors from many states and countries, this living collection furnishes a unique and fulfilling excursion into desert ecology.

Similar to the Arizona museum is the new Oregon High Desert Museum, near Bend. Combining natural and manipulated features of the fascinating ecosystem named in its title, this facility hopes to foster a new appreciation of the arid lands. From the beginning, the latest interpretive tools are being incorporated into the evolving site. Special interpretive themes are seasonality and natural resources. In a sense, these unconventional museums illustrate the ultimate in the use of collections of outdoor recreation interpretation.[2,3]

FIELD NOTES AND INFORMATIONAL COLLECTIONS

Outdoor recreation areas comprise many of the great repositories of ecological knowledge. The gathering and disseminating of that knowledge lies with the administrative agencies and more specifically with the interpretive branches.

Why does a park need an information system? For one thing, visiting scientists require available data to prevent duplication and to provide clues for further research. For another, the national and international bank of knowledge depends on wild areas to contribute information on unaltered ecosystems, against which to measure changes on the outside. However, our chief concern here is the application of park information to interpretation. Interpretive programs should be dynamic, growing along with the interpreters' understanding of the area. Only by continually acquiring data and by monitoring results from other, similar places will the staff be able to update interpretation. Also important in this context is the desire of some visitors to corroborate their own observations from park lists and files. Even if only a small number of visitors require this sort of personalized interpretation, presumably they derive deep satisfaction from their pursuits and they should be encouraged.

Occasionally intensive biological, geological, and anthropological investigations take place in parks and other reserves. The published results, no doubt, are collected and kept by the agencies involved. This is a fortuitous way of accumulating scientific information about an area, but this happens too infrequently and is usually too specialized to be relied on exclusively for informational collections. Therefore, published material should be augmented by actively accumulated field notes.

Field Notes

How are field notes obtained? Most interpretive specialists in the employ of park agencies will be in the habit of noticing events and natural features around them, and some will keep notes as a matter of course. These serious observers should be encouraged not only to deposit their own sightings in the park's files but also to teach novice personnel to be aware, to make accurate notes, and to deposit them likewise. This task and pleasure should not belong to the interpretive staff alone, for the enforcement and maintenance staffs spend just as much time in the woods and on the trails and roads. All park personnel are potentially valuable contributors to the data bank.

Field Observation

Type of observation: ✓ Zoological _____ Botanical _____ Geological _____ Anthropological

_____ Other

Order: *Lepidoptera* Family: *Nymphalidae* Species: *Polygonia satyrus and Cynthia annabella*

Date: *July 2, 1975* Time: *11am PDT*

Weather: *Clear and warm, 77°F, no wind*

Observer: *R. M. Pyle*

Location: *Big Soos Butterfly Reserve east side of Big Soos Creek, 1/4 mile north of Kent-Kangley Road, Kent, King County, Washington.*

Site details: *Dry exposed knoll of glacial till with gravel and cobbles. Bordered by wet meadow and stream on the west, open coniferous forest on the north and south, dry pasture on the east. Major plants on this knoll were yarrow, a daisy, chamomile, mallow, and nettle.*

Nature of Observation: *Polygonia satyrus (Satyr Angle Wing), a fresh female flew up the knoll exhibiting possible hilltopping behavior, common in butterflies. On the descent she alighted on a nettle. Six eggs, translucent green, were oviposited in a cluster on the ventral surface of a nettle leaf. Some minutes later a worn female Cynthia annabella (Western Painted Lady) arrived on the knoll from the east, flying rapidly. She stopped and landed on a mallow clump. Upon examination two eggs were found, laid singly on the dorsal surfaces of two leaves. Neither butterfly visited any of the surrounding flowers for nectar, nor did they encounter each other, other insects, or predators.*

FIG. 21-9. A sample card used in recording field observations.

Visitors, too, ought to help make up the body of knowledge, since they also draw from it. For obvious reasons, not all visitors' remarks about what they saw should be entered into the park's logs. When interested amateur, or visiting professional naturalists come into the visitor center, their observations should be accepted eagerly and gratefully. If questionable, these notes may then be checked out by a staff naturalist well-acquainted with the resource. Verification of rarities of unusual observations may include an interview with the donor of the information. Usually, outstanding or extraordinary sightings dhould be corroborated by a second observer.

Incorrect notes, like specimens with imprecise data, are worse than worthless because they can mislead. The components of proper field notes are standard. At the very least, they must include the date, precise location and nature of the sighting or finding, and who made it. Additional data might include latitude, longitude, altitude, weather, vegetation, and soil types.

In the western United States, the township, range, and section survey system provides an excellent shorthand for situating records with fair precision. More and more biological and other recording systems worldwide are going over to a 10-kilometer square grid based on the Universal Transmercator Grid, which appears on new editions of USGS (United States Geological Survey) topographic maps. Recorders should consider this, since vague or ambiguous locality data cause serious problems.

Floral notes are often accompanied by site descriptions and animal records include behavioral notations. Plant/animal associations and animal/animal encounters add interest and value. If a note comes in without a supporting specimen, and if there is any doubt as to the identity of the object observed, detailed descriptive notes will help convince skeptics.

Field notes may be written in various forms, although it is helpful to have printed a large supply of standard sheets with appropriate headings for entries (Fig. 21-9). All field notes need to be logically catalogued.

Data Retrieval Systems

Field notes must be subject to prompt data retrieval to be of value. Once a method of logging the information has been worked out, a scheme for storing the notes must follow. Card files may be the simplest and one of the most effective means of storing a limited quantity of material. Notebooks and logbooks do the job but are less flexible than card files. Innovation and improvisation serve the interpreter well in this task. It is highly unlikely that many systems will match the magnitude of the one employed by the British Biological Records Centre, Institute of Terrestrial Ecology. In this scheme, the data from hundreds of thousands of field note cards are computerized, later to be retrieved in the form of automatically printed maps at Monks Wood Experimental Station. Most interpretive areas will use something simpler. But should your information bank exceed the capacity of your system, microstorage might be considered. Both microfilm and microfiche (photographically printed plastic cards) allow for the storage of huge quantities of data in a small space.[7,8]

No one needs shoeboxes full of scraps of paper covered with illegible jottings. A properly executed set of field notes, in contrast, can render an interpretive program richer and stronger.

Film and Tape Collections

Without trespassing on the chapters dealing with photography and slide shows, it should be emphasized that collections of pictures, slides, movies, and sound tapes can be very valuable tools in outdoor recreation interpretation. Many of the most effective murals and flatwork exhibits in interpretive centers are made from photographs.

Slide presentations and film shows comprise a large part of the interpretive repertoire. Likewise, tape recordings of historic persons or events and of natural sounds find broad application in audio devices. Collections of these materials should be actively cultivated wherever they can be used and maintained.

The University of Washington has undertaken to assemble a vast new archive of tapes, films, photographs, and other materials pertaining to the recent eruptions of Mount St. Helens. This storehouse will prove immeasurably valuable to all who will be involved in the interpretation of the mountain and its activity in the future.

Maintenance is paramount with films and tapes. Scratched negatives, fingerprinted slides, broken movies, and accidentally erased tapes are the bane of interpreters who use audiovisual devices.

Slides, properly cared for, should be mounted and labeled as soon as they are received. That way they can be used again and again without damage. Glass-and-metal mounts are available from commercial suppliers, as are sets of slides if cameras and talent are not available to make a slide collection. Storage should be accessible but secure and away from dust, heat, and moisture. The best system is probably that in which slides are kept in multiple vertical trays in a cabinet. Each tray has several rows of slides and can be pulled out in front of a light panel for viewing. These cabinets are expensive, but they store many slides securely and very accessibly (Fig. 21-10).

Inexpensive storage systems can be built around almost any container that is dustproof and will accommodate a moderate number of slides. Agencies with access to a craftsman and materials can easily provide shallow trays with dividers in which 35-mm slides can be readily stored and indexed. Even cigar boxes work fairly well. Or, on a slightly more sophisticated level, various commercial boxes, trays, and clear plastic pocketed sheets are available at reasonable prices. The point is that nearly every interpretive area needs a slide collection and should be

FIG. 21-10. A storage cabinet which holds 6760 35mm slides on 52 steel holding-frames. The frames are pulled out in front of a lighted box for viewing. The cabinet is manufactured by Multiplex Display Fixture Company of St. Louis, Missouri. (Photo by John Spring.)

able to find a system of storage to meet its financial and spatial needs.

Once a system has been evolved, slides can be located when needed, and additions can be easily integrated.

In an area that uses slides, a growing collection ensures that when a particular view is needed for a presentation, for enlargement, or for publication, it will likely be available. One kind of incentive used in parks rewards employees with film for usable slides donated to the collection. Alternatively, photographers can be assigned a designated number of hours per week to pursue good shots. This is cheaper and better for morale than contracting for the work to be done, although that is another possibility.

Black-and-white photographs and color prints also require care and logical cataloguing to be useful. An effort should be made to secure for the collection any historical photos and in particular, old glass negatives, which might otherwise be destroyed. Historical recreation sites in particular rely on old photographs for interpretive resources. The photo files may come to have real significance for outside researchers as well as for publications.

Motion picture footage comes within the province of interpretive collections as well. Whether filmed in the area by park personnel, purchased from suppliers, or contracted out to a free-lance filmmaker or studio, films provide records of events and processes that cannot be adequately expressed in still photographs. In addition to programs in the visitor center, films provide grist for public relations and television shows. Films should be stored in the proper cannisters, repaired as soon as breaks occur, and should be reprinted periodically over the years (instead of using the master print for repeated showings). If raw stock is shot in the park at intervals, it should not be left in the camera for long periods before being developed. Prompt editing and indexing is imperative.

Sound tapes are just as useful and deserve equal care. Every effort must be made to secure historical tapes of old-timers, pioneers, eyewitnesses, and other interesting characters before they die. These will form an invaluable element of the oral history tape collection.

Equipment for recording natural sounds, including high-quality recorders, parabolic dishes, and microphones, is expensive. It constitutes a worthwhile investment, however, in an area where sounds play an important part in the interpretive story. The howls of wolves, songs of whales, and spring birdcalls greatly increase the interest in exhibits on those subjects. Excellent recordings from nature can be purchased, notably from the Cornell University Library of Natural Sounds.

Original Art, Articles, and Books

Original art depicting or relating to an outdoor recreation area might well be collected as an additional interpretive resource. Illustrative art for exhibits can be produced on demand. But fine art may have to be specially commissioned. Paintings and sculpture complement the decor of the visitor center as well as the interpretive theme. However, that theme should be respected. Oils by Thomas Moran enhance the fur-trade theme in the Moose Visitor Center in Grand Teton National Park. They also interpret, since Moran painted what he saw in Jackson Hole in the days when beaver was king. The lovely bas-relief woodcarving of dogwood foliage and flowers in the Yosemite Valley interpretive center tells the seasons of the trees; at the same time, it is intrinsically pleasing. Natural history societies and other parent bodies should consider establishing special funds for acquiring prints, paintings, sculptures, and other forms of original art that depict or originate in the areas with which they are concerned.

Libraries in park and recreation areas fill two essential needs. First, they provide references for visitors and interpretive staff. On many occasions the information needed to answer a visitor's question, to prepare an exhibit, or to give authority to a publication, walk, or talk can be found in the library. Second, park employees frequently are people with a taste for learning; however, they often find themselves in a provincial environment without bookstores or public libraries. Park

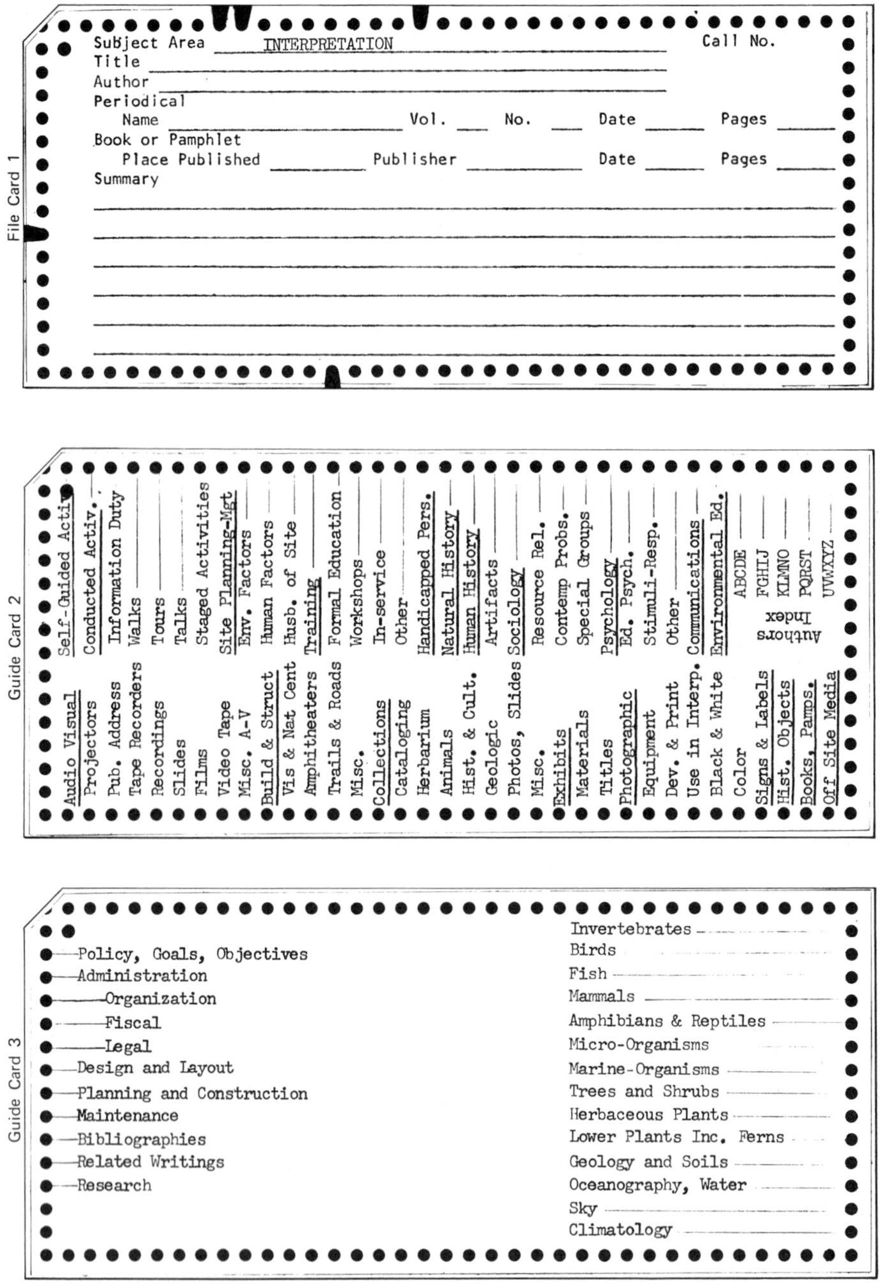

FIG. 21-11. A reference index system for the storage and retrieval of materials written on interpretation, utilizing the McBee Keysort marginal punch cards, a hand-operated v-punch (model #5201) and a sorting needle. All are manufactured by Litton Automated Business Systems, 600 Washington Avenue, Carlstadt, New Jersey 07072.

The system illustrated here was designed by interpretive students at the University of

libraries can fill a couple of shelves, like the tiny but adequate collection of books in remote Katmai National Monument, Alaska; or they can thoroughly cover the entire field of natural history and conservation in the region concerned as, for example, the experimental station library at Monks Wood National Nature Reserve in England.

A very important part of any research and interpretive library is the article and reprint collection. Keeping abreast of the current literature relating to the park and its resource should be a goal of interpretive specialists. This information is also frequently necessary for slide presentations, talks, walks, and publications. If you can bring together and efficiently organize this sort of literature, your program will benefit tremendously. The two necessary ingredients are an ongoing search of relevant journals and a workable indexing system. One example of such a system is illustrated here (Fig. 21-11).

Another kind of interpretive library consists of the books and papers of an individual who was intimately connected with the recreation area. In themselves, these may become inspirational interpretive exhibits. This is true of the leaf from John Muir's journal displayed in Yosemite National Park. In Kent and Hampshire, respectively, the homes and studies of English naturalists Charles Darwin and Gilbert White can be inspected just as the men left them. A visit to Down House or "The Wakes" assumes something of the spirit of a pilgrimage for the many modern-day nature enthusiasts who stop in during country rambles.

CONCLUSION

In this chapter no attempt is made to assay completely the entire realm of collections, and many excellent examples have been omitted. Instead, the reader has been apprised of some of the characteristics, types, and opportunities of collections as a part of the interpretive repertoire. Other viewpoints and detailed techniques may be found in natural history and museology texts, some of which are given in the references that follow. The importance of collections to interpretation,

---

Washington. New cards are blank, with factory-punched marginal holes. Top left: Card 1, a typical file card, showing a suggested organization of biographical data which has been mimeographed on the blank card. The reviewer reads an article, fills in the necessary information on this file card, and then, referring to Guide Cards 2 and 3 for topic assignments, hand punches over the appropriate holes on the margins of the file cards with a v-punch. Guide Card 2 shows the topic assignments for the side margins, and Guide Card 3 is for the upper and lower margins. The v-punching breaks the hole through to the edge of the card. The completed cards may be stacked in any order.

Retrieval is simple. After placing the appropriate guide card on top of the stack, the sorting needle is inserted through the desired classification hole. Because they have been v-punched, all cards under this classification will fall out when the stack is lifted by the needle. A separate needle thrust will be needed for each topic.

whether they are beetles or blue whales, should never be overlooked. For as many people find, a bird in hand definitely helps make sense out of the bush.

REFERENCES

General References

American Association for State and Local History. Numerous technical leaflets on administration and conservation of collections of historical materials. AASLH, 1315 Eighth Avenue, South Nashville, TN 37203.

Anderson, R. M. 1948. "Methods of Collecting and Preserving Vertebrate Animals," *Biol. Bull.*, No. 39, National Museum of Canada, Ottawa.

Bartlett, J. 1963. "Storage and Study Collections," *Museums Journal* **63**:62–63.

Bierne, B. P. 1955. *Collecting, Preparing, and Preserving Insects,* Canadian Department of Agriculture, Entomological Division Publication 932.

Brayshaw, T. C. 1973. *Plant Collecting,* The Provincial Museum, Victoria, British Columbia.

British Museum of National History. *Instructions for Collectors,* series in several parts covering all groups, Her Majesty's Stationery Office, London.

Burcaw, E. 1967. *"Active Collecting in History Museums," Museum News* **52**:46–48.

Cranstone, R. A. L. 1958. *Ethnography: Handbook for Museum Curators,* Museum Association, London.

Conrad, H. S. 1945. "The Bryophyte Herbarium, A Moss Collection: Preparation and Care," *The Bryologist* **48**:198–202.

Daifuku, H. 1960. "Collections: Their Care and Storage," *The Organization of Museums,* UNESCO, New York.

Davis, P. H. 1961. "Hints for Hard-Pressed Collectors," *Watsonia* **4**:283–289.

Dominick, Richard B. 1972. "Practical Freeze-Drying and Vacuum Dehydration of Caterpillars," *J. Lepid. Soc.* **26**:69–79.

Dunn, W. S. *Storing Your Collections* (technical leaflet), American Association for State and Local History, Nashville, TN.

Erwin, David G. 1975. "Collecting Methods in Biology," *Museum's Journal* **74**:164–165.

Gelder, R. G., and S. Anderson. 1967. "An Information Retrieval System for Collections of Mammals," *Curator* **10**:32–42.

Gray, Alice. (nd). "How to Collect Insects and Spiders for Scientific Study," "How to Mount and Label Hard-Bodied Insects"; and "How to Preserve a Collection of Soft-Bodied Insects and Spiders," Direction Leaflets three, four, and six, Department of Insects and Spiders, The American Museum of Natural History, New York.

Guldbeck, Per E. 1972. *The Care of Historical Collections.* American Association for State and Local History, Nashville, TN.

Holme, N. A., and A. D. MacIntire. 1971. *Methods for Study of the Marine Benthos,* IBP Handbook 16, Blackwell, Oxford.

Hurst, R. M. 1970. "Putting a Collection on Film," *Curator* **13:**199–203.

Knudsen, Jens, W. 1972. *Collecting and Preserving Plants and Animals,* Harper and Row, New York.

Lewis, G. D. 1965. "Obtaining Information from Museum Collections and Thoughts on a National Index," *Museums Journal* **65:**12–22.

Lewis, W. M. 1963. *Maintaining Fishes for Experimental and Instructional Purposes,* Southern Illinois University Press, Carbondale.

Manning, R. B. 1969. Automation in Museum Collections, *Proc. Biol. Soc. Wash.* **82:**686–691.

Neal, Arminta. 1969. *Help! For the Small Museum,* Pruett, Boulder, CO.

Nicholson, T. D. 1974. "Policy on Acquisition and Disposition of Collection Material," *Curator* **17:**5–9.

Owen, D. 1964. "Care of Type Specimens," *Museums Journal* **63:**288.

Peterson, G. E. 1958. "Artificial Plants," *Curator* **1**(3):12–35.

Peterson, G. E. 1966. "Artificial Mushrooms," *Curator* **9**(1):62–65.

Saville, D. B. O. 1962. *Collection and Care of Botanical Specimens,* Canadian Department of Agriculture, Ottawa.

Soper, J. H., and F. H. Perring. 1967. "Data Processing in the Herbarium and Museum," *Taxon.* **16:**13–19.

Stansfield, G. 1971. *Sources of Museological Literature,* Museums Association, London.

Stolow, N. 1966a. "Fundamental Case Design for Humidity-Sensitive Museum Collections," *Museum News Tech. Suppl.* **44:**1–6.

Stolow, N. 1966b. "The Action of Environment on Museum Objects. Part I: Humidity, Temperature, Atmospheric Pollution," *Curator* **9:**175–185.

Vance, D. 1970. "Museum Data Banks," *Information Storage and Retrieval* **5:**203–211.

Wagstaffe, R., and J. H. Fidler. 1968. *The Preservation of Natural History Specimens,* Withby, London.

Wood, A. A. 1958. *Preparing Insect Displays,* Canada Department of Agriculture, Entomology Division Publ. No. 1032, Ottawa.

References Cited

1. Alegre, Mitchell R. 1978. *A Guide to Museum Villages,* Drake, New York and London.

2. Anonymous. 1973. "The Internationally Known Arizona-Sonora Desert Museum," *Arizona Highways,* September, 1973.

3. Anonymous. 1978. *The Oregon High Desert Museum: Guide for Development,* OHDM, Bend, OR.

4. Heal, Henry George. 1973. "An Experiment in Conservation Education: The Drum Manor Butterfly Garden," *Intern. J. Environmental Studies* **4:**223–229.

5. Hudson, Kenneth. 1980. "Keep up the Good Works: Museums of Industrial Archaeology," *Sunday Times Magazine* (London) Aug. 24:31–42.

6. Pennyfather, Keith. 1975. *Guide to Countryside Interpretation: Part Two, Interpretive Media and Facilities,* Her Majesty's Stationery Office, Edinburgh (for the Countryside Commission).

7. Perring, F. H. 1971. "The Biological Records Centre—A Data Centre," *Biol. J. Linnean Soc.* **3:**237–243.

8. Squires, D. F. 1970. "An Information Storage and Retrieval System for Biological and Geological Data," *Curator* **13:**43–62.

CHAPTER 22

INTERPRETING THE SKY

Von Del Chamberlain

Two things fill my mind with ever new and ever greater
wonder and reverence the oftener and the longer I
allow my mind to dwell on them—The starry heavens
above and the moral law within me.

Kant

Sky Interpretation is the art and process of coupling direct observation with skilled communication for the purpose of informing people about the sky, its objects, and phenomena, with special emphasis on relationships of these to Earth and its occupants.

This chapter is intended to introduce a realm of natural interpretation that has generally been neglected. It will not be possible here to give detailed instruction about sky phenomena; it is possible to impart the importance of the sky in natural history interpretation and to make the reader aware of some useful procedures and materials. At the end of the chapter there is a study guide and selected references that will assist one in becoming knowledgeable about the sky and its interesting objects and events.

WHY INTERPRET THE SKY?

Interpreters seldom, if ever, question the relevance of biology, geology, and ecology in their work. It seems apparent that these subjects belong within the competence of any naturalist.

But why sky interpretation? Most objects of the sky seem removed from everyday life, and so unimportant compared with other things. What difference do they make in our lives? Does interpretation of the sky really belong in the list of abilities and duties of those who teach in the out-of-doors?

Let us briefly consider and list six reasons why sky interpretation *is* both appropriate and important for campfire programs, conducted walks, and other interpretive activities.

1. Sky Phenomena Are Part of the Scene

The cartoon (Fig. 22-1) illustrates an important point. What is the vertical boundary of the landscape? Does it end at the treetops or mountain tops? Would anyone wish to eliminate sunlight and starlight from its panoramic splendors? Stop to contemplate what it would be like to live on a planet with a perpetually clouded sky. Emerson wrote: "If the stars should appear one night in a thousand years, how would men believe and adore, and preserve for many generations the remembrance of the city of God." Indeed, parks are the only places where large numbers of people go where conditions allow them to see the pristine starry sky.

2. The Contrast Between City and Country Sky

Emerson's words come startlingly close to describing the situation for a goodly fraction of the population living in metropolitan areas. The viewing conditions existing in protected natural areas are becoming more and more special as populations grow, and the associated pollution problems increase in magnitude and complexity. City people seldom see the starlit sky as it can be seen from the country on a clear, dark night. It is one of the special features that can be best studied and enjoyed in our natural areas.

3. The Time Scale

In studying the stars we are becoming aware of the time scale and the physical processes going on in space to produce worlds like our own. By using telescopes and associated equipment we study stars in different stages of development. A picture is emerging. We are beginning to comprehend a fantastic transition that slowly occurred over billions of years of time, starting with dust floating between the stars and continuing to our present Sun and planet Earth. Contemplating the mechanisms of the universe and the vast time scale involved in producing the moment of human existence can alter our comprehension of ourselves and our place in the environment. Such awareness should result in deeper appreciation for our world and may help people improve their individual behaviors in ways that will protect and preserve our delicate planet.

4. The Earth and the Universe

We are so immersed within our immediate surroundings on the surface of our tiny planet, orbiting one star, that we are prone to forget that nearly all of the universe lies beyond. Thomas Henry Huxley wrote: "To a person uninstructed in natural history, his country or seaside stroll is a walk through a gallery filled with wonderful works of art, nine-tenths of which have their faces turned to the wall." Apply these words to the realm of the stars. Unless we are acquainted with the

FIG. 22-1. Artwork by Ron Miller.

starry sky, we really have little concept of the world and the vast universe. Astronomy has been the subject of intense human speculation and research for centuries, yet most humans are unaware or forgetful of even the elementary facts. Sky interpretation can help bridge this gap.

5. The Sky and Life Support Conditions

Perhaps we can better understand the magnitude and importance of the problems of preserving the conditions on the limited, thin surface of Earth by knowing the factors that produced and sustain these conditions and by contrasting them with the harsh emptiness beyond the protective atmosphere.

Modern astrophysics gives us even greater perspective of our own existence. Evidence suggests that the very elements composing our physical bodies are actually manufactured in the centers of stars through nuclear fusion processes. If people are directed to contemplate such possibilities while looking into the starry sky, they will see more than mere specks of light; and they should appreciate the miracle of their own existence more than they possibly could without interpretation of the sky.

6. Humans, Earth, and the Universe

Refer to the quotation from Immanual Kant at the beginning of this chapter and think about the intellectually stimulated emotions that can be kindled by a starlit sky. Recall the words of Plato: "Astronomy compels the soul to look upwards and leads us from this world to another." Astronomy has done exactly that, for man has stood on the surface of the Moon, looked back at Earth, and helped put humankind in better perspective.

Following a sky interpretive program, people often comment that they feel so insignificant looking into the starry night. Such comments are, perhaps, the most powerful reasons of all for interpreting the sky.

Summary

Posidonius (135–51 B.C.) defined Man as the beholder and expounder of the heavens. Throughout human history we have looked toward the stars and attempted to explain them. Simultaneously we attempt to explain ourselves. Our quest for understanding both ourselves and the stars continues. Where can this inquiry better take place than in natural areas removed from city lights and other distractions where one can see the stars in all their glory? And who can best assist people in enjoyment and understanding of the splendid sky? Probably no other group of people have a better combination of skills, interests, and opportunities than interpretive specialists and others who teach in the out-of-doors.

SUGGESTED PROCEDURES FOR SKY INTERPRETATION

Getting Started

How does one gain the ability to interpret the sky? Special instruction in sky interpretation is helpful but not essential. You can learn the basics quickly and adjust your presentation as your knowledge increases. Occasionally visitors will be a source of information.

Study the sky by careful and frequent observation. Contemplete the notions ancient people must have had as they pondered the objects and events of the sky.

Capture the thrill of the sky yourself and share your discoveries with visitors, being cautious not to claim abilities and offer explanations not yet clear in your own mind. Start with simple and brief samples of what the sky has to offer.

Suppose, for example, you have learned to identify a few bright stars in the current night sky and have learned a few facts about them. The night is clear and a thin cresent moon sets as twilight dissolves into a dark, crisp night with sharp, cleaming stars. Present your regular program as planned. As you conclude you should be at your best—completely confident and relaxed in the knowledge of having stimulated an awareness of one aspect of natural history. Don't let your audience go without drawing their attention to the "magic" of the sky. You might add a postscript essentially as follows:

You have heard what you came to hear and seen what you were promised this evening, but I want to call your attention to one more special feature of this area. Notice how the familiar surroundings on the landscape have melted away to become silhouettes, dark against the slightly brightened sky. And look at the stars! How long has it been since you last saw such a sky? Consider the distances you can see as you look off into deep space. What questions come to your minds? Let me hasten to say that I am not an astronomer and do not claim to be able to answer all the questions you might ask, but I would enjoy spending a few minutes speculating with you. It might be interesting if we just asked questions, even if we can find no definite answers to them.

I have learned to recognize a few of the brighter stars and can tell you some things about them. I also know a few native legends about the stars. Now I am going to walk over into that meadow and spend a few minutes reviewing the stars I know. You are invited to tag along. I am sure we can learn a few things together, share a few ideas, and become aware of things neither of us have ever noticed.

In this way you will have clearly stated you are not an "expert" in astronomy, but you have done it in a very positive way. You will probably not lose many from the audience except those who reluctantly carry sleeping babies back to camp. Those who go with you may never forget their brief introduction to a realm of nature in which they have previously felt little personal involvement, and you will have acquired experience and confidence in sky interpretation. From the questions asked you will also acquire additional interest in the sky.

As you gain experience you should begin to blend sky interpretation into your regular programs. Look for opportunities to relate objects of the sky to subjects included in programs. Such relationships are more numerous than you might think. Just being alert to the possibility of these relationships will help you discover them as you continue your study. Steadily work toward the time when you can prepare and present special programs about the sky. Plan the best sky program you can conceive and weave segments of it into your regular programs. Then, when you are ready, present your first complete program of sky interpretation.

The World's Finest Sky Theater

Planetariums are simulated sky theaters. Millions of people enter them each year in an attempt to comprehend the heavens, but planetarium educators can only imitate the setting available to interpreters in outdoor theaters. There is a distinct difference in the response of an audience to a good planetarium program and an equally good program presented under nature's stars. The one experience is make-believe—the other is real. Our national parks and other similar places contain the world's finest sky theaters.

In the outdoor amphitheater the interpreter can use slide and motion picture projection to bring meaning to the panorama of objects and events portrayed overhead on a clear, dark night. It is important to note that an illustrated amphitheater sky program more nearly resembles a conducted walk than it does other amphitheater programs. In the regular amphitheater, interpreters use pictures to discuss features of the region. But in the sky program the objects of interest are viewed directly and interpreted just as they are on a trail walk. This is why the night sky interpretive program is so memorable, especially to those who experience it for the first time. Most people have seldom, if ever, experienced the thrill of tutored contemplation of the universe.

The advantage of the amphitheater for sky interpretation is that it can accommodate up to several hundred people. Thus interpreters can handle larger audiences than can be accommodated on the trail and in other activities where the objects of nature are interpreted directly. (This advantage should be considered in planning other amphitheater programs. You may decide to use amphitheaters more frequently during daylight hours, interpreting natural surroundings which can be studied from that particular location.)

The illustrated sky program can take any direction the interpreter desires, ranging from simple identification of stars and planets to programs that identify objects of the sky in context with carefully selected information about them and their relationships to the more immediate environment. The importance of relating the sky to people and objects cannot be overemphasized. The relationships are not apparent to most people. They must be carefully studied by the interpreter and clearly pointed out to audiences.

The screen can be used to project photographs of star groups to assist in identifying constellations. In addition it can be used to extend vision beyond the ability of the naked eye by projecting photographs made with large telescopes. It is more exciting for people to learn about objects in deep space when they know approximately where they are located and can glance in that direction as they learn. Several of the most intriguing deep sky objects can faintly be seen with the naked eye. Discerning such an object, then glancing down to the screen and seeing its brilliance and detail revealed by one of the world's great telescopes is an exciting experience (Figs. 22-2 and 22-3). It is completed by providing an opportunity for individuals to use a small telescope (or even binoculars) to view the stars, planets, and other phenomena discussed during the program.

The Campfire Circle Sky Program

The basic difference between a campfire circle and an amphitheater is that the former lacks a projection screen. This is not necessarily an undesirable limitation. Indeed, a skillfully given campfire circle program can be a most entertaining and stimulating event. Generally, the audience is smaller. This and other factors provide the setting for an informal, provocative, interpreter-to-visitor experience.

The program might begin just as the stars are becoming visible. An effective opening is a legend about the stars. If possible use a story from the lore of native groups once occupying the region. Native American mythology abounds in sky legends as does the lore of most early cultures. What better way to start a program than to relate a story that might have been told to a different audience at that very place hundreds or thousands of years ago.

Choose for brief concentration a topic that relates to both the immediate environment and to visible features of the sky. For example, it is always fascinating to point out a star similar to the Sun and then raise the question of the possible existence of planets similar to Earth that are revolving about stars. What variation of intelligent creatures might exist and how many others have experienced problems similar to those with us now? How many eyes out there are turned in our direction at this very moment, speculating on the question, "Are we alone in the universe?" Even though you don't supply direct answers to such questions, this will provide a very stimulating review of the environmental factors that make our existence possible, the need to understand thoroughly these factors, and the importance of controlling our interactions with other elements of the ecosystem.

Be sure that a few important stars and planets are clearly identified so that

FIG. 22-2. The Great Galaxy in the constellation Andromeda (near center of photograph) as seen with binoculars. (Photo by Von Del Chamberlain.)

FIG. 22-3. The Great Galaxy in Andromeda (see Fig. 22-2) photographed with the 158-in. (4-m) Mayall telescope. (Photo courtesy of Kitt Peak National Observatory, Arizona.)

510

every member of the audience with vision can locate them. A powerful flashlight beam works well as a pointer if the audience is small and the sky is dark. Reference to distant landscape features is another method of identifying sky objects.

The program might end when it is dark enough to see fainter sky features such as the Milky Way and the Andromeda Galaxy. People should depart from the program with the ability to locate and identify several features of the sky and remember some significant information about each.

Perhaps the best indication of the success of the program is the number of trees bumped into and stones, roots, and logs stumbled over by members of the audience as they return to their camps with their senses still tuned to the sky.

In summary, start by learning about the sky, using selected bits of newly acquired knowledge and applying all you know about effective interpretation.

The Evening Stroll and the Sky Walk

The evening stroll can be a most enjoyable interpretive activity. Perhaps the most important reason to conduct evening strolls is to help people sharpen their senses so that they become aware of subtle changes in and relationships between various elements of the environment. This expands their concepts of the natural realm.

It is usually advisable to require registration prior to the walk and to limit the size of the group as appropriate for the location and other conditions. This also provides an easy way to distribute information about: (1) type of clothing suggested; (2) insect repellent (if needed); (3) flashlights; (4) time and place of departure; (5) duration and distance; (6) objectives of the activity; (7) weather and other factors that may lead to cancellation or modification of the activity.

Ideally the program should begin just before sunset while one can still see the day-star supplying our life-preserving energy. Beginning this early is difficult since it lengthens the activity considerably. In mountainous regions it may be very impractical, since the Sun may set behind mountains in the late afternoon several hours prior to darkness. In selecting the beginning time and place consider local conditions, length of twilight, schedules, program objectives, and other factors.

For purposes of illustration we will describe a program taking place during the late summer in the northern hemisphere at a place where the period of time between sunset and darkness is not extended by a high, mountainous horizon.

Participants meet at the appointed time and place on a clear, moonless evening as the Sun approaches the horizon. It is a carefully selected place which takes advantage of the beauty of the region. The interpreter calls attention to the Sun, reminding the group of its tremendous significance and explaining factors of Earth-Sun relationships which are most pertinent to that latitude, altitude, and time of year. He or she encourages the visitor to notice subtle relationships as well as those that are so apparent that they tend to be ignored.

Members of the group watch, listen, and comment as the Earth turns them

FIG. 22-4. Native American rock art frequently reminds us of Indian interest in the sky. This pictograph is at Chaco Canyon National Monument, New Mexico. (Photo by Von Del Chamberlain.)

512

away from the direct rays of the Sun. The sky and surrounding terrestrial features change color as the blue rays are scattered and the last yellow and red hues bathe the landscape.

The stroll begins along a carefully chosen path. Plants and animals may provide special interest. The first stop is made at a rocky outcrop where a member of the group discovers a native rock drawing that includes a sky symbol (Sun, Moon, star, cloud, rain, or lightning). Figure 22-4 is an example of such "rock art." The existence of this item is, of course, the reason for the stop. The group ponders the significance of this work, speculating about earlier concepts. Before moving on, the interpreter recites an Otoe tribal song about the coming of night:

One by one
The stars are lighted by the Sun
Before he retires to his lodge for rest
It is his last duty of the day.

Frequent stops are made to draw attention to the rapidly falling night. Differences in color, brilliance, and apparent form of landscape features are appropriate subjects for interpretation. Attention is drawn to the varying brightness of the sky in different directions around the horizon. The Earth's shadow may be visible as a slightly violet-gray region above the horizon opposite where the Sun has set.

The coming of night is a majestic and beautiful occurrence. This is especially true when it is experienced in a remote and scenic region. Changes occur rapidly and the interpreter attempts to awaken the sensitivity of the group to the continuum of changes.

At an appropriate time and place along the trail the party pauses quietly to listen to the sounds of evening, the breeze rustling leaves, the twittering birds, and the many other sounds that accompany nightfall. A reward, such as a free star map, may be offered to the first person in the group to see a star or planet. When it is dark enough to see the brighter stars, they are identified. This is the easiest way to learn to recognize them. Watching as it gets darker, people first see only the brightest stars and then notice greater and greater detail around them as dimmer features become visible in the darker sky. At the end they can still recognize the most prominent stars, now couched in groups of varying brightness and hue, and relate groups of stars to each other in order to establish patterns that will help them remember.

The main stop for sky interpretation has been planned for a location with outstanding sky visibility. This place is reached when it is dark enough to see many stars. Here the interpreter skillfully relates a native American sky legend (or other legend appropriate for the locale). This is especially appropriate in a natural setting, since it reminds people of the time when humans lived more intimately with nature. The contrast is noted between the ancient concept of the sky as an enclosed dome and our current realization that the sky opens toward infinity. The interpreter employs various comparisons to impart knowledge about distances, sizes, and separations of objects in space. Arcturus, a relatively nearby star, is identified. The naturalist asks if anyone in the group is willing to admit to an age of about 40 years and then explains that the light now entering the eyes, stimulating awareness of Arcturus, left the star about the time of this person's birth.

The star Antares is identified with the comment that if this star could be placed where the Sun is, leaving other objects of the solar system as they are, we would be inside the star!

A Sun-like star, such as Eta Cassiopeia, is identified and its distance is indicated. The possibility is raised that this star might be orbited by an Earth-like planet with intelligent creatures on it. Noting the time required for radio waves, which travel at the speed of light, to journey between here and there, the group speculates about the radio and TV programs that culture might be receiving from Earth.

Interpretation relating sky and Earth continues as long as is practical. The significance of the night stars is discussed, pointing out that they are energy sources like the Sun and that they are probably the chemical-element-producing factories of the universe. People are reminded of the necessity of these elements for the existence of the mineral and biological kingdoms. Hopefully, everyone will sense the relationship of the stars to the "miracle" of their existence.

The interpreter should be selective and brief, encouraging discussion and skillfully directing questions and comments toward the ideas he or she wishes to introduce.

On the return trip one more stop is made near the end of the walk. Now it is dark enough to see the Milky Way, clusters of stars, and nebulae (unless the Moon is bright). As people scan this star-speckled path across the sky, the interpreter helps them become acutely aware that they exist inside the galaxy, nurtured by one of its stars.

The interpreter helps people appreciate the details that can be seen by an eye coupled with an inquiring mind. A very distant feature, such as the galaxy in Andromeda (or the Magellanic Clouds in the southern hemisphere), is pointed out (Figs. 22-2 and 22-3). Visitors are made to realize the geological changes that have occurred since the light they see it by was given off by the object.

As the interpreter chants another Otoe song, they are again reminded of the concepts of previous people who once may have stood here looking out at this celestial ribbon:

The prairie is dark
But across the sky
Is a trail of light.
It is the ghost pathway
of the departed warriors.

The group walks on to the termination point. People are thanked for their participation and encouraged to continue interest in earth and sky and to take part in other interpretive activities wherever they go. A telescope available at the termination point offers an excellent "second feature" for those who wish to stay longer and see in greater detail.

The sky walk is a special variation of the evening stroll. The walk is taken on a trail that rises significantly in altitude. It need not be a long walk, but must be a climb upward "into the sky."

The trail is chosen to allow the stops described in the evening stroll. It should overlook the region that will be interpreted and should culminate in an open area when second magnitude stars are easily visible.

At the top the interpreter might recite an appropriate legend involving climbing into the sky (several native American legends are of this type). The most important distinction between the sky walk and the evening stroll is the use of the fact that the group has "climbed a little way into the sky." The major sky interpretation should take place at the top of the trail. Then the group carefully works back down the trail with a final stop at the bottom to look at the Milky Way and other dimmer features before terminating the activity.

SKY PHOTOGRAPHY WITH THE STATIONARY CAMERA

Color photographs (slides) are among the most effective aids for sky interpretation. Cameras with "fast" lenses combined with high-speed, color, photographic films make it possible to obtain high-quality night sky pictures with a stationary camera. Color slides of star patterns can show essentially what the eye sees and, when used effectively, greatly simplify identification of sky features.

The following equipment is desirable for obtaining constellation and other night sky pictures.

1. A camera with lens of $f/22.5$ or better and with "time" or "bulb" setting to permit long exposures.
2. Cable release.
3. A sturdy tripod.
4. Color film rated at ASA 200 or greater. Note that many films can be developed to effectively increase the "speed" of the film beyond the ASA rating.

The exact photographic procedures depend on the light conditions and the type of picture desired. Experience combined with records of the conditions, film, and camera settings will give you general knowledge of the factors that result in outstanding pictures. The following information will get you started. It is for film rated at ASA 200 or greater.

Constellation Photography

After loading the camera with the appropriate film place it securely on the tripod. Set the camera shutter for a time exposure (time or bulb). Focus to infinity. Open the lens to about $f/2.0$. The greater the aperture, the more stars you will capture in a given exposure time. However, when small f numbers are used, there will be some distortion of the star images at the edges of the field. This is especially noticeable when a bright star or planet is at the edge of the field.

Direct the camera toward the desired group and open the shutter using the cable release. Count off (or mechanically time) the appropriate number of seconds, and close the shutter.

The length of exposure time depends on sky lighting conditions and the range of star brightness you desire. The limitation for a 50-mm lens is about 30 seconds. Longer exposures produce star trailing due to rotation of the earth. The best all-around exposure time for pictures taken in the dark of night (after twilight has ended) is 20 seconds. Expose for less time to show fewer stars and more time to pick up fainter ones. An exposure of 20 seconds at $f/1.8$ will show more stars than the naked eye can see.

Earth and Sky Photography

This type of picture shows the starry heavens with landscape features in the foreground. Three techniques, each with different qualities, may be used.

1. Start photography in the evening just as the stars become visible. The sky is still bright enough to silhouette landscape features against the starry sky. Try exposures ranging from 1 to 15 seconds. As it grows darker, lengthen the exposure range to at least 20 seconds. Twilight photography can also be done in the early morning before sunrise. Start just as the sky begins to brighten.
2. Use moonlight to illuminate landscape features. From first quarter (half-full) to last quarter Moon there will be sufficient natural light to record moonlit landscape features with stars beyond. Try a range of exposures up to 30 seconds at about $f/2.0$.
3. Use a strobe light to illuminate selected landscape features. This technique will yield nearly any type of desired lighting of trees and other landscape features in the immediate neighborhood. Considerable experience is needed to obtain exactly the desired lighting. (Fig. 22-5.)

A tree, rock pinnacles, or the human figure silhouetted against the star-studded sky can produce a picture of breathtaking beauty, and at the same time make a striking statement about humankind and its relationship to the immensity of the universe.

FIG. 22-5. Two people silhouetted against a star-studded sky. The foreground was illuminated with a strobe light. (Photo by Von Del Chamberlain.)

Star Trails

Both artistic and illustrative pictures can be made by taking advantage of the Earth's rotation. A camera attached to a tripod on the earth's surface will move with the Earth as an exposure is being made. If the shutter is kept open longer than 30 to 45 seconds, star trailing will begin to be noticed. Stop the shutter down and leave it open longer to purposely draw light trails on the film. Try $f/2.8$ for 20-minute exposures and $f/5.6$ for exposures up to 2 hours. Stopping down beyond $f/8$ will eliminate all except the brightest stars.

In the northern hemisphere if the camera is directed toward the North Star and exposed for several minutes, the star trails will become arcs (Fig. 22-6). If directed to the east or west, the trails will be nearly straight. If directed toward the south, arcs will be apparent over the horizon since the south celestial pole is below the horizon.

Short exposures preceding or following longer ones on the same frame are especially interesting. For example, suppose one wants to show the rising of Orion. Start the exposure as Orion comes over the horizon and continue exposing as these stars move upward in the field of view. Before Orion passes out of the camera view, stop the exposure (by capping the lens) for 5 to 10 minutes, then expose again for 30 seconds. The resulting picture will show trails for each star in Orion and end with Orion in point outline.

FIG. 22-6. A 1-hour exposure of circumpolar star trails. Photographed on 35-mm high-speed Ektachrome film with a 50-mm lens. (Photo by Von Del Chamberlain.)

Star trail pictures are very useful for illustrating the Earth's rotation. If one describes how the picture is made, people should understand why the sky appears to move as the Earth rotates. The pictures are also very colorful, since each trail of light will show the color of the star that produced it.

Use of Sky Photography

Sky transparencies are useful both outdoors and indoors. Slides of star groups projected on an outdoor screen with clear night sky overhead can be very helpful in identifying sky features. Begin by describing the direction and appearance of the featured star group. Try to get members of the audience to locate the selected stars from your description. Follow this with the same star group projected on the screen. Now people can compare and confirm their identification. Using a pointer you can indicate each star in the group to make sure everyone is able to locate the features.

If weather prohibits direct sky interpretation, use slides and a projector to simulate what would be seen in the sky. You should be able to stimulate enough interest so that people will plan to study the sky on their own when weather permits.

Sky slides are also useful as supplementary material for lectures about any environmental topic. The most effective sky interpretation is that which is related directly to the surrounding region. The program need not be entirely devoted to the sky but should discuss the sky in context with other elements of the environment.

STUDY GUIDE FOR SKY INTERPRETATION

If possible, become familiar with different phenomena by observation. Locate and learn selected legends about each and study changes in concepts across cultures and through time. Be sure you understand the latest explanations for each. Begin files of information on each topic and start a picture and slide collection that includes your own photographs. The following is a suggested study list of sky phenomena.

Sky color and changes in sky color and lighting conditions
Clouds and cloud types
Lightning
Rainbows, solar and lunar halos, sun dogs
Aurorae
Eclipses of the Sun and Moon
Comets
Meteors, meteor showers, and fireballs

Each of the objects and features in the list below, except as noted, are visible to the naked eye. Begin your observations with the naked eye, then binoculars, and finally, where possible, a telescope. Use precaution when observing the Sun. Continue your observations, noting changes that occur through time, for example, changing midday altitude of the Sun, rising and setting directions of the Sun through the year, and changing positions of the planets (including those not visible to the naked eye). Learn all you can about the physical nature of each object. Collect and learn ancient concepts and legends about each. Learn enough Greek mythology to explain the origin of the names. Where appropriate, make several lists arranging the objects according to (1) brightness (order in which they will appear and disappear in the darkening and brightening sky), (2) distances (note that the distances of some are constantly changing), and (3) positions in the sky and visibility through the seasons. Be able to describe each, pointing out relationships to the Earth and humans and placing each in our current model of cosmic history. Begin files of information and pictures on each topic. Start a photographic slide file on each.

Moon
Planets, including Earth (Neptune and Pluto not visible to naked eye)
Milky Way
Stars
   Sun
   Sirius
   Canopus
   Alpha Centauri
   Arcturus
   Vega
   Capella
   Rigel
   Procyon
   Achernar
   Beta Centauri
   Betelgeuse
   Altair
   Aldebaran
   Alpha Crucis
   Antares
   Spica
   Fomalhaut
   Pollux
   Deneb
   Eta Cassiopeia
Star Clusters
   Pleiades
   Hyades
   Praesepe
   Double cluster in Perseus

Open clusters in Scorpius
Globular cluster in Hercules
Globular cluster in Centaurus (Omega Centauri)
Nebulae
Great Nebula in Orion
Lagoon Nebula in Sagittarius
Galaxies
Great Galaxy in Andromeda
Large and Small Magellanic Clouds
Other objects
Crab Nebula in Taurus (not visible to the naked eye)

Locate a list of all of the constellations. Learn to identify as many as possible at your home latitude. When you travel to latitudes where others are visible, add new ones to your list. Pay special attention to the constellations containing the objects listed above (including the zodiac through which the Sun, Moon, and planets move). Be prepared to reply to U.F.O. and astrology enthusiasts. Find out the origins of the names of the constellations and study constellation mythology from various parts of the world. Learn by your own observation to associate the constellations with the seasons. Obtain your own color slides of selected constellations. Begin a file of information about each constellation and objects within them. Be alert to information about constellations, star names, and ideas from cultures native to where you do your work.

Select a recent astronomy textbook and study the text in detail. Use other readings to supplement the text.

Enroll in astronomy, meterorology, and other courses related to sky interpretations as opportunities arise.

Attend planetarium programs whenever you can. In addition to noting the information presented, pay close attention to the methods used in presenting the programs. Afterward list the sequence of topics used and analyze this from the standpoint of effective interpretation. List ideas gleaned from the program that may be used in outdoor interpretation. What changes are necessary? Find out which classes or other activities offered by the planetarium staff might be useful to you.

REFERENCES

Additional Reading

The following references are carefully selected to direct students of natural history interpretation to some of the best sources of information about the sky, its objects, and phenomena. The student should watch for additional sources, especially current and revised ones. In addition to using this list for personal study, encourage the availability of such materials at park sales outlets for the benefit of visitors.

General References

Abell, George. 1969. *Exploration of the Universe,* Holt, Rinehart, and Winston, New York. (A widely used, comprehensive, elementary textbook in astronomy).

Allen, Richard H. 1963. *Star Names, Their Lore and Meaning,* Dover Publications, New York. (A handy reference source containing hard-to-find information about star names. Useful, but not meant to be read from cover to cover).

Battan, Louis J. 1961. *The Nature of Violent Storms,* Doubleday-Anchor, New York. (One of a number of books in the Science Study Series.)

Battan, Louis J. 1964. *The Thunderstorm,* New American Library, New York. (A Signet Science Book). (The title indicates the contents.)

Boeke, Kees. 1957. *Cosmic View of the Universe in 40 Jumps,* John Day Company, New York. (This little book presents an effective method for teaching the scale of the universe.)

Bragg, Sir William. 1959. *The Universe of Light.* Dover Publications, New York. (An outstanding book about sight and light. Topics range from vision to radiations from bodies in space. Comprehensive. Easy to read and fairly well illustrated.)

Brandt, John C., and Stephen P. Maran. 1972. *New Horizons in Astronomy,* W. H. Freemand and Co., San Francisco, CA. (Sensitive to the type of information the sky interpreter is apt to need in a reference source.)

Chandler, T. J. 1967. *The Air Around Us,* Aldus Books, London. (A well-illustrated book about the atmosphere and the forces within it that produce climate and weather phenomena.)

Davis, George A., Jr. 1944. *Pronunciations, Derivations, and Meaning of a Selected List of Star Names,* Sky Publishing Corp., Cambridge, MA. reprinted from Popular Astronomy. (Very important for anyone teaching sky features.)

Gregory, R. L. 1970. *Eye and Brain, The Psychology of Seeing,* McGraw-Hill, New York. (A very well written book on both the physiology and psychology of sight. Discusses light, the eye, the brain, brightness, movement, color, and illusions.)

Hartman, William K. 1978. *Astronomy: The Cosmic Journey,* Wadsworth Publishing Company, Inc., Belmont, CA. (An outstanding descriptive astronomy textbook).

Jastrow, Robert, and Malcolm H. Thompson. 1972. *Astronomy: Fundamentals and Frontiers,* Wiley Interscience, New York. (A new, easy-to-read, descriptive textbook. A reasonably complete reference source for the sky interpreter.)

Levitt, I. M., and Roy K. Marshall. 1964. *Star Maps for Beginners,* Simon and Schuster, New York. (A set of sky maps for each month of the year, and associated information.)

Mayall, R. N., M. Mayall, and J. Wyckoff. 1959. *The Sky Observer's Guide,* Golden Press, New York. (A pocket book with numerous illustrations on how to observe stars, Moon, Sun, and planets with unaided eye, binoculars, and telescope.)

Menzel, Donald H., Fred L. Whipple, and Gerard de Vaucouleurs. 1970. *Survey of the Universe,* Prentice-Hall, Englewood Cliffs, NJ. (A very comprehensive, descriptive text. An outstanding reference source for fundamental astronomical information.)

Martin, Martha Evans. Revised by Donald H. Menzel and William W. Morgan. 1964. *The Friendly Stars,* Dover Publications, New York. (An easy to read introduction to the sky. Excellent for the sky interpreter.)

Moche', Dinah L. 1978. *Astronomy,* John Wiley, New York. (A self-instructional book with a unique approach to teaching astronomy).

Mullaney, James, and Wallace McCall. 1966. *The Finest Deep-Sky Objects,* Sky Publishing Corp., Cambridge, MA. (An excellent booklet describing deep-sky objects for study with small telescopes.)

Norton's Star Atlas and Reference Handbook. 1969. Sky Publishing Corp., Cambridge, MA. (A detailed atlas and descriptive material for the serious observer. The combination is one of the best available.)

Olcott, William T. 1954. *Olcott's Field Book of the Skies,* revised by R. N. Mayall and M. W. Mayall, Fourth Edition, G. P. Putnam's Sons, New York. (An important guide for sky interpreters. Information about each constellation of the sky, emphasizing mythology and observation with unaided eye, binoculars, and telescope.)

Paul, Henry E. 1970. *Telescopes for Skygazing,* Amphoto, New York. (Information about the variety of small telescopes, how to select and use them.)

Paul, Henry E. 1970. *Outer Space Photography,* Amphoto, New York. (A guide to sky photography.)

Scorer, Richard. 1972. *Clouds of the World, A Complete Encyclopedia,* Stackpole Books, Harrisburg, PA. (A color-illustrated book about classification of clouds with brief descriptions of cloud development.)

Viemeister, Peter E. 1961. *The Lightning Book,* Doubleday and Company, Garden City, NY. (An interestingly written, descriptive book on lightning. An excellent source of ideas for the sky interpreter.)

Zadde, Arthur J. Revised by Theodore A. Smits. 1964. *Making Friends with the Stars,* Barnes and Noble, New York. (As title suggests.)

Zim, Herbert S., and Robert H. Baker. 1956. *Stars, A Guide to the Constellations, Sun, Moon, Planets and Other Features of the Heavens,* Golden Press, New York. (A highly illustrated pocketbook for the beginner.)

Periodicals

Astronomy, Circulation Services, 411 E. Mason St., 6th Floor, Milwaukee, WI 53202. (A beautiful astronomy magazine artistically describing the wonders of space. Excellent for sky interpreters.)

Graphic Time Table of the Heavens, Maryland Academy of Sciences, 7 West Mulberry Street, Baltimore, MD 21201. (A graphical chart for quick and easy determination of the times of visibility of astronomical objects. Includes times of rising and setting of the Sun and Moon and other objects. Published annually and designed for use at mid-northern latitudes. A very handy item for the sky interpreter.)

Griffith Observer, Griffith Observatory, P. O. Box 27787, Los Angeles, CA 90027. (A small, monthly magazine with popular astronomy articles.)

Sky Calendar, Abrams Planetarium, Michigan State University, East Lansing, MI 48824. (A monthly sheet highlighting the most interesting, visible, astronomical objects and events. Specially designed for teachers, sky interpreters, and others who want to be continually aware of what is going on in the sky.)

Sky and Telescope, Sky Publishing Corp., 49-50-51 Bay State Road, Cambridge, MA 02138. (A monthly magazine on astronomy and closely related subjects written for the amateur astronomer and others interested in astronomy.)

Sky Interpretation Resource Bulletin, published occasionally by the American Astronomical Society. For information write: Von Del Chamberlain, National Air and Space Museum, Smithsonian Institution, Washington, DC 20560. (A publication specifically for sky interpreters).

Star and Sky, 44 Church Lane, Westport, CT 06880. (Another colorful and informative astronomy monthly written for an audience with interests ranging from casual to serious amateurs.)

Native American Indian Sky Lore

Information about native American concepts of the sky is scattered in the literature of several disciplines (ethnology, anthropology, archaeology, history, astro-archaeology).

The following references include sky legends and illustrate the intriguing legends that can be found by searching the literature of the Americas and other continents.

Clark, Ella E. 1953. *Indian Legends of the Pacific Northwest,* University of California Press, Berkeley. (A wonderful collection of stories from the Northwest arranged in five sections: Myths of the Mountains; Legends of the Lakes; Tales of the Rivers, Rocks and Waterfalls; Myths of Creation, the Sky and Storms; Miscellaneous Myths and Legends.)

Clark, Ella E. 1966. *Indian Legends from the Northern Rockies,* University of Oklahoma Press, Norman. (An excellent collection with lots of sky lore.)

Judson, Katharine Berry. 1917. *Myths and Legends of British North America.* A. C. McClurg and Co., Chicago, IL. (Filled with information for the sky interpreter.)

Judson, Katharine B. 1914. *Myths and Legends of the Mississippi Valley and the Great Lakes,* A. C. McClurg and Co., Chicago, IL. (Lots of information for the sky interpreter.)

Parsons, Elsie Clews. 1939. *Pueblo Indian Religion* (2 volumes). University of Chicago Press. [One of the best sources on the Pueblos. Much information on ceremonies, cosmic notations, calendar, etc. See the index (stars, sky, thunder, lightning, solstice, winter solstice, Orion, Pleiades, Galaxy, Dipper, etc.)]

Thompson, Stith. 1929. *Tales of the North American Indians,* Indiana University Press, Bloomington, IN. (The comparative notes and references together with the text make this a valuable source.)

Wissler, Clark. 1956. *Star Legends Among the American Indians,* American Museum of National History, New York. (The title indicates the contents.)

Yazzie, Ethelou, editor. 1971. *Navajo History,* Navajo Curriculum Center, Rough Rock Demonstration School, Chinle, AZ 86503. (The emergence story told in word and picture. Includes the account of placement of the stars in the sky.)

CHAPTER 23

MARINE INTERPRETATION

Grant W. Sharpe

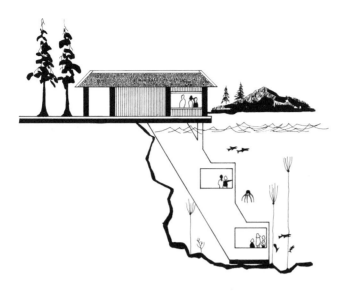

The seashores of the world, estimated at one million miles, are areas of great beauty and interest. Seventy percent of the planet is covered by water; most of this in four great oceans: the Pacific, Atlantic, Indian, and Arctic. There are few nations that do not have some shoreline on one of these bodies of water, yet most marine parks of the world lack interpretation or provide it only in the inter-tidal zone.

Since the emergence of the human race the oceans have provided a source of food and a means of transport for us. They modify climate and provide a rich resource for our recreational needs. There is a complex and fascinating story to be told anywhere land and water meet. This chapter, along with Chapter 22 (Sky Interpretation) calls attention to these aspects of the natural scene that have been slighted in common interpretive practice.

The marine environment is a fragile recreational resource; care and understanding is necessary to preserve it from harm. Those who interpret it must communicate this concern to the visitors. (The term "marine environment" here pertains primarily to salt water areas but will apply in part to large bodies of fresh water.)

THE MARINE ENVIRONMENT

Interest in the seashore usually begins with a family recreation visit. If the family is lucky, it will visit an area with some interpretation. My most enjoyable interpretive experiences were while working as a marine interpreter in Acadia National Park in Maine. Over the several summers I worked there, I must have taken several thousand people to the seashore to explain some of the ecological intricacies of the tidal zone.

I remember well a family who visited us in Maine. They lived a thousand miles (1600 km) inland, and it was their first visit to the ocean. Naturally on arrival they wanted to go down to the shore. I thought of the many things I had to tell them: how plants and animals survive in the pounding surf, what their enemies are, how each finds food, and how they reproduce in the sea. Where whould I begin, I wondered? When we reached the shore they had only one question—"Is the ocean really salty?" They scooped up a handful of water and answered their own question. I was amazed by their interest in something I had taken for granted. As so often happens, I learned from those I sought to teach.

Other than a place to bathe in the surf, feed seagulls, or bask in the sun, the marine environment is a strange one to most people. Like any complex subject, its multiplicity of relationships and actions cannot be grasped in one visit. Interpretation of these facts requires knowledge and enthusiasm, repetition, and patience—as does any interpretive challenge.

This chapter is meant to assist in realizing the interpretive potential of seashore areas. Greater familiarity will show relationships and patterns not at first evident. From these, interpretive themes may be suggested, such as shoreline erosion: The ocean gives and the ocean takes away; or plants along the shoreline: the effects of salt and wind.

Waves

Although they may not understand the physics involved, people love to watch waves. An interpretive specialist walking along the shore with a group of visitors would be remiss if he or she were to interpret only what was at their feet or in a nearby tidepool. The waves themselves are an integral part of the story, for they play a strong role in shaping the shoreline and determining what is able to live along the shore.

Waves can result from passing ships, landslides, changes in atmospheric pressure, earthquakes, or gravitational pull, but most waves seen along the shores of the world are caused by wind.

A wave has three dimensions: height (from trough to crest), length (the distance from the crest to that of the adjacent crest), and period (the time it takes for two adjacent crests to pass a fixed point). Knowing this we can study briefly how the major waves are formed.

Seismic Waves

Seismic waves, erroneously called "tidal waves," are extremely destructive. These are earthquake-related waves either from underwater landslides caused by earthquakes or from the sudden displacement of land as a result of fault slippage below the sea. The wave may be over 100 miles (161 km) in length, only 1 or 2 feet

(30 or 60 cm) in height, but with a period of 10 to 15 minutes. These waves travel for thousands of miles at speeds of several hundred miles per hour.

The crew of a ship at sea may not even be aware of the wave as it passes underneath. The catastrophe occurs when the seismic wave, sometimes called a "tsunami," reaches a populated shore. Entire cities have been covered, with thousands of lives lost, in historic seismic sea waves. The intensity of destruction varies with the shoreline shape and topography and the population density of the area. There is an average of three destructive tsunamis each year. Even though such waves travel at tremendous speeds, the distance traveled is great; and a warning service now permits evacuation of threatened areas.[1] Discussing seismic wave action is a dramatic part of marine interpretation.

Tides

The second kind of waves of interest to marine interpreters are those caused by the gravitational pull of the Sun and the Moon on Earth's oceans, specifically referred to as *the tides*.

An interpretive guide on coastal Maine states: "Spring tides, the highest and lowest tides, come twice a month, a full moon and new moon. At this time the sun, moon, and earth are all in line, or nearly so. Neap tides are smaller and occur when the sun and moon are at right angles to earth, their gravitational pulls partly canceling one another."[8]

Water bulges occur on the sides of the earth opposing and facing the moon (which is closer and has a stronger pull than the sun). As the earth rotates, the water masses are regularly subjected to these forces, giving shoreline areas a systematic high and low tide. In most areas this tidal cycle takes approximately 12 hours and 25 minutes. With each revolution of the earth two high and low tides occur, 50 minutes later each day. The effect of these tides is discussed in the section entitled "Intertidal Zone."

Wind Waves

In its simplest form a wind wave starts as a ripple on a mirrorlike surface of the sea. Once the ripple is formed, the wind has something to push against, energy is transferred from air to water, and small waves are formed. As the waves continue to enlarge the surface facing the wind, they become higher and steeper until a point of maximum steepness is reached. The steepness ratio is about 1:7. [A wave 7 ft (2 m) long can be no more than 1 ft (0.3 m) high; or a wave 21 ft (6.4 m) long can be only 3 ft (0.9 m) high, etc.]

If the wind continues, it causes the waves to break, forming whitecaps, known as "chop" to mariners. As the wind continues to produce more chop, smaller waves, which quickly reach their maximum height, are destroyed; the longer waves continue to grow. With time these longer waves reach their maximum size for that wind velocity. The distance the waves run in one direction while under the drive of the wind is called the *fetch*. In the fetch, which may be several hundred miles long, the waves reach their maximum period and height for the wind raising them; and the result is known as the *fully developed sea*. As the sea passes beyond the wind's influence, the wave height diminishes, the distance between crests increases, and the sea becomes a *swell*. These swells continue across the ocean for thousands of miles without much energy loss at speeds of 15 to 20 miles per hour (24 to 32 km/h) until they encounter land. There they break up in the *surf zone*. The drag on the bottom causes the waves' speed to slacken, crests of the preceding swells crowd in behind it, the wave form steepens, the crest curls forward, and the whole mass of water plunges with a booming, thundering roar of water, spray, and foam in a spectacular dying gasp.[1]

The wave that started at the beginning of the storm is not the same wave that breaks up on the beach thousands of miles away. Waves travel in groups. The lead wave is constantly using its energy to set previously undisturbed water in motion. As the lead wave disappears, a new wave is formed at the rear of the group, so that the number remains the same.

In the open sea where the fetch may cover several thousand miles, the largest waves are developed. A rule of thumb says that the height of the waves in feet will be one-half the speed of the wind in miles per hour. Thus, a 60 mph (96 km/h) wind could develop 30-ft (9-m) waves.

An interpreter standing on the shore can make a reasonable guess as to where the breakers originated. For example, the summer surf along California's shore-line could have originated in winter storms off New Zealand, 6000 miles (9656 km) away (Fig. 23-1).

FIG. 23-1. A surf watcher at Point Lobos State Reserve near Carmel, California. These waves could have originated near New Zealand, 6000 miles (9656 km) away. (Photo by Grant W. Sharpe.)

The Intertidal Zone

As we have seen, the tides are caused by the gravitational pull of the Sun and Moon on the Earth's oceans. This rising and falling of the sea every 12 hours and 25 minutes shapes the life pattern of intertidal zone plant and animal inhabitants. Those that live in the upper part of the zone have a long exposure to sun and air and a brief exposure to the sea; for those in the lower zone the exposures are just the opposite. Adapted to a twice-daily alternation of sea and air, these intertidal organisms live where conditions for their survival are best. The result is horizontal belts or colonies of similar species.

In some parts of the world the intertidal zone range may be only 1 or 2 ft (30 or 60 cm). In other areas it can be 20 ft (6 m) or more.

The intertidal zone should be of great interest to the marine interpreter for several reasons. There are many unusual forms of life in this zone, it is readily accessible, and visitors are keenly interested in a good intertidal program. Although rocky shores are generally more productive, sandy beaches, too, have a story to be interpreted.

Beaches

As Bascom points out, "beaches are everchanging, restless armies of sand particles, always on the move." Sand movement occurs mostly under water; and even though tons of sand shift each day, the short-term changes are not too obvious.

Seasonal changes, however, are dramatic. In winter when the wave action is greatest much of the sand is offshore in the form of bars. In the summer it is returned by waves to form a berm high on the beach. The forces that move the sand inshore or out or along the beach are in delicate balance. It is a matter of an individual grain of sand being lifted and transported with each wave and then being deposited in a slightly different location. With each wave, millions of grains of sand are relocated, and with more than 300 waves per hour, it is easy to see that a beach is in a constant state of flux. Beach migration is a story in itself, and the marine interpreter is encouraged to read Willard Bascom's *Waves and Beaches*. An entire beach geology walk could be centered around the story of berms and bars, beach profiles, storm surges, and minor beach features such as swash marks, backwash marks, rills, steps, cusps, domes, pinholes, and ripple marks.[1] A beach walk just after high tide is ideal, for the waves are like a huge eraser, removing all signs of human activity, making the entire beach a newly written story.

Life on Exposed beaches

With tons of water attacking the beach and millions of sand grains shifting position with each wave, it is a wonder anything can live in the surf zone. Rachael Carson in *The Edge of the Sea* tells us:

FIG. 23-2. A visitor to a beach in Maine looks at material drifting in from the sea. Such drift is a treasure chest of information for a marine interpretive story. Acadia National Park, Maine. (Photo by Grant W. Sharpe.)

Animals of open beaches are typically small, always swift-moving. Theirs is a strange way of life. Each wave breaking on the beach is at once their friend and enemy; though it brings food, it threatens to carry them out to sea in its swirling backwash. Only by becoming proficient in rapid and constant digging can any animal exploit the turbulent surf and shifting sand for the plentiful food supplies brought in by the waves.[3]

The marine interpreter has an unusual opportunity to point out the structural adaptations of the few animals that can live on exposed beaches. By using the life histories of such animals as the mole crab, ghost crab, beach hopper (sand flea), and certain burrowing clams, the story of survival in the battering surf and scraping sand is revealed.

The beach is often a depository for the unusual. Fishing gear, logs riddled with teredo, material from ships at sea, even plant life from deeper waters washes in (Fig. 23-2), contributing to the interpreter's story. Scavengers of the shore—the gulls, crows, crabs, and others—provide an opportunity to discuss the food chain and life and death on the seashore. The story of the producers, consumers, and decomposers is perhaps more clearly seen here than in a terrestrial environment.

Life Along the Rocky Shore

The rocky cliff and ledge area of the intertidal zone, even where exposed to heavy surf, is the home of a very large plant and animal population. Special adaptations include the ability to cling to solid surfaces and structurally dissipate the energy of the waves.

The barnacle, a close relative of the crab and lobster, is a delightful illustration of adaptation. Its low, cone-shaped form deflects the wave action, and a natural cement attaches it to the rock surface. Once attached in the larval stage it remains permanently fixed. The limpet, a primitive snail with a cone-shaped shell, represents a small improvement on this adaptation in that it can move about.[3]

Plants in the intertidal zone lack the root system of terrestrial plants but are anchored securely by means of holdfasts. Their rubbery fronds are elastic enough to withstand the pounding of the waves. As one soon discovers if the intertidal zone is visited at low tide, there are numerous niches where plants or animals can avoid the full impact of the waves. Here, where it lives a "sheltered" life, the same form that was encountered on a more exposed surface may take on a different appearance. A rocky shore is an asset to any interpretive program.

GEOLOGY OF THE SEASHORE

Although the seashore is constantly undergoing change, that change may not be readily apparent to visitors during their brief stay. The task of the marine interpreter is to point out these changes and show geology in action along the seashore.

Evidence of change is everywhere. On a sandy shore seek out long-range studies of the coast by geologists and coastal engineers. Review the historic records of shoreline occupancy. Bare cliffs may stand where houses once stood. The locations for two of the footings of the Marconi Wireless Telegraph antenna at Cape Cod National Seashore, once on land, are now several hundred feet from shore.

The town of Moclips, Washington, with its 350-room tourist hotel was almost wiped out in one night in 1913 when a combination of factors including high tides and wind waves caused the ocean to invade the town. Historical maps of coastal England reveal the location of entire towns that today are occupied by sandbanks far out to sea.[1]

In contrast, erosion on a rocky shoreline causes little obvious change over thousands of years. However, the evidence is still there. Here the interpreter looks for sea-cut cliffs, caves, chasms, seawalls, stacks, arches, cobble beaches, and other features to tell the story (Fig. 23-3). With the tide going out twice each day the visitor and interpreter have physical access to many of those features.

COASTAL EROSION AND ACCRETION

Willard Bascom tells us "either sand is being removed from some place that people wish it would stay or it is being deposited some place where it is not wanted, or both." Nearly every coastal country of the world is faced with the problem of wave erosion and deposition. Some shores of the world are retreating at average rates of 10 to 20 ft (3 to 6 m) a year and much more during great storm surges.[1]

Controlling erosion is the work of the coastal engineer. It is a fascinating subject and should be part of the marine interpreter's story. It is natural for sand to drift, for cliffs to erode, for harbors to fill, but as people occupy the shoreline in greater numbers, these changes interfere with their desires. Groins, jetties, or breakwaters are built; sand is pumped or dredged to protect valuable ocean frontage. Most action taken to correct one shoreline problem creates a new problem someplace else. Careful studies are necessary as there are legal and political considerations as well as financial concerns. Public understanding is essential, and the marine interpreter can assist by discussing the various human and natural forces at work.

OCEAN CURRENTS

In addition to the tidal currents mentioned earlier, there are huge oceanic rivers that influence shorelines. Cold water from the Earth's poles, being heavier and more dense, sinks and flows along the ocean bottom toward the tropics. It is replaced by the warmer, lighter water of the tropics that flows along the surface toward colder regions. Subterranean trenches, continents, and islands deflect these streams into irregular patterns. Prevailing winds, presumably caused by the Earth's rotation, also affect the direction of these currents. A map showing world currents will reveal the location and origin of streams and show why some areas enjoy a warmer climate than others in the same latitude.

Marine interpreters should comment on the influence these currents have on the immediate area, since they affect not only water temperature and marine life but also local climate.

THE ATMOSPHERE AND THE OCEAN

A strong relationship exists between the Sun, the air, and the ocean which oceanographers call the *atmospheric heat engine*. The power supply comes from the difference in the degree of solar heat absorbed by air over the land and that absorbed by air over the water. Because of evaporation and heat absorption of the sea, the colder, heavier air over the ocean flows toward the lighter, warmer, land air, pushing it up out of its path, causing a sea breeze.

FIG. 23-3. Geologic features illustrating erosion have great visitor interest. Here, a wave-cut chasm called Thunder Hole holds the visitors' attention. Acadia National Park, Maine. (Photo by Grant W. Sharpe.)

Water vapor from the ocean forms clouds that are carried landward. These clouds, forced to rise over the land mass, drop their moisture in the form of rain or snow. This water eventually returns to the ocean in streams and completes the "round-trip-of-the-raindrop," or hydrologic cycle. Reminding seacoast visitors about how the water cycle works is another possible theme for marine interpretation.

LIVELIHOODS

Interest in the sea should include what comes out of and what lies under the sea in the form of useful products. Coastal industry is therefore part of the interpretive story, even though it may not be found on park lands. Nearby fish canneries, seaweed processors, aquaculture sites, salt evaporators, mineral extracting plants, petroleum facilities, and energy power plants are examples.

FIG. 23-4. Watching a lobsterman hauling his trap gives the marine interpreter on board a tour boat an opportunity to inform visitors about an important coastal industry. Acadia National Park, Maine. (Photo by Grant W. Sharpe.)

These industries, including forestry and other land-use practices as seen from the sea, are interesting subjects to include in the interpretive narration on a boat cruise. Here, too, there may be an opportunity to watch commercial fishing, and there are sure to be questions as to the species caught and their eventual disposal (Fig. 23-4).

PIRACY AND SMUGGLING

Piracy has been going on since the development of ocean commerce and goes back at least to the Vikings who raided the coasts of Britain, Ireland, and France, and even before that to Roman times on the Mediterranean Sea. For many centuries the Barbary pirates operated out of the northwest coast of Africa. In later times sea robbers were active around the British Isles, where there existed a ready market for ill-gotten merchandise.

When life became too difficult in home waters, piracy ranged further afield to the West Indies and the east coast of the United States, where these plunderers operated for many years. The era was largely ended with the death of Blackbeard in 1718 on what today is Cape Hatteras National Seashore.

Piracy could exist only as long as there was a market for smuggled goods. Interpreters the world over should be able to find a port nearby where a pirate gang once landed and disposed of their plunder. Perhaps some would be lucky enough to have an interpretive link with such famous names as Captain John Avery, Bartholomew Roberts, or Edward Teach. Prohibition days left us a more contemporary legacy of rum-running, and even today smuggling of aliens, drugs, and arms is a timely topic when interpreting coastal areas almost anywhere in the world.

NAVIGATION AIDS

There are numerous navigation aids that assist ship captains and crews to guide their ships safely. On board these ships there are a variety of navigational aids and charts. In the water there are many kinds of buoys: can, nun, spar, lighted, whistle, and bell. On shore are range markers, radio beacons, light stations, and lighthouses. Each serves a particular function; each is a type of navigational traffic sign or signal.

Lighthouses are fascinating. These structures are strategically placed so as to be seen from far out at sea. Their shape, height, and markings provide identification during the day. At night each has a distinctive light that flashes in a certain pattern so that it may be distinguished from others. Most lighthouses are historical structures. The difficulty of constructing them and keeping them supplied, and the rigors of tending them have interpretive interest.

The drama of coast guarding agencies fits in with this interpretive theme, and it is well to be aware of their names and duties.

SHIPWRECKS

Some shorelines appear to have more than their share of shipwrecks. The shoals of sand off Nantucket, Massachusetts, shift constantly and have sunk over 2000 ships since 1900.[4] On the western shore of Vancouver Island, near Pacific Rim National Park in British Columbia, there are two sunken ships for every mile of open coast. The outer banks of North Carolina along Cape Hatteras National Seashore are known as the "Graveyard of the Atlantic" (Fig. 23-5).

Most ships wrecked along the coast are broken into fragments and scattered by storms. Many are repeatedly covered and uncovered by drifting sand. Even the remnants, however, have visitor interest. Marine interpreters should research the literature on ships wrecked in their area.

RECREATIONAL ACTIVITIES

A number of marine-related recreation activities can be brought into the interpretive program. It is not necessary that the visitor actually participate in the activity.

FIG. 23-5. The remains of the sailing vessel *Laura A. Barnes,* which went aground in 1921; one of several hundred ships now buried in the sands of the Atlantic Coast. Such wrecks have great visitor interest. Note the interpretive exhibit at right. Cape Hatteras National Seashore, North Carolina. (Photo by Grant W. Sharpe.)

FIG. 23-6. A surf-fishing demonstration given by the staff of the Cape Hatteras National Seashore, North Carolina. (Photo courtesy of National Park Service.)

FIG. 23-7. A surf rescue and swimming safety demonstration. Here a lifeguard illustrates for park visitors the method of approaching a drowning victim with a flotation device equipped with handles and a towline. Cape Hatteras National Seashore, North Carolina. (Photo courtesy of National Park Service.)

Surfboarding is a good case in point. Describing how the surfers wait for the right wave in the set, how they keep their balance while maneuvering, how they stay ahead of the break of the wave, and other fine points would be of interest to visitors. Other shore activities such as shellfish or seaweed gathering tours do permit visitor participation. Here is an opportunity to show visitors how to enjoy and utilize a harvest from the seashore and also stress conservation measures.

Surf fishing demonstrations are another activity to consider. The equipment needed and the techniques used are easily interpreted and are appreciated by visitors, especially those who aren't having much luck fishing (Fig. 23-6).

Swimmers and sun bathers are normally a difficult group to involve in an interpretive program. However, the staff at Cape Hatteras National Seashore has found a way. The lifeguards offer a surf rescue and swimming safety demonstration several times a week (Fig. 23-7). The scheduled activity is conducted on the beach, demonstrating the techniques for rescue and administering mouth-to-mouth resuscitation.

OTHER INTERPRETIVE OPPORTUNITIES

The imaginative marine interpreter will also include areas such as salt marshes, lagoons, estuaries, tide flats, and levees in the interpretive story. Along the shore many kinds of vegetation are restricted to the halophyte (salt-spray) zone, and above that are windswept and distressed trees. Sand dunes, both active and inactive, have interpretive interest. Include blowout areas, dune fences, dune invasion of forests, and the dune-holding power of natural or planted vegetation.

Offshore there is the migratory route of everything from birds to fur seals and whales to discuss with visitors. Major and minor shipping lanes could be mentioned also. The problems of pollution, its causes and effects, can tactfully be brought into the story. Another topic is "natural pollution" (sedimentation and glacial milk in rivers) and its effect on sea life.

Looking beyond the immediate area, there is the opportunity to discuss the origin of the oceans, the spreading mid-ocean floor, and continental drift. These theories take on new interest in a marine locale.

INTERPRETING THE MARINE ENVIRONMENT

The first part of this chapter dealt with what there is to be interpreted. This second part shows examples of how to carry out a marine interpretive program. Most terrestrial interpretive media such as talks, exhibits, guided walks, and publications have application in marine areas, and they are discussed elsewhere in this book. For our purposes marine environment will be divided into three basic components: surface, shorelines, and underwater areas.

SURFACE INTERPRETATION

Guided Boat Tours

Acadia National Park in the state of Maine is a fine example of an ocean-oriented park. Though there is considerable terrestrial interpretation in the park, only its marine activities will be described here. The first example is the guided boat tour as a means of interpreting the shoreline and the sea.

A privately owned excursion boat is made available to the National Park Service for a daily sea cruise out of Bar Harbor. The boat meets all U.S. Coast Guard regulations. The owner provides the crew, handles the tickets and reservations, and receives all passenger revenue. The National Park Service provides the interpreter and publicity for the cruise.

The sea cruise, which lasts 3 hours, follows the coast, and winds in and out of the offshore islands. A loudspeaker on board makes it possible to inform all passengers at once when an important feature is seen; however, care is taken to restrict announcements and comments so that visitors are not subjected to continuous chatter. Frequent stops are made for closer looks at shoreline features and

FIG. 23-8. A marine interpreter explores ashore with his party. The people were rowed in from the two cruise boats. A short walk on the beach makes this an unusually comprehensive interpretive activity. Acadia National Park, Maine. (Photo by Grant W. Sharpe.)

animal life. Navigational aids, lighthouses, and shipwrecks are also brought into the interpretive story. One of the highlights of the excursion is standing off from a lobster boat and watching a lobsterman haul in his trap (Fig. 23-4). A successful catch displayed to the floating audience usually results in a spontaneous cheer.

A second, less formal cruise is also available. This one includes the opportunity to go ashore on one of the small islands and explore. As the island does not have any dock, passengers are transported a few at a time in small rowboats, which further contributes to the adventure (Fig. 23-8). There follows a lighthouse visit and a walk to the exposed side of the island to view evidence of winter storms. When there are sufficient visitors to warrant a second boat, the interpreter rides out with the passengers on one boat and back with those on the other.

Marine Ferries

A second example of surface marine interpretation comes from Alaska, on the northwestern extreme of North America. This is a cooperative partnership between the U.S. Forest Service and the Alaska State Division of Marine Transportation. Here, the state of Alaska provides the ships and the interpreters' living quarters, and the federal government, through the Forest Service, provides the interpretive personnel (Fig. 23-9). In 1980, Forest Naturalists staffed seven vessels, that varied in length from 193 ft (58 m) (165 passengers, 54 cars) to 418 ft (127 m) (1000 passengers, 184 cars).

FIG. 23-9. A forest naturalist at his station aboard an Alaska State Ferry. (U.S. Forest Service photo by D. R. Hakala.)

The objectives of the interpretive programs are to provide understanding and appreciation of the natural and cultural resources of the national forest and adjacent areas; to assist management by providing feedback regarding management goals and guidelines; and to assist visitors in making wise and safe use of their national forest's recreation opportunities. Since the resource management interests of several state and federal agencies are involved, the programs the interpretive naturalists conduct are broadly environmental, with much cooperation among the agencies.[11]

The interpretive personnel working the ferries are seasonals, mostly college students or recent graduates who are residents of Alaska. Interpreters for this program should have a strong foundation in conservation education, natural resource management, and a broad range of communication skills. Because of the scope of the program, travel experience within Alaska is also desirable.[11]

Training

Before the season begins, each interpreter is sent two or more packets of job-related information. This material includes basic information about the Forest Service organization, forest resources, geography, communities, and other topics to allow interpreters to "get their sea legs" prior to the season's start.[11]

Training sessions, which include travel through the national forests to observe the country, people, and resource uses, are held before the working season begins. Numerous resource people contribute to the naturalists' training. Many are from outside of the Forest Service, representing fish and wildlife agencies, travel bureaus, historical libraries, museums, lumber and pulp companies, fish processing firms, chambers of commerce, and native Alaskan organizations.

Training continues through the remainder of the working season. The supervisors of the program, plus other Forest Service personnel traveling by ferry, help the naturalists by providing comments and information on resources within view of the ferry passengers. A newsletter is employed to keep naturalists informed about useful and current materials.

Onboard Resources

Interpreters have at their disposal at the forest naturalist station a lending library, maps, charts, specimens, publications for distribution, information files, and documentary records. Interpreters also use slides and motion pictures for presentations, and this necessitates use of projectors, screens, and a representative slide collection. Closed circuit video equipment on some vessels is used for showing "canned" programs featuring Alaska, its people, and resources. A bulletin board, with newspaper clippings on current Alaskan matters is also utilized. Exhibits are presently being planned that can be used year-round, providing interpretation in off-season.[12]

Carrying Out the Program

Interpretive activities are presented in any of the public areas on the vessel, wherever passengers are actively observing the passing scenes, without intruding on those individuals not interested in the program. Use of the ship's public address system, therefore, is limited to general announcements. Passengers are encouraged to participate in marine mammal surveys and bald eagle counts. Naturalists often go ashore while the ferry is in port and collect common plants and other specimens. When time in port permits, the naturalist may also conduct a walk on shore. Interpretive commentary is conducted in the ship's solarium.[12] A publication entitled *Interpreting the Tongass National Forest Via the Alaska Marine Highway* covers many of the subjects that are observed from the ferries.[5]

Feedback

Information on the successes and failures of the new program is solicited from the naturalists, ship's employees, and passengers. Each year new methods are implemented and the program continues to expand.

A second aspect of feedback is the means offered the public to express its concerns about the values and uses of national forest resources. Ideas received from the public are forwarded to the offices concerned and figure in the management decision process.[11]

SHORELINE INTERPRETATION

It would be difficult to single out one intertidal interpretive program since many areas are doing outstanding work in this phase of marine interpretation. For our purposes here we will review the method used in several of these areas.

The Methodology

Most intertidal zone programs have these features in common:

1. The activity begins at a designated time, usually from a parking lot located near the shore.
2. The shore area is reached by walking from this parking area.
3. The tide is out or going out at the time of arrival.

Because the convenient (daylight) low tide is 50 minutes later each day, the time of arrival at the seashore changes daily. These times can be calculated from tide tables and printed in advance of the visitor season. It is wise, however, to publicize the time of the activity daily on prominently located bulletin boards since this is one of the few activities whose starting time differs each day.

To avoid competition from the noisy surf and other features found there, the actual discussion of the shore environment takes place before reaching the shore. In Acadia National Park the interpreter takes the group to a rocky ledge above the surf zone, asks them to sit down, and for 20 minutes unfolds the story of the intertidal zone (Fig. 23-10). On days of very heavy surf, a portable, public address system is used.

In Olympic National Park, which has a sandy beach, the interpreter moves the group down onto the sand where a large circle is drawn; the participants are asked to watch and listen from outside the circle. Standing inside, the interpreter, using a stick, draws pictures of the Sun, Moon, Earth, and other features relevant to the tidal story. Questions are answered at this point.

At Acadia before approaching the shore the group is warned of the dangers involved at the next stop: the slippery rocks, the pounding surf, and the returning tide. For those visiting the seashore at other times, mention should be made of the possibility of being stranded on rocks when the tide comes in. The group is now taken down into the tidal zone to a preselected tidepool, and they seat themselves around the rim. In the meantime the interpreter has put on rubber hip

FIG. 23-10. An interpreter reveals the story of the intertidal zone to park visitors before taking them down to the tide pool. Acadia National Park, Maine. (Photo by Wenonah Sharpe.)

waders and stepped into the pool (Fig. 23-11). Within view of everyone the interpreter illustrates the talk by selecting live specimens from the tidepool. One by one their methods of locomotion, feeding, means of protection, interrelationships, and other pertinent data are discussed, using caution to handle all objects with care and respect. This develops in the group an attitude of respect and an understanding of the proper care of tidepool creatures. Each object is passed around for inspection, then it is carefully returned to the tidepool (Fig. 23-12).

During the presentation the interpreter must control the audience. If children are allowed to clamber over the rocks, they may slip on rockweed, fall into the tidepools, or get cut on barnacles. The result, to say the least, is disruptive. For this reason the interpreter must maintain control by asking children to return if they start to lose interest and wander. Saving some particularly interesting denizen of the tidepool for this moment is a good way to recapture their attention. After the tidepool presentation the visitors are invited to explore on their own. The interpreter remains with the group, answering questions. After a half hour of exploring, the tide should be returning, and the interpreter gathers the group for the return to the parking lot.

Other appropriate shoreline features may be interpreted on the return trip. Re-

FIG. 23-11.   Surrounded by his group, the interpreter reaches into the tidepool for specimens to illustrate his talk. Acadia National Park, Maine. (Photo by Wenonah Sharpe.)

turning at the designated time is important, however, since visitors often have other activities planned. A brief mention of other interpretive activities for the day is appropriate.

UNDERWATER INTERPRETATION

There are several ways of giving people a view of the bottom of the ocean. One is the self-propelled subsurface craft holding from 2 to 40 people. Such submarines presently see little use in most park areas, but the potential is there.

Fixed-location diving apparatus also have potential. Most are in use in harbors or ports at the end of piers and operate up and down in the same manner as an elevator.

Glass-Bottom Boats

Glass-bottom boats, which are already in use in fresh-water lakes, may be employed effectively in salt water, particularly over coral reefs. A fine example is at John Pennekamp Coral Reef State Park, Florida. The boat, owned by the con-

FIG. 23-12. The interpreter involves his group by passing specimens around for closer inspection. Here a visitor is smelling the very malodorous crumb-of-bread sponge. Acadia National Park, Maine. (Photo by Wenonah Sharpe.)

cessionaire, seats 124 people. It leaves the park marina and travels 1 hour to the coral reef.

Below the main deck is the observation room. The viewing windows are located along each side of the hull (Fig. 23-13). Visitors are not allowed in the observation room while the boat is underway, as viewing at this time causes dizziness.

On reaching the coral reef, half the visitors are allowed to use the observation room at one time. Total time over the reef is 20 minutes.

At present, interpretation over the reef is handled by the concessionaire. Taped messages, prepared by the park interpretive staff, are used en route to and from the reef.

To keep operational costs at a minimum, a large boat is needed. The boat must remain stable over the viewing area. If there is too much rocking, visitors may become seasick.[15]

Underwater Interpretation for Swimmers

Two of the most exciting approaches to underwater interpretation are the guided and self-guided activities found in Virgin Islands National Park.

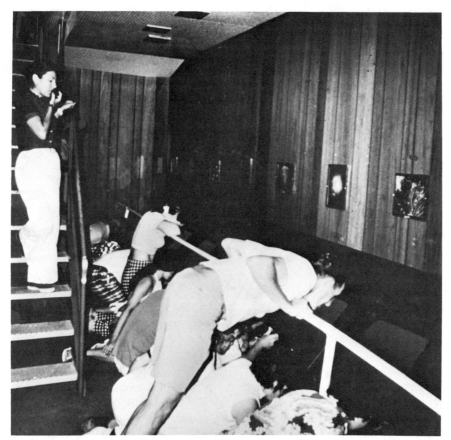

FIG. 23-13. The below-deck observation room of a boat with viewing windows located along the side of the hull. (Photo courtesy of John Pennekamp Coral Reef State Park, Florida.)

Guided Snorkel Tour

Snorkeling consists of floating face down on the water surface while wearing a faceplate, breathing tube (snorkel), and flippers. Each visitor must bring or rent this inexpensive equipment.

Usually 12 people is the optimum size for such a group. Two interpreters work together—one as the guide, the other as a lifeguard. The guide explains things just as he or she would on a terrestrial guided tour. Each trip lasts about 1 hour, and at the conclusion of each tour the interpreters switch duties. People need to be able to swim in order to participate. The interpreters show the visitors how to use the equipment before the trip (Fig. 23-14). There are problems with inexpe-

FIG. 23-14. A marine interpreter preparing his group for a guided snorkel tour. Each visitor is given instructions on the use of the faceplate, snorkel, and flippers. Virgin Islands National Park. (Photo by Donald H. Robinson.)

rienced swimmers not realizing their limitations or those of the equipment. Light rafts with handholds, towed by the leader, are a useful device where the water is deep or the bottom unsuited for standing because of sea urchin spines, biting fish, or eels.[7,13,16]

Self-Guided Activities: The Underwater Trail

At Trunk Bay on the Island of St. John in Virgin Islands National Park there is an example of a self-guided underwater trail. The course is triangular in shape with the starting angle on the shore. Two buoys are used to mark the other corners. A resting buoy is placed in the center for the convenience of tired swimmers.

On the shallow bottom are 24 markers made of cast concrete blocks, recessed in the middle to hold glass-covered labels. The hand-lettered and painted labels are covered by shatterproof glass held tightly in place with aquarium sealer. Because of marine growth and sediment the glass must be cleaned as needed with a wire brush. The labels themselves must be limited to a dozen words or less so swimmers can absorb the message quickly (Fig. 23-15).

The blocks are very heavy—about 125 lb (56 kg)—to prevent stormy seas from throwing them into sensitive areas such as coral beds. Twice a year the blocks are raised from the ocean floor by a winch and taken to shore. There the labels are replaced.

FIG. 23-15. An underwater label mounted on a large concrete block, located on the bottom in 25 ft (7.6 m) of water. Note the brief message, designed for swift and easy reading. Buck Island National Monument. (National Park Service photo by M. Woodbridge Williams.)

Experimentation with fired, ceramic-tile signs is planned for the near future. The signs will be easily removed from the concrete block, which will save the need for pulling up the block each time maintenance is needed. Another experiment planned is the use of cards on the rest floats, which would help visitors identify various marine life.[16]

Visitors on the underwater trail are under the watchful eye of a lifeguard. A beach sign shows a map of the trail and provides safe snorkeling tips.

At Buck Island National Monument 75 miles (120 km) away, there is a modification of the above trail. Off the eastern end of the small island a coral reef prevents the sea waves from entering a shallow 20 to 30 ft (6–9 m) deep turquoise-green lagoon. The lagoon flourishes with marine life and is so clear the bottom is easily visible.

Visitors are brought to the island by charter boats from Christiansted on the Island of St. Croix. They are taken in the morning by the charter skippers to the shallow, sheltered, western side of the island and given instructions in, and a

FIG. 23-16. Snorklers swimming over the self-guided underwater trail at Buck Island National Monument in the Virgin Islands. Note the life raft at left, and the charter boat at upper right. (Photo by Donald H. Robinson.)

chance to use, the faceplate, snorkel, and flippers. In the afternoon the charter boats move to the lagoon and tie up to a buoy. The visitors are assisted over the side and swim on their own along a marked trail.[14] For inexperienced swimmers a life raft may be towed over the underwater trail site by the charter crew (Fig. 23-16).

Most swimmers stay on the surface, looking through their faceplates and breathing through their snorkels. The experienced ones may dive to the bottom for a closer look at swimming fish and other features.

Problems

There are some problems inherent in such interpretive efforts. A careless skipper may drop anchor rather than use a buoy. This can break coral formations. Visitors may wish to collect coral, sea fans, and other specimens for sourvenirs. Enforcement of regulations is sometimes difficult; careful coordination with charter boat skippers is necessary in order to protect the marine environment from damage.

One of the major problems in managing any marine park and protecting its shipwrecks and marine life is that it cannot be fenced, and access may be difficult to control. When a park has been established for the protection of its marine life and associated attractions such as shipwrecks, regulations must be carefully written and enforced. Collecting, mutilating, or even anchoring to the bottom formations or growths should be prohibited. Tampering with wrecks or removing parts of wrecks from the park must be prevented if their interpretive value is to be realized.[7,13,14]

Artificial Reefs

Another opportunity for underwater interpretation, particularly in colder waters, is through the use of scuba: Self-Contained Underwater Breathing Apparatus.

Underwater trails for snorkelers should be of equal interest to the scuba diver. The personal investment for scuba gear, of course, is considerably greater than for the snorkeler. Interest in the sport, however, is growing rapidly and so are the number of underwater parks being established for this group. A popular approach to establishment of an underwater park for scuba use is through the development of artificial reefs.

The studies on artificial reefs were conducted in the interest of sports fishing to see what effect such reefs would have in attracting fish. The success of these programs has attracted another type of recreationist, the scuba diver. Interest in diving just to "look around" is growing, and the result has been the establishment of marine parks centered around artificial reefs.

The first artificial reef was constructed in the United States in 1935 off Cape May, New Jersey. Since that time they have been the subject of great interest and extensive experimentation. It is well known that fish are attracted to natural reefs as a source of food and shelter. Thus, artificial reefs are now regarded as a logical and effective way of creating conditions favorable for other marine animals as well.[2]

Coastal areas are often relatively barren. They offer their inhabitants very little food and no protective hiding places. Biologists have found that it takes only a small amount of relief to be of help to some species. However, the more relief offered by a reef, the better the chance of attracting larger fish. The main objective of the artificial reef has been to improve fishing by converting a relatively barren mud bottom into a thriving underwater community.

Experimental artificial reefs have been made from old tires, abandoned car bodies, concrete culverts, chunks of cement, or even sunken ships. At first the reef becomes covered with barnacles or other encrusting organisms. Soon many different varieties of fish, both juveniles and adults, are attracted.[10] Much work has been done experimentally with various reef materials. Old car bodies appear to be an obvious choice. The National Marine Fisheries Service, however, found them difficult to handle as they must be cabled together to assure stability on the bottom under storm surge, and they tend to rust away in about 6 years.[10]

Tires have been used with considerable success. Everything from single tires to multitire units composed of 4 to 10 tires stacked one upon the other have been tried. Devising ways of keeping the tires together has been taxing. Concrete, reinforcing rods, steel cables, and plastic straps have all been tried. In only a few weeks a multitire reef off New Jersey had an attached growth of polychaete worms. Later, shrimp, rock crabs, lobsters, and sea bass moved into the surrounding area. Another example of a tire reef is found off the Georgia coast in 55 ft (17 m) of water. Here thousands of tires in columnar stacks had a heavy, barnacle encrustation along with hydroids, sponges, and some sea feathers after 4 months.[9]

Steel-hulled ships have also been used as artificial reefs. Four donated vessels, stripped and cleaned to federal specifications, were sunk ¾ of a mile (1.2 km) off Palm Beach, Florida, in 90 ft (27 m) of water. After 4 months hydroids, soft corals, barnacles, and other encrusting organisms began to cover the hulls. Also reported on the reef were grunts, snappers, gray groupers, and jacks by the thousands. Even sea turtles appeared.[10]

These surplus metal ships, when available, provide the most desirable reef from the underwater park standpoint. Because of the large amount of relief that they provide, they attract larger fish and have more surface area for encrusting organisms. The ship itself has some interpretive interest for divers, such as its name, size, former ownership, and use.

In the United States before any material can be placed on a potential site a permit must be obtained from the U.S. Army Corps of Engineers, and an environmental impact statement must be approved by the state. All potentially toxic and floatable materials must be removed before the ships are taken to the reef sites. Before they are sunk the ships must meet Environmental Protection Agency standards.

Objections to artificial reefs can be minimized by:[6]

1. Not placing them in main navigation channels.
2. Not locating them in a commercial fishing area.
3. Notifying commercial fishermen of their exact locations.
4. Buoying them in accordance with approved U.S. Coast Guard standards for day and night navigational aids.

It is hoped that this chapter has introduced some new marine interpretive opportunities. The appendix contains an example of an interpretive program that might be offered in a seashore recreation area.

REFERENCES

General References

Bjorklund, Mona. 1974. "Achievements in Marine Conservation I: Marine Parks," Environmental Conservation **1**(3): 205–223.

Robinson, Alan H. 1971. "Marine Research and Resource Management in the Virgin Islands National Park," *Proceedings of American Association for The Advancement of Science,* December 1971, Philadelphia, PA.

Robinson, Alan H. 1973. "Natural vs. Visitor Related Damage to Shallow Water Corals—Recommendations for Visitor Management and the Design of Underwater Nature Trails for the Virgin Islands," Virgin Islands National Park Special Report, Denver, CO.

Robinson, Alan H. 1976. "Recreation, Interpretation and Environmental Education in Marine Parks; Concepts, Planning Techniques, and Future Directions," *An International Conference on Marine Parks and Reserves: Papers and Proceedings,* Tokyo, May 1975, IUCN Publication New Series No. 37.

Salvat, Bernard. 1976. "Guidelines for Planning Management of Marine Parks and Reserves," *An International Conference on Marine Parks and Reserves: Papers and Proceedings,* Tokyo, May 1975, IUCN Publication New Series No. 37.

Salvat, Bernard. 1979. "Trouble in Paradise, Part II: Coral Reef Parks and Reserves," *Parks Magazine* **4:**1.

Wallis, Orthello. 1971. "Establishing Underwater Parks Worldwide," Transactions of the 36th North American Wildlife and Natural Resources Conference, March 7–10, 1971, Tokyo, Japan.

References Cited

1. Bascom, Willard. 1964. *Waves and Beaches,* Anchor Books (Doubleday and Company, Inc.) Garden City, NY.

2. Betz, Frederick Jr. 1972. "Forward," *Proceedings of Sport Fishing Seminar,* Jekyll Island, GA.

3. Carson, Rachel L. 1955. *The Edge of the Sea,* Mentor Books (Oxford University Press, Inc.), New York.

4. Engel, Leonard. 1961. *The Sea,* Time Incorporated, New York.

5. Hakala, D. Robert. (nd). *Interpreting the Tongass National Forest Via the Alaska Marine Highway,* U.S. Department of Agriculture (Alaska Region).

6. Harrington, David L. 1971. "The Viewpoint of Commercial Fishermen on Artificial Reefs," *Proceedings of Sport Fishing Seminar,* Jekyll Island, GA.

7. Schultz, Paul E. 1968. "Public Use of Underwater Resources," *Park Practice Guideline,* reprinted from proceedings and papers of the International Union for the Conservation of Nature, tenth technical meeting, Lucerne, Switzerland, 1966.

8. Sharpe, Grant W. 1968. *Acadia National Park and the Nearby Coast of Maine,* Golden Press, New York.

9. Smith, Larry. 1971. "Construction and Studies of an Artificial Reef Off Brunswick, Georgia," *Proceedings of Sport Fishing Seminar,* Jekyll Island, GA.

10. Stone, Richard. 1971. "General Introduction to Artificial Reefs," *Proceedings in Sport Fishing Seminar.* Jekyll Island, GA.

Personal Communications

11. Hagadorn, Neil. Supervisory Naturalist, Tongass Marine Highway Interpretive Program, Forest Service, Juneau, AK.

12. Hakala, D. Robert. VIS Specialist, Regional Office, Forest Service, Juneau, AK.

13. Harriman, Walter. Regional Office, National Park Service, Seattle, WA.

14. Robinson, Donald H. Regional Naturalist, National Park Service (retired). Atlanta, GA.

15. Stevenson, James. Chief Naturalist, Florida Division of Recreation and Parks, Tallahassee, FL.

16. Webb, William. Superintendent, Virgin Islands National Park, St. Thomas, VI.

APPENDIX—SAMPLE PROGRAM

ROCKY HEAD

SEASHORE

RECREATION AREA

SUMMER

INTERPRETIVE

PROGRAM

Evening Programs

Offered Nightly in the Amphitheater at 8:30 PM in June and July; 8:00 PM in August and September.

Sunday: The Changing Salt Marsh
Monday: The Intertidal Zone
Tuesday: Geology of the Coast
Wednesday: Birds, Mammals, and People
Thursday: Fishing and Shellfishing
Friday: The Underwater World
Saturday: Life of the Seashore

Evening Campfires 8:30 PM in June and July; 8:00 PM in August and September. Meet at Beach Campfire Circle.

Friday: Night Sky Interpretation
Saturday: "Rap" with a Ranger, topics of your choice.

Self-Guided Activities

ROCKY HEAD LIGHT—A do-it-yourself trip to a 100-year-old lighthouse built after several maritime disasters took place off this coast.
SEASHORE BIRD WALK—Pick up a bird checklist at the ranger station. The brief descriptions will help you identify most of the common sea birds.
SNORKEL TOUR—A tour of Blue Lagoon. Must bring or rent your own snorkel, facemask, and flippers. See lifeguard for instructions.

Seashore Publications

The Beachcombers Book
A Guide to Fishes
A Guide to Seashells
Life of the Salt Marsh
Life of the Seashore
Where the Land Meets the Sea
Trees, Shrubs, and Wildflowers of the Coast
Shipwrecks of the Coast

SEASHORE ACTIVITIES	TIME	LENGTH	S	M	T	W	T	F	S
GUIDED TOURS									
BOAT TOUR—A cruise along the coast and to nearby islands with a park interpreter. History, birdlife, mammals, and fish resources will be interpreted. Tickets must be purchased and reservations made in advance at Fisherman's Dock.	9:00 AM	3 h	*	*	*	*	*	*	*
BICYCLE TOUR—A park interpreter-led trip along the coastal road to nearby marshes and headlands. Shore birds and other animal life will be observed. Meet at ranger station.	9:00 AM	3 h	*		*		*		*
OLD FORT TOUR—A brief visit with a park historian through the remains of Fort Smith, which played a prominent role in the settlement of this area. Meet at fort flag pole.	Hourly 9:00 AM to 4:00 PM	3/4 h	*	*	*	*	*	*	*
GUIDED WALKS	TIME	LENGTH	S	M	T	W	T	F	S
TIDE POOL WALK—A visit to the rocky shoreline at low tide to observe plant and animal life found in the intertidal zone. Meet at parking lot Number 3.	VARIES† w / tides	2 h	*	*	*	*	*	*	*
BEACH WALK—A leisurely walk along the beach to observe marine life and its relationship with the land and sea. Meet at ranger station.	2:00 PM	1½ h		*		*		*	
SHORELINE TO FOREST WALK—An ecology walk through the various habitats of plants and animals from the salt water to the forest. Meet at ranger station.	10:00 AM	2 h	*		*		*		*
SALT MARSH WALK—A look at the rich, fascinating life of the salt marsh. Meet at parking lot Number 4.	10:00 AM	2 h		*		*		*	
GEOLOGY WALK—A look at the erosive effects of waves: arches, stacks, wave-cut beaches, caves, cliffs, and blowholes. Meet at parking lot Number 2.	2:00 PM	3 h	*		*		*		*
SUNSET WALK—A leisurely walk to observe wildlife at dusk. Ends at campground amphitheater in time for evening program. Meet at ranger station.	7:30 PM	1 h						*	*
NIGHT PROWL—1½ hours of discovering the sights and sounds of twilight. Bring a flashlight. Meet at ranger station.	8:00 PM	1½ h		*		*			
DEMONSTRATIONS									
SURF FISHING—Presented by a park ranger, who explains the use of equipment, baiting the hook, and surf casting techniques. Meet at ranger station.	9:00 AM	1 h		*		*		*	
SURF RESCUE—Presented by lifeguards using the equipment and techniques of rescuing a victim from the surf. Meet at parking lot Number 1.	10:00 AM	1 h	*	*	*	*	*	*	*

† Check at ranger station or campground bulletin boards for times.

CHAPTER 24

HISTORICAL
INTERPRETATION

Lawrence Rakestraw

AN OVERVIEW OF HISTORICAL INTERPRETATION

Historical interpretation in the United States had its genesis in the preservation of historic sites. Associated with the growth of American nationalism, the preservation movement sought to preserve as shrines the homes or public buildings associated with great individuals or heroic deeds of the past. It paralleled similar movements in Europe, where Sweden passed an act to preserve antiquities as early as 1660. France, in 1830, set up a commission to inventory French monuments worth preserving. These monuments (meaning buildings or other evidences of the past) were listed in several priorities: those of absolute prime value, those of historic significance, those of regional significance, and those of technological significance. In England, the work was initiated by individuals. John Ruskin and William Morris were prime movers, setting up a Society for the Protection of Ancient Monuments. By 1895 a National Trust was set up to preserve houses of great historical interest or those connected with great national events. At Skansen, in Stockholm, Sweden, a living museum was set up in 1891. Here crafts of the past were interpreted by farmers, craftsmen, and informed guides.

In the United States also the preservation movement was initiated through private groups. Thus, preservation of the Old State House in Philadelphia was undertaken between 1830 and 1850, and Fort Ticonderoga in 1816. A preservation program was initiated for Monticello, Jefferson's home, in 1830, and for Andrew Jackson's home, the Hermitage, in 1856. The preservation movement spread to cover a variety of buildings, including pioneer landmarks like Bent's Fort in Colorado, Spanish missions in California, and early churches and synagogues. Organizations such as the Daughters of the American Revolution, Colonial Dames, Sons of the Golden West, and state and local historical societies were active in this work. During the early period some help was received from the individual states, but little from the federal government.

Such interpretation as existed was voluntary in nature; it was much the same kind of interpretation that guides gave to their parties in lodges in Maine, or that fishermen gave the summer cottagers on Isle Royale, that is, a combination of tall tales, factual material, and anecdotes delivered in a historical setting.[18] Rather than consisting of a carefully researched and comprehensive account of an event, or of the life of a famous person, "interpretation" tended to be related to such artifacts as were available.

The "history" of a historic site often follows a typical pattern. Over the years the ownership changes, and with it the use; the idea of preservation comes almost too late. Bent's Old Fort illustrates this pattern. A large adobe trading post built by Charles and William Bent and Ceran St. Vrain in eastern Colorado, Bent's Fort was completed in 1834. It became an army post and, later, a way station on the Santa Fe Trail. After the fur trade died out, the fort served as a way station for a stagecoach line that ran from Kansas City to Santa Fe until 1891. Then, for a time, it was used as a cattle corral. In 1912 the Daughters of the American Revolution, mindful of its importance in the Santa Fe trade, acquired the site and placed a granite marker at the sadly dilapidated fort. In 1934, the state of Colorado took over title to the site and gave custody of it to the Colorado State Historical Society. Six years later it was designated a National Historic Site. In 1963 the National Park Service assumed its administration, and began the reconstruction of the fort in 1975 (Fig. 24-1). A year later, in time for the Nation's bicentennial and the Colorado centennial, an interpretive program was initiated, with costumed interpreters cast as trappers, *vaqueros,* blacksmiths, or other fort characters who demonstrate their skills and answer questions.[3]

In the late nineteenth and early twentieth centuries there was a heavy investment in preservation and restoration through private philanthropy. Businessmen endowed museums and other cultural endeavors and made gifts to cities to aid in preservation work. Two major figures in private philanthropy were Henry Ford and John D. Rockefeller, Jr. Henry Ford, a man who valued the rural life his Ford car had done so much to change, was particularly interested in the lives and tools of pioneer craftsmen. At Greenfield Village near Detroit he collected and displayed working models of early agricultural machinery and rare musical instruments as well as much other Americana, in addition to restoring homes of great public figures. At Menlo Park, New Jersey, the site of Edison's laboratory, Ford set up electrical exhibits using working models of Edison's old equipment. Rockefeller funded the restoration of Old Williamsburg, Virginia to its eighteenth-century glory. The restoration involved a great deal of archeological work, and combined the research of archeologists, historians, architects, and craftsmen in a noteworthy manner. It is an outstanding example of living history as a means of interpretation, as well as of the excellent result produced when private funding and research are possible.[18]

FIG. 24-1. An aerial view of Bent's Old Fort National Historic Site, located in southeastern Colorado, near La Junta. This was a principal outpost of civilization on the Southern Plains in the early 1800s, and later became the center of a vast fur-trading empire in the West. (Photo courtesy of National Park Service.)

Another turn of the century development was that of federal legislation to assist in historic site preservation. This began in the 1890s with the reservation of various battlefield sites and the establishment of national cemeteries. In 1906, the passage of the Act for the Preservation of American Antiquities gave the president authority to reserve areas of scientific or historic value as national monuments. Many of the areas so designated were historical or archeological in nature (Fig. 24-2). The Forest Products Laboratory, established in Madison, Wisconsin in 1910, rendered valuable service by developing methods of preserving old wooden structures and stabilizing stone or adobe.[7,19,29] The history of interpretation of these historic sites paralleled that of interpretation in natural history. As is described in Chapter 2, interpretation began in the national parks about 1920. It should be noted that early interpretive programs included human as well as natural history. Pioneering work in this field was done by C. Frank Brockman in Mount Rainier National Park, and by Harold C. Bryant in Yosemite National Park, as well as other national park interpreters (Fig. 2-6, page 45). On the state level, the work was largely carried on by state historical societies, and by local historical museums. The Forest Service was slow in developing interpretive pro-

FIG. 24-2. Although not within a national monument, these petroglyphs on Forest Service land near Wrangle, Alaska also received protection under the Antiquities Act. (Photo courtesy of the U.S. Forest Service.)

grams; however, in 1962 the Visitor Information Service (VIS) was organized on the model of the National Park Service. In 1980, Interpretive Services became the new name for this program.[4,8,16,35,40] Major activity in expanding state, county, and local park areas occurred in the late 1920s, and these areas developed rapidly during the 1930s with the help of the New Deal programs, particularly the Works Progress Administration (WPA) and Civilian Conservation Corps (CCC). State parks sometimes contain historic or archeological remains. The Porcupine Mountains State Park in Michigan has significant geological and botanical attractions and was also the scene of prehistoric, as well as more recent, human activity. Historical sites under state jurisdiction may involve buildings connected with individuals or events, historical villages, existing towns that mirror the past, or former sites of industrial activity. Administration of these areas varies. Many states combine management of historical sites and parks with the management of natural parks, usually through a Department of Natural Resources. In Colorado, however, sites are managed by a state historical society, in New Mexico by the New Mexico Museum, and in New York by the State Education Department.[5]

A study made in 1976 indicated that the National Park Service had under its jurisdiction 300 historical or archeological sites whereas the states had 800 to 900 associative monuments, the cities and counties 300 more, and roughly 10,000 sites were under private management. These figures will have increased by now.[33]

THE PROFESSIONAL HISTORIAN AS INTERPRETER

The larger parks and monuments containing historic resources may employ a historian. Professional historians who seek careers in interpretation will find that they need training that goes far beyond the usual training of academic historians. They will need to develop skills in the related fields of cultural resource management, such as restoration, museology, and preservation. They will also need to know how to use the skills of the architectural historian, the historian of industrial archeology, and those required by natural resource history. They must acquire some knowledge of the economics of historic site management. They must have knowledge of natural history as well, for historical interpreters may deal with matters that relate to both natural and cultural history. The interpreter of the fishing site may need to explore fish species and habitat as well as the evolution of fishing practices from the spears of the native Americans to the pound net of the commercial fishermen.

The normal academic training of the historian has in the past often been inadequate to meet the demands of public work such as interpretation. Several colleges and universities, including the University of Washington, Seattle, the University of California, Santa Barbara, and Northern Michigan University, Marquette, have developed programs in what is called public history. These programs are designed to bring the historian into the field of public affairs. They include some training in museum management and techniques, public finance, and natural history as well as the traditional history curriculum.[6,8,36,37] One of the most important skills required is the ability to communicate effectively with the public, as is emphasized in Part II of this book, "The Techniques of Interpretation."

THE INTERPRETER ATTEMPTING HISTORICAL INTERPRETATION

Much historical interpretation is done by nonprofessional historians, either interpreters who find themselves interpreting historical areas—certainly not all parks have historians—or by dedicated amateurs from local historical societies. These persons must learn something of the methods of the historian, and how historians think and arrive at their conclusions. They must examine the site to be interpreted, handle the artifacts, and examine photographs and drawings. They may need to delve into archives and may have to learn the filing system of the agency involved. They must learn how records are used, for instance, the relationship of licensing laws to old taverns or of mineral land laws to old mining claims. They must use maps, and know something of map making, especially the records of surveyors, who not only surveyed the area, but described vegetation, settlements, trails, and roads. The amateur historian must learn to seek out bibliographical guides and locations of manuscript materials.[7]

Above all, the quality of work done by both the professional and the non-professional historian will be enhanced by their experience in life. A historian has written:

> *History is concerned with life, and he who wished to understand or interpret human activity must himself have participated in affairs, and the richer his experience the better. That is what Gibbon said when, referring to his own brief military career, he said that the captain of the Hampshire Grenadiers was of use to the historian of Rome. . . . Scholarly training and much learning are not adequate substitutes for experience. They can produce technicians but not the rich, wise minds from which alone great history can be expected.*[17]

LIVING INTERPRETATION (ROLE PLAYING)

Living interpretation is discussed in Chapter 10. It has been in use for many years, particularly in reconstructed historic sites or villages. The bicentennial of 1976 led to a great increase in these projects. Living interpretation, unfortunately, has sometimes been vulgarized and commercialized by being used as a vehicle for entertainment rather than education. On the other hand, if carefully planned and executed, it is a highly effective method of presenting the past to the visitor. It is, at the same time, a method that takes exhaustive preparation, and demands a great deal from the interpreter. It requires the ability to judge the audience well and gear the presentation to their level of understanding, and it requires that the interpreter not only know about the past but know it well enough to be able to act it out with some degree of verve and spontaneity.[12,27,39]

HISTORICAL INTERPRETATION

In traditional historical interpretation, the nature of the program and the depth of the interpretation will depend on several factors. The interpreter must bear in mind that the visitors to a historical area or a historic site often will be more sophisticated, but less well-informed, than their nineteenth-century counterparts. The sites of the nineteenth century were set up to commemorate the great, and since the heroic deeds of the Founding Fathers and other patriots were part of every school curriculum in the days of *McGuffey's Readers,* not a great deal of explanation was needed. Today, for various reasons, this is no longer true, and a carefully weighed amount of skillfully presented information *is* needed.

Similarly, the farmer or artisan laborer of the 1890s would know and understand the life of the eighteenth century. Techniques of harnessing horses, making soap, or of carpentry had not changed greatly over the years. This is not necessarily the case for the city housewife, the farmer from a mechanized farm, or the factory worker. These people may find themselves quite puzzled by the tools and techniques of the past. On the other hand, the interpreter may find among the audience the professional historian or the hobbyist who knows more about the subject than the interpreter. For this reason interpreters must, above all, be adaptable. They must gear the interpretive presentation to the understanding of the majority of the audience, yet be prepared to gracefully handle any specialist's comments.

The nature and depth of the interpretive program on any historic site will depend in part on the knowledge, understanding, and motivation of the visitors themselves. The visitors to a purely historic site, like Cowpens National Battlefield, South Carolina, or Saint-Gaudens National Historic Site, New Hampshire, will likely go there because they are interested in the history of the area or the person it commemorates. They will probably have done some preliminary study on whatever they plan to see. In this instance, the task of the interpreter is to vitalize the scene and answer the perhaps rather specialized questions of a motivated audience. It is far otherwise with a roadside museum or site where the audience has come for a short time and then only incidentally. For these people the interpreter must plan a program that is informative on the popular level. The area that combines natural history with human history, on the other hand, must strike a balance, with the stress perhaps being on human influence in changing the face of the earth, or on human use and misuse of the bounty of nature.

Terminology

At this point, something needs to be written about the terms we use in regard to interpretation and related activities.

A *historic site* is the place or setting for an event—a house, or a structure, usually. *Historic* and *historical* are used interchangeably among agencies, but *historical site* is properly applied to a larger area than the site of a single building. One may speak of the historic Fayette opera house, but historical Fayette. Another distinction drawn between *historic* as meaning of actual importance in history, and *historical* as meaning merely *from the past.* The term *archeological site* is applied to sites in which the chief interest belongs to a prehistoric period, though the usage again varies. Some state historical sites are in reality primarily archeological in nature. *Historic landmark* is an official designation by the National Park Service to identify structures of national significance. *Historical preservation* involves preservation of a given area or site, and is generally considered to include interpretation. *Cultural Resource Management* (CRM) is a catchall term used by the Forest Service and National Park Service to underscore the fact that there is no legal distinction between archeological and historic resources. The term *management* emphasizes the reality that the federal responsibility only begins with the discovery of the resource, and that protection and maintenance are vital. *Cliology* has been suggested as a term to identify the interpreter specializing in historical interpretation, much as *cliometrics* has been coined to define those who work with historical statistics.

Preservation, restoration, and conservation are also terms that are used frequently by those involved in historical interpretation. *Preservation* is defined as "the protection, rehabilitation, restoration, and reconstruction of districts, sites, buildings, structures and objects significant in American history, architecture, archeology or culture." Historic *restorations* have secondary meanings in identifying a structure in which the original fabric is repaired or duplicated. *Conservation,* to museologists, means the various techniques used to prevent artifacts from deteriorating, such as that for keeping cloth from fading, the preservation of leather bindings, or preventing the growth of fungi in wood.[1,6,8,18,22]

Categories of Interpretive Sites

Historic or historical sites tend to fit into three broad categories depending on their primary purposes. The first of these is the *documentary site,* whose prime objective is to document an important historic event, or the life of a prominent person or family. Sagamore Hill, New York, the home of Theodore Roosevelt, is an example of this category. Restored to the conditions of Roosevelt's time, it is an effective document for the life, character, and tastes of its owner. A second category is the *representative site.* Here, the prime objective is to help the visitor to understand a period of history or a way of life. Like the documentary site, it is based on the lives of individuals, but instead of being focused on an individual, it focuses on the characteristics of a period of the past. The geologist, by drilling and extracting the drill core, gets a good picture of the subsurface stratigraphy. Similarly, the individual visiting a representative site gets a representative sample of the past in a given area. Village preservation, like that in Bayfield, Wisconsin, is an example. There much of the appearance and flavor of a nineteenth-century fishing village is preserved. Port Gamble, Washington, which preserves the appearance of an early west coast lumber town, is another. A third category of *historical buildings* exhibits typical rooms of a period with examples of furnishings, artifacts, and fixtures. Some historic buildings are adapted for this purpose, for instance, historical museums like the Burt House in Marquette, Michigan or the Pittock Mansion in Portland, Oregon.

FIG. 24-3. This self-guiding trail through a reconstructed mountain farm utilizes both signs and a leaflet and marker system of interpretation. Here a visitor learns the importance of pignut hickory (at his right) from the leaflet. At left, a sign points out a wooden hopper for holding ashes used in the manufacture of lye soap. Humpback Rocks, Blue Ridge Parkway, Virginia. (Photo by Grant W. Sharpe.)

Secondary objectives are usually developed at these sites. There are several things interpreters would like visitors to learn. A site may not only demonstrate the life of the individual, but life on a plantation in antebellum days, the difficulties of the fur trade in the West, the early use of irrigation in the arid lands of eastern Washington, or how our great-grandparents utilized trees or made soap (Fig. 24-3). It can provide a glimpse of the heritage of the people and the nation. The home of a mining company owner, or a mining site, should not be regarded as an isolated phenomenon, but as an entity rooted in the nation's demand for silver and copper, the result of mining law and mining business methods, and representative of the heterogeneous makeup of people and ideas typical of the time and place. As well as information, the site should provide visitors with insight into the nation's history.[1,38]

Where Historical Interpretation Takes Place

Museums.   A commonly used interpretive device at a historical site is the museum. Traditionally, it is the place where exhibits are housed. Properly used, the museum exhibit is an important adjunct to the whole interpretive effort. These exhibits help to orient the visitor who has arrived on a site but has not yet started the tour, or may enrich the visit by providing an extension of the tour. They are also the place where publications are sold, and tours begin.[1]

There are a variety of types of museums. Some are of national or regional significance, such as the Museo Nacional de Antropologia in Mexico City, which has both indoor and outdoor exhibits (Fig. 24-4), the Smithsonian Institution, with its complex of buildings and hundreds of exhibits, and the Montana State Historical Museum, with its dioramas and other exhibits of regional history. County or local museums exhibit events in local history. Often the potential of a museum is wasted or dissipated when, for political resons, it must house a collection of historical or other objects that the members of the community have donated, few of which are of significance locally. Some museums in this situation have been able to separate the two collections tactfully but effectively. Education of the community is the eventual answer to this quandry, especially when funding is dependent on local sources.

There is a growing tendency to integrate the museum into the community, rather than to isolate the building. In urban areas, it may be linked with a walking tour that places the museum and its exhibits in their historical setting. In rural areas, the exhibits often are combined with outdoor exhibitions of the life of the people. Logging museums, for example, combine exhibits with living interpretation, requiring interpreters to dress as loggers, conduct history walks, and interpret rides on logging locomotives. Living history farms are among the most rapidly growing types of outdoor-indoor museums. Like other kinds of museums, they give permanent safekeeping to tangible objects while preserving the values and folkways associated with them. Tracing their origins to European open-air museums established to perserve farm buildings and folk traditions, they have had a rapid growth since the establishment of the Pliny Freeman Farm in Old Sturbridge Village, Massachusetts, in 1952. Today, there are about 50 living historical farms in the United States and Canada. Here the visitor finds exhibits on handicrafts and technology of the past as well as historical interpreters in period dress who perform tasks such as plowing, churning butter, or harvesting hay.[10,11,12,21,23,27,29]

Visitor Centers.   A visitor center might be called a giant label for a site. The center will contain interpretive exhibits plus an auditorium for lectures or slide programs, rest rooms, sales and information desks, and administrative offices. Because such buildings are new and are designed for these specific purposes, they can meet professional standards of exhibit display. They often have an advantage

FIG. 24-4. A reconstructed native Mexican village, located adjacent to the Museo Nacional de Antropologia, Chapultepec Park, Mexico City. (Photo by Grant W. Sharpe.)

in this respect over historic buildings used as museums, since exhibits will, unless skillfully positioned, detract from the historic integrity of the building. Visitor centers are ideally suited for the sale of publications.[1,11]

On-Site Areas. Archeological digs in progress are frequently associated with historical sites. Archeologists at an old fort site, for example, will often be busy during the visitor season excavating the locations of old stables or privies to recover artifacts and to fix the pattern of settlement. Such "digs" in progress often offer an opportunity to interpreters to broaden the program by showing how the archeologist works and how findings are incorporated into the programs. Signs or conducted walks are commonly used, depending on which will be best suited to interpretation without interrupting the work of the archeologist.

An interpreter coming to an unfamiliar area should be alert for signs of former human habitation such as cellar holes, stone fences, fruit trees, chimneys, barbed wire, or artifacts. These relics suggest that there are opportunities for historical interpretation. Generally speaking, such traces should be left in place unless there is anger of loss of valuable artifacts from foraging visitors. The appropriate method of interpretation could be selected by following the Media Selection Matrix (see Fig. 5-10, page 120).

Where old buildings are in good repair, they are often used as part of the interpretive program, as the setting for living interpretation, as a museum, or for a self-guided or conducted tour (Fig. 24-5). Where the original fabric of the house is relatively sound, the house should be restored, using original material as much as possible. In some instances buildings have been rebuilt completely. Such was the case with Theodore Roosevelt's original homestead cabin at Theodore Roosevelt Birthplace National Historic Site, New York, and with St. Michael's Church, Sitka, Alaska. When rebuilding is required, the original dimensions and style of the building should be carefully followed. Modification should be primarily for the sake of safety and fire protection. Where old buildings are beyond repair, and are not sufficiently important, or where funds for restoration are lacking, photographs and measurements of the building should be taken before the structures are razed and should be kept on file by the agency.[1,8,16,18,24]

Methods of Research

Research is the life blood of history and is necessary in all stages of the historical interpretive process. It is necessary to evaluate the site for its potential for preservation and conservation. Research is also necessary in planning the interpretive program, and in determining what type of interpretation is most desirable. It will be necessary, too, in evaluating the program, bringing it up to date in the light of new findings, and in measuring its effectiveness.

Research is carried on in libraries and archives and in the field. Historical interpreters must be able to use a compass, to pace accurately, and to do rough mapping. Familiarity with the site in all its aspects is needed to translate what has been read or heard about the site into factual data. Field notes should be transcribed as soon as possible while the impressions of the researcher are still fresh.

Interpreters accustomed to working with natural history may find less difficulty with the techniques of field research, once they are convinced of the necessity of an unbiased approach and meticulous care, than with effectively utilizing library and archival resources.

Libraries, Archives, Special Collections.   In using libraries, archives, and special collections, the interpreter should first find out where the material needed is to be found. There are many reference guides available. The Forest History Society, for example, has published two excellent bibliographies, one listing published works and the other listing libraries and archives where this material may be found. These bibliographies are of great assistance to anyone dealing with logging or forest history. Most historical societies publish catalogs of their holdings, many with some descriptions. General histories of a state or region will have citations and references to collections. In using collections, interpreters must become acquainted with the filing system used, either of the agency in the case of

FIG. 24-5. A blacksmith shop, reconstructed in the style of an earlier day. Here a blacksmith demonstrates his trade daily and sells his products to visitors. Note the fire in the forge visible through the side door. Mabry Mill, Blue Ridge Parkway, Virginia. (National Park Service photo by Fred Bell.)

federal or state papers, or of the museum or archive itself. Librarians and archivists are universally helpful to interpreters, who should make full use of their services.[9,20,32,36]

Newspapers. Newspapers are a valuable source for the historical interpreter. They give a day-to-day account of events that fills in the general history of the area and supplies the names of individuals important in the area of the site. Formerly, newspaper files were to be found in the newspaper office. Increasingly now, however, newspaper files are microfilmed and placed in libraries or research centers.[20]

Courthouse Records and Other Sources. Courthouse records are valuable for the surveyor's description of the site and the detail that they supply regarding land transactions. Many business firms or local organizations have papers that have not been catalogued and remain in storage; the interpreter should be diligent in seeking out such possibilities.[15,20,]

Oral History

Interviews are carried on either in controlled environments or under field conditions. The interviewer working at a university will generally have access to a controlled environment, that is, a room free from noise or distractions, such as bells or telephone calls. Such an interview will generally use fairly bulky equipment with large reels to preserve fidelity of voice quality. The person conducting interviews in the field, on the other hand, can best use a portable recorder, that operates either with batteries or house voltage. The tape will often pick up background sounds like telephones ringing, motor noises, a cat meowing, or sounds from the kitchen. These matters may be beyond the interviewer's control, but he or she should take all means possible to minimize the effect of distractions.

In either type of interview the important thing is to establish a rapport with the person interviewed (Fig. 24-6). It is necessary to discuss the interview in advance, to inform the person of the need and importance of the interview, and the nature of the questions to be asked. The interviewer will need to obtain permission for use of the interview, and the person interviewed should be allowed to read a transcript of the tape before it is used.[9,31]

FIG. 24-6. The interviewer, having successfully established a friendly, comfortable atmosphere, is using a cassette tape recorder to record the voice of the 98-year-old pioneer. (Photo by Grant W. Sharpe.)

FIG. 24-7. The technology of the day is seen in this 1896 photo of a river drive crew waiting for the sluice gate, at right, to open. With their aid, the "flushing" action of the head of water so released will carry the logs on down the river, perhaps through more ponds and gates, to the mill. Sturgeon River, near Chassell, Michigan. (Photo courtesy of Michigan Technological University Archives.)

Photographs

The value of photographs as an interpretive tool is covered in another chapter, and Hume, in his book on historical archeology, has dealt with archaeological photography. However, something should be said about the collection and use of historical photographs.

Historical photographs are visual artifacts. They range from old daguerreotypes and glass plate negatives to studio portraits and snapshots, to 35-mm shots. A primary consideration is that they have value for planning and conducting interpretation. They should be considered a multiple-use resource. At first glance an old photograph may seem merely strange or puzzling. A little research on a picture like that of Figure 24-7 will tell us why there are so many men standing on logs as though they were waiting for something to happen. This photograph of a river drive in the Lake States provides the interpreter with many fascinating items of information about logging and milling technology, work clothing, dam and sluice construction, and vegetative patterns. Photographs not only inform, they

FIG. 24-8. A historical photograph such as this commands attention in exhibits and slide presentations. This photo of touring cars in Glacier National Park was taken during the 1920s. (Photo by Hileman, courtesy of the National Archives.)

enliven the message and engage the viewer, whether in historical exhibits, or in slide presentations (Fig. 24-8).

The search for photographs should be as diligent as the search for manuscript sources. Museums and federal and state agencies usually have published guides to their photographic collections. The individual who acquires historical photographs should record the source of the collection. Photographs should be dated as accurately as possible. Everything that can be of use in interpretation—the individuals in the photo, landmarks, what is happening in the scene, the location from which the picture was taken—should be identified. The photographs must be copied and returned or carefully preserved, if donated.

Preservation, conservation, and care of historical photographs are usually the task of the archivist or curator rather than the interpreter. For interpreters with these duties, the best guide is that by Weinstein and Booth.[34]

COMMUNITY INVOLVEMENT

Because local residents often have a proprietory interest in the area, the interpreter will often find within the community the most receptive audience for presentations and publications about the site. Local inhabitants are often a good source of information for research activities, as well as the most responsive source of funds for carrying out the project. Seasonal interpreters and museum docents are also drawn largely from this source as are donations of artifacts for museums.

Dealing with community members calls for enthusiasm, tact, and judgment. The interpreter must learn, for example, how to deal with the gift of a 1902 Oliver typewriter when there are already four on hand, how to correct inaccurate folklore that has grown up over the years, or how to persuade the old-timer to allow memories to be taped for posterity (Fig. 24-6). Each community presents its own challenges.[1,15,39,41,42]

Public hearings are often held on matters relating to preservation, and the historical interpreter may be involved in them. Hearings may relate to the preservation of old buildings, to development in historic areas, or to rights-of-way over private property for historic trails. Needless to say, the interpreter should become familiar with the situation well in advance of the meetings. As a participant, he or she needs to know how to make a presentation in its historical context and must know the site well. Publicity must be handled skillfully in order to get people to attend. Participants must refrain from attacking personalities and operate by challenging ideas, not individuals. In the presentation the interpreter-historian should be assisted with slides and other aids to clarify the situation.[30]

Special mention should be given to youth projects in history. Young people are frequently attracted to historical programs. They have a sense of wonder, curiosity, and a desire to learn, and are often among the most enthusiastic observers of living history programs. A number of state historical societies have set up workshops, history clubs, and history fairs for children. Indiana and Texas began special programs for children in the 1930s, with New York, Minnesota, and Pennsylvania following. Such programs involve all levels from elementary to senior high school. History Day, involving grades six to twelve, includes research and the writing of papers. High school students can often serve as docents in museums during the summer.[13,14,28]

The student field trip, in which the students visit a local museum or historic house, is common during the school year. This gives the students a chance to use all of their senses—to see, touch, and hear. In preparation for such visits, the museum staff should first define the educational objectives of the trip and make certain that the students have preliminary information about why they are visiting the site and what to look for. For the rest, the visit should not be overscheduled; there should be arrangements for a change of pace, and problems should be anticipated and emergencies planned for.[2]

FUNDING

General financing of programs is discussed in Chapter 6, "Management of the Interpretive Program." As is noted above, community participation is very important to funding, through membership fees, admission fees, donations, or corporate assistance. The success of continuing permanent funding may depend to a great extent on the relationship of the organization to the community. Strong support from the community may in its turn bring in state or federal aid. There are at present more funds available for cultural history interpretation than for natural history. Grants and aid from private foundations may also be available. (Refer to the general references and bibliographic notes at end of this chapter.)

Small museums should avail themselves of the services of the Museum Assessment Program, operated by the American Association of Museums (1055 Thomas Jefferson Street, N.W., Washington, DC 20007). This service offers an assessment of a museum's strengths and weaknesses, and suggests sources of technical and financial assistance. Application is uncomplicated, and the costs of the examination can be covered by a nonmatching block grant from the Institute of Museum Services. The museum will be surveyed by a museum professional, who will file a written report, designated as a starting point for the formulation of long-range plans.[5,25]

PROFESSIONAL ACTIVITIES

Organizations

Historians, like other professional groups, have many organizations with a variety of purposes but with generally two main objectives: to have meetings at regular intervals where members may exchange ideas, and to publish professional journals wherein accounts of research and other material of general interest may appear.

The interpreter of historic sites, whether a professional historian or not, will find membership in these organizations and attendance at their meetings rewarding. Each state has a historical society, and the interpreter should join that society. Members of the society are not predominately professional scholars, but the journal is usually edited by a professional historian, and the publications contain a mixture of articles by professionals and amateurs. Some of the national organizations, such as the Western History Society, welcome papers at their meetings by those outside the field of history. Whether attending as an observer or as a participant, the interpreter will receive a warm welcome.

Meetings of professional historians usually include tours and workshops. The tours are generally arranged with the help of the city in which the conference is held and include historical buildings and other sites of interest. Walking tours are often available. The tours offer a good opportunity for the interpreter to observe innovative methods and trends in interpretation.

The Association for State and Local History holds regular regional seminars for historians or nonhistorians on such matters as conservation of materials, publications, and interpretation of history by museums. These seminars are usually limited to 20 or 30 participants, and consist of an intensive three- or four-day meeting directed by experts in the field.

The base of research and participation can be broadened by holding meetings. These are often planned on the state level, through the state historical society or other state divisions. In Alaska, for example, the Division of Parks has a series of regional workshops. They deal with the historical values of a given area, state and federal legislation regarding preservation, methods of putting historic buildings on the National Register, and the inventory of local historical resources. Periodically they also sponsor conferences combined with workshops on, for example, subjects like "Mining in Alaska's Past." Some off-site and off-season work is carried on through workshops. The Forest Service visitor center at Mendenhall Glacier near Juneau, Alaska, for example, is used during the winter for a fireside series, involving Indian dances, slide programs, and talks on the history of the area (Fig. 19-2, page 423). This is a cooperative venture involving not only the Forest Service but the National Park Service, state agencies, and units of the city government. At Voyageurs National Park, International Falls, Minnesota, during the spring and winter, scholars give a series of talks on various aspects, including the historical, of Voyageurs National Park. These talks are sponsored in part by the Minnesota Council for the Humanities, and the series is published.[15,20]

In preparing a conference, a theme must be chosen. Then it must be decided whether the treatment should be broad or narrow, and whether for the specialist or the generalist. Financing sources should be sought out; very often several groups, such as a university or a state agency, can cooperate to fund the project. The project should be organized with both overall direction and a committee on local arrangements. Visiting participants should be invited early and encouraged to meet deadlines for submitting copies of their papers. More than one reminder may be necessary. Audiovisual aids should be on hand if they are needed. The mind can absorb only what the seat can endure, so sessions should not extend over two hours without a break.[26]

Publications

While engaged in research, the interpreter should consider how relevant material can best be presented to the public. Sources are abundant for publication. They include the official publications of the agencies with which the interpreter is associated, local, state and regional newsletters and magazines, and magazines of national circulation. Contributions will be of value to other interpreters and would-be interpreters.[20]

Most of the material in Chapter 13, "Interpretive Publications," applies to historical writing, but some additional points may be made here. There is a great variety of publications useful in the interpretation of historic sites. The interpreter may wish to narrate the history of the site, or to edit documents such as diaries or business records, or to build the story around historical photographs. The article may be written as a pamphlet for the visitor, or as a monograph to appeal to a wider audience, or it may be intended for regional or national circulation. Whatever the nature of the publication, it should be a self-contained unit, and also should fit into a wider pattern, with the meshing made clear. A study of historic mining in a national park, for example, should be related to the history of mining booms and technology in the region and in the nation. Studies should be regional without being provincial.

The writing should be done with a definite audience in mind. As noted in Chapter 13, writing for children is a specialized field and is an art in itself. It also takes a good deal of talent to write on scientific matters for the layman, and many historical studies are of a specialized nature. The interpreter should cultivate an ability to write well, composing with clarity and picturesqueness without sacrificing logic, objectivity, or accuracy.[20]

CONCLUSION

Interpreters may find themselves charged with the responsibility of dealing with evidences of the past. Historical interpretation requires special care and accuracy and must be approached with deliberation. Resources must be inventoried, researched, and recorded. Then, decisions must be made on how best to present these resources to the public. The community will be involved, probably more so than when natural history is the subject matter. Not only are there traditional and perhaps personal ties of the people and way of life being considered, but there is a new interest generally in historical themes and in our forebears.

This chapter has briefly described the development of historical interpretation, has noted the rigorous standards of professional historians, and has considered the various means of presenting historical interpretation. It has suggested some procedures and sources of help in order that, despite the difficulties, the pleasures and fascination of exploring the past may be reflected in its interpretation.

REFERENCES

General References and Bibliographic Notes

The standard text for historical site interpretation is William T. Alderson and Shirley Payne Low, *Interpretation of Historic Sites* (Nashville, TN, The American Association for State and Local History, 1976). It is available in paperback. This is a practical book, dealing with the problems of developing and conducting interpretive programs at historical sites.

For the story of historical preservation, which has some material on interpretation, Charles E. Hosmer, *Presence of the Past: A History of the Preservation Movement in the United States Before Williamsburg* (New York, G. P. Putnam's Sons, 1965) is a good historical account. A second volume, dealing with preservation over the past 50 years, will be forthcoming. John Ise, *Our National Park Policy: A Critical History* (Baltimore, Johns Hopkins Press, 1961) has some material on the development of interpretation in historical parks. C. Frank Brockman's "Park Naturalists and the Evolution of National Park Service Interpretation Through World War II," *Journal of Forest History* **22**:1 (January 1978) pp. 24–43 is a good account by a pioneer in the field. Robert M. Utley, "A Preservation Ideal," *Historic Preservation* **28** (June 1976) is a brief but valuable article. Individual parks or museums often have published accounts of the development of their interpretive programs. For example, *Yosemite Nature Notes* **39**:7 (1960) has a series of articles on such development. On the state level a representative article is Thomas G. Friggens "History Comes Alive at Fort Wilkins," *Chronicle: The Magazine of the Historical Society of Michigan* **15**:3 (Fall 1979) pp. 13–15, 20–24.

Since this chapter is built around the fact that not all historical interpretation is done by professional historians, several books giving background information on the nature of history and historical research may be recommended for amateur historians. W. Stull Holt, *Historical Scholarship in the United States and Other Essays* (Seattle and London, The University of Washington Press, 1967) is a classic work on historiography. Allen Nevins, *The Gateway to History* (Boston, D. C. Heath and Co., 1938) is a standard text in historiography. It has been reprinted many times. Jacques Barzun and Henry F. Graff, *The Modern Researcher* (New York, Harcourt, Brace and Co., 1962) is a manual on how the historian gathers and organizes facts, checks their accuracy, and reports the findings. Robin W. Winks (ed.), *The Historian as Detective* (New York, Harper and Row, 1969) is a charming set of essays on how the historian evaluates evidence.

There are a number of organizations whose peridoicals have articles on interpretation. The American Association for State and Local History is the most valuable of these organizations for the historical interpreter to join. They publish a large number of technical leaflets, some noted in References Cited; their periodical, *History News,* has articles on preservation and interpretation, news of grants, and a job register. The National Trust for Historic Preservation, 740-748 Jackson Place, Washington, DC 20006, issues two publications: *Historic Preservation,* which has articles on interpretation, and *Preservation News,* a newsletter that also contains a listing of jobs. Historical interpreters involved in preservation should request a checklist of their books and articles. Of other journals, *Trends* deals with National Park Service activities in interpretation; *Parks and Recreation* has some good articles, usually from the management point of view; and the *Journal of Forest History* presents articles on forest and logging museums, and contains a section dealing with museum activity. The Forest History Society also has two good bibiliographical aids: Ronald J. Fahl, *North American Forest and Conservation History,* a bibliography listing published articles, books, and theses; and Richard C. Davis, *North American Forest History: A Guide to Archives and Manuscripts in the United States and Canada.* Both were published in 1977 by Clio Press, Santa Barbara, California. Richard J. Cox, "An Annotated Bibliography of Basic Readings on Archives and Manuscripts", *AASLH Technical Leaflet 150* (September 1980) is a convenient compilation". William T. Alderson, "Preserving America's Heritage: The American Association for State and Local History," *Journal of Forest History* **15**:4 (October 1974) gives a brief summary of the Association's work, and suggestions as to how the interpreter can best use it.

On funding, *Grants and Fellowships of Interest to Historians,* published annually by the Institutional Service Program of the American Historical Association, 400 A Street S.E., Washington, DC 20003, lists some grants for archival or museum work, and contains a list of internships in history. The National Historical Publications and Records Commission (NHPRC) has a great program. Details can be obtained from NHPRC, National Archives and Records Service, Washington, DC 20408. *History News, Preservation News,* and historical journals generally, have a listing of pending grants and awards. *The Annual Register of Grant Support,* published by Marquis Academic Media, 200 East Ohio Street, Chicago, Il 60611, gives detailed information on sources for funding.

References Cited

1. Alderson, William T., and Shirley Payne Low. 1976. *Interpretation of Historic Sites,* The American Association for State and Local History, Nashville, TN. (Hereinafter abbreviated as AASLH.)

2. Benedict, Paul L. 1971. "Historic Site Interpretation: The Student Field Trip," *AASLH Technical Leaflet 19.*

3. Briggs, Walter. 1979. "Castle in the Desert," *American West* **XIII**:5, 10−18.

4. Brockman, C. Frank. 1978. "Park Naturalists and the Evolution of National Park Interpretation Through World War II," *Journal of Forest History* **22**:1, 24−43.

5. Buchanan, John Edward, Jr. 1980. "An Applicant's Map to the Museum Assessment Program," *History News* **35**:9, 16−17.

6. Clary, David L. 1978. "Historic Preservation and Environmental Protection: The Role of the Historian," *The Public Historian* **1**:1, 61−80.

7. Clary, David A. 1977. "Historic Preservation on Federal Lands," *Periodical Journal of the Council on Abandoned Military Posts* **9**:2, 16−22.

8. Clary, David A. 1980. "Cultural Resource Management and History: A Partnership," *The Forest Service History Line,* Winter, 4−5.

9. Cox, Richard J. 1980. "An Annotated Bibliography of Basic Readings on Archives and Manuscripts," *AASLH Technical Leaflet 130*.

10. Davis, Douglas F. 1975. "Port Gamble—Unique Historical Restoration Project," *Journal of Forest History* **19:**3, 137–139.

11. Davis, Douglas F. 1974. "Logging, Lumbering and Forestry Museums: A Review," *Journal of Forest History* **17:**4, 11–28.

12. Elder, Betty Doak. 1979. "Behind the Scenes at Living History Farm," *History News* **34:**12, 331–349.

13. Elder, Betty Doak. 1980. "Youth Projects in History," *History News* **35:**3, 5.

14. Foster, Olive. 1980. "Junior Historians," *History News* **35:**3, 6, 8–9.

15. Frederic, Robert A. 1975. "Preservation in the Great Land," *Historical Preservation* **27:**1, 4–12.

16. Hakala, Robert. 1976. "Historic Preservation as a Responsibility of Resource Management," paper presented at Association of Interpretive Naturalists Annual Meeting, Seattle.

17. Holt, W. Stull. 1967. *Historical Scholarship in the United States,* University of Washington Press, Seattle.

18. Hosmer, Charles B. 1965. *Presence of the Past: A History of the Preservation Movement in the United States Before Williamsburg,* G. P. Putnam's Sons, New York.

19. Ise, John. 1961. *Our National Park Policy: A Critical History,* Johns Hopkins Press, Baltimore, MD.

20. Jordan, Philip H. 1968. *The Nature and Practice of State and Local History,* American Historical Association, Washington, DC. Service Center Publication 14.

21. Kirk, Ruth, and Louis Kirk. 1980. "The Pompeii of the Northwest," *Historic Preservation* **32:**2, 2–9.

22. Low, Shirley P. 1965. "Historic Site Interpretation," *AASLH Technical Leaflet 20*.

23. Lynn, John A. 1976. "Reconstructing a Maine Lumber Camp of 1900: The Diorama as a Historical Medium," *Journal of Forest History* **20:**4, 190–202.

24. Mentes, J. D., A. N. Glick, and W. Bell. 1979. "A Solution to Recreation and Resource Management in Remote Areas," *Parks and Recreation* **14:**8, 25–32, 48.

25. Pizer, Laurence R. 1977. "Financing Your History Organization: Setting Goals," *AASLH Technical Leaflet 106*.

26. Richman, Irwin. 1967. "A Guide to Planning Local History Institutes," *AASLH Technical Leaflet 43*.

27. Ripton, Michael J. 1973. "Pennsylvania Lumber Museum," *Journal of Forest History* **17:**3, 29–32.

28. Scharf, Lois. 1980. "History Day," *History News* **35**:3, 2–10.

29. Sherrer, G. Terry. 1980. "Hitching History to the Plow," *Historic Preservation* **32**:6, 42–50.

30. This, Leslie E. 1975. "Public Hearing Practice (and Pitfalls)," *Historic Preservation* **27**:6, 36–40.

31. Tyrell, William G. 1966. "Tape Recording Local History," *AASLH Technical Leaflet* **35,**88–101. Also published in *History News* **21**:5.

32. Tyrell, William G. 1964. "Methods of Research for the Amateur Historian," *AASLH Technical Leaflet 21.* Also published in *History News* **19**:8.

33. Utley, Robert M. 1976. "A Preservation Ideal," *Historic Preservation* **28**:3, 40–44.

34. Weinstein, Robert A., and Larry Booth. 1977. *Collection, Use and Care of Historic Photographs,* AASLH, Nashville, TN.

Personal Communications

35. Brockman, C. Frank. Professor Emeritus, University of Washington, Seattle.

36. Bromberg, William (National Park Service) Retired Superintendant, Apostle Islands National Park.

37. Burke, Robert. Professor of History, University of Washington.

38. Carstensen, Vern. Professor of History, University of Washington.

39. Friggens, Thomas. Historian, Fort Wilkins State Park, Copper Harbor, MI.

40. Hakala, D. Robert. Retired VIS Specialist, Regional Office Forest Service, Juneau, AK.

41. Kennedy, Michael. Alaska Division of Parks, Anchorage, AK.

42. Scheffner, Charles. Naturalist, Fayette State Park, Fayette, MI.

CHAPTER 25

PROBLEMS: VANDALISM AND DEPRECIATIVE BEHAVIOR

Anne Harrison

Whether planning a new visitor center or completing a self-guided trail, many interpreters have one nagging worry in common: will the facility survive vandals?

In most areas vandalism is a much greater problem today than it has ever been in the past. This is expected because there are many more people than before; thus, there are more potential vandals and more facilities (generally more expensive ones at that) to be vandalized. However, the reasons behind vandalism involve much more than sheer numbers of people.

Because the problems of vandalism and depreciative behavior are complex, the reader who is looking for foolproof cures will be greatly disappointed. There are no magic formulas; there are just too many variables. Preventive measures that succeed in one setting may fail miserably in another. Vandalism labeled severe by one area may be brushed off as a minor incident elsewhere; it may be nonexistent in one park and yet devour 10 percent (or more) of another's annual budget in repairs alone.[23]

This chapter is primarily concerned with vandalism as it relates to interpretive activities. It can only provide some guidelines for analyzing various situations. Interpreters should experiment with new preventive measures to find the best solutions.

WHAT IS VANDALISM AND DEPRECIATIVE BEHAVIOR?

In recent studies, Campbell, Hendee, Clark, and others[3,5,17] define *depreciative behavior* as any act that detracts from the social or physical environment. This definition includes many activities that were once commonplace and approved or overlooked.[6] Explorers left their names on stone gateways to ancient Asian palaces. The Conquistadors left their marks on rocks beside native American pictographs. Daniel Boone carved his name and the date on a tree. This depreciative behavior eventually came to be looked on as worthy of preservation and such places became historical shrines.

Today, because of the vast numbers of people, activities like these now have a serious impact. Growing numbers of *nuisance acts,* such as loose pets, littering, sanitary offenses, noise, rock throwing in swimming areas, and violations of privacy are but one part of the problem. *Legal violations,* including theft and violations of traffic and campground regulations form another part of the problem. A third area of depreciative behavior, and the principle concern of this chapter, is *vandalism.* This is defined as any willful act of physical damage that lowers the aesthetic or economic value of an object or area. In contrast to other categories of depreciative behavior, vandalism results in visible scars on the resource.

HISTORICAL DEVELOPMENT

Vandalism in recreation areas became a major problem about the time of World War II, but it has appeared in one form or another for centuries. The word itself is derived from the Vandals, an Eastern Germanic tribe remembered for its destructive expeditions in the fifth century A.D. A ravaged, burned trail marked the path of these people to Italy, where they destroyed many monuments and works of art.[9] They saw it differently, no doubt.

Until recently, damage was for the most part associated with civic or political causes. The rebellion of the Luddites against technology at the dawn of the Industrial Revolution is a prime example. The Boston Tea Party was inspired by real or imagined threats arising from the political situation.[9] Although most damage was done by adults, there were some teenagers involved. However, in those days they were considered adults. In the past it was rare to find property destroyed for no apparent reason. World War II appears to mark a significant turning point. The war played a dramatic role in the disruption of the family unit. Mothers entered the working force, and a great many children were left on their own. By this time many agencies were beginning to respond to the demand for more public recreation areas. As more areas became accessible, vandalism seemed to increase.

Many countries have experienced a similar trend. Prior to the 1960s, vandalism was mainly politically inspired and was associated with violent demonstrations, attacks on embassies, and graffiti protests appearing on everything from state memorials and synagogues to Stonehenge slabs. Nonpolitical or at least less easily categorized vandalism grew in Europe and the middle East during the late 1960s. Invasions of coastal resorts by teenagers (England), decapitation of the Little Mermaid statue in Copenhagen, and smashing of train windows and seats by fans returning from soccer matches in England are further manifestations of the growing problem.[9]

IMPACT ON THE INTERPRETIVE PROGRAM

In interpretive areas the effects of vandalism may be significant and have both physical and psychological impacts. The most obvious result is seen in physical destruction. Interpretive facilities (message repeater stations, exhibits, labels, signs, and buildings) suffer greatly and can be very expensive to repair. The interpreter must divert funds from an often meager budget to make these repairs. Consequently, the time and money required to restore damages must be subtracted from the production of new programs and facilities.

Facilities can be replaced, but the stolen collections or unusual specimens the naturalist may have worked for years to acquire cannot be. (This is a good argument for the use of replicas when originals are irreplaceable.)[26] It is often the creative product, the personal investment of the naturalist, that is vandalized and causes the greatest trauma.[22] The cost of this type of destruction cannot be computed in dollars.

Unfortunately, due to destruction or defacement, some natural features are beyond restoration. The vents of Yellowstone's geysers are clogged with coins and logs; giant saguaro cacti have been dug up or shot down; natural tourist attractions have been cut down and hauled off.[1] Indeed, a naturalist may one day discover that the focal point of the program has disappeared. Depending on the agency or administrative policy of the area, naturalists may also find that they are spending less time on interpretation and more time in crime prevention or law enforcement work.

With this background, it is easy to understand the pessimistic attitude of so many interpreters. Believing a proposed trail or exhibit will be vandalized, they often feel it is pointless to construct it. This may be a carryover from the long-accepted attitude that vandalism is largely unexplainable and unavoidable. Yet, however complex the vandalism issue is, attempts to analyze, reduce, and ultimately eliminate it must persist.

The first step should involve an analysis of where, when, and by whom most vandalism is carried out. This should be followed if possible by careful evaluation of the underlying reasons for the damage. This information will aid the interpreter in designing a prevention plan to fit the situation.

WHEN TO EXPECT VANDALISM: THE PHYSICAL FACTORS

Exposure

The classic invitation to the vandal is a dark, hidden, or isolated facility that appears poorly maintained. Vandals often operate in seclusion, thus selecting a locale where there is little enforcement of regulations or chance for observation. A section of a park that is poorly lit and rarely patrolled is a good target. One would expect that most damage would occur after dark, but a poorly patrolled area is almost as vulnerable in daylight as at night. Areas with entrances controlled by a contact station and manned with uniformed personnel often suffer less vandalism.[22,24] Visitors can also be a deterrent to vandalism. Areas receiving heavy use and offering a full schedule of structured activities receive less damage. In the off-season when visitation lessens and the self-policing effect is lost vandalism increases.

Recreation fee systems, periodically in and out of effect in federal recreation areas, also have an impact. The abolishment of fees in 1973 at almost all U.S. National Forest areas eliminated the need for uniformed rangers to issue or check permits. The subsequent loss of patrol personnel left no one to supervise or enforce regulations, and several National Forests reported a significant increase in vandalism.[15,21]

Accessibility

Very often the annual costs of repairs directly reflect the *distance of the site* from population centers. National Forests adjacent to population centers such as Los Angeles, Albuquerque, and Portland (Oregon) are heavily vandalized, as are many urban parks (Fig. 25-1). Yellowstone National Park, which has in a sense attracted its own city, also receives heavy damage.

Another factor is the *ease of access*. As an example, the opening of a new coastal highway in Oregon was followed by an increase in the number of buoys and signal marker lights shot out.[1] The increase in off-road-vehicles (ORVs) such as snowmobiles, jeeps, motorcycles, has so improved visitor mobility that previously inaccessible wildlife and unique features (i.e., ancient native artifacts) are now threatened. In contrast, consider Isle Royale National Park in Lake Superior. Accessible only by boat or seaplane, Isle Royale is noted for almost complete absence of vandalism.[23]

Another factor influencing accessibility is the boundary of the interpretive area. Long, narrow fingers of land are especially vulnerable to vandalism. In determining boundaries during land acquisition programs, special consideration should be given to the ease of protection of the site.[20]

Other Factors

The appearance of facilities themselves may invite or deter destruction. A collection of amateurish, flimsy devices or those not immediately repaired when damaged are an open invitation to vandalism.

The calendar provides another means for anticipating vandalism. Interpreters have learned, for instance, to intensify their patrols on weekends, graduation nights, Halloween, and during the first warm months when people finally get outdoors after winter confinement.

FIG. 25-1. A section of boardwalk trail showing where the handrail and boards have been removed by vandals. Much other vandalism has occurred in the same park, located in Bellevue, Washington. (Photo by Grant W. Sharpe.)

WHO IS THE VANDAL?

This is a good question and a difficult one to answer. Since very few vandals are caught, many "profiles" of the typical vandal are based more upon feelings than on documented evidence. Most people can remember at least some mildly vandalic acts from their own childhood.

There are two factors that should be remembered. First, only a small percentage of the population is involved in vandalism. The cyclic nature of incidents (speaking now of vandalism and not other classes of depreciative behavior), which is commonly noted, indicates that a few individuals may be responsible for many incidents of damage.[26]

Secondly, we find different classes of users in different facilities. Situations and motives for vandalism vary greatly between inner city parks, private nature centers, and distant forest campgrounds. For instance, some sites are within walking or bicycling distance whereas others are accessible only by car. Some areas function to serve families (or others) camping far from home (requiring a certain economic status to afford the means to do this), whereas others serve as a neighborhood backyard for residents. Others serve only those groups with educational purposes. With these variables it is obvious that there is no "typical" vandal.

The effects of these differences are reflected in various studies of depreciative behavior. For instance, some studies[3,5] indicate that most vandalism in campgrounds is done by young children at play and by adults. On the other hand, police reports[14] and many other sources[1,19,25] indicate that, of those vandals caught, most are males between the ages of 9 and 21 years.*

Consequently, it is very important to find out *who* the vandals are *in each individual situation*. Preventive measures depend on the interpreter's knowledge of the target groups—and they may range from delinquents to uninformed adults, the boys—beer—car group, rich or poor, law abiding or rebellious, to local or distant visitors. After discovering who the culprits are the next step is to take a close look at possible motives, an analysis that may be quite complex as is in the next section.

UNDERSTANDING VANDALISM: THE PSYCHOLOGICAL FACTORS

There was a time when violence was a means of last resort. Now it is a method of communication.

(Whatever Became of Sin, *by Karl Menninger*)

In analyzing vandalism it is evident that there are two aspects to the problem. One is behavioral: the complex, inner elements that are discussed herein. The other is physical: the external, environmental factors discussed in a later section.

Wilson[25] believes the behavioral aspect of vandalism is determined by controls from within an individual. In some individuals these controls are quite strong whereas in others they break down at a lower threshold. What is needed, he feels, is a greater understanding of how and why the internal controls are reinforced in some people and not in others. Through an understanding of human nature and behavioral psychology the interpreter can have an effect on these controls. Depreciative behavior can also be influenced through careful handling of external factors, minimizing those conditions under which the threshold is reached and the controls from within break down.

What factors might affect these internal controls?

In America, both increased population and the contemporary way of life have

---

*Petty, Paul E., in *Vandalism in National Forests and Parks,* (unpublished condensation of master's thesis, Colorado State University, Nov. 1966) indicates about 90 percent of the offenders are teenage boys. This group is also found responsible for much damage in a recent study by the Institute for Juvenile Research in Chicago (quoted in the newsletter, "Howdy's Happenings").

been blamed. In an extremely short time the era of small towns, where everyone knew what everyone else was doing, has been left behind. This in itself was a control. Citizens at one time identified with their communities. The effects of the complex changes that have occurred since then, perhaps in the span of one life-time, have been the subject of countless books and studies. Dr. John M. Martin of Fordham University states in his book, *Juvenile Vandalism,* that vandalism is an index of social stresses.[11] He finds that in New York it tends to concentrate in parts of the city where tensions among adults are greatest. Likewise, other re-asearchers link school vandalism with tensions or morale problems in the schools.[2,9,12]

Another study was conducted in Israel where vandalism and crime are growing problems. Dr. Judith T. Shuval of the Israel Institute of Applied Social Research[9] attributes the rise in crime to (a) increased affluence, (b) rebellion against authority, (c) resentment by immigrant children of the gap between them and the affluent, (d) the change in the structure of Israeli families from large, cohesive, paternal groups to western-type small families, and (e) the altering of the overall values of the country as the challenges that faced earlier immigrants disappear.

The loss of community roots, depersonalization of urban life, increased tensions, changed attitudes toward the family unit and moral values, drugs, the effect of mass media on individual attitudes, and countless other factors have psychological implications well beyond the scope of this chapter.

Types of Vandalism

Depending on the motivation, most acts of vandalism fall into one of three categories: erosive, fun, or vindictive.[9] They are often hard to separate but give good clues for prevention programs.

Erosive Vandalism.   Erosive vandalism includes many acts of depreciative behavior and vandalism that by themselves might not be damaging, but when multiplied by the increasing numbers of users involved, add up to a costly erosion of resources. This misuse is often a result of thoughtlessness or ignorance on the part of visitors, and offenders seldom view their actions as vandalism.

With little tie to the land, many visitors have no commitment to care for it and don't understand the consequences of their carelessness. Perhaps they have even been "trained" in the art of depreciative behavior. Children have been educated to enjoy destruction,[9] many interpreters report incidents of parents encouraging children in vandalistic acts.[17,20] Every day they see advertisements promoting throwaway containers or commercials demonstrating miracle cleaners that erase anything children might smear on walls or floors. They needn't worry about their carelessness; someone will be there to clean up after them.

Sometimes a camper who lacks some basic need, such as firewood or a tent pole, resorts to vandalism to obtain this necessity. Other damage may result when newly imposed restrictions interfere with the goals of visitors.[3,5] Remembering the old days, when rangers overlooked loose dogs and late night parties, campers and other users rebel against restrictive regulations. What were then small annoyances are now major problems. They may express themselves with erosive or other types of vandalism and feel fairly safe from apprehension since onlookers very rarely interfere.

The problem of non-involvement is not limited to erosive vandalism. One research team[3,5] reported that 80 percent of the depreciative behavior they observed was done when others were present, but that the witnesses almost never reacted. This studious disregard for others is used in park settings, just as it is in cities, as a means of creating privacy and freeing oneself from any responsibility for the behavior of others. Ignoring an incident also eliminates the witness's fear of being identified as the informant and later being a victim of reprisal. However, the witness is likely to open up and report all incidents to the park staff on leaving, no longer fearing retaliation by the offenders.[22]

Fun Vandalism.   Fun vandalism includes incidents such as using signs for target practice and chasing wildlife with snowmobiles until the animals collapse from exhaustion. Destructive play by children also takes its toll. Often their urban background does not prepare them for the freedom of the outdoors. When parents, looking forward to quiet privacy, turn children loose, the children create their own "fun"[3,5] (Fig. 25-2).

Vandalism is often described as a group activity, especially when the motive is to have a good time. A carload of teenagers who are drinking and looking for adventure will often do anything just for some action. They may be dominated elsewhere, but when they're together, teens get a feeling of power. This feeling may be especially important to them since this is the age when they long for independence. Any feelings of boredom or restlessness, rebellion against excessive restraints at home or school, the desire for attention, or need for thrills may be expressed more safely in a group. In past eras many human drives had survival value; aggressiveness and energy were a necessity for defense or the chase for food.[16] These urges have persisted, but many of the outlets are no longer socially acceptable. However, as will be pointed out in the section on Personal Involvement, there are *positive* ways to channel these drives, and the wise interpreter will capitalize on them.

Vindictive Vandalism.   Of the three categories of vandalism, the vindictive type is the most understandable and possibly the most difficult to eliminate. The causes are complex and certainly not limited to young offenders.

A fisherman in Virginia finds his favorite stream crossed by a guide rope for

FIG. 25-2. Children are often turned loose to do as they wish in outdoor recreation areas. Interpretative signs must be of rugged materials to withstand children's play. Mount Rainier National Park, Washington. (Photo by Grant W. Sharpe.)

a disabled person's interpretive trail, and he repeatedly cuts the rope.[21] Animosity over condemnation of private land for a large recreation area may be the cause of the repeated destruction of an isolated visitor observation station in West Virginia. Incidents of damage occurring when a new park development infringes on the territory of neighborhood youth are common. There also have been incidents of vandalism that apparently were in reaction to unfriendly members of park staff, but that suddenly discontinued when the staff member left the job and a friendlier replacement was found.[13]

Youthful aggression today has been explained in part as a result of the lengthened dependence of youth on their parents.[9] The granting of privileges and responsibilities of adulthood are now withheld long beyond physical maturity. Tied by laws that require attendance at school, a young adult cannot hold a job that would offer income and much-needed self-esteem. The young person today is dependent and, therefore, in the power of parents. Without encouragement to channel resulting aggressiveness into positive releases, he may resort to vandalism.* Some police officers work with youths in athletic activities or help older boys build motorbikes in an effort to direct their energies toward constructive projects. Without this type of program, energies may be turned to envious or malicious destruction of property (Fig. 25-3).

MINIMIZING VANDALISM

To be effective, prevention measures for vandalism should be tailored to the type of vandalism, its motives, and the conditions affecting it. Motives may be hard to determine, but the previous discussion should provide clues. One good aid is to develop open communication with nearby residents—especially teenagers. If it is found that neighboring youth frequently cause trouble, then they are probably the best source of ideas for solutions.

Preventive techniques can be classified under (1) facilities (design and maintenance), (2) attitudes (education, personal involvement, and regulations), and (3) enforcement. Each has its place and each has met with some success when used in the appropriate situations. For greater detail the reader should consult some of the suggested references at the end of the chapter. Of particular help are George T. Wilson's booklet, *Vandalism: How to Stop It,* and the Park Practice series, which includes *Grist* and *Guidelines.*

The many interpreters who shared their successes in vandalism control with this writer know that there is no magic formula and that much work remains to be done before the problem is fully understood. But, thanks are due to them for their insights and suggestions.

Facilities (Design and Maintenance)

Paging through vandalism articles reveals enough ingenious gimmicks designed to keep garbage cans, flagpole ropes, cannon balls, and gate locks in place to show that there are many interpreters and maintenance people determined to outsmart the vandals.

There is probably no recreation facility or interpretive device that is completely vandal-proof. However, good initial design goes far toward lessening vandalism. Do the job right the first time because it is this initial design that often regulates

---

*The pronoun *he* is used because females, whether because of a lack of opportunity, culturally-induced passivity, or concerns that are antithetical to violence, have not participated in serious vandalism in statistically significant numbers.

FIG. 25-3. Vandalism affects everyone, including the interpretive specialist. Repairs for this incident alone may cost the equivalent of the salary for a seasonal interpreter, an exhibit, or some much-needed projection equipment. (Photo courtesy of the Racine, Wisconsin, Department of Parks and Recreation.)

the amount of maintenance needed later. Give careful consideration to location, function, durability, operational and supervisory procedures, ease of circulation, maintenance, appearance, and human nature.[13] Developments that do not meet the specific needs of visitors (for example, a secluded interpretive trail in an urban park where local residents might rather have a sports field) may be vandalized out of existence. Remember that *high-quality, durable, attractive facilities* are basic deterrents to vandalism. If the site is well-maintained and looks as if the interpreter really cares about it, visitors will have more respect for it too.

It does help to have equipment and devices as unpryable, unbendable, unuprootable, unchoppable, and unsledge-hammerable as possible. But, to make a building almost prisonlike or mount a trail label on a 3 ton monument as a means of keeping it intact has no effect on the attitude that causes destruction in the first place. Design measures are short-term solutions; they attack the result rather than the source of the problem. Whenever possible, design aspects should be coupled with protection measures that are more attitude-oriented (i.e., education, personal involvement, and regulation). Until responsible attitudes are developed, repair costs will continue to mount, and funds available for new facilities and programs will decrease.

Self-Guiding Trail.   Because of their seclusion, trails are particularly vulnerable to vandalism. The ideal situation, of course, is the use of interpretive personnel where the budget permits. However, to provide a full spectrum of interpretive offerings, a self-guided trail may be desirable.

Assuming vandalism is a problem, which type of interpretation should be employed? In Chapter 14 the labeled trail was identified as the one most subject to vandalism, with the leaflet and marker trails experiencing the least. Many labeled trails have received such extensive damage that some areas have had to abandon them in favor of leaflets.

The *leaflet-marker trail* offers less opportunity to vandals and provides the additional advantage of the leaflet's value as a souvenir and reference. It has greater versatility in length, content, and format of message. A fee for brochures not only pays printing costs, but assigns some value so that they will be taken home rather than discarded. The main requirement is a dispensing point for brochures that is regularly and frequently checked and restocked. The coin box may well be irresistible to vandals and thieves, of course.

As pointed out in Chapter 14, the numbered trail markers themselves are subject to some vandalism. One solution is the landmark trail approach. Here there are no labels or posts along the way. The visitor is given a leaflet that describes obvious landmarks and their locations and may even include line drawings or photographs of each. The visitor hunts for them from the written descriptions or illustrations.[8] This idea has a double advantage. It provides the excitement of a treasure hunt and leaves the trail in a natural condition. However, without clear landmarks such as stumps, rock outcrops, or ponds, this type of trail may be difficult to develop.

Should the trail be in a remote area or in a situation where brochures cannot be kept in supply, then a *labeled trail* could be used. The stakes and label mounts devised for withstanding damage to these trails show a wide range of inventiveness. Stakes should be sturdy and well anchored with rocks or concrete. They should have two crossbars, one at the lower end of the post to prevent uprooting and the other at right angles to the first, just below ground level, to prevent loosening. Variations on this theme are endless. Sections of telephone poles, so thick that vandals can't get enough leverage to uproot them, are effective. One of the more interesting posts, though, is that used at Pinnacles National Monument in California. Cast in concrete, this post is reinforced with two vertical steel rods through the center and fine mesh wire embedded under the outer surface of the concrete. Rounded corners prevent chipping, and posts can be dipped in fiberglass to resist pounding by rocks (Fig. 25-4).

Other alternatives for trailside interpretation are nonprint media such as tape cassettes, radios transmitting to visitor's (rented) headsets, or message repeater stations. Audio stations and other devices in secluded spots are vulnerable to abuse and should be of sturdy construction.

If vandalism is a problem, caution is urged in using visitor-manipulated devices. Because of the difficulty of designing buttons, dials, and switches that are tamper-proof, many interpreters only use such equipment if it is to be under supervision.

Both trail layout and means of interpretation may invite or deter vandalism. If the trail is adjacent to a manned center or is regularly patrolled, it is less likely to be damaged. When possible, trails should be routed to avoid temptations such as smooth-barked ("graffiti") trees, loose rocks, which may invite smashing of labels, and sensitive features. A boardwalk trail through a marsh or skirting a hotsprings lets people know where they are supposed to walk and also keeps them from approaching too closely. This cuts down on trampling, and makes it difficult for visitors to throw coins and other objects in the water. If attention is called to rare

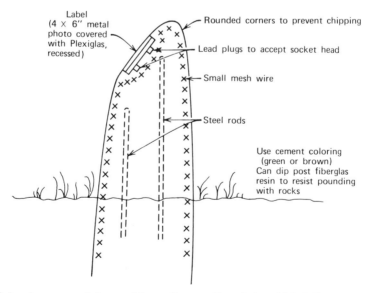

FIG. 25-4. An approach to vandal-proofing a self-guided trail label. From Pinnacles National Monument, California. Illustrated in *Grist*.

or unusual plants, visitors may be tempted to remove them. Also, by pointing out fragile situations (e.g., "Don't collect petrified wood" or "Don't mark on algae"), the interpreter may be giving the visitor ideas. In designing special trails for disabled visitors don't use long pieces of rope for guidelines. A long piece of rope is handy on any camping trip and useful at home, too. Remove the temptation to steal it by cutting the rope in short sections and mounting it between posts; or use strong, coated cables, such as those used by telephone companies.[21]

Labels and Signs.   To discourage damage, all labels should appear professionally done. However, those labels with catchy phrases or unusual design may have a high souvenir value and may disappear as fast as those that are poorly designed. *Grist,* a Park Practice publication, provides a good source of label ideas, from casting trailside markers in molten lead to coating the backs of signs with thick, gloppy grease to discourage theft. Many interpreters prefer to use labels that are cheap and easily replaced. These can be made in quantity, sometimes for just a few cents each, and the stolen or vandalized label can be quickly replaced. Labels of this kind are economical when used repeatedly on several trails but become expensive when each text is tailored to one specific site. Labels may be printed on cardboard, vinyl, or mylar. The entire label—text and artwork—may be a photographic reproduction. This photographic technique is best if the labels are to be laminated with liquid plastics or similar coatings, as such substances smear printing ink.[19] Mounting labels on solid backings, such as fiberglass, metal, or wood, improves their ruggedness and permanency. However, plywood has a disadvantage in some forested areas. The glue in the plywood is a delicacy to squirrels and porcupines, and they will relish these labels. Also, damp wood may discolor labels, so it helps to coat the wood with waterproofing.[19]

If trails are not patrolled frequently, labels should be of a more permanent nature. Utilize labels of ceramic tile, metal photo (although it is rather easily scratched), metal baked enamel, fiberglass with silkscreened messages (relatively cheap replacement cost), cast aluminum or bronze (very durable), and routed or painted wood signs (permanent until they're carved up or used for firewood).

Security.   The protection of buildings and grounds from damage offers a sizable challenge to many park personnel.

Glass windows are replaced with Lexan and tough plastics that cannot be shot out. Some buildings are designed with *no* windows but have fiberglass roofs that admit light. Doors are strategically reinforced with metal. Roofs are bordered with extruding metal spikes so vandals cannot climb up and tear off shingles. Special lighting systems and removal of shrubbery near buildings leave vandals no place to hide. Damage has also been minimized where a naturalist or caretaker lives on the site, facilities are locked at night, the entrance is controlled by a manned station, or chain-link fence materials are used (Fig. 25-5).

FIG. 25-5. Although not aesthetically pleasing, a chain link fence is one means of reducing vandalism. Gas Works Park, Seattle, Washington. (Photo by Grant W. Sharpe.)

Vandals can be discouraged in other ways. In Arizona a Forest Service Visitor Center, while still under construction, had its large windows shattered with rocks. When they were replaced, a burglar alarm was installed with a metal tape visible on all the new windows. There has been no trouble in the 10 years since, even though the building is left unoccupied for months at a time during the off-season.

One exasperated naturalist had a similar, but less costly, approach to the matter. One night his collection of native artifacts and some mounted animals were stolen from his urban nature center. After some thought, he discarded any idea of turning the center into a fortress. He decided to leave all the shutters open and the building exposed. But, he tacked up wires all around the center. These wires led into a box that he painted red and labeled. "ALARM." The box *didn't do anything*—but it did stop his vandalism problem. He later left that particular park, and his successor—a nonbeliever—removed the box. The center has had several break-ins since.

Graffiti and Park Design. Graffiti can also be minimized through proper planning. Consider first the reason behind it. Observations support the idea that graffiti is a matter of identity—the urge to leave one's mark behind.[7] How can proper facility design satisfy this urge?

The guest book is one outlet. Visitors can leave their names there legally. Other pacifiers are "carving logs" or "graffiti slabs" (Fig. 25-6).

FIG. 25-6. A graffiti pacifier, such as this sandstone slab, gives visitors an outlet for the urge to leave their mark and helps to protect sensitive features. Walnut Canyon National Monument, Arizona. (National Park Service photo by Parker Hamilton.)

Some walls, particularly those in rest rooms, attract graffiti. Epoxy tile, cement enamels, or very smooth, plasticized walls are hard to write on and are easily cleaned when necessary. Some areas have experimented with rough, sandy surfaces, but these are difficult to clean and don't deter the charcoal or lipstick artists. Another approach is used by the East Bay Regional Parks in California.[24] They cover graffiti on the walls and tunnel entrances to some parks with colorful murals. Their theory is that if they replaced the negative action (graffiti) with a positive one (murals), they discourage defacement. Thus far, the murals have been a success.

FIG. 25-7. A litter can shaped like an animal has considerable appeal to children who look for litter to feed it. This one is called the "Garbage Gobbler." Okanagan Lake, British Columbia. (Photo by Grant W. Sharpe.)

Litter. Some success in decreasing litter has been achieved through equipment design. Litter cans decorated with marsh scenes (at lakeside areas), or shaped like miniature silos (at an interpretive site with a farm theme), or even designed as animals, which are "fed" litter, have all enticed people to deposit litter in the containers[10] (Fig. 25-7).

Indiana Dunes National Lakeshore operates a combination control and recycling program.[10] As a result of advertising the program, visitors deposited 23.5 tons (21.3 t) of cans during the first month alone. Park personnel took these cans to collection points to be recycled.

FIG. 25-8. The thin metal braille sign at left has been vandalized. Neglect will attract more vandalism. San Bernardino National Forest, California. (Photo by Jacque Beechel.)

Preventive Maintenance. It is said that the maintenance budget of a park is often the main factor standing between the area and the vandal. Prompt repair of facilities is an important deterrent to further damage. Unkempt facilities have a look of neglect that attracts vandalism (Fig. 25-8). For this reason trails, exhibits, and other facilities should be inspected several times weekly and cleaned or repaired as soon as possible. With today's recreation budgets this may be asking too much. The all-too-familiar situation is one where funds are available for new construction but not for maintenance. Many areas are building new interpretive facilities, even though they are unable to properly maintain those already in existence.

Attitudes (Education, Involvement, and Regulations)

One of the original reasons for initiating interpretive programs was that they would be a vital factor in reducing vandalism and lessening visitor impacts. When people feel an area is their own, they are more likely to protect it whether it is a park, school, or apartment compound. Certainly, a prime objective of interpretation is to cause the visitor to fully identify with the land so that a feeling of personal commitment for its care develops. However, the present alienation between humans and their natural environment, along with other sociological variables, makes this an increasingly difficult task.

Clark reports that studies show visitors may profess a protective attitude toward the environment and yet exhibit an opposite behavior. (Almost everyone is against littering, but almost everyone litters.[17]) They indicate that education geared toward developing positive attitudes does not automatically result in a lessening of depreciative behavior. Nonetheless, the following attitudinal activities are the interpreter's best means of influencing the internal controls discussed earlier.

Education.   The interpreter's impact on visitor attitudes is often concentrated in scheduled on-site programs. Educational activities are aimed at giving the visitor an appreciation of the park and a feeling of responsibility toward it.

In addition to using the traditional lecture programs, interpreters develop many other methods for gaining visitor cooperation. Puppet shows on littering and vandalism for younger children, followed by discussions and group participation have been used.[24] Michigan State Parks and 4-H have an experimental, cooperative agreement that enables that agency to hire program leaders.[22] They supplement the regular program by supervising workshops and nature activities for children. Such activities as berry picking and fishing safaris teach visitors how to use the resources of the park with minimum impact. The Michigan Department of Natural Resources also makes a point of discussing park problems during evening programs. By showing visitors the consequences of depreciative behavior, patrons are encouraged to be more careful.

One problem with many on-site programs is that very often the people who attend are not those who create problems or who need to be contacted. An aggressive program that reaches out to many parts of the community is a real asset, especially when it contacts the types of people who represent the basis of the problems. Several national parks attribute their low vandalism to their active, *off-site* naturalist programs. Naturalists in or near urban areas are especially well situated to work with these groups, whether youth, local citizen, or special interest clubs (see Chapter 17.)

An urban nature center near Washington, D.C. has plans to meet this challenge through a wide-reaching Urban Nature Project.[18] They propose converting old residential area stores into "Storefront Nature Centers," staffed in part by trained volunteers from scout groups, universities, and local community groups. Other sections of the community would be served by a trailer outfitted with exhibits and equipment for programs. This trailer would operate similarly to a bookmobile, changing locale regularly. Their "Bio-Van," a mobile field lab, is equipped for soil and water quality tests and other environmental analyses and is used by small groups of high school students or adults. "Open Air Seminars" (discussions on urban environmental concerns) are also planned for park areas, shopping centers, and town halls.

Park personnel in Milwaukee, Wisconsin, have been successful in reaching out into the community. They hired a retired park supervisor to contact residents in neighborhoods where vandalism was common. He discussed with families their attitudes toward the park department, whether or not they thought vandalism was a problem, and if they had ever witnessed it. He explained that the park facilities are theirs, and they should police them. He also told them how to report vandalism without the danger of being identified as the informant.

Other areas have encouraged the development of positive peer images by working with high school students on neighborhood surveys of vandalism and prevention campaigns. These efforts include public meetings, radio dramas, and programs for preteens, all carried out by the older students.[9]

Personal Involvement.   This subject, which includes the personal involvement of visitors in planning, programs, or patrolling, might fit more easily under the education section. However, it is placed here to emphasize the value of active visitor participation in encouraging cooperation.

A good place to start is by involving members of the community in the planning stage of the development of an area. This greatly increases both their understanding of the problems and their commitment to care for the site. It can also help the staff meet visitors' needs. A nature center in Wisconsin[20] set up an Advisory Committee, giving patrons a voice in evaluating and planning the kinds of programs the center offers.

Another good deterrent to vandalism is the involvement of youth. Older teens, particularly, are often a forgotten group. Often all they need is responsibility. Some areas offer teen training courses where the teenagers volunteer or sometimes are hired for antivandalism patrols. Washington, D.C., has its "Rebels with a Cause"[14], another city its T.O.P.s (Teens on Patrol).[11]

Teenagers trained to function as junior naturalists can set an example and a goal for preteens. A nature center in a metropolitan area of Maryland[18] has a program in which children progress through a series of nature clubs and other activities toward a goal of assistant naturalist on reaching high school age. As beginning naturalists they lead activities, prepare exhibits, help with research, and aid in the operation of the center. This same center gives special privileges to neighborhood youth. They are given an identification card and may participate in both a center-sponsored pet exchange and trading post. Through these programs, participants may exchange their excess hamsters for a kitten or trade an unusual fossil for an arrowhead. In addition these youths informally patrol the surrounding park. In an area which would be heavily vandalized the staff has designed a program that keeps problems to a minimum.

Some parks have resident school camps and work with student volunteers building trails and working on conservation projects.[22] At others, annual spring cleanup days are sponsored by local service clubs with various special interest and youth groups helping to prepare the park for the summer season[10] (Fig. 25-9). Carried further, it was total community involvement that produced the West Rock Nature Center in New Haven, Connecticut. Hundreds of thousands of

FIG. 25-9. A volunteer youth group cleaning up a pond in a metropolitan park in Ohio. Such activities can instill a sense of pride in the park. (Photo courtesy of Cleveland Metropolitan Park District, Cleveland, Ohio.)

volunteer hours have gone into actual building, maintenance, and program activity at the urban center which, incidentally, has suffered very little vandalism. These types of friendly, shoulder-to-shoulder partnerships strengthen the tie between youth, adults, and the park. Then it often becomes a personal responsibility to care for the area.

Littering is an example of a problem where education may have affected attitudes, but it took an involvement technique to actually change behavior. In a series of experiments a Forest Service research team[3,4] showed that with a tangible reward for an incentive, litter could be reduced by 70 to 80 percent. Children in selected campgrounds were given litter bags and offered their choice of a Junior Ranger badge, arm patch, or other incentive if they returned full litter bags. The main value of this incentive system, other than the fact that the children almost entirely cleaned up the areas, was that its positive effect on littering behavior was long lasting and didn't disappear as soon as the reward was received (Fig. 25-10). Incidentally, incentive programs offering money for beverage containers have been sponsored by various companies with many so successful that some companies have paid 10 times what they expected in rewards.

Regulations. Many interpreters feel the authoritarian attitude reflected in the wording of numerous regulations incites retaliation by visitors. Regulations could offer another opportunity to educate and gain visitors' cooperation. Instead, they often challenge people to see how much they can get away with. It would be good to spend some time reading such signs with an open mind. Is each restriction imposed absolutely necessary? Are signs clearly and concisely written? Are opportunities for humor capitalized on? Does wording not only state but also *interpret* the regulation? This last point is very important—and often overlooked.

FIG. 25-10. Children displaying awards received for participating in the "Incentive System for Litter Control." The sacks of litter collected by the children are seen in the foreground. Wenatchee National Forest, Washington. (Photo by Wallace C. Guy.)

If these criteria are met, chances are regulations will be more easily administered and have effective results. If not, printed regulations may be contributing to instead of eliminating troubles.

Another important factor is the attitude of the staff administering the regulations. Remember: vandalism may be a form of rebellion against the impatient or officious patrolman. Evaluate staff approaches: are officials trained to use a friendly, understanding approach and exercise a sense of humor, especially in difficult situations? During patrols, which should be frequent when vandalism is a problem, do officers exploit the opportunity to contact visitors and interpret regulations to them? Do they try to educate rather than police? The attitude of staff can play a vital part in stopping vandalism and encouraging cooperation.

A good example of this positive attitude exists in Rochester, New York, which has had notable success in curbing vandalism. There, vandalism is treated as a symptom of social stress.[11] The police regularly visit recreation areas as friends, not as disciplinarians. On the basis of visits with youth and parents, they have made changes in programs and personnel and have minimized vandalism.

Enforcement

Facility design, education and other attitudinal measures, and the presence of uniformed staff deter the average visitor from depreciative behavior. But a certain amount will persist and can only be checked with effective enforcement, apprehension, and restitution of damages. Without these, vandalism problems will be compounded.

For sites that continually receive heavy damage, extensive, unscheduled patrols or even continual surveillance may be needed for apprehension. Although costs may be high for these measures, they can be less than the long-run costs of continual repairs.

In some areas interpreters are expected to serve as enforcement officers. When this is not the case and when staff are not trained in enforcement, it is particularly important to maintain good relations with law enforcement agencies. Interpreters should meet with the local judge and enforcement officers and should take them on a "show-me" trip so they can see the extent of the problem. This offers an opportunity for interpreters to encourage effective fines, especially those involving payment through work or money to repair damages. (When the vandal comes from a home where a monetary fine is no problem, labor may be the more effective sentence. The opposite is true for those from lower income families.)

Finally, follow up through publicizing court actions, damages, and their costs to taxpayers, and by stressing the need for improved enforcement. The public needs to see that this is a problem that affects everyone, and the vandal must see that it will not be tolerated.

SUMMARY

The problems of vandalism and other depreciative actions are more than a matter of delinquent behavior. Their complexity demands preventive measures designed to fit the situation. Approaches taken depend on:

    a. What is vandalized.
    b. Where and when the incident occurs.
    c. Who the vandal is.
    d. The motive (erosive, fun, vindictive, or other).
    e. Attitudinal factors.

The internal and external aspects of the problem give depreciative behavior two facets. The interpreter effects the internal controls in people through educational activities (including visitor involvement and interpretation of regulations). The physical, external aspect of depreciative behavior is influenced by proper planning, design, and maintenance of facilities. However, regardless of preventive measures used by interpreters, a certain amount of criminal or malicious vandalism persists. To control this element, an effective enforcement program is needed. Administrators of interpretive areas should encourage staffs to experiment with new preventive techniques to minimize problems.

REFERENCES

General References

Alfano, Sam S., and Arthur W. Magill. 1976. *Vandalism and Outdoor Recreation: Symposium Proceedings.* Pacific Southwest Forest and Range Experiment Station, Berkeley, CA.

Christianson, Harriet H., and Roger N. Clark. 1978. "Understanding And Controlling Vandalism And Other Rule Violations In Urban Recreation Areas," *Proceedings of the National Urban Forestry Conference,* Washington, DC.

Muth, Robert M., and Roger N. Clark. 1978. *Public Participation in Wilderness and Backcountry Litter Control: A Review of Research and Management Experience.* Pacific Northwest Forest and Range Experiment Station, Seattle, WA.

References Cited

1. Bennett, Joseph W., 1969. *Vandals Wild,* Metropolitan Press, for the Bennett Publishing Co., Portland, OR.
2. "Boredom May Be Cause of School Vandalism," 1960. *Science Newsletter* Vol. 78.

3. Campbell, Frederick L., John C. Hendee, and Roger Clark. 1968. "Law and Order in Public Parks," *Parks and Recreation.*

4. Clark, Roger N., John C. Hendee, and Robert L. Burgess. 1968. "The Experimental Control of Littering," *The Journal of Environmental Education,* **4** (2).

5. Clark, Roger N., John C. Hendee, and Frederick Campbell. 1971. *Depreciative Behavior in Forest Campgrounds: An Exploratory Study,* U.S. Forest Service, Pacific Northwest Forest Experiment Station, Bulletin: PNW-161.

6. Cohen, Stanley. 1968. "Politics of Vandalism," *The Nation,* **207.**

7. "An Identity Thing: Graffiti in New York and Philadelphia," 1972. *Time,* **99.**

8. Knudsen, George. (moderator), 1967. "Summary of A.I.N. Workshop on Vandalism," and "Techniques to Reduce Vandalism," Annual Workshop of the Association of Interpretive Naturalists, Oglebay Park, Wheeling, WV.

9. Madison, Arnold, 1970. *Vandalism—The Not-So-Senseless Crime,* The Seabury Press, New York.

10. Park Practice Program. *Grist.* (numerous entries), National Recreation and Parks Association, National Conference on State Parks, and National Park Service. Arlington, VA.

11. "Surging Vandalism—Its Expense to America," 1969. *U.S. News and World Report,* **67**(8).

12. "The Vandal: Society's Outsider," 1970. *Time,* **95**(3).

13. Wilson, George T. 1961. "Vandalism—How to Stop It," American Institute of Park Executives (now National Recreation and Park Association), Management Aides, Bulletin No. 7.

14. "Wreckcreation: What Can Teenagers Do About Vandalism?" 1967. *Senior Scholastic,* **90**(14).

Personal Contacts

15. Barnacastle, Robert. U.S. Forest Service; Sabino Canyon Visitor Center, Coronado National Forest, Tucson, AZ.

16. Bishop, Norman. Interpretive Services, National Park Service; Regional Office, Atlanta, GA.

17. Clark, Dr. Roger. Pacific Northwest Forest Experiment Station, U.S. Forest Service, Seattle, WA.

18. Griffeth, Blaine. Clearwater Nature Center, Wheaton, MD.

19. Knudsen, George, Chief Parks Naturalist, Wisconsin Department of Natural Resources, Madison, WI.

20. Larsen, Andrew. Director, Riveredge Nature Center, Newburg, WI.

21. Leichter, William. U.S. Forest Service, George Washington National Forest, VA.

22. Nagel, Roland. Regional Interpreter, Michigan Department of Natural Resources, Lansing, MI.

23. National Park Service, letters (on vandalism) to Ms. Renee Renninger, graduate student, University of Washington, Seattle, from 32 units of the NPS.

24. Nelson, Christian. East Bay Regional Parks, Oakland, CA.

25. Wilson, Dr. George. Assistant Superintendant, Milwaukee Public Schools, Division of Municipal Recreation and Adult Education, Milwaukee, WI.

26. Yeager, Donald. Monroe County Parks, Rochester, NY.

PART IV

PROFESSIONAL DEVELOPMENT

Find out your audience's frame of reference before
you try to bring them into your own.

John M. Good

CHAPTER 26

EDUCATING FOR INTERPRETER EXCELLENCE

Paul H. Risk

Since the early 1900s North American park and recreation agencies have made some effort to provide information and answer questions about their resources. Much of the impetus for this movement had its origins in the national parks in the United States.

Early interpreters were selected almost exclusively from the ranks of natural scientists. Although this choice is still widespread throughout the interpretive field, it is based on two debatable concepts. First, it is doubtful that people come to parks with the idea of being educated. Second, there is no correlation between possession of a degree in natural sciences and the ability to communicate. If anything, there may be a negative correlation, and communication is the name of the game. For interpretation to be effective in its goals of developing sensitivity, awareness, understanding, enthusiasm, and commitment, communication skill is of paramount importance.

PERSONAL ATTRIBUTES OF THE INTERPRETER

A great deal has been said and written regarding the formal education of interpreters, but little attention has been directed to the basic building blocks—personal characteristics of the interpreter. Although Freeman Tilden has alluded to the fact that interpretation is, to some degree, a teachable art,[3] the fact remains that some individuals possess certain attributes that seem to make them more successful in this field. Since interpretation is a limited field and can have profound effects on public environmental attitudes, it is important for those who administer these programs to have clearly in mind a number of personality characteristics as indices to use in their selection process. Furthermore, these same attributes should be strongly considered in counseling prospective students investigating this academic pursuit.

The first reaction to a listing of the qualities desirable in an interpreter may be that this is pure idealism. It is! Idealism brought to reality is "the stuff" of which quality interpretation is made.

Although "sparkle" may be a rather nebulous term to use in the description of personality characteristics, it nevertheless seems the sum of a series of desirable qualities. Certainly, it is a visceral-level explanation of what is desired. Don't get trapped in the old argument that "we can't all have sparkle." This may be true, but we can't all be interpreters either, and if that is what you are trying to educate or to hire, take the time to evaluate and choose those who match your criteria.

Here is a list of qualities that may be included in the definition of the term "sparkle." It gives some idea of the direction to go in selection criteria.

Enthusiasm

Enthusiasm can help to minimize the problems when difficulties arise. It presupposes zeal and drive to produce desirable ends. Here at least it is possible to detect a *literal* sparkle in the eyes that will betray the characteristic you are seeking. Smiling easily and elaborating on ideas, the enthusiastic person is usually a "self-starter" requiring minimal supervision.

Sense of Humor and Perspective

The two go hand in hand. Nothing is more deadly than the person who never sees the humor in a situation unless it is an individual who, when the joke is on him or her, perceives it as an affront. A sense of perspective helps remind one not to take oneself too seriously. (Others don't!)

A sense of both humor and perspective can be of great aid on those days when things don't seem to be going well and the interpreter gets "peopled"—crushed by a mass of rushed, unhappy visitors with incessant demands. An inability to maintain perspective can easily result in a serious public relations problem.

Articulateness

Essentially this means that the interpreter should be able to communicate and express ideas clearly and smoothly, using phrases easily with words in pleasing and proper order. Practice during the course of employment will increase this ability, but the flair for articulate speech is something that is detectable even before experience molds it. Look especially for this as it has a strong influence on interpreter credibility and agency image in the eyes of the public.

Self-Confidence

Self-confident people instill this same quality in those around them. In addition they won't have to be hand-led into new enterprises. They will instead look on newness as a challenge and generally prove to be an asset to the agency as they successfully launch new projects. One indicator of this trait is the person's ability to maintain eye contact.

Warmth

Does the individual make you feel comfortable as you talk? Remember that people like people who like them. Lack of warmth is frequently the single most important factor in the determination of a visitor-perceived image in public contact work. It gives a rather clear idea as to whether or not the person likes to work with people.

Poise

Poise really is a composite of several traits including maturity, confidence, and warmth. People with poise meet strangers easily, giving the feeling that they are in control of themselves and the situation. It is a trait that will grow with experience and age.

Credibility

Perhaps *perceived* credibility is a better way to put this. It is related to the fact that some people in their style of communication give the feeling that they are to be believed. Others, such as those who "put the mouth in gear without the brain being engaged," don't. We often refer to this type as a "know-it-all" who is merely trying to cover up inadequate knowledge with a barrage of words and the attempt to impress. In either case the result is undesirable. Frequent hesitations and verbal discontinuities along with overuse of words such as "maybe," "perhaps," "probably," "I guess," or "you know" also shake confidence and destroy credibility.

Pleasant Appearance and Demeanor

This again is a complex of conditions relating to those characteristics of physiognomy, movement, and dress that others use to determine their own sense of comfort with the person. We all are aware that there are some people who don't even need to speak to make us feel drawn to them and that there are others who repel us for various reasons. Careful consideration of dress standards together with physical appearance, habitual expression, and personal peculiarities should give an accurate assessment of how this person will affect others.

Although this is not intended to be an exhaustive list of personal attributes to be sought in interpreters it can provide general guidelines. You will surely find other characteristics that you consider important.

FORMAL EDUCATION

Rather than total or overriding emphasis on the sciences, the formal education of the interpreter should be one stressing a balance. If interpreters are anything, they are *communicators* in, for, and about the environment. Communication presupposes an audience of other humans. Therefore, there must be sufficient communication and human behavior courses to provide a nucleus of proficiency. All too frequently students seeking jobs that will allow them to "hunt, fish, trap, live in a log cabin, and carry heavy loads up slippery trails" enter educational programs in interpretation with an isolationist attitude. Certainly, counseling prior to enrollment will go a long way to avoid future problems, but it must be assured through intelligent curriculum development that budding interpreters receive adequate exposure to people-oriented disciplines.

In North America the Association of Interpretive Naturalists[1] stated basic needs in the education of interpreters when they identified five broad areas recommended for study.

1. Knowledge and understanding of the natural and man-made environment.
2. Effective use of communicative skills.
3. Human behavior.
4. Program planning and administration.
5. Integrative final seminar considering humans and their relationship to all the above.

In the first category are those courses in natural resources and science that provide a basis for understanding the ecosystem. Field courses are an important part of this curriculum (Fig. 26-1). Emphasis throughout should be oriented toward a broad ecological understanding rather than a series of unrelated bits of information. Later this information must be transmitted to the visiting public in a manner calculated to produce a behavior change, and skill in communication is of utmost importance. Often it is not *what* is said but *how* it is said that dictates whether or not the interpretive goals are met. To plan wisely to attain these goals presupposes a clear knowledge of the principles of human interaction. The person who administers and plans the program of studies must understand the field of interpretation and its relation to other disciplines and activities. Otherwise, imbalances will result, often in the form of overemphasis of particular facets.

FIG. 26-1. College interpretive education should include direct exposure to interpretive facilities through field trips. Here an outdoor recreation class from the University of Washington visits and evaluates a self-guiding trail and entrance exhibit in the Mt. Baker-Snoqualmie National Forest, Washington. (Photo by Grant W. Sharpe.)

Furthermore, it must be realized that an effective interpreter making satisfactory progress within the profession will ultimately be promoted to more responsible positions in which overall responsibility for the operation of interpretive activities will be important. Person-to-person contact between the interpreter and the public will tend to progressively decrease as more administrative responsibilities come between the visitor and the rising interpretive manager. In a sense this may be unfortunate, since excellence in communication and interpretation does not guarantee similar abilities in management. Nevertheless, this is true, and a well-conceived college curriculum ought to provide budding interpreters with education in the fields of administration and management of interpretive operations as well as with courses in interpretive planning. This chapter, however, will be limited to discussions pertaining mostly to the beginning interpreter and will therefore not attempt to detail the needed administrative and planning training.

A study conducted in 1971 by Ben Mahaffey[2] singled out two curricula, one at the University of Michigan and one at Michigan State University, for examination as to the balance of course work leading to degrees specializing in the field of interpretation. Based on his study another slightly different balance was determined and presented as a third example. The three are reproduced here to give an idea of these approaches. Certainly, they are not to be construed as "best," but rather are to be used as a starting place from which to work.

1	2	3
University of Michigan	**Michigan State University**	**Study Curriculum**
Biology 17%	Biology 19%	Biology 11%
Physical Sciences 17	Physical Sciences 17	Physical Sciences 9
Natural Resources 20	Natural Sciences 17	Natural Sciences 26
Social Sciences 13	Social Sciences 11	Social Sciences 11
Communication 8	Natural Resources 11	Natural Resources 11
Other 25	Communication 12	Communication 19
———	Other 13	Administration
100%	———	and Policy 6
	100%	Other 7
		———
		100%

Mahaffey goes on to suggest that cultural history, government philosophy and operations, as well as social problems, should be included in the curriculum.

The list of courses with which an interpreter might come into contact in an ideal scholastic setting is almost limitless. A partial list of the more specialized ones includes the following:

Historical Interpretation

Interpretation of military areas
Interpretation of colonial and pioneer areas
Acting in living history interpretation
How to research the historical site
Conducted activities in historical and archaeological sites
Use of demonstrations in historical areas
Historical interviewing

Museology

Accession, cataloging, storage, and preservation
Exhibit design and construction

Media

Visual media in interpretation
Audio media in interpretation
Use of radio and TV in interpretation
Signs and signing

Design

Design of self-guided trails
Visitor center design
Amphitheater design

Natural Area Interpretation

Conducted activities

Communication Skills

Interpretation—speaking
Interpretation—writing

Interpretation in Special Situations

Interpretation for the deaf
Interpretation for the blind
Interpretation for the physically handicapped

Urban Interpretation

The natural history of the city and its suburbs
Gutters and supermarkets—interpretive challenges

Others

Off-season, off-site opportunities
Interpretation for children
Interpretation for senior citizens

No matter how comprehensive the formal course list, the student should have the opportunity to work with the public before permanent employment is secured. Some institutions approach this goal by requiring at least one summer of approved work experience, but this amount is marginal. Ideally, students would have the opportunity to make repeated interpretive presentations under supervision during an extended period of their schooling. One way to accomplish this is to develop cooperative agreements with park and recreation agencies near the college or university (Fig. 26-2). This enables student interpreters to relieve some of the agency's burden of public demand and at the same time to gain experience. Such arrangements can form the basis for experiences similar to the on-the-job training required of student teachers. Properly supervised, these public-contact ventures can provide an important core of the academic training as well as a realistic indication of what interpretation is all about before four years are invested.

EMPLOYEE SELECTION

Agencies may make selections while the students are still completing their education or wait until they have graduated. Some agencies, to promote acquiring

FIG. 26-2.   A student on information duty in a national park. Through cooperative agreements between park staffs and nearby colleges offering interpretive courses, students can gain experience in interpretive work as part of their professional training. Mount Rainier National Park, Washington. (Photo by Grant W. Sharpe.)

the highest quality employees, establish student traineeships. These programs provide promising students a job during the summer months with a guarantee of permanent employment following satisfactory seasonal evaluation and completion of schooling. In this way substantive training occurs while the interpreter is working during the summer, paving the way for smoother assimilation on graduation and minimizing required intake training.

Whenever selection is made, it is important that careful evaluation of all possible criteria be carried out. Although an application form is a rather sterile and ineffective mode of personality assay, many agencies still confine themselves to this or to an intake test to determine fitness for interpretive service. As long as this inadequate selection practice continues, these agencies will flounder along with mediocre personnel.

A personal interview should be arranged if at all possible. The Canadian National Parks routinely use this technique, and the high quality of their interpreters shows it.

The Interview

Although the interview may be conducted by a single person, it is far more desirable that two or more people be involved, giving an opportunity for several opinions to be expressed.

Use this setting to the best advantage in acquiring insight into the individual's personality and capability. But be aware that the interviewee will be under stress and responses are likely to be more awkward and stiff than would be the case under ordinary circumstances. Nevertheless, look for those attributes that were discussed in the earlier part of this chapter. Does the person maintain eye contact? Is his or her countenance pleasant and mobile? Does the person have a sense of humor? What are his or her hobbies and interests? Does he or she seem to be enthusiastic? Is the person an articulate and smooth conversationalist? Do you feel comfortable with him or her? Ask the interviewee what his or her strong points are and the reasons he or she should be considered for this job. Such responses can go a long way toward indicating degree of confidence, credibility, realism, and candor.

The Telephone Interview

Distance may make it impossible to personally interview each applicant. In these cases a telephone interview is an acceptable alternative. Plan this interview more carefully than you would one conducted personally. Not only is this important to minimize the phone bill, but it will assist in breaking the ice and in moving the interview along. Find out about the person's interests and hobbies. How effectively are they able to describe these activities. Some of this information may be on the application forms, but you are attempting to loosen up the interviewee and to get a conversation going that will allow you to determine something about those traits discussed in the first part of this chapter. Once an easy give and take is established, you will be able to determine enthusiasm, communication ability, poise, sense of humor, and other factors.

Videotaping

Videotape can be used for interviews. The interviewer and applicant, seated comfortably in familiar surroundings, proceed through the usual format using questions or topics that the employer has supplied. Not only can the camera provide overall views of both the subject and the interviewer, but it can zoom in for close-up shots of expression. In this manner an actual interview can be conducted without the expense of a long trip. The tape is mailed to the employer for review.

An extension of this procedure would be to tape the applicant giving an interpretive presentation. However, this should be a live taping with an audience rather than a studio session in which the interpreter is expected to interpret for a camera only. Such artificial situations usually tell little about the responses of the interpreter to a real audience and may give a very erroneous impression.

AGENCY IN-SERVICE TRAINING

Permanent Personnel

Although formal academic training will go a long way toward producing the type of interpreter desired, it cannot do everything. A well-conceived intake training program in interpretive skills and procedures related to your agency is important. The interpreter should be literally immersed in an intensive program covering every aspect of communication skills. Certainly, some of this will repeat material covered in college. However, a major shortcoming of academic training is that it occurs prior to employment and thus at a time of low relevance to the interpreter. Once on the job, information presented will be more immediate and better assimilated.

Take advantage of resource people both from within and without the agency to expose interpretive trainees to examples of interpretive skill. Remember that examples are far better than discussions of principles. If possible, have the resource people provide example programs in a general public setting so that the trainees can observe the effect of public contact.

Videotaped presentations by the trainees will provide the basis for clinical evaluation sessions and allow close examination of strong and weak points inherent in style and delivery. It is important that trainees also receive information on the agency itself so that they can begin to acquire and develop esprit de corps, a feeling of enthusiasm for agency goals. This is vital in maintaining high-quality services.

Although intake training is important, it will not by itself insure good interpretation. Maintenance of desirable proficiency levels will require that the interpreter periodically have the opportunity to participate in short, in-depth experiences of a training nature. Not only will this serve to maintain skill levels, but it will also expose the interpreter to innovative methods and current thinking on interpretive matters.

In addition, some retraining and exposure to new information should come from contact with professional organizations such as the Association of Interpretive Naturalists, Western Interpreters Association, and Interpretation Canada, at their annual meetings and at regional workshops.

Colleges and universities can make an important input toward maintaining interpretive excellence by providing conferences, workshops, and short courses designed specifically to meet the needs of currently employed interpreters. These must be as short as possible to minimize the time lost from the job and will necessitate in-depth, concentrated approaches that utilize most of the hours of each workshop day to permit as much material to be covered as possible. There have been a few such workshops but more are needed, and it may be largely up to the agencies to provide the catalyst of request in order to see more of them developed.

Topics could include innovative media techniques, as well as different approaches to various aspects of interpretive activities. Ideally, they should be directed to a wide variety of agencies to maximize cross-pollination or sharing of ideas. Workshops and short courses directed toward and staffed by members of the same agency often reinforce the status quo, instead of broadening the outlook and stimulating the imagination.

Seasonal Employees

For many agencies the seasonal employee is an important part of the overall program. The following suggestions can assist in the training of these interpreters and will also have application to permanent personnel.

Preseason Training

Once the season is under way, time is at a premium. Often the seasonals report and are on the job almost immediately. The training they do receive is on a hit-and-miss basis, jammed into an already impossible schedule. Therefore, efforts should be made to provide training prior to the season.

Information Packets

Prepared and mailed to each seasonal during the winter or spring, the packets should include: basic park statistics (how high, how long, how often, how many, how difficult), park area policies and regulations, administrative chains of command, plant and animal checklists, geological information, communication skills guidelines, uniform requirements, and housing information. The use of such a packet can reduce greatly the material presented in formal sessions during the season.

Preseason Meetings

Group meetings should be scheduled in central locations for interpreters living close enough to attend. These could take place on weekends during winter months although this may represent a difficult logistical problem.

Tape Checkout

Each area should maintain a file of tape recordings of exemplary programs. These files, enlarged to permit a loan system, would be of great help in easing the sharp transition that occurs when a new seasonal arrives.

Audio-Tutorial Material

Slide-tape copies of actual programs could also be prepared. These, too, should be available on loan to seasonals at their homes before seasonal duty begins.

Seasonal On-Site Training

Provide training in communications skills useful in interpretation. Steer away from long, involved descriptions of the administrative chains of command. Stick to the subject of interpretation. If the training is to be meaningful, it must include actual demonstration. Walks especially should be demonstrated on-site by the permanent staff or by knowledgeable, seasonal personnel (Fig. 26-3). The seasonals should have the opportunity to witness demonstrators presenting evening pro-

FIG. 26-3. The chief of the park interpretive staff (in the white cap) listens intently as an experienced seasonal interpreter leads a group of new interpreters on a guided-walk demonstration. Mount Rainier National Park, Washington. (Photo by Grant W. Sharpe.)

grams to the general public so that they can see the full scope of interpreter-audience interaction. Formal evening program and walk demonstrations can provide many opportunities to question, observe, and ascertain reasons for the inclusion or omission of various materials as well as to evaluate the approaches used.

When an employee shows great ability, training should be scheduled to permit all seasonals to attend a program given by him or her, followed by a session at which program content and format could be discussed.

QUALITY CONTROL

Just because a great deal of time and money has been spent to create the finest interpreter possible, there is no guarantee that the goal has been met, or that once met, it will forever sustain itself. Periodic samples must be taken to assure that things are as the supervisor assumes and desires. Some sampling methods are better than others.

Auditing, Critiques, and Coaching

Critiques, auditing, and evaluations—the words carry a built-in threat. No amount of reassurance can eliminate this overtone entirely. (And perhaps that isn't *all* bad.) However, it must be realized that quality control when wrapped in such labels may yield misleading results.

The term "coaching" implies far less threat, and the techniques employed tend to promote *cooperative* interaction. Effective coaching must be preceded by detailed and careful explanation to all concerned. The goal is enhanced interpretive quality, something "in which we are all interested." It is couched in terms of "we are all working together toward a common goal."

Coaching implies interaction. It can involve seasonals interacting with permanents or seasonals interacting with other seasonals. The main problem associated with seasonal/permanent coaching is the inhibitory effect that the presence of permanent personnel may have. It must be clearly established that the permanent employee is there only to function as part of the group and to make a contribution to improved interpretation, the common goal. To get the most out of coaching, seasonal/seasonal coaching groups should also be set up. Seasonals can usually take criticism from a peer with less resentment than from a superior.

Whatever arrangement is used, each member of the group must have contact with the subject under discussion. In other words, it is important for seasonals to observe each other in action. The whole idea of coaching is cooperative exchange or discussion relating to programs and program content.

For example: What did you like or dislike about the programs observed in the last few days? What have you tried in your own programs in an effort to improve them? Did these innovations work? Why? Why not? What does the group think? What did observers notice about audience responses that you missed?

Coaching can be a very rewarding enterprise. It not only strengthens weak points in delivery but also builds rapport among personnel.

Self-Improvement

No matter what action is taken on the part of trainers, supervisors, administrators, and groups of seasonals, the responsibility for improved interpretive programs falls on the individual. After all, this person is the one giving the programs, responding to feedback from visitors, innovating (or not), learning about the area (or not), and showing enthusiasm (or not).

One of the most effective ways for individuals to assess the quality of their programs is to record them . . . and then *listen* to them. Difficulties arise because most of us do not like to listen to our own voices. However, interpreters must make a definite effort and force themselves to record and to listen. Recorders don't lie, flatter, or mask. Personal peculiarities in delivery such as "uh's" and "ah's," mispronounced or improperly used words, frequently repeated words and phrases, and other distracting mannerisms will be appallingly evident.

Another effective procedure is to ask a respected observer to criticize program content and delivery. Acceptance of criticism is always difficult, but when you seek it yourself from an authoritative source, the implication is that you are ready to hear it.

Critique from Without

Any organization can become inbred and suffer from deterioration brought about by the perpetuation of inefficient practices.

Groups within organizations can also suffer from the same malady. It is easy to say, "We've been doing it this way for 15 years, and there's no reason to change now." In such cases participants are too close to the action. They lose perspective. Their personal preferences, prejudices, and concerns prevent a clear, evaluative look at the situation. Input from outside the organization can serve the important purpose of providing fresh perspective and new points of view.

Continuance and Rehire

An important factor in the perpetuation of mediocre interpretation is a softhearted attitude on the part of supervisors. The interpretive job market is not a therapeutic organization designed to rehabilitate inadequate communicators. Yet, year after year, in spite of marginal (or less) performance ratings, ineffective interpreters continue to be rehired. Better personnel are available. Long delay in taking the corrective steps will result in some of those poor interpreters becoming permanent personnel, perhaps eventually supervisors in their own right. The quality of interpretation will surely not be maintained or improved should this happen.

The operation of the best possible interpretive services in park and recreation areas is a difficult and challenging task. One of the most controversial discussions centers on the training and education of interpreters. The chief naturalist, or chief of visitor information services, or whoever hires the seasonal naturalists for outdoor recreation areas, should choose carefully from the growing crop of eager, well-educated, and highly motivated aspirants. Interpretive specialists must be special people.

REFERENCES

References Cited

1. Association of Interpretive Naturalists. *Preparation of the Interpretive Naturalist—A Statement by the Association of Interpretive Naturalists,* Jean S. Replinger report, Needwood, MD.
2. Mahaffey, Ben D. 1973. *Curricular Recommendations for Environmental Interpreters,* Department Technical Report No. 73-5, Texas Experiment Station, Texas A & M University.
3. Tilden, Freeman. 1967. *Interpreting Our Heritage,* The University of North Carolina Press, Chapel Hill.

CHAPTER 27

RESEARCH IN INTERPRETATION

J. Alan Wagar

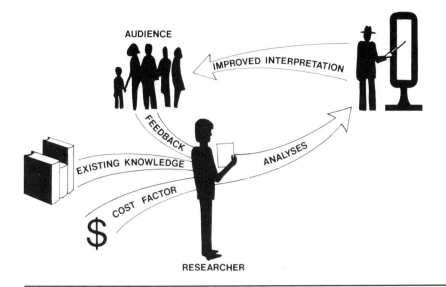

AUDIENCE

IMPROVED INTERPRETATION

FEEDBACK

EXISTING KNOWLEDGE

ANALYSES

COST FACTOR

$

RESEARCHER

Within the context of interpretation, research often means studies to discover new information that can be presented to visitors, for example, descriptive studies of geological phenomena or the life histories of plants and animals. These studies are important. However, as used in this chapter, research refers only to studies designed to improve the effectiveness with which information is presented.

The purpose of this chapter is to provide a framework within which useful research results might be obtained and applied, not to summarize findings. Attention is therefore focused on the kinds of studies that are likely to be useful and on procedures for doing sound research.

USEFUL KINDS OF STUDIES

Three kinds of studies can be especially useful for increasing the effectiveness with which natural and cultural resources are interpreted. These are: (1) studies to provide the interpreter with summaries of existing knowledge from such disciplines as psychology, sociology, anthropology, communications, and education; (2) studies to evaluate the costs and effectiveness of alternative interpretive procedures; and (3) studies to develop feedback methods that interpreters can use to evaluate audience response to their work.

Making Existing Knowledge Available

As an applied art, interpretation must draw on the knowledge and insights of many disciplines. However, few interpreters have received formal training in all of the disciplines that could help them. As a result, most interpreters are not prepared to delve into the research literature of diverse disciplines in search of valuable insights.

Researchers can help remedy this situation in two ways. First, they can write summaries that draw together useful principles from pertinent disciplines in understandable terms. Examples covering education and communications, respectively, are found in works by Boulanger and Smith and by Dick, McKee, and Wagar.[3,4] Second, researchers can undertake studies to adapt known principles to specific interpretive situations or settings. For example, behavioral and educational psychologists have shown that people tend to persist in doing the things they find rewarding.

In examining the implications of this principle for exhibits, Washburne and Wagar identified a number of factors associated with high levels of visitor interest or reward.[15] For example, above average interest was found for dynamic presentations that included motion, changing lighting, and recorded sound. Violent subject matter also created above average interest, as did holistic presentations that included cause-and-effect relations or stories going beyond mere identification and isolated facts.

Evaluating Costs and Effectiveness

Evaluating the costs of reaching a visitor with various interpretive procedures requires information on both costs and visitor contacts.[13] For facilities, costs will normally include construction, depreciation, interest, and maintenance and operation. For person-to-person interpretation, costs may include salaries, travel, and specimens, visual aids, and projection equipment. Procedures need to be developed and data compiled to document typical costs for alternative approaches to interpretation.

Defining the actual accomplishments of interpretation is much more difficult than identifying costs. The number of visitors contacted is only a crude measure of what has been accomplished. Vistor-minutes of contact might better reflect exposure, but they still do not define the effectiveness of that exposure. It is reasonable to assume that visitors will gain the most from presentations that hold their attention, and attention is most likely to be held by presentations they enjoy. Measures of attention and enjoyment can therefore indicate possible levels of effectiveness. However, such measures still do not identify what has been accomplished.

Evaluating effectiveness requires clear objectives; unless we have defined precisely what we want to do, we can not determine how well we have done it.[8,9] However, objectives for interpretation have seldom been specified in terms that permit effectiveness to be measured. Too often, they are stated in terms of actions to be taken rather than effects to be achieved. A typical example is "Interpret the natural and scenic attractions of Sycamore Valley."

The effects normally intended for interpretation are increased visitor enjoyment, awareness, and understanding. Measurement of these effects requires that visitors be observed or questioned. As Mager has pointed out, objectives for education are best stated in "behavioral" terms; that is, they must define what a person should be able to do as a result of a specific experience.[8]

For an interpretive setting, an example of a behavioral objective would be "After hearing the naturalist talk at Sycamore Valley, the visitor will be able to name and discuss the three major forces that shaped the valley." Formal or informal questioning can show how well a specific objective has been achieved. Many objectives will usually be needed to define what visitors should be able to do as a result of the interpretation they are provided.

Developing Feedback Methods

By evaluating the effectiveness of selected interpretive presentations, formal research can identify general principles for increasing the effectiveness of interpretation. But interpretive settings and situations differ so much that every presentation needs evaluation, especially while it is still being developed or before and after it is changed in some way.

To avoid making a major research undertaking out of every evaluation, simple feedback procedures and systems are needed by interpreters. One approach to obtaining feedback is to develop self-testing devices that determine what visitors gain from presentations. For example, a recording quizboard was developed to record answers to four questions based on interpretive presentations, and procedures were developed for its use.[12] Then, to avoid the complexity, power requirements, and limited capacity of the quizboard, a mechanical self-testing device was developed, based on early teaching machine designs (Figs. 27-1 and 27-2).

A second approach to feedback is to record the behavior of visitors. When visitors are free to walk among the parts of a presentation, time-lapse photography can show where they are stopping and thus what is holding their attention.[14] Visitor attention to a presentation can also be recorded by direct observation.[5] By periodically scanning an audience to determine how people's eyes or heads are directed, observers can quickly identify changes in audience attention or differences between audience reactions to different presentations (Fig. 27-3).

RESEARCH IN INTERPRETATION

Many books have been written about how to conduct research; these should be studied by anyone proposing to conduct research in interpretation.[1,2,10,11,16] Only the major steps of a research undertaking are repeated here to orient researchers and to help others judge the adequacy of research that is either proposed or

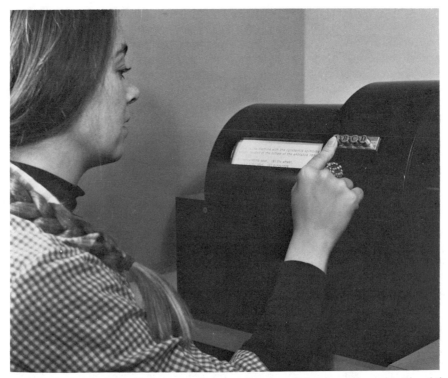

FIG. 27-1. Mechanical self-testing machine in operation. A knob on the right side of the machine is turned to uncover the correct answer and advance to the next question. The machine can be used for interpretive presentations in addition to testing. (Photo by John Spring.)

published. These steps concern existing information, objectives, research design, data collection, and communicating results.

For each step, detailed information should be written in a study plan. Writing a review of pertinent literature, specifying objectives, and writing down how a study will be conducted usually allow an amazing number of minor difficulties to be uncovered and corrected. A written study plan also facilitates review by others, thereby helping to identify any additional flaws in logic or methodology before it is too late to correct them.

Review of Existing Information

Research is a collective enterprise, and a competent researcher will normally start a study by examining what is already known about the problem and the methodologies other researchers have devised to uncover new information about similar problems. For interpretation, this is a challenging task.

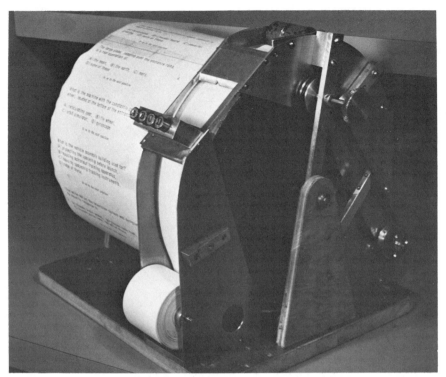

FIG. 27-2. A self-testing machine with its case removed. A paper with multiple-choice questions or interpretive materials is mounted on the large cylinder. Pushing an answer button punches an A, B, C, or D into adding machine tape. Used answer tape can be removed and summarized to determine the proportion of correct responses for each question. (Photo by John Spring.)

Although very little research has been specifically labeled "interpretation," an enormous amount of research bears directly on interpretation. Pertinent fields and subfields include psychology (motivation, perception, operant and classical conditioning); sociology and anthropology (small groups, human ecology, origin and transmission of values, public opinion); communications (journalism, advertising, marketing, radio-television, cinema); and education (learning theory, programmed instruction).

Objectives

Just as interpretive undertakings need clear objectives, so does each study need one or more specific objectives. Study objectives identify the critical elements of the problem. In a sentence or two, each objective should define precisely what question is to be answered or what hypothesis is to be tested.[6] Too often, the

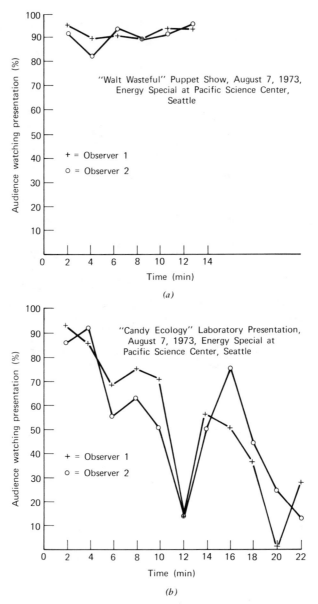

FIG. 27-3. Plotted observations showing the attention-holding effectiveness of presentations.[14] Tape recording the presentations permits later study of the reasons for high or low attention.

beginning researcher collects data with only a vague idea of how they might bear on a specific problem. One of the researcher's most important tasks is to break a nebulous problem into pieces of manageable size and for which precise objectives can be written. The quality of proposed research and the competence of the researcher can often be judged by the clarity and specificity with which objectives are stated.

The objectives for research in interpretation will nearly always concern such practical or "applied" problems as identifying procedures by which an interpreter can increase interest among the visitors he or she contacts. "Basic" research is much better suited to the parent disciplines on which interpreters must draw. For example, really new information about the ways people remember or how they respond to varied stimuli is likely to come from neurology or psychology. Research in interpretation might then show how to apply this information in interpretive settings or might identify the settings in which known principles are most applicable.

Research Design

Unless studies are conducted according to well established principles of research design, they can produce erroneous or misleading results. Two common mistakes resulting from inadequate understanding of research design are (1) generalizing as if results apply to situations substantially different from those sampled, and (2) reporting apparent relationships without determining their dependability. Avoiding these mistakes requires careful design of both sampling and analysis procedures. The factors that can distort research results are so numerous and sometimes so subtle that even the most experienced researcher will normally consult specialists when formulating study procedures.* Depending on the study, they may be specialists in sampling, statistical design and analysis, computer handling of data, interviewing, questionnaire construction, or other fields.

Data Collection

If a study has been carefully designed, data collection can be a routine implementation of previously defined procedures. However, sloppy application of excellent plans can demolish a promising investigation. The researcher should guard especially against incomplete or disorderly records, interjection of personal bias, and departures from rigorous procedures.

---

*Length-of-stay bias is one example of an easily overlooked source of error.[7] If an investigator goes to a selected location on a random or periodic schedule and records data for the people found there, visitors present for extended periods are almost certain to be sampled while those staying only a few minutes are rarely sampled. Therefore, unless special sampling and computational techniques are used, such studies overestimate average length of stay and also give erroneous estimates for factors correlated with length of stay. Such factors may include age, education, occupation, and interest or activity patterns. Overestimation can be substantial, sometimes several hundred percent.

DATA FORM FOR STUDY OF AUDIENCE ATTENTION TO INTERPRETIVE PRESENTATIONS,
PNW–1902–15

Title and description of presentation:					Attention defined as		Observer:	
Informal naturalist talk in small amphitheater, Higgins Pass Visitor Center (Speaker: J.R.Brown Male 25± yrs.					Eye contact ✓ Head direction ___		*I. M. Smith* Date: *July 12, 1974*	
TIME	ATTENTION		AUDIENCE SIZE [2]				REMARKS	
Started	Number showing		At beginning ___*17*___			Percent giving attention		
2:18 p m Plus	attent.[1]	inattent.[1]	arr.	dep.	Subtotal			
02	*11*	*6*			*17*	*65*	*Slow start, no clear introduction*	
04	*9*	*8*			*17*	*53*		
06	*14*	*3*			*17*	*82*		
08	*17*	*0*			*17*	*100*	*pointing at avalanche chute*	
10	*15*	*5*	*3*		*20*	*75*	*audience distracted by new arrivals*	
12	*18*	*2*			*20*	*90*		
14	*13*	*7*			*20*	*65*		
16	*14*	*6*			*20*	*70*	*audience fidgetting*	
18	*10*	*10*			*20*	*50*	*speaker running down*	
20	*10*	*8*		*2*	*18*	*56*		
22	*4*	*9*		*5*	*13*	*31*		
24	*7*	*6*			*13*	*54*		
26	*5*	*4*		*4*	*9*	*56*		
28	*2*	*7*			*9*	*22*	*Talk seemed too long for audience*	
60								

Ended

2:46 p m *CK*

Audience size

at end: ___*9 CK*___

Additional remarks (Identify by time interval
and use back of form if necessary):

[1] Record attention or inattention, whichever is smaller

[2] Subtotals and percentages should be computed in office with calculator.

FIG. 27-4. A sample data collection form used to study audience attention to interpretive presentations. Labeled spaces remind project personnel to make complete records.

Each data collection record should include the date, the name(s) of person(s) collecting the data, the title of the study, a clear record of measurements or observations, and a record of conditions that could affect interpretation of the data. Usually it is good practice to mimeograph data collection forms with spaces labeled to remind data collection personnel to take complete information (Fig. 27-4). When data are placed on computer cards, each card should include enough identifying information that the data "deck" can, if dropped, be reassembled in correct order.

The biases of research personnel can be a major problem whenever social data are involved, as is true when the effects of interpretation are evaluated. For example, sampling procedures may be compromised because an interviewer finds some visitors easier to approach than others. Also, many people are so suggestible or so willing to be agreeable that their answers will be affected by any clues the investigator gives concerning preferred answers. In addition, interviewers whose appearance or behavior is in some way unusual or objectionable may affect the responses of the people interviewed.

Procedures designed to avoid biases and to insure complete and accurate records should be followed precisely. Although it is sometimes necessary to modify predetermined procedures because of unforeseen circumstances, rigor should not be abandoned. This is especially important when data are collected by personnel who are not fully familiar with research techniques. In such cirumstances, written instructions, careful training, and frequent monitoring may be essential.

Analysis of Data and Interpretation of Results

The analysis of data, like data collection, can be a routine implementation of previously designed procedures. However, investigators must guard against shaping the analysis to fit desires for clear-cut results or their commitment to specific propositions. Their attitude must be "to determine if . . ." rather than "to prove that . . ." In all but exploratory studies, investigators should use data to test hypotheses developed *before* the data were collected. If the data suggest conclusions different from the original hypotheses, such conclusions should be considered tentative until supported by additional data. Investigators must also resist the temptation to reject data that do not fit their hypotheses.

The analysis itself will often involve statistical manipulation of data by computer. This requires care to insure that errors do not occur in the transcribing or keypunching of data or in the computer instructions that define the form of input and the labeling of output.

A key step in almost every "applied" research effort is to interpret the meaning of results—often in terms of their implications for management procedures and decisions. Uninterpreted results are often too abstract or limited to illuminate management problems. The researcher, however, can often recast information in terms that are meaningful to managers. At the same time, researchers can often integrate other sources of information with their results. In this way one can provide guidelines that reflect the support or contradictions supplied by other studies or observations. The researcher can also reflect the risks of proceeding with imperfect information as well as the risks of not using the best information available.

Developing the implications of research results is not an easy task, and too many researchers avoid it. Consequently, their results go largely unused.

Communicating and Applying Results

Unless research results are communicated to others, they serve little purpose. Communication almost always includes publishing to make results widely available to potential users. Stoltenberg et al. have provided an excellent summary of basic principles for writing up research.[11] Because most publishers receive far more material than they can use, a manuscript is most likely to be published if it presents findings of obvious importance, is brief, and is easy to read. Many research organizations employ professional editors to help researchers put results into understandable form.

Results are most likely to be applied if publication is supplemented with graphic and personalized communication. The ideal is to have researchers and interpreters work together to identify useful lines of research, carry it out, and apply the results. Demonstrations, informal discussions, presentations at meetings, field trips, slide-tapes, and videotapes are also useful ways to convey research findings and can increase the chances of such findings being put into practice.

An important step in developing publications and other presentations is to have them reviewed by professional colleagues, including people in a position to apply the information presented. Most experienced researchers consider review essential. Reviewers should examine the validity of procedures and inferences and the clarity with which they are expressed. A good reviewer will question anything that is apparently wrong or unclear and will offer specific suggestions for improvement.

Discussion with interpreters who have applied research findings indicates that such findings are most likely to be applied (1) when they demonstrate convincingly that specific procedures are especially effective, (2) when they provide readily applied evaluation techniques, and (3) when interpreters and researchers work together or communicate often enough to maintain good rapport. At Fort Langley, British Columbia, for example, researchers from the head office of Parks Canada teamed up with planners from the regional office and interpreters from the local site in using surveillance photography to analyze the effectiveness of an orientation exhibit. Results were used to identify difficulties and to justify modification and relocation of the exhibit.* In the Pacific Southwest Region of the U.S. Forest Service, observation of audience attention[5] was recognized as a very concrete and readily applied system for evaluating effectiveness and was adapted for analyzing guided walks. The technique quickly showed that most interpretation was at an adult level and ineffective with children, even though they comprised a significant portion of the audience. Observation also showed that the level of attention, especially of children, dropped when interpreters discussed resource management issues.†

---

*Personal communication with Scott Meis, Socio-economic Division, Parks Canada, Department of Environment, Ottawa, Canada. October 28, 1980.
†Field test of techniques described in: "Audience attention as a basis for evaluating interpretive presentations," USDA Forest Service Research Paper PNW-198. Unpublished report by Nord Whited, Interpretive Services Coordinator, U.S. Forest Service, Pacific Southwest Region, San Francisco. September 1976.

CONCLUSION

Researchers and interpreters need to recognize that their skills and interests are complementary. Researchers, for example, should understand that the effectiveness of many interpreters involves such difficult-to-measure factors as a contagious enthusiasm for subject matter and an intuitive feel for the mood of an audience. Interpreters, in turn, need to recognize that the methodical approach of researchers is not a straitjacket on creativity; principles and evaluation techniques developed by research can aid creative interpretation.

To increase the effectiveness of interpretation, researchers and interpreters must work together to identify the problems that need study and to translate study results into improved practice.

REFERENCES

References Cited

1. Bachrach, Arthur J. 1965. *Psychological Research: An Introduction,* Random House, New York.
2. Blalock, Hubert M., Jr. 1970. *An Introduction to Social Research,* Prentice-Hall, Englewood Cliffs, NJ.
3. Boulanger, F. David, and John P. Smith. 1973. *Educational Principles and Techniques for Interpreters,* USDA Forest Service Gen. Tech. Rep. PNW-9, Pacific Northwest Forest and Range Experiment Station, Portland, OR.
4. Dick, Ronald E., David T. McKee, and J. Alan Wagar. 1974. "A Summary and Annotated Bibliography of Communications Principles," *Journal of Environmental Education* **5**(4), 8–13.
5. Dick, Ronald E., Erik Myklestad, and J. Alan Wagar. 1975. *Audience Attention as a Basis for Evaluating Interpretive Presentations,* USDA Forest Service Res. Pap. PNW-198, Pacific Northwest Forest and Range Experiment Station, Portland, OR.
6. Krathwohl, David R. 1966. *How to Prepare a Research Proposal,* Syracuse University Bookstore, Syracuse, NY.
7. Lucas, Robert C. 1963. "Bias in Estimating Recreationists' Length of Stay from Sample Interviews," *Journal of Forestry* **61**(12), 912–914.
8. Mager, Robert F. 1962. *Preparing Instructional Objectives,* Fearon Publishers, Belmont, CA.
9. Putney, Allen D., and J. Alan Wagar, 1973. "Objectives and Evaluation in Interpretive Planning," *Journal of Environmental Education* **5**(1), 43–44.
10. Selltiz, Claire, Marie Jahoda, Morton Deutsch, and Stuart W. Cook, 1959.

Research Methods in Social Relations, Holt, Rinehart, and Winston, New York.

11. Stoltenberg, Carl H., Kenneth D. Ware, Robert J. Marty, Robert D. Wray, and J. D. Wellons, 1970. *Planning Research for Resource Decisions,* Iowa State University Press, Ames.

12. Wagar, J. Alan, 1972. *The Recording Quizboard: A Device For Evaluating Interpretive Services,* USDA Forest Service Res. Pap. PNW-139, Pacific Northwest Forest and Range Experiment Station, Portland, OR.

13. Wagar, J. Alan, 1974. "Interpretation to Increase Benefits for Recreationists," Pages 101–106 in *Outdoor Recreation Research: Applying the Results,* USDA Forest Service Gen. Tech. Rep. NC-9, North Central Forest Experiment Station, St. Paul, MN.

14. Wagar, J. Alan, Gregory W. Lovelady, and Harlan Falkin. 1976. *Evaluation Techniques for Interpretation: Study Results from an Exhibition on Energy,* USDA Forest Service Res. Pap. PNW-211, Pacific Northwest Forest and Range Experiment Station, Portland, OR.

15. Washburne, Randel F., and J. Alan Wagar, 1972. "Evaluating Visitor Response to Exhibit Content," *Curator* **15**(3), 248–254.

16. Webb, Eugene J., Donald T. Campbell, Richard D. Schwartz, Lee Sechrest, 1966. *Unobtrusive measures: Non-Reactive Research in the Social Sciences,* Rand McNally, Chicago.

PART V

THE WORLD SCENE

Our interpretive efforts must be designed to complement an area, to tell its story, and at the same time utilize the purpose and values of the area to stimulate better understanding and the appreciation of this place—earth—our home.

Tom D. Thomas

CHAPTER 28

INTERPRETATION AROUND
THE WORLD

Myron D. Sutton

INTRODUCTION

Cuando la tecnología no tenga nada más que ofrecer al hombre, aun continuará la naturaleza mostrándole sus maravillas.

Eduardo Arango

This sign is displayed as panel number one in the exhibit room at a visitor center in Isla de Salamanca National Park on the northern coast of Colombia. Translated, it reads: "When technology has nothing more for man, then nature will go on showing him her wonders." Such a thought, and such a visitor center, and such a national park were rare in developing countries a dozen years ago. Interpretation, if any, was rudimentary. Few skilled interpreters were available, even if a park could afford them. Some countries scarcely had biological curriculums in their universities, much less courses in public land administration or interpretive studies. The closest approaches, perhaps, were schools for tourist guides. Trip leaders, licensed by the national tourism bureau, served in a sense as interpreters. But all too often they merely recited names of important places and eminent people and made witty remarks that had little of what we now deem "interpretation."

The scant finances of emerging park systems seldom allowed for interpretation, since priorities more often went to land acquisition and park protection. Indeed, the hiring of an "educated" ranger was considered inappropriate because the principal duties of rangers were to confront poachers, vandals, thieves, and other lawbreakers, and for this the administrators felt they needed rough-and-tumble men schooled in mountain warfare rather than in science and public relations.

History has proved them right as well as wrong, and eventually a few signs began to appear at the most obvious tourist attractions. Record trees, for example, were surrounded by fences and supplied with signs stating age, height and diameter (Fig. 28-1). Personal interpretation was simply not yet feasible because authorities remained preoccupied with problems such as villages annexing parts of a park and settlers moving in.

Some parks had little support at the highest government levels if they happened to have petroleum in the ground beneath them. Others have been plagued by war, official apathy, government instability, inflation, and pollution.

Another problem was the lack of printed or audiovisual reference materials. Quite often the only materials available in local languages were North American or European texts, and while these might have covered the general principles of ecology, they had little or nothing to do with interpretation and bore scant relation to the country's own parks.

Given this lack of background and only a limited buildup of public interest in natural resources, it is little wonder that a national consciousness of conservation was slow to materialize. Only when local groups and inspired amateurs pressured the government, or the facts became officially known that other countries relatively advanced in the park field were earning foreign exchange from it, could parks have a fair opportunity to take their place in the national economic structure.

Now, throughout the world, the conservation movement is burgeoning, though a bit unevenly, and of the more than 120 countries with systems of national parks, dozens are undertaking interpretive programs (Fig. 28-2). Nevertheless poaching is still rampant and vandalism is common; consequently, law enforcement and the protection of parks continue to have the higher priority. Political threats must still be met, and demands for wholesale intrusion of tourism facilities to earn immediate economic benefits must be moderated or rejected.

But officials from tourism and conservation ministries have viewed the extraordinary success of interpretive activities in New Zealand, Australia, Canada, the United States, and elsewhere, and have accordingly modified or reversed some of their philosophies. Wildlife management and park administration officials are discovering that interpreation is an effective adjunct to law enforcement and are no longer delaying interpretive plans for some mythical day when protection problems are solved. There is, indeed, an increasing awareness of the American philosophy that "interpretation leads to appreciation, and appreciation leads to protection."

Even so, administrators may misunderstand the values of interpretation, or possess little scientific background on which to base an interpretive program. Museums may exist, but in consonance with early philosophies some of them display objects unrelated to the natural or historic features in the park. Guidebooks in several languages may be offered for sale, but this kind of interpretation is

FIG. 28-1. An interpretive sign on a huge plane tree in Uludag National Park, Turkey. The five lines read: "My name is chinar (plane tree), my age is 550 (years), I will live until 1,000, I am this country's tree, I enjoy plentiful water and soil." (Photo by Myron Sutton.)

frowned on in some quarters because it allegedly reduces the amount of revenue that could be earned by private guides for hire.

Specialists in countries where interpretive programs have achieved success on national, state, and local levels might view with alarm some of the interpretive activities being developed abroad. For example, one Latin American visitor center

FIG. 28-2. A small but adequate museum of natural history, built by the Park Administrator (at left) in his spare time. The natural history of the park is exhibited inside. Rio Simpson National Park, Chile. (Photo by Grant W. Sharpe.)

has a portion of its grounds devoted to captive wild animals, and even though the animals are retained in open areas surrounded by moats, the confinement of live animals is usually considered inappropriate in nature parks.

Social and developmental philosophies vary, not only with respect to local cultural traditions, but because public appreciation of geology, wildlife, and natural habitats is not equally advanced on all continents. It is difficult to engender a broad base of public support for wildlife until citizens have an opportunity to observe such life close at hand. As soon as wildlife can be readily viewed in surrounding natural habitats, animal compounds at visitor centers might be phased out.

Apart from such local differences, however, interpretive programs have certain similarities from country to country. Many are based on successful techniques pioneered and tested in the last 50 years, and one finds instances of superior thought and innovative techniques even where training has been minimal.

Some examples of these techniques show the ingenuity with which interpretive programs are organized with a minimum use of funds. The enlistment of competent artists to prepare materials for exhibits and trail guides has saved thousands of dollars because the artists were willing to contribute to the public cause, were the wives of rangers and thus already interested in conserving the heritage, or for some other reason lent their talents gratis. Retired professors of history, less interested in income than in public service, have conducted tours, explained battlefield events, or written exhibit plans and guidebooks.

Popular local legislators or civic leaders have been enlisted to conduct campaigns for acquisition of exhibit specimens. Scores of U.S. Peace Corps Volun-

FIG. 28-3. Participants from around the world attending the annual International Seminar on Administration of National Parks and Equivalent Reserves pick up an interpretive idea at Blue Ridge Parkway, Virginia. Here they learn of the utilization of noninterpretive personnel in the interpretive program. The man at the right, a member of the park maintenance staff, demonstrates two homemade musical instruments, a guitar and dulcimer, to the visitors. (Photo by Grant W. Sharpe.)

teers have been pressed into service to design trail systems, construct boardwalks from available materials, teach local inhabitants, conduct tours, and even serve as park administrators.

Many countries have made full use of training funds and travel grants awarded by international organizations such as the United Nations (especially UNESCO and FAO), and the Organization of American States. One of the most popular training courses for world park experts is the International Seminar on Administration of National Parks and Equivalent Reserves, sponsored annually by the University of Michigan, Parks Canada, and the United States National Park Service. Interpretive programs in several agencies and of differing scope are studied in this month-long traveling seminar which, between 1965 and 1980, was attended by some 500 persons from 95 countries (Fig. 28-3).

The "education center," located in a national park, has been effective in attracting public interest to park features or to scientific and historic principles. Likewise, restoration of prehistoric ruins is an example of work done by ministries

FIG. 28-4. Visitors to Spain's Canary Islands off northwest Africa transported by camel up the slopes of the volcanoes in Timanfaya National Park. (Photo by Myron Sutton.)

FIG. 28-5. The turtle house, Darwin Biological Station, Galapagos National Park, Ecuador. (Photo by Myron Sutton.)

other than those related to natural resources, such as a Ministry of Education.

Camels are used in the Canary Islands to take visitors up cinder hills in volcanic national parks (Fig. 28-4). A scientific center in the Galápagos Islands is a focal point for explanations of natural phenomena to park visitors (Fig. 28-5).

Thus there are numerous ways to inaugurate interpretive programs on slender budgets and with few local experts available. The following paragraphs provide a limited summary of world progress in different fields of public interpretation. The work is rapidly expanding, however, and a detailed international review of this subject would fill a volume of its own.

SHIPBOARD INTERPRETATION

A common means of explaining natural or historical phenomena involving water, especially on lakes or among islands, is interpretation aboard motor vessels. This is essential when the resources are fragile and little protection or interpretation is available on land. For example, the usual method of visiting islands in Galápagos National Park, Ecuador, is a government-chartered cruise ship on which tourists live for a week or two. Each evening competent bilingual guides present lectures on features that will be seen the following day. Together with a study of maps, this prepares the passengers for travels by launch and foot when the vessel anchors offshore.

In Japan, hydrofoils provide a rapid means of seeing points of interest; river excursions on the Nara River in Honshu are made to observe archaic and vanishing methods of fishing with cormorants. Tours of the Thames, the Seine, and other major rivers of the world are well known.

CONDUCTED TOURS

Walking tours through places such as the Tower of London are conducted by experienced guides, but the concept of tours through wild natural scenes is only beginning and is expected to grow as visits to parks and reserves increase. Many thousands of school children participate in conducted walks throughout Japan. In Thailand, rangers at Khao Yai National Park take visitors by truck on night excursions to "spot" animals. Night walks to observe tigers are carried out in Royal Chitwan National Park, Nepal. Escorted daylight walks are also provided for school groups at several other parks and game sanctuaries. Costa Rica has helped to pioneer this activity in Latin America. Rangers in the Province of Chubut, Argentina, are required to accompany visitors to fragile sea lion rookeries. For the most part, though, such efforts are uncommon and in the developing countries have their best success where groups of interested students form a substantial percentage of visitors. In most countries, interpretation is still largely by guides employed on commercial tours.

VISITOR CENTERS

The concept of visitor centers and museums (or sometimes education centers) is more widespread, and excellent examples have been constructed in Colombia, Costa Rica, Australia, Canada, Argentina, Italy, Switzerland, Thailand, Japan, Kenya, and Uganda. An innovation of special value is an exhibit guide leaflet in several languages, useful in places like the Swiss National Park, where many languages prevail.

Some of the world's most advanced and sophisticated visitor centers have been constructed in Australia, especially in the State of New South Wales. Sydney enjoys the advantage of several national parks in its environs, but from the point of view of park authorities this means the extra challenge of serving many people. Accordingly, patterns of visitor circulation are carefully planned, satellite interpretive centers are designed to spread public use, and trail systems provide some relief from congestion.

In the Kalkari Visitor Center at Ku-ring-gai Chase National Park, the auditorium program has achieved a "state of the art" by utilizing a computer-programmed three-screen, eight-projector presentation that's scored with music composed for this production. These efforts are not intended to produce a dazzling multimedia extravaganza but rather a low-key, effective, and dramatic educational experience. In the lobby, a television screen is installed to show a visitor-actuated videotape of the birth of the kangaroo, material provided by local broadcasting sources. Outside the museum, visitors see kangaroos and other aspects of the coastal mountain ecosytem by walking a self-guiding trail.

BOARDWALKS AND TRAILS

Some national parks have been established where wild ecosystems are inhabited by animals dangerous to man. It is a little disconcerting to hike along a wild stream in Khao Yai National Park, Thailand and come upon tiger tracks only a few minutes old. Under such conditions, the construction of trails and even of campgrounds is discouraged unless the installation can be provided with some security. Certain African park officials, if they permit overnight stays, require that visitors remain in protected compounds. Of course, it is virtually impossible in any country to ward off all attacks by wild animals in parks and refuges, but where public safety is a primary consideration, care is taken to afford the visitor protection through design, interpretation, and law enforcement. However, some degree of hazard is a proper part of the park experience, and dangers from wildlife do not prohibit public use altogether.

The famed Iguazú Falls, on the boundary between Argentina, Brazil, and Paraguay, consist of 278 separate cataracts, most of them on the Argentine side. The National Park Service of Argentina has developed trails to important points of interest, including boardwalks that traverse the brink of the falls for more than 500 yd (460 m). The Colombian National Park Service experimented with boardwalks leading into brackish lagoons, through coastal forests, and out to mangrove swamps at the edge of the sea. Foreign park officials have been inspired by the success of such boardwalks as the Anhinga Trail in Everglades National Park, Florida.

UNDERWATER INTERPRETATION

Few segments of park development have captured the interests of worldwide park administrators more than underwater parks, or "marine-terrestrial" parks as they are sometimes called. Experiments at Virgin Islands National Park and Buck Island Reef National Monument have been carefully observed. The Kenya Government has installed underwater viewing capability at Mazima Springs, where hippos may be seen swimming. Japan has facilities for viewing ocean reefs at Shirahama and Kushimoto Marine Parks. Oceanographic laboratories and exhibit aquariums may be found at numerous localities around the world.

BLINDS

The construction of special facilities for public concealment where large animal populations are present has gained in popularity. The so-called "Treetops," in Aberdari National Park, Kenya, is well known, though it is more than a blind because it provides visitor accommodations. A similar example is Tiger Tops in Nepal. At Khao Yai National Park, Thailand, there is a large concrete blind observation tower. Visitors look out across a sloping meadow to a pond with a salt lick. Here gaur (a colorful wild Asian oxen), Sambar deer, and occasionally wild elephants and tigers may be seen. The experience is worthwhile, especially at sunset, when flocks of hornbills fly from tree to tree enroute to roost for the night, and the trumpeting of elephants can be heard through the tropical forest. The popularity of these kinds of installations is beneficial to the international tourism industry; many park visitors now have high-quality cameras and easy-to-use "zoom" telescopic lenses. There is danger, of course, that the "blind" concept could expand into hotel accommodations where visitors observe wild scenes from their rooms. The addition of amenities, support systems and service activities

could, through improper planning, constitute an undesirable encroachment on
the wilderness.

SELF-GUIDED TRAILS

North American experience has convinced other governments of the need to develop self-guided trails, and the idea has been put into practice in modest and
economical ways. Large signs have been installed along a path that leads into a
dry tropical forest in Santa Rosa National Park, Costa Rica. Colorful motmot birds
are common along the trail; iguanas and armies of marching ants may be observed; and white-faced monkeys peer down through trees at visitors. Self-guided
trails through Roman Empire ruins in the mountain massif at Termessus National
Park, Turkey, present authoritative explanations of structures and concepts that
time has largely erased. American Peace Corps and German Volunteer Service
workers have helped build self-guided nature walks in several parks and game
sanctuaries in Thailand. Self-guided trails have also been developed and refined
in Canada, Great Britain, New Zealand, Chile, and elsewhere.

CONDUCTED TRIPS

Conducted trips, as distinguished from commercial tours, achieve success where
parks have become well developed, as in Canada and Japan. An underlying consideration in lesser developed countries is the ability of the public to get to parks.
If comparatively few citizens have automobiles, then bus trips become a common
mode of access, but the arrival of bus groups may not coincide with the availability of park tour leaders. Costa Rica is experimenting with conducted trips, and
other nations are inaugurating variations of this technique. Where parks lie closer
to urban areas, guided tours may enjoy greater success owing to the proximity of
school groups and convenient bus transportation.

EXHIBITS FOR THE BLIND

These are not yet as widespread as in North America, but at Seto Inland Sea
National Park, and the Oita Marine Palace, Japan, visitors may handle models of
fish that inhabit local marine environments.

OUTSIDE PUBLICATIONS

General interest in natural and historical features has been widely stimulated. Of
course it is true that in a few places, such as southeast Asia where religious shrines

FIG. 28-6. Two natural history publications. At left, the guide to Stelvio National Park in Italy; at right, a handbook on the national parks of Uganda. Both are profusely illustrated with photographs. (Photo by John Spring.)

are common, public interpretation remains dependent chiefly on guides hired by tour agencies. In such cases, printed descriptions of the religion or the shrine are seldom available and if so, consist of perhaps a single sheet. As for natural phenomena, publishers in several countries are producing wildlife identification manuals. For example, bird guides covering individual continents and specific countries are now available, including Africa, Europe, North and South America, West Indies, Central America, Trinidad and Tobago, Colombia, Argentina, Japan, Thailand, Nepal, Australia, and New Zealand. Although publishers' experience in the United States suggests that the public is far more interested in birds than in any other kind of wildlife, large mammals are of greater general interest in Africa, and all aspects of nature are receiving attention. Commercial interest in the desires of tourists vis-à-vis national parks seems to be expanding.

Only in a few countries, such as Canada, Great Britain, Switzerland, and Australia, are there easily available guides to trees, wild flowers, and other parts of the natural environment. The British have produced paperbound volumes on individual national parks, which summarize all aspects of park resources. Several countries, including Peru, Venezuela, Costa Rica, France, Australia, and New Zealand, have produced volumes on their entire national park system. These examples suggest that a growing body of literature does exist and that these references will support the rapid development of an international consciousness of conservation.

IN-SERVICE PUBLICATIONS

Several Australian states have issued attractive publications describing their national parks. Fine ones have also been issued in Canada, New Zealand, Italy, and Uganda (Fig. 28-6). The quality of language and illustrations in New Zealand self-guided trail booklets is especially commendable. In other countries, small park budgets permit few publications of this sort, and at early stages of development they are usually only experimental. Nevertheless, examples of trail guides are circulating widely among park staffs, and new publications have increased. One recent example is a combined natural and historic trail guide booklet in Port-Cros National Park, France. Australian park authorities have produced an abundant list of interpretive publications, such as a comprehensive study of rain forests.

AUDIOVISUAL DEVICES

Apart from sound-and-light programs, which reach a fine degree of sophistication in England, France, Greece, Spain, and Italy, audiovisual programs have either been rejected as an interpretive device or are as yet poorly developed in countries where park interpretive programs are starting. Importation of electrical machines is sometimes embargoed to support local industries, but local industries often do not produce audiovisual instruments of sufficient quality to withstand heavy use. In some parks that generate their own electricity, power is not even regularly available during daylight hours. There is also the problem of qualified maintenance technicians. All of this is generally regarded as too expensive to be worthwhile during the early stages of interpretive development. Nevertheless, some visitor centers have small auditoriums where transparencies can be shown, usually by a park biologist, to visiting groups. In Canada and Australia, audiovisual programs have reached an extraordinary level of good taste and effectiveness.

MOTION PICTURES

Several countries have produced exceptional films relating to parks. In cooperation with a leading banking establishment, Japanese park officials produced a series of four films with a total running time of two hours, depicting the scenic and aesthetic values of Japanese national parks throughout the year. Both Canada and Japan have been especially successful in reproducing, as nearly as a film can, the aesthetic values of natural areas. The utilization of color, microscopic views, and seasonal variations has been brought to a high state of art by film producers in those countries. South African and East African authorities have been notably successful in producing wildlife films, most of which avoid production cliches and bring out not only the subtle ecological relationships in natural habitats, but also the values of wildlife observations to human beings.

Widespread high-quality publications and public television programs throughout Australia nearly guarantee better educated visitors to parks. For optimum professionalism, as in visitor center motion pictures, park authorities engage the services of the best production organizations. For example, South Australian park authorities have two exceptional films, "Kangaroo Island," and "Long Time Journey," that were produced by the South Australian Film Corporation, a studio of international fame.

PRESS, RADIO, AND TELEVISION

A press campaign interpreting the significance and values of parks can have extraordinary results. The public reaction to news reports, feature articles, and editorials in Costa Rica helped encourage the presidency, the legislative assembly, the provinces, and the public to support park establishment and operation. Youth groups worked in the parks on weekends. The College of Biologists at the University of Costa Rica issued timely reports and scientific calls to action. International organizations helped to solve problems related to squatters, and conservation groups contributed funds for land management and acquisition. All of these developments were fully reported by the media. Within less than two years a prevailing philosophy of unwise utilization of prime parklands was reversed. When parks were established, squatters were promptly and judiciously removed, a sensitive issue in a country where voting is compulsory.

Park authorities often give wide distribution to the remarks of visiting specialists or important personalities. These pronouncements are not only published in national newspapers but may be issued as government documents and incorporated as training materials in school curricula. Another common practice is the radio and television interview with university specialists, prominent visitors, or eminent local citizens who make news with regard to parks and conservation. One technique that has proved rather startling to audiences in developing countries has been the playing of recorded wildlife sounds, which serves to stress the values and importance of life forms usually taken for granted.

Australian broadcasters inaugurated a television series, "In the Wild with Harry Butler," characterized by unassuming, personal, down-to-earth approaches. It became one of the most popular programs in Australian television history, and books based on the series became best sellers.

All in all, the printed and electronic media may serve effectively in interpreting park values and features to a wide audience while there is still little on-site interpretation available in the parks themselves.

OUTDOOR EXHIBITS

Outside the United States, governments are concerned with the variety of languages spoken by visitors and often provide booklets, texts, museum explanations, and guides in perhaps half a dozen languages. With outdoor exhibits this is a little more difficult, but the Swiss have resolved the problem to some degree. In the Swiss National Park, where no facilities are permitted inside the boundaries, trailside exhibits are installed at various entrances to the park (Fig. 28-7). These are signs constructed of weather-resistant baked enamel and installed under a rustic canopy; the colors are bright and, being shaded, seem fairly durable. The exhibits describe park trail systems and explain park regulations. Though worded in Romansch and the other official languages of Switzerland, as well as other languages, the accompanying illustrations are so clear that visitors have little doubt of their meaning. For example, a large white "X" is superimposed across an illustration of a hand picking a flower, meaning that such an action is prohib-

FIG. 28-7.   A trailside exhibit shelter in Swiss National Park, Switzerland with information in several languages. (Photo by Michael Sutton.)

FIG. 28-8. A visitor center under construction in Isla de Salamanca National Park, Columbia. (Photo by Myron Sutton.)

ited. This use of symbols conforms in a way to the international scheme of road signs and highway construction indicators, which are designed to be understandable regardless of language.

In some localities, outdoor exhibits are unsuccessful because of vandalism; they have been dismantled by park visitors and utilized for domestic purposes. As appreciation for wild environments increases, however, such abuses tend to diminish. Argentina has simple but effective wooden signs in remote localities, and these have endured for years.

MUSEUMS

We still see in many places the traditional "storage house" museums where glass cases contain abundant items related only by provenience or era, with labels that identify but do very little to explain. Such facilities are slowly being modified, and North American techniques have often served as guidelines. Among the newer examples are visitor centers in the Swiss National Park; in Stelvio National Park, Italy; and in Isla de Salamanca National Park, Colombia (Fig. 28-8). Usually a large wall map of the park introduces the exhibits. This is followed by simple displays of plants, animals, and geologic features, but the historical story is seldom well developed. This may be because the history of the region has already been described in book form, or because the national park administration does not include historic sites. There has been little interest in the aboriginal inhabitants of natural areas, although several countries are redefining their policy in this field. Canada, Turkey, Guatemala, and Costa Rica have major historical and archeological parks with museum exhibits that include displays on early inhabitants, conflicts, settlement, and the paraphernalia of civilization.

RESTORED SITES

Pressed by international organizations such as UNESCO, national tourism agencies and ministries of education or culture, several countries are restoring or stabilizing prehistoric ruins or are planning large-scale programs centering in or near ancient cities. The cliff-bound ruins of Machu Picchu in Peru are well known. On the high altiplano of Bolivia, at 13,000 ft (3962 m), the Ministry of Education has restored an attractive sunken court at the pre-Inca site of Tiahuanaco and installed a museum nearby. The Nepalese and Thais are obtaining data on the deterioration of religious and historic shrines. The Indonesians are attempting to stabilize the remarkable ruins of Borobudur, a Buddhist temple. Many ancient ruins in the once elegant Roman Empire have been placed under public protection, but some Mediterranean sites such as Carthage are either being washed away or encroached upon by human settlements. The government of Greece protects classic sites such as Delphi and is planning for the proper protection and use of Ancient Olympia and similar sites as well as natural areas.

One unusual challenge will be interpretation of Ancient Troy National Park in western Turkey. Archeologists have discovered that at least 15 cities functioned on the same spot, and for this reason the interpretive story may well be among the world's most complex. The ruins have nearly all been leveled, and a small museum at the site attempts to reconstruct at least a portion of the story. But a great deal of activity and thought will be required before the history of ancient Troy can be made more comprehensible to the general public.

At Sovereign Hill, in the old Australian gold fields at Ballarat, Victoria, an entire village has, through living history interpretation, come to life as has the program at Columbia State Historical Park in California.

SCIENTIFIC AND HISTORICAL BACKGROUND

The scientific data required to make sound planning decisions or build interpretive programs is fairly advanced in certain countries. Argentina, for example, has for years been producing a series of scientific journals entitled *Anales de los Parques Nacionales*. Papers in this series help to analyze before and after ecological situations that have a direct bearing on park management decisions.

Biologists in local universities are occasionally called on to produce such general interpretive information as the number of species of orchids in a country. Church scientists in Latin America have become leading experts in fields like ornithology, a substantial accomplishment where 1600 species of birds exist. The Spanish have comprehensive volcanic and water resource studies on which to base their geologic interpretation of the Canary Islands. Scientific background for parks and reserves has also been well developed in Zaïre, Rhodesia, Tanzania

(Serengeti Research Station), Ecuador (Galápagos National Park), Poland, Czechoslovakia, and the Soviet Union.

MASTER PLANNING

The most sought-after expertise in national park management today is that pertaining to planning for the development and use of fragile natural and historical areas. To some degree this stems from urgent proposals by pressure groups to utilize parks for inappropriate purposes, or to install such complex and elegant tourist facilities that the values for which the park was set aside would be destroyed. It is to the lasting credit of presidents, bureau executives, and legislators that they have often withstood these pressures and have halted development until a proper plan could be prepared. In that way, certain valuable swamps, reefs, and unique wildlife habitats have been saved.

Nevertheless, park lands must eventually provide something more than heritage benefits, and master plans for the conservation and use (including tourism) of parks have proliferated. Examples include Jordan (Qumran, Jericho, Amman, Jerash, and Samaria National Parks); Turkey (Göreme, Troy, Ephesus, Koprulu Canyon, Pergamum, Pamukkale, Termessus, Kovada Lake, Olympus Seashore, Boğazköy-Alacahöyük, and Halicarnassus Seashore); Venezuela (Canaima, which includes Angel Falls, highest in the world); Tanzania (Kilimanjaro); Guatemala (Tikal); Panama (Portobelo and Volcan Barú); and general surveys in Kenya, Ethiopia, Costa Rica, Argentina, Chile, Korea, Thailand, Indonesia, and Greece.

These plans contain details on the significance of a park: history, natural history, and archeology; management objectives; boundary considerations; access; circulation; administrative facilities; interpretive installations; utilities; visitor data; staffing; organization; and maps. In the parts devoted to visitor information and interpretation, a typical plan would have sections dealing with the story to be told, visitor arrival, visitor centers (museums, auditorium, exhibit gallery), trails, park tours, duties of the chief of visitor services, and base maps related to vegetation, geology, archeology, and similar resources.

TRAINING

A substantial interchange of interpretive training specialists and trainees has been underway for many years, and special training schools have adopted interpretation in their curricula. Museum specialists have frequently studied techniques and installations in the United States, Mexico, Europe, and other notable localities and have taught at the UNESCO Regional Training Center, Jos, Nigeria. Wardens in training at the College of African Wildlife Management in Tanzania, East Africa, receive an introduction to herbarium management, public relations programs, and related techniques. A similar college in French-speaking West Africa at Garoua, Cameroon, provides instruction in park and conservation methods. Several wildlands management courses are offered by the Food and Agriculture Organization of the United Nations (FAO) in Chile and Argentina. Interpretation has been emphasized in the annual Seminar on Natural Areas and Tourism, hosted by the Argentine Province of Chubut. Australia, New Zealand, Costa Rica, and Canada conduct training programs.

This emphasis on training is a response to the absence of formal interpretive training in most colleges and universities. Hence, the requirements of park interpretive personnel, guides, and exhibit specialists must be met in local, regional or international training courses, or through matriculation in foreign universities where such studies are offered.

CONCLUSION

Since protection against poaching, vested interests, political pressures, and other threats is the first order of business in new national park systems, interpretive installations are not generally as advanced in developing countries as in those nations where park systems have been established for a number of years. Nevertheless, imaginative interpretive programs, executed with diligence and skill, have been placed at the disposal of the public, and the number of installations is increasing.

The need for interpretation is especially acute in countries where national consciousness of conservation has not fully manifested itself. Legislative officers concerned with environmental degradation often lament that little or nothing is available to explain to their citizens the values of the national heritage. Hence, scant public appreciation ensues. Foreign officials visiting the United States see in roadside exhibits and small field museums the key to their problem. They maintain that if such facilities were available along highways in their own countries the buildup of grassroot support could significantly influence conservation legislation.

One can dwell at length on the need for interpretation, but perhaps the most fundamental is the need for education. It often happens that when students in other countries arrive at a site where there is a field exhibit or small regional museum, they make extensive notes, often copying entire exhibit texts verbatim. Since this has been observed on all continents where parks and at least limited interpretive facilities exist, it is safe to suggest that the hunger for education is universal and constitutes one of the most compelling reasons for installing interpretive facilities. The cultural and economic advantages of a well-planned interpretive program are becoming more apparent on an international scale.

REFERENCES

Aldridge, Don. 1975. *Guide to Countryside Interpretation: Part One, Principles of Countryside Interpretation,* Her Majesty's Stationery Office Edinburgh, for Countryside Commission, Scotland.

Pennyfather, Keith. 1975. *Guide to Countryside Interpretation: Part Two, Interpretive Media and Facilities,* Her Majesty's Stationery Office, Edinburgh, for Countryside Commission.

INDEX

Page numbers in **bold face** refer to photographs or other illustrations.